kayās nōhcīn

ᑲᔮᐢ ᓅᐦᒌᐣ

I Come from a Long Time Back

OUR OWN WORDS 1

kayās nōhcīn

ᑲᔮᐢ ᓅᐦᒌᐣ

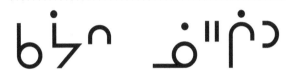

I Come from a Long Time Back

as told by

Mary Louise Rockthunder, wēpanākit

Edited and translated by
Jean L. Okimāsis and Arok Wolvengrey

FIRST NATIONS UNIVERSITY OF CANADA

COVER AND TEXT DESIGN: Duncan Noel Campbell
COPY EDITOR: Donna Grant
PROOFREADER: Kelly Laycock
COVER PHOTO: Portrait of Mary Louise Rockthunder, courtesy of the Rockthunder family
MAP: Weldon Hiebert

Library and Archives Canada Cataloguing in Publication

TITLE: kayās nōhcīn = I come from a long time back / as told by Mary Louise Rockthunder, wēpanākit; edited and translated by Jean L. Okimāsis and Arok Wolvengrey.

OTHER TITLES: I come from a long time back

NAMES: Rockthunder, Mary Louise, author. | Okimāsis, Jean L., 1938- editor, translator. | Wolvengrey, Arok, 1965- editor, translator. | Container of (work): Rockthunder, Mary Louise. kayās nōhcīn. | Container of (expression): Rockthunder, Mary Louise. kayās nōhcīn. English.

DESCRIPTION: Series statement: Our own words ; 1 | Syllabics in title could not be transcribed. | Text in nēhiyawēwin (Cree) syllabics, nēhiyawēwin (Cree) roman orthography, and in English translation.

IDENTIFIERS: Canadiana (print) 20210308729 | Canadiana (ebook) 20210309091 | ISBN 9780889778375 (hardcover) | ISBN 9780889778368 (softcover) | ISBN 9780889778382 (PDF) | ISBN 9780889778399 (EPUB)

SUBJECTS: LCSH: Rockthunder, Mary Louise. | LCSH: Cree language—Texts. | CSH: First Nations women—Saskatchewan—Biography. | CSH: First Nations—Saskatchewan—Biography. | CSH: First Nations—Saskatchewan—Social life and customs. | LCGFT: Autobiographies.

CLASSIFICATION: LCC E99.C88 R6313 2021 | DDC 971.24/400497323—dc23

University of Regina Press

University of Regina, Regina, Saskatchewan, Canada, S4S 0A2
TEL: (306) 585-4758 FAX: (306) 585-4699
WEB: www.uofrpress.ca

We acknowledge the support of the Canada Council for the Arts for our publishing program. We acknowledge the financial support of the Government of Canada. / Nous reconnaissons l'appui financier du gouvernement du Canada. This publication was made possible with support from Creative Saskatchewan's Book Publishing Production Grant Program.

Canada Council for the Arts | Conseil des arts du Canada
Canada
creative SASKATCHEWAN

Contents

kayās nōhcīn
I Come from a Long Time Back

Preface and Acknowledgements

A funny thing happened on the way to the completion of this book. Many funny things, actually, as you will read in some of the texts herein. But also some more serious. Not least of these is the long delay in getting this volume out to honour the life and memory of a beautiful woman and storyteller. Of course, it began with Mary Louise Rockthunder a long time back, but many others have helped on the journey to bring her stories back for all of us to share, and we wish to thank and acknowledge everyone who shared this journey.

The first recording was made a quarter of a century (!) ago now, and was facilitated through Jean's introduction to Mary Louise by Doreen Oakes of Nekaneet First Nation. Doreen, as a graduate of the Education program at the Saskatchewan Indian Federated College (now First Nations University (FNUniv)), was just beginning her own Cree teaching career, and she participated in that first recording at Mary Louise's home at Piapot (see chapters 1 and 2). Following this, sections of this book were recorded on three more occasions: once in our home (see chapter 6), once again at Mary Louise's home (see chapter 5), and once at a Language

Teachers' Workshop hosted by the Saskatchewan Cree Language Retention Committee (see chapters 3 and 4). We are grateful to all who participated at this latter event, especially our long-serving colleagues on that committee, all of whom inspired so much work towards Cree language revitalization in each other and in us. We could name names, but we would undoubtedly forget someone and regret it forever. We (*niyanān*) know who we (*kiyānaw*) are and the memories are beautiful.

The last of the recordings was made in 2002, and work on the transcription and translation of the texts continued to progress until Mary Louise's passing in 2004. That is perhaps the best and the worst explanation for the many delays that beset the work for the next fifteen years. Work did continue intermittently, bringing the basic transcription to near completion, but many other projects came and went in the meantime. Finally, in 2018–2019, during a sabbatical from teaching granted to Arok from FNUniv, we were able to return to the manuscript in earnest and prioritize its completion. Arok would particularly like to thank Jean for her indulgence in spending a four-month research period at the University of Amsterdam, where we nevertheless made considerable progress towards completing the translations and began work on the final organization of the book.

Still, much work remained when teaching duties resumed in 2019, so it is perhaps one of the few positive aspects of the isolation imposed during the "summer of Covid" (2020) that we were able to concentrate fully on bringing the manuscript to a form that we could finally submit for publication. Jean would particularly like to thank Arok for the work on the Syllabics section — something essential in a book by and for Mary Louise — and the Cree-English Glossary. These features of the final book follow those established in the Cree text publications of Freda Ahenakew and H.C. Wolfart, and we can never adequately express our gratitude for their monumental contributions.

Though the manuscript was essentially complete by this point, there were still some unresolved questions and the need for expert eyes on the Cree sections, and we have two additional people to thank for their knowledge. Our friend and colleague Solomon Ratt proofread the entire manuscript thoroughly and paid special attention to the synchronization of the Syllabics and roman orthography sections. Elder Barry Ahenakew helped to identify certain vocabulary, *ispi-nēhiyawēwin* (high Cree), and plant names that would otherwise have remained obscure to us. We are extremely grateful to both Solomon and Barry for their help. Any remaining issues are entirely our own responsibility and we can only hope that we have done all we can to accurately represent Mary Louise's words.

We also have several people, not to mention the entire organization, to thank once the manuscript was submitted to the University of Regina Press (URP). We are grateful to Karen Clark, Kelly Laycock, David McLennan, Donna Grant and Duncan Campbell for all the encouragement and technical work of prepping a book for publication. Donna and Kelly in particular went through the manuscript meticulously, smoothing out our English and further synchronizing the three main sections of the book — no mean feat that. Duncan Campbell is owed much gratitude for his patience with us and for once again coming through with a beautiful cover design, highlighting our beautiful Elder. The URP in general continues to be tremendously supportive of Indigenous Language publications, including a growing number of language textbooks, the First Nations Language Readers series, and now, the Our Own Words series. It is an honour to have this book as the first volume within this new series of larger Indigenous language texts.

Finally, we wish to express our gratitude to the family of Mary Louise Rockthunder, for sharing their wonderful mother, *kōhkom*, and *cāpān* with us, and their patience in awaiting this book.

We are particularly grateful to Mary Louise's eldest surviving daughter, Margaret Rockthunder, for conversations about her mother's legacy, Margaret's son Jeff Cappo for confirmation of family contacts, and to Mary Louise's two other surviving daughters, Barbara Borkowski and Marie Smith, and grandson Lorne Rockthunder, for their encouragement and support of this project. We dedicate this book to all Mary Louise's children, grandchildren, great-grandchildren, and generations to come. We are sure they will all join us in extending our most heartfelt thanks to our beloved Elder, *wēpanākit*.

mistahi kinanāskomitinān, Mary Louise.
kākikē ka-kiskisitotātinān.

Jean Okimāsis *ēkwa* Arok Wolvengrey
opāskāwēhowi-pīsim, 2021

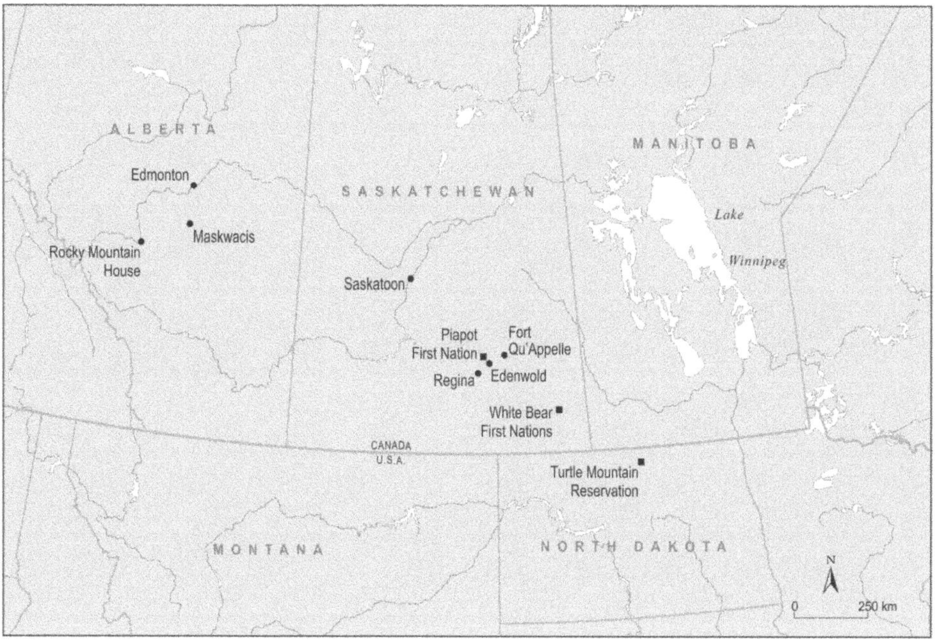

Locations mentioned in Mary Louise Rockthunder's narration.

Introduction

otācimow / The Narrator

Mary Louise Rockthunder (née Bangs), *wēpanākit*, was an Elder of Cree, Saulteaux, and Nakoda (Assiniboine) descent, born, raised, and married at *nēhiyawipwātināhk* / Piapot First Nation. She was born on October 16, 1913, and left for the spirit world over ninety years later, on July 2, 2004. She spoke with respect for her parents, grandparents, and her great-grandfather, and she had many children, grandchildren, and great-grandchildren, all of whom she spoke of so proudly. A partial family tree, highlighting those mentioned in her narratives, is provided on the following page as Figure 1.

Mary Louise also had a long lifetime of experiences, which she shared as a consummate and much-loved storyteller. Jean had the privilege of meeting and getting to know her in the last decade of her life, and she shared her memories, stories, and knowledge with Jean, and with her colleagues in Cree language education, revealing her personal humility and her deep love and respect for her family and her Cree language and culture. What might seem an odd omission in the family tree illustrates her deep respect for her mother, who, following Cree tradition, she never refers to by name.

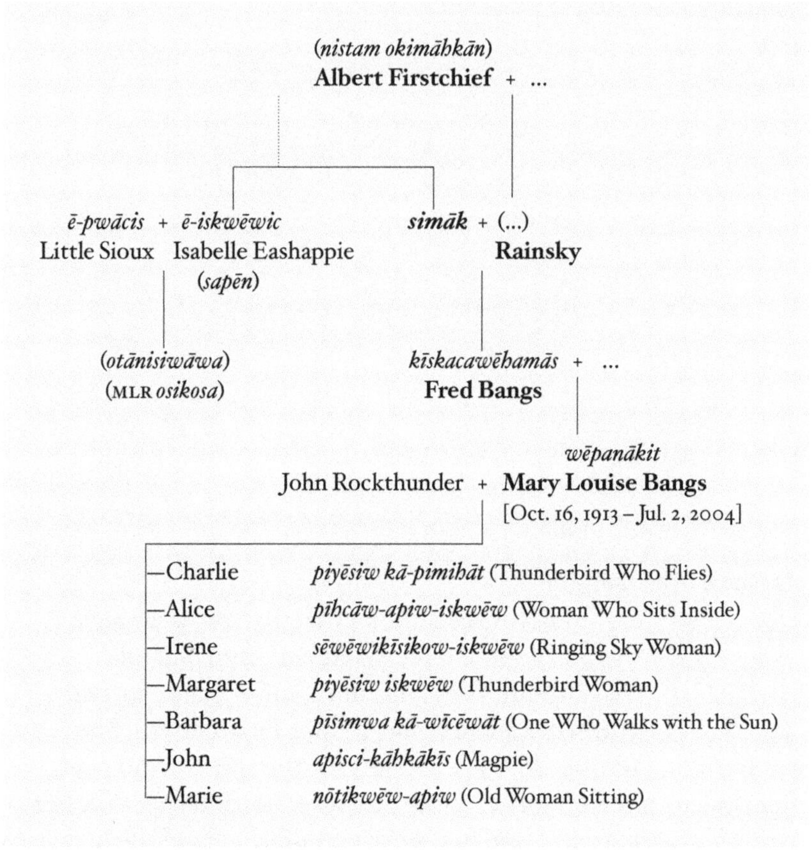

FIGURE 1: Immediate family of Mary Louise as referenced in the texts

Mary Louise was an amazing Elder who, even in her eighties, was filled with vigour and remarkably clear memories of her life as a child and young woman as she dutifully supported her parents, and as an adult with a grown family of her own, living and working in Regina in the 1960s and '70s. Her memories often included the precise dates, days of the week, and even the time of day or hour of the clock when events in her life occurred. She was so precise, it seemed that she stored her diary in her mind. Yes, she had her good memories and some sad ones as well, but she preferred to remember and speak of the good, as she had been instructed by her father. And to be sure, she delighted most in making her family and wider audience laugh, imparting many hilarious escapades from her own life, making fun of herself but disparaging no-one else. It is our privilege to help make these narratives and teachings available to a new audience and to let the reader share in Mary Louise's life, laughter, and language.

kā-itācimot / The Narration

Mary Louise was recorded on four separate occasions, resulting in the six texts included in this collection. Each session was preceded by the appropriate protocol and offering of tobacco. Within these texts, you will occasionally encounter references to aspects of Cree spirituality and ceremonies. It is not appropriate for the editors of this book to provide explanation of these matters beyond those offered by Mary Louise herself. Those who are inspired to learn more are welcome to bring their questions to appropriate elders following culturally acceptable protocols.

Recording Session 1: May 10, 1995

On this day, Jean Okimāsis and Doreen Oakes visited Mary Louise at her home at Piapot Reserve. The two sides of the 120-minute cassette tape that was recorded that day constitute the two large texts that begin this collection, which we have titled:

1. **kayās ēkwa anohc / Long Ago and Today**, and
2. **nēhiyawiskwēw opimohtēhowin / A Cree Woman's Life.**

We have also divided each of these texts into numerous topical subsections, with appropriate subheadings assigned by the editors. In some cases, there are minor breaks or pauses in the recording that led to natural section breaks, but at other times new sections have been introduced editorially where Mary Louise transitioned seamlessly between topics.

As with most of the texts in this collection, the first text, **kayās ēkwa anohc**, is almost exclusively Mary Louise's narration, with very little input from others present during the recording.

In order to detract as little as possible from the presentation, even those instances of backchannel agreement evident on the recording (e.g., āha, yes, oh, etc.) have largely been omitted from this text. The sole exceptions occur when the interaction has an obvious impact on the narration itself, and those are indeed very few on the first side of the cassette recorded on May 10, 1995. Otherwise, the only common editorial intrusions evident are the (very) occasional indications of [*pāhpināniwan / laughter*]. In this first text, there is also a long aside by Mary Louise herself. Although an interruption to the main text, it is still important to the text and is presented as an indented block of text with an em dash (—) at the beginning and end of the text block.

The second part of this narration, presented here as the second text, **nēhiyawiskwēw opimohtēhowin**, begins in the midst of narration, due to a recording problem that obscured the initial minutes of the tape. Hence, a small part of the text is missing, although it continues much as the first side ended. As the recording progresses, there are increasing instances of interaction with both Jean and Doreen, identified by the speaker codes JO and DO respectively. Minor backchannel interactions are coded like editorial intrusions (see also the Note on Editorial Insertions on page xxvii). More extensive interactions are represented by including speech from Jean and Doreen indented within the text and preceded by the appropriate speaker's code, while Mary Louise's speech remains unindented and usually unmarked by the speaker code MLR (except when her responses are themselves backchannel responses to Jean and Doreen). As in the first text, here there are also several instances of longer asides by Mary Louise, each of which, again, is presented as an indented text block with an em dash at the beginning and end.

Recording Session 2: November 23, 1997

On this date, Mary Louise was a visitor in the home of Jean Okimāsis. In addition to an enjoyable social visit, Mary Louise answered Jean's questions, expanding on a topic that was touched upon in the earlier recording of May 10, 1995 (see text 2, section 4), the traditional use of plants. This recording forms the final text presented in this collection:

6 **ocēpihkwa, maskihkiya ēkwa mīnisa / Roots, Herbs, and Berries**

Editorially, we have chosen to present this text last because of two features of the text itself.

First, this text is somewhat different from the other texts in this collection, as it much more closely approaches a conversational tone rather than straight narration. In this text, Jean poses a series of questions about the traditional uses of various plants, sometimes including follow-up questions and answers. As such, the speech of both Jean [JO] and Mary Louise [MLR] are coded with appropriate speaker codes throughout their interaction.

Second, and most importantly from our standpoint, is the beautiful way that Mary Louise ended the recording. She simply provides a most fitting way to conclude the entire collection, and one that never ceases to evoke our most heartfelt memories of our much loved Elder.

Recording Session 3: March 23, 2001

On this day, the Cree Language Retention Committee (CLRC) organized a Language Teachers' Workshop in Saskatoon. We had the privilege of driving Mary Louise to this workshop, where she participated as an Elder sharing both sacred stories (*ātayōhkēwina*) and humorous, autobiographical episodes (*wawiyatācimisowinisa*). We present the two main recordings here as:

3 **cahkatahikēwin / Bingo**

4 **kā-ātayōhkēhk / Telling a Sacred Story**

In the third text, Mary Louise provides her audience with a much elaborated version of an episode that she refers to briefly in the second text (see text 2, section 1), as well as restating the context of her coming to work in Regina, where she would first discover her love for bingo (see text 1, section 9).

In the fourth text, she provides a wonderful introduction to the genre of *ātayōhkēwina* (sacred stories), and provides an example that was touched upon in her earlier discussion of traditional plants, specifically *okiniyak* (rosehips; see text 2, section 4). Telling this story to her Cree audience at the workshop was appropriate, as there was still snow on the ground, something which she had avoided six years earlier in May, when the story could not be told. The *ātayōhkēwin* itself was previously published as a separate chapter in *wawiyatācimowinisa / Funny Little Stories* (Wolvengrey, ed. 2007). It is presented again here, but now within the fuller context of Mary Louise's experiences of hearing the stories told in a traditional setting and her introduction of the main character (who we will not name, as we write this in summer).

Recording Session 4: February 22, 2002

The final recording that Mary Louise shared with Jean was made the year following the CLRC workshop. In all of her shared teachings and stories, one topic area that had not fully been touched upon was her knowledge of traditional Cree cultural activities, customs, and sayings. For this reason, Jean once again visited Mary Louise at her home to record a series of texts on a variety of topics. These are presented together here as the fifth text:

5 nēhiyaw-isīhcikēwina / Cree Customs

The first of the four sections of this text and recording begins with Mary Louise offering a more formal prayer (*kākīsimowin*) for guidance in the proper conduct of the teachings to be offered, and this is followed immediately by her discussion of the Thirst Dance (*nipākwēsimowin*; also sometimes referred to as both a Sundance or a Raindance) as well as the ceremony's concluding sweatlodge (*matotisān*). The next two parts of the recording give details of Cree funerary rites (*awiyak kā-nahiniht*), also indicating the loss of certain activities in more modern times. Further details on this are included in the final section of this text, where Mary Louise also discusses some additional features of Cree life (*nēhiyawātisiwin*), most prominently a young woman's coming of age (*kīsiskwēwiwin*) and the importance of good relations (*miyo-wīcēhtowin*).

ācimowina / The Texts

Beyond this short introduction, this book follows the format established in a number of the Cree text collections compiled by Freda Ahenakew and H.C. Wolfart (e.g., Whitecalf 1993, Kâ-Nîpitêhtêw 1998). It consists of three main sections. First, all of the texts are presented in Cree Syllabics, themselves very important to Mary Louise, as she describes in text 2, section 2. The second section presents each text in both Cree in the standard roman orthography (SRO, or standard Cree alphabet) and English translation on facing pages. A final section provides a glossary of all Cree vocabulary found within the texts. Features of these three sections are briefly introduced below.

1) Syllabics

The Cree Syllabary or "Syllabics" is a very important writing system that differs considerably from the alphabetic system that English readers are familiar with. Instead of necessarily representing each individual consonant or vowel with a separate symbol, a syllabary in general consists of symbols that represent the possible syllables of a language, at least minimally the inventory of possible combinations of consonant and vowel together (e.g., ᐯ = pē, ᑎ = ti, ᑯ = ko, ᒐ = ca, etc.). As Mary Louise describes in text 2, section 2, her father taught her the use of the Cree syllabary in a matter of two evenings and she was well practised in their use.

The system of Syllabics in use in this book differs slightly from that used by most literate elders, and the main difference is illustrated in comparing the two Syllabic charts offered here as Figures 2 and 3 on the following two pages. In Figure 2, the basic symbols are displayed in the traditional order that Mary Louise herself gives, in four main columns corresponding to the four basic

	ē	i	o	a	Finals
	ᐁ	ᐃ	ᐅ	ᐊ	ᐦ ᕽ h hk
w	ᐍ	ᐏ	ᐓ	ᐘ	ᐤ
p	ᐯ	ᐱ	ᐳ	ᐸ	ᑊ
t	ᑌ	ᑎ	ᑐ	ᑕ	ᐟ
k	ᑫ	ᑭ	ᑯ	ᑲ	ᐠ
c	ᒉ	ᒋ	ᒍ	ᒐ	ᐨ
m	ᒣ	ᒥ	ᒧ	ᒪ	ᒼ
n	ᓀ	ᓂ	ᓄ	ᓇ	ᐣ
s	ᓭ	ᓯ	ᓱ	ᓴ	ᐢ
y	ᔦ	ᔨ	ᔪ	ᔭ	ᐩ

FIGURE 2: Traditional Western Cree Syllabics

	ē	i	ī	o	ō	a	ā	Finals
	ᐁ	ᐃ	ᐄ	ᐅ	ᐆ	ᐊ	ᐋ	ᐦ ᕽ h hk
w	ᐌ	ᐎ	ᐐ	ᐒ	ᐔ	ᐗ	ᐙ	ᐤ
p	ᐯ	ᐱ	ᐲ	ᐳ	ᐴ	ᐸ	ᐹ	ᑊ
t	ᑌ	ᑎ	ᑏ	ᑐ	ᑑ	ᑕ	ᑖ	ᐟ
k	ᑫ	ᑭ	ᑮ	ᑯ	ᑰ	ᑲ	ᑳ	ᐠ
c	ᒉ	ᒋ	ᒌ	ᒍ	ᒎ	ᒐ	ᒑ	ᐨ
m	ᒣ	ᒥ	ᒦ	ᒧ	ᒨ	ᒪ	ᒫ	ᒼ
n	ᓀ	ᓂ	ᓃ	ᓄ	ᓅ	ᓇ	ᓈ	ᐣ
s	ᓭ	ᓯ	ᓰ	ᓱ	ᓲ	ᓴ	ᓵ	ᐢ
y	ᔦ	ᔨ	ᔩ	ᔪ	ᔫ	ᔭ	ᔮ	ᐩ

FIGURE 3: Pointed Western Syllabics

vowel qualities of *nēhiyawēwin* / Plains Cree. To read the chart, each symbol corresponds to the combination of the consonant at the head of its row, and the vowel at the top of its column (e.g., ᑌ occurs in the ***t*** row under ***ē*** vowel, and therefore ᑌ = tē).

The Plains Cree sound system actually utilizes seven distinct vowels, but for three of the basic vowels listed in Figure 2 there is a difference of vowel length between short (i, o, a) and long (ī, ō, ā) vowels. However, for fluent Cree elders, this distinction (along with the occurrence of the special "final" symbol for ***h*** (ᐦ)) is rarely marked.

As in the SRO, this distinction of vowel length can certainly be marked in Syllabics — by adding an overposed dot to the basic symbol (e.g., ᐃ = i; ᐄ = ī) — as is shown in Figure 3. This seems to expand the chart considerably, but really only adds the possibility of marking all vowels as long (with the exception of ***ē*** (ᐁ), which is always long but never marked as such in Syllabics). A similar expansion of the chart could be made for each consonantal row to indicate that adding a dot after the basic symbol marks a ***w*** sound before the vowel (e.g., ᐊ = a, ᐘ = wa; ᐯ = pē, ᐻ = pwē; ᑖ = tā, ᑤ = twā, etc.).

The Syllabics found in the texts follow the full "pointed" system of Figure 3 (on the previous page), marking the important distinction of vowel length. Though this would not have been necessary for a fluent speaker like Mary Louise, it is useful both for learners of Cree and for speakers who are just learning Syllabics themselves, as many of the readers of this book will be.

Additionally, punctuation marks utilized in the Cree SRO texts are largely matched in the Syllabics, as this too can be useful for indicating naturally occurring breaks and intonational rises and falls that would not otherwise be represented in syllabic or alphabetic writing systems. The two main differences you will find between English punctuation and that in use in the Syllabics section, are 1) the occurrence of a small x for the period, and 2) the use of French guillemets « » for quotation marks.

The preparation of the Syllabics section of this book has been greatly facilitated by the online Syllabics conversion tool and "Syllabics App" (https://syllabics.app/) created by Eddie Santos as part of the 21st Century Tools for Indigenous Languages research project. This project includes partners at First Nations University of Canada, the University of Alberta, and Carleton University, among other institutions, as well as community partners, most prominently at Maskwacis [formerly Hobbema], Alberta. The Maskwacīs Education Schools Commission and the four communities that make up the Maskwacīs Cree Tribal Council are strong proponents of Cree language education and the use of Cree Syllabics. As found in her narrative, Mary Louise had strong family and cultural ties to the Maskwacīs community.

2) Cree SRO and English Translation

The second main section of this book presents Mary Louise's texts in both standard roman orthography (SRO, or the standard Cree alphabetic writing system) and English translation. These are on facing pages for ease of reference for learners. Again, this has been a common practice in Indigenous language text publications, particularly those of Freda Ahenakew and H.C. Wolfart (e.g., Vandall and Douquette 1987, Bear et al. 1998, etc.) after whose work this volume is modelled (as are the University of Regina Press's First Nations Language Reader series and Our Own Words series).

Each chapter is preceded by a title page that includes comments specific to that text, but see above for more details on the circumstances of the recording of each text. As the texts presented here were recorded directly from spoken narrative, attempts have been made to retain many of the features of that narration. This means that false starts are generally included and an additional punctuation marker, the tilde (~), is used to indicate when Mary Louise breaks off a word or hesitates during her narration.

Another feature of fluent speech is the process of "sandhi." A common example of sandhi in Cree speech is the contraction of adjacent vowels within compound words or across word boundaries. This process is abundant in Mary Louise's speech and a great many examples can be found within the texts.

When vowels contract, there are several common patterns, the most important of which are illustrated by the examples in Figure 4 on the following page. Generally, two like short vowels combine to a single long vowel (e.g., /a + a/ > [ā]), while two dissimilar short vowels tend to merge into a long vowel of the quality of the second vowel (e.g., /i + a/ > [ā]). If the second vowel is already long, it will often subsume the preceding short vowel (e.g., /a + ō/ > [ō]) as if the short vowel is simply dropped (with fewer such examples included in the chart for brevity). Contractions involving an initial short /o/ usually retain a [w] before the resulting long vowel (e.g., /o + a/ > [w ā]) unless it is subsumed in a long [ō] (e.g., /o + o/ > [ō]). Two long vowels do not generally contract at all. None of the contractions are in fact obligatory, so examples of both contracted and uncontracted vowel combinations are common in the texts. Sometimes, instead of vowel sandhi, vowels are separated by an inserted [y], [h], or [w] (depending on the vowels involved; e.g., kēhtē-aya > kēhtē[h]aya or kēhtē[y]aya). However, this is generally left unmarked in the SRO.

Finally, a very prominent instance of contraction occurs which can obscure an important grammatical distinction. Either the preverb *ka-* or, exceptionally, the preverb *kā-*, can contract with a following short /o/ or long /ō/. In all cases, /ka-o.../, /kā-o.../ /ka-ō.../ and /kā-ō.../ can and frequently do contract to a form that is pronounced as [kō] and thus represented in the text as *k-ō...* (e.g., ka-ohpikicik > k-ōhpikicik; kā-ōh-tōtamān > k-ōh-tōtamān). The meaning context alone will determine whether *ka-* or *kā-* was intended.

The representation of these two features — hesitations and sandhi — are presented somewhat differently in the Syllabics section, where most false starts and virtually all sandhi have been removed for the benefit of a smoother albeit fuller representation for readers of Syllabics. There are a couple of exceptions that can

VOWEL SANDHI	UNCONTRACTED EXAMPLES	RESULT OF SANDHI
a + a > **ā**	awa ayi	aw **ā**yi
	anima ayi	anim **ā**yi
	ōma ayis	ōm **ā**yis
a + i > **ī**	awa iskwēw	aw **ī**skwēw
	ōma itē	ōm **ī**tē
	awa itwēw	aw **ī**twēw
	ōma iyikohk	ōm **ī**yikohk
a + o > **ō**	ōma ohci	ōm **ō**hci
	anima ocēpihk	anim **ō**cēpihk
a + ē > **ē**	ōma ēkwa	ōm **ē**kwa
a + ō > **ō**	ōma ōta	ōm **ō**ta
	ōma ōtē	ōm **ō**tē
i + a > ā	anihi ayi	anih **ā**yi
	ēkosi anima	ēkos **ā**nima
	ē-ati-ayāt	ē-at-**ā**yāt
i + i > ī	ēkosi isi	ēkos **ī**si
	aniki iskwēwak	anik **ī**skwēwak
	nitati-itēyihtēn	nitat-**ī**tēyihtēn
i + o > ō	ati-otinam	at-**ō**tinam
i + ā > ā	kā-ati-ākwā-pipohk	kā-at-**ā**kwā-pipohk
i + ē > ē	ēkosi ē-kī-...	ēkos **ē**-kī-...
o + a > **w ā**	ēwako anima	ēwak**w** **ā**nima
	piko awiyak	pik**w** **ā**wiyak
	miyo-ayāwak	miy**w**-**ā**yāwak
	nīso-askiy	nīs**w**-**ā**skiy
o + i > **w ī**	piko ispīhk	pik**w** **ī**spīhk
	piko itē	pik**w** **ī**tē
o + o > **ō**	ēwako ohci	ēwak **ō**hci
	nimiyo-ohpikihāwak	nimiy-**ō**hpikihāwak
o + ē > **w ē**	ēwako ēkwa	ēwak**w** **ē**kwa
o + ō > **ō**	ēwako ōma	ēwak **ō**ma

FIGURE 4: Sandhi (Vowel Contraction) in the Texts

be mentioned here. First, a hesitation is generally only retained in the Syllabics text when it is obviously different from what follows (i.e., the word is not simply restarted and completed, but replaced by something quite different). In such instances the tilde (~) is introduced as extra punctuation even within the Syllabics texts to mark the hesitation. Similar in both texts, though, is the use of the tilde (~) to also indicate when one speaker's speech is interrupted by another. Second, although most sandhi is undone and the vowels represented in full in the Syllabics text (e.g., ᐁᐊᐧᑯ ᐊᓇ = *ēwako ana*, even when the SRO text records *ēwakw āna*), the aforementioned occurrence of *k-ō...* is represented simply as ᑰ ([kō]) in Syllabics, since the entire point of this writing system is to represent full syllable combinations of consonant and vowel together, not to separate consonants from following vowels.

3) Cree-English Glossary

The final section of this volume is a Cree-to-English glossary or word list containing all the nouns, verbs, particles, and pronouns found within the Cree texts, with accompanying word class and translation. The form of this glossary again closely follows Wolfart and Ahenakew's (1987) lead. As such, the glossary includes Cree entries listed in their base or stem form (as indicated with verbs, nouns, preverbs, and prenouns by a following hyphen; e.g., *wāpam-* VTA; *pōni-* IPV), and these stems may or may not match the actual spoken form of a full word recognized by a fluent speaker and as produced in the context of Mary Louise's texts. This is particularly the case with many kinship terms and body parts, which, as "bound stems," are listed at the beginning of the glossary in their uninflected stem forms (e.g., *-kāwiy-* NDA2 "mother"). Such stems will never be found in such a bare state in spoken Cree, but must always occur with one or another person-marking or possessive prefix (e.g., *nikāwiy* "my mother," *kikāwiy* "your mother," etc.).

To a certain extent, then, it is unavoidable with this type of glossary that some knowledge of Cree grammar is required to find the parts of words isolated in the entries. It is simply a fact of the structure of the Cree language that a single noun or verb can occur in a great variety of forms, each of which would fill one or more pages. However, all of these grammatically predictable forms are not typically entered into a print dictionary or glossary as traditionally understood. It is fortunate then that today we have begun to see the development of smart dictionaries that not only recognize the basic forms of nouns or verbs, et cetera, but can also analyze all their inflected forms and point learners to the correct stem. The *itwēwina* dictionary, developed as part of our colleague Dr. Antti Arppe's "21st Century Tools for Indigenous Languages" research partnership is an example of this type of advanced online dictionary (https://itwewina.altlab.app/), and it can help learners to understand the various parts of complex words, such as many found within these texts. Additional helpful resources are listed at the beginning of the glossary itself.

References

Print

Bear, Glecia, et al. 1998. *kôhkominawak otâcimowiniwâwa / Our Grandmothers' Lives as Told in Their Own Words.* Edited by Freda Ahenakew and H.C Wolfart. Regina: Canadian Plains Research Center.

Kâ-Nîpitêhtêw, Jim. 1998. *ana kâ-pimwêwêhahk okakêskihkêmowina / The Counselling Speeches of Jim Kâ-Nîpitêhtêw*. Edited by Freda Ahenakew and H.C Wolfart. Winnipeg: University of Manitoba Press.

Vandall, Peter, and Joe Douquette. 1987. *wâskahikaniwiyiniw-âcimowina / Stories of the House People*. Edited by Freda Ahenakew. Winnipeg: University of Manitoba Press.

Whitecalf, Sarah. 1993. *kinêhiyâwiwininaw nêhiyawêwin / The Cree Language Is Our Identity*. Edited by H.C. Wolfart and Freda Ahenakew. Winnipeg: University of Manitoba Press.

Wolfart, H.C., and Freda Ahenakew. 1987. "Notes on the Orthography and the Glossary." 113–125 in Freda Ahenakew, ed., *wâskahikaniwiyiniw-âcimowina / Stories of the House People*. Winnipeg: University of Manitoba Press.

Wolvengrey, Arok, ed. 2007. *wawiyatācimowinisa / Funny Little Stories*. Regina: University of Regina Press.

Online

Syllabics App. https://syllabics.app/

The *itwēwina* Online Dictionary. https://itwewina.altlab.app/

A Note on Editorial Insertions in the Texts

Readers will find a number of editorial insertions in the texts that follow; all editorial insertions are in square brackets. Following is a summary of the various kinds of editorial insertions found in the three sections of the book — the Cree Syllabics, the SRO transcriptions, and the English translations — along with examples of each and some information about the particulars of formatting. We begin with the English translation section, since most of the editorial insertions occur in this section.

In the English translations:

1. Subheadings assigned by the editors, which divide the texts into numerous topical subsections (described above in the Introduction).

2. Editorial explanations of particular words or phrases in the narrative

e.g. ...as he peeled these eyes of mine [i.e., he removed cataracts from my eyes] ...

...when our Grandfather had disappeared [i.e., when the Sun set] ...

3. Translation of Cree terms

e.g. *mistaskosīmina* ["big-grass-berries"]

wēpināsona [ceremonial cloths]

4. Corrections

e.g. He was from Turtle Mountain, Monta-- [North Dakota], oh, my father was from over there in the States.

5. Missing words

e.g. There were perhaps twelve [cans] in each box ...

... they take me and we go to midnight [mass] ...

6. Parts of the audio recording that are not part of the narrative proper, including pauses in the recording, responses from Mary Louise's listeners, external interruptions to the narrative, minor asides by Mary Louise herself, non-verbal aspects of the interactions between Mary Louise and her listeners, and occasional instances when words are inaudible and therefore untranscribable. *These are always in a smaller font*, in order to draw attention to the fact that they are outside the narrative. In these insertions, speakers are identified with their initials and their words are in quotes, while descriptions are in italics.

e.g. [*pause in recording*]

[*laughter*]

[*A telephone rings.* MLR: *"Take it."*]

Oh my, they did taste good though.
[JO: *"Marshmallows?"*]

We sewed upstairs — [*aside,* MLR: *"If you want to drink coffee…"*] — we sewed.

… they do like this [*MLR gestures*].

Ah, hold on. [*the sound of rustling papers*] I guess that's it.

This is our [*inaudible*], like when there is a Thirst Dance …

In the Cree SRO transcriptions:

1. Subheadings (described above under English translations and in the Introduction)

2. Editorial explanations

e.g. ōm ōhci, *you know*, kā-is-āyān [otēh ē-itahk, *pacemaker*]

3. Corrections and/or Standardizations

e.g. kitapahikan [*sic*: kitipahikan]

[ni]nihtā-ayamihcikān

4. Parts of the audio recording that are not part of the narrative proper (described above under English translations)

e.g. [*aciyaw ē-nakipitamihk*]

[*pāhpināniwan*]

In the Cree Syllabics:

1. Subheadings (described above under English translations and in the Introduction)

2. Editorial explanations

e.g. *Agency at the Fort* [ᑭᐸᐦᐃᑲᓂᕽ]

3. Corrections and/or Standardizations

e.g. ᑭᑕᐸᐦᐃᑲᐤ [*sic:* ᑭᑎᐸᐦᐃᑲᐤ]

4. Parts of the audio recording that are not part of the narrative proper (described above under English translations)

e.g. [ᐊᒋᔭᐤ ᐁ ᓇᑭᐱᑕᒥᕽ]

[ᐹᐦᐱᓈᓂᐘᐤ]

[ᒪᑘ ᓭᐍᐱᒋᐸᔨᐤ]

ᑲᒫᐣ ᐧᒑᐦᒌᑐ

1
ᑲᔮᐢ ᐁᑲᐧ ᐊᓄᐦᐨ

ᐦᐋᐤ, ᐊᓄᐦᐨ ᑳ ᑮᓯᑳᐠ, ᓅᓯᓯᒪᐠ ᐆᑕ ᐁ ᐯ ᑲᑫᐧᒋᒥᒋᐠ, ᓂᔭ, *Mary Louise Rockthunder*᙮ ᐊᓄᐦᐨ ᑳ ᑮᓯᑳᐠ ᒫᑲ, ᐁ ᒥᔦᐧᔨᐦᑕᒫᕽ ᐁ ᐚᐸᐦᑕᒫᕽ ᐁ ᒥᔽᓯᐠ ᐁ ᐄᐧ ᐊᐢᑭᐦᑕᑲᐧᐢᑲᒥᑳᐠ, ᐁ ᐄᐧ ᓅᐱᓂᓯᔮᕽ ᑳᓂᑲᓈ ᓅᓯᓯᒥᓈᓂᐠ, ᓂᑕᐚᐧᓯᓯᒥᓈᓂᐠ ᑫᐧᔭᐢᐠ ᑲ ᐅᐦᐱᑭᒋᐠ, ᐁᑳᐩ ᑮᑲᐧᐩ ᑕᒫᔮᑕᕽ ᐆᑌ ᑫ ᓃᑳᓃᔨᐠ᙮ ᐁᑯᓯ ᐁ ᐱᒥ ᐃᓯ ᓂᑐᑕᒫᐣ ᐊᓄᐦᐨ᙮ ᓂᑕᐚᐧᓯᒥᓴᐠ ᐆᑕ ᐁ ᑲᑫᐧᒋᒥᒋᐠ ᐆᑕ ᓀᐦᐃᔭᐃᐧᐹᐧᑎᓈᕽ ᐊᔨᐢᐠ ᐆᒪ ᐁ ᐅᐦᒌᔮᐣ ᐆᑕ ᑳ ᐹᐦ ᐲᑭᐢᑫᐧᔮᐣ ᑳ ᐄᐧ ᐋᒋᒧᐢᑕᐊᐧᑭᐠ ᐆᑭ᙮

[1. ᓂᐚᐦᑰᒪᑲᓇᐠ]

ᑲᔮᐢ, ᓅᐦᑖᐃᐧᐩ, ᑮᐢᑲᒐᐁᐧᐦᐋᒫᐢ ᑮ ᐃᓯᔨᐦᑳᓱᐤ ᐁᑲᐧ ᓃᐢᑕ *Mary Louise Bangs* ᓂᑮ ᐃᓯᔨᐦᑳᓱᐣ᙮ ᐁᑯᓯ ᓂᑮ ᓀᐃᐧᓈᐣ ᓂᒥᓴᐠ, ᓂᐢᑐ ᓂᑮ ᐊᐧᓂᐦᐋᐊᐧᐠ, ᓂᔭ ᐱᑯ ᐁ ᐱᒫᑎᓯᔮᐣ᙮ ᓂᑮ ᓃᐢᑎᓈᐣ ᓅᐦᑖᐃᐧᐩ ᐁᑲᐧ ᓂᔭ ᐁᑲᐧ ᓂᑳᐃᐧᐩ, ᓇᒨᔭ ᐅᐦᒋ ᐚᐱᐤ ᓂᑳᐃᐧᐩ, ᓂᑮ ᐸᒉᔨᒫᐤ ᓂᑳᐃᐧᐩ, ᓂᑮ ᐸᒥᐦᐋᐤ᙮ ᓇᒨᔭ ᓅᐦ ᐃᑐᐦᑖᐣ ᑭᐢᑭᓇᐧᐦᐋᒫᑐᐃᐧᑲᒥᑯᕽ; ᓂᑮ ᐃᑐᐦᑖᐣ ᐊᔦᓈᓀᐤ ᐁ ᐃᑕᐦᑐᐱᐳᓀᔮᐣ, ᒫᑲ ᓅᐦᑖᐃᐧᐩ, ᒨᐩ ᐅᐦᒋ ᓂᑕᐁᐧᔨᐦᑕᐨ

ᑕ ᑭᐢᑭᓇᐧᐦᐊᒫᑯᓯᔮᐣ ᓂᑳᐃᐧᐩ ᓈᐊᐧᐩ ᑕᓇᑲᑕᐠ, ᑮ ᐸᑳᐧᑕᑦ ᓅᐦᑖᐃᐧᐩ᙮ ᐁᑯᓯ ᓂᑮ ᐯ ᑮᐋᐧᐣ᙮

ᐦᐋᑦ, ᐊᓄᐦᐨ ᐁᑲᐧ, ᓂᒥᐦᑖᑌᐣ, ᐃᔨᑯᕽ ᒨᓂᔮᐤ ᐃᔨᓂᐤ ᐁᑲᐧ ᐊᓄᐦᐨ, ᑳ ᐄᐧᒋᐦᐃᑯᔮᕽ, ᓇᒪ ᑮᑲᐧᐩ ᓂᔭ ᒥᐢᑕᐦᐃ ᑭᐢᑫᔨᐦᑖᓯᐃᐧᐣ ᓂᑕᔮᐣ, ᐊᐱᓰᐢ ᐱᑯ, ᐁᑕᑕᐤ! ᒫᑲ ᐁᔨᐁᐧᕽ ᓂᐄᐧᒋᐦᐃᓱᐣ, ᓂᐄᐧ ᑲᑫᐧ ᐄᐧᒋᐦᐃᓱᐣ ᑮᑲᐧᐩ᙮ ᐁᑯᓯ, ᐆᑕ ᐁ ᑮ ᑕᓯ ᓂᐦᑖᐃᐧᑭᔮᐣ᙮ ᐁᑯᓯ ᒦᓇ ᓂᒐᐋᐧᓯᒥᓴᐠ ᑲᐦᑭᔮᐤ ᐆᑕ ᐁ ᑕᓯ ᓂᐦᑖᐃᐧᑭᒋᐠ, ᒣᑐᓂ ᓂᓇᓈᐢᑯᒫᐤ ᑰᐦᑖᐄᐧᓇᐤ ᐊᓄᐦᐨ — ᑭᓴᒪᓂᑐᐤ — ᑳ ᑮᓯᑳᐠ᙮ ᑫᑳᐨ ᑲᐦᑭᔮᐤ ᓂᑕᐋᐧᓯᒥᓴᐠ ᐁ ᐅᐦᑎᓂᑫᔮᐣ, ᓃᓯ ᓂᑮ ᐊᐧᓂᐦᐋᐊᐧᐠ ᒫᑲ; ᓃᓯ ᐃᐢᑫᐧᓯᓴᐠ ᓂᑮ ᐊᐧᓂᐦᐋᐊᐧᐠ᙮ ᐊᔦᓈᓀᐤ ~ ᑫᑳ ᒥᑖᑕᐦᐟ ᑕ ᑮ ᐊᔮᐊᐧᑭᐠ ᐊᐋᐧᓯᓴᐠ, ᓃᓯ ᓂᐊᐧᓂᐦᐋᐊᐧᐠ, ᑌᐸᑯᐦᑊ ᐱᒫᑎᓯᐊᐧᐠ, ᓂᔮᓇᐣ ᐃᐢᑫᐧᐊᐧᐠ, ᓃᓯ ᓈᐯᐊᐧᐠ᙮ ᑫᑳᐨ ᒣᑐᓂ ᓂᒥᔪ ᐅᐦᐱᑭᐦᐋᐊᐧᐠ ᓂᑕᐋᐧᓯᒥᓴᐠ, ᓇᒨᔭ ᐁ ᒪᒥᐦᒋᒧᔮᐣ, ᒫᑲ ᐁᑐᑫ ᐁ ᐯ ᓂᑐᐦᑕᐃᐧᒋᐠ ᑖᓂᓯ ᐁ ᐯ ᐃᑌᐧᔮᐣ, ᓂᔭ ᓂᑕᐋᐧᓯᒥᓴᐠ ᐃᐧᔭ ᐁᐊᐧᑯᓂᐠ; ᓇᒨᔭ ᐁ ᓂᑕᐤ~ ᓇᒨᐩ ᓅᓯᓯᒪᐠ ᐆᑭ ᐆᑌ — ᓅᓯᓯᒪᐠ ᓂᓴᐁᐧᔨᒫᐊᐧᐠ, ᒦᓇ ᑲᐦᑭᔮᐤ ᓂᐋᐧᐦᑰᒫᑲᓇᐠ ᓂᓴᐁᐧᔨᒫᐊᐧᐠ᙮

ᐆᒪ ᑫ ᐃᐢᐲᐦᑎᓰᔮᐣ, ᓇᒨᐩ ᐄᐧᐦᑳᐨ ᐊᐃᐧᔭᐠ ᐁ ᐯ ᒫᔨ ᐃᑕᐠ ᐊᐢᐱᐣ ᓂᐯ ᐅᐦᐱᑭᐣ, ᓇᒨᐩ ᐄᐧᐦᑳᐨ ᓂᐯ ᓇ ᓅᑎᓂᑳᐣ ~, ᐁ ᐯ ᐊᐋᐧᓯᓰᐃᐧᔮᐣ ᒦᓇ ᓇᒨᐩ ᐄᐧᐦᑳᐨ ᓅᐦ ᐯ ᓅᑎᓂᑳᐣ᙮ ᐋᐧᐄᐧᐢ ᐁᑲᐧ ᐆᒪ ᐁ ᑫᐦᑌ ᐊᔨᐃᐧᔮᐣ ᓅᐦᑖᐃᐧᐩ ᐁ ᑲᑫᐢᑭᒥᐟ, « ᐁᑳᐩ ᐊᐃᐧᔭᐠ ᒫᔨ ᐄᐧᒣᐤ᙮ ᐱᑮᐧᑕ ᑭᑲ ᐲᐦᑐᑳᐧᐣ ᐁᑳ ᐊᐃᐧᔭᐠ ᒫᔨ ᐄᐧᒣᐊᐧᒋ᙮ ᑲᑫᐧ ᒥᔪ ᐱᒫᑎᓯ, » ᓂᑮ ᐃᑎᐠ ᒫᓇ ᓅᐦᑖᐃᐧᐩ᙮ ᐁᐊᐧᑯ ᓂᓴᑭᓀᐣ ᐊᓄᐦᐨ᙮ ᓇᒨᐩ ᐄᐧᐦᑳᐟ ᓂᒫ~, ᐊᐃᐧᔭᐠ ᓈᓂᑕᐤ ᑳ ᐃᑌᐧᐟ ᓇᒨᐩ ᓂᓅᐦᑌ ᓇ ᓂᑐᐦᑌᐣ, ᓂᑲᓇᐁᐧᔨᐦᑕᒫᓱᐣ᙮ ᒨᔭ ᐄᐧᐦᑳᐨ ᑮᑲᐧᐩ ᓂᑲᑫᐧ ᒫᔨ ᐅᐦᐱᓀᐣ ᐁ ᐄᐧ ᑲᑫᐧ ᒥᔪ ᐱᒫᑎᓯᔮᐣ᙮ ᑮᑲᐧᐩ ᑳ ᐆᐦ ᑑᑕᒫᐣ? ᓂᑕᐋᐧᓯᒥᓴᐠ, ᓅᓯᓯᒪᐠ, ᓂᐋᐧᐦᑰᒫᑲᓇᐠ ᑕ ᑲᑫᐧ~ ᐄᐧᐢᑕᐋᐧᐤ ~ᒥᔪᑌᐦᐁᒋᐠ ᐊᓄᐦᐨ ᑳ ᑮᓯᑳᐠ ᐆᒪ ᑫ ᐃᓯᓈᑲᐧᕽ ᑭᑕᐢᑮᓇᐤ, ᐁ ᐄᐧ ᐊᐢᑭᐦᑕᑲᐧᐢᑲᒥᑳᐠ᙮ ᐦᐋᐤ, ᐊᓄᐦᐨ ᓂᐄᐧ ᐱᒥ ᐋᒋᒧᐣ᙮

ᑲᔮᐢ ᐆᑕ ᐁ ᐅᐦᒌᔮᐣ, ᑲᔮᐢ᙮ ᐁ ᑮ ᓂᐦᑖᐃᐧᑭᔮᐣ, ᓂᑲ ᐄᐧᐦᑌᐣ ᒫᑲ ᓂᑲ ᐋᑲᔮᓰᒧᐣ, *nineteen thirteen* ᐁ ᑮ ᓂᐦᑖᐃᐧᑭᔮᐣ, ᐄᐦ, ᑖᓂᒪᔨᑯᕽ

ᐆᒪ ᒣᑳᐧᐨ ᐁᑐᑫ? ᒣᑐᓂ ᓂᑐᐢᑭᓃᑭᐢᑫᐧᐃᐧᐣ ᐊᓄᐦᐨ᙮ ᒣᑐᓂ ᐁ ᐅᐢᑭᓃᑭᐢᑫᐧᐃᐧᔮᐣ ᐊᓄᐦᐨ ᐆᒪ ᑳ ᑮᓯᑳᐠ᙮ ᑫᔮᐱᐨ ᒫᑲ, ᑫᔮᐱᐨ ᓂᐸᐹᒧᐦᑖᐣ, ᐃᐢᑯ ᐹᐧᑕᐃᐧᐦᑖᔮᓂ ᑕ ᐱᒧᐦᑌᔮᐣ ᐁᑐᑫ ᓂᑲ ᐊᐱᐣ; ᓂᑲ ᐊᐱᐣ ᐁᑐᑫ ᓂᐯᐃᐧᓂᕽ᙮ ᒨᔮ ᐁᑯᑐᐃᐧᕽ ᐁ ᓂᑐᑕᒫᑫᔮᐣ ᒫᐠ~, ᓇᒨᔮ ᐁᑯᑐᐃᐧᕽ ᐁ ᓂᑕᐁᐧᔨᐦᑕᒫᐣ ᐁᑯᓯ ᐃᑕ ᐯᔭᑲᐧᓄᕽ ᑕ ᐊᐱᔮᐣ ᐊᐦᐴ ᐁᑐᑫ ᓂᑲ ᐸᐹᒥᑖᒋᒧᐣ ᑖᓂᓯ ~ [ᐹᐦᐱᓈᓂᐊᐧᐣ] ᐁᑯᓯ᙮

ᐁᑲᐧ ᐆᑕ, ᐆᑕ ᐁ ᑮ ᑕᓯ ᓂᐦᑖᐃᐧᑮᔮᐣ, ᓃᐦᒑᔨᕽ ᐆᒪ ᐆᑕ *down the valley* ᐁ ᑮ ᑕᓯ ᓂᐦᑖᐃᐧᑮᔮᐣ᙮ ᐁᑯᐢᐲᕽ ᑲᔮᐢ *nineteen thirteen, sixteenth of Feb~* ᐋᐦ, ᐋᐦ, ᐋᐦ, *October* ᑳ ᑮ ᓂᐦᑖᐃᐧᑮᔮᐣ, *nineteen thirteen*᙮ ᐃᔨᑯᕽ ᐆᒪ ᐊᓄᐦᐨ ᑳ ᐃᐢᐲᐦᑎᓰᔮᐣ᙮ ᐁᑲᐧ ᑖᓂᓯ ᐁ ᑮ ᐯ ᐃᓯ ᐋᐧᐸᐦᑕᒫᐣ ᐊᓄᐦᐟ ᓅᓯᓯᒪᐠ ᓂᐄᐧ ᐋᒋᒧᐢᑕᐋᐧᐊᐧᐠ᙮

ᓇᒨᔮ ~, ᓇᒨᔮ ᓂᔭ ᐋᑳᐧᐢᑲᒼ ᐆᑕ ᑕ ᑮ ᐃᑌᐧᔮᐣ ᐆᑕ ᓅᐦᑖᐃᐧᐩ ᓇᒨᔮ ᐋᑳᐧᐢᑲᒼ ᐆᑕ ᐁ ᑮ ᐅᐦᒌᐟ, ᐁ ᑮ ᒧᐢᒋ ᐲᐦᑐᑲᐧᐦᐃᐦᐟ ᐁᑐᑫ ᓅᐦᑖᐃᐧᐩ *Bangs*; ᐆᑌ ᐁ ᐅᐦᒌᐟ *Turtle Mountain*, *Monta~* ᐅᐦ, *States* ᐁᑯᑌ ᐁ ᐅᐦᒌᐟ ᓅᐦᑖᐃᐧᐩ᙮ ᐁᑯᑌ ᐁᑐᑫ ᐊᓂᒪ ᐊᐢᑭᐩ ᐁ ᑎᐯᔨᐦᑕᒫᐣ ᓃᐢᑕ᙮ ᓂᑮ ᐅᐦᑎᓯᓈᐣ *nineteen ~ nineteen thirty-six* ᓂᑮ ᒫᒨᐦᑎᓯᓈᐣ ᐊᓂᒪ ᐊᐢᑭᐩ, ᓂᑮ ᓂᐢᑎᓈᐣ ᓂᔭ ᐁᑲᐧ ᓂᑳ~, ᓂᑳᐃᐧᐩ ᐁᑲᐧ ᓂᑖᓂᐢ ᐁᑲᐧ ᓂᔭ ᓂᑮ ᓂᐢᑎᓈᐣ ᐁ ᐅᐦᑎᓰᔮᕽ ᐊᓂᒪ ᐊᐢᑭᐩ᙮ ᐁᑯᑌ ᓂᐢᑕᒼ ᐅᑭᒫᐦᑳᐣ, ᓂᒧᓲᒼ, *Albert Firstchief* ᑮ ᐃᓯᔨᐦᑳᓱᐤ, ᐁᐊᐧᑯ ᐊᓇ ᐅᑕᐢᑭᐩ᙮ ᓅᐦᑖᐃᐧᐩ ᐁᐤ~ ᐁᑯᓂ ᓅᐦᑖᐃᐧᐩ ᐅᐦᑖᐃᐧᔭ *Rainsky* ᑮ ᐃᑖᐤ ᐁᓴ ᓂᒧᓲᒼ; *Rainsky* ᐅᐦᑖᐃᐧᔭ ᐆᐦᐃ *Fra~ Albert Firstchief* ᐁᐊᐧᑯ ᐊᓇ ᓂᒧᓲᒼ ᓂᑖᓂᐢᑰᐦᐱᒋᑲᐣ ᐁᐊᐧᑯ᙮ ᐁᑯᑌ ᐊᐢᑭᐩ ᐁᑐᑫ ᐊᐱᓲᐢ ᓂᑲᓇᐋᐧᐸᒥᑯᐣ ᒫᑲ ᓂᐄᐧ ᑲᑫᐧᒋᐦᑫᒧᐣ ᐆᑌ, *States* ᐊᓂᒪ ᐁ ᐄᐧ ᑲᑫᐧᒋᐦᑫᒨᔮᐣ ᑮᑳᐧᐩ ᐊᓂᒪ ᐃᓂᑐ ᓲᓂᔮᐤ ᑳ ᑮ ᐅᑎᐦᑎᑯᔮᕽ᙮ ᐊᐢᑭᐩ ᐃᐧᔭ ᓂᑎᐯᔨᐦᑌᐣ ᐁᑯᑌ ᒨᐩ ᐄᐧᐦᑳ~ ᒨᐩ ᒫᑲ ᒣᑐᓂ ᓂᑭᐢᑫᔨᐦᑌᐣ᙮

ᐁᑯᓯ, ᐁᑯᓯ ᐆᑕ ᓂᑮ~ ᓂᑮ ᑕᓯ ᓂᐦᑖᐃᐧᑭᐣ ᓅᐦᑖᐃᐧᐩ ᐆᑕ ᑮ ᐲᐦᑐᑲᐧᐦᐋᐤ ᐊᔨᐢᐠ ᐸᔨᐹᐧᑎᐢ ᐆᑕ᙮ ᐆᑌ ᓃᐦᒑᔨᕽ ᓂᑎᓯᔨᐦᑳᑌᓈᐣ, ᐁᑯᑌ ᐁ ᑮ ᑕᓯ ᓂᐦᑖᐃᐧᑮᔮᐣ᙮ ᐁᑲᐧ ᓂᒧᓲᒼ ᐁ ᐹᐧᒥᐢ ᑮ ᐃᑖᐤ, *Little*

Sioux ᑮ ᐃᑖᐤ ᓂᒧᓲᒼ᙮ ᐁᑲᐧ ᓅᐦᑯᒼ, ᓅᐦᑯᒼ *Isabelle* ᑮ ᐃᑖᐤ ᓅᐦᑯᒼ, ᓴᐯᐣ ᓂᑮ ᐃᑖᓈᐣ ᒫᓇ ᓅᐦᑯᒼ ᐁ ᓀᐦᐃᔭᐃᐧᐦᑳᓯᐟ; ᐃᐧᔭ ᐁᐊᐧᑯ ᐅᒫᒥᐦᑫᐧᐤ ᑮ ᓂᐦᑖ~ ᐊᐦᓯᓂᐹᐧᐣ [*Assiniboine*] ᑮ ᐃᓯ ᐲᑭᐢᑫᐧᐤ᙮ ᑮ ᐹᐧᔩᒧᐤ ᓅᐦᑯᒼ, ᐁᑯᓯ ᒫᓇ ᓂᑮ ᑭᐢᑭᓇᐧᐦᐊᒫᑯᓈᐣ ᓂᔭ ᐁᑲᐧ ᓂᓯᑯᐢ, ᐁ ᑮ ᐹᐧᔩᒧᔮᕽ ᐁ ᑮ ᐃᑌᔨᐦᑕᒫᕽ ᐁ ᑮ ᐃᓯ ᓂᓯᑐᐦᑕᐋᐧᔮᕽ ᓅᐦᑯᒼ, ᒫᑲ ᑲᔮᐢ ᑳ ᓇᑲᓯᐟ ᓅᐦᑯᒼ, *a hundred and four* ᑮ ᐃᑕᐦᑐᐱᐳᓀᐧᐤ ᓅᐦᑯᒼ ᐁ ᑮ ᐸᓈᑎᓯᐟ, ᑫᔮᐱᐨ ᑮ ᑲᑳᔨᐋᐧᑎᓯᐤ ᓅᐦᑯᒼ᙮ ᑳᓂᑲᓈ ᑲ ᐅᑎᐦᑕᒫᐣ, ᑳᓂᑲᓈ ᓅᐦᑯᒼ ᓇᐢᐱᑕᐊᐧᐠ ᑳᔭᑳᐧᑭ~ ᒨᐩ, ᒨᐩ ᒫᑲ ᒣᑐᓂ ᑕ ᓇᐢᐱᑕᐊᐧᐠ ᒨᐩ ᐊᔨᐢᐠ ᐅᐦᒋ ᐋᐧᐱᐤ, ᒫᑲ ᐃᐧᔭ ᓂᔭ ᓂᐋᐧᐱᐣ ᐊᔨᐢᐠ᙮ ᒫᑲ ᐊᔨᐢᐠ ᒨᓂᔮᐤ ᑯᐦ ᐋᐧᐱᔮᐣ ᐁ ᑮ ᐹᐦ ᐲᐦᑐᓇᕽ ᓂᐢᑮᓯᑲᐧ ᐆᐦᐃ, ᐁ ᑮ ᐄᐧᒎᐦᑲᒪᐃᐧᐟ᙮

ᐁᑲᐧ ᒦᓇ, ᐆᒪ ᓃᐢᑕ ᐆᒪ ᐆᑕ ᑳ ᐋᔮᔮᐣ ᐆᑕ ᓃᐢᑕ ᒦᓇ ᒨᓂᔮᐤ ᐁ ᐃᑖᒧᔮᐣ ᐁ ᓈᓇᐹᒋᐦᐃᐟ᙮ ᓃᐢᑕ ᓇᒨᔭ ᑫᐧᔭᐢᐠ ᒥᔮᐧᓯᐣ, ᒨᐩ ᓂᑌᐦ ᐆᒪ ᐲᐋᐧᐱᐢᐠ ᓃᐢᑕ ᐊᔨᐢᐠ, *a pacer* ᐁ ᐋᔮᔮᐣ ᓂᑌᐦᐃᕽ᙮ ᒫᑲ ᓂᐄᐧᒋᐦᐃᑯᐣ, ᓂᓇᓈᐢᑯᒫᐤ ᒨᓂᔮᐃᐧᔨᓂᐤ ᐁ ᑮ ᐄᐧᒎᐦᑲᒪᐃᐧᐟ, *a pacer* ᐁ ᐋᔮᔮᐣ᙮ *Two years* ᐁᑲᐧ ᐁᑯᓯ ᐁ ᐋᔮᔮᐣ ᓃᓱ ᐊᐢᑭᐩ ᐁᑲᐧ ᐆᒪ, ᐁ ᑭᑭᐢᑳᒫᐣ ᐆᒪ᙮ *My will* ᓂᑮ ᐅᓰᐦᑖᐣ ᐆᑕ ᐋᐦᑯᓰᐃᐧᑲᒥᑯᕽ, *my will* ᓂᑮ ᓂᑕᐆᐧᓰᐦᑖᐣ᙮ ᐸᓈᑎᓯᔮᓂ ᐁ ᓂᑕᐁᐧᔨᐦᑕᒫᐣ ᑕ ᑫᒋᑯᓇᐦᑭᐠ ᐁᑯᓯ ᒪᓯᓇᐦᐃᑳᑌᐤ *my will* ᐊᓂᒪ ᐁᐊᐧᑯ ᐁ ᑮ ᐅᓰᐦᑖᔮᐣ᙮ ᑮᐢᐱᐣ ᐊᔨᐢᐠ ᑕᑯᐦᑌᔮᓂ ᐆᑌ ᑖᓂᑌ ᑳ ᑌᐹᐧᓯᐟ ᒪᓂᑐᐤ ᑕᑯᐦᑕᐦᐃᒋ ᐁᑯᑌ, ᑕᑯᐦᑌᔮᓂ ᒨᐩ ᑲ ᒌᐦᑫᔨᐦᑕᒼ ᐆᒪ ᐲᐋᐧᐱᐢᐠ ᐆᑕ ᓈᐢᑭᑲᓂᕽ ᑳ ᑭᑲᒧᐠ, ᓂᑲ ᐯ ᓃᐦᑕᒋᐁᐧᑎᓴᐦᐅᐠ, ᓂᑲᑳᐧᑕᑭᐦᑖᐣ ᐆᑕ, ᐁᐊᐧᑯ ᐅᐦᒋ ᑯᐦ ᑮ~ ᐅᓯ ᐄ~ ~ᐃᐧᔭᐢᒋᑫᔮᐣ᙮

[2. ᑲᔮᐢ ᐱᒫᒋᐦᐅᐃᐧᐣ]

ᐦᐋᒼ ᐁᑲᐧ, ᑲᔮᐢ ᐊᔨᓯᔨᓇᐧᐠ ᑖᓂᓯ ᐁ ᑮ ᐃᓯ ᐱᒫᒋᐦᐅᒋᐠ, ᒣᑐᓂ ᑮ ᒥᔪ ᐊᔮᓂᐃᐧᐤ ᑲᔮᐢ᙮ ᑲᐦᑭᔭᐤ ᑮᑲᐧᐩ ᐁ ᑮ ᒦᒋᕽ, ᐊᔨ ᐆᒪ *wild meat* ᑫ ᐃᑕᒥᕽ, ᑖᐱᐢᑰᐨ ᒨᓯᐃᐧᔮᐢ ᑮ ᒦᒋᓈᓂᐃᐧᐤ ᐁᑲᐧ ᒦᓇ ᐊᐱᓯᒨᓯᐢ ᑮ ᒨᐋᐧᐤ; ᑳᐦᑫᐊᐧᑲᐧ ᓂᑮ ᐅᓰᐦᑖᓈᐣ᙮ ᓇᒨᔭ ᐊᓂᒪ ᐆᐟ~ ᓇᒨᔭ ᐊᓂᒪ ᐁ ᐅᐦᒋ ᐅᓯ~ ᐁᑯᑕ ᐆᒣᐊᐧᐠ ᐁ ᐅᐦᒋ ᐊᔮᒋᐠ ᐁ ᑮ ᑲᐢᑳᐸᓴᐦᑭᐠ ᓅᑐᑫᐧᐊᐧᐠ,

ᑮ ᔩᑲᑌᔮᐸᓱᐘᐠ᙮ ᐁᐘᑯ ᐁᑎᑫᐧ ᐊᓂᒪ *spray* ᐑᐢᑕᐚᐤ ᐁ ᑮ ᐃᑑᑕᐦᑭᐠ ᓅᑐᑫᐧᐘᐠ ᑲᔮᐢ᙮ ᑮ ᐅᓰᐦᑖᐘᐠ ᑳᐦᑫᐘᑲᐧ ᐁᑲᐧ ᒦᓇ ᔩᐘᐦᐃᑲᓇ ᒦᓇ ᑮ ᐅᓰᐦᐁᐘᐠ ᑫᐦᑌ ᐊᔭᐠ, ᐁ ᐅᓰᐦᑖᒋᐠ ᐱᒦᐦᑳᐣ ᑳ ᐃᑕᒥᕽ᙮ ᐑᐦᑲᐧᐩ, ᓅᐦᑯᒼ ᒫᓇ ᐑᐦᑲᐧᐩ ᑮ ᑲᐢᑭᑳᐧᑕᒼ ᐁᑯᑕ ᐁ ᐊᓯᐘᐦᐚᐟ ᐆᐦᐃ ~ ᐆᒪ ᐱᒦᐦᑳᐣ ᐆᒪ ᐁ ᑲᐢᑭᐱᑕᕽ᙮

ᐁᑲᐧ ᓂᒧᓲᒼ ᐊᐘ ᑖᓂᓯ ᑳᐦ ᐃᓰᐦᒋᑳᑕᒧᑫᐧ ᒫᓇ ᐊᐳᔭ ᑮ ᑕᐦᑯᓀᐤ; ᑮ ᓯᐯᐧᐦᑌᐤ ᒫᓇ ᐁ ᓯᐯᐧᐦᑕᑖᒋᐠ ᐆᒪ ᑮᑳᐧᐩ ᐁᑐᑫ ᐆᒪ ᐱᒦᐦᑳᐣ ᐆᒪ, ᐁᑯᑌ ᐁ ᓂᑕᐘᐢᑖᒋᐠ᙮ ᒪᑖᐧᐣ ᒌ ᒫᓇ ᐁ ᑮ ᐊᔭᐦᐊᐦᑭᐠ ᒨᐩ ᓂᑳᐦ ᑭᐢᑫᔨᐦᑌᐣ, ᒫᑲ ᓂᑮ ᑭᐢᑫᔨᐦᑌᐣ ᒫᓇ ᐲᐚᐱᐢᐠ, ᐲᐚᐱᐢᐠ ᐊᓂᒪ ᒥᐢᑎᑯᐘᐢ ᐁᑯᑕ ᒫᓇ ᐁ ᑮ ᐊᐢᑖᒋᐠ ᐊᓂᒪ ᐊᔨ ᐱᒦᐦᑳᐣ᙮ ᐁᑲᐧ ᑳ ᐊᑎ ᐋᑳᐧ ᐱᐳᕽ ᓈᓂᑕᐤ ᐁᑐᑫ, ᓈᓂᑕᐤ ᐁᑐᑫ ᑳ ᐋᐱᐦᑖ ᐱᐳᕽ, ᓂᔭᓈᐣ ᐋᐱᐦᑖ ᐱᐳᓂ ᐲᓯᒼ ᓂᑎᑖᐧᓈᐣ, *January* ᐁᐘᑯ; ᐁᑯᑕ ᒫᓇ ᐁ ᑮ ᓈᑕᐦᑭᐠ ᐊᓂᒪ ᓅᐦᑯᒼ ᐁᑲᐧ ᐁ ᒦᒋᔮᕽ ᑖᐱᐢᑰᐨ ᒣᑐᓂ ᐊᓄᐦᐨ ᐁ ᑮ ᑮᓯᐦᑖᕽ᙮ ᑖᐱᐢᑰᐨ, ᑖᐱᐢᑰᐨ ᐆᒪ ᐊᓄᐦᐨ *canning* ᑳ ᑑᑕᒪᕽ ᐁᑯᓯ ᐁ ᑮ ᑑᑕᐦᑭᐠ ᒫᑲ *Indian way* ᐑᐢᑕᐚᐤ᙮ ᓇᒨᐩ ᓅᐦᐋᐦᑯᓰᐢᑳᑯᓈᐣ ᐊᓂᒪ, ᓇᒨᐩ ᐑᐦᑳᐟ ᓅᐦᐋᔮᓈᐣ *cancer* ᐚᓭᑲᒣ ᐆᒪ ᐊᑎ~ ᐁᐘᑯ ᓀᒪ, ᓈᐘᐩ ᓀᒪ *nineteen - nineteen twenty* ᐊᐘᓯᑌ᙮ ᓇᒨᔭ ᐑᐦᑳᐨ ᑮᑳᐧᐩ *cancer* ᐊᐃᐧᔭᐠ ᑕ ᐊᔮᐟ᙮ ᓇᒨᐩ ᐑᐦᑳᐨ ᐊᐃᐧᔭᐠ ᑕᒥᔨᐃᐧᐟ, ᓇᒪ ᑮᑳᐧᐩ᙮ ᒪ ᑮᑳᐧᐩ ᐊᐃᐧᔭᐠ *whooping cough* ᑳ ᐃᑌᐧᕽ, ᒪ ᑮᑳᐧᐩ᙮ ᒥᐢᑕᐦᐃ ᓲᐢᑳᐧᐨ ᐁ ᑮ ᐅᐦᐱᑮᔮᕽ, ᓲᐢᑳᐧᐨ ᐁ ᑮ ᒪᒥᔭᐧᔮᕽ᙮

ᑳ ᐊᑎ ᑎᐱᐢᑳᐠ, ᑳ ᐊᑎ ᑎᐱᐢᑳᐠ ᑖᐱᐢᑰᐨ ᐊᐘ ᑭᒧᓲᒥᓇᐤ ᑳ ᑮᓯ ᐊᐘᓭᐍᐟ, ᐁᐘᑯ ᐁᑐᑫᐧ ᐊᓂᒪ ᑳ ᐃᑕᒪᕽ ᐊᓄᐦᐨ *six o'clock* ᐁᐘᑯ ᑳ ᐃᑕᒪᕽ ᑭᔮᓇᐤ, ᑮ ᑎᐸᐦᐋᑫᐘᐠ ᐲᓯᒪᐧ ᑫᐦᑌ ᐊᔭᐠ᙮ ᐁ ᐊᑎ ᐊᐘᓭᐍᐟ « ᐲᐦᑐᑫᐠ, ᐯᔭᐦᑕᐠ~ ᐯᔭᑲᐧᓄᕽ ᐊᔮᐠ ᐚᐢᑲᐦᐃᑲᓂᕽ! » ᑖᐱᐢᑰᐨ ᓂᑮ~ ᓇᒨᐩ ᓅᐦ ᐃᑌᔨᐦᑌᐣ ᑖᐯᐧ ᐆᑭ ᓂᑲᑳᐧᑕᑭᐦᐃᑲᐧᐠ ᓂᑫᐦᑌ ᐊᔨᒪᐠ, ᓇᒨᐩ ᓅᐦ ᐃᑌᔨᐦᑌᐣ᙮ « ᓂᐹᐠ, ᑫ ᐚᐸᕽ ᑮᑭᓭᐹ ᐑᐸᐨ ᑲ ᐘᓂᐢᑳᔦᐠ᙮ ᑲ ᐸᐹᒥ ᒣᑕᐚᓈᐚᐤ ᑫ ᐚᐸᕽ, » ᓂᑮ ᐃᑎᑲᐏᓈᐣ ᒫᓇ᙮ ᑖᐯᐧ ᐁ ᐊᑎ ᐅᑖᑯᓯᑭ ᓂᑮ ᑲᐏᓯᒨᓈᐣ ᐁ ᓂᐹᔮᕽ, ᐁ ᓇ ᓂᐹᔮᕽ᙮ ᐏᔮᐸᐦᑭ, « ᐊᐦᐋ, ᒦᒋᓱᑖᐣ᙮ » ᓂᒦᐨ~, ᓂᑮ~, ᓇᒨᔭ ᑮᑳᐧᐩ ᐃᐧᔭ *porridge*

ᒪ ᑮᑲᐧᐩ, ᐁ ᐃᓂᑐ ᒦᒋᓱᔮᕽ ᒦᒋᒫᐳᐩ ᐁ ᑭᐢᐟ~ ᐁ ᒦᒋᔮᕽ ᑮᑲᐧᐩ ᐆᐦᐃ ᐅᑎᓰᐦᑳᓇ᙮ ᐊᐦᐴ ᑳᐦ ᒦᒋᔮᕽ ᐊᔨ *wild turnips, on a hill* ᒫᓇ ᐃᐦᑕᑯᓇᐧ᙮ ᒥᐢᑕᐢᑯᓰᒥᓇ ᒫᓇ ᓂᑮ ᐃᓯᔨᐦᑳᑌᓈᐣ ᐁᑲᐧ ᐁ ᒨᓇᐦᐊᐦᑭᐠ ᐆᑭ ᑫᐦᑌ ᐊᔭᐠ ᐁ ᓯᑲᐧᑕᐦᐊᐦᑭᐠ, ᐁ ᐹᓴᐦᑭᐠ, ᒦᒋᒫᐴᕽ ᐁ ᐸᑳ~᙮ ᐊᐧᐦᐋᐧ, ᐄᐧᐦᑲᓯᐣ ᒦᒋᒫᐳᐩ *wild turnip* ᐁᐊᐧᑯ ᑳ ᐃᑕᒥᕽ ᑭᔮᓇᐤ ᐊᓄᐦᐟ *turnips* ᑳ ᐃᑕᒪᕽ᙮

ᐁᑲᐧ ᐆᒪ ᑳ ᐹᐦ ᐲᑭᐢᑳᐧᑎᑕᑯᐠ ᐊᓄᐦᐨ, ᓇᒨᔭ ᑮᑲᐧᐩ, ᒪ ᑮᑲᐧᐩ ᐁ ᒫᔮᑕᕽ, ᐁ ᒥᔮᐧᓯᐠ ᐁ ᐯ ᓂᒎᐢᑲᒣᐠ ᐁᐊᐧᑯ ᑰᐦ ᐄᐧᐦᑕᒫᑕᑯᐠ, ᓅᓯᓯᒼ ᐊᐊᐧ ᑭᔭ ᒦᓇ ᓅᓯᓯᒼ ᑰᐦᑯᒥᐋᐧᐤ ᑳ ᐯ ᐋᐧᒋᒼ~, ᓇᒨᔭ ᐃᐧᔭ ᐁ ᑭᔮᐢᑭᔮᐣ ᐁ ᑖᐯᐧᔮᐣ ᐆᒪ ᑳ ᐃᑌᐧᔮᐣ᙮ ᒨᐩ ᓂᑳᐦ ᑮ ᑭᔮᐢᑭᐣ ᐆᒪ ᑫ ᐃᑖᒋᒧᐢᑖᑕᑯᐠ, ᐁᑯᓯ ᐁ ᑮ ᐯ ᐃᓯ ᐅᐦᐱᑭᔮᕽ ᓈᐊᐧᐩ ᓀᒪ᙮

[3. ᐊᓄᐦᐨ ᒫᔨᓂᑫᐃᐧᐣ]

ᐊᓄᐦᐨ ᐁᑲᐧ, ᓂᐋᐧᐸᐦᑌᐣ ᑖᓂᓯ ᐊᓄᐦᐨ ᐁ ᐃᐢᐸᔨᐠ, ᓂᑕᐋᐧᓯᒥᓴᐠ, ᓅᓯᓯᒪᐠ, ᓂᑖᓂᐢᑯᐦᐱᒋᑲᓇᐠ, ᑖᓂᓯ ᐊᓄᐦᐨ ᐁ ᐃᓯ ᐅᐦᐱᑭᒋᐠ, ᑳ ᑎᐱᐢᑳᐠ ᐅᑮᓯᑳᒥᐊᐧᐠ ᐊᓄᐦᐨ ᐊᐋᐧᓯᓴᐠ, ᐁᐊᐧᑯ ᐅᐦᒋ ᑰᐦ ᒫᐦ ᒫᔨᓂᑫᒋᐠ ᑭᑕᐋᐧᓯᒥᓯᓇᐊᐧᐠ ᑰᓯᓯᒥᓇᐊᐧᐠ᙮ ᐃᐧᔮᐸᐦᑭ ᑳ ᐯᐦᑕᒪᕽ ᐁ ᑮ ᓂᐸᐦᐃᐦᐟ ᑰᓯᓯᒥᓇᐤ, ᑭᑕᐋᐧᓯᒥᓯᓇᐤ ᑮ ᑕᐦᑳᒫᐤ, ᒥᔮᑐᔭᕽ ᐁᑯᑕ᙮ ᐋᑕ ᐊᓂᒪ ᐁ ᐅᐦᒋᒫᐊᐧᓲᔭᕽ, ᒨᐩ ᒫᑲ ᓂᓯᑐᐦᑕᒪᐧᐠ ᐊᓄᐦᐟ, ᐊᓄᐦᐨ ᑖᓂᓯ ᑫ ᐃᓯ ᐅᐦᐱᑭᒋᐠ ᐊᓄᐦᐨ᙮ ᑭᓵᐢᑕᐤ, ᑭᓵᐢᑕᐤ ᐊᓄᐦᐨ ᐆᒪ ᓇᐊᐧᒋᑯ ᐊᐱᓲᐢ ᐁ ᒫᔨ ᐅᐦᐱᑭᕽ, ᓇᒨᐩ ᑖᐱᐢᑰᐟ ᓀᒪ ᑲᔮᐢ, ᒥᐢᑕᐦᐃ ᑲᔮᐢ ᑮ ᒥᔮᐧᓯᐣ᙮ ᓇᒨᐩ ᐄᐧᐦᑳᐨ ᒫᒥᕽ ᐊᔨᓯᔨᓂᐤ ᐅᐦᒋ ᑮᐢᑫᐧᐯᐤ᙮

ᑮᑳᐧᐩ ᑳ ᐃᑌᐧᕽ ᐁ ᑮᐢᑫᐧᐯᕽ, ᐁ ᑲ ᑮᐢᑫᐧᐟ ᐊᐃᐧᔭᐠ᙮ « ᐊᐦᐋᒼ, » ᑮ ᐃᑌᐧᐊᐧᐠ ᒫᓇ ᑫᐦᑌ ᐊᔭᐠ, « ᐊᓇᐦᐊ [*sic*: ᐊᓇ ᓈᐦᐊ] ᑳ ᐋᐧᐸᒪᐟ ᑲᒥᓂᐦᑫᐧᐟ, ᒪᑖᐧᐣ ᒌ ᑭᑖᐦᒥᓭᐧᔨᐦᑕᒼ ᐊᓇ ᐆᒪᑐᐊᐧᕽ ᑕ ᐸᑲᒪᐦᐅᐦᐟ ᐅᐢᑎᑳᐧᓂᕽ, ᑲᐯ ᑮᓯᐠ ᐃᐢᑯ ᐁ ᐊᐊᐧᓴᐁᐧᐟ ᑕ ᐸᐹᑲ ᑮᐢᑫᐧᐟ, ᓇᒪ ᑮᑲᐧᐩ ᑕ ᑭᐢᑫᔨᐦᑕᒼ, ᓇᒨᔭ ᑖᐦᒥᓭ~ ᑖᐦᒥᓭᓈᑲᐧᐣ ᐁᐊᐧᑯ, » ᑮ ᐃᑌᐧᐊᐧᐠ ᒫᓇ

ᑲᔮᐢ᙮ ᐃᐧᔮᐸᒫᑖᐧᐃᐧ ᐊᐃᐧᔭ ᓇᐊᐧᒋᑯ ᐁᑯᓯ ᑳ ᐄᐧ ᐃᐢᙾ᙮ ᑲᔮᐢ ᐁᑐᑫ ᑮ ᐅᔦᓰᐦᑖᐊᐧᐠ ᒫᓇ ᑮᒨᐨ ᑮᑲᐧᐩ, ᓇᒨᐩ ᓂᑳᐦ ᑮ ᒪᒥᐦᒋᐦᑌᐣ ᐁᐊᐧᑯ ᐊᓂᒪ᙮ ᑮᑲᐧᐩ ᐁᑐᑫ ᒫᓇ ᑮ ᒥᓇᐦᐃᓱᐊᐧᐠ ᐆᑭ᙮ ᐁᑯᓯ ᐊᓂᒪ ᒫᓇ ᑳᐦ ᐃᑌᐧᒋᐠ, « ᓇᒨᐩ ᑖᐦ ᒌᐦᑫᖬᐦᑕᒼ ᑕ ᐸ ᐸᑲᒪᐦᐅᐦᐟ ᐅᐢᑎᑳᐧᓂᕽ ᐊᖬ ᑕ ᐸ ᐹ ᑲ ᑮᐢᑫᐧᐟ, » ᐁᑯᑐᐊᐧ ᐊᖬᐢᐠ ᐊᓂᒪ ᑳ ᑮᐢᑫᐧᐯᕽ, ᑳ ᐃᑌᐧᕽ᙮ ᐊᖬ ᑭᖬᑎ‴ ᐊᓂᒪ ᓇᒨᔭ ᐁᒥᔮᐧᓯᐠ, ᓇᒨᔭ ᐁᒥᔮᐧᐹᐊᐧᑖᔭᐣ ᐁᐊᐧᑯ ᐊᓂᒪ ᐅᑮᐢᑫᐧᔮᐸᒧᕽ ᑳ ᒥᓂᐦᑫᐧᕽ᙮ ᓂᑭᐢᑫᖬᙾ ᓂᑮ ᐸ ᐯ ᒥᓂᐦᑳᐧᐣ ᓃᐢᑕ ᑲᔮᐢ, ᒨᐩ ᒫᑲ ᒥᐢᑕᐦᐃ, ᓂᑮ ᐸ ᐴᔦᓈᐣ᙮ ᓂᑮ ᐯ ᒥᓂᐦᑳᐧᓈᐣ ᐊᐱᓰᐢ, ᒨᔭ ᒥᐢᑕᐦᐃ ᑳᐦ ᑲ ᑮᓯᙾ ᐁᑯᓯ ᓂᑮ ᐸᑭᑎᓈᐣ᙮ ᑲᔮᐢ ᑳ ᐴᓂ ᒥᓂᐦᑫᐧᔮᐣ, ᓂᑭᓭᖬᓃᒼ ᒦᓇ ᑲᔮᐢ᙮ ᑲᔮᐢ ᒦᓇ ᑳ ᐴᓂ ᐲᐦᑖᐧᔮᐣ᙮

ᐲᐦᑖᐧᐃᐧᐣ ᐆᒪ, ᐁᐊᐧᑯ ᒦᓇ ᑳ ᓂᐸᐦᐃᑯᕽ ᐲᐦᑖᐧᐃᐧᐣ, ᐊᖬᓯᖬᓂᐤ ᒥᐢᑕᐦᐃ ᑳ ᐅᑎᓇᕽ᙮ ᐆᑌ ᐆᒪ, ᑭᐦᐸᓇᐠ [*sic*: ᑰᐦᐸᓇᐠ] ᐆᑭ, ᑭᑎᒪᐦᐋᐊᐧᐠ, ᑭᑭᑎᒪᐦᑖᐣ ᑭᖧᐦᐁᐃᐧᐣ᙮ ᐄᐦ, ᑖᓂᒪᙾ ᑖᓂᑐᐊᐧᕽ ᐁ ᐋᐸᒋᐦᑕᒨᐦᐃᑲᐃᐧᔭᕽ ᐊᓅᐦᐨ *spray* ᐊᓅᐦᐨ ᒨᓂᔮᐊᐧᐠ ᑲᒥᔦ ᖧᐦᐁᔭᕽ᙮ ᐁᑯᑐᐊᐧᕽ ᓂᑖᐸᒋᐦᑖᐣ, *spray* ᓂᑑᓂᕽ ᓂᑖᐸᒋᐦᑖᐣ, ᒫᑲ ᐆᒪ ᓂᔭ *my heart* ᑰᐦ ᒥᖬᑲᐃᐧᔮᐣ, ᑕ ᑲᑫᐧ ᒥᔦᑯᑌᐠ ᐆᒪ *my cord* ᐆᑌ᙮ ᓂᑖᐸᒋᐦᑖᐣ ᐊᓂᒪ ᓃᓵᐧᐤ, ᓃᓵᐧᓂᐢᙾ ᐊᖬ, ᐊᖬ, ᓂᑎᐢᐱᑕᒫᓯᑊ *air, you know,* ᐁᐊᐧᑯ ᐊᓂᒪ ᓂᒥᔦ ᑑᑖᑯᑊ, ᒫᑲ ᐃᐧᔭ ᓂᔭ ᐊᓂᒪ ᐊᖬ ᐆᒪ ᐁᑐᑫ ᓂᑌᐦ ᐅᐦᒋ᙮

ᐁᐊᐧᑯ ᐊᓂᒪ ᐊᓅᐦᐨ ᐁ ᐱᒥ ᐋᒋᒧᐢᑖᑕᑯᐠ, ᑲᔮᐢ ᒥᐢᑕᐦᐃ ᑮ ᒥᔮᐧᓯᐣ, ᒣᑐᓂ ᐅᑎ ᑲᔮᐢ᙮ ᐊᓅᐦᐨ ᐁᑲᐧ ᐊᐋᐧᓯᓴᐠ, ᒪ ᑮᑲᐧᐩ ᑭᓂᑐᐦᑖᑯᓇᐊᐧᐠ, ᐊᖬᐢ ᐸᐦᑳᐣ ᐃᓯᑭᐊᐧᐠ, ᐸᐦᑳᐣ ᑭᑎᓯ ᐅᐦᐱᑭᐦᐋᓇᐊᐧᐠ, ᓇᒨᐩ ᑖᐱᐢᑰᐨ ᑲᔮᐢ᙮ ᓇᒨᔭ ᐁ ᒪᒥᐦᒋᒨᔭᐣ ᐆᒪ ᐁ ᐯ ᑭᐢᑫᖬᐦᑕᒫᐣ ᐊᓂᒪ ᑰᐦ ᐋᒋᒧᐢᑖᑕᑯᐠ, *you know,* ᑖᓂᓯ ᐁ ᐯ ᐃᐢᐸᖬᐠ ᐊᓅᐦᐨ ᐁᑲᐧ ᑳ ᑕᑯᐦᑌᔭᕽ ᐊᓅᐦᐨ ᐁᑲᐧ ᓂᐋᐧᐸᐦᑌᐣ ᓃᐢᑕ᙮ ᑕᐦᑐ ᑮᓯᑳᐤ ᑫᑳᐟ ᓂᒨᐢᑯᑌᐦᐋᐣ ᓅᓯᓯᒪᐠ ᐅᐦᒋ, ᓂᑕᐋᐧᓯᒥᓴᐠ᙮ ᐯᔭᐠ ᓃᐢᑕ ᓂᑕᐋᐧᓯᒥᐢ, ᒨᐩ ᑖᐯᐧ ᑮᑲᐧᐩ ᐁ ᑖᐯᐧᐦᑕᕽ, ᐁ ᐃᓯᙾ ᐁ ᐃᐦᑕᓯᔮᕽ ᐋᑕ ᐊᓇ ᐁ ᓴᐯᐧᖬᒫᔮᕽ ᐁ ᓵᑭᐦᐋᔮᕽ ᐊᓇ ᐋᑕ᙮ ᐁᑳ ᓴᐯᐧᖬᒫᔮᕽ ᓇᒨᐩ ᓂᑳᐦ ᑭᑐᑖᓈᐣ, ᑭᔮᒼ ᓂᑳᐦ ᐃᑌᖬᐦᑌᓈᐣ, ᒫᑲ ᐁ ᓴᐯᐧᖬᒫᔮᕽ ᐯᔭᐠ ᓃᐢᑕ ᓂᑕᐋᐧᓯᒥᐢ; ᓂᔭ, ᓂᔭ, ᓂᔭ, ᓂᑐᐦᐱᑭᐦᒋᑲᐣ,

ᐁᐊᐧᑯ ᐊᓂᒪ᙮ ᓇᒨᔭ ᒣᑐᓂ ᐋᑕᐃᐧᔭ ᒥᑐᓂ ᒥᐢᑕᐦᐃ ᑎᑕ ᒨᐦᒍᐃᐧᐟ ᒫᑲ ᓇᐊᐧᒋᑯ ᓴᓰᐱᐦᑕᑦ᙮ ᑮᑲᐧᐩ ᒫᑲ ᐊᓂᒪ ᑳ ᐄᐧᐦᑕᒫᐦᐟ ᐋᐧᐸᐦᑕᑦ: « ‘ᑳᐃᐧᔭ’, ᑮᑲᐧᐩ ᐊᓂᒪ, ‘ᑳᐃᐧᔭ’? » ᐋᐧᐸᒣᐤ ᐊᐄᐧᓂᐊᐧ ᐊᓂᐦᐃ ᓇᐊᐧᒋᑯ ᐊᔨᐋᐧᐠ ᐁᓴ ᐁ ᑎᐯᔨᒥᑯᐟ, ᓯᒫᑲᓂᐢ ᐊᔨᐢ ᐊᓄᐦᐨ ᑭᑎᐯᔨᒥᑯᓇᐤ ᐁᑲᐧ ᐊᓄᐦᐨ ᑳ ᑮᓯᑳᐠ᙮ ᓈᓂᑕᐤ ᑫ ᐃᓯ ᒪ ᒫᔨᓂᑫᕽ ᐋᓴᐩ ᐁᑯᑕ ᓯᒫᑲᓂᐢ᙮ ᒥᔪ ᐅᑭᒫᐤ ᑭᑎᑌᔨᐦᑌᓈᓇᐤ, ᓇᒨᔭ᙮ ᓈᓂᑕᐤ ᐁ ᐊᔨᑎᓂᑫᕽ, ᐋᓴᐩ ᐆᑕ, ᐯ ᐊᔮᐤ, ᐁᑲᐧ ᑭᓂᑐᑕᒫᑯᓇᐤ ᐊᐄᐧᓇ ᑳ ᒪ ᒫᔨᓂᑫᐟ ᑕ ᐄᐧᒎᐦᑲᒪᐋᐧᔭᕽ ᓲᓂᔮᓈᕽ ᐅᐦᒋ᙮

ᑖᓂᑌ ᑫ ᐅᐦᑎᓇᐠ ᓲᓂᔮᐤ? ᓇᒨᐩ ᓂᑕᑐᐢᑳᐣ, ᓂᑫᐦᑌ ᐊᔨᐃᐧᐣ᙮ ᑮᑲᐧᐩ ᐱᑯ ᐁ ᐯᐦᑖᔮᐣ ᓂᒪᓯᓇᐦᐃᑲᐣ ᑕᐅᑎᐦᑎᑯᔮᐣ, ᐁᐊᐧᑯ ᐱᑯ ᓂᔭ᙮ ᑲᔮᐢ ᐁᔨᐁᐧᕽ ᓂᑮ ᓲᓂᔮᐦᑫᓯᐣ᙮ ᐊᓄᐦᐟ ᓂᐄᐧᑲᑫᐧ ᓲᓂᔮᐦᑳᐣ, ᐁᑕᑕᐤ ᒫᑲ ᓂᑲᐢᑭᐦᑖᐣ ᐁ ᓲᓂᔮᐦᑫᔮᐣ᙮ ᓂᓲᓂᔮᐦᑫᓯᐣ ᒨᐩ ~ ᒨᐩ ᒫᑲ ᐁᐊᐧᑯᔨᑯᕽ, ᓂᑲᐢᑭᐦᑖᐣ ᒫᑲ ᐊᐱᓰᐢ ᐁ ᐚᐸᒪᐠ ᐊᓇ ᒨᓂᔮᐢ ᑳ ᑕᑲᐦᑫᔨᒫᒋᐠ ᐃᑐᐊᐧ ᓲᓂᔮᐊᐧ᙮ ᐁᐊᐧᑯᓂ ᐊᔨᐢ ᐃᐧᔭᐋᐧᐤ ᑌᑲᐦᑫᔨᒫᒋᐠ, ᒨᓂᔮᐊᐧᐠ ᐆᑭ᙮

[ᐊᒋᔭᐤ ᐁ ᓇᑭᐱᑕᒥᕽ]

[4. ᐸᔨᐹᐧᑎᓈᕽ]

ᓂᑲ ᒫᒋ ᐋᒋᒧᐣ ᑮᑲᐧᐩ ᐁ ᐯ ᐃᓯ ᑲ ᑭᐢᑫᔨᐦᑕᒫᐣ᙮ ᑲᔮᐢ, ᑲᔮᐢ ᓂᔭᓈᐣ ᐁᑯᓯ ᐁ ᑮ ᐯ ᐃᑖᒋᐦᐅᔮᕽ ᐆᑭ ᐊᐋᐧᓯᓴᐠ ᑳ ᐯ ᐄᐧᐦᑕᒪᐊᐧᑭᐠ᙮ ᐁᔨᐁᐧᕽ ᓂᑮ ᐯ ᒦ~ ᑮ ᐯ ᒥᔪᑭᐊᐧᐠ ᐊᐋᐧᓯᓴᐠ, ᑕ ᑮ ᐃᑌᐧᔮᐣ, ᐁ ᑮ ᐯ ᒥᔪᑭᒋᐠ᙮ ᓇᒨᔭ ᐄᐧᐦᑳᐨ ᐊᐃᐧᔭᐠ ᓅᐦ ᐯᐦᑌᓈᐣ « ᐁᐊᐧᑯ ᐊᓇ ᒥᓯᐊᐧᓈᒋᐦᐃᐁᐧᐤ, ᓂᐸᐦᑖᑫᐤ, » ᒨᐩ ᐄᐧᐦᑳᐨ ᓅᐦᒋ ᐯᐦᑌᓈᐣ, ᒣᑐᓂ ᐊᔨᐢ ᑮ ᑯᐢᑌᐊᐧᐠ ᒨᓂᔮᐃᐧᔨᓂᐊᐧ ᐆᑭ ᓂᔭᓈᐣ ᐃᔨᑯᕽ ᑳ ᐯ ᐃᐢᐲᐦᑎᓰᔮᐣ᙮ ᐊᐦᔮ ᒫᓇ ᑳ ᐯ ᐃᑎᓵᐸᒪᑭᐠ ᓂᔭ ᐁ ᐃᐢᑫᐧᓯᓯᐃᐧᔮᐣ ᑳᐦ ᑕᐸᓰᔮᐣ, ᓂᑮ ᓴᑳᐧᒧᐣ ᓈᓂᑕᐤ ᐊᑖᒥᕽ ᐁᑳᐩ ᑕ ᐚᐸᒥᐟ ᒨᓂᔮᐢ᙮ ᐁ ᑮ ᐃᓯ ᑯᐢᑖᔮᐦᑯᐠ ᒨᓂᔮᐊᐧᐠ, ᒪᐢᑭᒧᑕ ᐁ ᑮ ᑯᐢᑕᒫᕽ᙮ ᑮ ᑕᐦᑯᓇᒪᐧᐠ ᐊᔨᐢ ᒫᓇ ᒪᐢᑭᒧᑕ ᐆᐦᐃ᙮ ᑫᔮᐱᐨ ᐊᓂᒪ ᓂᑲᓇᐁᐧᔨᐦᑌᐣ ᐊᓂᒪ ᐃᑐᐊᐧᕽ ᑳ ᑮ ᑯᐢᑕᒫᐣ ᐁ ᐃᐢᑫᐧᓯᓯᐃᐧᔮᐣ

ᐊᓂᒪ ᐊᔨ, ᐊᓂᒪ, ᑖᐱᐢᑰᐨ *big purse*, ᒥᓵᐤ, *black one*᙮ ᑫᔮᐱᐨ ᓂᑲᓇᐁᐧᔨᐦᑌᐣ *for souvenir* ᐁ ᐃᑖᐧᑕᒫᐣ᙮ ᐁ ᑮ ᓂᐸᐦᐃ ᑯᐢᑕᒫᐣ ᐊᓂᒪ ᒫᓇ, ᒪᐢᑭᐦᑮᐃᐧᔨᓂᐤ ᒫᓇ ᐁ ᑮ ᑯᐢᑕᐠ, ᓂᑮ ᓴᑳᐧᒧᐣ ᒫᓇ ᐊᔨ ᐊᑖᒥᕽ ᐆᒪᑐᐊᐧᕽ ᓂᐯᐃᐧᓂᕽ᙮ ᐁᑲᐧ ᐊᓅᐦᐨ ᐊᐋᐧᓯᓴᐠ ᒨᓂᔮᐃᐧᔨᓂᐤ ᑳ ᐯ ᑕᑯᐦᑌᐟ ᒨᓂᔮᐢ, ᑳ ᐄᐧᐦᑫᐧᑳᐸᐃᐧᒋᐠ ᐊᐋᐧᓯᓴᐠ ᐁ ᑭᑐᑖᒋᐠ ᒨᓂᔮᓴ᙮ ᒨᐩ ᐊᓂᒪ ᑮᑲᐧᐩ ᓂᔭᓈᐣ ᑲᔮᐢ, ᓂᑮ ᑯᐢᑖᓈᓇᐠ ᒨᓂᔮᓴᐠ᙮

ᐊᓅᐦᐨ ᐁᑲᐧ ᓇᒨᐩ ᑮᑲᐧᐩ ᑕ ᑯᐢᑕᐦᑭᐠ ᐊᐋᐧᓯᓴᐠ᙮ ᐋᑲᔮᔩᒧᐊᐧᐠ ᐊᔨᐢᐠ, ᓂᓯᑐᐦᑕᒪᐧᐠ ᐊᔨᐢ, ᒫᑲ ᓂᔭᓈᐣ ᒨᐩ ᓅᐦᐋᐦᐋᑲᔮᔩᒧᓈᐣ, ᐃᔨᑯᕽ ᐊᐋᐧᓯᓴᐠ ᑳ ᑮ ᐯ ᐊᐩ~ ᒨᐩ ᒫᐦ ᒥᐦᒉᐟ ᐁ ᐅᐦᒋ ᐊᔮᐋᐧᒋᐠ ᐊᐋᐧᓯᓴ, *parents*, ᒨᐩ ᐃᐧᔭ ᒫᐦ ᒥᐦᒉᐟ, ᐋᑎᐦᐟ ᓄᐅᐧ, ᓂᐢᑐ ᐱᑯ ᐋᑎᐦᐟ᙮ ᐄᐦ, ᑖᐱᐢᑰᐨ ᐆᒪ ᓂᔭ ᓂᑮ ᓄᐃᐧᐣ ᐱᑯ, *four, four … three sisters, but* ᑮ ᐸᓈᑎᓯᐊᐧᐠ ᓃᑎᓵᓇᐠ, ᐁᑲᐧ ᐋᑎᐦᐟ ᑮ ᓃᓰᓴᐊᐧᐠ ᓇᓭᐢᑕᐤ᙮ ᐁᑲᐧ ᐁᑐᑫ ᐊᓇ ᑲᔮᐢ ᓂᑮ ᐸ ᐯᐦᑌᐣ ᑭᑦ~ ᓂᒧᓲᑦ~ ᓂᒧᓲᒥᓈᐣ, ᐅᑭᒫᐦᑳᐣ ᐆᑕ, ᐁᐊᐧᑯ ᐊᓇ ᑳ ᑮ ᒥᐦᒉᑑᐢᑫᐧᐁᐧᐟ, ᒥᑖᑕᐦᐟ ᐄᐧᐊᐧ, ᐁ ᑮ ᒥᑖᑕᐦᑑᐢᑫᐧᐁᐧᐟ ᐊᓇ *Chief* ᐸᔨᐹᐧᐟ ᑮ ᐃᑖᐤ, ᐁ ᑮ ᐅᑭᒫᐦᑳᓂᐃᐧᐟ, ᒥᑖᑕᐦᐟ ᐃᐢᑫᐧᐊᐧ ᐁ ᑮ ᐄᐧᑭᒫᐟ᙮ ᐁᑯᓯ, ᐁᑯᓯ ᑮ ᐃᑌᐧᐤ ᒫᓇ ᑳ ᑮ ᐅᔦᐦᑖᐃᐧᔮᐣ᙮ ᓇᒨᔭ ᐁ ᑮ ᒥᐦᒉᑑᓯᐟ ᐊᓇ ᐊᔨ, ᐅᑭᒫᐦᑳᐣ ᐊᓇ᙮ ᐊᓭᓈᓄᐤ ᐱᑯ ᐅᑕᐋᐧᓯᒥᓴ ᐁ ᑮ ᐃᐦᑕᓯᔨᐟ ᐃᔨᑯᕽ ᒥᐦᒉᐟ ᐁ ᑮ ᐊᔮᐋᐧᐟ …

> — ᒪᑖᐧᐣ ᒌ ᐊᓇ ᑭᓴᔨᓂᐤ ᐁ ᑮ ᐅᐦᑕᒥᐣ~, ᐁ ᑮ ᐊᔨ~
> ᐁᐩ, ᒫᐢᑰᐨ ᐊᓇ ᑭᓴᔨᓂᐤ ᐁ ᑮ ᑎᔭᐄᐧᐟ, *you know,*
> ᑎᑕ ᐸᐹᐄᐧᒉᐋᐧᐟ ᐆᐦᐅ ᐅᑎᐢᑫᐧᒪ; ᐁᑲᐧ ᐊᐦᐴ ᐁᑐᑫ ᒦᓇ
> ᐁᑯᐟ~, ᐊᐦᐴ ᒌ ᑮ ᑳᐦ ᑳᐦᑫᐧᔨᐦᑐᐊᐧᐠ ᐊᓂᑭ ᐃᐢᑫᐧᐊᐧᐠ᙮
> [ᐹᐦᐱᓈᓂᐊᐧᐣ] ᓇᒨᔭ ᐊᓂᒪ ᑕ ᐹᐦᐱᕽ, ᑲ ᐹᐦᐱᐦᑖᓈᐋᐧᐤ᙮ —

ᐁᑯᓯ ᐊᓂᒪ ᒫᓇ ᑳᐦ ᐃᑌᐧᕽ, ᐊᓭᓈᓄᐤ ᐱᑯ ᐁ ᑮ ᐃᐦᑕᓯᒋᐠ ᐊᐋᐧᓯᓴᐠ ᐁᑲᐧ *ten wifes* ᐁ ᑮ ᐊᔮᐋᐧᐟ᙮ ᐁᑲᐧ ᐊᓇ *the old ~* ᒫᒪᐊᐧᒋ ᐄᐧᐃᐧᒫᐤ ᐊᓇ, ᐁᐊᐧᑯ ᑳᑭᑫ ᑲ ᐸᐹᐄᐧᒋᐦᐃᐁᐧᐟ, ᓈᓂᑕᐤ ᑲ ᐃᓯᑖᐹᓰᐃᐧᐦᐟ, ᑲ ᓂᑯᐦᑌᐃᐧᐦᐟ, ᐁᑯᓯ ᐁᓴ ᑳᐦ ᐴᓯᐟ ᐁᐊᐧᑯ᙮ ᐁᐊᐧᑯ ᐁᓴ ᑮ ᐸᐹᐄᐧᒋᐦᐃᐁᐧᐤ, ᑭᐦᒋ ᐄᐧᐃᐧᒫᐤ ᐊᓇ᙮ ᐁᑲᐧ ᐆᑭ ᐆᑌ

ᑫᑳ ᒥᑖᑕᐦᐟ ᐁᐊᐧᑯᓂᐠ ᐁ ᑮᓯᑌᐳᒋᐠ, ᐁ ᐸᒥᓇᐊᐧᓱᒋᐠ ᑲᐦᑭᔭᐤ ᑮᑲᐧᐩ ᑲᐦᑫᐊᐧᐠ ᐁ ᐅᓰᐦᑖᒋᐠ, ᒥᐦᑕ ᐁ ᐋᐊᐧᒋᑖᐯᒋᐠ, ᐁ ᓂᑯᐦᑌᒋᐠ᙮ ᐅᒥᐦᐟ~ ᒥᐦᑎᑭᐋᐧᐦᐸ ᑲᔮᐢ ᑮ ᐅᓰᐦᑖᐊᐧᐠ ᒫᓇ ᑮ ᐃᑌᐧᐤ ᓅᐦᑖ~ ᑳ ᑮ ᐃᐧᔦᐦᑖᐃᐧᔮᐣ᙮ ᐁ ᒋᒪᑖᒋᐠ ᐊᔨ, ᒥᐦᑕ, ᑲᔮᐢ ᐁᐊᐧᑯ ᐁᑳ ᑕ ᐊᔭᐦᐋᑯᓂᔨᑭ᙮ ᐁᑲᐧ ᒦᓇ ᐁᑯᑌ ᑮᑲᐧᐩ ᐊᐢᑖᓯᐃᐧᑲᒥᑯᐦᑫᒋᐠ ᐁ ᐋ~ ᐅᒥᓯ ᐁ ᐃᑕᐦᐱᑕᐦᑭᐠ ᐊᔨ ᒥᐢᑎᑲᐧ᙮ [ᐁ ᐃᓯᓂᐢᑫᐟ] ᐁᑯᑌ ᐁ ᑌᐦᑕᐢᑖᒋᐠ ᐊᔨ, ᐅᒦᒋᐃᐧᓂᐋᐧᐊᐧ ᑖᐱᐢᑰᐨ ᐆᒪ ᒨᓯᐃᐧᔮᐢ, *deer meat*, ᐁᑯᑌ ᐁ ᐊᐢᑖᒋᐠ, ᑮ ᐃᑌᐧᐊᐧᐠ ᒫᓇ ᐁ ᑮ ᑖᐱᑎ ᐯᐦᑕᐊᐧᑭᐠ ᒫᓇ᙮ ᐁᐊᐧᑯ ᐊᓂᒪ ᐄᐧᐢᑕᐋᐧᐤ ᐅᑕᐢᑖᓯᐃᐧᑲᒥᑯᐋᐧᐤ ᐊᓂᒪ *same time* ᐁ ᑮ ᐅᓰᐦᑖᒋᐠ ᒥᐦᑕ ᐊᓂᐦᐃ ᐅᐦᒋ᙮ ᐃᐢᑫᐧᐊᐧᐠ ᒫᑲ ᐁᓴ ᐆᑭ ᐁ ᑮ ᐅᓰᐦᑖᒋᐠ ᐁᐊᐧᑯᓂᐠ ᐆᑭ ᐆᑭ *ten - nine wives* ᐆᑭ ᐆᑌ ᑳ ᓇᑲᑎᐦᒋᐠ *behind* ᐊᔨᐢᐠ ᐯᔭᐠ ᐊᐊᐧ ᐄᐧᒋᐦᐃᐁᐧᐤ ᑮᑳᐧᐩ ᐸᐹᓈᑕᒧᐋᐧᑫᐧ᙮ ᒪᑖᐧᐣ ᒌ ᐁᐊᐧᑯ ᐊᓇ ᓇᐊᐧᐨ ᐁᑐᑫ ᐊᐦᐴ ᐃᐧᔭ ᐁᐊᐧᑯ ᐁ ᑮ ᓵᑭᐦᐃᐦᐟ ᓂᐢᑕᑦ ᐄᐧᐃᐧᒫᐤ ᐊᐦᐴ ᒦᓇ ᐁᑯᓯ, ᐁᑯᓯ ᐁ ᑮ ᐃᐢᐸᔨᐠ᙮

ᐁᑯᓯ ᒫᓇ ᓂᑮ ᐃᑎᐦᑌᐣ ᐊᔨᐢᐠ ᒫᓇ ᓂᑮ ᐊᔨ~ᓇ ᓂᑐᐦᑕᐋᐧᐊᐧᐠ ᓂᒧᓲᑦ ᐁᑲᐧ ᒦᓇ ᓅᐦᑯᑦ, ᐊᐊᐧ *Little Sioux* ᐁ ᐲᐦᑐᑳᐧᐦᐟ ᐆᑭ ᑫᐦᑌ ᐊᔭᐠ ᐆᑕ ᓂᔭᓈᐣ ᑲᔮᐢ᙮ ᐁᑯᓯ ᒫᓇ ᓂᑮ ᐸ ᐯᐦᑕᐋᐧᐊᐧᐠ ᐁ ᐃᑖᒋᒧᒋᐠ ᐁ ᐸᑦ~ ᐁ ᓇ ᓂᑐᐦᑕᒫᐣ ᐁᑲᐧ ᐁ ᐹᐦᐱᒋᐠ ᒫᓇ᙮ ᑫᑕᐦᑕᐁᐧ ᒫᓇ ᐁ ᑮ ᐊᐧᐃᐧᔭᓵᒋᒧᐟ ᐊᐊᐧ ᐊᔨ, ᐊᐊᐧ ᓂᒧᓲᑦ ᐊᐊᐧ, *Little Sioux* ᑮ ᐃᑖᐤ, ᐁ ᐹᐧᒋᐢ ᑮ ᐃᑌᐊᐧᐠ᙮

ᐁᑲᐧ ~ ᑎᐱᔭᐁᐧ ᐃᐧᔭ ᐊᐊᐧ ᓅᐦᑯᑦ ᐊᐊᐧ ᐁ ᑮ~ ᓅᐦ~ ᓅᐦᑖᐃᐧᐩ ᐊᔨ, ᑎᐱᔭᐁᐧ ᐅᑳᐄᐧᓴ, ᑳ ᑮ ᐃᐧᔦᑳᐄᐧᐟ ᓅᐦᑖᐃᐧᐩ ᐁ ᑮ ᐅᒥᓯᐟ ᐆᐦᐃ᙮ ᐆᑭ ᐊᔨ, ᓅᐦᑯᑦ ᐁᐊᐧᑯ ᐊᐊᐧ, ᓅᐦᑯᑦ ᐁᓴ ᓯᒫᐠ ᑮ ᐃᑖᐤ ᑲᔮᐢ ᐁᐊᐧᑯ ᐅᐄᐧᐦᐅᐃᐧᐣ ᓅᐦᑯᑦ ᓅᐦᑖᐃᐧᐩ ᐊᐊᐧ ᐅᑳᐃᐧᔭ, ᓯᒫᐠ ᑮ ᐃᑖᐤ ᐁᓴ ᓅᐦᑯᑦ, ᐁᐊᐧᑯ ᑎᐱᔭᐁᐧ ᓅᐦᑯᑦ᙮ ᐁᑲᐧ ᐊᐊᐧ ᓅᐦᑯᑦ, *her sis--* ᐆᐦᐃ ᐄᐧᒋᓵᓇ ᐆᐦᐃ *Mrs. Little Sioux* ᐁᐊᐧᑯ, ᒫᑲ ᐁᐊᐧᑯ ᐊᓇ ᑮ ᐃᑖᐤ ᓅᐦᑯᑦ ᐁ ᐃᐢᑫᐧᐃᐧᐨ ᑮ ᐃᑖᐤ᙮ ᑳ ᐃᐢᑫᐧ~, ᐁ ᐃᐢᑫᐧᐃᐧᐟ ᑖᐱᐢᑰᐨ, ᐁᑯᓯ ᑮ ᐃᓯᔨᐦᑳᓱᐤ᙮ ᐁᑯᓯ ᐊᓂᒪ ᐁ ᑮ~ ᑳ ᐃᐢᐸᔨᐠ᙮

[5. ᒦᒋᐃᐧᐣ]

ᑲᔮᐢ ᐁᐊᐧᑯ ᐆᒪ ᑳ ᐄᐧᐦᑕᒫᑕᑯᐠ, ᒫᑲ ᐁᑎᑫᐧ ᓇᒪ ᑮᑲᐧᐩ ᓂᑮᔮᐢᑭᐣ, ᐁ ᑖᐯᐧᔮᐣ ᐆᒪ ᑳ ᐃᑖᒋᒧᔮᐣ ᐁ ᑮ ᐯ ᓀᐦᐃᔭᐃᐧ ᐱᒫᑎᓯᕽ; ᐊᐦᐴ ᒦᓇ ~᙮

ᒥᐦᑕ ᐁ ᑮ ᐅᐦᑖᒋᐦᐅᕽ ᐁᑯᑕ ᐁ ᑮ ᐅᐦᒋ ᒦᒋᓱᕽ ᐁᑲᐧ ᒦᓇ ᐁ ᑮ ᑲᐊᐧᐦᐃᑫᒋᐠ ᓈᐯᐊᐧᐠ᙮ ᒣᑐᓂ ᑮ ᒥᓯ ᓴᑳᐤ ᐆᒪ ᐆᑕ ᐸᔨᐹᐧᑎᐢ᙮ ᐁᐊᐧᑯ ᐊᓂᒪ ᐁᑐᑫ ᐁ ᑮ ᑭᑖᒋᐠ ᐁ~ ᐆᐦ~ ᒥᐦᑕ ᐆᐦᐃ ᓇᒪ ᑮᑲᐧᐩ ᐁᑲᐧ ᑳ ᐊᔮᑭ᙮ ᐁ ᑮ ᐋᐦᐃᐢᐹᐢᑫᐧᔮᐠ ᐁᓴ ᐆᑕ ᒫᑲ ᒋᒪᒣᓴ ᐆᐦᐃ ᐁ ᑮ ᐅᓰᐦᑖᒋᐠ ᐁᑯᓂ ᐁ ᐊᑖᐋᐧᑫᒋᐠ᙮ ᑲᐦᑭᔭᐤ ᑮᑲᐧᐩ ᐁ ᐊᑖᐁᐧᒋᐠ: ᑭᐢᑎᑳᓇ, ᐃᐧᔮᐢ, ᐁᑲᐧ ᐆᐦᐃ ᐆᑕ, ᑲᐦᑭᔭᐤ ᑮᑲᐧᐩ ᐆᐦᐃ ᐅᐦ~ ᐅᐦᐱᑭᐦᒋᑲᓇ ᐆᐦᐃ, ᐋᐧᐊᐧ ᒦᓇ ᐁᑯᑕ, ᐱᒥᐩ — ᓰᑯᓴᑲᓇ, ᒨᓂᔮᐊᐧᐠ ᐆᑭ ᑳ ᐅᓰᐦᐋᒋᐠ — ᐁᑯᓂ ᐁ ᐅᐦᑎ ᐊᑖᐁᐧᒋᐠ᙮ ᓂᑮ ᒪᒥᔭᐧᐦᒋᑳᓈᐣ ᒫᓇ᙮ ᐁᑲᐧ ᒦᓇ ᐁ ᑮ ᒥᔨᑲᐃᐧᔮᕽ ᒫᓇ ᑲᔮᐢ ᐊᔨ~ ᑮ ᐃᑖᐧᓂᐤ ᒫᓇ « ᐊᓴᐦᑐᐃᐧᐣ », ᑭᔮᓇᐤ *rations* ᑮ ᐃᑖᐧᓂᐤ᙮ ᐊᔨ ᒫᓇ ᐁ ᑮ ᒥᔨᑲᐃᐧᔮᕽ ᐊᔨ, ᐊᔭ ᐊᐊᐧ, *bacon* ᐊᐊᐧ᙮ ᓲᐢᑳᐧᐨ ᒫᓇ ᐯᔭᐠ ᑭᑕᐸᐦᐃᑲᐣ [*sic*: ᑭᑎᐸᐦᐃᑲᐣ] ᐁ ᐁᐧᐁᐧᑭᓂᑲᑌᐠ ᐁ ᒥᔨᑲᐃᐧᔮᕽ᙮ ᐃᐧᔮᐢ, ᓰᐃᐧᓂᑲᐣ, ᐁᑲᐧ ᑲ~ ᐊᐦ, *prunes* ᐆᑭ, *prunes* ᐁ ᑮ ᐊᓴᒥᑲᐃᐧᔮᕽ᙮ ᓰᐃᐧᓂᑲᐣ, ᓂᐦᑎᐩ, ᐁᑲᐧ ᒋᐢᑌᒫᐤ, ᐁ~ ᑕ ᐃᓯ ᐋᐸᒋᐦᑖᕽ! ᐊᐧᐦᐋᐧ, ᑖᐱᐢᑯᐨ ᐁ ᑮ ᓂᑕᐤᒥᓯ ᐊᑖᐁᐧᕽ ᒫᓇ᙮ ᐁᑯᓂ ᐊᓂᐦᐃ ᐁ ᐊᓴᒥᑲᐃᐧᔮᕽ, ᐁᐊᐧᑯᓂ ᐊᓂᐦᐃ ᐁ ᒦᒋᔮᕽ᙮ ᐁᑲᐧ ~

ᐋᐢᑕᒥᑕ ᐁᑲᐧ, ᑮᑳᐧᐩ ᐁ ᑮ ᐄᐧᒋᐦᐃᑲᐃᐧᔮᕽ, ᑮᑳᐧᐩ ᐁᑎᑫᐧ ᐸᐦᑫᐧᓯᑲᓇᐠ ᒫᓇ ᓂᑮ ᐄᐧᒋᐦᐃᑲᐃᐧᓈᐣ᙮ *Nineteen twenty-two* ᐁᐊᐧᑯ, ᓂᑮ ᐄᐧᒋᐦᐃᑲᐃᐧᓈᐣ ᑳᐢᐱ ᐸᐦᑫᐧᓯᑲᓇᐠ, ᒣᑐᓂ ᐁ ᑮ ᒪᐢᑲᐃᐧᓯᒋᐠ᙮ ᒣᑐᓂ ᒫᑲ ᑮ ᐄᐧᐦᑭᒋᓯᐊᐧᐠ ᒫᓇ, ᐁ ᑮ ᓯᑲᐧᒋᐊᐧᓴᐧᑭᐠ ᒫᓇ ᓂᔭ ᐁᑲᐧ ᓲᒥᓂᓴᐠ ᐁ ᑕᑯᓇᑭᐠ᙮ ᓂᑕᐋᐧᓯᒥᓴᐠ ᐆᑭ ᐁ~ ᐁ~ ᑐᐦᑑᓵᐳᐩ ᐁ ᑕᑯᓇᐦᑭᐠ᙮ ᑮ ᒥᔪᒦᒋᓱᐊᐧᐠ ᒫᓇ ᐆᑭ ᐊᐋᐧᓯᓴᐠ᙮ ᐁᐊᐧᑯ ᐊᓂᒪ ᐁ ᓰᐃᐧᐳᐦᐋᐊᐧᓱᔮᐣ, ᐁ ᒦᒋᓱᒋᐠ ᐁᑯᑕ᙮

ᐁᑲᐧ ᓂᑮ ᒥᔨᑲᐃᐧᓈᐣ ᒦᓇ ᓵᐦ ᓲᐢᑳᐧᐟ ᐯᔭᐠ ᒥᐢᑎᑯᐊᐧᐢ ᐆᒪ ᐊᔨ, *canned meat*, ᑳ ᐴᐢᑲᐧᐦᐊᒪᕽ ᒫᓇ, ᐋᐢᑲᐤ ᓃᓱ ᒥᐢᑎᐠ~ ᐁ ᐃᐦᑕᓯᔮᕽ

ᐃᔨᑯᕽ ᐁ ᐃᓯ ᒥᔨᑲᐃᐧᔮᕽ᙮ ᐊᐧᐦᐋᐧ, ᐁᑲᐧ ᒫᓇ ᐁ ᓵᓵᐱᐢᑭᓴᒫᕽ ᐁᐊᐧᑯ᙮ ᓂᑮ ᐊᑎ ᓯᑲᑌᔨᐦᑌᓈᐣ ᐊᓂᒪ, *canned meat* ᐊᓂᒪ, ᑭᑭᐢᑫᔨᐦᑌᐣ, ᓂᑮ ᒥᓯ ᒥᔨᑲᐃᐧᓈᐣ ᐊᓂᒪ ᐋᐢᑲᐤ *eight boxes* ᐆᐦᐃ᙮ ᒪᑖᐧᐣ ᒌ ᐊᓂᐦᐃ *twelve* ᒫᓇ ᐁ ᑮ ᐊᓯᐊᐧᑌᑭ, ᑫᐦᒋᓈ, *twelve*, ᐁᐩ, ᐃᑐᓂ ᑮ~᙮ ᐊᐧᐦᐋᐧ, ᓂᑮ ᒪ ᒥᔪᐸᑦ~ ᓂᑮ ᒥᔪ ᐸᒥᐦᐃᓱᓈᐣ, ᓂᑮ ᒥᔪ~᙮

ᐊᓄᐦᐨ ᐆᒪ ᐁᑲᐧ, ᓲᓂᔮᐤ ᐱᑯ, ᓲᓂᔮᐤ ᐱᑯ ᐊᓄᐦᐨ, ᓲᓂᔮᐤ ᐁ ᐊᔮᐊᐧᐟ ᑳ ᒦᒋᓱᔭᐣ᙮ ᐁᑲᐧ, ᐁᑲᐧ ᐁᐊᐧᑯ ᐆᒪ ᒦᒋᐃᐧᐣ ᐊᐱᓰᐢ, ᐊᐱᓰᐢ ᓈᓂᑕᐤ ᑭᑑᑖᑯᓈᓇᐤ, ᒫᑲ ᐊᔨᐢᐠ ᐅᐦᑎᑕᐤ ᑕ ᒦᒋᔭᕽ᙮ ᐁᑲᐧ ᒦᓇ, ᓰᓰᐸᐠ ᒦᓇ ᑲᔮᐢ ᓂᑮ ᒧᐋᐧᓈᓇᐠ, ᐁᑲᐧ ᒦᓇ ᐁᐧᐢᑲᒫᓂᓯᐸᐠ ᓂᑮ ᒧᐋᐧᓈᓇᐠ᙮ ᐋᐧᐊᐧ ᓂᑮ ᒦᒋᓈᐣ, ᐁᐊᐧᑯᔨᑯᕽ ᐆᒪ ᑫ ᐃᐦᑭᕽ ᐆᒪ *this month* ᐊᐊᐧ, ᓂᑮ ᒦᒋᓈᐣ ᐋᐧᐊᐧ᙮ ᐁᑲᐧ ᐊᓄᐦᐨ ᑳ ᐅᐦᒋᒥᑲᐃᐧᔮᕽ ᐁᑲᐧ, ᑕ ᐅᐦᒋᒥ~ ᓅᐦᒋᒥᑲᐃᐧᓈᐣ ᐁᑲᐧ ᓰᓰᑊ ᑕ ᒧᐋᐧᔮᕽ᙮ ᑖᓀᐦᑭ ᐅᐦᒋ ᑲ ᐅᐦᒋᒥᑲᐃᐧᔮᕽ? ᑮᑳᐧᐩ ᐊᓂᒪ ᐁ ᒥᔪᓯᐟ ᐊᐊᐧ ᓰᓰᑊ, ᑖᓀᐦᑭ ᐁᑎᑫᐧ? ᑮᑳᐧᐩ ᒫᑲ ᑳ ᐅᐦᒋᒥᑯᔨᐦᑯᐠ ᒨᓂᔮᐊᐧᐠ? *Spray* ᐊᓂᒪ ᐆᑕ ᑳ ᐊᐢᑖᒋᐠ *in a field*, ᑳ ᑭᐢᑎᑫᒋᐠ *spray*᙮ ᐁᑯᑕ ᐆᐦᒋ ᓰᓰᐸᐠ ᐁ ᒦᒋᓱᒋᐠ, ᒨᔭ ᒥᔪᐸᔨᐤ ᐆᑌ ᐃᐧᔭᐃᐧᐋᐧᕽ ᑕ ᐊᑎ ᒧᐋᐧᔭᐦᑯᐠ ᓰᓰᐸᐠ᙮ ᐊᓄᐦᐨ ᐁᑲᐧ ᒨᐩ ᓂᑲᐢᑭᐦᑖᓈᐣ, ᐁᑲᐧ ᐁ ᐄᐧᐦᑭᒋᓯᒋᐠ ᐊᓂᑭ ᓰᓰᐸᐠ᙮ ᒣᑐᓂ! ᒦᒋᒫᐳᐩ, ᐸᐦᑫᐧᓯᑲᐣ ᑳ ᑕᑯᓇᐟ, ᐸᐦᑫᐧᓯᑲᐣ, ᒥᑐᓂ ᐊᐋᐧᓯᓴᐠ ᒫᓇ ᐁ ᑮᐢᐳᒋᐠ᙮ ᐊᓄᐦᐨ ᐁᑲᐧ ᓇᒨᐩ ᑮᑳᐧᐩ ᓂᐸᑭᑎᓇᒫᑲᐃᐧᓈᐣ ᑳ ᐊᔨᓯᔨᓃᐃᐧᔮᕽ ᑕ ᒧᐋᐧᔮᕽ ᐱᓯᐢᑮᐢ, ᐊᐦᔮ *deer* ᒦᓇ ᐊᐦᔮ ᐁᑐᑫ ᓅᐦᒋᒥᑲᐃᐧᓈᐣ ᐁᑲᐧ ᑕ ᒧᐋᐧᔮᕽ, ᒣᑳᐧᐨ ᐆᒪ; ᐊᔨᐢᐠ ᒦᒋᓱᐤ, ᐸᐹᒦᒋᐤ ᐆᒪ *spray* ᐄᐧᐢᑕ ᐱᐢᑕᐦᑕᑦ᙮ ᐁᑯᑕ ᐁᑐᑫ ᐊᐦᔮ ᐋᐦᑯᓯᐃᐧᐣ ᓂᑳᐦ ᑮ ᐅᐦᒋ ᑳᐦᒋᑎᓀᓈᐣ᙮ ᐄᐦ, ᐊᓄᐦᐨ ᐆᒪ ᐋᐧᐳᓴᐧᐠ ᒫᓇ ᐁ ᑮ ᒥᔦᐧᔨᒪᑭᐠ, ᓇᐊᐧᒋᑯ ᐁᑲᐧ ᓂᑯᐢᑖᐊᐧᐠ, ᐊᓂᒪ ᐁ ᐋᐧᐦ ᐃᑌᐧᕽ, *you know*, ᓈᓂᑕᐤ ᐃᓯ ᑖᐯᐧ, *you know*, ᐆᒪ *spray* ᐄᐧᐢᑕᐋᐧᐤ ᐱᑯ ᑮᑳᐧᐩ ᒦᒋᐊᐧᐠ, *grass* ᐊᔨᐢᐠ ᐆᑭ ᐋᐧᐳᓴᐧᐠ᙮ ᓂᑯᐢᑖᐊᐧᐠ ᒦᓇ ᐁᐊᐧᑯᓂᐠ ᓃᐢᑕ, ᓇᒨᔭ, ᓇᒨᔭ ᐋᑕ ᐁ ᑭᐦᒋ ᐃᑌᔨᒨᔭᐣ, *but* ᓇᔦᐢᑕᐤ ᐁᐊᐧᑯ ᐅᐦᒋ᙮ ᑮᐢᐱᐣ ᐁᑳ ᐁᑯᓯ ᑮ ᐃᐢᐸᔨᐠ, ᑫᔮᐱᐨ ᐆᒪ ᐋᐧᐳᓴᐧᐠ ~ ᓂᑮ ᓂᐦᑖ ᑖᐸᑳᐧᐣ ᒫᓇ ᑲᔮᐢ ᒫᑲ ᐁᑲᐧ ᒨᐩ ᓂᑳᐦ ᑲᐢᑭᐦᑖᐣ ᑕ ᑖᐸᑫᐧᔮᐣ᙮ ᐸᐦᑭᓯᓂᔮᐣ ᓈᓂᑕᐤ

ᐁᑯᑕ ᓂᑳᐦᐸᐱᒥᓯᓂᐣ, ᓇᒨᔭ ᐊᔨᐢᐠ ᒥᔮᐧᓯᓇᐧ ᓂᐦᒋᑲᐧᓇ, ᐆᒪ *arthritis* ᐁ ᐊᔮᔮᐣ, ᐁᑲᐧ ᐁ ᓴᐢᑲᐦᐅᐦᑌᔮᐣ᙮

[6. ᒦᓂᓴ, ᐸᐦᑫᐧᓯᑲᐣ ᐁᑲᐧ ᓂᐦᑎᐩ]

ᐊᐧᐦᐋᐧ, ᓃᐱᓅᕽ ᐆᒪ, ᒦᓂᓴ ᐆᑕ ᒣᑐᓂ ᐁ ᑲᑳᐧᔭᑫᔭᑎᑭ, ᒣᑐᓂ ᐁ ᓅᐦᑌ ᒦᒋᔮᐣ ᒦᓂᓴ, ᒣᑐᓂ ᐅᒥᓯ ᐁ ᐃᑖᐢᑭᐢᑯᑌᑭ᙮ *Walker* ᓂᑖᔮᐣ, ᐊᔭ ᐁ ᑮ ᒥᔨᐟ ᐊᓂᒪ, *Jean* ᐊᔭ, ᐋᑲᒐᐨ [*Akachuk*], ᐊᔨ, ᐁ ᑮ ᐄᐧᒋᐦᐃᐟ᙮ ᐁᐊᐧᑯ ᐁᑲᐧ ᒪᐦᑎ, ᐆᑕ ᐁᑲᐧ *my apron* ᓂᑳᐦ ᑭᐸᐧᐦᐱᑌᐣ, ᓂᑖᔩᑕᐦᐱᑌᐣ᙮ ᓂᓈᑕᐋᐧᐱᐣ ᒪᐦᑎ ᑌ ᐯ ᐃᑕᑯᑌᐠ, ᓴᐦᑫᐢ ᑕ ᐯ ᐃᑕᑯᒋᐠ, ᒨᐩ ᐊᐃᐧᔭᐠ᙮ ᓂᓯᐯᐧᐦᑖᐣ ᐁᑲᐧ ᐆᑕ ᐆᒪ ᓴᑳᕽ ᑭᓯᐋᐧᐠ, ᐁᐊᐧᑯ ᐆᒪ *walker*᙮ ᐊᐧᐦᐋᐧ, ᒦᓂᓴ ᐅᒥᓯ ᐁ ᐃᑖᐢᑭᐢᑯᑌᑭ᙮ ᒣᑐᓂ ᐁᑲᐧ ᐁ ᒪᐃᐧᓰᔮᐣ ᐁᑲᐧ, ᐊᐧᐦᐋᐧ, ᒥᐢᒐᐦᐄᐢ, ᐊᐧᐦᐋᐧ! ᓂᐯ ᐲᐦᑐᑳᐧᐣ ᐁᑲᐧ ᐅᔮᑲᐣ ᓂᐱᐩ ᓂᓰᑭᓀᐣ, ᐁ ᒫᔮᑕᐦᑭ ᐊᐧᐢᑭᒋᐸᔨᓇᐧ, ᐁᐊᐧᑯᓂ ᐁᑲᐧ ᓂᐁᐧᐱᓀᐣ ᐁᑲᐧ, ᓂᐁᐧᐱᓀᐣ ᐆᒪ ᓂᐱᐩ᙮ ᐊᐧᐦᐋᐧ, ᓂᓵᓵᐱᐢᑭᓴᐣ ᐁᑲᐧ ᒦᓂᓴ, ᐃᔨᓂᑐ ᐸᐦᑫᐧᓯᑲᐣ ᒦᓇ ᐊᐊᐧ ᒣᑐᓂ ᒥᔦᐦᑲᓯᐤ ᐊᔨᐢᐠ ᐁᔨᐁᐧᕽ ᓂᓂᐦᑖᓇᐊᐧᒌᐣ ᑫᔮᐱᐨ᙮ ᐁᐊᐧᑯ ᐆᒪ *muscles* ᑰᐦᐊᔮᐊᐧᑭᐠ ᐃᔨᑯᕽ ᐁ ᒫᐦᒫᑯᓇᐠ *bannock*᙮ [ᐹᐦᐱᓈᓂᐊᐧᐣ]

ᐁᑯᓯ, ᐁᑲᐧ *bannock* ᐁᑲᐧ ᐊᐊᐧ ᐃᔨᓂᑐ ᐸᐦᑫᐧᓯᑲᐣ ᓂᑳᐦ ᑮᐢᑭᓵᐧᐤ᙮ ᐁᐩ! ᐁ ᒪ ᒧᐊᐧᐠ ᐁᑲᐧ ᒦᓂᓴ ᐆᐦᐃ, *you know*᙮ ᒨᐩ ᐋᐃᐧᔭᐠ, ᓂᑫᒋᑯᓀᐣ ᐆᐦᐃ ᓃᐱᑎᐦᑲᓇ ᐁ ᑯᐢᑕᒫᐣ ᑕ ᐊᑎᓴᒫᐣ, *you know*, ᒨᔭ ᐊᐃᐧᔭᐠ᙮ ᒣᑐᓂ ᓂᑮᐢᐳᐣ ᒦᓂᓴ ᐁ ᒦᒋᔮᐣ᙮ ᐁᑲᐧ ᐃᐧᔮᓯᐢ ᐆᒪ ᐁ ᑕᑲᐧᐦᑕᒫᐣ ᐃᐧᔮᐢ, *you know*᙮

ᓂᐦᑎᐩ: ᑮᑲᐧᐩ ᐊᔨᐢ ᐆᒪ ᒦᓇ ᐁ ᐸᑳᐧᑕᒫᐣ ᓂᔭ᙮ ᓂᑮ ᐋᐸᒋᐦᑖᐣ ᒫᓇ ᓂᐦᑎᐩ ᐊᓂᐦᐃ ᑳ ᐊᓯᐊᐧᑌᑭ ᒪᐢᑭᒧᒋᓯᕽ ᒥᐢᑕᐦᐃ ᓂᑮ ᓇᐸᐦᑖᐃᐧᐢᐱᑌᐣ ᒫᓇ, ᑖᐱᐢᑰᐨ ᒫᓇ ᐸᑭᐊᐧᔮᓂᐢ ᐁ ᑭᑭᒥᓂᐦᑫᐧᔮᐣ ᐁ ᑮ ᐃᐢᐱᑕᒫᐣ ᐆᒪ ᓂᐦᑎᐩ᙮ ᐋᐧ, ᓂᑫᐧᐢᑮᐣ ᓂᑕᐋᐧᐨ᙮ *Loose tea* ᐁᑲᐧ ᓂᒪᒥᓂᐦᑳᐧᐣ ᑳᔮᐢ ᐅᐦᒋ᙮ ᒪ ᑮᑲᐧᐩ ᐁᐊᐧᑯ ~ ᒪ ᑮᑲᐧᐩ ~ ᒪ ᑮᑲᐧᐩ ᑕ~ ᑎᑕ ᐃᐢᐱᑕᒪᐣ ᐸᑭᐊᐧᔮᓂᐢ

ᐁᑯᑕ, ᓇᒎᔭ ᐊᔨᐢᐠ ~ *loose tea* ᐊᓂᒪ ᓂᑕᑖᐊᐧᐣ᙮ *Blue Ribbon* ᒫᓇ ᐊᓂᒪ ᐁᐊᐧᑯ ᐊᓂᒪ ᓂᑕᑖᐊᐧᐣ, ᓂᒪ ᒥᓂᐦᑳᐧᐣ ᐁᐊᐧᑯ᙮ ᒫᑲ ᒦᐢᑯᐟ ᓂᐋᐧᓂᐦᐃᑯᐣ ᐊᓂᐦᐃ ᐊᔭ *leaves, you know*, ᒫᑲ ᒫᓇ ᑫᐧᔭᐢᐠ ᐁ ᐁᐧᐱᓇᒫᐣ ᐊᓂᑕ ᒫᓇ ᐊᔨ, ᐊᓂᒪ ᐊᔨ ᐃᑕ ᑳ ᑭᓰᐯᑭᔮᑲᓀᔮᐣ, ᐁᑯᑕ ᐃᐢᐸᔨᓇᐧ᙮ ᓂᐁᐧᐱᓀᐣ ᒫᑲ ᒫᓇ, *you know*᙮ *Loose tea* ᐆᒪ ᐁ ᒪ ᒥᓂᐦᑫᐧᔮᐣ᙮

[7. ᒪᐃᐧᒍᐢᒋᑫᐃᐧᓇ]

ᐁᑯᓯ ᐊᓂᒪ ᑳ ᐊᔨᑖᒋᒧᐢᑖᑕᑯᐠ ᑲᔮᐢ ᑮ ᒥᔮᐧᓯᐣ᙮ ᐁᑲᐧ ᒦᓇ ᓂᑳᐃᐧᐩ, ᓂᑳᐃᐧᐩ ᑮ~ ᑭᔦ~ ᒎᐩ ᐅᐦᒋ ᐚᐱᐤ᙮ ᒣᑐᓂ ᑮ ᒥᔦᐧᔨᐦᑕᒼ, ᑮ ᓵᑭᐦᑖᐤ ᐆᒪ ᐸᐦᑯ ᐊᔭᒥᐦᐋᐃᐧᐣ, *Catholic* ᐆᒪ ᑫ ᐃᑌᐧᔭᕽ, ᐁᑲᐧ ᒦᓇ ᐆᒪ ᓀᐦᐃᔭᐃᐧ ᐊᔭᒥᐦᐋᐃᐧᐣ ᑮ ᓵᑭᐦᑖᐤ᙮ ᐅᒥᓯ ᒫᓇ ᓂᑮ ᐃᑎᐠ, « ᓂᑖᓂᐢ, ᐁ ᓃᓯᑭ ᐆᐦᐃ ᐱᑯ ᑭᒪᐃᐧᒍᐢᒋᑫᐃᐧᓂᓇᐊᐧ, » ᑮ ᐃᑌᐧᐤ ᒫᓇ᙮ « ᐆᒪ ᐊᔨ, ᐸᐦᑯ ᐊᔨᓴᐠ ᐆᑭ — ᐸᐦᑯ ᐊᔨᓴᐠ ᑫ ᐃᑎᐦᒋᐠ *Catholic* ᐊᓂᑭ — ᐁᑲᐧ ᐆᒪ ᑳ~ ᐆᒪ ᑳ ᓂᐹᑫᐧᓯᒧᕽ ᐁᑲᐧ ᒦᓇ ᑳ ᒪᑐᑎᓯᕽ, ᓃᓯ ᐊᓂᐦᐃ ᐁᐊᐧᑯᓂ ᑭᔮᓇᐤ, » ᐁ ᑮ ᐃᑌᐧᐟ ᒫᓇ᙮ ᐁᐊᐧᑯ ᐅᐦᒋ ᑰᐦᓰᑭᐦᑖᔮᐣ, ᑳᑭᑫ ᓂᑮ ᐃᑐᐦᑕᐦᐋᐤ ᓂᑳᐃᐧᐩ *communion* ᑫ ᐃᑐᐦᑌᐟ ᓂᑮ ᐋᐧᒣᐋᐧᐤ *communion* ᐁ ᐅᑎᓇᕽ᙮ ᑫᑳᐟ ᑕᐦᑖᐧᐤ ᐊᔭᒥᐦᐁᐃᐧᑮᓯᑳᐤ ᐁ ᑮ ᐲᐦᑐᑫᐧᔮᕽ *church* ᐆᑕ᙮ ᑮ ᒥᔦᐧᔨᐦᑕᒼ ᓂᑳᐃᐧᐩ ᐁᑯᑐᐃᐧ ᐁ ᐃᓯ ᐊᔭᒥᐦᐋᐟ ᑮ ᓵᑭᐦᑖᐤ ᐁᑲᐧ ᒦᓇ ᐆᒪ ᓀᐦᐃᔮᐃᐧᐃᐧᐣ ᒦᓇ ᑮ ᓵᑭᐦᑖᐤ, ᓃᓯ᙮

ᐁᑲᐧ ᑫ ᐃᑎᑯᐟ ᐁᑲᐧ ᐊᔭᒥᐦᐁᐃᐧᔨᓂᐤ ᐃᐢᑫᐧᔮᐨ ᑳ ᐯ ᐲᐦᑐᑳᑯᔮᕽ, ᐋᐧᐦᑕᒫᐠ, « ᓇᐊᐧᐨ, ᓇᐊᐧᐨ *once a year* ᐱᑯ ᑮ ᐅᑎᓇᒪᐣ ᐆᒪ ᐊᔨ, ᑕ ᓂᑕᐃᐧ ᓴᐢᑲᒧᔭᐣ, » ᑮ ᐃᑎᐠ᙮ « ᑖᓂᑕ ᑕ ᐅᑎᓇᒪᐣ, *Easter time*᙮ ᐁᑯᑕ ᑕ ᐅᑎᓇᒪᐣ, ᐯᔭᑲᐧᐤ ᑲᓇᑫ᙮ ᐁᑲᐧᔨᑯᕽ ᑭᑭᑎᒫᑭᓯᐣ ᐁᑳ ᐁ ᐋᐧᐱᔭᐣ, » ᑮ ᐃᑎᐠ ᓂᑳᐃᐧᐩ᙮ « ᑭᐋᐧᐸᒥᐠ ᐁᑐᑫ ᒪᓂᑐᐤ ᐁᑳ ᐁ ᐋᐧᐱᔭᐣ, ᐯᔭᑳᐧᐤ ᐱᑯ ᐯᔭᑳᐧᐤ ᐅᑎᓇ, ᑕ ᓴᐢᑲᒧᔭᐣ᙮ » ᐁᑯᓯ ᓂᑮ ᐃᑑᑌᓈᐣ ᓂᑳᐃᐧᐩ᙮ ᐯᔭᑳᐧᐤ, ᐯᔭᐠ ᐲᓯᒼ ᐯᔭᑳᐧᐤ ᐁ ᐊᔭᒥᐦᐋᔮᕽ ᓂᑮ ᓂᑕᐃᐧ ᓴᐢᑲᒧᓈᐣ ᓂᑳᐃᐧᐩ᙮

ᐦᐋᑦ, ᑫᔮᐱᐨ, ᑫᔮᐱᐨ ᐊᐢᐱᐣ ᓂᑳᐃᐧᐩ ᐁ ᑮᐢ~ ᐁ ᑮ ᐃᓯ ᑭᐢᑭᓇᐧᐦᐊᒪᐃᐧᐟ ᑫᔮᐱᐨ ᓂᑲᓇᐁᐧᔨᐦᑌᐣ ᐊᓂᒪ, ᑫᔮᐱᐟ ᓂᓴᐢᑲᒧᐣ᙮ ᐃᐢᐲ ᒉᔪᐸᔨᑭ *communion* ᓂᑎᑐᐦᑖᐣ, *confession* ᐆᒪ, ᑭᑭᐢᑫᔨᐦᑌᐣ, ᓂᑎᑐᐦᑖᐣ ᐯᔭᑳᐧᐤ᙮ ᒉᔪᐸᔨᑭ ᐃᑕ ᓂᑎᑐᐦᑖᐣ, ᐯᔭᑳᐧᐤ᙮ ᐁᑲᐧ ᐆᒪ ᒦᓇ ᑳ ᒪᐃᐧᒍᐢᒋᑫᕽ ᐱᑯ ᐃᐢᐲ ᐃᐧᔭ ~ ᐱᑯ ᐃᐢᐲᕽ ᐃᐧᔭ ᐁᐊᐧᑯ ᓂᑎᑐᐦᑖᐣ᙮ [ᒨᐩ ᑲᐧᔭᐢᐠ ᐯᐦᑖᑲᐧᐣ] ᐆᒪ ᑭᔮᓇᐤ ᑳ ᐊᐩ~᙮ ᑖᑊ~ ᑖᐱᐢᑰᐨ ᑳ ᓂᐹᑫᐧᓯᒧᕽ ᐁᑲᐧ ᒦᓇ ᐁᑯᓯ ᐆᒪ ᑳ ᐊᔨ~, ᑳ ᒪᐃᐧᒍᐢᒋᑫᕽ ᐃᐧᔭ ᐁᐊᐧᑯ ᓂᑎᑐᐦᑖᐣ, ᒨᔭ ᑲᑖᐨ ᐯᔭᑳᐧᐤ ᐯᔭᐠ ᐊᐢᑭᐩ᙮ ᒫᑲ ᐃᐧᔭ ᐊᓇ ᓂᑳᐃᐧᐩ ᐁ ᑮ ᐱᒥᑎᓴᐦᐊᐧᐠ ᐊᓂᒪ ᐯᔭᐠ ᐊᐢᑭᐩ ᐱᑯ ~ ᐯᔭᐠ ᐊᐢᐠ~, ᑫᑕᐦᑕᐁᐧ ᓂᑮ ᐃᑐᐦᑖᓈᐣ *not every Sunday* ᒫᑲ ᒫᓇ *every Sunday* ᓂᑮ ᐃᑐᐦᑕᐦᐋᐤ ᐁ ᓴᑳᐯᑭᓇᐠ ᐁ ᐃᑐᐦᑌᔮᕽ ᓂᑕᐃᐧᓴᐢᑲᒧᐟ, ᑕ ᓂᑕᐤ ᓴᐢᑲᒧᔮᕽ᙮ ᐁᑯᓯ ᐁ ᑮ ᐃᓯ ᐊᔭᒥᐦᐋᐟ ᓂᑳᐃᐧᐩ᙮

ᐦᐋᑦ, ᐁᑲᐧ ᐆᑭ ᓂᒐᐋᐧᓯᒥᓴᐠ, ᐁᑯᓯ ᐁ ᐃᓯ ᐄᐧᐦᑕᒪᐊᐧᑭᐠ, ᐁᐊᐧᑯ ᓴᑭᓇᒪᐧᐠ᙮ ᓵᑭᐦᑖᐊᐧᐠ ᐆᑭ *Catholic* ᓂᒐᐋᐧᓯᒥᓴᐠ ᒥᔦᐧᔨᐦᑕᒪᐧᐠ᙮ ᐁᑲᐧ ᒦᓇ ᐆᒪ ᑳ ᓂᐹᑫᐧᓯᒧᕽ, ᑳ ᓀᐦᐃᔭᐃᐧ ᒪᐃᐧᒍᐢᒋᑫᕽ ᒦᓇ ᓵᑭᐦᑖᐊᐧᐠ, ᐄᐧᒉᐦᑕᒪᐧᐠ ᒦᓇ ᐁᐊᐧᑯ, ᐁ ᓃᓯᑭ ᐱᑯ᙮

ᑫᑕᐦᑕᐁᐧ ᐯ ᓇᑮᐊᐧᐠ ᐆᑕ, ᑮᑲᐧᔭᐠ ᐁᑐᑫ, *preachers* ᐆᑕ᙮ ᓇᒨᔭ ᓂᑲᐢᑭᐦᑖᐣ ᐁᑯᑌ ᑕ ᐃᓯ ᐄᐧᑫᐊᐧᑭᐠ, ᐋᑕᐃᐧᔭ ᐄᐧᐢᑕᐋᐧᐤ ᐁᓴ ᐁ ᒥᔦ ᓂᑐᑕᐦᑭᐠ ᑮᑲᐧᐩ, *you know*, ᒫᑲ ᐄᐧᐢᑕᐋᐧᐤ ᐸᐦᑳᐣ, ᐄᐧᐢᑕᐋᐧᐤ ~ *but* ᐄᐧᐢᑕᐋᐧᐤ ᐸᐦᑳᐣ᙮ ᐁᑯᓯ ᒫᓇ ᐁ ᐃᑌᔨᐦᑕᒫᐣ, ᒨᐩ ᐁ ᐸᑳᐧᑕᑭᐠ, *you know, but* ᒪ ᑮᑲᐧᐩ ᓂᔭ ᐁᑯᑕ ᐄᐧᐢᑕᐋᐧᐤ ᐊᔨᐢᐠ ᐸᐦᑳᐣ᙮ ᓃᐢᑕ ᐆᑭ ᓂᑕᐋᐧᓯᒥᓴᐠ ᐁ ᐃᓯ ᐄᐧᐦᑕᒪᐊᐧᑭᐠ, ᐃᑑᑕᒪᐧᐠ ᐁᐊᐧᑯ᙮ ᐁᐊᐧᑯ ᐆᒪ ᑫᑕᐦᑕᐁᐧ ᓴᐢᑲᒧᐊᐧᐠ ᐆᑭ ᐁᑲᐧ ᒦᓇ ᐆᒪ ᑳ ᐊᔨ~ ᑖᐱᐢᑰᐨ *Christmas, midnight mass* ᐃᑐᐦᑌᐊᐧᐠ ᐆᑭ ᓂᑯᑖᐧᐤ᙮ ᐋᐢᑲᐤ ᓂᐄᐧᓵᒥᑲᐧᐠ ᓂᑎᑐᐦᑕᐦᐃᑲᐧᐠ *midnight* ᐆᒪ ᐁ ᐃᑐᐦᑌᔮᕽ, ᐁ ᒪᐃᐧᒍᐢᒋᑫᕽ ᐊᔨᐢᐠ ᐊᓂᒪ ᒦᓇ ᐁᐊᐧᑯ, *you know*, ᑲᔮᐢ᙮ ᑲᔮᐢ ᐁᐊᐧᑯᓂ ᐊᓂᐦᐃ ᓃᓱ, ᓃᓱ ᐊᔭᒥᐦᐋᐃᐧᓇ ᐁ ᑮ ᐊᔮᔮᕽ᙮

[8. ᐱᒫᑎᓯᐎᐣ ᐘᔭᐑᑎᒥᕽ ᐁᑿ ᐊᐢᑮᐦᑳᓂᕽ]

ᐁᑯᓯ ᐊᓂᒪ ᒣᑐᓂ ᐁ ᑕᑲᐦᑫᔨᐦᑕᒫᐣ ᐆᒪ ᐁ ᐯ ᐃᓯ ᑲᑵᒋᒥᔭᐠ, ᐋᑕ ᒥᐢᑕᐦᐃ, ᐊᔨ, ᑿᔭᐢᐠ ᐁ ᑲᑵ ᐑᒋᐦᐃᑕᑯᐠ᙮ ᑳᔮᐢ, ᑖᓂᓯ ᐁ ᑮ ᐯ ᐸᐸᒥᐦᐅᕽ, ᐊᐦᐴ ᒫᓇ ᐘᔭᐑᑎᒥᕽ ᒦᓇ ᐁ ᑮ ᐘ ᐑᑭᕽ ᒦᑭᐚᐦᐱᕽ᙮ ᐊᓄᐦᐨ ᐁᑿ ᓴᓴᐢᑫᔨᐦᑖᑿᐣ ᐊᐎᔭᐠ ᑕ ᐱᐢᒋᐸᔨᐦᑖᐟ ᑮᑭ, ᒥᑐᓂ ᑕ ᓂᐸᐦᐃᐢᑰᐦᐃᐢᐠ ᐁᑯᑕ, ᐊᓄᐦᐨ ᐁᑿ ᐁᐘᑯ᙮ ᐁᑯᓯ ᐁ ᐃᐢᐸᔨᐠ, ᐁᐦᐊ᙮ ᐘᔭᐑᑎᒥᕽ ᐁ ᑮ ᓇ ᓂᐹᕽ, ᑳ ᓂᐹᔮᐣ ᐱᔦᓰᓴᐠ ᐁ ᐯᐦᑕᐘᒋᐠ ᑳ ᐊᑎ ᐚᐸᕽ᙮ ᐁᑿ ᐁ ᑯᑕᐌᔭᐣ ᐲᐦᒫᔨᕽ, ᑯᒐᐚᓈᐱᐢᑯᐢ ᐁ ᐑ ᐸᐢ~, ᐆᒪ ᐁ ᓂᑐᐦᑕᒪᕽ *fire*᙮ ᐋᐦ, ᑮ ᒥᔫᐧᓯᐣ ᑳᔮᐢ, ᐊᓄᐦᐨ ᐁᑿ ᓇᒨᔭ᙮ ᐘᐦᐚ, ᒥᑐᓂ᙮ ᐁᑿ ᒦᓇ ᑳᔮᐢ ᒦᓇ ᒫᓇ ᐁ ᑮ ᓇᐘᒌᔮᕽ ᑳᐦᑫᐘᐠ ᐆᒪ ᐊᔨ, *dry meat*, ᐁ ᓇᐘᒌᔮᕽ, *we roast it*, ᐘᐦᐚ, ᐁᑿ ᐱᒥᐩ ᐁᑯᑕ, ᐃᔨᓂᑐ ᐱᒥᐩ᙮ ᐘᐦᐚ, ᐁᑿ *bannock* ᒣᑐᓂ ᒫᓇ ᐁ ᑮ ᐑᐦᑲᓯᐠ ᑖᐱᐢᑰᐨ ᐆᒪ *dry meat*, ᑳ ᐹᓴᒥᕽ ᐆᒪ ᑳᐦᑫᐘᐠ᙮ ᒣᑐᓂ ᒫᓇ ᓂᑮ ᑕᑲᐦᑫᔨᐦᑌᓈᐣ᙮

ᐊᓄᐦᐨ ᐁᑿ ᐸᐦᑳᐣ᙮ ᑮᒁᐩ ᐅᒪᑭᓰᓴ ᐁᑿ ᐊᓂᐦᐃ ᐊᔨ ᑳ ᑮᓯᓴᐦᑭᐠ? ᐅᑖᑯᓰᕽ ᐁᑯᓯ ᓂᑮ ᓂᑕᐎ ᐃᑑᑌᓈᐣ᙮ ᐁᑿ ᒦᓇ ᑮᒁᐩ ᐁᑐᑫ ᐚᐚᐱᐢᑳᓯᓇᐧ ᐁᑯᓂ ᒦᓇ ᐁ ᓇᐘᒌᔮᕽ ᐊᓂᐦᐃ᙮ ᐘᐦᐚ, ᐑᐦᑲᓯᓇᐧ ᐎᔭ ᐋᑕᐎᔭ᙮ [JO: *Marshmallows?*] ᐁᑯᑐᐘ, ᐊᐚᓯᓴᐠ, ᑭᔮᑦ ᒣᑐᓂ ᐁ ᐱᐦᑲᐦᑌᑭ ᑮ ᓵᐦ ᓰᐸᐦᑕᒷᐠ, ᓃᐢᑕ ᒦᓇ ᐁᑯᓯ ᐁ ᐃᓯ ᒦᒋᔮᐣ ᐊᔨᐢᐠ ᐑᐦᑲᓯᓈᐧ᙮ [ᐹᐦᐱᓈᓂᐘᐣ] ᐘᐦᐚ! ᐘᐎᔭᑌᔨᐦᑖᑿᐣ ᐆᒪ ᐊᓄᐦᐨ ᑳ~

ᐋᐦ, ᐁᑿ ᒦᓇ ᐊᐚᓯᓴᐠ ᐊᓄᐦᐨ᙮ ᐘᐦᐚ! ᒨᔭ ᑮᒁᐩ ᑳᔮᐢ ᐁᐘᑯ᙮ ᐆᐦᐃ ᑫᐦᒐᐹᒋᑲᓂᓴ, ᐋᐦ, ᐁ ᐊᑎ ᐱᒪᑯᒋᐦᑭᐠ᙮ ᐘᐦᐚ, ᑖᓂᐢᐲᕽ ᐁᑐᑫ ᐱᑯ ᑕ ᐋᐳᒋᒁᓃᒋᐠ, ᑕ ᓂᐸᐦᐃᓯᐦᑭᐠ᙮ ᒫ ᑮᒁᐩ ᑳᔮᐢ᙮ ᑮᒁᐩ ᒫᓇ ᓂᔭᓈᐣ ᐁ ᑮ ᐋᐸᒋᐦᑖᔮᕽ? ᒥᐢᑎᐠ ᐁ ᑮᐢᑲᑕᐦᐊᒫᕽ, ᒥᐢᒋᑯᐢ, ᑕᑿᐦᐃᒥᓈᓈᐦᒋᑯᐢ, ᐁᐘᑯ ᐁ ᐸᐹᑌᐦᑕᐲᔮᕽ ᑖᐱᐢᑰᐨ ᑖᐺ᙮ ᑳᔮᐢ ᐁᐘᑯ ᐊᓂᒪ, ᐁᑿ ᐊᓄᐦᐨ ᑲ~ ᐅᐢᑳᑎᓯᐚᐘ ᑯᓂᑕ ᑳ ᐃᑕᑯᑌ~ [ᐹᐦᐱᓈᓂᐘᐣ] ᐁᐘᑯ ᐊᐣ~ ᑳᔮᐢ ᓂᒣᑕᐌᐎᓈᐣ ᓂᔭᓈᐣ ᒥᐢᒋᑯᓴ ᐁ ᑮ ᑌᐦᑕᐹᑕᒫᕽ ᐋᐦᑭ ᐃᑖᐟ ᑖᐱᐢᑰᐨ ᒥᓴᑎᑦ ᐊᓇ ᐁ ᐸᐹᒥᐸᐦᑖᔮᕽ᙮ [ᐹᐦᐱᓈᓂᐘᐣ] ᐘᐦᐚ, ᐁᐘᑯ ᐘᐎᔭᑌᔨᐦᑖᑿᐣ᙮

ᒣᑐᓂ ᐁᑯᓯ ᐊᓂᒪ, ᐊᓄᐦᐨ ᐁᑲᐧ ᒦᓇ ᐃᐧᔭ ᐋᑕ ᐃᐧᔭ ᐁᑲᐧ ᐸᐦᑳᐣ ᒦᓇ ᐆᒪ ᐊᓄᐦᐨ ᓂᑕᑎ ᐃᑌᔨᐦᑌᐣ ᐆᒪ ᐆᑕ ᑳ ᐊᔮᔮᕽ ᐸᔨᐹᐧᐟ's᙮ ᒥᑐᓂ ᑲᒫᐧᑕᐣ ᐆᑕ᙮ ᓇᒪ ᑮᑲᐧᕀ ᐁ~ ᒨᕀ ᐋᑳᐧᐢᑲᑦ ᐊᐃᐧᔭᐠ᙮ ᓂᔭ ᐃᐧᔭ ᐁ ᐃᓯ ᑭᐢᑫᔨᐦᑕᒫᐣ, *you know*, ᑎ~ ᑕᒥᓯ ᓵᐢ~ ᐊᐃᐧᔭᐠ ᑕ ᓴᓰᐦᑌᔨᐦᑕᒫᐣ ᐆᒪ *next door*, ᒨᔭ᙮ ᒣᑐᓂ ᓰᐢᑳᐧᐨ *at night*, ᒪ ᑮᑲᐧᕀ *no noise*, ᑲᐧᔭᐢᐠ ᓂᓇ ᓂᐹᓈᐣ᙮ ᒨᕀ ᑮᑲᐧᕀ ᐁᑲᐧ ᒦᓇ ~ ᓰᐢᑳᐧᐨ ᐊᔨ *nice and quiet* ᑳ ᐃᑌᐧᕽ, ᓰᐢᑳᐧᐨ ᒥᑐᓂ ᒥᔮᐧᓯᐣ ᐊᐢᑮᐦᑲᓂᕽ ᐊᐃᐧᔭᐠ ᑕ ᐊᔮᐟ᙮ ᐁᑯᑕ ᐊᔨᐢᐠ ᐆᒪ ᐁ ᐅᐦᑕᐢᑳᓂᓯᔭᕽ ᐊᐢᑮᐦᑳᓂᕽ᙮ ᒫᑲ ᐊᔨᐢᐠ ᑮᑲᐧᕀ ᑳ ᐃᑌᐧᔮᐣ, ᓰᓂᔮᐤ ᐁᑲᐧ ᐊᓄᐦᐨ, ᐁᐊᐧᑯ ᐆᒪ ᑰᐦᐊᔮᔦᐠ ᐆᑌᓈᕽ, ᑭᑕᑐᐢᑳᓈᐚᐤ ᐊᔨᐢ, ᓰᓂᔮᐤ ᐁ ᑲᐢᑭᐦᐋᐧᔦᐠ᙮ ᐊᓄᐦᐨ ᐁᑲᐧ ᓰᓂᔮᐤ ᑳ ᐲᑭᐢᑫᐧᐟ, ᑭᔭᐚᐤ ᐆᒪ ᐊᓄᐦᐨ ᑳ ᐅᐦᐱᑭᔦᐠ᙮ ᐁᑲᐧ ᒫᑲ ᓂᔭᓈᐣ ᐆᒪ ᑳ ᑫᐦᑌ ᐊᔨᐃᐧᔮᕽ, ᒪ ᑮᑲᐧᕀ ᐁᐊᐧᑯ, *you know*, ᓇᒨᕀ~ — ᐁᐊᐧᑯ ᐅᐦᒋ ᐁᑐᑫ ᐆᑕ ᑐᓂ ᑰᐦ ᑕᑲᐦᑫᔨᐦᑕᒫᐣ ᓂᔭ, *you know*, ᑭᓄᐧᓰᐣ ᐆᒪ ᑳ ᑮ ᓯᐯᐧᐦᑌᔮᕽ ᐆᑕ ᐅᐦᒋ *nineteen sixty-six* ᑳ ᑮ ᐅᐦᒋ ᐱᒥᔮᕽ᙮

[9. ᓰᓂᔮᐦᑫᐃᐧᐣ]

ᑮᑲᐧᕀ ᐊᓂᒪ ᑳ ᑮ ᐅᐦᒋ ᐱᒥᔮᕽ? ᑮ ᒣᑕᐚᓂᐃᐧᐤ ᒫᓇ ᐊᐧᔭᐄᐧᑎᒥᕽ *cars* ᐁ ᓂᑕᐃᐧ ᒣᑕᐁᐧᔮᕽ *bingo* ᐁ ᓂᑕᐤ ᒣᑕᐁᐧᕽ᙮ ᑲᔮᐢ ᐁᐊᐧᑯ ᐊᓂᒪ ᐊᐧᔭᐄᐧᑎᒥᕽ ᐁ ᑕᓯ ᒣᑕᐁᐧᕽ᙮ *Edenwold* ᐆᑕ, ᐁᑯᑌ ᓂᑎᑐᐦᑖᓈᐣ ᓂᑭᓭᔨᓃᑦ ᓂᐄᐧᒉᐚᐤ, ᓂᐆᓯᐦᐃᑲᐃᐧᓈᐣ, ᐁ ᒧᐦᒋ ᐆ~ ᐁ ᒧᐢᒋ ᒧᐢᑐᐦᑌᔮᕽ ᒫᑲ ᓂᐆᓯᐦᐃᑲᐃᐧᓈᐣ᙮ ᐁᑲᐧ ᐊᔨ ᐱᑯ ᐁ ᐅᓰᓂᔮᒥᔮᕽ, *fourteen dollars* ᐱᑯ ᐁ ᐊᔮᐋᐧᔮᕽ ᑳ ᓂᑕᐤ ᒣᑕᐁᐧᔮᕽ *Edenwold*᙮ *Nineteen -- nineteen sixty-six, twelfth of May -- July, July*, ᓇᒨᔭ ᐃᐧᔭ *May*᙮ *July* ᐁ ᒣᑕᐁᐧᕽ *Edenwold* ᐆᑕ᙮ ᐁᑯᑌ ᐁ ᒣᑕᐁᐧᕽ, ᓂᑭᓭᔨᓃᑦ ᑳ ᐅᑕᐦᐅᐁᐧᐟ *thousand dollars*᙮ ᐊᐧᐦᐊᐧᐦ! ᓂᐯ ᑮᐋᐧᓈᐣ᙮ ᓂᐯ ᑮᐋᐧᓈᐣ *a thousand* ᐁ ᐊᔮᐋᐧᔮᕽ, ᓃᐦᒑᔨᕽ ᐁᑯᑌ ᐁ ᐊᔮᔮᕽ᙮ ᓅ~ ᓂᑭᓭᔨᓃᑦ ᑮ ᐊᑐᐢᑫᐤ ᑭᐢᑭᓇᐧᐦᐊᒫᑐᐃᐧᑲᒥᑯᕽ ᐁ ᐁᐧᐸᐦᐃᑫᐟ, ᐁ ᐊᑐᐢᑫᐟ ᐊᓂᑕ ᐁ ᐯᐦᑭᐦᒋᑫᐟ᙮ ᓃᐢᑕᓇᐤ ᑕᐦᑖᐧᐱᐢᐠ ᐁ ᒥᔨᐦᐟ, ᐁ ᑎᐸᐦᐊᒫᐦᐟ *every two weeks* ᐁᐊᐧᑯ, *twenty dollars* ᐁ ᒥᔨᐦᐟ᙮ ᑮ ᐁᐧᐦᑕᑭᐦᒌᑲᓂᐃᐧᐤ ᐊᔨᐢᐠ ᑲᔮᐢ᙮

ᐄᐦ, ᐁ ᑭᐢᑫᔨᐦᑕᐦᑭᐠ ᐆᑭ *welfare*, ᓂᔭᓈᐣ *welfare*, ᓂᔭ ᐁᑲᐧ *Johnny* ᐁᑲᐧ *Marie* ᐁ ᓂᐢᑎᔮᕽ᙮ ᑳ ᑮᐢᑭᓯᑲᐃᐧᔮᕽ *our welfare*, ᓇᒨᐩ ᓅᐦᒥᔨᑲᐃᐧᓈᐣ᙮ ᐁᑯᓯ ᑳ ᐃᑌᐧᐟ *old man*, « ᓂᑕᑭᓴ ᐊᐊᐧ *thousand dollars*, » ᐃᑌᐤ᙮ « ᑭᔮᒼ, ᐱᒋᑖᐣ, » ᐃᑌᐤ᙮ « ᑲ ᓂᑕᐃᐧ ᐄᐧᒑᔮᒫᓇᐤ *Barbara*᙮ » ᑮ ᐊᑐᐢᑫᐤ ᐊᓂᑕ *eleven block Albert Street* ᐊᐊᐧ *Barbara*, ᑮ ᐊᑐᐢᑫᐤ ᐊᔨᕽ ᐋᐦᑯᓯᐃᐧᑲᒥᑯᕽ᙮ *Nurse* ᐆᒪ ᐁ ᐃᑕᑐᐢᑫᐟ᙮ ᓇᒨᔭ ᐃᐧᔭ ᐁ *nur*ᓯᐃᐧᐟ, *you know*, ᒫᑲ ᐁ ᐄᐧᒋᐦᐋᐧᐟ *nur*ᓴ᙮ ᐁᑯᓯ ᓂᑎᑖᐤ ᐊᐊᐧ *Barbara*, « ᑲ ᐯ ᐄᐧᒑᔮᒥᑎᓈᐣ, ᒥᓴᐋᐧᐨ ᑭᑕᑐᐢᑳᐣ, ᓂᑲ ᐯᐦᑲᐢᒋᑳᐣ ᓂᔭ ᐁᑲᐧ ᒦᓇ ᓂᑲ ᑮᓯᑌᐳᐣ ᐁᑲᐧ ᒦᓇ ᑲ ᐊᐢᑕᒫᑎᓈᐣ ᑕᒦᒋᔭᕽ, ᑕᒦᒋᔭᕽ, ᑕᒦᒋᔭᐣ, » ᓂᑎᑖᐤ᙮ « ᐁᐦᐊ, » ᐃᑌᐤ᙮ « ᐁᑯᓯ ᐃᐢᐲ ᒥᐢᑲᒫᓂ ᐋᐧᐢᑳᐦᐃᑲᐣ, ᐁᑯᐢᐲ ᓂᑲ ᓯᐯᐧᐱᒋᓈᐣ, » ᓂᑎᑖᐤ᙮ « ᐆᑕ ᓂᑲᑫᐧ ᐊᔮᓈᐣ ᐆᑌᓈᕽ, » ᓂᑎᑖᐤ᙮ « ᐁᐦᐊ, » ᐃᑌᐤ᙮ ᑖᐯᐧ ᓂᑕᐃᐧ ᐊᑐᐢᑫᐤ᙮

ᐁᑲᐧ ᒦᓇ ᐊᐊᐧ ᑭᓴᔨᓂᐤ ᒥᐢᑲᒼ *chickens* ᐁ ᐊᑐᐢᑳᑖᒋᐠ ᐃᐧᔭ ᐁᑲᐧ ᓂᑯᓯᐢ, *Johnny* ᐊᐊᐧ, ᐊᐊᐧ *Johnny Rockthunder, my son* ᐊᐊᐧ, *you know*᙮ ᐁᑯᑕ ᑮ ᐊᑐᐢᑫᐊᐧᐠ *chickens* ᐁ~ ~ᐱᒥ ᐊᑐᐢᑳᑖᒋᐠ, *you know*, ᑳ ᐱᒪᑯᒋᐦᑭᐠ *chickens* ᐁᑯᑐᐊᐧ, ᑮ ᓲᓂᔮᐦᑫᐊᐧᐠ᙮ ᐁᑯᓯ ᐁᑲᐧ ᐁ ᐴᔦᐟ, ᐁ ᐴᔦᐟ ᐁᑲᐧ ᐊᐊᐧ ᓂᑭᓴᔨᓃᒼ ᓂᑯᓯᐢ ᒦᓇ᙮ ᐊᐧᐦᐋᐧ, ᓂᔭᐢᑯᑕᒼ ᐁᑲᐧ᙮ ᐱᑕᒫ ᓂᑌᐹᐧᑌᐣ ᐊᔨ ᐋᐧᐢᑳᐦᐃᑲᐣ ᒪᐦᑎ ᑕᒥᐢᑲᒫᐣ᙮ ᓂᒥᐢᑫᐣ ᐯᔭᐠ, ᐁᑯᑕ *hundred and ten* ᓂᑎᑲᐃᐧᐣ ᑕᑎᐸᐦᐊᒫᐣ᙮ ᐁᑯᑌ ᓂᑎᐢᐱᒋᓈᐣ᙮

ᐁᑯᑌ ᐁᑲᐧ ᐁ ᐃᐢᐱᒋᔮᕽ, ᐊᐧᐦᐋᐧ, ᓇᒪ ᑮᑲᐧᐩ ᐁᑲᐧ ᓲᓂᔮᐤ ᑳ ᐲᑭᐢᑳᐧᑕᐠ ᐯᔭᐠ, ᐋᐦ, *Sister* ᐁ ᑭᐢᑫᔨᒪᐠ, *at Sacred Heart*᙮ *I phone her* ᐁᐊᐧᑯ᙮ ᐁᐊᐧᑯ ᑖᐯᐧ ᓂᐯ ᐋᓯᑌᒥᐠ᙮ « ᐊᐦᐋᒼ, » ᐃᑌᐤ᙮ « ᐯ ᐊᑐᐢᑫ ᐆᑕ, » ᐃᑌᐤ᙮ « ᓇᒨᔭ ᒫᑲ ᐃᐧᔭ *by the hour*, » ᐃᑌᐤ᙮ « ᑲ ᒧᐢᒋ ᑎᐸᐦᐊᒫᑎᐣ ᓲᓂᔮᐤ ᐁᑲᐧ ᒦᓇ ᑭᑲ ᒧᐢᒋ ᒥᔨᑎᐣ ᑮᑲᐧᐩ ᑕᒦᒋᔭᐣ ᑖᐱᐢᑰᐨ ᑮᑲᐧᐩ ᐆᒪ ᐱᒥᐩ ᐁᑲᐧ ᓵᓯᑲᓇᐠ ᐆᑭ ᐁᑲᐧ ᒦᓇ ᐸᐦᑫᐧᓯᑲᐣ ᐁᑲᐧ ᒦᓇ ᐊᐊᐧ ᐊᔭ, ᐆᐦᐃ ᓲᐃᐧᐦᑲᓰᓴᐠ᙮ ᐁᐊᐧᑯᓂᐠ ᑭᑳᐦ ᑮᐁᐧᐦᑕᐦᐋᐊᐧᐠ ᐁᑲᐧ *a little bit money*, » ᐃᑌᐤ᙮ ᑖᐯᐧ, ᑳ ᐃᑐᐦᑌᔮᐣ᙮ ᑖᐯᐧ ᐁ ᐅᑖᑯᓯᐠ

ᑳ ᐯ ᑮᐁᐧᐦᑕᐦᐃᒋᐠ ᒥᓯ ᐴᓯᐦᒋᑫᐊᐧᐠ ᓈᐊᐧᐩ᙮ ᐱᒥᐩ ᐁ ᒥᓯ ᒥᔨᒋᐠ, *Sisters* ᐆᑭ, *you know*᙮ ᑖᓂᑌ ᐁᐧᑎᓇᒧᐋᐧᑫᐧ, ᒪᑖᐧᐣ ᒌ ᐊᓂᑭ ᑳ ᑭᐢᑭᓅᐦᐊᒫᐦᒋᐠ ᓀᑭ ᐊᔭᒥᐦᐁᐃᐧᐦᑳᓇᐠ ᐁᑯᑌ ᐅᐦᒋ᙮ ᓂᒥᓯ ᐯ~ ᓂᐯ~ ᓂᒥᓯ ᐯ ᑮᐁᐧᑐᓇᐋᐧᐣ ᑮᑲᐧᐩ ᑕᒥᓯ ᒦᒋᔮᕽ, ᐸᐦᑫᐧᓯᑲᐣ, *pastry, cakes* ᐆᑭ ᓇᓈᑐᕽ᙮ ᓂᐦᑎᐩ ᒦᓇ ᓂᒥᔨᐠ, ᑳᐢᐱᓯᑲᐣ ᒦᓇ ᐯᔭᐠ ᓂᒥᐩ~᙮ ᐊᐧᐦᐋᐧ, ᒣᑐᓂ ᐁᑲᐧ ᒦᓇ ᐊᐊᐧ ᓲᓂᔮᐢ ᐊᐊᐧ ᐆᑕ, ᒣᑐᓂ ᓂᒥᔮᐧᒋᐦᐅᓈᐣ᙮ ᐁᑲᐧ ᐆᒪᔨᑯᕽ ᐁᑲᐧ ᐃᐧᔮᐸᐦᑭ ᒫᓇ ᐁ ᐃᑐᐦᑌᔮᐣ ᐁ ᒧᐢᑐᐦᑌᔮᐣ *Sacred Heart*, ᐁᑲᐧ ᐋᐦ, *ten block McTavish* ᐁ ᐋᔮᔮᐣ ᐁᑯᑌ ᐅᐦᒋ ᐁ ᒧᐢᑐᐦᑌᔮᐣ᙮ *St. Mary's* ᐊᓂᒪ, ᐋᐦ, ᐁᑯᑌ ᐁ ᐃᑐᐦᑌᔮᐣ *every morning*᙮

ᐱᔨᐢᐠ ᓂᑕᑎ ᒥᐦᒉᑎᓈᐣ ᐃᐢᑫᐧᐊᐧᐠ ᐁ ᐊᑐᐢᑫᔮᕽ᙮ ᒥᐦᒉᐟ ᐁᑯᑕ ᓅᐦ ᑭᐢᑫᔨᒫᐊᐧᐠ ᐆᑭ *young people* ᐆᑭ, ᐅᐢᑭ ᐃᐢᑫᐧᓯᓴᐠ ᐆᑭ; ᐁ ᐊᑐᐢᑫᔮᕽ, ᐁ ᐃᐧᔦᓴᒫᕽ ᐆᐦᐃ ᒪᐢᑭᓯᓇ᙮ ᐁᑲᐧ ᒦᓇ *jack-shirts* ᐆᐦᐃ ᐁ ᐃᐧᔦᓴᒫᕽ, ᐁᑲᐧ ᒦᓇ *mukluks* ᐁ ᐃᐧᔦᓴ~, ᐁ ᐊᑎ ᑲᐢᑮᑳᐧᑖᔮᐦᑯᐠ᙮ ᐱᔨᐢᐠ ᒣᑐᓂ ᒥᐢᑕᐦᐃ ᑮᑲᐧᐩ ᓲᓂᔮᐦᑫᐤ ᐊᐊᐧ ᐊᔭ *Sister*᙮ ᐊᑎ ᓲᓂᔮᐦᑫᐤ, ᓂᑎᐸᐦᐊᒫᑯᓈᐣ ᒨᐩ ᐃᐧᔭ *by the hour* ᓲᓂᔮᓴ ᐅᒥᓯ ᐃᓯ᙮ ᑲᐦᑭᔭᐤ ᑮᑲᐧᐩ ᐊᐦᐴ ᐱᑯ ᒦᓇ ᒪᓂᓯᑲᓂᓴ ᒦᓇ ᒥᓯ ᓈᑎᑎᓴᐦᐊᑦ ᒥᑐᓂ ᐁ ᒥᔮᐧᓯᑭ᙮ ᐁᑯᓂ ᒦᓇ ᐹᐦ ᐯᔭᐠ ᐁ ᒥᔨᑯᔮᕽ, ᐁᑯᓂ ᐊᓂᐦᐃ *seven dollars* ᐁ ᑎᐸᐦᐊᒫᕽ ᐊᓂᐦᐃ ᒪᓂᓯᑲᓂᓴ ᐸᐦᑫᑭᐣ ᐅᐦᒋ᙮ ᑎᐱᔭᐁᐧ ᐆᐦᐃ ᑫᔮᐱᐨ ᐊᓂᒪ ᒥᓯ ᒪᓂᓯᑲᓂᐢ ᐆᑕ ᓂᑖᐸᒋᐦᑖᐣ ᑳ ᑲᐢᑮᑳᐧᓲᔮᐣ᙮ ᒥᑐᓂ ᓂᒥᔪ ᓲᓂᔮᐦᑳᓈᐣ᙮

ᐁᑯᓯ ᐁᑲᐧ, ᐁᑯᓯ ᐁᑲᐧ, ᐃᐢᐱᒥᕽ ᐁᑲᐧ ᑳ ᐋᐦᑐᑫᔮᕽ ᐁᑲᐧ *eighteen twenty-one Scarth Street*᙮ *Scarth Street*, ᐁᑯᑕ ᐁᑲᐧ ᒦᓇ ᑳ ᐊᑐᐢᑫᔮᕽ᙮ ᒥᑐᓂ ᐁᑲᐧ, ᓂᔭ ᐁᑲᐧ *Mrs. Fourhorns, Violet* ᐃᑖᐤ᙮ ᐁᑲᐧ ᒦᓇ ᑮ ᐸᓈᑎᓯᐤ ᐯᔭᐠ ᐊᔭ *Dorothy Francis*, ᐊᐦᐴ ᐁᑐᑫ *you know her, that's the one*, ᐁᑲᐧ ᓂᔭ, ᓂᓂᐢᑎᓈᐣ᙮ ᓂᑲᐢᑮᑳᐧᓲᓈᐣ ᐃᐢᐱᒥᕽ [ᐁ ᐄᑲᑌ ᐃᑌᐧᐟ: *coffee* ᐄᐧᒥᓂᐦᑫᐧᔦᑯ], ᓂᑲᐢᑮᑳᐧᓲᓈᐣ᙮ ᐊᐧᐦᐋᐧ, ᒥᑐᓂ ᐱᑯ! ᓂᒫᐦᒥᔨᑲᐃᐧᓈᐣ ᐆᐦᐃ ᑮᑲᐧᐩ ᐆᐦᐃ ᐃᑖᐸᒋᐦᒋᑲᓇ ᐊᐦᐴ ᐱᑯ *aprons* ᐆᐦᐃ ᑕ ᑭᑭᐢᑭᑲᒫᕽ ᑳ ᑲᐢᑮᑳᐧᓲᔮᕽ, ... ᑳ ᑲᐢᑮᑳᐧᓲᔮᕽ᙮ ᐊᐧᐦᐋᐧ, ᒥᑐᓂ ᓂᑕᑲᐦᑳᒋᐦᐅᓈᐣ᙮

ᑫᑕᐦᑕᐁᐧ ᑳ ᐅᐃᐧᔭᓯᐁᐧᕽ᙮ « ᐄᐧ ᐅᔭᓯᐋᐧᓂᐃᐧᐤ, » ᐃᑖᐧᓂᐤ᙮ ᐄᐧ ᐅᔭᓯᐁᐧᐤ *Co-op Company* ᐃᑌᐧᐊᐧᐠ ᐆᑭ *Violet* ᐃᐧᔭᐋᐧᐤ, *Violet*᙮ ᑭᐢᑫᔨᐦᑕᑦ ᐊᐊᐧ ᐃᐧᔭ ᓂᐢᑎᑦ ᐊᐊᐧ ᐆᑕ *Violet*, ᐊᔭ ᐊᐊᐧ *Fourhorns*᙮ ᑭᐢᑫᔨᐦᑕᑦ ᐊᓂᒪ ᑲᐦᑭᔭᐤ, ᓇᒨᔭ ᐆᒪ ᐁ ᑭᔮᐢᑮᐋᐧᒋᒧᔮᐣ, ᑫᐧᔭᐢᐠ ᐁ ᐋᒋᒧᔮᐣ᙮ ᑖᐯᐧ, *Co-op* ᐊᓂᒪ ᑲ ᐅᑎᓇᕽ ᐆᒪ *shop* ᐆᒪ ᑳ ᐊᔮᔮᕽ᙮ *Co-op* ᑮ ᐅᑎᓇᑦ, *by the hour* ᐁᑲᐧ ᐁ ᐄᐧ ᒥᔨᑲᐃᐧᔮᕽ᙮ « ᐁᐦᐊ, » ᓂᑎᑖᐧᓈᐣ᙮ ᐊᐦᐋᑦ ᐁᑲᐧ ᓄᑌ ᑫ ᐃᐢᐱᒋᔮᕽ ᐁᑲᐧ ᐋᐦ, ᐋᐦ, *Victoria Avenue, way up east*, ᐁᑲᐧ ᓄᑌ ᐁ ᐊᔮᔮᐣ ᓄᒪ ᐊᔨ *Connaught Street, seventeen block, west side* ᐁ ᐊᔮᔮᕽ, ᐋᐧᐦᔭᐤ᙮ *Four miles* ᐁ ᐃᑐᐦᑌᔮᐣ ᒫᓇ᙮ ᒨᐩ ᐃᐧᔭ ᐁ ᐱᒧᐦᑌᔮᐣ, *bus* ᐁ ᐴᓯᔮᐣ᙮ ᑳ ᐅᑎᓇᕽ ᐁᑲᐧ *company* ᐊᐊᐧ ᐊᓂᒪ, *by the hour* ᐁᑲᐧ *five dollars* ᓂᑎᑲᐃᐧᓈᐣ ᐁ ᐄᐧ ᑎᐸᐦᐊᒫᑲᐃᐧᔮᕽ᙮ ᑖᐯᐧ᙮

ᒥᑐᓂ ᒥᓯ-*machines* ᐯ ᐹᐦ ᐲᐦᑐᑲᐧᑖᓂᐃᐧᐤ ᑲᐢᑭᑳᐧᓯᓈᑲᓇ, ᓂᑳᐦ ᑯᒌᐦᐃᑲᐃᐧᓈᐣ, ᓂᑳᐦ ᑲᐢᑭᐦᑖᓈᐣ᙮ ᒣᑐᓂ ᐁᑲᐧ ᐃᐢᑫᐧᐊᐧᐠ ᒥᓴᐦᑲᒥᐠ ᐁᑯᑕ ᐁ ᐅᑎᓂᐦᒋᐠ ᐁᑲᐧ ᐊᔨᐢ ᐁᑲᐧ *by the hour* ᐁᑲᐧ ᐁ ᐃᓯ ᒥᔨᑲᐃᐧᔮᕽ, *company* ᐊᐊᐧ ᐁ ᒥᔨᑯᔮᕽ, ᐋᐦ, *Co-op*᙮ ᐋᐦ, ᓂᑕᑐᐢᑳᓈᐣ, *eight o'clock* ᓂᒫᑕᑐᐢᑳᓈᐣ, *four o'clock* ᓂᐴᔪᓈᐣ᙮ *Bus* ᒫᓇ ᓂᑑᑎᓈᐤ ᓃᐢᑕ, *four miles* ᐁ ᐃᑐᐦᑌᔮᐣ *every morning*᙮ *Every morning* ᐊᓂᒪ ᐁᑯᑕ ᐁ ᐅᐦᑐᐦᑌᔮᐣ ᐊᔨ ᐁ ᑲᑫᐧ ᓰᓂᔮᐦᑫᔮᐣ᙮ ᐱᔨᐢ ᐁᑲᐧ, ᐋᐦ, *five dollars and thirty cents* ᑳ ᒥᔨᑲᐃᐧᔮᕽ᙮ ᐱᔨᐢᐠ ᐁᑲᐧ *thirty-five cents* ᓂᔭᐦᑭ ᒥᔨᑲᐃᐧᓈᐣ, *five thirty-five* ᓂᔭᐦᑭ ᒥᔨᑲᐃᐧᓈᐣ᙮ ᐋᐦ, ᓂᓰᓂᔮᐦᑳᓈᐣ ᑐᓂ, *every two weeks* ᓂᒥᔨᑲᐃᐧᓈᐣ *money*᙮

ᐁᑯᑕ ᐁᑲᐧ ᐃᔨᑯᕽ ᐁ ᓰᐢᑯ~ ᑲᐦᑭᔭᐤ ᑮᑲᐧᐩ ᐁ ᐅᓰᐦᑖᔮᕽ, *mukluks*, ᐸᑲᐧᐦᑌᐦᐅᓇ, *beadwork*, ᑲᐦᑭᔭᐤ ᑮᑲᐧᐩ ᐁ ᐃᐧᔪᓴᒫᕽ *jack-shirts*, ᐋᐦ! ᐊᐧᐦᐋᐧ, ᒥᓯ ᒥᐢᑎᑯᐊᐧᑕ ᒫᓇ ᐊᐊᐧ ᐁ ᑮ~ ᐁᐊᐧᑯ ᐊᐊᐧ ᓂᑑᑭᒫᒥᓈᐣ *Roger* ᑮ ᐃᑖᐤ, *Roger, Howard; Roger* ᒫᑲ ᑮ ᐃᑖᐤ᙮ ᐁᐊᐧᑯ ᒫᓇ ᐁ ᑭᐸᐦᐊᕽ ᐆᐦᐃ ᒥᐢᑎᑯᐊᐧᑕ, ᓂᑕᑐᐢᑫᐃᐧᓂᓈᐣ ᐆᒪ ᐁ ᓯᐯᐧᑎᓴᐦᐊᕽ᙮ ᑲᐦᑭᔭᐤ ᑮᑲᐧᐩ ᔨᔩᑲᐢᑎᓴᐠ ᒦᓇ, ᐁᑲᐧ ᒦᓇ ᑳ ᒫᓯᐦᑫᒋᐠ ᐊᓂᐦᐃ

ᐁ ᐯ ᐊᑐᐢᑫᒧᒋᐠ ᐊᔨ, *jackets* ᐊᓂᐦᐃ, *fringes* ᐆᑭ᙮ ᐁᐘᑯᓂᐠ ᐊᓂᑭ ᒦᓇ ᐁ ᑮ ᒥᓯ ᐅᓰᐦᑕᒪᐚᔮᐦᑯᐠ ᐊᓂᐦᐃ *jackets*, ᑮᐦ ᑳᐦ ᑭᑭᐢᑲᒪᐧᐠ ᒫᓇ ... ᐸᐦᑫᑭᓀᐧ *jackets*, ᓂᔭᓈᐣ ᐊᓂᐦᐃ ᐁ ᑮ ᐅᓰᐦᑖᔮᕽ᙮ ᐁ ᑮ ᐊᑐᐢᑫᒧᒋᐠ ᒫᑲ ᐏᔭ ᐁ ᐅᐦᑎᓯᐟ ᐊᐘ ᓂᑑᑭᒫᒥᓈᐣ, *you know*, ᒫᑲ ᒣᑐᓂ ᒥᐢᑕᐦᐃ ᓂᑮ ᓰᓂᔮᐦᑫᐢᑕᒪᐚᓈᐣ᙮ *Company* ᐁᐘᑯ ᐑᐢᑕ ᐊᔨᐢᐠ ᐁ ᐅᑑᑭᒫᒥᐟ ᐊᓂᐦᐃ, *you know*, ᐁᑲᐧ ᓃᐢᑕᓈᐣ ᐊᐘ ᓂᑑᑭᒫᒥᓈᐣ᙮

ᐚᐦᐚ, ᒥᑐᓂ ᐱᑯ ᓂᑮ ᒥᔪᐸᔨᓈᐣ ᐊᓂᒪ ᐃᔨᑯᕽ ᐃᐢᑯ ᓃᐢᑕ *sixty-five year old* ᑳ ᑮ ᐴᔪᔮᐣ᙮ *My last, my last day* ᓂᑮ ᓂᑕᐚᑐᐢᑳᐣ *sixty-five*᙮ ᑳ ᐯ ᒥᔨᐟ ᓂᑑᑭᒫᑦ ᐊᔨ ᐊᓯᐘᒋᑲᐣ ᐊᓯᓰᐍᑭᐣ ᐁᑯᑕ ᐯ ᐊᐢᑖᐤ, « *For your birthday,* » ᓂᑎᐠ᙮ ᑮᑳᐧᐩ ᐁᑐᑫ, *I thought* ᓂᔭ *a card* ᐁ ᒥᔨᐟ, *you know*, ᓂᑐᐦᑕᒪᐦᑲᒥᑭᓯᐣ ᐆᑌ; *las- my last day* ᐆᒪ ᐁ ᓂᑕᐘᑐᐢᑫᔮᐣ᙮ ᐁᑲᐧ ᐆᒪ ᓂᔫᐦᑌᓀᐣ ᐆᒪ *my* ~ ᑮᑳᐧᐩ ᑳ ᐯ ᒥᐩ~ ᐊᐑᓇ ᐊᐘ ᒥᑖᑕᐦᑐᒥᑕᓇᐤ ᑕᐦᑖᐧᐱᐢᐠ, *a hundred* ᐁᓴ ᐆᒪ *for my birthday*᙮ ᐚᐦᐚ, ᓂᑕᑕᒥᐦᐃᐠ ᐁᑯᑕ ᐁᑲᐧ ᐅᐦᒋ ᐁ ᐚᐦ ᐚᐢᑎᓇᒪᐘᐠ, « *Thank you,* » ᐁᑯᑌ ᐅᐦᒋ ᐁ ᐃᑕᐠ, *you know*, ᐁ ᓇᓈᐢᑯᒪᐠ ᐁ ᑎᐸᐦᐊᒪᐏᐟ, ᐁ ᒥᔨᐟ ᐆᒪ *for my birthday* ᐊᐘ ᓂᑑᑭᒫᒥᓈᐣ᙮ ᐁᑯᓯ ᐃᐢᑫᐧᔮᐨ ᐁᑲᐧ ᓂᑮ ᐃᑎᐠ, « ᓇᒨᔭ ᐁ ᐸᑭᑎᓂᑖᐣ, » ᓂᑎᐠ, « ᑮᐢᐱᐣ ᓈᓂᑕᐤ ᐆᑕ ᐃᐢᐸᔨᑭ ᑭᓇᑲᒋᐦᑖᐣ ᑮᑳᐧᐩ, ᑭᑲ ᑌᐹᐧᑎᑲᐏᐣ, ᑭᑲ ᐯ ᐊᔨ~, ᑭᑲ ᐯ ᐅᑎᓀᐣ *a little bit work* ᑭᑲ ᑎᐸᐦᐊᒫᑲᐏᐣ, » ᐁ ᑖᐯᐧᐟ ᒫᑲ᙮

ᐁᑲᐧ, ᐁᑯᓯ ᐁᑲᐧ ᓀᑌ ᓂᑎᑐᐦᑖᐣ ᐁᑲᐧ ᓀᒪ ᐊᔨ, *Grey Nuns* ᓀᒪ ᓂᑮ ᐃᓯᔨᐦᑳᑌᓈᐣ, *Grey Nuns* ᒫᓇ ᐁᐘᑯ ᐆᒪ, *Pasqua* ᐁᑲᐧ᙮ ᐁᑯᑌ ᓂᑕᐱᐣ *x-ray* ᐁ ᓂᑕᐏᐅᑎᓇᒫᐣ, ᐋᓴᐩ ᐁ ᑮ ᑮᓴᑐᐢᑫᔮᐣ, ᐆᒪ ᐊᔨᐤ ᐊᓂᑕ *shop* ᐊᓂᒪ ᐋᓴᐩ ᐁ ᑮ ᐴᔪ~᙮ ᐁᑯᑕ ᐊᐘ *x-ray man* ᐊᐘ, ᒥᑐᓂ ᓂᑕᑲᐦᑫᔨᒥᐠ, *you know*, ᒥᑐᓂ ᓂᐹᐦ ᐲᑭᐢᑳᐧᑎᐠ, ᓂᑲᑫᐧᒋᒥᐠ ᑖᓂᓯ, ᓂᐚᐦ ᐑᐦᑕᒫᐠ ᑖᓂᓯ ᐆᑭ ᐊᔨᓯᔨᓂᐘᐠ, ᓂᑳᐦ ᑭᐢᑫᔨᒥᒫᐘ, *you know*᙮

ᐁᑲᐧ ᐆᒪ ᐃᑌᐧᐤ, « ᑫᔮᐱᐨ ᒌ ᐆᒪ *shop* ᐁ ᐱᒥᐸᔨᐦᑖᐟ? » ᐃᑌᐧᐤ᙮ ᐁᑯᓂ ᐆᐦᐃ ᐑᐦᐁᐤ ᐆᐦᐅ ᐆᑕ ᓂᐢᑎᒪ ᐆᐦᐃ *Violet* ᐊᐘ᙮ « ᓇᒨᔭ ᐁᑲᐧ ᓂᔭ, » ᓂᑎᑖᐤ᙮ « ᓂᑮ ᐴᔪᐣ, » ᓂᑎᑖᐤ, « *but* ᓂᑑᑎᓀᐣ ᒫᑲ

ᑫᔮᐱᐨ *a little bit work* ᐁᑯᑌ ᐅᐦᒋ, » ᓂᑎᑖᐤ᙮ « *Mr. Rogers* ᐊᓇ ᓂᑑᑭᒫᑦ᙮ » « ᐁᐊᐧᑯ ᐊᓇ ᐁ ᑮ ᑭᑐᑕᐠ, » ᐃᑌᐤ᙮ « ᐁᑲᐧ ᐆᒪ ᐁ ᑮ ᐄᐧᐦᑕᒪᐃᐧᐟ ᐁᑲᐧ ᐆᒪ ᐁ ᐃᓯᔨᐦᑳᓱᔭᐣ *Mary Louise Rockthunder,* ᑭᔭ ᐁᒋᑯᒫ, » ᓂᑎᐠ᙮ « ᐁᐦᐊ, » ᓂᑎᑖᐤ᙮ « ᑭᔭ ᒌ ᑲ ᐅᑎᓇᒪᐣ ᐊᔨ, » ᐃᑌᐤ, « ᐊᔨ ᐊᐱᓰᐢ ᐊᑐᐢᑫᐃᐧᐣ ᐊᐧᔭᐄᐧᑎᒥᕽ? » ᓂᑎᐠ᙮ « ᐁᐦᐊ, » ᓂᑎᑖᐤ, « ᓂᔭ᙮ » « ᐊᔨ, » ᐃᑌᐤ, « ᐁ ᓅᐦᑌ ᐊᑐᑎᑖᐣ, » ᐃᑌᐤ᙮ « ᒣᑐᓂ ᒥᓴᐦᑲᒥᐠ ᐆᑕ ᑮᑲᐧᐩ ᓂᑕᔮᓈᐣ, » ᐃᑌᐤ, « *nurses* ᐁᑲᐧ ᒦᓇ *doctors* ᐆᑭ, ᐁ ᐹᐦ ᐲᑯᐸᔨᓂᔨᑭ ᐊᔨ, » ᐃᑌᐤ, « ᐁᑯᑐᐊᐧᕽ ᐆᐦᐃ, » ᐃᑌᐤ, « ᐆᐦᐃ ᐅᑭᑭᐢᑭᑲᓂᐋᐧᐊᐧ ᑖᐱᐢᑰᐨ ᐆᒪ ᐋᔨ *jacket* ᐆᒪ, *ripping,* ᐁᑲᐧ ᒦᓇ ᐅᑖᓯᐋᐧᐊᐧ, *patching,* ᐁᑲᐧ ᒦᓇ ᐅᒪᐢᑭᓯᓂᐋᐧᐊᐧ, *patching,* » ᐃᑌᐤ᙮ « ᐁᑯᑐᐊᐧᕽ ᐁ ᓅᐦᑌ ᐊᑐᑎᑖᕽ, » ᐃᑌᐤ᙮ « ᒨᐩ ᒌ, ᓇᒨᐩ ᒌ ᓈᓂᑕᐤ ᐅᑎᓇᒪᐣ? » ᐃᑌᐤ᙮ « ᑖᐯᐧ, » ᓂᑎᑖᐤ᙮ « ᐁᑯᓯ ᐊᓂᒪ ᐁ ᐃᑕᑐᐢᑫᔮᐣ, » ᓂᑎᑖᐤ᙮ « ᓂᑳᐦ ᑮ ᐅᑎᓀᐣ, » ᓂᑎᑖᐤ᙮ « ᒫᑲ ᑭᑲ ᐃᑑᑌᐣ, » ᓂᑎᑖᐤ, « ᑮᐢᐱᐣ, ᑮᐢᐱᐣ ᐊᐃᐧᔭᐠ ᐁ ᐄᐧ ᐊᑐᓯᐟ ᑳᐦᑭᔭᐤ ᒪᓯᓇᐦᐃᑲᓇ ᐅᑕᔨᐃᐧᓂᐋᐧᐊᐧ ᐊᐄᐧᓇ ᐊᓇ ᐅᒪᐢᑭᓯᓇ, ᐁᑯᑕ ᑭᑲ ᐊᑯᐢᑕᐦᐁᐣ, » ᓂᑎᑖᐤ᙮ « *You paste it* ᐁᑯᑕ, ᑳᐦᑭᔭᐤ᙮ ᐁᑯᓯ ᐊᑎ ᑮᓯᐦᑖᔭᓂ ᑳᐦᑭᔭᐤ ᐆᐦᐃ ᐁᑯᑕ ᓂᑲ ᐊᑎ ᑭᑲᒍᐦᑖᐣ, *which ones* ᐊᓂᐦᐃ᙮ » « ᐁᑯᓯ ᓂᑲ ᐃᑑᑌᐣ, » ᐃᑌᐤ᙮ « ᑭᑫ ᐃᑐᐦᑕᑕᒫᑎᐣ, *you wait for me about, oh, about* ᓃᓱ ᑮᓯᑳᐤ ᐆᑕ ᐅᐦᒋ, » ᐃᑌᐤ᙮ « *You wait* ~᙮ » ᓂᑲᑫᐧᒋᒥᐠ, « ᑖᓂᑌ ᐅᐦᐟ~ ᐁ ᐋᔮᔮᐣ? » — ᓀᑌ ᓂᑮ ᐋᔮᐣ *2nd Avenue,* ᓀᑌ ᓀᒪ ᐋᔨ *street* ᐊᓂᒪ᙮ — « ᐁᑯᑌ ᓂᑕᔮᐣ, » ᓂᑎᑖᐤ ᐁᑲᐧ ᒦᓇ *my phone number* ᓂᑑᑎᓀᐣ, ᓂᒥᔮᐤ, ᐁᐊᐧᑯ ᒦᓇ ᐅᑎᓇᑦ᙮ « *I phone you,* » ᐃᑌᐤ, « ᒪᔭᐤ ᐄᐧ ᓯᐯᐧᐦᑌᔮᓂ᙮ » « *Okay*᙮ »

ᑖᐯᐧ, ᑫᑕᐦᑕᐁᐧ ᑳ ᐯ ᓴᐁᐧᐱᒋᑫᐟ *next day:* « ᑫ ᐋᐧᐸᕽ, ᑫ ᐋᐧᐸᕽ *you wait for me,* » ᐃᑌᐤ, « *about four o'clock,* » ᐃᑌᐤ᙮ « ᓂᑲ ᑮᓴᑐᐢᑳᐣ ᐆᑕ, » ᐃᑌᐤ, « *half past four*᙮ *You wait for me*᙮ » « ᐁᐦᐊ, ᐁᐦᐊ, » ᓂᑎᑖᐤ, « ᑲ ᐯᐦᐃᑎᐣ᙮ » ᐊᔨᐢᐠ ᓂᑲ ᒥᓭᐧᔨᐦᑌᐣ *bingo, any time* ᑕ ᓲᓂᔮᐦᑫᔮᐣ *for my bingo, you know*᙮ ᑖᐯᐧ! ᑳ ᑕᑯᐸᔨᐠ ᐆᑕ *nice*

ᐊᔨ, ᐊᔨ, ᐊᔨ ᐆᒪ *van* ᒥᑐᓂ ᐘᐦᐚ, ᐯ ᒪ ᒪᑘᐦᐃᑫᐤ ᐁᐘᑯ ᐊᐘ, ᐁᐘᑯ ᐊᐘ *x-ray man* ᐊᐘ, ᓂᓂᓯᑕᐍᔨᒫᐤ᙮ « ᓂᐯᑖᐣ ᐆᑕ ᐊᓂᐦᐃ, » ᐃᑘᐤ, « ᑳ ᐑ ᐊᑐᑎᑲᐏᔭᐣ, » ᐃᑘᐤ᙮ « ᓂᑲ ᓈᑌᐣ, » ᐃᑘᐤ᙮ « ᒎᔭ ᒌ ᓈᐣ~ ...? » «ᐯ ᐲᐦᑐᑿᑖ! » ᓂᑎᑖᐤ᙮ ᐘᐦᐚ, ᒥᓯ ᒥᐢᑎᑯᐘᐢ ᒉᑐᓂ ᐊᓂᒪ ᐁ ᒦᓴᐠ ᑳ ᐯ ᐲᐦᑐᑵᑕ~ ᐯ~ ᐯ ᐊᐢᑕᒪᐏᐟ᙮ ᐘᐦᐚ, ᑖᐣ ᐆᐟ ᐋᓂ ᑕᒦᓴᐦᐃᑫᔮᐣ! ᐊᐦᐴ ᒥᑖᓴᐠ ᒫᑲ ᐆᑭ ᐊᔭ *buckskin pantses* ᐆᑭ, ᑭᑭᐢᑫᔨᐦᑌᐣ, *hide* ᐆᒪ, *you know*᙮ ᐁᑿ ᒦᓇ ᐆᐦᐃ *jackets* ᐁ ᐋᐦ *rip*ᐃᐏᑭ᙮ « ᐁᐘᑯᓂ ᐆᐦᐃ, » ᐃᑘᐤ᙮ « ᑲᐦᑭᔭᐤ ᒪᓯᓇᐦᐃᑲᓇ ᑭᑲᒍᐘ ᐅᐑᐦᐅᐏᓂᐚᐘ, » ᐃᑘᐤ᙮ « ᐁ ᐊᑎ ᐃᓯ ᑮᓯᐦᑖᔭᐣ, ᐁᑯᓯ ᐃᓯ ᐊᑎ~... » « ᐁᐦ, ᑭᐑᐦᑕᒫᑎᐣ ᐁ ᐑ ᐊᑎ ᐊᑿᐦᐊᒫᐣ, » ᓂᑎᑖᐤ᙮ ᑖᐻ᙮ ᐁᑿ ᒥᔮᒋᑳᐧᓯᔮᐣ ᐁᑿ, ᓂᑮᓯᐦᑖᐣ ᐯᔭᐠ ᓂᑕᑎ ᐊᑯᐢᑕᐦᐁᐣ ᐊᓂᐦᐃ, ᐅᐦᐱᒉ ᓂᑕᑎ ᐊᓯᐚᑖᐣ ᑲᐦᑭᔭᐤ ᐆᐦᐃ᙮ « ᐁᑿ ᒪᔭᐤ ᑮᓯᐦᑖᔭᓂ, » ᐃᑘᐤ, « *you phone me,* » ᐃᑘᐤ᙮ « ᑲᐦᑭᔭᐤ ᓂᑲ ᒫᐘᓴᑿᓯᓇᐦᐁᐣ ᑖᓂᓯ ᐁ ᐃᑕᑭᐦᒋᑫᔭᐣ, » ᐃᑘᐤ᙮ ᓂᐑᐦᑕᒪᐚᐤ ᑖᓂᓯ ᐁ ᐃᑕᑭᐦᒋᑫᔮᐣ᙮ ᑮᑿᐩ ᐆᒪ, ᐊᐱᓰᐢ ᑮᑿᐩ ᐁ ᐲᑯᐸᔨᐠ ... [ᒪᑘ ᓴᐍᐱᒋᐸᔨᐣ] ᐊᐱᓰᐢ ᐁ ᐲᑯᐸᔨᐠ ᑮᑿᐩ ᐁᔨᐍᕽ ᐊᐱᓰᐢ ᑖᐱᐢᑰᐨ *seven dollars,* ᐁᑿ ᒥᐢᑕᐦᐃ ᑮᑿᐩ ᐁ ᐲᑯᐸᔨᐠ ᒥᐢᒐᐦᐄᐢ᙮ ᓂᑕᑎ ᒪᓯᓇᐦᐁᐣ ᐁᑯᑕ ᓂᑕᑎ ᒪᓯᓇᐦᐁᐣ, ᓂᑕᑎ ᒪᓯᐣ~ ᓂᒪᓯᓇᐦᐃᑳᐣ ᐊᔨᐢ ᐏᔭ, *you know*᙮ « ᐁᑯᓯ ᒪᔭᐤ ᑮᓯᐦᑖᔭᓂ, » ᐃᑘᐤ, « *you phone me,* » ᐃᑘᐤ᙮ ᓂᓇᑲᑕᒫᐠ ᐊᔨᐢ *phone number*᙮

ᒪᔭᐤ ᐁ ᑮᓯᐦᑖᔮᐣ ᑲ ᑕ~ ᐋᓴᐩ ᑳ ᐯ ᑕᑯᐸᔨᐟ᙮ ᐘᐦᐚ *two hundred and fifty* ᓂᑮ ᓲᓂᔮᐦᑳᐣ, *two hundred and fifty* ᓇᓭᐢᑕᐤ *repairing work* ᐁ ᐃᑑᑕᒫᐣ᙮ *You know,* ᐁ ᒦᓴᐦᐃᑫᔮᐣ ᐆᒪ᙮ ᐁᑯᓯ ᒫᑲ ᐊᓂᒪ *two fifty, lots* ᐁ ᑮ ᐅᓰᐦᐊᐠ, *you know,* ᓃᑭᕽ ᐁ ᒪ~ ᓇᒎᔭ ᐊᐏᔭᐠ ᑎᐸᐦᐃᑫᓯᒎᔭᐣ ᐁᑯᓯ, ᑌᐱᔮᕽ ᓂᒦᓴᐦᐃᑫᐏᐣ, *you know,* ᐋᑎᐦᐟ ᐊᐱᓰᐢ, *you know, seven dollars* ᐁᐘᑯᓂ ᒪᐢᑭᓯᓇ ᒦᓇ ᐊᐱᓰᐢ ᐋᑎᐦᐟ ᒫᑲ ᒫᐦ ᒥᐢᑕᐦᐃ, *you know, ripping* ᒥᐢᑕᐦᐃ ᐁᐘᑯ ᐊᓂᒪ᙮ ᒫᑲ ᑲᐦᑭᔭᐤ ᑮᑿᐩ ᐊᔨᐢ ᓂᑕᔮᐣ, *you know,* ᐊᓂᒪ ᑖᐱᐢᑰᐨ ᐊᔨ ᓵᐳᓂᑲᐣ ᐁᑿ ᒦᓇ *threa-,* ᐊᓂ ᐊᔨ, *string* ᒦᓇ ᐊᓂᒪ, *you know*᙮ ᑲᐦᑭᔭᐤ ᑮᑿᐩ, *pliers,*

ᒪᓂᓯᑲᓂᓴ, ᒣᑐᓂ ᓰᐢᑳᐧᐨ ᓂᑕᐱᐣ *one room* ᐊᓂᒪ ᐁ ᐊᔮᔮᐣ ᐁᑲᐧ ᒦᓇ ᐊᓂᒪ ᐊᑯᐢᑭᐊᐧᐦᐃᑲᐣ ᐁᐊᐧᑯ ᓂᑕᑎ ᐋᐧᐸᒥᐦᒑᐣ ᐁᑲᐧ ᐁ ᑲᐢᑭᑳᐧᓲᔮᐣ, *no time* ᓂᑮᓯᐦᒑᐣ᙮ *Two fifty* ᑳ ᐯ ᒥᔨᐟ ᑲᐦᑭᔭᐤ ᐆᒪ ᐁ ᒫᐊᐧᓴᑯᐯᐦᐊᕽ ᑖᓂᒣᔨᑯᕽ ᐁ ᑮ~ ᐄᐧᐢᑕᐋᐧᐤ ~ᑎᐸᐦᐃᑫᐦᐃᐦᒋᐠ ᐊᓂᑭ *people*, ᐊᐄᐧᓇ ᐊᓇ ᑳ ᐊᑐᓯᐟ, *you know*᙮ ᐁᑲᐧ ᑳ ᐯ ᓴᐁᐧᐸᔨᐠ *phone* ᐁ ᐊᑕᒥᐦᐋᐧ~ ᐁ ᐊᑕᒥ~ ᐁ ᐊᑕᒥᓈᒋᐠ ᐊᓂᑭ ᑳ ᐄᐧᐣ~ ᐆᑯ ᑳ ᐄᐧᒋᐦᐊᑭᐠ, *you know*᙮ ᒣᑐᓂ ᐁᔨᐁᐧᕽ ᓂᑮ ᓰᓂᔮᐦᑳᐣ ᐁᑯᐢᐲᕽ, ᒫᑲ *bingo* ᐊᔨᐢᐠ ᒥᐢᑕᐦᐃ ᐁ ᒥᓭᐧᔨᐦᑕᒫᐣ᙮ [ᐹᐦᐱᐤ] ᓇᒨᔭ ᓂᐲᐦᑖᐧᐣ, ᓇᒨᔭ ᒦᓇ ᓂᒥᓂᐦᑳᐧᐣ, *you know*᙮ [ᐹᐦᐱᐤ]

[ᐊᒋᔭᐤ ᐁ ᓇᑭᐱᑕᒥᕽ]

[10. ᓂᓃᑭᐦᐃᑲᐧᐠ]

ᓂᑮ ᐯ ᐯᔭᑯ ᐱᒫᑎᓯᐣ, ᓂᒥᓴᐠ ᐊᔨᐢᐠ ᓂᐢᑐ ᑳ ᐋᒋᒧᐢᑖᑕᑯᐠ ᑮ ᐸᓈᑎᓯᒋᐠ᙮ ᓂᑮ ᐯᔭᑯᐣ ᐁᑲᐧ ᒫᓇ ᓅᐦᑖᐃᐧᐩ ᐊᐊᐧ ᐁ ᑮ ᐃᓯᐟ, « ᑮᑲᐧᐩ ᑑᑕ ᐆᑕ, ᑲᐢᑭᑳᐧᓯ, ᑲᑫᐧ ᐅᓰᐦᑖ ᑕ ᐊᑲᐧᓇᐦᐅᔭᐣ᙮ ᑲᐢᑭᑳᐧᓯ, ᓂᑖᓂᐢ, ᐁᑲᐧ ᒦᓇ ᑮᑲᐧᐩ ᐆᑕ ᑑᑕᒪᐤ ᑭᑳᐃᐧᐩ ᐁ ᐄᐧ ᓇᑲᑕᒫᐣ᙮ ᒥᐦᑕ ᓂᑕᐢᑖᐣ ᐆᑕ, ᑭᐯᑕᒫᑎᓈᐋᐧᐤ ᑕ ᐴᓇᒣᐠ᙮ ᑭᑳᐃᐧᐩ ᓈᑲᑐᐦᑫ, ᑳᔭ, ᐁᑳᔭ ᓈᐦ ᓇᑲᒋᐸᐦ᙮ ᐁᑲᐧ ᒦᓇ ᓇᒨᔭ ᒥᔮᐧᓯᐣ ᑕ ᐸᐹᑳᐦ ᑭᔪᑫᔭᐣ᙮ ᐯ ᐃᑎᓵᐸᒫ~ ᐯ ᐃᑎᐢ~᙮ » ᑯᓂᑕ ᒫᓇ ᐁ ᑮ ᓴᑭᒥᐟ ᓅᐦᑖᐃᐧᐩ, « ᐯ ᐃᑎᓵᐸᒥᑲᐃᐧᔭᓂ ᓄᑌ ᐃᐢᑳᐧᐦᑌᒥᕽ, ‘ᑮᑳᐧᐩ ᐱᓭᓈᑕᕽ ᐊᐊᐧ?’ ᑭᑲ ᐃᑎᑳᐧᐠ᙮ ᓇᒨᐩ ᑲ ᐯᐦᑕᐋᐧᐤ ᐊᐃᐧᔭᐠ, » ᑕ ᐃᓯᐟ, « ᐃᐢᑳᐧᐦᑌᒥᕽ ᑭᑲ ᓃᐸᐃᐧᐣ ᑭᔭ, ᑭᑲ ᓇ ᓃᐸᐃᐧᐣ᙮ ᐁᑳᐩ ᐁᑯᓯ ᑑᑕ! ᐯᔭᑲᐧᓅᕽ ᑲᑫᐧ ᐊᔮ, ᑭᑳᐃᐧᐩ ᑲᓇᐁᐧᔨᐨ᙮ » ᓂᑮ ᓴᑭᒥᐠ ᒫᓇ ᐁ ᑮ ᐃᓯ ᑭᐢᑭᓇᐧᐦᐊᒪᐃᐧᐟ ᓅᐦᑖᐃᐧᐩ, *you know*, ᑯᓂᑕ ᒫᑲ ᐁᑐᑫ ᒫᓇ ᐁ ᑮ ᐃᓯ ᓴ ᓴᑭᒥᐟ ᐊᓂᒪ, *you know*᙮

ᐁᑯᓯ ᒫᓇ ᒧᐩ~, ᐁᑯᓯ, ᐁᑯᓯ ᓂᑮ ᐄᐧ ᑲᑫᐧ ᐃᑑᑌᐣ, ᑭᐢᐯᐤ *eight year old* ᐁ ᐊᔮᔮᐣ᙮ *nine year old* ᐁᑲᐧ, ᐁ ᑮ ᑌᐦᒋᑳᐸᐃᐧᔮᐣ ᒫᓇ

ᒥᐢᒋᑯᐊᐧᒋᐢ *bannock* ᒫᓇ ᐁ ᓇᐊᐧᒌᔮᐣ, ᐃᔨᓂᑐ *bannock* ᐊᐊᐧ ᓂᑳᐃᐧᐩ ᐁ ᐅᓰᐦᑕᒪᐊᐧᐠ᙮ ᓂᑮ ᓂᐦᑖ ᓇᐊᐧᒌᐣ ᐸᐦᑫᐧᓯᑲᐣ, ᐊᓴᓈᓀᐤ ᐁ~, ᑫᑳ ᒥᑖᑕᐦᐟ ᐁ ᐃᑕᐦᑐᐱᐳᓀᔮᐣ, *bannock* ᓂᑮ ᐅᓰᐦᐋᐤ ᐃᔨᓂᑐ ᐸᐦᑫᐧᓯᑲᐣ ᐁ ᓇᐊᐧᒌᔮᐣ ᑳ~᙮ ᒥᐦᑕ ᐊᔨᐢ ᒦᓇ ᐁ ᐴᓇᒫᕽ᙮ ᒥᐦᑕ ᐁ ᒪᓇ~, ᒎᐩ ᐁ ᓅᐦᑌ ᒣᐢᑎᓯᓯᔮᐣ, *you know*, ᓂᑕᐢᐱᓂᑳᐣ ᑮᑲᐧᐩ᙮ ᑮᑳᐧᐩ ᐁᑐᑫ ᓅᐦᑖᐃᐧᐩ ᑳᐦᐊᐢᑕᒪᐃᐧᐟ ᐋᑕᐃᐧᔭ ᐁᑯᑕ, ᑮᑳᐧᐩ ᐁᑐᑫ ᑳᐦᐊᐢᑖᐟ? ᒪᑖᐧᐣ ᒌ ᐊᓇ ᐁᑲᐧ ᐊᐢᑎᓯᐦᑳᐣ ᑳ ᐊᔮᐋᐧᔭᕽ, ᒪᑖᐧᐣ ᒌ ᐁᑯᑐᐊᐧᕽ ᐊᓇ, ᒎᐩ ᓂᑭᐢᑫᔨᐦᑌᐣ᙮

ᐁᑲᐧ ᐊᐊᐧ ᓂᒫᒫ ᒫᓇ ᐁ ᐊᐧᔭᐄᐧᐦᑕᐦᐊᐧᐠ, *washroom* ᐊᔨᐢᐠ ᐊᐧᔭᐄᐧᑎᒥᕽ ᐆᒪᑐᐊᐧᕽ ᐁ ᑮ ᐅᓰᐦᑖᕽ᙮ ᐁ ᓴᑳᐯᑭᓇᐠ ᓂᑳᐃᐧᐩ ᐁ ᐊᐧᔭᐄᐧᐦᑕᐦᐊᐧᐠ᙮ ᑳ ᑎᐱᐢᑳᐠ ᒦᓇ ᑳ ᐄᐧ ᓃᐹ ᐊᐧᔭᐄᐧᐟ, ᐱᑯ ᑕ ᐊᐧᓂᐢᑳᔮᐣ ᐁ ᑌᐹᐧᓯᐟ, ᐱᑯ ᑕ ᐳᐢᑕᔭᐃᐧᓂᓴᔮᐣ ᐁ ᓴᑳᐯᑭᓇᐠ ᐁ ᐊᐧᔭᐄᐧᐟ᙮ ᐁᐊᐧᑯ ᓂᑳᐃᐧᐩ ᐁ ᑮ ᐃᓯ ᐯ ᐸᒥᓇᐠ᙮ ᐊᓅᐦᐨ ᑳ ᑮᓯᑲᐠ ᓇᒎᐩ ᓂᒥᐦᑖᑌᐣ ᓂᑳᐃᐧᐩ ᐁ ᑮ ᐸᒥᐦᐊᐧᐠ᙮ ᓇᒎᔭ ᐄᐧᐦᑳᐟ ᓅᐦ ᑭᓰ ᑭᑐᑖᐤ ᓂᑳᐃᐧᐩ᙮ ᓇᒎᐩ ᐄᐧᐦᑳᐟ ᓅᐦ ᑭᓯᐋᐧᐦᐃᐠ ᓂᑳᐃᐧᐩ᙮ ᐁᐩ, ᒪᓂᑐᐤ ᓂᓂᑐᐦᑖᐠ, ᐁᑯᓯ ᐁ ᑮ ᐃᓯ ᐸᒥᐦᐊᐧᐠ ᓂᑳᐃᐧᐩ᙮ ᒎᐩ ᐄᐧᐦᑳᐟ ᓅᐦ~, ᒎᐩ ᐄᐧᐦᑳᐟ ᓇ~ ᑕᑲᑫᐧᑭᓰᒥᐟ ᓂᑳᐃᐧᐩ, ᓇᒎᔭ᙮ ᐁ ᑮ ᑭᑎᒫᑭᓇᐊᐧᐠ ᐁᑳ ᐁ ᐋᐧᐱᐟ ᓂᑳᐃᐧᐩ᙮ ᓂᑮ~ ᐊᓅᐦᐨ ᐁᑲᐧ ᓂᒥᓭᐧᔨᐦᑌᐣ ᐁ ᑮ ᐃᓯ ᐸᒥᐦᐊᐧᐠ ᓂᑳᐃᐧᐩ, ᐁᑳ ᐄᐧᐦᑳᐨ ᐁ ᑮ ᐯ ᑭᓰ ᑭᑐᑕᐠ ᐁ ᑮ ᐯ ᐃᓯ ᓇᑲᓯᐟ᙮

ᓅᐦᑖᐃᐧᐩ, ᐄᐧᐸᐨ ᓂᑮ ᓇᑲᑎᑯᓈᐣ᙮ ᓅᐦᑖᐃᐧᐩ, ᑲᔮᐢ ᑳ ᐸᓈᑎᓯᐟ ᐁᐊᐧᑯ *nineteen thirty-two, seventh of January* ᓅᐦᑖᐃᐧᐩ ᑳ ᐊᐧᓂᐦᐋᔮᕽ, ᐁᑲᐧ ᓂᒫᒫ ᑫᐦᒋᓈ *after about - about five years*, ᓂᔮᓇᐣ ᐊᐢᑭᐩ ᑫᐦᒋᓈ ᓂᑳᐃᐧᐩ ᐁᑳ ᒌ, *or* ᐁᑳ ᒌ ᓂᑯᑖᐧᓯᐠ ᐊᐢᑭᐩ ᓂᑳᐃᐧᐩ ᑳ ᑮ~ ᐋᐦ ~ᑮ ᐋᐢᑯᐦᐋᐧᐟ ᓅᐦ~ ᐅᑭᓴᔨᓃᒪ, ᓂᑳᐃᐧᐩ ᐊᐊᐧ, *you know*᙮ ᐁᑯᓯ᙮

ᐁᑯᐢᐲ ᐁ ᑮ ᐅᐦᒋ ᐯᔭᑯᔮᐣ, *nineteen thirty-eight* ᐁ ᑮ ᐅᐦᒋ ᐯᔭᑯᔮᐣ, ᐁ ᑮ ᐅᐦᒋ ᐯᔭᑯ ᐱᒫᒥᐦᐅᔮᐣ ᐆᒪᑐᐃᐧᕽ ᐋᐧᐢᑳᐦᐃᑲᐣ ᐁ ᑮ ᐊᔮᔮᐣ᙮ ᐁᑯᓯ ᐁᑯᑕ ᐅᐦᒋ ᓂᑮ ᐸ ᐯᔭᑳᐧᒋᐦᐅᐣ᙮ ᐱᔨᐢᐠ ᐊᐊᐧ ᑳ ᑮ ᒪᒥᐢᑲᐊᐧᐠ ᓂᑭᓴᔨᓃᑦ,

ᐁᑯᑕ ᐁ ᑮ ᐅᐦᒋ ᐊᐧ ᐄᐧᒉᐊᐧᐠ *nineteen thirties, my old man* ᐊᐊᐧ᙮ ᐁᑯᐢᐲᕽ ᐁ ᐅᐦᒋ ᐯᔭᑳᐧᒋᐦᐅᔮᕽ᙮

ᐁᑯᐢᐲᕽ ᐁ ᑮ ᐃᓯᐟ ᐆᒪ, ᐁᑳᐩ ᑕᑲᑫᐧ ᐁᐧᐱᓇᒫᐣ ᓂᐋᐧᐢᑳᐦᐃᑲᐣ ᐁ ᐄᐧ ᓇᑲᓯᐟ᙮ ᑫᔮᐱᐨ ᓂᑲᓇᐁᐧᔨᐦᑌᐣ ᓂᐋᐧᐢᑳᐦᐃᑲᐣ ᐁ ᑮ ᐃᓯ ᑭᐢᑭᓇᐧᐦᐊᒪᐃᐧᐟ ᑫᔮᐱᐨ ᓂᑑᑌᐣ᙮ « ᓇᒨᔭ ᐋᑳᐧᐢᐠ~ » ᓅᐦᑖᐃᐧᐩ ᐁ ᑮ ᐃᓯ ᑭᐢᑭᓇᐧᐦᐊᒪᐃᐧᐟ, « ᓇᒨᔭ ᐋᑳᐧᐢᑲᒼ ᐸᐹ ᑲ ᑭᔪᐠ~᙮ » ᑫᑕᐦᑕᐁᐧ ᓂᑭᔪᑳᐣ, ᑭᑭᐢᑫᔨᐦᐟ~, ᑫᑕᐦᑕᐁᐧ, ᑫᑕᐦᑕᐁᐧ, ᒫᑲ ᑲᐧᔭᐢᐠ ᐁ ᑭᔪᑫᔮᐣ᙮ ᓇᒨᔭ ᑮᑲᐧᐩ ᐁ ᓂᑕᐤ ᒫᔮᑕᕽ ᐁ ᐯᐦᑕᒫᐣ ᒦᓇ ᓇᒨᔭ ᑮᑲᐧᐩ ᐁ ᓅᐦᑌ ᒪ ᒫᔨ ᐋᒋᒧᔮᐣ, ᐁ ᓅᐦᑌ ᓂᑐᐦᑕᒫᐣ ᑮᑲᐧᐩ ᑕ ᐹᐦᐱᕽ ᑌᐱᔮᕽ, *you know*᙮

[11. ᒥᔪ ᐄᐧᒉᐦᑐᐃᐧᐣ]

ᐁᐊᐧᑯ ᐅᐦᒋ ᑳᐦᑭᔭᐤ ᐊᔨᓯᔨᓂᐤ ᑰᐦᒋ ᒥᔪ ᐄᐧᒉᐊᐧᐠ᙮ ᓇᒨᔭ ᐊᐃᐧᔭᐠ ᓂᒫᔨ ᐄᐧᒉᐋᐧᐤ᙮ ᓇᒨᔭ ᓈᓂᑕᐤ ᓂᓄᐯᐃᐧᓯᐣ ᑕ ᐃᑐᐦᑌᔮᐣ᙮ ᓇᒨᐩ ᐄᐧᐦᑳᐨ ᐊᐃᐧᔭᐠ ᓂᐯ ᑮᐦᑳᒥᐠ, ᓇᒨᐩ ᐄᐧᐦᑳᐨ ᐊᐃᐧᔭᐠ ᓂᑮᐦᑳᒫᐤ᙮ ᓇᒨᐩ ᐄᐧᐦᑳᐨ ᓂᒪ ᒫᔨ ᐋᒋᒧᐣ, ᓇᒨᔭ ᐁ ᒪᒥᐦᒋᒥᓱᔮᐣ, *you know, but* ᐁᑯᓯ ᐁ ᑮ ᐯ ᐃᑖᒋᐦᐅᔮᐣ ᐁ ᐋᒋᒧᐢᑖᑕᑯᐠ, ᐁᑯᓯ ᑕᑲᑫᐧ ᐃᑑᑕᒣᐠ ᑮᐢᑕᐋᐧᐤ᙮ ᐱᑯ ᐊᐃᐧᔭᐠ ᐃᐧᔮᐸᒫᓴᑯ ᑕᑲᑫᐧ ᐋᐧᐦᑰᒫᓴᐠ ᐋᑕ ᐁᑳ ᐁ ᓂᓯᑕᐁᐧᔨᒫᓴᐠ ᐊᐃᐧᔭᐠ᙮ ᓇᐊᐧᐨ ᐁᐊᐧᑯ ᑲᒥᔪᐦᑕᐦᐃᑯᓈᐋᐧᐤ, ᐁᑯᓯ ᒫᓇ ᓂᑮ ᐯ ᐃᑎᑲᐃᐧᐣ ᐁᑲᐧ *same time* ᒦᓇ ᐁ ᑲᑫᐢᑭᒥᑕᑯᐠ, *you know*, ᐱᑯ ᐊᐃᐧᔭᐠ᙮ ᐁᑳᐃᐧᔭ ᐊᐃᐧᔭᐠ ᓄᐯᐃᐧᓰᐢᑖᕽ! ᓇᒨᔭ ᒥᔮᐧᓯᐣ ᑕ ᓄᐯᐃᐧᓯᕽ ᐊᔨᐢ ᓇᒨᔭ ᑭᑭᐢᑫᔨᒫᓇᐤ ᐊᐄᐧᓇ ᐊᓇ ᐁ ᐋᐧᐸᒫᔭᕽ, ᑕᑲᑫᐧ ᑭᑐᑖᔭᕽ ᓇᐊᐧᐨ ᐁᑯᓯ ᑕ ᐃᓯ ᒥᓴᐧᔨᐦᑕᒼ: « ‘ᐁᐊᐧᑯ ᑳ ᑮ ᑭᑐᓯᐟ ᐁᑯᑌ ᑳ ᑮ ᐋᐧᐸᒪᐠ,’ ᑫᑕᐦᑕᐁᐧ ᑭᑫ ᐃᑎᐠ, » ᓂᑮ ᐃᑎᑲᐃᐧᐣ ᒫᓇ ᓃᐢᑕ᙮ ᑖᐯᐧ ᐊᓂᒪ ᐁᑯᓯ ᐁ ᐃᐢᐸᔨᐠ᙮ ᐁᑯᓯ ᓂᑑᑌᐣ ᐊᓅᐦᐨ᙮

ᐱᑯ ᐊᐃᐧᔭᐠ, ᓅᓯᓯᒪᐠ ᑳ ᐋᐧᐸᒥᒋᐠ ᑳ ᐯ ᓭᑭᑫᐧᓂᒋᐠ ᐁ ᐯ ᐅᒉᒥᒋᐠ᙮ ᒣᑐᓂ ᐊᓂᒪ ᐁ ᒥᓴᐧᔨᐦᑕᒫᐣ ᐁ ᓭᐁᐧᔨᒥᒋᐠ ᓅᓯᓯᒪᐠ᙮ ᓂᔭ ᒦᓇ

ᐁᓴᐍᔨᒪᑭᐠ᙮ ᓇᒨᔭ ᐊᐃᐧᔭᐠ ᓂᒪᓈ ᐄᐧᐦᑕᒪᐋᐧᐤ ᑮᑲᐧᐩ, ᐁ ᒥᔮᐧᓯᓂᔨᐠ ᐅᑎ ᑮᑲᐧᐩ ᑭᑭᐢᑫᔨᐦᑌᐣ ᓇᒨᔭ ᐃᐧᔭ ᐁ ᒫᔮᑕᕽ ᑮᑲᐧᐩ᙮ ᒥᐦᒉᑎᐊᐧᐠ ᓅᓯᓯᒪᐠ᙮ ᐋᑕ ᒦᓇ ᐁᑳ ᐁ ᓂᓯᑕᐍᔨᒪᑭᐠ ᓅᓯᓯᒪᐠ ᐊᓂᑭ, ᐊᐦᐴ ᒨᓂᔮᐊᐧᐠ ᓅᓯᓯᒪᐠ᙮ « ᐋᐦ, ᑯᐦᑯᒼ, *Grandma*! » ᐱᑮᐧᑕ ᓂᑎᑲᐧᐠ ᐁ ᓂᓯᑕᐍᔨᒥᒋᐠ ᒨᓂᔮᓴᐠ ᐊᔨᐢᐠ ᒥᐦᒉᐟ ᓂᓇᑲᔮᐢᑲᐋᐧᐊᐧᐠ᙮ ᒥᐦᒉᐟ ᓂᑭᑐᑖᐊᐧᐠ ᒨᓂᔮᓴᐠ᙮ ᐁᑯᑐᐊᐧᕽ ᒦᓇ ᐆᒪ ᐁ ᐸᐸᐹ ᐄᐧᑕᐱᐦᑫᒧᔮᐣ, ᐊᐋᐧᓯᐢ ᑳ ᑲᑫᐢᑭᒥᐦᐟ, ᑭᑭᐢᑫᔨᐦᑌᐣ, ᑳ ᐄᐧᐦᑫᐧᐱᕽ ᐊᓂᒪ ᐁᑯᑕ ᐊᓂᒪ ᒦᓇ ᐁ ᐸᐸᐹ ᐲᐦᑐᑫᐧᔮᐣ, ᐁ ᐸᐸᐹ ᐄᐧᒎᐦᑲᒪᐊᐧᑭᐠ ᐆᑭ ᓅᓯᓯᒪᐠ᙮ ᓂᔭ ᐊᔨᐢᐠ ᐁᑲᐧ ᐱᑯ ᓂᑫᐦᑌ ᐊᔨᐃᐧᐣ᙮ ᓇᒨᔭ ᐁᑯᓯ ᐁ ᐃᓯ ᓂᑐᑕᒪᐊᐧᑭᐠ ᑕ ᐃᓯ~ ᑕ ᐃᓯ ᐄᐧ~ ᑕ ᐃᓯ ᓰᐦᑭᒥᒋᐠ ᒫᑲ ᓃᐢᑕ ᐁ ᑲᑫᐧ ᐄᐧᒎᐦᑲᒪᐊᐧᑭᐠ, ᐁᓯᑖᐧᐃᐧ ᑕ ᐄᐧᒎᐦᑲᒪᐊᐧᑭᐠ ᓂᐄᐧᒎᐦᑲᒪᐋᐧᐊᐧᐠ ᓅᓯ~, ᐁᑯᑕ ᐆᒪ ᑳ ᐄᐧᐦᑫᐧᐱᕽ ᐊᓂᒪ ᐆᑭ ᓅᐢ~᙮

ᐁᑲᐧ ᒣᑐᓂ ᓂᒥᔦᐧᔨᐦᑌᐣ ᑳ ᑭᑐᑕᐠ, ᑳ ᑭᑐᐟ~ ᓂᓄᐦᐃᔭᐋᐧᐣ ᒫᓇ, ᐱᑯ ᑕ ᐃᑌᐧᐢᑕᒪᐃᐧᔦᐠ ᓂᑎᑖᐊᐧᐠ ᒫᓇ ᐊᐃᐧᔭᐠ ᐁ ᓂᐦᑖ ᓄᐦᐃᔭᐍᐟ ᓂᑲ ᐃᑌᐧᐢᑕᒫᐠ᙮ ᐯᔭᐠ ᒫᓇ ᐆᑕ *Mr. Lavallee* ᐊᓇ, *Alphonse*, ᐁᐊᐧᑯ ᒫᓇ ᓂᑎᑌᐧᐢᑕᒫᐠ ᐊᓇ ᓂᑎᐦᑲᐧᑎᒼ, ᐆᒪ ᐁ ᑫᐧᐢᑲᐢᑖᐟ, *you know, how,* ᐁ ᐋᑲᔮᔩᒧᐟ᙮ ᓂᐄᐧᐦᑕᒪᐋᐧᐊᐧᐠ ᑖᓂᓯ ᐁ ᐃᑌᔨᐦᑕᒫᐣ, ᐊᑎ ᐄᐧᐦᑕᒼ᙮ ᐁᑲᐧ ᓂᑎᑖᐊᐧᐠ ᓇᒨᔭ ᐁᐊᐧᑯ ᐃᔨᑯᕽ ᐁ~ ᐆᑭ ᒨᓂᔮᐊᐧᐠ, ᓂᐄᐧᑕᐱᒫᓈᓇᐠ *lawyers* ᐆᑭ, ᐁᑲᐧ ᒦᓇ ᐆᑭ *welfare people*, ᓇᓈᑐᕽ ᐃᓯ᙮ ᓂᐄᐧᐦᑕᒪᐋᐧᐊᐧᐠ ᐁᑯᑕ, ᓂᑎᑖᐊᐧᐠ, ᓇᒨᔭ ᐆᒪ ᐁ ᓂᐦᑖ ᐋᑲᔮᔩᒧᔮᐣ᙮ ᓂᑖᑲᔮᔩᒧᑐᑕᐋᐧᐊᐧᐠ, « ᓇᒨᔭ ᐁ ᓂᐦᑖ ᐋᑲᔮᔩᒧᔮᐣ᙮ ᒣᑐᓂ ᐁ ᐸᐸᑳ ᐋᑲᔮᔩᒧᔮᐣ᙮ ᐁᐊᐧᑯᔨᑯᕽ ᐁ ᑮ ᐃᑐᐦᑌᔮᐣ ᑭᐢᑭᓇᐧᐦᐋᒫᑐᐃᐧᑲᒥᑯᕽ, ᒪ ᑮᑲᐧᐩ ᓂᑭᐢᑫᔨᐦᑌᐣ᙮ ᑯᓂᑕ ᓂᑖᐦᐋᑲᔮᔩᒧᐣ, ᒫᑲ ᓂᑯᐢᑌᐣ ᒫᓇ ᑕ ᐊᐧᓂᑐᓈᒧᔮᐣ, » ᓂᑎᑖᐊᐧᐠ᙮ « *A little bit* ᐆᒪ ᑖᐱᐢᑯ-ᑳᒥᓯ ᐲᑭᐢᑫᐧᕽ ᐆᒪ *high words* ᐁᑯᑕ ᓂᓇᑳᓯᓂᐣ᙮ » ᓂᑎᑖᐊᐧᐠ᙮ « ᒫᑲ ᓂᐄᐧ ᓄᐦᐃᔭᐋᐧᐣ, ᒫᑲ ᓈᐦᐊ ᓂᑲ ᐃᑌᐧᐢᑕᒫᐠ᙮ » « ᐁᐦᐊ, » ᓂᑎᑲᐧᐠ, « ᑕ ᑮ ᐲᑭᐢᑫᐧᔭᐣ ᐆᒪ ᑕ ᐋᑲᔮᔩᒧᔭᐣ, » ᓂᑎᐠ ᒫᓇ *lawyer* ᐆᑕ, « ᑭᓂᐦᑖᐋᐧᐣ᙮ » « ᒨᔭ, » ᓂᑎᑖᐤ᙮ « ᒨᔭ ᑭᐄᐧᐦᑕᒫᑎᓈᐋᐧᐤ ᓈᓂᑕᐤ

ᐃᓯ, ᓈᓂᑕᐤ ᐃᓯ ᐊᐧᓂᑐᓈᒧᔮᓂ ᓂᑲ ᒫᔨ ᐃᑑᑌᐣ᙮ » « *Okay, okay, okay, Grandma, okay*᙮ »

ᐁᑲᐧ ᒫᓇ ᐁᑲᐧ ᐊᐊᐧ *Alphonse* ᒫᓇ ᓂᑎᑌᐧᐢᑕᒫᐠ, ᐁ ᑫᐧᐢᑲᐢᑖᐟ ᑫᐧᔭᐢᐠ ᐁ ᐄᐧᐦᑕᒪᐊᐧᐠ ᐊᐊᐧ ᓅᓯᓯᒥᓈᐣ ᑳ ᐯ ᐃᑐᐦᑕᐦᐃᐦᐟ᙮ « ᐄᐦ, » ᓂᑎᑖᐤ ᒫᓇ, ᒫᑲ ᐁᑲᐧ ᐁ ᐋᑲᔮᓰᒧᔮᐣ ᒫᓇ ᐁ ᐋᑲᔮᓰᒧᑕᐊᐧᐠ ᐁᐊᐧᑯ ᐊᐊᐧ᙮ « ᓂᑐᐦᑕᐃᐧᐠ, » ᓂᑎᑖᐊᐧᐠ ᒫᓇ᙮ « ᐊᐱᓰᐢ ᓂᐄᐧ ᐲᑭᐢᑳᐧᐣ, ᓇᒨᔭ ᒥᐢᑕᐦᐃ ᐁ ᐄᐧ ᑭᑐᑕᐠ ᐊᐊᐧ ᓅᓯᓯᒼ᙮ » ᓂᑖᑲᔮᓰᒧᑕᐋᐧᐤ, « ᑖᓂᓯ ᐁ ᐃᓯ ᒌᐦᑫᔨᐦᑕᒪᐣ, ᑕ ᒌᐦᑫᔨᐦᑕᒪᐣ, » ᐁ ᐃᑕᐠ ᒫᓇ᙮ « ᐚᐸᐦᑕ ᐃᔨᑯᕽ, ᑖᓂᒣᔨᑯᕽ ᐆᑕ ᐁ ᐊᐱᔮᕽ᙮ *You know why we come here, we want to help you,* ᑕ ᓂᑐᐦᑕᐃᐧᔮᕽ, ᑕ ᑲᑫᐧ ᓴᐁᐧᔨᒥᔮᕽ, ᐁ ᓴᐁᐧᔨᒥᑖᕽ᙮ ᑮᐢᐱᐣ ᐁᑳ ᐁ ᓴᐁᐧᔨᒥᑖᕽ ᓇᒨᔭ ᐆᑕ ᓂᑳᐦᐊᔮᓈᐣ᙮ ᑖᓂᓯ ᐆᒪ ᑳ ᐃᑑᑕᒪᐣ? ᐸᑭᑎᓇ ᐁᐊᐧᑯ! ᓇᐊᐧᐟ ᑕᒥᔪᐦᑕᐦᐃᑯᔭᐣ ᑕᑭᐢᑭᓇᐧᐦᐊᒫᑯᓯᔭᐣ᙮ ᓇᒨᔭ ᑕᒥᔮᐧᓯᐣ ᑮᑯ~ ᑭᔭ *Dojack* ᐊᓂᒪ ᑕ ᐃᑐᐦᑌᔭᐣ, ᓇᒨᔭ ᐁᐊᐧᑯ ᑕᒥᔮᐧᓯᐠ ᑭᔭ ᐅᐦᒋ, ᓇᐊᐧᐟ ᑕ ᓂᑐᐦᑕᐃᐧᔮᕽ, ᓇᐊᐧᐟ ᑕ ᑲᑫᐧ ᑫᐧᐢᑭᓇᒪᐣ ᑭᒫᒥᑐᓀᔨᐦᒋᑲᐣ᙮ ᒪᓂᑐᐤ ᑭᑲ ᐄᐧᒋᐦᐃᐠ ᐁᑯᓯ ᐃᓯ ᑭᑲᒥᔪᑭᐣ ᐊᐦᐴ ᒌ ᑭᑲᒥᔪ ᓰᓂᔮᐦᑳᐣ ᐊᐦᐴ ᒌ ᑭᑲ~ ᑭᑲ ᐚᐸᒋᐦᐅ~ ᑳ ᐚᐸᒋᐦᑖᔭᐣ ᐊᐧᔭᐄᐧᑎᒥᕽ *car* ᐊᐦᐴ ᒌ ᑭᑲ ᑲᐢᑭᐦᑕᒫᓱᐣ᙮ ᐁᑳᐩ ᑭᑕᐅᑎᓇᒪᐣ ᐊᓂᒪ ᐁ ᒫᔭᑕᕽ, ᐁᑳᐩ ᑮᑲᐧᐩ ᑕ ᒌᐢᑕᐦᐃᓱᔭᐣ᙮ ᓇᐊᐧᐨ ᐅᒥᓯ ᐃᓯ ᑕ ᑭᑎᒫᑭᐦᑕᐃᐧᔮᕽ ᐁ ᓵᑭᐦᐃᑖᕽ ᐆᒪ, *we love you, that's why we here,* » ᓂᑎᑖᐊᐧᐠ ᒫᓇ ᐊᓂᑭ ᐊᐋᐧᓯᓴᐠ᙮ ᔮᐦ ᓈᒥᐢᑫᐧᐃᐧᐊᐧᐠ, ᐋᐢᑲᐤ ᐯ ᐃᐢᐸᔨᐦᐅᐊᐧᐠ ᐁ ᒫᑐᒋᐠ, ᑭᑭᐢᑫᔨᐦᑌᐣ, ᐁ ᐅᒣᒥᒋᐠ᙮ ᓃᐢᑕ ᒫᓇ ᓂᒫᑐᐣ ᐊᔨᐢᐠ ᓂᒨᐢᑯᒥᑲᐧᐠ, ᑖᐱᐢᑰᐨ ᐁ ᒨᐢᑯᒧᔮᐣ ᐁ ᒥᔦᐧᔨᐦᑕᒫᐣ ᑖᐱᐢᑰᐨ ᐁ ᐄᐧ ᑖᐯᐧᐦᑕᐦᑭᐠ᙮ ᑖᓂᑕᐦᑐ ᐁᑯᓯ ᓂᑎᑑᑕᐤ~ ᓂᐄᐧᒋᐦᐃᐋᐧᐣ᙮

ᓈᓂᑕᐤ ᑳ ᐚᐸᒪᑭᐠ ᐊᓂᑭ ᐊᐋᐧᓯᓴᐠ ᑳ ᐯᒫᐢᑕᒧᐦᑌᒋᐠ᙮ ᑭᔮᒼ *a lot of people* ᐆᑌ ᐯᒫᐢᑕᒧᐦᑌᒋᐠ ᐁ ᐯ ᓴᑭᑫᐧᓂᒋᐠ, « *Grandma, you here*᙮ » ᐁ ᐯ ᐅᒣᒥᒋᐠ᙮ ᐄᐦ, ᑖᓂᓯ ᒫᓇ ᐁ ᐃᑌᔨᐦᑕᒫᐣ, *my heart,* ᒥᐢᑕᐦᐃ ᒫᓇ ᓂᒥᔪᑌᐦᐋᐣ, ᐋᐧᐄᐧᐢ ᐁᑐᑫ ᒪᓂᑐᐤ᙮ ᐋᐧᐄᐧᐢ ᐁᑐᑫ ᒪᓂᑐᐤ

ᓴᐍᔨᒣᐤ ᐊᓂᐦᐃ ᐁ ᐃᑑᑕᒥᔨᐟ, ᐊᐦᐴ ᐁᑐᑫ ᒥᑐᓀᔨᐦᑕᒼ, « ᐦᐋᒼ, ᓅᓯᓯᒼ ᓂᑲ ᑫᐧᐢᑭᓈᐤ, ᐸᐦᑳᐣ ᑕ ᐃᑌᔨᐦᑕᒼ᙮ » ᐃᐧᐩ~ ᐊᐦᐴ ᐁ~ ᐊᐦᐴ ᐁᑐᑫ ᐁᑯᓯ ᐃᑌᔨᐦᑕᒼ ᒪᓂᑐᐤ, ᐊᐦᐴ ᓂᔭ ᐁᑯᓯ ᐁ ᐃᑌᔨᐦᑕᒫᐣ ᓂᒨᓯᐦᑖᐣ ᐊᓂᒪ ᒫᓇ, *I feel it*, ᑳ ᐯ ᓴᑭᑫᐧᓂᒋᐠ᙮ ᑳᓂᑲᓈ ᐁᑯᓯ ᐃᓯ ᒥᔪᑭᒋᐠ ᑳ ᐃᑖᔮᐦᑯᐠ, ᑖᐯᐧᐦᑕᐦᑭᐠ, ᐁᑯᓯ ᒫᓇ ᐁ ᐃᑌᔨᐦᑕᒫᐣ᙮

ᐄᐦ, ᐊᓄᐦᐨ ᐆᒪ ᒦᓇ ᓂᑮ ᐃᑐᐦᑖᐣ ᐆᑕ *last week* ᐆᑕ ᐆᑌᓈᕽ᙮ ᐁᑯᓯ ᐆᒪ ᐁ ᐃᑕᐱᔮᕽ ᐁ ᐚᓴᑳᐱᔮᕽ᙮ ᓂᑭ ᐲᑭᐢᑳᐧᐣ ᒦᓇ, ᒨᐩ ᐋᐃᐧᔭᐠ ~ ᒨᐩ ᐊᐃᐧᔭᐠ ᑭᑖ~ ᒨᔭ ᐊᐃᐧᔭᐠ ~ ᒨᐩ ᐊᐃᐧᔭᐠ ᑕ ᓄᐯᐃᐧᓰᐢᑕᐊᐧᐠ, ᓇᒨᔭ᙮ ᓇᒨᔭ, ᓇᒨᔭ ᓂᓄᐯᐃᐧᓯᐣ ᐊᔨᐢᐠ ᐁ ᒥᔮᐧᓯᐠ ᐊᓂᒪ, *you know*᙮ ᑮᑲᐧᐩ ᑕ ᓄᐯᐃᐧᐦᐃᑯᔮᐣ ᑕ ᒫᔨ ᐃᑕᐠ ᐊᔨᓯᔨᓂᐤ᙮ ᐦᐋᒼ, ᑕ ᒫᔨ ᐃᑕᐠ ᐊᔨᓯᔨᓂᐤ ᑭᑕ ᐃᑐᐦᑌᔮᐣ ᓄᑌ, ᓇᒨᐩ ᓂᑳᐦ ᑲᐢᑭᐦᑖᐣ ᑕ ᐃᑐᐦᑌᔮᐣ ᓂᔭ ᐊᔨᐢᐠ ᓂᑳᐦ ᓄᐯᐃᐧᐦᐃᓱᐣ ᐁᐊᐧᑯ ᐊᓂᒪ ᑳ ᐃᑌᐧᕽ᙮ « ᐁᑳᐩ ᐊᐃᐧᔭᐠ ᑲᑫᐧ ᒫᔩ~ ᒫᔨᐄᐧ~ ~ᒫᔨ ᐃᓯ᙮ ᐁᑳ ᑮᑲᐧᐩ ᐁ ᒫᔭᑕᓂᔨᐠ ᑮᒋ ᐊᔨᓯᔨᓂᐤ ᑎᑕ ᐃᑕᐟ᙮ ᓇᒨᔭ ᒥᔮᐧᓯᐣ᙮ ᓇᐊᐧᐨ ᐁ ᒥᔮᐧᓯᐠ ᑕ ᐃᑕᐟ, ᓇᒪ ᑮᑲᐧᐩ ᑲ ᓄᐯᐃᐧᐦᐃᑯᐣ ᐱᑮᐧᑕ ᑲ ᐲᐦᑐᑳᐧᐣ᙮ » ᐁᑯᓯ ᓂᑮ ᐃᑎᑲᐃᐧᓈᐣ ᒫᓇ ᑳ ᑲᑫᐢᑫᐧᒋᐠ ᐆᑭ ᑫᐦᑌ ᐊᔭᐠ, ᐁ ᑖᐯᐧᒋᐠ᙮ ᑮᐢᐱᐣ ᐊᔨᓯᔨᓂᐤ ᐁᑳ ᑲᐧᔭᐢᐠ ᐁ ᐃᓯᑌᐦᐁᐟ, ᐁᑳ ᑲᐧᔭᐢᐠ ᐁ ᐃᓯ ᐸᒥᓈᐟ ᐅᐄᐧᒉᐚᐧᑲᓇ, ᓄᐯᐃᐧᐦᐅᐤ ᐊᓇ᙮ ᒨᐩ ᑲᐢᑭᐦᑖᐤ ᑕ ᐃᑐᐦᑌᐟ ᒥᐦᒉᑎᓈᓂᕽ, ᒨᐩ ᑲᐢᑭᐦᑖᐤ ᑕ ᑭᑐᑖᐟ ᐊᔨᓯᔨᓂᐊᐧ, ᑯᓯᑐᓈᐦᑫᒧᐤ, ᑯᓯᐟ~ ᑯᐢᑌᐤ, ᑮ ᐯᐦᑕᒼ ᐁᑐᑫ ᐊᐊᐧ ᐁ ᑮ ᐃᑕᐟ, ᐁᑯᓯ ᐃᑌᔨᐦᑕᒼ, ᐁᑳ ᑲᐧᔭᐢᐠ ᑳ ᐱᒫᑎᓯᐟ ᐊᔨᓯᔨᓂᐤ᙮

ᓇᒨᔭ ᐁ ᒪᒥᐦᒋᒧᔮᐣ ᐆᒪ ᑳ ᐃᑌᐧᔮᐣ ᑲᐧᔭᐢᐠ ᐁ ᐄᐧᐦᑕᒫᐣ ᑖᓂᓯ ᐁ ᐃᐢᐸᔨᐠ ᑳ ᓄᐦᐃᔮᐃᐧᔭᕽ᙮ ᐱᑮᐧᑕ ᐁ ᐃᑐᐦᑌᕽ, ᓇᐊᐧᐨ, ᓇᐊᐧᐨ, ᓇᐊᐧᐨ ᑭᑑᑑᑌᒥᐣ ᐊᔨᓯᔨᓂᐤ, ᓇᐊᐧᐨ ᑭᐚᐦᑯᒥᐠ ᐊᔨᓯᔨᓂᐤ᙮ ᐁᐊᐧᑯ ᐊᓂᒪ ᑳ ᐃᑌᐧᕽ « ᐁ ᐅᑑᑌᒥᕽ, » ᐁ ᐚᐦᑯᒥᐢᐠ ᑲᐧᔭᐢᐠ ᑳ ᓄᐦᐃᔮᐃᐧᕽ᙮ ᒫᑲ ᒣᑐᓂ ᑲᐧᔭᐢᐠ ᐁ ᐲᑭᐢᑫᐧᔭᐣ, ᑖᐱᐢᑯᐨ ᐆᒪ ᑳ ᐋᑲᔮᓰᒧᔪᐠ *high words*᙮ « ᐁ ᐅᑑᑌᒥᕽ, » ᓇᒨᐩ ᑭᓂᓯᑐᐦᑌᓈᐚᐤ ᒫᑲ ᐁ ᐚᐦᑯᒥᐢᐠ ᐁᐊᐧᑯ ᐊᓂᒪ ᑳ ᐃᑌᐧᕽ᙮ ᐁᑯᑕ ᒫᐣ ᐋᓂᒪ ᑳ ᐃᑕᒫᐣ ᑳ ᓄᐦᐃᔭᐍᕽ, ᐊᐱᓰᐢ

ᒦᓇ ᐁ ᐋᐦᐃᐢᐱ ᐲᑭᐢᑵᕽ᙮ ᐋᑎᐦᐟ ᓇᒨᐩ ᓂᓯᑐᐦᑕᒷᐠ, ᐯᔭᑿᐤ ᐆᒪ ᑳ ᐋᑲᔮᓰᒧᓴᐠ ᐁ ᐃᐢᐱ ᐲᑭᐢᑵᐟ ᐊᐎᔭᐠ᙮ ᐁᑯᑕ ᒫᓇ ᓃᐢᑕ ᓂᑖ~ ᓂᑖ~ ᓂᑖᒋᓯᓂᐤ, *you know*, ᐁᑿ᙮ [ᐹᐦᐱᓈᓂᐘᐤ]

[ᐊᒋᔭᐤ ᐁ ᓇᑭᐱᑕᒥᕽ]

2
ᓀᐦᐃᔭᐃᐧᐢᑫᐧᐤ ᐅᐱᒧᐦᑌᐦᐅᐃᐧᐣ

[1. **ᐁ ᐊᐧᐃᐧᔭᑖᒋᒧᕽ**]

... ᐁᑲᐧ ᒫᓇ ᐆᑭ, ᒪᔭᐤ ᑮᑲᐧᐩ ᑳ ᑲᑫᐧᒋᒥᒋᐠ, ᐁᑯᓯ ᐁ ᒫᑖᒋᒧᐢᑕᐊᐧᑭᐠ, ᐁᑯᓯ ᒫᓇ ᐁ ᐄᐧ ᓂᐸᐦᐋᐦᐱᒋᐠ, ᐁ ᑖᐦ ᑌᐯᐧᔮᐦᐱᒋᐠ ᒫᓇ᙮ [ᐹᐦᐱᓈᓂᐊᐧᐣ] « ᒪᐦᑎ ᐯ ᑭᔪᑫᐦᑲᐣ ᓀᑌ ᓅᐦᑯᒼ ᑭᑲ ᐯ ᓈᑎᑎᓈᐣ ᐃᒋ, ᐯ ᒦᒋᓱᐦᑲᐣ᙮ » « ᐁᐦᐊ, » ᓂᑎᑖᐤ ᐊᓇ ᓅᐢ~, ᐆᑌ ᐁ ᑭᔪᑫᔮᕽ ᐆᑕ ᐊᔮᐤ ᐊᓇ ᓅᓯᓯᒼ, ᐊᔭ, ‘ ᒫᔭ ’ ᐃᓯᔨᐦᑳᓱᐤ, *Lorraine Bear* ᐃᓯᔨᐦᑳᓱᐤ ᓅᓯᓯᒼ ᐊᓇ, ᐁᑯᑌ ᐁ ᑮ ᑭᔪᑫᔮᐣ ᐁᑲᐧ ᐅᑳᐃᐧᔭ ᑮ ᐸᓈᑎᓯᔨᐊᐧ, *Mrs- Blanche* ᐊᓇ, *you know, she passed away* ᑲᔮᓭᐢ, ᒫᑲ *Lorraine* ᐊᐊᐧ ᐱᒫᑎᓯᐤ, ᐁᑯᑕ ᐊᓂᒪ ᐁ ᑭᔪᑫᔮᐣ᙮

« ᓂᑳᐃᐧᐢ, » ᐃᑌᐧᐤ ᐊᐊᐧ ᐊᔭ, *Blanche*, « ᒪᐦᑎ ᐋᒋᒧ ᐊᓂᒪ, » ᐃᑌᐧᐤ, « ᑳ ᑮ ᐋᐧᐦ ᐊᐧᐃᐧᔦᓯᔨᓃᐦᑫᔮᐣ, » — ᑐᓂ ᐊᔨᐢᐠ ᓀᐦᐃᔭᐁᐧᐊᐧᐠ, — « ᑳ ᑮ ᐋᐧᐦ ᐊᐧᐃᐧᔭᐢ~, ᑳ ᑮ ᐋᐧᐦ ᐊᐧᐃᐧᔭᓯᑑᑕᒪᐣ, ᒪᐦᑎ ᐁᐊᐧᑯ ᐋᒋᒧ᙮ » « ᐁᐦᐊ » ᓂᑎᑖᐊᐧᐠ, « ᑲᐦᑭᔭᐤ ᐆᒪ ᑭᔭᐋᐧᐤ ᒥᓴᐋᐧᐟ ᓅᓯᓯᒪᐠ, ᓈᐦᐊ ᐱᑯ ᓂᑎᐦᑲᐧᑎᒼ, ᓇᒨᔭ ᒫᑲ ᓈᓂᑕᐤ ᐯᐦᑕᐃᐧᒋ ᑌᐱᔮᕽ ᑭᑕ ᐹᐦᐱᐟ ᐆᒪ ᑳ ᐄᐧ ᐋᒋᒧᔮᐣ᙮ » ᐁᑲᐧ ᐁᑲᐧ ᐆᒪ ᐁ ᐋᒋᒧᔮᐣ ᐁᑲᐧ, ᐋᐧᐦᐊᐧᐩ, ᐁᑲᐧ

ᐃᔨᑯᕽ ᑳ ᐄᐧ ᓂᐸᐦᐋᐦᐱᐦᐃᒋᐠ ᒣᑐᓂ ᐁ ᒫᐦ ᒎᐢᑳᐧᐦᐱᒋᐠ ᐁ ᐊᐧᐃᐧᔭᐢ~, ᐁ ᐊᐧᐃᐧᔭᓯᐦᑕᐃᐧᒋᐠ ᑖᓂᓯ ᐆᒪ ᐁ ᐊᔨᑎᓂᑫᔮᐣ᙮

— ᑖᐯᐧ ᐊᔨᐢ ᐆᒪ, ᐆᒪ ᑳ ᐃᐢᐲᐦᑎᓰᔮᐣ ᑳ ᐋᒋᒧᐢᑖᑕᑯᐠ, ᒪ ᑮᑲᐧᐩ, ᒪ ᑮᑲᐧᐩ ᐁ ᐊᔭᒥᐦᒋᑫᔮᐣ; ᓂᑕᔭᒥᐦᒋᑳᐣ, ᓇᒨᔭ ᒦᓇ ~ ᓂᑕᔭᒥᐦᒋᑳᐣ, ᓂᓂᓯᑕᐃᐧᓀᐣ ᐋᑎᐦᐟ ᒨᐩ ᒫᑲ ᑲᒫᐟ [*sic; cf.* ᑲᑖᐨ] ᓂᓈᐦᑌ ᐊᔭᒥᐦᒋᑳᐣ; ᑯᓂᑕ ᑮᑲᐧᐩ ᓂᑕᑎ ᐃᓯ ᓇ ᓇᐊᐧᑎᓀᐣ, ᑭᑭᐢᑫᔨᐦᑌᐣ, ᐊᓂᒪ ᐊᔨᐢ ᑲᒫᐟ ᐊᔭᒥᐦᒋᑫᔮᐣ, ᐋᐦ, ᑭᔮᒼ ᐁᑯᓯ᙮ —

ᐄᐦ, ᓂᐋᐧᐦ ᐊᐧᓂ ᐅᑎᓀᐣ ᑮᑲᐧᐩ ᐁᑯᓂ ᐆᐦᐃ ᐊᐧᐁᐧᔩᐦᐅᐃᐧᓂ ᐊᔨᓴ ᐁᐊᐧᑯ ᐊᓂᒪ ᑳ ᐹᐦ ᐱᐢᒋ ᐊᐢᑖᔮᐣ; ᒥᐦᒉᐟ ᑮᑲᐧᐩ ᐆᒪ ᐁ ᐱᐢᒋ ᑑᑕᒫᐣ ᐁᐊᐧᑯ ᒫᑲ ᑳ ᐋᒋᒧᐢᑖᑕᑯᐠ ᑳ ᓯᓯᐯᑲᐦᐅᔮᐣ ᐊᓂᒪ ᐊᔨ, *marker* ᐊᓂ, *bingo marker* ᐁᐊᐧᑯ ᐁ ᐱᐢᒋ ᑑᑕᒫᐣ ᐁᑲᐧ ᒦᓇ ᐊᓂᒪ ᑳ ᓯᓯᐯᑲᐦᐅᔮᐣ ᐆᑕ ᓂᐢᑎᑳᐧᓂᕽ ᐊᔨ ᐊᓂᒪ *toothpaste*, ᐁᑲᐧ ᒦᓇ ᒨᔭ ᐁ ᐊᔭᒥᐦᑖᔮᐣ, ᐁᑲᐧ ᒦᓇ ᐊᐊᐧ ᓂᑖᓂᐢ ᐊᐊᐧ *Barbara* ᐁᐊᐧᑯ ᑳ ᐋᒋᒨᔮᐣ ᐁ ᐊᔨ~ ᐁ ᑲ ᑲᓇᐁᐧᔨᐦᑕᒫᕽ ᐆᒪ *suite*᙮ ᓂᐋᐧᐸᒫᐤ ᒫᓇ ᐊᐊᐧ ᓂᑖᓂᐢ ᑳ ᐄᐧ ᓯᐯᐧᐦᑌᐟ ᐁ *spray*ᐃᐃᐧᐟ ᐆᒪ ᐅᐢᑎᑳᐧᐣ ᐊᔨᐢ, ᐊᔨᐢ ᐊᔭ ᑕ ᑎᑎᐸᐁᐧᐦᐃᑫᐟ ᑖᐱᐢᑰᐨ; ᓂᐋᐧᐸᒫᐤ ᒫᓇ ᐁ *spray*ᐃᐃᐧᐟ ᐆᒪ, ᐆᒪ ᐅᐢᐟ~᙮

— ᐁᑲᐧ ᐆᒪ ᐁᐊᐧᑯᓂᐠ ᐯᔭᑲᐧᐣ ᐆᑭ *Joe Carrier* ᓂᑎᐦᑲᐧᑎᒼ ᐊᐊᐧ ᐁᑲᐧ ᒦᓇ ᓂᐢᑎᒼ ᐊᐊᐧ *Alice Carrier* ᑳ ᑮ ᐃᑎᐦᐟ ᐅᐄᐧᑭᒫᑲᓇ ᐆᐦᐃ, *couple* ᐆᑭ᙮ ᐁᐊᐧᑯᓂᐠ ᐆᑭ ᐁ ᐯ ᓈᑎᑯᔮᐦᑯᐠ᙮ ᐁᑲᐧ *Barbara* ᐄᐧᐢᑕ ᐄᐧ ᐄᐧᒋᐦᐃᐁᐧᐤ, ᑳᔮᐢ ᒫᓇ ᐆᐦᐃ ᐊᔭᐦᐊ *purses* ᐆᑕ ᑭᑮ ᑖᐱᐢᑫᓈᐋᐧᐤ ᐁ ᒥᔮᐧᓯᑭ, ᑖᐱᐢᑰᐨ *saddle* ᐆᑕ ᐁᑯᑐᐊᐧ, ᐁᑯᑐᐊᐧ, ᐊᑐᐢᑫᐤ ᐊᔨᐢ ᒫᑲ ᐄᐧᐢᑕ ᐁᑲᐧ ᐁ ᐄᐧ ᓂᑕᐃᐧ ᒣᑕᐁᐧᐟ᙮ —

ᐄᐦ, ᓂᐋᐧᐸᒫᐤ ᒫᓇ ᐊᐊᐧ ᓂᑖᓂᐢ ᐁ ᓯᓯᐹᑕᕽ ᐆᒪ ᐅᐢᑎᑳᐧᐣ, ᐁ *spray*ᐃᐃᐧᐟ ᐆᒪ, ᐁ ᓯᓯᐹᑕᕽ᙮ ᒣᑐᓂ ᒫᓇ ᐄᐧᐦᑭᒫᑯᐢᑎᑳᐧᓀᐤ;

ᐁᑯᐢᐲ ᓃᐢᑕ ᓄᐢᒐᑳᓭ ᓇᐊᐧᒋᑯ ᓂᑮ ᐄᐧ ᑲᑫᐧ ᒨᓂᔮᐢᑫᐧᐁᐧᐊᐧᐦᐃᑫᓯᐣ, ᐁ ᑮᐢᑲᐦᐋᒫᔮᐣ, ᐊᓄᐦᐨ ᐁᑲᐧ ᓇᒨᔭ, ᓂᐸᑳᐧᑌᐣ ᐁᑯᓯ ᑕ ᐃᓰᐦᐆᔮᐣ ᐊᔨᐢ ᓂᑕᑎ ᑫᐦᑌ ᐊᔨᐃᐧᐣ, ᒨᐩ ᐁᑯᓯ, ᓇᐊᐧᐟ ᐁ ᐊᐱᐦᑫᔮᐣ ᓂᒥᔦᐧᔨᐦᑌᐣ᙮ ᓂᐋᐧᐸᒫᐤ ᒫᓇ ᐆᒪ ᐁ *spray*ᐃᐃᐧᐟ *her hair* ᐆᑕ, « ᒪᐦᑎ ᓂᑲ ᑭᒧᑕᒪᐋᐧᐤ, » *in the bedroom* ᓄᑌ ᑕᑕᐦᑲᒥᑭᓯᐤ [ᒪᑌᐧ ᓭᐁᐧᐱᒋᑳᓂᐊᐧᐣ᙮ MLR: ᐅᑎᓇ᙮], ᑕᑕᐦᑲᒥᑭᓯᐤ ᐁᑯᑕ [MLR: *I have no time* ᐃᐧᔭ ᓂᔭ᙮ [ᓭᐁᐧᐱᒋᑲᐣ ᐊᓂᒪ ᑳ ᐃᑕᕽ]] ᑕᑕᐦᑲᒥᑭᓯᐤ, ᓂᐋᐧᐸᒫᐤ ᒫᓇ ᐁ *spray*ᐃᐃᐧᐟ ᐆᒪ ᐅᐢᑎᑳᐧᐣ; ᐄᐦ, « ᓂᑲ ᑭᒧᑕᒪᐋᐧᐤ, » ᓂᓂᑕᐃᐧ ᐲᐦᑐᑳᐧᐣ *washroom*, ᐄᐦ, ᑲᑳᐧᔭᑲᑯᑌᐊᐧ ᐆᐦᐃ ᐆᑌ *containers* ᐆᐦᐃ ᓇᓈᑐᕽ ᐁ ᐃᓯᓈᑲᐧᐦᑭ, ᐋᑎᐦᐟ ᐁ ᑲᐢᑭᑌᐋᐧᑭ᙮ ᐄᐦ, ᑖᓂ ᐁᐊᐧᑯ ᐁᑎᑫᐧ ᑫᐅᑎᓇᒫᐣ? ᐯᔭᐠ [ᐸᐦᐱᓈᓂᐊᐧᐣ] ᐯᔭᐠ ᓃᑑᑎᓄᐣ, ᐁ ᒥᓵᐠ᙮ ᐊᐧᐦᐋᐧ, ᓂᐸᓴᑳᐧᐱᐣ, ᓂᐋᐧᐸᒫᐤ ᒫᓇ ᐁ ᐃᑑᑕᕽ᙮ ᒥᓯᐁᐧ, ᑐᓂ ᒥᓯᐁᐧ, ᑖᐯᐧ ᒣᑐᓂ ᐊᔨ, ᔩᐦᑕᐋᐧᐊᐧ ᓄᐢᑕᑲᔭ᙮ « ᑭᔨᐸ, *mom*, » ᐃᑌᐤ, « ᐋᓴᐩ ᐆᒪ *outside* ᑭᐯᐦᐃᑲᐃᐧᐣ, » ᐃᑌᐤ, « ᐋᔨᒫᐨ ᐁ ᐄᐧ ᐴᓯᐦᐃᑲᐃᐧᔭᕽ᙮ » « ᐊᐦᐋᒼ᙮ » ᐯ ᐊᐧᔭᐄᐧᐤ᙮ « *Mmm mmm*, » *she told me*, « *you put too much*᙮ » ᐄᐦ, ᐁ ᑭᐢᑫᔨᐦᑕᕽ ᐁ ᑭᒧᑕᒪᐊᐧᐠ [ᐹᐦᐱᓈᓂᐊᐧᐣ], ᐁ ᑭᐢᑫᔨᐦᑕᕽ ᐁ ᑭᒧᑎᔮᐣ᙮ « ᐊᐦᐋᒼ, ᐁᑯᓯ ᓵᒫᐠ᙮ » « ᐊᐧᐦᐋᐧ *mom*, *you put too much*᙮ » « ᑮᑳᐧᐩ *too much* ᒫᑲ ᐁ ᐊᐢᑖᔮᐣ? » « *You put too much house spray*, » ᑳ ᐃᓯᐟ᙮ *House spray* ᐁᓴ ᐆᒪ ᑳ ᓯᓯᐦ~ [ᐹᐦᐱᓈᓂᐊᐧᐣ] ᑳ ᓯᓯᐹᑕᒫᐣ ᓂᐢᑎᑳᐧᐣ, ᓇᒨᐩ ᓂᑭᐢᑫ~ « ᑖᓂᑕ, ᑖᓂ ᐁᐊᐧᑯ ᐁᐧᑎᓇᒪᐣ, ᑖᓂ ᐁᐊᐧᑯ᙮ » « ᐋᐢᑕᒼ, ᒫᒋᑰᑎᑖᐠ᙮ » *Washroom*, *a black tube* ᐊᓂᒪ, *house spray* ᐁᓴ ᐆᒪ ᑳ ᓯᓯᐹᑕᒫᐣ ᓂᐢᑎᑳᐧᐣ᙮ ᐊᐧᐦᐋᐧ! [ᐹᐦᐱᓈᓂᐊᐧᐣ] ᒣᑐᓂ ᐁ ᐄᐧ ᓂᐸᐦᐋᐧᐦᐱᐟ᙮ ᑯᓂᑕ ᒦᓇ ᐁᑲᐧ ᐊᓂᒪ ᐁ ᑭᒧᑎᔮᐣ᙮ [ᐹᐦᐱᓈᓂᐊᐧᐣ] ᐁᑲᐩ ᐊᓂᒪ ᐁ ᐊᔭᒥᐦᒋᑫᔮᐣ, *you know*᙮ ᐊᐧᐦᐋᐧ, ᓃᐢᑕ ᒦᓇ ᐁᑯᑕ ᓂᑮ ᐹᐦᐱᐣ, ᐁ ᑭᒧᑎᔮᐣ ᐊᓂᒪ; ᒨᐩ ᓂᑕᔭᒥᐦᒋᑳᐣ, ᑯᓂᑕ ᓂᑎᓯᐅᑎᓄᐣ *spray* ᐊᓂᒪ, *house spray* ᐁᓴ ᐊᓂᒪ ᑳ ᓯᓯᐹᑕᒫᐣ, ᑖᐯᐧ ᒫᑲ ᔩᑕᐤ᙮ [ᐹᐦᐱᓈᓂᐊᐧᐣ] ᐊᐧᐦᐋᐧ, ᒥᑐᓂ ᓂᒪ ᒫᔨᓂᑫᐢᑭᐣ, ᒥᑐᓂ ᐁ ᐃᓯ ᑑᑕᒫᐣ᙮

ᐁᐊᐧᑯ ᒦᓇ ᐊᓂᒪ ᓂᑭᓭᔨᓃᒼ ᐊᓇ, ᐁᐊᐧᑯ ᒦᓇ ᐁ ᑮ ᑕᑲᐦᑳᐸᒪᐠ ᒫᓇ ᐁ ᐄᐧᐦᑭᒫᑯᐢᑎᑳᐧᓄᐟ, ᐁᐊᐧᑯ ᐊᓂᒪ ᐊᐩ~ ᐊᓂᒪ; ᑖᓂᓯ ᐁᑎᑫᐧ

ᒫᓇ ᐁ ᑮ ᐃᓯᔨᐦᑳᑌᐠ ᐁ ᑲᐢᑭᑌᐚᐠ *tube* ᒫᐣ ᐋᓂᒪ ᐅᐢᑎᑳᐧᓂᐚᕽ ᓈᐯᐊᐧᐠ ᐁ ᐋᐸᒋᐦᑖᒋᐠ᙮ ᐁᐊᐧᑯ ᐊᓂᒪ ᐁ ᑭᒧᑎᔮᐣ ᐁ ᐃᑕᑭᐦᒋᑫᔮᐣ ᑳ ᐊᐧᓂ ᐅᑎᓇᒫᐣ ᐊᓂᒪ ᐊᔨ *toothpaste* ᐁᓴ ᐆᒪ ᑳ ᒥᓯ ᐊᐢᑖᔮᐣ ᑳ ᐋᒋᒧᐢᑖᑕᑯᐠ᙮ ᐋᐦ, ᒣᑐᓂ ᑳ ᒥᓯ ᑲᑳᐧᔭᑭᐦᐅᔮᐣ ᐆᒪ *bingo* ᐁ ᐄᐧ ᑌᐯᐧᕽ, ᐱᑕᒫ ᒦᓇ ᐁ ᓂᑕᐃᐧᑭᓰᐯᑭᐢᑎᑳᐧᓅᔮᐣ᙮ ᐊᐧᐦᐋᐧ! *Foam, no towel,* ᒪ ᑮᑲᐧᐩ ᐊᓂᑭ *paper towels, nothing*᙮ ᐋᐦ, *my shirt* ᐁᑲᐧ ᑳ ᐋᐸᒋᐦᑖᔮᐣ ᐁᑲᐧ᙮

> — ᓂᑯᐢᑖᐤ ᐊᔨᐢᐠ ᓂᑭᓭᔨᓃᒼ ᑕ ᑭᓰ ᑭᑐᓯᐟ, ᓂᑮ ᑯᐢᑖᐤ ᐊᓇ᙮ ᐊᔨᐢᐠ ~ ᐊᔨᐢᐠ ᑳ ᐄᐧᑭᒪᐟ ᓈᐯᐤ ᑭᑯᐢᑖᐤ, *you know,* ᐊᔨᐢᐠ ᑭᑭᐦᒋ ᐄᐧᑭᒫᐤ, *you know,* ᑭᑮ ᐊᓱᑌᐣ ᑖᓂᓯ ᐁ ᐄᐧ ᑑᑕᒪᐣ ᐁ ᑲᑫᐧᒋᒥᐢᐠ, ᐁ ᑲᑫᐧᒋᒥᐢᐠ ᑳ ᐄᐧᑭᐦᑕᐦᐃᐢᐠ ᐊᓇ, « ᑭᐄᐧ ᑑᑌᐣ ᒌ ᑖᓂᓯ ~᙮ » ᐁ ᐃᑎᐢᐠ ᐊᓇ᙮ « ᐁᐦᐊ, ᓂᑲ ᑑᑌᐣ᙮ *I will, I will,* » ᑭᑎᑖᐧᐣ ᐁ ᐊᓱᑕᒪᐊᐧᐟ ᐊᐊᐧ ᒦᓇ ᒪᓂᑐᐤ᙮ ᐋᐦ, ᑖᐯᐧ᙮ ᑭᑯᐢᑖᐤ ᐊᓇ ᓈᐯᐤ; ᓂᔭ ᓂᑮ ᑯᐢᑖᐤ, ᑮᑲᐧᐩ ᓈᓂᑕᐤ ᑕ ᐃᓯ ᑭᓯᐋᐧᐦᐊᐠ, *you know,* ᑖᐱᑕᐤ ᐁᑎᑫᐧ ᐁ ᓂᑕᐁᐧᔨᐦᑕᒫᐣ ᐊᔨ ᑭᑕᒥᔮᐧᑎᓯᐟ, ᑭᑭᐢᑫᔨᐦᑌᐣ, ᐁ ᑲᑫᐧ ᑌᐱᔭᐁᐧᐦᐊᐠ ᐅᒥᓯ ᐃᓯ, ᐁᑲᐧ ᑳ ᐄᐧ ᑭᓰ ᑭᑐᓯᐟ ᑖᐱᐢᑯᐨ ᒫᓇ ᐁ ᑮ ᒐᒋᐦᒋᐱᐸᔨᔮᐣ, *you know,* ᐁ ᑮ ᐃᓯ ᑯᐢᑕᐠ᙮ ᓂᑮ ᑯᐢᑖᐤ, ᐁ ᑖᐯᐧᔮᐣ ᓂᑮ ᑯᐢᑖᐤ᙮ —

ᐄᐦ, ᐊᓂᒪ, ᐊᓂᒪ *bingo* ᐊᓂᒪ ᐁ ᑑᑖᑯᔮᐣ ᑳ ᑑᐢᑭᓇᐠ, « ᑭᔮᒪᐱ᙮ » ᐦᐊ, ᑖᓂᓯ ᒫᐠ~ ᐄᐦ, ᐊᓂᒪ, ᐁ ᑭᓰᐯᑭᐢᑎᑳᐧᓅᔮᐣ ᓂᑭᒧᑎᐃᐧᐣ ᐁᑳ ᐁ ᐊᔭᒥᐦᒋᑫᔮᐣ᙮ [ᐹᐦᐱᓈᓂᐊᐧᐣ]

ᐊᐧᐦᐋᐧ, ᐊᓂᒪ ᒦᓇ ᑳ ᓯᓱᐯᑲᐦᐅᔮᐣ ᑳ ᐋᒋᒧᐢᑖᑕᑯᐠ, ᐊᐦᐋᐧ, ᐁᑲᐧ ᐊᓂᒪ ᒦᓇ ᐊᐧᐃᐧᔫᐢ ᐊᓂᒪ ᒦᓇ ᐁᐊᐧᑯ᙮ ᐄᐦ, ᐊᓂᒪ ᐁ ᐄᐧ ᐊ ~ ᓂᑕᐃᐧ ᐊᑐᐢᑫᔮᐣ ᓂᑑᒋᐱᑎᑯᐣ ᐁᑯᓯ ᐁᑲᐧ ᐱᑯ ᒪᐢᑭᐦᑭᐩ ᓂᑮ ᐊᑖᐁᐧᐢᑕᒫᐠ ᐊᓂᒪ *green medicine*᙮ ᐋ, ᒥᑐᓂ ᐁᑲᐧ *half asleep* ᑳ ᐅᑎᓇᒫᐣ, ᐁ ᒥᓯ ᐅᒋᐱᑎᑯᔮᐣ ᒣᑐᓂ ᐁᑲᐧ ᓂᐢᑳᑕ ᐆᐦᐃ, ᐁᑲᐧ

ᐁ ᐊᑎ ᐋᐱᓯᐦᑲᐧᓯᔮᐣ ᐊᐄᐧᓇ ᐆᒪ ᓂᑮ ᑕᐦᑯᓅᐣ *bingo marker*, ᒣᑯᓂ ᑳ ᒫᐦ ᒥᓯ ᐊᐢᑭᐦᑕᑯᑳᑌᔮᐣ᙮ [ᐹᐦᐱᓈᓂᐊᐧᐣ] ᐊᐧᐦᐋᐧ! ᓂᑲᑳᐧᔭᑭᐦᐃᓯᐣ; ᒫᑲ ᓂᑖᐢᑌ ᐊᔮᐣ, ᐁ ᒥᔮᐧᓯᐠ ᐁᑎᑫᐧ ᐊᓂᒪ ᓂᑖᐢᑌᐢᑳᑯᐣ, ᑕᐦᑭᑲᒫᐳᐩ ᐊᔨᐢᐠ, ᑕᐦᑭᑲᒥᐤ [JO: ᐋᐦᐊ᙮], ᓂᐴᓂ ᐅᒋᐱᑎᑯᐣ᙮ ᐁᑯᓯ ᐁᑲᐧ ᑕ ᓂᑕᐃᐧ ᐊᑐᐢᑫᔮᐣ, *my bus any time coming* ᒫᑲ *snowing* ᐯᐢᑭᐢ, ᑭᒥᐊᐧ~, ᒪᒥᐢᐳᐣ᙮ ᐋᐦ, ᐊᐧᐦᐋᐧ, ᑕ ᓂᑕᐃᐧ ᑯᐢᑯᓇᐠ ᓂᑭᓴᔨᓃᑦ, ᓂᑭᐢᑫᔨᐦᑌᐣ ᑕ ᑭᓰ ᑭᑐᓯᐟ, ᐊᐧᐦᐋᐧ ᐦᐊᐩ, « ᐋᐦ! » ᑖᐯᐧ ᓂᑭᓰ ᑭᑐᑎᐠ᙮ ᐱᑯ ᐁᑯᓯ ᑲ ᐃᓯ ᐴᓯᔮᐣ ᐁ ᐊᐢᑭᐦᑕᑯᑳᑌᔮᐣ ᐊᓂᒪ; ᓅᑌ ᑲ ᐃᑐᐦᑌᔮᐣ ᓂᑑᑭᒫᑦ ᑫᑳᐨ ᑳ ᓂᐸᐦᐃ ᐹᐦᐱᐟ, ᓂᑑᑭᒫᐢᑫᐧᑦ ᒦᓇ ᐊᐊᐧ᙮ ᐋᐧᐦᐋᐧ, ᑫᑳᐨ ᓂᑮ ᓂᐸᐦᐋᐊᐧᐠ *bingo marker* ᐁ ᓇᓈᑕᐃᐧᐦᐋᐧᑫᔮᐣ ᒫᐠ ᐋᔨᐢᐠ ᓂᑮ ᒥᔦᐧᐢᑳᑯᐣ, ᐁ ᒥᔮᐧᓯᐠ ᐊᓂᒪ᙮ [ᒥᓯ ᐹᐦᐱᓈᓂᐊᐧᐣ] ᐋᐧᐦᐊᐩ!

ᓇᒨᔭ ᐆᒪ ᐁ ᑭᔮᐢᑮᐋᐧᒋᒨᔮᐣ, ᐁ ᑖᐯᐧᔮᐣ, ᒥᓯᐁᐧ ᒥᓴᐋᐧᐨ ᓂᐯᐦᑖᑲᐃᐧᐣ᙮ ᐊᐦᐴ ᐆᑯ ᐆᑌ ᐆᑌᓇᐃᐧᔨᓂᐊᐧᐠ, ᐆᑯ ᑭᐦᒋ ᐅᑭᒫᐊᐧᐠ, ᑲᐦᑭᔭᐤ ᐊᓂᒪ ᑭᐢᑫᔨᐦᑕᒪᐧᐠ, ᓂᐯᐦᑖᑲᐧᐠ᙮ ᐆᑭ ᒦᓇ ᓂᑕᐋᐧᓯᒥᓴᐠ, ᐁ ᐊᐧᐃᐧᔭᑌᔨᐦᑕᐦᑭᐠ ᓇᓭᐢᑕᐤ ᐁ ᐹᐦᐱᐦᐃᑲᐃᐧᔮᐣ, ᒥᑐᓂ ᓂᑕᑲᐦᑫᔨᐦᑌᐣ, ᐊᔨᐢᐠ ᒫᑲ ᓂᑮ ᒪ ᒫᔨᓂᑫᐢᑭᐣ ᐁᑳ ᐁ ᓂᐦᑖ ᐊᔭᒥᐦᒋᑫᔮᐣ᙮

[2. ᑭᐢᑭᓇᐧᐦᐊᒫᑐᐃᐧᐣ]

ᐁᐊᐧᑯ ᑳ ᐃᑕᒫᐣ ᐁ ᐋᔨᒪᕽ ᐁᑳ ᑳ ᐊᔭᒥᐦᒋᑫᐟ ᐊᔨᓯᔨᓂᐤ, ᐁᐊᐧᑯ ᐅᐦᒋ ᑰᐦ ᐃᑕᑭᐠ, « ᐃᑐᐦᑌᐠ ᑭᐢᑭᓇᐧᐦᐊᒫᑐᐃᐧᑲᒥᑯᕽ, ᑮᑲᐧᐩ ᑕ ᑭᐢᑫᔨᐦᑕᒣᐠ, » ᓂᑎᑖᐊᐧᐠ ᐊᐋᐧᓯᓴᐠ ᐁ ᑖᐯᐧᔮᐣ᙮ ᐁᑯᑐᐊᐧᕽ ᐊᔨᐢᐠ ᐁᑲᐧ ᐱᓯᓯᐠ ᒨᓂᔮᐊᐧᐠ ᐁᑲᐧ ᑭᔭᐋᐧᐤ ᐁᐊᐧᑯ ᐊᓂᒪ ᒨᓂᔮᓴᐠ ᐁ ᑭᐢ~, ᑕ ᑭᐢ~, ᐁ ᑭᐢᑭᓇᐧᐦᐊᒫᑯᔦᑯᐠ ᑮᑲᐧᐩ, ᓂᔭᓈᐣ ᑲᔮᐢ ᓇᒪ ᑮᑲᐧᐩ, ᑮ ᐁᐧᐦᒐᓯᐣ ᐃᑌᔨᐦᑖᑲᐧᐣ ᒫᑲ ᐁᒋᑳᓇ ᐁ ᑮ ᑭᑎᒪᐦᐃᓯᔮᕽ, *you know*, ᐊᓅᐦᐨ ᐁᑲᐧ, ᑭᑎᒫᑲᐣ᙮ ᓂᔭ ᐅᐦᒋ, ᓂᑭᐢᑫᔨᐦᑌᐣ ᓂᔭ, ᐁᑕᑕᐤ ᑳ ᐋᑲᔮᓰᒨᔮᐣ, ᓂᑲᐢᑭᐦᑖᐣ ᐁ ᐲᑭᐢᑫᐧᔮᐣ ᒨᐩ ᒫᑲ *high words* ᐆᐦᐃ, ᓂᐹᐧᑕᐃᐧᐦᐅᐣ ᐁᑯᑕ᙮ *But* ᐁᑲᐧ ᒦᓇ ᐊᐱᓰᐢ ᓂᑭᐢᑫᔨᐦᑌᐣ ᑕ ᐃᓯ ᐊᔭᒥᐦᒋᑫᔮᐣ, ᐊᐱᓰᐢ

ᒎᔦ ᒥᐢᑕᐦᐃ᙮ ᑮᑳᐤ ᐅᐦᒋ ᑯᐦ ᑭᐢᑫᔦᐦᑕᒫᐣ ᑲ ᐄᐧᐦᑖᒪᑎᓈᐚᐤ, ᑮᑳᐤ ᑰᐦ ᐋᑲᓭᔩᒎᔧᐣ ᓂᑲ ᐄᐧᐦᑌᐣ ᒦᓇ ᐁᐊᐧᑯ, ᑭᑲ ᐄᐧᐦᑖᒪᑎᓈᐚᐤ ᒦᓇ ᐁᐊᐧᑯ᙮

ᓂᑕᐚᐧᓯᒥᓭᐠ ᐁ ᑭᐢᑭᓇᐧᐦᐊᒪᐃᐧᐦᒋᐠ᙮ ᓂᑕᐚᐧᓯᒥᓭᐠ, ᓂᔧᓇᐣ ᐃᐢᑫᐧᐊᐧᐠ ᓂᑕᔦᐚᐧᐊᐧᐠ, ᐁᑲᐧ ᑲᐦᑭᔦᐤ ᐁ ᐋᑲᓭᔩᒍᒋᐠ ᐁᑲᐧ ᐋᑎᐦᐟ ᐁ ᓃᐦᐃᔦᐁᐧᒋᐠ᙮ ᑮᑳᐤ ᐁᒪᒫᐹᔫᐣ ᐱᑭᐢᑫᐧᐃᐧᓂˣ ᓂᑫᐧᐢᑭᐁᐧᐱᓂᑲᐧᐠ, ᓂᑫᐧᐢᑲᐢᑖᒪᑲᐧᐠ᙮ « ᐁᑯᓯ ᐊᓂᒪ ᑕ ᐃᑌᐧᔦᐣ, ᒫᒫ, ᑭᐊᐧᓂᑐᓈᒍᐣ᙮ » ᐦᐋᐤ, ᐁᑯᑕ ᓂᑭᐢᑫᔦᐦᑌᐣ ᑮᑳᐤ, ᑖᓂᓯ ᑭᑕ ᑮ ᐃᑌᐧᔦᐣ, ᓂᑕᑎ ᑭᐢᑫᔦᐦᑌᐣ ᐁᑯᑕ, ᐁᑯᓂᐠ ᐆᑭ ᐁ ᑭᐢᑭᓇᐧᐦᐊᒪᐃᐧᒋᐠ ᐁᑲᐧ ᒦᓇ ᓅᒋᐢᑫᐧᓯᓴᐠ ᑳᓭᐣ ᓂᐢᑕᐟ ᐁᐊᐧᑯ, ᐁᐊᐧᑯ ᐆᒪ *a, b, c, d* ᐁᑲᐧ ᒦᓇ *1,2,3* ᓂᑮ ᑭᐢᑭᓇᐧᐦᐋᒫᑲᐧᐠ ᐁ ᐯ ᑮᐁᐧᒋᐠ *from Lebret*, ᓅᒋᐢᑫᐧᓯᓴᐠ᙮ ᐁᑯᑕ ᓂᑮ ᐅᐦᒋ ᑭᐢᑫᔦᐦᑌᐣ ᐁᐊᐧᑯ᙮ ᐁᑲᐧ ᐆᒪ ᐁ ᐊᑎ ᐃᓯ ᑫᐦᑌ ᐊᔦᐃᐧᔫᐣ ᓂᑕᐚᐧᓯᒥᓭᐠ ᐁᑲᐧ ᓂᑫᐧᐢᑭᓂᑲᐧᐠ, ᐁᑯᓂᐠ ᓂᐄᐧᐦᑖᒪᑲᐧᐠ ᑮᑳᐤ ᑳ ᐄᐧᒫᒫᐹᔫᐣ᙮ ᓂᑲᐢᑭᐦᑖᐣ ᐁ ᐋᑲᓭᔩᒎᔧᐣ, ᓂᑲᐢᑭᐦᑖᐣ ᐁ ᐲᑭᐢᑫᐧᐢᑖᒪᐧᔫᐣ, ᐊᐦᔮ ᐅᑭᒫᓈˣ ᓂᑲᐢᑭᐦᑖᐣ ᐁ ᐃᑐᐦᑌᔫᐣ ᐁ ᓂᑖᐤ ᐲᑭᐢᑫᐧᐢᑖᒪᐧᔫᐣ ᐁ ᐋᑲᓭᔩᒎᔧᐣ᙮ ᒫᑲ ᓂᐄᐧᐦᑕᒪᐚᐧᐊᐧᐠ ᐃᑕ ᐁᑳ ᑲ ᓂᓯᑐᐦᑕᐊᐧᑭᐠ *high words* ᐆᐦᐃ, ᒫᑲ ᑫᐧᐢᑲᐢᑖᐊᐧᐠ ᐁᑯᑐᐊᐧ ᐁᑯᓯ ᐁ ᐃᑎᑖᐣ, ᐁᑯᑕ ᓅᐦᐊᔥ ᑭᐢᑫᔦᐦᑌᐣ᙮ ᐁᑯᓯ, ᐁᑯᓯ ᐁ ᐃᓯ ᓇᔦᐦᑖᐄᐧᔫᐣ᙮ ᐁᑲᐧ ᒦᓇ ᓂᑳᐦ ᑭᐢᑭᓅᐦᐋᒫᑳᐣ ᐆᒪ ᓂᓂᐦᑖ ᓃᐦᐃᔦᐊᐧᔦᒥᐦᒋᑳᐣ, ᓂᓂᐦᑖ ᓃᐦᐃᔦᐤ~ … [MLR: *Margaret!* … *oh.*] ᐋᐦ, ᓂᐦᑖ~, ᓂᐦᑖ ᐊᔦᒥᐦ-~, [ᓂ]ᓂᐦᑖ ᐊᔦᒥᐦᒋᑳᐣ ᐆᒪ ᐁ ᓃᐦᐃᔦᐁᐧˣ, ᐊᓂᐦᐃ ᐊᔥ ᐊᓂᐦᐃ, *half, half-diamond* ᐊᓂᒪ [JO: ᐆᐦ, *Syllabics*᙮] ᐁᐊᐧᑯ ᐊᓂᒪ [JO: ᐋᐦᐊ], ᓂᓂᐦᑖ ᐊᔦᒥᐦᒋᑳᐣ [JO: ᐆᐦ!], ᓂᓂᐦᑖ ᐊᔦᒥᐦᒋᑳᐣ, ᓂᓂᐦᑖᐊᐧᓯᓇᐦᐃᑳᐣ ᓂᓂᐦᑖ ᐊᔦᒥᐦᒋᑳᐣ ᐁ ᓃᐦᐃᔦᐁᐧˣ᙮ ᓂᑳᐦ ᑭᐢᑭᓅᐦᐋᒫᑳᐣ ᐆᒪ, ᓂᑳᐦ ᓈᓂᔮᐦᑳᐣ, ᒫᑲ ᐁᐊᐧᑯ ᐱᑯ ᐆᒪ ᐁ ᐃᑌᐧᔦᐣ, *you know*᙮

ᑖᐱᐢᑯᐨ ᐆᒪ: « ᐋᐦᐋᐧᐤ, ᑫ ᐚᐧᐸˣ ᐁᑯᑌ ᐯ ᐃᑐᐦᑌᐦᑲᐣ, ᐁᐊᐧᑯ ᐄᐧᑭᐚᐧˣ, » ᑎᑕ ᐃᐤ~ ᑎᑕ ᐃᑕᐢᑖᔦᐣ, « ᐋᐦᐋᐧᐤ, ᐆᑌ ᐯ ᐃᑐᐦᑌᐠ ᑮᑭᐚᐧˣ᙮ » « ᐦᐋᐧᐤ, ᐆᑕ ᑖᐦ ᒪᓯᓇᐦᐊᐤ ᐊᐃᐧᔦᐠ ᑕ ᒎᓂᔮᐃᐧᐯᐦᐊˣ᙮ ᐁᑯᓯ ᐆᒪ ᐁ ᐃᑌᐧᐟ ᐊᐊᐧ᙮ » [*e.g.*, ᐊ] [JO: *mhm.*] ᑭᓂᓯᑐᐦᑌᐣ ᑳ ᐃᑕᒫᐣ? [JO: *mhm.* ᐋᐦᐊ᙮] ᐁᑯᑕ ᑲ ᐅᐦᒋ ᑭᐢᑫᔦᐦᑌᐣ ᑕ ᒉ~ ᑕ~ ᑕ ᐊᔦᒥᐦᑖᔦᐣ

ᐆᒪ, ᒫᑲ ᐁᑯᓯ ᐁ ᐃᑎᑖᐣ, « ᐦᐋᑦ, ᐁᑯᑌ ᐯ ᐃᑐᐦᑌᐦᑲᐣ ᐁᐊᐧᑯ ᐄᐧᑭᐋᐧᕽ᙮ » [JO: *mhm.*] ᒫᑲ ᐊᔨᐢᐠ ᓂᑳᐦ- ᓂᐦᑖᐊᐧᓯᓇᐦᐃᑫᔮᐣ ᓂᑳᐦ ᒪᓯᓇᐦᐁᐣ ᐁᑯᓯ ᐆᒪ ᐁ ᐃᑌᐧᔮᐣ, ᒫᑲ ᐁᐊᐧᑯ ᓂᓵᑯᐦᐃᑯᐣ᙮

JO: ᐋᐦᐊ᙮ ᓂᐦᑖ- ᓂᐦᑖᐊᐧᓯᓇᐦᐃᑫᐤ ᐄᐧᐢᑕ ᐊᐊᐧ᙮

ᒪᓯᓇᐦᐃᑫᐤ?

JO: ᐋᐦᐊ᙮

ᐁᑯᑐᐊᐧ ᒌ ᑳ ᑭᐢᑫᔨᐦᑕᒪᐣ?

DO: ᐋᐦᐊ᙮

ᐁᑯᑐᐊᐧ ᐊᓂᐦᐃ ᒣᑐᓂ ᐁ ᓇᑲᒋᐦᑖᔮᐣ, ᒣᑐᓂ ᑐᓂ ᐁ ᓂᐦᑖ- ᐁ ᓂᐦᑖ ᒪᓯᓇᐦᐃᑫᔮᐣ, ᐁᑲᐧ ᐁ ᓂᐦᑖ- ᐁ ᓂᐦᑖᐃᐧᐯᐦᐃᑫᔮᐣ [JO: ᐋᐦᐊ᙮], ᑲᐦᑭᔭᐤ ᐁ ᑭᐢᑫᔨᐦᑕᒫᐣ, ᑲᐦᑭᔭᐤ ᐆᑭ ᒦᓇ ᐆᑭ, ᐆᑭ ᒦᓇ ᐆᑭ ᐊᔭᑲᐠ, ᐆᑭ ᐊ-, ᐆᑭ ᐊᔨ, ᐆᑭ ᒐᐦᑭᐯᐦᐃᑲᓂᓴᐠ [JO: ᐋᐦᐊ᙮], ᑲᐦᑭᔭᐤ ᐊᔨᐢᐠ ᐆᑕ ᑕ ᐄᐧᒋᐦᐃᐁᐧᒋᐠ ᑲᐦᑭᔭᐤ᙮ ᐄᐦ, ᑖᐱᐢᑰᐨ ᐊᐊᐧ: ᐋᐧ, ᐱ, ᑎ, ᑭ, ᒋ, ᒥ, ᓂ, ᓯ, ᔨ; ᔨ ᐊᐊᐧ᙮ [JO: ᐋᐦᐊ᙮] ᐁᑯᓯ ᐊᓂᒪ ᐁ ᐃᓯ ᐊᔨ- ᑭᑭᐢᑫᔨᐦᑌᐣ? [DO: *ya.*] ᐁ ᐃᓯ ᐊᔭᒥᐦᒋᑫᕽ, ᐁᐦᐊ᙮ ᓂᑳᐦ ᑭᐢᑭᓇᐧᐦᐊᒫᑳᐣ ᐆᒪ, ᓂᑳᐦ ᑭᐢᑭᓇᐧᐦᐊᒫᑳᐣ, *but* ᐁᐊᐧᑯ ᓂᓇᐸᐦᑖᐄᐧᐣ ᑕ ᐊᑎ ᐃᑕᐢᑖᔮᐣ ᐊᓂᒪ ᑕᐦᑕ- ᑕ ᐊᑕ- ᑖᓂᓯ ᐊᓂᒪ ᐁ ᐃᑌᐧᔮᐣ᙮ [JO: *mhm, mhm, yeah,* ᑲᐧᔭᐢᐠ᙮]

JO: ᐁ ᑮ-, ᐊᐄᐧᓇ ᐁ ᑮ ᑭᐢᑭᓇᐧᐦᐊᒫᐢᐠ?

ᑳ ᑮ ᐃᐧᔦᐦᑖᐃᐧᔮᐣ, ᑳ ᑮ ᐃᐧᔦᐦᑖᐃᐧᔮᐣ, ᐋᐦ — ᐋᓴᐩ ᒌ ᐱᒪᑯᑌᐤ? — ᑳ ᑮ ᐃᐧᔦᐦᑖᐃᐧᔭᐣ ᐁ ᑮ ᑭᐢᑭᓇᐧᐦᐊᒪᐃᐧᐟ ᑮ ᓂᐦᑖᐃᐧᐯᐦᐃᑫᐤ, ᐁ ᓀᐦᐃᔭᐃᐧᐯᐦᐃᑫᐟ, ᐁ ᓀᓂᐦᐋᐤ- ᐁ ᓀᐦᐃᔭᐊᐧᔭᒥᐦᒋᑫᐟ, ᐁᑲᐧ ᓂᑮ ᐊᐱᓈᐣ ᐁ ᑎᐱᐢᑳᐠ, *two nights* ᓂᑮ ᐊᐱᓈᐣ᙮ ᐯᔭᐠ, ᐯᔭᐠ ᓅᒋᐢᑫᐧᓯᐢ ᐄᐧᐢᑕ ᐁᑯᑕ, ᑮ ᐸᓈᑎᓯᐤ ᒫᑲ, ᐁ ᑭᐢᑭᓇᐧᐦᐊᒫᑯᔮᕽ ᓅᐦᑖᐃᐧᐩ᙮ ᓂᑮ ᑭᐢᑫᔨᐦᑌᐣ,

two nights ᐋᓴᐩ ᓂᑮ ᓂᐦᑖᐊᐧᓯᓇᐦᐃᑳᐣ᙮ [JO: ᐆᐦ᙮] ᐁᐧᐦᒐᓯᐣ ᐊᓂᒪ, ᒌ? ᐁᐧᐦᒐᓯᐣ, ᐁᐧᐦᒐᓯᐣ᙮

[3. ᐚᐦᑰᐦᑐᐃᐧᐣ]

JO: ᐁᑲᐧ *Turtle Mountain* ᑰᐦᑖᐃᐧᐩ ᐁ ᑮ ᐅᐦᒌᐟ?

ᐁᑯᑌ ᐁ ᑮ~ ᐁᐊᐧᑯ ᑳ ᐋᒋᒧᐢᑖᑖᐣ, ᑳ ᐃᐧᔐᐦᑖᐃᐧᔮᐣ ᐊᐊᐧ ᐁ ᑮ ᐅᒧᓲᒥᐟ *Albert Firstchief* ᑮ ᐃᓯᔨᐦᑳᓱᐤ ᓂᒧᓲᒼ ᐁᑯᑌ, ᐅᒧᓲᒪ ᐊᐊᐧ ~, ᒫᒋᑰᒋᒑᐣ, ᓂᔭ ᐆᒪ ᐁᑲᐧ ᐊᐊᐧ ᓈᐦᑖᐃᐧᐩ ᐁᑲᐧ ᓈᐦᑖᐃᐧᐩ ᐅᐦᑖᐃᐧᔭ ᐁᑲᐧ ᐊᐊᐧ ᓂᒧᓲᒼ ᐅᐦᑖᐃᐧᔭ ᐆᐦᐃ *Albert Firstchief* ᐁᐊᐧᑯ᙮ *Albert Firstchief* ᐅᑯᓯᓴ ᐆᐦᐃ *Rainsky*, ᐁᑯᑕ ᐅᐦᒋ ᓈᐦᑖᐃᐧᐩ *Bangs* ᑮ ᐃᓯᔨᐦᑳᓱᐤ, ᐁᑯᑕ ᐅᐦᒋ ᐆᒪ ᓂᔭ *Mary Louise*᙮ ᐄᐦ, ᐁᑲᐧ ᐊᐊᐧ ᓈᐦᑖᐃᐧᐩ ᐊᐊᐧ *Fred, Fred Rainsky* ᑕ ᑮ ᐃᓯᔨᐦᑳᓱᐟ *but* ᑮ ᒨᐦᒍᐃᐧᐊᐧᐠ ᑲᔮᐢ ᓀᐦᐃᔭᐊᐧᐠ, ᒨᐩ ᐅᐦᒋ ᓇᑲᐟ~ ᒨᐩ ᐅᐦᒋ ᓈᑲᑐᐦᑫᐊᐧᐠ *last names*, ᒨᐩ ᐅᐦ-~ ᒨᐩ ᐅᐦᒋ ᐅᑎᓇᒪᐧᐠ ᐁᑯᑐᐊᐧ, ᐅᐄᐧᐦᐅᐃᐧᓂᐚᐤ ᑮ ᐋᐸᒋᐦᑖᐊᐧᐠ᙮ ᐄᐦ, ᐁᐊᐧᑯ ᐊᐊᐧ ᓈᐦᑖᐃᐧᐩ ᐊᐊᐧ *Bangs* ᐁ ᐃᓯᔨᐦᑳᓱᐟ, ᐁ ᐊᑎ ᑫ~, ᐁ ᐊᑎ~ ᐊᔭ ᐆᒪ, ᐁ ᐊᑎ ᒪᓯᓇᐦᐃᑳᓱᔮᐣ ᐅᑭᒫᐃᐧᐃᐧᐣ, ᓃᐢᑕ ᐁᑲᐧ *Bangs* ᓂᑖᐸᒋᐦᑖᐣ᙮ ᓂᑮ ᐋᐸᒋᐦᑖᐣ *his name* ᐊᓂᒪ, *his nickname* ᐊᓂᒪ ᑳ ᐋᐸᒋᐦᑖᔮᐣ, ᑮᐢᑲᒐᐁᐧᐦᐊᒫᐢ, ᐁᐊᐧᑯ ᐊᓂᒪ ᑳ ᐋᐸᒋᐦᑖᔮᐣ, *Bangs, Mary Louise Bangs*, ᓂᔭ ᐁᐊᐧᑯ᙮ ᐄᐦ, *Rainsky* ᐊᓇ ᑕ ᑮ ᐃᑎᐦᐟ ᓈᐦᑖᐃᐧᐩ, ᑕ ᑮ ᐋᐸᒋᐦᑖᐟ ᐆᐦᐃ ᐅᐦᑖᐃᐧᔭ ᐅᐄᐧᐦᐅᐃᐧᓂᔨᐤ, ᐊᐁᐧᑳ ᒌ ᐊᐊᐧ, *Albert* ᐊᐊᐧ, *Firstchief* ᑕ ᑮ ᐋᐸᒋᐦᑖᐟ ᐊᐊᐧ *Rainsky, Firstchief* ᐅᐦᒋᑕᐤ ᑕ ᑮ ᐋᐸᒋᐦᑖᔮᕽ, ᑭᑭᐢᑫᔨᐦᑌᐣ? [JO: ᐋᐦᐊ᙮]

ᐁᑯᑌ ᐆᒪ ᐆᑌ ᐊᐢᑭᐩ ᐁ ᑎᐯᔨᐦᑕᒫᐣ; ᐁ ᐃᑌᔨᐦᑕᒫᐣ ᑖᓀᐦᑭ ᐅᐦᒋ ᑰᐦ ᑮ ᐅᐦᑎᓯᔮᕽ, ᐁ ᓂᐢᑎᔮᕽ, ᓂᔭ ᐁᑲᐧ ᓂᑳᐃᐧᐩ ᐁᑲᐧ ᓂᑖᓂᐢ, ᐁ ᓂᐢᑎᔮᕽ᙮ ᐁᑯᑌ ᐁ ᑮ ᐅᐦᑎᑎᓴᐦᐊᒫᑲᐃᐧᔮᕽ ᓲᓂᔮᐤ᙮ ᐁ ᑮ ᐊᐃᐧᐦᐃᐁᐧᐟ ᐁᓴ ᓂᒧᓲᒼ ᐊᔭ [ᐅᐢᒍᐢᒍᒐᓯᐤ; *Excuse me.*], ᐁ ᑮ ᐊᐃᐧᐦᐃᐁᐧᐟ ᐁᓴ ᐊᔭ, ᐊᔭ, *to rent* ᐊᔭ, ᑖᐱᐢᑰᐨ ᒥᓴᑎᒪᐧᐠ ᐃᑕ ᑳ ᐊᓯᐊᐧᓯᒋᐠ, ᐁᑲᐧ ᒦᓇ ᐃᑕ ᑳ ᒣᑕᐁᐧᒋᐠ ᑳ ᑳᐧᐢᑫᐧᓂᑐᐁᐧᒋᐠ, *golf ground*, ᐁ ᑮ ᐊᐃᐧᐦᐃᐁᐧᐟ ᐁᓴ

ᓂᒧᓲᒼ᙮ ᐁᑲᐧ ᒦᓇ ᐃᑕ ᑳ ᓅᒋᑭᓄᓴᐁᐧᒋᐠ ᓵᑲᐦᐃᑲᐣ, ᐁ ᑮ ᐊᐃᐧᐦᐃᐁᐧᐟ ᐁᓴ ᐅᑭᒫᐦᑳᐣ ᐁᐊᐧᑯ; ᐁ ᓅᒋᑭᓄᓴ~ *renting, rent*᙮ ᐁᑲᐧ ᐋᐧᐢᑳᐦᐃᑲᓂᓴ ᒦᓇ ᐆᐦᐃ ᑳ ᓯᓲᓀᐢᑌᑭ ᓯᓲᓀᑲᒦᕽ, *you know*, ᓯᓲᓀ ᓵᑲᐦᐃᑲᓂᕽ᙮ ᐁᑯᓯ ᐁᓴ ᐁ ᑮ ᐃᓯ ᐊᐃᐧᐦᐃᐁᐧᐟ ᓂᒧᓲᒥᓈᐣ᙮ ᐁᐊᐧᑯ ᐊᐊᐧ ᓲᓂᔮᐤ ᐊᐊᐧ ᐁ ᑮ ᒫᐊᐧᓴᑰᐟ *Washington* ᐆᑌ ᐊᔭ, ᓀᑌ ᐅᑭᒫᓈᕽ ᐁᐊᐧᑯ ᐊᐊᐧ ᑳ ᑮ ᒥᔨᑲᐃᐧᔮᕽ ᐊᓂᒪ ᐊᐢᑭᕀ᙮ ᐁᑲᐧ ᐊᐊᐧ ᑳ ᑮ ᐅᒧᓲᒥᔮᐣ, *Albert Firstchief*, ᐁ ᑮ ᒪᓯᓇᐦᐊᒨᐦᐃᐦᐟ ᐁᓴ, ᑲᔮᐢ, ᑲᔮᐢ ᐁᐊᐧᑯ *law*, ᐲᐋᐧᐱᐢᐠ ᐁ ᓇᐸᑳᐠ, ᐁ ᓲᐦᑲᕽ ᐲᐋᐧᐱᐢᐠ, ᐁᑯᑕ ᐁ ᒪᓯᓇᐦᐊᒧᐦᐟ ᐃᔨᑯᕽ *sections* ᐁ ᐊᔮᐟ ᐊᐊᐧ ᓂᒧᓲᒼ *Albert Firstchief*᙮ *Fifty-five, two fives* ᐁᓴ ᐁ ᑮ ᒪᓯᓇᐦᐊᒧᐦᐟ; ᒪᑖᐧᐣ ᒌ ᐊᓂᒪ *fifty-five sections* ᐁ ᑮ ᐊᔮᐟ ᓂᒧᓲᒼ, ᐊᐢᑭᕀ᙮ ᐁᐊᐧᑯ ᐊᐊᐧ *Albert Firstchief*, ᐃᔨᑯᕽ, ᐃᔨᑯᕽ ᑕ ᑮ ᑎᐯᔨᐦᑕᕽ ᐊᐊᐧ *Albert Firstchief, fifty-five section[s]* ᐁ ᑮ ᓴᑲᐦᐊᒧᐦᐟ ᐊᐢᑭᕀ᙮ ᐃᑖᒥᕽ ᐁᓴ ᐊᓂᒪ ᑫᔮᐱᐨ ᐁᑎᑫᐧ ᑭᑲᒧᐣ ᐊᓂᒪ ᐁᑯᑌ ᐊᓂᒪ ᐊᐢᑮᕽ᙮

JO: ᐄᐧᐦᑳᐨ ᒌ ᐁᑯᑌ ~?

ᓇᒨᔭ ᐄᐧᐦᑳᐨ ᐆᒪ ᓂᑎᑐᐦᑖᐣ, ᒨᕀ ᑮ~ ᒨᕀ ᐋᐃᐧᔭᐠ ᓂᑭᐢᑫᔨᐦᑌᐣ ᑕ ᐄᐧᒎᐦᑲᒪᐃᐧᐟ᙮

[ᐊᒋᔭᐤ ᐁ ᓇᑭᐱᑕᒥᕽ]

ᓂᔭ ᐃᐧᔭ ᐊᓂᒪ ᐁᑯᑌ ᓅᐦᑖᐃᐧᕀ ᐊᓂᒪ ᐁᑯᑌ ᐁ ᑮ ᐅᐦᒌᐟ, ᓂᐋᐧᐦᑰᒫᑲᓂᓈᓂᐠ ᐆᑭ᙮ ᐁᑲᐧ, ᐆᒪ ᒣᑳᐧᐨ ᐁ ᑭᐢᑫᔨᒪᑭᐠ ᐊᓂᑭ ᑲᐦᑭᔭᐤ ᐁ ᐃᓯᔨᐦᑳᓱᒋᐠ ᓂᒧᓲᒼ ᐁᑲᐧ ᓅᐦᑯᒥᓈᐣ᙮

[ᐊᒋᔭᐤ ᐁ ᓇᑭᐱᑕᒥᕽ]

ᐆᑌ ᐊᓂᒪ ᐊᐢᑌᐤ ᓃᐢᑕ ᐊᔭ, ᐊᐦ, *States* ᐊᓂᐦᐃ ᓂᒪᓯᓇᐦᐃᑲᓇ, ᐁᑯᑌ ᐊᓂᒪ ᐊᐢᑌᐊᐧ᙮ *Nineteen, nineteen forty-five* ᐁᑯᐢᐲᕽ ᑳ ᒥᓯ ᓅᑎᓂᑐᕽ, ᑳ ᓅᑎᓂᑫᒋᐠ ᒨᓂᔮᓴᐠ, ᐁᑯᐢᐲᕽ ᓂᑮ ᐯ ᐃᑎᓴᐦᐊᒫᑲᐃᐧᐣ ᐊᔭ ᒪᓯᓇᐦᐃᑲᐣ, *letter* ᓂᑮ ᐯ ᐃᑎᓴᐦᐊᒫᑲᐃᐧᐣ᙮

— *Jean*, ᓇᒨᐩ ᑕ ᑖᐯᐧᐦᑕᒪᐣ ᒣᑐᓂ ᐁ ᑮ ᓵᐹᐧᐢᑌᐠ *like this, like this* [ᐁ ᑭᑐᐁᐧᔦᑭᐦᒋᑫᐟ], ᒣᑐᓂ ᐁ ᑮ ᓵᐹᐧᐢᑌᐠ᙮ [JO: *Oh, yeah, I remember those.*] ᐁ ᑮ~, ᐁ ᑮ ᐋᔮᒪᕽ *paper* ᐃᐢᐲᕽ ᑳ ᓅᑎᓂᑐᕽ᙮ ᑌᐱᔮᕽ ᐊᓂᐦᐃ *letters* ᐊᓂᐦᐃ ᐁ ᐊᔭᒥᐦᑖᕽ, ᑖᓂᓯ ᐁᑎᑫᐧ ᑳᐦ ᐃᑕᐢᑌᐠ᙮ —

ᑲᐦᑭᔭᐤ ᐊᓂᐦᐃ ᐁ ᑮ ᐊᐧᓂᐦᑖᔮᐣ᙮ ᑲᐦᑭᔭᐤ ᓂᒪᓯᓇᐦᐃᑲᓇ ᐁ ᑮ ᐊᐧᓂᐦᑖᔮᐣ, ᑲᐦᑭᔭᐤ ᐁ ᑮ ᑲᓇᐁᐧᔨᐦᑕᒫᐣ ᐁᑲᐧ ᐆᒪ ᓂᑲᒥᔪ ᐋᐸᒋᐦᑖᐣ᙮ ᐁᑲᐧ ᐆᒪ ᐯᔮᑳᐧᐤ ᐁ ᓂᑑᐢᑲᒫᐣ ᐁᑯᑌ ᐃᓯ, ᓇᒨᔭ ᐅᐦᒋ ᑭᐢᑫᔨᐦᑕᒪᐧᐠ ᐆᓵᒼ ᓇᒨᔭ ᒥᐢᑕᐦᐃ ᑮᑲᐧᐩ ᐊᔨ, ᑭᐢᑫᔨᐦᑖᓯᐃᐧᐣ ᓅᐦᐊᐢᑖᓈᐣ ᐊᓂᒪ, ᑭᑭᐢᑫᔨᐦᑌᐣ? [JO: ᐋᐦᐊ᙮] ᑌᐱᔮᕽ, ᑌᐱᔮᕽ ᐁ ᑮ ᐃᓯ ᓈᑎᑎᓴᐦᐊᐧᐠ ᐊᓇ ᓲᓂᔮᐤ, ᐁ ᑮ ᐃᓯ~ ᐁ ᑮ ᐃᓯ ᑭᐢᑭᓇᐧᐦᐊᒫᑫᔮᐣ, ᑮ ᓈᑎᑎᓴᐦᐋᐧᐤ᙮ ᐁ ᓈᑎᑎᓴᐦᐅᐦᐟ, ᐁ ᐯ ᐃᑎᓴᐦᐅᐦᐟ ᓲᓂᔮᐤ *Agency at the Fort* [ᑭᐸᐦᐃᑲᓂᕽ]᙮

ᓇᒨᔭ ᓂᔭ ᓅᐦ ᐄᐧᒉᑲᐃᐧᐣ᙮ ᓇᔦᐢᑕᐤ ᓂᒍᓰᒼ ᐁ ᑮ ᐱᐢᑎᐢᑲᐊᐧᐠ, ᑳ ᑮ ᐃᐧᔪᐦᑖᐃᐧᔮᐣ ᐁᓴ ᐁ ᑮ ᐅᑯᓯᓯᐦᑳᐦᐟ ᐆᐦᐃ ᐁ ᑮ~ ᐆᐦᐃ ᓅᐦᑖᐃᐧᔭ ᐆᒪᑐᐃᐧ ᐁᓴ ᐁ ᑮ ᐊᐢᑖᒋᐠ *in a paper* ᐆᒪ ᐁ ᑖᐹᐦᑰᒫᐟ ᐆᐦᐃ, ᐆᐦᐃ ᐊᔨ ᓅᐦᑖᐃᐧᔭ᙮ ᓂᑮ ᐱᐢᑎᐢᑲᐋᐧᐤ ᐊᓇ ᓂᒍᓰᒼ ᐄᐧᐢᑕ ᑮ ᑎᐸᐦᐊᒪᐋᐧᐤ᙮ ᓅᐦᑖᐃᐧᔭ ᓇᔦᐢᑕᐤ ᐁ ᑮ ᑖᐹᐦᑰᒫᐟ, ᐁᑲᐧ ᓂᑳᐃᐧᐩ, ᓂᒍᓰᒼ ᐁᑲᐧ ᓂᑳᐃᐧᐩ, ᐃᐧᔭᐋᐧᐤ ᐱᑯ ᑮ ᐃᑐᐦᑌᐊᐧᐠ *Agency* [ᑭᐸᐦᐃᑲᓂᕽ] ᐁ ᓈᑖᒋᐠ ᐊᓂᐦᐃ ᓲᓂᔮᐊᐧ᙮ ᒫᑲ ᓂᑮ ᑎᐸᐦᐊᒫᑲᐃᐧᐣ ᓃᐢᑕ, ᓂᑖᓂᐢ ᐁᑲᐧ ᓂᔭ; ᓂᑮ ᓂᐢᑎᓈᐣ ᐊᓇ ᓲᓂᔮᐤ ᐁ ᒥᔨᑲᐃᐧᔮᕽ ᐁᑯᑌ ᐊᓇ ᐁ ᐅᐦᒌᐟ, ᓂᑳᐃᐧᐩ ᐁᑲᐧ ᓂᒍᓰᒼ ᐄᐧᐢᑕ, *Little Sioux*, ᓇᒨᔭ ᐊᓇ ᑎᐱᔭᐤ ᐁ ᐋᐧᐦᑯᒪᐠ *Little Sioux*, ᒨᐩ ᑖᐯᐧ᙮ ᑌᐱᔮᕽ ᓅᐦᑯᒼ ᐁ ᑮ ᐄᐧᑭᒫᐟ; ᑭᓂᓯᑐᐦᑌᐣ ᒌ? [JO: ᐋᐦᐊ, ᐋᐦᐊ᙮] ᓇᒨᔭ ᐃᐧᔭ, ᓅᐦᑯᒼ ᐊᐊᐧ, ᐊᐊᐧ ᐊᔭ, ᐊᔭ, ᐁ ᐃᐢᑫᐧᐃᐧ- ᑳ ᑮ ᐃᑎᐦᐟ ᑎᐱᔭᐁᐧ ᓅᐦᑯᒼ, ᓅᐦᑖᐃᐧᐩ ᐊᓂᐦᐃ *his aunt*, ᐅᑳᐄᐧᓴ ᑎᐱᔭᐁᐧ, ᓅᐦᑖᐃᐧᐩ ᐁ ᑮ ᐅᔪᑳᐄᐧᐟ *her sister* ᐊᓂᐦᐃ ᓂᒫ~, *you know*, ᑭᑭᐢᑫᔨᐦᑌᐣ? [JO: *yeah*, ᐋᐦᐊ᙮] ᓅᐦᑖᐃᐧᐩ ᐅᑳᐃᐧᔭ *her sister* ᐆᐦᐃ, *Mrs. Little Sioux*᙮ ᐁᑯᓂ ᐊᐊᐧ ᐁ ᑮ ᐄᐧᑭᒫᐟ ᐊᐊᐧ ᓅᐦᑯᒼ ᐊᐊᐧ, ᐆᐦᐃ ᐊᔭ *Little Sioux*, ᒨᐩ ᑖᐯᐧ ᓂᒍᓰᒼ ᐊᓇ, *you know*᙮ [JO: ᐋᐦᐊ᙮] ᐊᐊᐧ ᐱᑯ ᑎᐱᔭᐁᐧ ᓅᐦᑯᒼ

ᐊᐊᐧ, *the old lady* ᐊᐊᐧ, ᐊᔮ, ᑳ ᑮ ᐃᐧᐋᐦᑖᐃᐧᔫᐣ ᐅᑳᐄᐧᓴ, ᐁᑯᓯ ᐊᓂᒪ ᐁ ᑮ ᐃᐢᐸᐦᐣᐠ×

ᓂᑮ ᐱᐢᑎᐢᑲᐚᐊᐧᐠ ᐊᓂᑭ, ᑮ ᑎᐸᐦᐊᒪᐚᐊᐧᐠ; ᑮ ᑎᐸᐦᐊᒪᐚᐤ ᐊᓇ ᓂᒍᓰᐨ× ᒫᑲ ᐁᑳᐧ ᐊᓇ ᓂᒍᓰᐨ, ᒨᔮ ᐊᐃᐧᔮ ᐁᑳᐧ ᐅᐚᐦᑰᒫᑲᓇ, ᓇᒨᔮ ᐊᐃᐧᔮ ᐱᒫᑎᓯᐦᐊᐧ× ᐯᔮᐠ ᐁ ᑮ ᐅᐦᐱᑭᐦᐚᕆᐠ, ᐁᐊᐧᑯ ᐱᑯ, ᒨᐩ ᒫᑲ ᐁᑯᑕ ᐃᐧᔮ ᑮ ᐅᐦᑎᓰᐤ× ᒨᐩ ᐁᑯᓯ ᐃᐢᐸᐦᐤ×

ᓂᔮ ᐱᑯ ᐊᓂᒪ, ᓂᔮ ᐱᑯ ᐁᑳᐧ ᐁᑳᐧ ᐁ ᐱᒫᑎᓰᔫᐣ× ᐁᑳᐧ ᐁ ᒪᓈ ᑑᑕᒫᐣ, *you know*, ᐊᐦᐣ ᐆᒪ ᐃᐦᑯᕽ ᓂᑎᐦᑕᓯᐣ, ᑖᐱᐢᑰᐨ ᑌᐸᑯ''' ᐆᒪ ᐁᑳᐧ ᓂᑎᐦᑕᓯᐣ× ᑲᐦᑭᔮᐤ ᓂᑕᐚᐧᓯᒥᓴᐠ, ᓃᓯ ~ ᐯᔮᐠ ᓂᑯᓯᐢ *Charlie* ᐃᑖᐤ, ᐁᑳᐧ ᐯᔮᐠ *Johnny* ᐃᑖᐤ, ᐁᑳᐧ ᐯᔮᐠ ᐊᔮ, ᐊᔮ ᐃᑖᐤ *Irene*, ᐁᑳᐧ ᐊᐊᐧ ᐯᔮᐠ ᐋᐦ, ᐊᐊᐧ, ᐊᔮ ᐊᐊᐧ, ᐋᐦ *Pearl*, ᐊᔮ ᐊᐊᐧ *Pearly*, ᐁᑳᐧ ~ *No, Alice, Alice* ᐊᐊᐧ ᓂᑖᓂᐢ; ᑖᐱᐢᑰᐨ ᐆᒥᓯ ᓂᑫ ᐃᑖᐧᐣ, ᐊᔮ ᐊᐊᐧ, *Charlie* ᐊᐊᐧ, ᐁᑳᐧ *Alice*, ᐁᑳᐧ ᐁᑳᐧ ᐊᔮ, ᐊᐊᐧ *Margaret*, ᐁᑳᐧ ᐊᔮ, *no, Irene, Margaret, Barbara*, ᐁᑳᐧ ᐊᔮ, ᐊᔮ *Marie*, *no, Johnny* ᐁᑳᐧ *Marie*; ᐁᑯᓯ ᐁ ᐃᐦᑕᓯᕆᐠ; ᐊᐊᐧ ᐆᑕ ᓂᑯᓯᐢ ᐊᐊᐧ *Johnny*, ᐆᐦᐃ ᐁ ᐅᓰᒥᐟ ᐆᐦᐃ *Marie*ᐊᐧ× ᓂᑖᓂᐢ ᐁᑳᐧ ᐊᐊᐧ ᓂᐯᐲᓯᐨ ᓃᐢᑕ *thirty-nine* ᐃᑕᐦᑐᐱᐳᓈᐤ, *Marie* ᐁᐊᐧᑯ× ᐁᑳᐧ ᐊᐊᐧ, ᐊᐊᐧ, ᐊᐊᐧ ᓂᐢᑕᒎᓴᐣ *sixty-one* ᐃᑕᐦᑐᐱᐳᓈᐤ, *sixty-one Alice*, ᐁᐊᐧᑯ *my first one*, ᐁᐊᐧᑯ ᓂᐢᑕᒎᓴᐣ×

[ᐊᒥᔮᐤ ᐁ ᓇᑭᐱᑕᒥᕽ]

[4. ᓇᓈᑐᕽ ᑳ ᐅᐦᐱᑭᐦᑭ]

JO: *Cactuses* ᐊᓂᐦᐃ, ᐊᑎᒍᓯ~, ᐊᑎᒍᓯᑕ×

ᐊᐣ ᐁᓴ ᐊᓂᐦᐃ ᑳ ᑳᓭᑭ ᐃᓯᐣᐦᑳᑌᐊᐧ× [JO: ᑳᓭᑭ, ᐆᐦ×] ᑳ ᑳᓭᑭ, *yeah* [JO: ᐆᐦ, ᐋᐦᐋ×], ᑳ ᑳᓭᑭ× ᐁᑯᓂ ᐊᓂᐦᐃ ᑳ ᐊᐢᑭᐦᑕᑳᐧᑭ, ᑳ ᑳᓭᑭ ᐃᓯᐣᐦᑳᑌᐊᐧ ᐁᓴ ᐊᓂᐦᐃ× [JO: ᐆᐦ×] ᑳ ᐊᐢᑭᐦᑕᑳᐧᑭ ᐊᓂᐦᐃ ᑳ ᑳᓭᑭ,

ᐁᑯᓂ᙮ ᐁᑲᐧ ᒦᓇ ᐯᔭᑲᐧᐣ ᐁᑯᑕ ᒦᓇ ~, ᐁᑯᑕ ᒦᓇ ᐯᔭᑲᐧᐣ, ᐁᑯᑕ ᒦᓇ ᐯᔭᑲᐧᐣ ᐁᐧᐦᐱᑭᐦᑭ ᐊᓂᐦᐃ ᐊᔨ, ᐊᔨ ᐊᓂᐦᐃ, ᐁᑯᓂ ᒦᓇ ᑳ ᓅᐦᑌ ᐄᐧᐦᑕᒫᑖᐣ ᐊᓂᐦᐃ, ᒦᓇ ᐁᑯᓂ ᐊᐦᐴ ᐁᑎᑫᐧ ᐊᐃᐧᔭᐠ ᑖᐦ ᓅᐦᑌ ᑭᐢᑫᔨᐦᑕᑦ, ᐊᔨ ~ ᐊᐩ, ᑖᓂᓯ ᐁ ᐃᓯᔨᐦᑳᓱᐟ, ᐁᐩ, ᐦᐁᐩ! ᓂᐊᐧᓂᐦᑳᐣ ᐊᓂᒪ, ᓂᐊᐧᓂᐦᑳᐣ ᓈᓂᑕᐤ ᓂᐢᑎᑳᐧᓂᕽ ~

JO: ᐊᒋᒧᒣᔨᓯᒥᓇ?

ᐊᒋᒧᒣᔨᓯᒥᓇ! [ᒪᑌᐧ ᐹᐦᐱᓈᓂᐊᐧᐣ] ᑭᑭᐢᑫᔨᐦᑌᐣ ᒦᓇ ᐁᑯᓂ, ᒌ?

JO: ᐅᑖᑯᓰᕽ ᑭᑮ ᐄᐧᐦᑕᒪᐃᐧᐣ᙮

ᐋᐦ, ᐊᒋᒧᒣᔨᓯᒥᓇ, ᑳᓵᐊᐧ ᒫᓇ ᐯ ᓵᑭᑭᓇᐧ ᐊᓂᐦᐃ, ᐄᐧᐦᑲᓯᓇᐧ ᒫᓇ ᐊᒋᒧᒣᔨᓯᒥᓇ, ᒫᑲ ᐊᔨ ~ ᐃᐢᐸᑎᓈᕽ ᐅᐦᐱᑭᓇᐧ᙮

JO: ᐋᐦᐊ᙮ ᐁᑯᓂ ᐊᓂᐦᐃ, ᐋᐦᐊ᙮

ᐊᒋᒧᒣᔨᓴ ᐄᐧᐦᑲᓯᓇᐧ ᑳ ᑕᑳᐧᑭᐠ ᒫᓇ, ᑭᑭᐢᑫᔨᐦᑌᐣ? ᐁ ᐸᐹ ᐅᑎᓇᒥᕽ, ᑳᓵᐊᐧ ᐸᑎᐦᑕᑯᓈᓴᐠ, ᑭᑭᐢᑫᔨᐦᑌᐣ, *stem* ᐁ ᐅᐦᒋ ᐅᒋᐱᑕᒪᐣ, ᑳ ᑮ~ ᐄᐧᐦᑲᓯᓇᐧ᙮ ᓇᒨᔭ ᒫᑲ ᓈᓂᑕᐤ ᑮ ᐃᓯ ᑮᓯᓯᑳᑌᐊᐧ, ᐄᐧᓂᓈᑲᐧᓇᐧ ᑕ ᑮᓯᓴᒥᕽ, *you know*᙮ ᐸᓴᑳᐧᐊᐧ ᒦᓇ᙮ [ᐹᐦᐱᓈᓂᐊᐧᐣ]

JO: ᐊᓇ ᐁ ᑲᑫᐧᒋᒥᐟ, *"There's a willow,"* ᐃᑌᐧᐤ [MLR: ᐁᐦᐊ᙮], ᓇᐊᐧᒋᑯ ᐋᐧᐱᐢᑳᐧᐊᐧ [MLR: ᐁᐦᐊ᙮], ᐁᑲᐧ ᒦᓇ ᐊᓂᐦᐃ ᓃᐱᔭ ᒦᓇ ᐋᐧᐱᐢᑳᐧᐊᐧ, ᐁᑲᐧ ᒦᐣ ᐋᓂᐦᐃ, *ah*, *"white berries,"* ᐃᑌᐧᐤ᙮ [MLR: ᐁᐦᐊ᙮] ᑖᓂᓯ ᑲᓂ ~

ᐁᑯᓂ ᐊᓂᐦᐃ ᒦᓇ, ᐁᑯᓂ ᐊᓂᐦᐃ ᒦᓇ ᐄᐧᐦᒋᑳᑌᐊᐧ ᐁ ᐃᓯᔨᐦᑳᑌᑭ; ᐋᐧᐱᐢᑳᐧᐊᐧ ᐁᑲᐧ ᐁ ᔫᐢᑲᐧᐦᑕᒪᐣ *green* ᐃᓯᓈᑲᐧᓇᐧ᙮ [JO: ᐋᐦᐋ᙮] ᐁᑲᐧ ᐆᒪ ᐁ ᐄᐧᐦᑕᒪᐃᐧᐟ *Alice* ~, — ᒫᒋᑰᐨ ᐆᒪ ᐊᔭᒥᐦᑖ, ᐁᐊᐧᑯ ᐊᓂ ᐁ ᒪᓯᓇᐦᐊᒪᐊᐧᐠ ᑖᓂᓯ ᑳᐦ ᑮ ᐃᑖᐧᐣ ᐁ ᐃᑕᐠ᙮

JO: ᐅᑲᒪ~ ᐅᑳᑦ~

ᐅᑳᒥᓇᑲᓰᐚᐦᑎᑿᐠ [JO: ᐅᑲᑦ~], ᐅᑳᒥᓇᑲᓰᐚᐦᑎᑿᐠ᙮ ᑭᑭᐢᑫᔨᒫᐘᐠ ᐊᓂᑭ ᑮᑿᔭᐠ ᐅᑳᒥᓇᑲᓰᐚᐦᑎᑿᐠ? [JO: ᒨᔭ᙮] ᐅᑳᒥᓇᑲᓯᔭᐠ? ᐊᔨ ᒫᓇ, ᓴᑳᕽ ᒫᓇ ᒥᑐᓂ ᐅᐦᐱᑭᐘᐠ ᐅᑳᒥᓇᑲᓯᔭᐠ, ᒫᐣ~ ᑳᐦᑭᓈᐘ ᒫᓇ ᐁ ᑳᓵᑭ, ᐁᑯᐟ~ ᐁᑯᑐᐘ ᒥᐢᑎᐠ ᐊᓇ [JO: *Oh, thorns.*] ᐁᐦᐊ, ᐁᑯᑐᐘ᙮ [JO: *Thorn trees.*] ᐁᑯᑐᐘ, ᒫᐦᒥᓵᐘ ᒫᓇ ᐊᔨ [JO: ᐋᐦᐊ᙮ *Red berries.*], ᐁᑯᑐᐘ ᒥᐦᑳᐘ, ᐁᑯᓂ ᐊᓂᐦᐃ, ᐅᑳᒥᓇᑲᓰᐚᐦᑎᑿᐠ ᐁᐘᑯᓂᐠ, ᐅᑳᒥᓇᑲᓰᐚᐦᑎᑿᐠ᙮

JO: ᒪᐦᑎ ᐁᓴ, *do you have a ~*

ᑫᐢᑿ, ᐆᑕ ᓂᑖᔮᐣ ... [ᒪᑌᐧ ᑕᐦᒋᐱᒋᑫᐤ] ...,

ᐅᑳᒥᓇᑲᓰᐚᐦᑎᑿᐠ: ᐯᔭᐠ ᐁᑯᑕ ᒪᓂᓯ~ [ᒨᐩ ᑿᔭᐢᐠ ᐯᐦᑖᑿᐣ] ᑫᐢᑿ᙮ ᑫᐢᑿ, ᑫᐢᑿ, ᑫᐢᑿ᙮ ᐅᑳᒥᓇᑲᓰᐚᐦᑎᑿᐠ, ᐅᑳᒥᓇᑲᓰᐚᐦᑎᑿᐠ, ᒥᓯᑭᑎᐘᐠ ᒫᓇ, ᒥᑐᓂ ᑳᐦᑭᓈᐘ ᒫᓇ ᐊᔨ, ᒑᐱᐢᑰᐨ ᐊᔨ, ᓵᐳᓂᑲᓇ, ᐁᑯᑕ, ᐁᑯᑕ ᓵᑲᒧᐘᐠ ᒫᓇ ᐁ ᒥᐦᑯᓯᒋᐠ *berries* ᒑᐱᐢᑰᐨ, ᒫᑲ ᐱᐦᐁᑯᓯᐘᐠ ᐊᔨ ᑳ ᒧᐘᒋᐠ ᒑᐱᐢᑰᐨ ᐁ ᐱᐦᐁᑳᐧᐠ᙮ ᐁᑯᓂᐠ ᐊᓂᑭ ᐅᑳᒥᓇᐠ~ ᐅᑳᒥᓇᐠ~, ᑖᓂᓯ? [JO: ᐅᑳᒥᓇᓰᐚᐦᑎᐠ~] ᐅᑳᒥᓇᐠ~, ᐊᐩ ᓴᐩ! [JO: ᐅᑳᒥᓇᓰᐚᐦᑎᑿᐠ [*sic*]] ᐋ, ᐅᑳᒥᐣ~, ᐁᐩ, ᐁᑯᓯ ᐊᓂᒪ᙮

DO: ᐁᑲᐧ ᓂᔭᓈᐣ ᑫᐦᑎᓈ ᐅᑭᓂᔭᐠ ᐃᓯᔨᐦᑳᓱᐘᐠ᙮

Yeah, ᐁᐘᑯᓂᐠ ᑭᔭ ᐊᓂᑭ ᐸᐦᑳᐣ, ᐅᑭᓂᔭᐠ ᑳ ᐃᑕᒋᐠ ...

DO: ᐸᐦᑳᐣ ᒌ?

... ᒋᒥᓯᓯᐘᐠ ᒫᓇ᙮

JO: *Those are small ones.* [DO: ᐆᐦ᙮] [MLR: ᐁᐘᑯᓂᐠ᙮] *There's other thorn berries* ᒦᓇ᙮

ᑯᑕᐠ ᒦᓇ, ᒋᒥᓯᓯᐘᐠ ᐏᔭ ᐊᓂᑭ ᐅᑭᓂᔭᐠ ᑳ ᐃᑕᒋᐠ᙮ [JO: *mhm.* DO: *mm.*] ᐊᔨ ᐊᔨᓯᔨᐦᑳᓱᐘᐠ ᒫᓇ ᐅᑫᔨᑭᒋᐢᑫᐦᐃᐍᓰᓴᐠ

[ᑌᐯᐧᔮᐦᐱᓈᓂᐊᐧᐣ], ᑳ ᒥᓯ ᒧᐊᐧᒋᐠ ᑭᑫᔭᑭᒥᐢᑳᐣ; ᑖᐯᐧ ᑳ ᐊᐧ~ ᐁ ᒥᓯ ᒧᐊᐧᒋᐠ ᐁ ᐊᐧᔭᐄᐧᔭᐣ, ᓈᓈᑫᐢ ᑭᒨᓯᐦᑖᐣ ᐁ ᐄᐧ ᑫᔭᑭᒥᐢᑫᔭᐣ, *you know*᙮ [ᐹᐦᐱᓈᓂᐊᐧᐣ] ᐁᑯᓂᐠ ᐊᓂᑭ ᐅᑫᔭᑭᒥᐢᑫᐦᐃᐁᐧᓰᓴᐠ ᐃᑖᐊᐧᐠ᙮ [ᑌᐯᐧᔮᐦᐱᓈᓂᐊᐧᐣ] ᐁᑯᓯ ᐃᓯᔨᐦᑳᓱᐊᐧᐠ, ᑖᐯᐧ!

JO: ᒪᐦᑌᓴ ᓂᑲ ᒪᓯᓇᐦᐁᐣ, ᑖᓂᓯ ᑲᓂᕽ, ᐅ~?

ᐅᑫᔭᑭᒥᐢᑫᐦᐃᐁᐧᓰᓴᐠ [ᐹᐦᐱᓈᓂᐊᐧᐣ], ᐅᑫᔭᑭᒥᐢᑫᐦᐃᐁᐧᓰᓴᐠ ᐃᑖᐊᐧᐠ ᐊᓂᑭ, ᐅᑳᒥᓇᑲᓯᔭᐠ ᐁᐊᐧᑯᓂᐠ᙮ [DO: *oh?*] ᓇᒨᔭ, ᒨᔭ, ᒨᔭ, ᒨᔭ [DO: ᐅᑭᓂᔭᐠ᙮], ᐅᑭᓂᔭᐠ ᐁᐊᐧᑯᓂᐠ, ᐅᑭᓃᐋᐧᐦᑎᑲᐧᐠ ᐃᐧᔭ ᐃᓯᔨᐦᑳᓱᐊᐧᐠ ᐊᓂᑭ, ᒥᐢᒋᑯᓴᐠ ᐊᓂᑭ, ᐅᑭᓃᐋᐧᐦᑎᑲᐧᐠ ᐁᐊᐧᑯᓂᐠ; ᐅᑭᓃᐋᐧᐦᑎᑲᐧᐠ, ᐁᑯᑕ ᑭᑲᒧᐊᐧᐠ ᐊᓂᑭ ᐅᑫᔭᑭᒥᐢᑫᐦᐃᐁᐧᓰᓴᐠ [ᐹᐦᐱᓈᓂᐊᐧᐣ]

JO: ᐅᑫᔭᑭᒥᐢ~ ᑫ [ᐦᐅ] ᐁᐧ [MLR: ᓰᓴᐠ] ᓰ [MLR: ᓴᐠ] ᓴᐠ᙮ [MLR: ᐁᐦᐊ᙮] [ᒥᓯ ᐹᐦᐱᓈᓂᐊᐧᐣ]

ᒫᑲ ᐊᔨᐢ ᑭᓅᐦᑌ~ [ᐊᒋᔭᐤ ᐁ ᓇᑭᐱᑕᒥᕽ ᐁᑯᓯ ᒨᔭ ᒪᓯᓇᐦᐃᑳᑌᐤ] … ᐁ ᐃᓯᔨᐦᑳᑌᐠ ᑮᑲᐧᐩ [JO: *Ya.*] ᑐᓂ ᐁ ᐊᐧᐃᐧᔭᑌᔨᐦᑖᑲᐧᕽ ᐊᓂᑭ ᐅᑭᓂᔭᐠ᙮ ᐅᑭᓃᐋᐧᐦᑎᑲᐧᐠ ᐃᑖᐊᐧᐠ ᐊᓂᑭ; ᐅᑭᓂᔭᐠ ᐊᓂᑭ ᑳ ᓵᑭᑭᒋᐠ ᒥᑐᓂ ᑲ~, ᒫᑲ ᐊᐱᓵᓯᓇᐧ ᐊᔨ, *pins, you know*, ᐊᐱᓵᓯᓇᐧ ᒫᑲ ᒣᑐᓂ ᑳᓵᐊᐧ, *you know*᙮ ᒫᑲ ᓇᒨᔭ ᑕᒥᓯ ᒧᐊᐧᒋᐠ ᐊᓂᑭ ᐊᔨᐢ ᐅᑭᓂᔭᐠ ᑭᑫᔭᑭᒥᐢᑫᐢᑳᑲᐧᐠ, ᒪᓵᓂᐃᐧᐊᐧᐠ ᐊᓂᑭ, *you know*, ᒪᓵᓂᐃᐧᐊᐧᐠ᙮ ᒫᑲ ᒥᐢᑕᐦᐃ ᐁ ᑕᑯᓇᒪᐣ ᐱᒥᐩ, ᓇᒨᐩ ᐁᑯᓯ ᑭᑎᑎᐢᑳᑲᐧᐠ᙮ *You put* ~

JO: ᑖᓂᓯ ᒫᑲ ᐁ ᐃᓯ ᐊᔨ~,

ᐁ ᐃᓯ ᑮᓯᓴᐧᒋᐠ? [JO: ᐋᐦᐊ᙮]

ᐊᐩ, ᑭᓯᑲᐧᐦᐋᐧᐊᐧᐠ, ᑭᓯᑲᐧᐦᐋᐧᐊᐧᐠ ᐁᑲᐧ ᑭᑫᒋᑯᐱᑌᐣ *stems* ᐊᓂᐦᐃ ᐊᔨᐢᐠ *leaves* ᐅᒥᓯ ᐃᑕᒧᓇᐧ, ᐁᑯᓂ ᑲᐦᑭᔭᐤ, ᑖᐱᐢᑰᐨ *apples*᙮ ᑲᐦᑭᔭᐤ ᑭᒪᓂᐱᑌᐣ ᐊᓂᐦᐃ, ᒣᑐᓂ ᑭᐯᐦᑭᐦᐋᐊᐧᐠ ᑭᑭᓰᐯᑭᓈᐊᐧᐠ ᑫᐧᔭᐢᐠ, ᑭᓵᑲᒥᑌᐋᐧᐴᕽ, ᐊᐦᐴ ᐁᑎᑫᐧ *worms* ᐁᑯᑕ ᑭᑲᒧᐊᐧᐠ ᐊᐧᔭᐄᐧᔮᐸᐁᐧᐊᐧᐠ

ᐁᐊᐧᑯᓂᐠ, ᑭᓀᐧᓰᐢ ᐁ ᐊᑲᐧᒧ~ ᐁ ᐊᓯᐊᐧᐦᐊᒋᐠ ᓂᐲᕽ ᐁ ᑭᓯᑌᐠ᙮ ᐁᑯᓯ ᐁᑲᐧ ᑭᐹᐦᑲᐧᐦᐋᐧᐊᐧᐠ, ᐁᑯᓯ ᐁᑲᐧ ᑭᑎᓯ ᐸᑳᓯᒫᐊᐧᐠ ᐱᒦᕽ, ᑭᓯᑲᐧᐦᐋᐧᐊᐧᐠ ᐊᔨᐢᐠ, ᑭᓯᑲᐧᐦᐋᐧᐊᐧᐠ ᐊᓂᑭ ᐱᒥᐩ ᒫᑲ ᑭᑕᑯᓀᐣ ᐁᑲᐧ ᓰᐃᐧᓂᑲᐣ, ᒥᐢᑕᐦᐃ ᐄᐧᐦᑭᑎᓯᐊᐧᐠ᙮ ᐄᐧᐦᑭᑎᓯᐊᐧᐠ ᐊᓂᑭ, ᓀᐦᐃᔭᐃᐧ *fruit* ᐊᓂᒪ, *you know*᙮ [DO: *mhm.*]

JO: *But how do you take out those seeds?*

ᐁᑯᓯ ᐃᓯ ᑭᑮᓯᓴᐣ, ᐁᑯᓯ ᐃᓯ᙮ [JO: ᐆᐦ᙮] ᐁᐊᐧᑯ ᑰᐦ ᑑᒥᓇᒪᐣ ᐁᐊᐧᑯ ᑰᐦ~, ᑮᐢᐱᐣ ᐊᓂᒪ ᐲᐦᒑᔨᕽ ᐊᓂᑭ ᓇᔦᐢᑕᐤ ᐁ ᐋᐸᒋᐦᐊᒋᐠ, ᐁᑳ ᐁ ᑑᒥᓇᒪᐣ ᐊᓂᒪ, ᐁᑯᑕ ᑳ ᑫᔭᑭᒋᐢᑫᐢᑳᐢᑭᐠ᙮ ᒣᑐᓂ ᑭᑳᐦ ᐹᐦ ᐲᑯᐱᑌᐣ ᑭᒋᐢᐠ ᑭᔭ᙮ [ᑭᓀᐧᐢ ᒥᓯ ᐹᐦᐱᓈᓂᐊᐧᐣ] ᒫᑲ ᐃᐧᔭ ᒥᓯ ᑑᒥᓇᒋᐠ, ᓇᒨᔭ ᑭᑖᐦᑯᐦᐃᑲᐧᐠ, *you know*, ᐊᔨᐢ ᑑᒥᓯᐊᐧᐠ᙮

JO: ᐋᐦᐊ, ᓅᐦᑯᒼ ᐊᓇ ᐁ ᑮ ᐋᒋᒧᐟ ᒫᓇ ᐊᔨ, ᐋᐦ, ᐅᐦᑯᒪ ᐁᑎᑫᐧ ᒫᓇ ᐁ ᑮ ᐊᔨ~ ᐁ ᑮ ᐸᐹᒨᒥᓀᒋᐠ ᐁᑲᐧ ᒫᑲ ᐅᐦᑯᒥᐋᐧᐊᐧ ~ [MLR: ᐁᐦᐊ᙮] ᒫᑲ ᒨᐩ ~ ᒨᐩ ᑮ ᐄᐧᐦᑕᒼ ᑖᓂᓯ ᐁ~

ᐁ ᐃᑎᐦᑲᓵᐧᒋᐠ᙮

JO: *Yeah* [MLR: ᐁᑯᓯ ᐊᓂᒪ ~], ᑖᐱᐢᑰᐨ ᐁ ᑮ~ ᒨᔭ, ᒨᔭ ᑮ ᑮᓯᓴᐧᐤ᙮

ᓇᒨᔭ, ᑮᓯᓵᐧᐊᐧᐠ ᐊᓂᑭ, ᐁ ᓯᑲᐧᐦᐊᐧᒋᐠ᙮

JO: ᐁᑲᐧ ᐁ ᑮ ᓴᑯᓇᐦᑭᐠ *in a bag*᙮

ᐁᐦᐊ; ᐃᐧᔭᐋᐧᐤ ᐁᑎᑫᐧ ᐸᐦᑳᐣ, ᓂᔭᓈᐣ ᒫᓇ ᐃᐧᔭ ᑳ ᐃᓯ ᐊᓴᒥᑲᐃᐧᔮᕽ ᑳ ᑮ ᐃᐧᔦᐦᑯᒥᔮᐣ, ᑮ ᓂᑕᐤ ᒪᐃᐧᓱᐤ ᐊᓂᐦᐃ ᒫᐣ~, ᒨᐩ ᐃᐧᔭ ᒌᐳᑭᓂᔭᐠ ᐊᓂᑭ᙮ ᒌᐳᑭᓂᔭᐠ ᐋᑎᐦᐟ [JO: ᐋᐦᐊ᙮], ᒌᐳᑭᓂᔭᐠ ᒌᐳᓯᐊᐧᐠ, ᒫᑲ ᐊᓂᑭ ᑳ ᐋᐧᐃᐧᔦᓯᒋᐠ ᐁᑯᑐᐊᐧ᙮ ᑮ ᒥᓯ ᒪᐃᐧᓱᐤ ᒫᓇ ᓅᐦᑯᒼ; ᐁᑲᐧ ᐊᓂᐦᐃ ᑲᐦᑭᔭᐤ ᐊᓂᐦᐃ *stems* ᐊᓂᐦᐃ ᑲᐦᑭᔭᐤ ᐁ ᑮ ᐁᐧᐱᓈᐟ ᐁᑲᐧ ᑭᓵᑲᒥᑌᐋᐧᐴᕽ ᐁ ᐊᑯᐦᒋᒫᐟ᙮ « ᑖᓀᐦᑭ ᑰᐦᐊᑯᐦᒋᒪᒋᐠ ᐆᑭ, » ᐁ ᐃᑖᔮᕽ ᒫᓇ ᓅᐦᑯᒼ᙮

« ᐊᐳ ᐊᓂᑭ ᑕ ᐊᐧᔭᐄᐧᔮᐹᐁᐧᒋᐠ ᐋᑎᐦᐟ ᒧᐦᒉᓴᐠ ᐲᐦᒑᐳᕽ ᑭᑲᒧᐊᐧᐠ, ᐁ ᐊᐧᔭᐄᐧᔮᐹᐁᐧᒋᐠ, ᐊᐧᐢᑭᒋᑭᐸᐳᐤ ᐁᑯᓂᐠ ᑭᐁᐧᐱᓈᐊᐧᐠ, ᐁᐧᐱᓈᐊᐧᐠ᙮ ᐁᑲᐧ, ᐁᑲᐧ, ᐁᑲᐧ ᐁ ᐊᑎ ᑮᓯᓴᐧᒋᐠ ᐁᑲᐧ, ᐱᒥᐩ ᐁᑯᑕ ᑭᑕᑯᑐᐣ, ᐱᒦᕽ ᐁᑲᐧ ᐁ ᑮᓯᓴᐧᒋᐠ ᐁ ᓂᐸᐦᐃᐦᑲᓴᒪᐣ ᐊᓂᒪ ᐊᐳ, ᐊᓂᒪ ᑑᐦ ᑫᔭᑭᒋᐢᑫᔭᐣ ᐁ ᓂᐸᐦᐃᐦᑲᓴᒪᐣ, » ᐊᓂᒪ ᐃ~ ᑮ ᐃᑌᐧᐤ ᒫᓇ᙮ ᐁᑲᐧ ᐁᑯᓯ ᔩᐃᐧᓂᑲᐣ ᐁ ᑕᑯᓇᒪᐣ, ᑭᑕᐢᐸᐦᒋᑳᐣ ᐄᐧᐦᑭᒋᓯᐊᐧᐠ ᒣᑐᓂ ᐄᐧᐦᑭᒋᓯᐊᐧᐠ᙮ ᐁᑲᐧ ᒨᐩ, ᒨᐩ ᑭᑫᔭᑭᒋᐢᑫᐢᑳᑲᐧᐠ ᐱᒥᐩ ᐁ ᒥᓯ ᑕᑯᓇᒪᐣ, *you know*᙮ ᒫᑲ ᐃᐧᔭ ᐁᑳ ᐁ ᑕᑯᓇᒪᐣ ᐱᒥᐩ, ᑭᑫᔭᑭᒋᐢᑳᐣ ᑭᐹᐦ ᐸᑯᐱᑌᐣ ᑭᒋᐢᐠ᙮ ᐁᑲᐧ ᑭᑖᐸᒋᐦᑖᐣ *after, vaseline, you know,* ᐁ ᑑᒥᒋᐢᑫᔭᐣ᙮ [ᐹᐦᐱᓈᓂᐊᐧᐣ] ᐊᐧᐦᐋᐧ!

DO: ᐄᐧᓴᐦᑫᒑᕽ᙮

ᐊᐊᐧᐢ, ᐁᑳᐩ! [ᐹᐦᐱᐤ] ᐁᑳᔭ ᑕᓯᑦ ᐄᐧᓴᐦᑫᒑᕽ, ᑲ ᐯ ᓈᓂᑕᐃᐧᑑᑖᑯᓇᐤ ᐆᑕ ᑕ ᐯ ᐲᐦᑐᑫᐤ ᐊᔭ, ᐊᔭ, ᐅᓯᑭᔮᐄᐧᐢ᙮ [ᐹᐦᐱᓈᓂᐊᐧᐣ]

[5. ᑖᓂᓯ ᑰᐦ ᐃᓯᐳᐦᑳᓱᒋᐠ ᐱᓯᐢᑭᐊᐧᐠ]

ᐅᓯᑭᔮᐄᐧᓴᐠ! ᐊᐧᐦ, ᐅᓯᑭᔮᐄᐧᓴᐠ ᐊᐳᐢ ᐆᑭ ᓂᐦᑖ ᓅᑎᐢᑫᐧᐁᐧᐊᐧᐠ᙮ ᐊᐧᔭᐄᐧᑎᒥᕽ ᑳ ᐊᔮᕽ ᐁᓴ ᐃᔮᔭᐤ ᐁ ᑲᑫᐧ ᑮᒥᓂᑫᒋᐠ ᐊᐳᐢ, *you know*᙮ ᐁᑲᐧ ᐁᓴ ᒫᓇ ᐁᑯᓯ ᐆᒪ [ᐁ ᐃᓯᓂᐢᑫᐟ] ᐁ ᑑᑕᐦᑭᐠ ᐅᓯᑭᔮᐄᐧᓴᐠ, ᑖᐱᐢᑰᐨ ᐁ ᐋᑲᐋᐧᓯᓇᒫᒋᐠ ᐁ ᑲᑫᐧ ᐋᐧᐸᒥᐢᑭᐠ ᑖᐣ~, ᐁᑲᐧ ᐁᓴ ᒫᓇ ᐅᒥᓯ [ᐁ ᐃᓯᓂᐢᑫᐟ] ᐁ ᑑᑕᐦᑭᐠ᙮ ᑖᐱᐢᑰᐨ ᐁ ᑕᐦᑭᓂᐢᑭᐠ, ᑭᐢᑫ~, ᐁ ᒥᔮᐦᑕᐦᑭᐠ ᐅᒋᐦᒌᓯᐋᐧᐤ ᐃᑖᐧᓂᐤ ᒫᓇ, ᐁ ᑮᒥᓂᑫᐢᑭᒋᐠ ᐊᐳᐢ ᐊᓂᑭ ᐅᓯᑭᔮᐄᐧᓴᐠ᙮ ᐁᑯᓯ ᐃᑕᒋ ᐊᐃᐧᔭᐠ « ᐅᓯᑭᔮᐄᐧᐢ! », ᐁ ᑮᒥᓂᑫᐢᑭᐟ ᐊᓇ᙮ [ᐹᐦᐱᓈᓂᐊᐧᐣ]

ᐁᑲᐧ ᒦᓇ, ᐁᑲᐧ ᒦᓇ, ᐁᑲᐧ ᒥᓇ ᑳ ᑮᐦᑳᐃᐧᑐᕽ, ᑫᑕᐦᑕᐁᐧ ᐊᐃᐧᔭᐠ ᑭᑮᐦᑳᒥᐠ, ᑭᓇ ᓂᑐᐦᑕᐋᐧᐤ ᐊᐃᐧᔭᐠ ᐁ ᑮᐦᑳᒥᐢᐠ ᑭᒐᐋᐧᐢ~, ᑭᐄᐧᑭᒫᑲᐣ ᐊᐁᐧᑳ ᒌ ᒦᓇ ᑯᑕᐠ ᐊᐃᐧᔭᐠ, *you know*, ᑭᔮᑦ ᑕ ᓂᑐᐦᑕᐊᐧᐟ ᓈᓂᑕᐤ ᐁ ᐃᑎᐢᐠ ᐊᐃᐧᔭᐠ᙮ ᓈᓂᑕᐤ ᐅᒥᓯ ᐃᑎᐢᑭ, « ᐊᑎᑦ » ᐃᑎᐢᑭ, ᐁᑳᐩ ᑲ ᑭᓰᒥᐠ, ᐁᑳᐩ ~ ᐁᑳᐩ ᑲ ᑭᓯᐋᐧᓯᔭᐣ, ᐁ ᒪᒥᐦᒋᒥᐢᐠ ᐊᓂᒪ᙮ ᑖᐱᐢᑰᐨ ᒥᑐᓂ ᐊᐳ ᐁ ᒦᐦᑲᐃᐧᑮᔭᐣ, *you know*, ᑖᐱᐢᑰᐨ

ᐊᐃᐧᔭᐠ ᐁ ᐊᑎ ᓯᐯᐧᐸᐦᑖᐟ, ᑖᐱᐢᑰᐟ ᑕ~ ᐋᐦ ~ ᑕ ᐊᑎᒪᐟ, ᑖᐱᐢᑰᐨ *you* ~ ᑕ ᐊᑎᒪᐟ ᐁ ᐃᑎᑲᐃᐧᔭᐣ, ᑖᐱᐢᑰᐨ ᐁ ᒦᐦᑲᐃᐧᑮᔭᐣ ᐁ ᐃᑎᐢᐠ ᐊᓂᒪ ᐊᐃᐧᔭᐠ᙮ « ᐊᑎᒼ » ᐃᑎᐢᑭ, ᒨᐩ ᑕ ᑭᓯᐋᐧᓯᔭᐣ, ᑖᐱᐢᑰᐟ ᓂᔭ ᑭᑎᑌᔨᐦᑌᐣ ᐊᒋᒧᓯᐢ ᐁ ᐊᐢᐱ ᑮᐦᑳᒥᐟ ᐁ ᐃᑌᔨᐦᑕᒪᐣ, ᓇᒨᔭ᙮ ᑖᐱᐢᑰᐨ ᐊᓂᒪ ᐁ ᒪᒥᐦᒋᒥᐢᐠ, *you know*, ᐃᑌᔨᐦᑕᒼ ᐃᐧᔭ ᐊᐊᐧ ᐊᔨᓯᔨᓂᐤ ᐁ ᒥᓯ ᐃᑕᕽ ᐊᓂᒪ ᐁ ᑮᐦᑳᒪᐠ « ᐊᑎᒼ » ᑳ ᐃᑕᐠ᙮ ᒨᔭ! ᐁ ᒪᒥᐦᒋᒥᐢᐠ ᐊᓂᒪ, ᐁ ᐃᑎᐢᐠ ᐊᓂᒪ ᐁ ᒦᐦᑲᐃᐧᑮᔭᐣ, *you know*? [JO: *Ooooh.*] ᑭᓂᓯᑐᐦᑌᓈᐋᐧᐤ ᒌ ᐁ ᐊᑎᒪᐟ ᐊᐃᐧᔭᐠ? [DO: *mhm.*]

ᐁᑲᐧ ᒦᓇ ᐊᓇ ᒥᓅᐢ ᑳ ᐃᑎᐦᐟ; ᒥᓅᐢ ᑭᑎᑖᓇᐤ ᐴᓰᐢ; ᒥᓅᐢ ᑭᑎᑖᓇᐤ᙮ ᐁ ᑖᐯᐧᒫᔭᕽ ᐊᓇ ᒥᓅᐢ ᑳ ᐃᑖᔭᕽ ᐄᐧᐦᐅᐃᐧᐣ ᐊᔨᐢ ᐊᓂᒪ ᒥᓅᐢ᙮ ᐆᑕ ᐁ ᐃᑎᓇᐟ ᐅᐢᑳᑎᓯᕽ ᐁ ᐸᑭᒋᐁᐧᐱᓇᐟ, ᒦᓅᐤ ᐊᓇ, ᑭᑭᐢᑫᔨᐦᑌᐣ? ᒦᓄᑯᒋᐣ [JO: *Ooooh.*], ᓃᐸᐋᐧᑯᒋᐣ, ᒦᓇ ᐁᐋᐧᑯ ᐊᓂᒪ᙮ ᐁᐦᐊ, ᐁᑯᓯ ᐊᓂᒪ ᒦᓇ ᐁ ᐃᑌᐧᕽ᙮

ᐁᑲᐧ ᒦᓇ ᓰᓰᑊ ᐁ ᐋᐧᐸᒪᐟ, « ᐄᐦ, ᓈᐦᐊ ᓰᓰᑊ! » ᐁ ᐃᑌᐧᔭᐣ ᑫᐧᔭᐢᐠ ᐊᓂᒪ ᐁ ᐄᐧᐦᐊᐟ ᐊᓇ ᓰᓰᑊ᙮ ᑭᑭᐢᑫᔨᐦᑌᐣ ᑖᓂᓯ ᐊᓇ ᐁ ᐃᓯᔨᐦᑳᓱᐟ ᓰᓰᑊ ᑳ ᐃᑎᐦᐟ, ᓰᓰᐸᐠ ᐆᑭ᙮ ᑭᑭᐢᑫᔨᐦᑌᐣ ᑖᓀᐦᑭ ᐅᐦᐃᓯᔨᐦᑳᓱᐟ, ᓰᓰᑊ? [JO: ᓇᒨᔭ᙮] ᑳ ᐄᐧ ᐅᐦᐸᐦᐅᐟ, ᐱᓯᓯᐠ ᐁ ᓰᐲᐟ, *see!* [ᐁ ᐃᓯᓂᐢᑫᐟ] [JO: ᐆᐦ᙮] ᑭᓂᓯᑐᐦᑌᐣ? [JO & DO: ᐋᐦᐊ᙮]

ᐁᑲᐧ ᒦᓇ, ᑖᓂᓯ ᐊᓇ ᒦᓇ, ᑖᓂᓯ ᐊᓇ ᒦᓇ ᑰᐦ ᐃᓯᔨᐦᑳᓱᐟ ᐊᓂ ᐊᔭ, ᓯᐦᑯᐢ ᑳ ᐃᑖᔭᕽ, ᓯᐦᑯᐢ, *a weasel*, ᑖᓂᓯ ᐊᓂᒪ? ᓯᐦᑯᐢ ᐊᓇ ᑖᓂᓯ ᐊᓇ ᐁ ᐄᐧ ᐃᓯᔨᐦᑳᑕᐟ? ᓯᐦᑯᐢ ᑳ ᐃᑕᐟ? ᒨᐩ ᑭᓂᓯᑐᐦᑌᐣ? [DO: ᒨᔭ᙮] ᑲ ᐄᐧᐦᑖᒫᑎᐣ ᑮᑳᐧᐩ ᐊᓂᒪ᙮ ᓯᐦᑯᐢ ᐊᐊᐧ *weasel* ᑭᓄᓯᐤ, ᓇᒨᔭ ᐊᓇ ᐁ ᐅᐃᐧᔭᐃᐧᐟ ᓇᓴᐢᑕᐤ ᒉᑐᓂ ᐁ ᓰᑯᓯᐟ ᐊᓇ, *you know*᙮ ᐁ ᓰᑯᓯᐟ ᐊᓇ ᓯᐦᑯᐢ, ᓇᒪ ᑮᑳᐧᐩ ᐆᑌ ᐊᔨ, ᓇᒨᐩ ᒥᐢᑕᐦᐃ ᑮᑳᐧᐩ ᐆᑌ ᐁ ᐊᔮᐟ᙮ [DO: *Oh, yeah.*] ᐁ ᓰᑯᓯᐟ ᓯᐦᑯᐢ ᑳ ᐃᑖᔭᕽ᙮ ᐆᑭ *weasels* ᐆᑭ ᑳᐦ ᑭᓅᓯᐋᐧᐠ, ᓇᒨᔭ ᐊᓂᑭ ᑖᐯᐧ ᑮᑳᐧᐩ ᐆᑌ ᐁ ᐊᔮᒋᐠ᙮ ᐁ ᓰᑯᓯᐟ, ᑭᓂᓯᑐᐦᑌᐣ? [JO: ᐋᐦᐊ᙮ DO: *Yeah.*] ᐄᐦ, ᐁᐋᐧᑯ ᒦᓇ ᐊᓂᒪ ᑕᑲᐦᑭ ᐋᒋᒧᐃᐧᐣ, *you know*᙮ ᓯᐦᑯᐢ ᑳ ᐃᑖᔭᕽ ᐊᓂᒪ ᐁᑲᐧ, ᐁ ᓰᑯᓯᐟ ᐊᓂᒪ ᐁ ᐃᑌᐧᔭᕽ, ᑫᐧᔭᐢᐠ

ᐊᓂᒪ ᐁ ᐄᐧᐦᐋᔮᕽ, *you know*᙮ ᑖᐯᐧ ᐊᓂᑭ ᑳᐦᑭᓄᓯᐊᐧᐠ, ᒪ ᑮᑲᐧᐩ
ᐆᑌ ᐁ ᐊᓯᐊᐧᑌᐳᐠ, ᐁᑕᑕᐤ, ᐁᑕᑕᐤ ᐊᐱᔫᐢ ᐱᑯ; ‘ᔫᑰᐢ’ ᐁ ᐃᑖᔮᕽ,
ᐁ ᔫᑯᓯᐟ᙮ [ᐹᐦᐱᓈᓂᐊᐧᐣ] [JO: *Geez,* ᑖᐯᐧ ᐁᓴ᙮]

ᐁᑯᓯ ᐊᓂᒪ ᒦᓇ, ᐁᐊᐧᑯ ᐊᓂᒪ ᒦᓇ, ᐁᑲᐧ ᐊᓂᒪ ᒦᓇ ᐋᒋᒧᐃᐧᐣ
ᐊᓂᒪ, ᐁᑯᓯ ᐊᓂᒪ ᒦᓇ᙮ ᐄᐦ, ᐊᓇ ᒥᓅᐢ ᐊᓇ, ᐁ ᑖᐯᐧᒥᐦᐟ ᐊᓇ᙮
ᐅᐢᑳᑎᕽ ᑯᒋᐦᐋᐦᑲᐣ, ᐅᐢᑳᑎᕽ ᑲᓇᐯᐧ~, ᐅᒥᓯ ᑭᑲ ᐃᑎᓈᐤ, ᑲ ᐸᑭᒋᐁᐧᐱᓈᐤ,
ᑕ ᑫᐧᐢᑮᐤ, ‘ᒦᓅᐢ’, ᐁ ᒦᓅᐟ! ᑭᓂᓯᑐᐦᑌᐣ ᒌ? [DO: ᐋᐦᐊ᙮ JO: ᐋᐦᐊ᙮]
ᐁᑯᓯ ᐊᓂᒪ, ᐁᑯᓯ ᐊᓂᒪ ᒦᓇ ᐁ ᐃᑌᐧᕽ ᐊᓂᒪ᙮ ᐁᐊᐧᑯ ᐊᓂᒪ ᒦᓇ,
ᐁᐊᐧᑯ ᐊᓂᒪ ᒦᓇ ᐋᒋᒧᐃᐧᐣ ᐁ ᐊᐧᐃᐧᔭᑌᐳᐦᑖᑲᐧᕽ, *you know*᙮

ᔫᔫᑊ ᒦᓇ ᐊᓇ, ᔫᔫᑊ ᑳ ᐃᑖᔮᕽ, ᐁ ᔫᐲᐢᑭᐟ ᐊᓇ [ᐁ ᐃᓯᓂᐢᑫᐟ], ᑭᐋᐧᐸᒫᐤ
ᐱᓯᓯᐠ ᐁ ᔫᐲᐟ [DO: ᐋᐦᐊ᙮] ᔫᔫᑊ ᑭᑎᑖᓇᐤ᙮ ᐁᐊᐧᑯ ᐊᓂᒪ ᒦᓇ, ᐁᐋᐧᑯ
ᐊᓂᒪ ᒦᓇ ᑕᑲᐦᑭ ᐋᒋᒧᐃᐧᐣ᙮ [JO: *mhMMM.*] [ᑮᐦᑖᐧᑦ ᐹᐦᐱᓈᓂᐊᐧᐣ]
ᐅᑫᔭᑭᒋᐢ~ ᑫᔭᑭᒋᐢᑫᔫᓴᐠ, ᐅᑫᔭᑭᒋᐢᑫᐦᐃᐁᐧᔫᓴᐠ … [ᐹᐦᐱᓈᓂᐊᐧᐣ;
ᐋᐧᐦᐅᐢᑐᐢᑐᑕᑦ] … ᐊᐧᐃᐧᔭᑌᐳᐦᑖᑲᐧᐣ!

[6. ᐊᑯᐦᐸ ᐁᑲᐧ ᐯᐧᑭᒋᒥᓇᐠ]

ᐁᑲᐧ ᒦᓇ ᐆᒪ ᑳᒥᐳᐟ ᐆᒪ ᑳᐊᑕᒥᐦᐃᐟ ᐊᓇ ᑳᐃᑎᑖᐣ᙮
« ᑭᑕᑕᒥᐦᐃᐣ » ᑳᐃᑕᐠ ᐆᒪ, ᑕ ᐊᑲᐧᓇᐦᐅᔫᐣ ᐊᐳᐢ ᐆᒪ ᐁ ᓂᑕᐁᐧᐳᒥᐟ
ᑕ ᑮᓰᐦᑳᐧᒥᔫᐣ᙮ ᒎᐩ ᑲᓛᐨ ᓂᑲ ᒉᐧᐢᑖᒌᐦᑲᐋᐧᐊᐧᐠ ᐯᐧᑭᒋᒥᓇᐠ ᑕ ᒍᐊᐧᑭᐠ᙮
[ᑌᐯᐧᔫᐦᐱᓈᓂᐊᐧᐣ] ᓂᑲ ᑮᓰᐦᑳᐧᒥᐣ ᑲᐧᔭᐢᐠ᙮

JO: ᒫᒋᑰᑎᑖᐣ, *is it* - ᑖᓂᓯ ᐆᒪ ᑳ ᐃᓯᐳᐦᑲᑌᐠ?

DO: *Foot warmer.*

JO: *Oh. Foot warmer* ᐃᓯᐳᐦᑳᑌᐤ ᐆᒪ [MLR: ᐋᐦᐊ, ᐋᐦᐊ᙮], *it will warm your feet.* [MLR: ᐁᐦᐊ, ᐁᐦᐊ᙮] [ᐹᐦᐱᓈᓂᐊᐧᐣ]

ᐁᑯᓯ ᐃᓯᔨᐦᑳᑌᐤ; ᒫᑲ ᐁᑲᐧ ᒦᓇ ᐆᑕ ᑕ ᑮᓲᐢᑳᑯᔮᐣ ᐆᑕ, ᐁᑲᐧ ᑮᐢᐱᐣ ᒥᑐᓂ ᐁ ᓅᐦᑌ ᑮᓲᐦᑳᐧᒥᔮᐣ, *beans* ᓂᑲ ᒥᓯ ᑮᓯᓵᐧᐊᐧᐠ᙮ ᒨᐩ ᑯᓂᑕ ᓂᑲ ᐊᑲᐧᓇᐦᐅᐣ, *you know*᙮ ᒫᑲ ᐃᐧᔭ ᐆᒪ, ᒨᐩ ᑲᒫᐨ *beans* [ᐹᐦᐱᐤ], ᒨᐩ ᑲᒫᐨ ᐯᐧᑭᒋᒥᓇᐠ ᑕ ᒧᐊᐧᑭᐠ᙮ [ᐹᐦᐱᓈᓂᐊᐧᐣ] ᑭᑕᑕᒥᐦᐃᐣ᙮

ᐊᐧᐦᐋᐧ ᐦᐊᐩ!

JO: ᑫᐦᒋᓈᐨ ᐊᐊᐧ ᐁ ᐹᐦᐱᐦᐃᐟ᙮

ᐁᐦᐊ, ᐁᑯᓯ᙮ [ᐹᐦᐱᐤ]

ᐊᐧᐃᐧᔭᑌᔨᐦᑖᑲᐧᐣ ᐊᓂᒪ ᐋᒋᒧᐃᐧᐣ, ᒣᑐᓂ ᒥᓴᐦᑲᒥᐠ ᑮᑲᐧᐩ ᐆᒪ ᑭᑳᐦᐋᒋᒧᐢᑖᑎᓈᐚᐤ, ᒣᑐᓂ ᑲᐯ ᑮᓯᐠ ᓂᑳᐦ ᐹᐦ ᐲᑭᐢᑳᐧᐣ ᑮᑲᐧᐩ ᑕ ᐄᐧᐦᑕᒫᑕᑯᐠ, ᐁᒥᔮᐧᓯᐠ ᐅᑎ, ᒨᐩ ᐃᐧᔭ ᐁᒫᔭᑕᕽ, ᐁ ᐊᐧᐃᐧᔭᑌᔨᐦᑖᑲᐧᕽ ᒦᓇ ᐁᑲᐧ ᐁ ᐹᐦᐱᕽ᙮ ᐁ ᐊᐧᐃᐧᔭ~ ᐁ ᐊᐧᐃᐧᔭᑌᔨᐨ~, ᐁ ᐊᐧᐃᐧᔭᓯ ᐋᒋᒧᕽ ᑕᑲᐦᑫᔨᐦᑖᑲᐧᐣ, ᑭᐹᐦᐱᐣ ᐊᔨᐢ᙮

[7. ᐁ ᐹᐦ ᐸᑲᒪᐦᐃᑫᐟ]

ᐄᐦ, ᐅᑭ ᓅᓯᓯᒪᐠ ᐆᑭ, ᒨᓂᔮᐊᐧᐠ ᐆᑭ, ᐊᐧᐦᐋᐧ, ᒥᐢᑕᐦᐃ ᒦᓇ ᓂᑮ ᐹᐦᐱᐣ ᐆᒪ᙮ ᐱᑯ ᐃᑕ ᒫᓇ ᐆᒪ ᐊᔨᐢ ᐁ ᐴᓯᔮᐣ, ᐆᒪ ~, ᐆᒪ ᐊᐩ~, ᐱᑯ ᐃᑕ ᐁ ᐴᓯᔮᐣ ᐊᔨᐢ ᓂᒥᔦᐧᔨᐦᑌᐣ *bingo*᙮ ᑮᐢᐱᐣ ᑳ ᐅᓲᓂᔮᒥᓯᔮᐣ, ᐊᐦᐋᐧ, ᐋᓴᐩ ᑳ ᐊᑎ ᐅᑖᑯᓯᐠ ᐆᒪ ᒫᓇ ᒣᑳᐧᐨ ᒨᔭ ᓂᑮ ᒥᔦ ᐱᒧᐦᑖᐣ, ᐁᑕᑕᐤ ᓂᐸ ᐱᒧᐦᑖᐣ᙮ ᒫᑲ ᑫ~ ᒥᑐᓂ ~ ᓂᑯᑖᐧᓯᐠ ~ ᓂᑯᑖᐧᓯᐠ ᑎᐸᐦᐃᑲᐣ, ᓂᑯᑖᐧᓯᐠ ᑳ ᐊᑎ ᐃᐢᐸᔨᐠ ᒣᑐᓂ ᓂᔭᐦᑮᐣ ᐆᑌ ᐁ ᐸᐹᒧᐦᑌᔮᐣ, *bingo* ᐊᔨᐢ ᐆᒪ ᑕ ᐃᑐᐦᑌᔮᐣ; ᒣᑐᓂ ᓂᔭᐦᑭᑯᒋᓂᐣ ᓇᒨᔭ ᐊᐃᐧᔭᐠ ᐁᑲᐧ ᓂᐄᐧᒨᐦᑲᒫᐠ᙮ ᐁᑲᐧ, ᐁᑲᐧ, ᐁᑲᐧ ᑕ ᑲᑫᐧ *hitchhike*ᐃᐃᐧᔮᐣ ᐁᑲᐧ, ᑖᐯᐧ! ᓂᑲᐢᑭᐦᐅᐣ ᐆᑌᓈᕽ ᑕ ᐃᑐᐦᑌᔮᐣ, ᒫᑲ ᐁ ᒋᐸᐦᐃᑫᓯᔮᐣ ᑫᐧᔭᐢᐠ, *you know*, ᐁ ᑲᑫᐧᒥᔭᐠ ᑮᑲᐧᐩ, *gas money* ᐊᐊᐧ, ᐃᔨᑯᕽ ᐁᐧᓲᓂᔮᒥᓯᔮᐣ ᐋᐢᑲᐤ *twenty, ten dollars, five dollars*, ᐃᔨᑯᕽ ~ ᐃᔨᑯᕽ ᐁ ᑌᐯᔨᒧᔮᐣ ᐃᔨᑯᕽ ᐁ ᐅᓲᓂᔮᒥᔮᐣ᙮

ᐁᑲᐧ, ᓂᑯᓯᐢ ᐊᐊᐧ ᒫᑲ ᓇᓂᐍ~ ᓂᓇᓅᔭᒋᒥᐠ ᓇᐘᒋᑯ ᒫᓇ ᐁ ᐃᓯᐟ ᓂᑯᓯᐢ ᐊᐊᐧ *Johnny* ᐊᐊᐧ, « ᒫᒫ! » « ᑮᑿᐩ? ᑮᑿᐩ? » ᓂᑎᑖᐤ᙮ « ᐘᐦᐚ, *you hitch-- you hitchhike* ᒫᓇ ᐱᓯᓯᐠ, » ᐃᑌᐤ, « *bingo all the time* ᐱᑹᑌ ᐁ ᐴᓯᔮᐣ᙮ ᐱᑹᑕ ᑳᐦ ᑮ ᓂᐹᐣ ᐋᑕᐏᔭ, » ᐃᑌᐤ᙮ « ᓂᑭᐢᑫᔨᐦᑌᐣ ᐏᔭ ᐱᑹᑕ ᑕ ᓂᐹᔮᐣ, » ᐃᑌᐤ, « ᓇᒨᐩ ᓈᓂᑕᐤ, » ᐃᑌᐤ, « ᐊᔨᐢ *you hitch-- you hitchhiking all the time,* » ᓂᑎᐠ ᐁ ᐋᑲᔮᔩᒧᐟ᙮ « ᐁᐦᐊ᙮ »

— ᐁ ᐱᒥᐸᔨᔮᕽ ᐆᒪ ᓴᐦᑫᓯᕽ᙮ ᒋᒪᑌᐘ ᐆᑕ *number six* ᐊᔨ ᓃᓯ ᐃᓂᑐ ᒪᒉᑭᓅᐦᑳᓇ, ᑭᐚᐸᐦᑌᓈᐚᐤ? [DO & JO: ᐋᐦᐊ᙮] —

« ᒫᒫ, » ᐃᑌᐤ, « ᑫᑕᐦᑕᐍ ᐱᒥ ᓃᐹᐦᑌᔭᓂ, » ᐃᑌᐤ, « ᑲᑫᐧ ᐲᐦᑐᑫᔮᐦᑕᐑᐦᑲᐣ ᐆᒪ ᒉᓂᑲᐣ, » ᐃᑌᐤ, « ᐁᑯᑕ ᑲ ᓂᑕᐏ ᓂᐹᐣ, » ᐃᑌᐤ, « ᓇᒨᐩ ᐋᐏᔭᐠ ᓈᓂᑕᐤ ᑲ ᐃᑎᐠ᙮ » [ᐹᐦᐱᓈᓂᐘᐣ] ᐁᑲᐧ ~ ᐁᑲᐧ ᒦᓇ ᐁ ᐊᑎ ᐹᐦᐱᐦᐃᐟ ᐁᐘᑯ, ᑖᐱᐢᑰᐟ ᑖᐻ ᑕ ᐲᐦᑐᑫᔮᐣ ᐆᒪ ᒥᓯ~, ᓂᑲ ᓵᑭᑳᑌᓯᓂᐣ, ᓂᑭᓄᓯᐣ ᐊᔨᐢᐠ᙮ [ᐹᐦᐱᓈᓂᐘᐣ] ᐚᐦᐊᐩ, ᓇᐘᒋᑯ ᒫᐣ ᐁ ᐃᓯᐟ, ᐁ ᐹᐦᐱᐦᐃᐟ ᒫᑲ ᐊᓂᒪ, *you know*᙮

ᐋᐦ, ᐁᑯᓯ ᒫᓇ ~ ᐁᐩ, *bingo* ᐁ ᒥᔻᔨᐦᑕᒫᐣ, *you know*, ᐁ~, ᑌᐱᔮᕽ ᐁ~, ᐋᐢᑲᐤ ~ ᐋᐢᑲᐤ ᐊᔨ, ᓂᑮ ᒥᔦᐸᔨᐣ ᐆᒪ ᓇᒨᐩ ᑳᔮᐢ᙮ *Fifth of March* ᑳ ᒥᔦ~, ᑳ ᑕᑲᐦᑭᐸᔨᔮᐣ, ᐋᑕᐏᔭ ᓂᓅᑎᑫᐏᐣ, *you know*, ᒫᑲ ᑫᔮᐱᐨ ᓂᑕᑲᐦᑭᐸᔨᐣ, ᐁᐁᐦ! [ᐹᐦᐱᓈᓂᐘᐣ] ᒨᔭ, ᑵᔭᐢᐠ ᐆᒪ ᐁ ᐃᑎᓂᑫᔮᐣ, *you know*᙮

ᐊᔨ, ᓂᐢᑎᑦ ᐊᐊᐧ ᐯᔭᐠ ᐆᑕ, « *Auntie,* » ᐃᑌᐤ, « ᐯᔭᐠ ᒌ ᐊᑯ‴ ᑭᑕᑖᒥᑎᐣ? » ᐃᑌᐤ᙮ ᐁᑯᑐᐘ ᐆᒪ, *you know*᙮ « ᐋᐦᐊ, » ᓂᑎᑖᐤ᙮ *Forty* ᐊᔨᐢ ᐆᐦᐃ, « ᐯᔭᐠ ᓂᑲ ᐅᑎᓈᐣ᙮ » ᐘᐦᐚ, *I phone her now, I phone,* « ᓂᐢᑎᑦ, » ᓂᑎᑖᐤ, « ᐊᑯᐦᐸ ᐆᑕ ᐊᐢᑌᐘ, ᐯ ᓇᐘᓴᐚᐸᒧᐤ *which one you like,* ᑲ ᐯ ᐅᑎᓈᐣ᙮ » « ᐁᐦᐊ, » ᐃᑌᐤ, « *You wait for me*᙮ » ᐁ ᓅᐦᑌ ᐃᑐᐦᑌᔮᐣ *bingo*᙮ « ᑖᐻ, » ᐃᑌᐤ᙮ ᐋᓴᐩ ᐆᑕ *car,*

ᐦᐋ, ᐦᐋ ᓇᒨᐩ ~, ᐋᓴᐩ ᒣᑳᐧᐨ ᐊᔨ *my - springtime, you know*᙮ ᐁᑯᓯ ᐅᒪ ᐁ ᐃᓯ ᐯᐦᑲᐢᑌᐠ ᓃᑭᐢ᙮ ᓇᒨᔭ ᐄᐧ ᐯ ᐲᐦᑎᑫᐧᐤ, ᓀᑌ ᓃᐸᐃᐧᐤ ᐊᓂᒪ ᐊᔨ, *carpet* ᐊᓂᒪ ᐁ ᐊᐢᐱᑳ~, ᓇᒨᐩ ᐁ ᓅᐦᑌ ᑫᑕᐢᑭᓯᓀᐟ; « ᐊᐧᐦᐋᐧ, ᓂᓯᑯᓴ, ᑖᓂ ᐁᐊᐧᑯ? » ᐊᓂᑕ ᐆᐦᐃ ᐊᐢᑌᐊᐧ᙮ « ᐋᐦ, ᐱᑯ ᐊᓂᒪ, » ᓂᑎᑖᐤ, « ᐅᑎᓇᒪᓂ, ᐊᓂᒪ ᑲ ᒥᔪᑳᐧᑌᐤ᙮ » *Half* ᐆᐦᐃ ᒫᓇ ᐆᒪᑐᐊᐧ, ᑭᑭᐢᑫᔨᐦᑌᐣ [JO: ᐋᐦᐊ᙮], ᐅᒥᓯ ᐃᓯ, ᒥᑐᓂ ᓂᒥᔪ~, ᓂᒥᔪᑳᐧᑌᐣ᙮ « ᐁᐊᐧᑯ ᐆᒪ, » ᐃᑌᐧᐤ᙮ ᓇᐊᐧᒋᑯ, ᓇᐊᐧᒋᑯ *green* ᐃᓯᓈᑲᐧᐣ᙮ « ᐁᐊᐧᑯ᙮ » *Forty dollars* ᓂᐯ ᒥᔨᐠ᙮

ᐊᐦ, ᐁᑲᐧ ᐁ ᓂᑑ ᓯᐯᐧᐦᑌᔮᐣ, ᐊᐧᐦᐋᐧ, ᑳ ᐊᑎ ᓯᐯᐧᐦᑌᐟ ᒪᔭᐤ ᓵᒫᐠ *phone* ~

— ᐊᔨᐢ ᓂᑕᔮᐣ *phone; I have to have a phone here* ᐆᒪ ᐅᐦᒋ, *you know*, ᑳ ᐃᓯ ᐊᔮᐣ᙮ [ᐅᑌᐦ ᐁ ᐃᑕᕽ, *pacemaker*] —

ᓵᒫᐠ ᓂᑌᐹᐧᑖᐤ ᐊᐊᐧ ᓂᑯᓯᐢ᙮ « *Johnny*, » ᓂᑎᑖᐤ, « *you pick me up*, » ᓂᑎᑖᐤ, « *I have a little bit money here*᙮ » « *Okay*, » ᐃᑌᐧᐤ, « *You wait for me, about half an hour's time*᙮ » « *Okay*᙮ » ᐋᓴᐩ ᐆᑕ ᓂᑯᓯᐢ *half an hour outside*; ᐋᓴᐩ ᐃᐧᔭ ᓂᑮᓯ ᐯᐦᑭᐦᐅᐣ, ᓂᐯᐦᑭᐦᐅᐣ ᒫᓇ, *you know*, ᒨᓂᔮᓈᕽ ᐊᔨᐢ᙮ ᐊᐦ, ᓂᑕᐤ ᐴᓯᐣ, ᓂᑕᑎ ᐄᐧᑫᐋᐧᐊᐧᐠ; ᓀᒪ ᐁᑲᐧ ᐊᔨ *Queen City* ᐁᑲᐧ ᐁ ᐃᑐᐦᑌᔮᕽ *bingo*᙮

ᐁᑳ ᑳ ᐲᐦᑖᐧᕽ ᓂᑕᑎ ᓇᐦᐊᐱᐣ, *first table* ᐊᓂᒪ ᒫᓇ ᑳ ᐊᑎ ᐲᐦᑎᑫᐧᕽ, ᐃᐧᔭᐋᐧᐤ ᐋᐧᐦᔭᐤ ᓀᑌ; ᒨᔭ ᐊᐃᐧᔭᐠ ᐊᔨᐢ ~, ᓇᒨᔭ ᐊᐃᐧᔭᐠ ᓂᒥᒋᒥᓂᐠ, ᓂᑲᐢᑭᐦᐅᐣ ᐁ ᐊᑎ ᐲᐦᑎᑫᐧᔮᐣ, ᓂᑕᐋᐧᐱᐣ ᐁᑯᑕ᙮ ᐄᐦ, *forty dollars* ᐊᐊᐧ ᓂᑕᔮᐋᐧᐤ, *ten* ᓂᒥᔮᐤ, *thirty* ᐁᑲᐧ ᐱᑯ ᓂᑕᔮᐋᐧᐤ, *cards* ᐁ ᑎᐸᐦᐊᒫᐣ *thirty*, ᓂᑕᐤ ᓇᐦᐊᐱᐣ᙮ ᐋᐦ, ᐆᑌ *behind* ᐋᐱᐦᑕᐃᐧᑯᓯᓵᓂᐢ ᓂᓂᓯᑕᐁᐧᔨᒫᐤ, *behind* ᐊᐱᐤ᙮ ᐁᑲᐧ ᐆᒪ ᐁ ᐄᐧ ᒫᒋ ᒣᑕᐁᐧᕽ ᐆᒪ *Queen* ᐊᓂᐦᐃ ᒫᓇ *yellow ones* ᐊᓂᐦᐃ, ᐁ ᐄᐧ ᒫᒋ ᒣᑕᐁᐧᕽ ᐊᐢᐱᐣ ᓃᓱ ᐁ ᑮ ᐊᑖᐁᐧᔮᐣ *two dollars* ᐅᐦᒋ, *three dollars* ᐅᐦᒋ *52 Bonanzas* ᐁ~᙮ ᐋᐦ, ᐁᑲᐧ ᓂᑲ ᒫᒋ ᐸᑲᒪᐦᐃᑳᐣ ᐁᑲᐧ ᐄᐧ ᒫᒋ ᒣᑕ~, ᐊᐦ, ᓂᓂᑐᓀᐣ *my paper*,

ᓇᒫᐧ- ᑮᑲᐧᐩ! ᐁᐩ!! ᐁᓴ ᑳᐦ ᒨᓴᐦᑭᓇᐦᑭᐠ ᐆᑭ ᐅᐁᐧᐸᐦᐃᑫᐊᐧᐠ ᐊᓂᑭ ᒫᓇ *paper* ᑳ ᐅᑎᓇᐦᑭᐠ; ᐊᐦ, ᓇᒪ ᑮᑲᐧᐩ *my paper*, ᑲᐦᑭᔭᐤ ᐁᓴ ᒪᓴᐢᑯᓇᒪᐧᐠ!

ᐊᐧᐦᐋᐧ! ᐆᑌ ᐊᐊᐧ ᐋᐱᐦᑕᐃᐧᑯᓯᓵᐣ ᓅᓯᓯᒼ ᐊᐊᐧ, « ᓅᐦᑯᒼ, » ᓂᑎᐠ ᒫᓇ᙮ « ᑯᐦᑯᒼ, *what you doing now?* » ᐃᑌᐧᐤ᙮ « *You know what,* » ᓂᑎᑖᐤ, « *I lost all my paper here,* » ᓂᑎᑖᐤ᙮ ᑖᐯᐧ, ᓇᒪ ᑮᑲᐧᐩ ᐊᐢᑌᐤ, *you know*, ᐊᐦᐴ, *you know just my purse* ᐆᑕ ᐁᑲᐧ *my kerchief* ᐆᑕ, ᓇᒪ ᑮᑲᐧᐩ, ᒧᐢᒑᔨᕽ ᒦᓇ ᓇᒪ ᑮᑲᐧᐩ, ᓇᒨᔭ ᓂᓂᐦᑖ ᑲ ᑲᕋᔨᓯᐣ, *you know*, ᒪ ᑮᑲᐧᐩ᙮ ᒪ ᑮᑲᐧᐩ, ᑲᐦᑭᔭᐤ ᐁᓴ ᑳᐦ ᒨᓴᐦᑭᓇᐦᑭᐠ᙮ « *Here's this girl, call her,* » ᓂᑎᐠ, « ᐊᐦᐴ ᐁᑎᑫᐧ ᑮ ᐅᑎᓇᒼ᙮ » *I call this girl now, I call her,* « *Come here!* » ᐊᐧᐦᐋᐧ! ᐋᓴᐩ ᐆᑕ, « ᑖᓂᓯ, *Grandma?* » ᐃᑌᐧᐤ᙮ « *You know what?* » ᓂᑎᑖᐤ, « *I lost all my paper* ᐆᑕ, » ᓂᑎᑖᐤ᙮ « ᑖᓂᒉᔨᑯᕽ ᑳᐦᐅᐦᒋ ᐅᑎᓇᒪᐣ ᐊᔨ *Bonanzas,* » ᓂᑎᐠ᙮ « ᓇᒨᔭ ᒥᐢᑕᐦᐃ, » ᓂᑎᑖᐤ, « *just five dollars' worth, two dollars' worth of yellow ones, Queen* ᐊᓂᐦᐃ, » ᓂᑎᑖᐤ, « ᐁᑲᐧ ᐃᐧᔭ *three dollars' worth of 52*᙮ » « ᐦᐊᐩ, » ᐃᑌᐧᐤ, « *I'll help you, fif-- ah, three dollars' worth* ᐊᔨ, » ᐃᑌᐧᐤ, « ᐆᐦᐃ ᐊᔨ 52᙮ » *So* ᐆᑕ ᐯ ᐊᐢᑖᐤ *six, six* ᐊᔨᐢ᙮ « ᐁᑲᐧ ᐊᓂᐦᐃ *yellow ones* ᑭᓂᑕᐁᐧ~ » ᐋᓴᐩ ᒫᑲ ᐄᐧᒫᒋ ᒉᑕᐁᐧᐊᐧᐠ ᐁᑲᐧ᙮ ᐁ ᐅᑕᑕᒥᐦᐃᐟ [*sic;* ᐁ ᐅᑕᒥᐦᐃᐟ] ᓃᓱ, *you know, two dollars* ᐅᐦᒋ ᐊᔨ, *ya*, ᓃᓱ ᐸᑲᐦᑲᒼ᙮

ᐋᓴᐩ ᐁᑯᑕ ᑳ ᐯ ᑕᑯᐦᑌᐟ ᐯᔭᐠ ᐃᐢᑫᐧᐢ ᐊᐢᐱᐣ ᐁ ᓈᒋᐸᐦᑖᐧᐟ *yellow ones* ᐁ ᐄᐧᒥᔨᐟ᙮ ᑳ ᐯ ᐄᐧᒉᐋᐧᐟ ᐊᐤ ᐆ~ ᐁᐊᐧᑯ ᐊᐊᐧ ᐅᑭᒫᐤ ᐊᓇ ᑳ ᐅᑭᒫᐦᑳᐣ~ ᐊᓂᑕ, ᐋᐦ, *manager* ᐁᑎᑫᐧ ᐆᑕ ᓃᐸᐃᐧᐤ ᐁᑲᐧ ᓂᑲᑫᐧᒋᒥᐠ, « *Grandma, what's wrong with you?* » ᓂᑎᐠ, « *You lost something?* » « *Yeah,* » *I told him,* « *I lost all of my paper,* » ᓂᑎᑖᐤ, « ᑲᐦᑭᔭᐤ ᐅᑎᓇᒪᐧᐠ ᐊᓂᑭ ᐃᐢᑫᐧᓯᓴᐠ, *I don't know which one,* » ᓂᑎᑖᐤ᙮ ᐯᔭᐠ ᓂᐯ ᐋᐧᐸᐦᑕᐦᐃᐠ *but* « *my marker red* ᓂᔭ, » ᓂᑎᑖᐤ, « *all blue* ᐊᓂᐦᐃ, » ᓂᑎᑖᐤ᙮ « *Well,* » ᐃᑌᐧᐤ, « *what do you -, if you want,* » ᐃᑌᐧᐤ, « *I replace it for you,* » ᐃᑌᐧᐤ, « *that money, how much you*

~ ᑳ ᐆᐟ~ ᑳ ᐃᓯ ᒉᐣᑎᓂᑫᔮᐣ, » ᓂᑎᐠ᙮ « *Just five dollars.* » ᓇᒨᔭ ᐊᔨᐚᐠ ᓂᓅᐦᐅ ᐃᑖᐤ᙮ « *Five dollars.* » « *Okay,* » ᐃᑌᐤ᙮ *This girl,* « *Help her,* » ᐃᑌᐤ; « *I need* ᐊᔨ, » ᓂᑎᑖᐤ, « *two dollars* ᑫᔮᐱᐨ ᐅᐦᒋ, » ᓂᑎᑖᐤ᙮ ᒑᐯᐧ ᐋᓴᐩ᙮ ᐁᑯᓯ ᐁᑲᐧ *five dollars* ᐅᐦᒋ ᐊᓂᐦᐃ᙮ ᒥᓭᐧᔨᐦᑕᐨ ᐊᐊᐧ ᐆᑕ ᐋᐱᐦᑕᐃᐧᑯᓯᓵᐣ᙮ « ᐊᐧᐦᐋᐧ! » ᐃᑌᐤ, ᐃᑌᐤ ᐆᐦᐃ ᐅᑭᒦᐊᐧ᙮ « ᐁᐊᐧᑯ ᐊᓂᒪ ᑳ ᐸᑳᐧᑕᒦᐣ, » ᐃᑌᐤ, ᐃᑌᐤ ᐊᐊᐧ ᐋᐱᐦᑕᐃᐧᑯᓯᓵᐣ, « ᑕ ᑮ~, ᐆᑭ ᐅᑕᑐᐢᑫᐊᐧᐠ ᑳ ᐋᐧ ᐯᐦᑭᐦᒋᑫᒋᐠ, ᑕ ᑮ ᑲᑫᐧᒋᒫᒋᐠ ᐊᓂᐦᐃ, *which ones* ᐊᓂᐦᐃ ᐁᑳ ᐁ ᓂᑕᐁᐧᔨᐦᑕᒥᔨᐟ᙮ » ᐋᐦᒋ ᐱᑯ ᐊᐊᐧ ᑭᓴᔨᓂᐤ ᐅᑑᐢᑭᓃ~, ᓈᐯᐤ ᐊᐊᐧ ᐃᑌᐤ, ᐋᓴᐩ ᒫᑲ ᓂᐋᐧᒋᐦᐃᑳᐧᐠ᙮ « *Well, that's okay,* » ᐃᑌᐤ ᐊᐊᐧ ᐊᔭ *manager* ᐊᐊᐧ᙮ « *You,* ᐁᑯᓯ ᒌ? » ᓂᔭ « ᐁᑯᓯ, » ᓂᑎᑖᐤ᙮

ᐁᑲᐧ ᐁ ᐯ ᐸᑲᒪᐦᐃᑫᔮᐣ ᐁᑲᐧ ᐁᐊᐧᑯ ᐆᒪ ᐊᔨ ᐆᐦᐃ *52s* ᐁᑲᐧ᙮ ᓀᒪ ᓂᑲᓇᐋᐧᐸᐦᑌᐣ ᓀᑌ᙮ ᐊᐧᐦᐋᐧ, *sixty-seven* ᐆᑕ, ᓇᒨᔭ ᑌᐹᐧᒋᑳᑌᐤ᙮ *Sixty-eight* ᒦᓇ᙮ ᓅᓯ ᓂᒪᓀᓯᐣ᙮ « ᐋᐦᐋ, » ᓂᑌᔨᐦᑌᐣ᙮ *I know this girl,* ᐯᔭᐠ ᐊᐊᐧ *Linda* ᐃᓯᔨᐦᑳᓱᐤ᙮ *I call her,* « *Come here,* » ᓂᑎᑖᐤ, « *come and help* ᑯᐦᑯᐨ *here*᙮ » « ᑮᑳᐧᐩ? » ᓂᑎᐠ᙮ « ᒪᐦᑎ ᐆᐦᐃ *check it* ᐆᐦᐃ, » ᓂᑎᑖᐤ᙮ « *My pa-- my 52* ᐆᒪᑐᐃᐧ, ᒑᐱᐢᑰᐨ *I need just two,* » ᓂᑎᑖᐤ᙮ ᓅᓯ ᐊᔨᐣᐠ ᐁ ᐸᑕᐦᐊᒫᐣ᙮ ᐁᑲᐧ, ᐃᔺᐸᐦᑕᕽ ᐁᑲᐧ ᐁᑲᐧ ᐊᐊᐧ, *you know,* ᓂᐋᐧᒎᐦᑳᒪᐠ ᐆᐦᐃ᙮ ᐯᔭᐠ ᐁᑯᑕ ᐯ ᓅᐸᐃᐧᐤ, « ᐋᐧᐦ! ᑮ ᑌᐹᐧᒋᑳᑌᐤ ᐊᓂᒪ *sixty-eight,* » ᐃᑌᐤ ᐆᐦᐃ ᐃᐢᑫᐧᓯᓴ᙮ « ᐊᐦ, ᒑᐯᐧ, » ᐃᑌᐤ, « *Grandma, you need just one*᙮ » [ᐁ ᐅᐢᑐᐢᑐᑕᕽ] « *You need just one, sixty-- sixty-seven* ᐱᑯ᙮ » ᐯᔭᐠ ᓂᓂᑕᐁᐧᔨᐦᑌᐣ᙮ [ᒨᐩ ᑲᐧᔭᐣᐠ ᐯᐦᒑᑳᐧᐣ] ... *next table* ᐊᐱᐊᐧᐠ᙮ ᓂᑕᑲᐧᓇᐦᐁᐣ ᐁᑲᐧ ᐆᒪ ᐁᑲᐧ *my purse on top*; ᒣᑐᓂ ᐁᑲᐧ ᓂᑲᓇᐁᐧᔨᐦᑌᐣ᙮ ᐊᐧᐦᐋᐧ, *N-34* ᐯ ᐊᐧᔮᐃᐧᐤ, *N-45*; ᒨᐩ ᑮᑳᐧᐩ *'O'*᙮ ᑫᑕᐦᑕᐁᐧ ᑳ ᐯ ᑫᐧᐢᑭᐸᔨᐦᐅᐟ « *Grandma, Mrs. Rockthunder, you need, you need, that's your number!* » ᓂᑎᐠ, ᐁ ᐋᐧᐸᐦᑕᕽ [ᐁ ᐅᐢᑐᐢᑐᑕᕽ] *sixty-seven*᙮ « ᐋᓴᐩ ᐯᔭᐠ *one winner,* » ᐃᑌᐤ ᐊᐊᐧ᙮ « ᑫᔮᐱᐨ ᐯᔭᐠ, » ᑳ ᒥᓯ ᑌᐯᐧᔮᐣ᙮ *A thousand dollars* [JO: *Oooo.*] [ᒨᐩ ᑲᐧᔭᐣᐠ ᐯᐦᒑᑳᐧᐣ] ... ~ᐆᔮᓂ *forty dollars* ᐆᒪᑐᐊᐧ

ᓂᒥᓯ ᐚᒋᐦᐃᑯᐣ, *thirty* ᐁ ᑮ ᐅᓲᓂᔮᐦᑫᓯᔮᐣ᙮ *Forty,* ᒫᑲ ᐁ ᑮ ᐚᒋᐦᑖᓱᔮᐣ *ten dollars᙮*

ᐁᑯᓯ ᓂᐯ~, ᓃᓱ ᓂᐯ ᑎᐸᐦᐊᒫᑲᐧᐠ ᐆᑕ, *five hundred a piece* ᑕᐦᑯᓄᐊᐧᐠ, *you know,* ᓂᐸ ᐯᔭᑲᐧᐱᐣ ᐊᔨᐢᐠ᙮ [JO: *mhm.*] ᐆᑕ ᓂᐯ ᑎᐸᐦᐊᒫᐠ ᐊᐊᐧ᙮ ᐁᑲᐧ ᐊᐊᐧ ᑳ ᑮ ᐚᒋᐦᐃᐟ ᐊᐊᐧ ᓅᓯᓯᑦ, « *Come here,* » ᓂᑎᑖᐤ, « *I'm going to help you, a little money for you, twenty dollars,* » « *No, Grandma,* » ᐃᑘᐤ᙮ « *Keep it, keep it,* » ᓂᑎᐠ᙮ « ᓇᒨᔭ, » ᓂᑎᑖᐤ, « *for your smokes,* » ᓂᑎᑖᐤ, « *You help me lots᙮* » « *Okay, okay᙮* » ᐯ ᐅᑎᓄᐤ *twenty dollars᙮* ᒨᓂᔮᐢ ᐊᐊᐧ: « *Grandma, me too, I smoke,* » ᐁ ᓇᓅᔭᒋᒥᐟ ᒨᓂᔮᐢ ᐊᐊᐧ᙮ [ᐹᐦᐱᓈᓂᐊᐧᐣ] ᐁ ᒫᐦ ᒣᑭᐊᐧᐠ ᐆᒪ ᓲᓂᔮᐊᐧ᙮ [ᐹᐦᐱᓈᓂᐊᐧᐣ]

ᐁᑯᓯ ᐁ ᑮᓯ ᑎᐸᐦᐊᒪᐏᐟ, ᐁ ᑎᐸᐦᐊᒪᐏᐟ ᒣᑳᐧᐨ ᐁᑲᐧ᙮ ᐊᐄᐧᓇ ᐊᐊᐧ ᐋᓴᐩ ᐆᑕ ᓂᑯᓯᐢ *Johnny* ᑮ ᓃᐸᐏᐤ, ᐁ ᐯ ᓈᓯᐟ ᐁᑲᐧ ᐊᔨᐢᐠ ᓂᐄᐧᒉᐋᐧᐊᐧᐠ, ᐁ ᑮ ᓇᑲᓯᒋᐠ ᐆᒪ ᐋᐧᐦᔭᐤ [ᐹᐦᐱᓈᓂᐊᐧᐣ] ᐁ ᐊᐧᐃᐧᔭᑌᔨᒪᐠ, ᓂᐊᐧᔭᐄᐧᓈᐣ᙮ [ᐹᐦᐱᓈᓂᐊᐧᐣ] ᒣᑐᓂ ᐁᑲᐧ ᓂᑭᐦᒋ ᐃᑌᔨᒥᑲᐧᐠ ᐆᒪ ᐁ ᒥᓯ ᐅᑕᐦᐅᐁᐧᔮᐣ᙮ [ᐹᐦᐱᓈᓂᐊᐧᐣ]

[8. ᐁ ᐱᒧᐦᑌᐦᐅᐟ]

ᐄᐦ, *fifth of- fifth of March* ᐊᓂᒪ ᑳ ᑮ ᐅᑕᐦᐅᐁᐧᔮᐣ᙮ *Fifth of March* ᑳ ᑮ ᐅᑕᐦᐅᐁᐧᔮᐣ, ᑲᐦᑭᔭᐤ ᒪᓯᓇᐦᐃᑳᑌᐤ ᓄᑌ᙮ ᑖᐱᐢᑰᐨ ᒦᓇ ᐊᓂᑕ ᐊᓂᐦᐃ ᑲᐦᑭᔭᐤ ᑮᑲᐧᐩ ᓂᒪᓯᓇᐦᐁᐣ ᒫᓇ, *you know,* ᐆᒪ ᑖᓂᓯ ᐁ ᐊᔨᑕᐦᑲᒥᑭᓯᔮᕽ᙮ ᐆᑌ ᓂᑮ ᐃᑐᐦᑕᐦᐃᑲᐏᐣ ᒦᓇ ᐅᐲᒪ ᐁᑲᐧ ᒦᓇ ᐃᔨᑯᕽ ᐁ ᒣᐢᑎᓂᑫᔮᐣ, ᑲᐦᑭᔭᐤ ᒪᓯᓇᐦᐃᑳᑌᐤ᙮ ᐁᑯᑌ ᐊᔨᐢᐠ ᒫᓇ ᐁ ᐃᑐᐦᑌᔮᐣ, *Hobbema᙮* ᑲᔮᐢ ᒫᓇ ᓂᑮ ᐅᑎᓈᐤ *plane,* ᒨᔭ ᒫᑲ ᐁᑲᐧ, *you know,* ᐋᐦᑲᐧᑭᓱᐤ ᐁᑲᐧ ᐊᔨᐢᐠ᙮ ᑲᔮᐢ ᐃᐧᔭ *a hundred and seventy* ᒫᓇ *one way, plane* ᐊᐊᐧ, *you know?* [JO: ᐋᐦᐊ᙮] ᓂᐢᑖᐧᐤ ᐁᑯᑐᐊᐧ ᓂᐴᓯᐣ ᐆᑕ ᐅᐦᒋ, *an hour and ten minutes* ᐋᓴᐩ ᓄᑌ ᐊᔨ, *Edmonton*

ᑕᑲᐧᑯᑌᐤ᙮ ᐊᒋᔭᐤ ᐱᑯ ᐁ ᐊᐱᔮᐣ, *you know*, ᓇᒨᔭ ᑭᓀᐧᐢ᙮ ᒫᑲ ᐁᑲᐧ ᒫᓇ ᓇᒨᔭ, *bus* ᓂᑐᑎᓈᐤ ᐋᐢᑲᐤ, ᐋᐢᑲᐤ *car* ᐊᐃᐧᔭᐠ ᓂᐴᓯᐦᐃᐠ, *you know*᙮

JO: ᐋᐢᑲᐤ ᒫᓇ ᐊᓂᒪ *seat sale* ᐊᔮᐊᐧᐠ᙮ [MLR: ᐁᐦᐊ᙮] ᐁᐧᐦᑕᑭᐦᑌᐤ᙮

ᐁᑯᓯ ᐊᓂᒪ ᐋᐢᑲᐤ᙮ ᐊᔨ ᐊᓂᒪ, ᐃᐢᐲᕽ ᑳ ᐯ ᑮᐁᐧᔮᐣ, ᒣᐧᐦᒋ ᐊᓂᒪ *New Year's Day, on the first,* ᑳ~ *next day* ᑖᐱᐢᑰ- ᑳ ᐄᐧ ᐯ ᑮᐁᐧᔮᐣ, *New Year's Day* ᑳ ᐯ ᑮᐁᐧᔮᐣ, ᒣᑐᓂ ᐁ ᐋᐦᑲᐧᑭᐦᑌᑭ ᐁᑲᐧ ᐁᑯᑕ ᐊᓂᒪ ᐊᔨ, ᐊᓂᐦᐃ ᐊᔭ *fare money* ᐊᓇ, *you know*᙮ ᓇᑲᒫ, ᒥᓴᐦᑲᒥᐠ ᐁ ᒣᐢᑎᓇᐦᑭᐠ ᐊᓂᐦᐃ ᑳ ᐁᐧᐦᑕᑭᐦᑌᔨᑭ, ᐁᑲᐧ ᐅᐦᒋᑕᐤ ᑕ ᐅᑎᓇᒫᐣ ᐊᓂᒪ ᑳ~, *first class* ᐊᔨ, ᐊᓂᒪ ᐊᔨ ᒪᓯᓇᐦᐃᑲᐣ ᓂᑮ ᐅᑎᓀᐣ ᐁ ᐯ ᑮᐁᐧᔮᐴᔫᔮᐣ, *plane* ᐁ ᐯ ᑮᐁᐧᔮᐣ᙮

ᓈᓇᐦᐃ ᑫᓷᐧᐣ ᒦᓇ ᐁᑯᑕ ᐁ ᐅᑕᐦᐅᐁᐧᔮᐣ *that night, fifty-two hundred* ᐁ ᐃᐢᐸᔨᐟ ᐊᔭ *Bonanzas*, ᒫᑲ ᓂᑮ ᓂᐢᑎᓈᐣ, ᑕ ᑮ ᓀᐃᐧᔮᕽ ᒫᑲ ᐊᐊᐧ ᐯᔭᐠ ᒪ ᑮᑲᐧᐩ *forty-six* ᐁ ᐊᔮᐟ᙮ ᓂᐢᑐ ᐱᑯ ᓂᔭᓈᐣ ᑫᐧᔭᐢᐠ, ᐁᑯᓯ ᐊᓇ *fifty-two, fifty-two hundred* ᐊᓇ ᓲᓂᔮᐤ; *seventeen hundred and thirty-three dollars and thirty-three cents a piece* ᓂᑮ ᒥᔨᑲᐃᐧᓈᐣ [JO: *Ooooh.*], ᐁ ᓂᐢᑎᔮᕽ᙮ ᐦᐋ, ᐊᑭᐦᒋᑫᔭᐣ ᐁᐊᐧᑯᔨᑯᕽ [JO & DO: *mhm.*], ᐁᐊᐧᑯᔨᑯᕽ ᓂᐢᑐ᙮ *Fifty-two hundred*, ᐁᐊᐧᑯ ᐊᓂᒪ ᐁ ᑮ ᒥᓯ ᐅᑕᐦᐅᐁᐧᔮᐣ ᐁᑯᑌ ᒦᓇ, *you know*᙮ ᑮᐦ ᐯᔭᑯᔮᐣ ᒥᐢᑕᐦᐃ ᓂᑲ ᑮ ᐅᑕᐦᐅᐋᐧᐣ᙮ *Lions* ᐊᓂᑭ ᐁ ᐅᓰᐦᑖᒋᐠ ᐊᓂᒪ *bingo* ᐁᑯᐢᐲᕽ, ᐁᑲᐧ ᐊᐊᐧ ᓃᑦ ᐁ ᓂᑕᐃᐧᓈᑖᐟ ᐊᓂᐦᐃ ᓲᓂᔮᐊᐧ, *Lloyd Buffalo* ᐃᑖᐤ᙮ « ᓂᔭ ᓂᑲ ᓈᑖᐤ, ᓃᑦ, » ᐃᑌᐧᐤ᙮ « ᐯ ᐊᐢᑯᐃᐧᐣ, » ᓂᑎᐠ᙮ *Lions* ᐆᑭ ᒥᑐᓂ ᒫᓇ *yellow* ᑳ ᐃᓰᐦᐅᒋᐠ [JO: ᐋᐦᐊ᙮], ᑎᐸᐦᐊᒪᐃᐧᐟ, ᐁ ᒥᔨᐟ ᐊᓂᐦᐃ ᓲᓂᔮᐊᐧ᙮ « ᐁ ᐅᑕᐦᐅᐁᐧᐟ ᐊᐊᐧ, » ᐃᑌᐧᐤ, « *from Regina,* » ᐃᑌᐧᐤ᙮ « *Well,* » ᐃᑌᐧᐤ, « *first class* ᑭᑲ ᐅᑎᓄᐣ *plane here*᙮ » « ᐁᑯᑐᐊᐧ ᒫᑲ ᐊᓇ ᐁ ᑮ ᐯ ᐴᓯᐟ, » ᐃᑌᐤ ᐊᐊᐧ ᓃᑦ᙮ « ᐁᑯᑐᐊᐧ ᐊᓇ ᐁ ᑮ ᐅᑎᓈᐟ, ᐁᑲᐧ ᒦᓇ ᐁᑯᑐᐊᐧ ᑕ ᐊᑎ ᑮᐁᐧᐟ ᐆᒪ ᐁ ᐄᐧᐅᑎᓈᐟ

ᐁᑯᑐᐊᐧ ᐅᒐᐋᐧᓯᒥᐢ ᐁ ᐄᐧᑲᑫᐧ ᐅᑎᐦᑖᐟ *New Year, New Year's Day,* » ᐃᑌᐤ᙮ ᐄᐦ, ᑖᐯᐧ ᐊᓂᒪ ᓂᑮ ᐅᑎᓈᐤ ᐊᓇ [ᐁ ᐅᐢᑐᐢᑕᕽ] *a hundred* ~ *okay,* ᑫᑳᐟ *two hundred* ᐸᑲᐦᑲᒼ ᑳ ᑮ ᑎᐸᐦᐃᑫᔮᐣ ᐊᓂᒪ ᐋᔨ, ᑭᑭᐢᑫᔨᐦᑌᐣ, ᐁ ᐋᐦᑲᐧᑭᐦᑌᐠ ᐁ ᒣᐢᑎᓇᒥᕽ ᐊᓂᐦᐃ ᐊᔨ ᒪᓯᓇᐦᐃᑲᓇ, ᐅᐴᓯᐊᐧᐠ ᐆᑭ ᐁ ᒣᐢᑎᓇᐦᑭᐠ᙮

[ᐊᒋᔭᐤ ᐁ ᓇᑭᐱᑕᒥᕽ]

ᓃᑎᒼ ᐊᓇ ᐁᐊᐧᑯ ᐊᓇ, ᐁ ᑮ ᐅᔪᒋᐋᐧᒥᐟ ᐊᐊᐧ ᑳ ᑮ ᐄᐧᑫᐊᐧᐠ᙮ ᐁᑲᐧ ᐊᓂᑭ ᐁᑯᑌ ᐋᐧᐦᑰ~, ᐁ ᑮ ᐋᐧᐦᑰᒫᐟ ᐊᐊᐧ ᑳ ᑮ ᐅᔪᑭᓭᔨᓃᒥᔮᐣ, *Rabbits* ᐊᓂᑭ᙮ *Rabbits* ᐃᑖᐊᐧᐠ ᐁ ᑮ ᐋᐧᐦᑰᒫᐟ ᑳ ᑮ ᐄᐧᑫᐊᐧᐠ ᐊᐊᐧ *John,* ᑭᓭᔨᓂᐊᐧ ᐊᓂᐦᐃ *Joe Rabbit* ᑮ ᐃᑖᐤ, ᑮ ᐸᓈᑎᓯᐤ ᒫᑲ, *you know*᙮ ᐁᑲᐧ ᐁᑯᓂ ᐁᐊᐧᑯ ᒫᓇ ᐆᒪ ᑰᐦ ᐃᑐᐦᑌᔮᐣ ᐁᑯᑌ, ᓂᑎᐦᑲᐧᑎᒪᐠ ᐊᓂᑭ ᐁᑲᐧ ᒦᓇ ᓂᐢᑎᒪᐠ, ᒫᑲ ᓂᑭᓭᔨᓃᒼ ᐊᓇ ᐁ ᑮ ᐋᐧᐦᑰᒪᐟ, *you know*᙮ ᒫᑲ ᒣᑐᓂ ᓂᓇᑲᔮᐢᑲᐋᐧᐊᐧᐠ, *you know,* ᐁᑲᐧ ᒦᓇ ᒣᑐᓂ ᓂᓴᐍᔨᒥᑲᐧᐠ᙮ ᐃᐧᔭᐋᐧᐤ ᐆᑭ ᓂᑕᐋᐧᓯᒥᓴᐠ ᐁ ᐋᐧᐦᑰᒪᒋᐠ, *you know*᙮ [JO: *mhm.*]

ᑳᑭᑫ ᐁᑯᑌ ᓂᑎᑐᐦᑖᐣ, ᐁᑯᑌ ᐆᒪ ᐁ ᑮ ᐃᑐᐦᑌᔮᐣ ᐆᒪ, ᐆᑌ *north*᙮ ᐁᑲᐧ ᒦᓇ ᐆᒼ ᐆᑌ ᐊᔭ, ᐊᔭ ᐊᓇ, ᐁᑯᓂᐠ ᐊᓂᑭ ᑖᓂᓯ ᐁ ᐃᓯᔨᐦᑳᓱᐟ ᐊᓇ ᑳ~ ᐊᓅᐦᐨ ᑳ ᐄᐧᐦᐊᐟ ᐊᓇ, ᐋᐦ, ᐊᐧᐦᐋᐧ ᐦᐊᐩ, ᓂᐊᐧᓂᐦᑳᐣ᙮ *Carrieres* ᐊᓂᑭ ᑳ ᐋᐧᐦᑰᒪᒋᐠ ᐊᓂᐦᐃ ᐁᑎᑫᐧ ~ [JO: *Daniels.*] *Daniels!* [JO: ᐋᐦᐊ᙮] *Henry* ᐃᑖᐤ ᐊᓇ, *Henry Daniels* ᐃᑖᐤ ᐊᓇ ᑳ ᑮ ᐯ ᓈᑎᑎᓭᐦᐅᐟ᙮ ᐆᑌ ᐊᓇ ᐅᑭᒫᐦᑳᐣ ᐊᔨ ~ [JO: ᑯᑕᑲᐠ ᐊᓂᑭ ᑫᐢᒋᓈᐨ᙮] ᑯᐟ~, ᐸᐦᑳᐣ, ᐸᐦᑳᐣ᙮ [JO: ᐋᐦᐊ, ᐸᐦᑳᐣ᙮] ᐄᐧᐢᑕᐋᐧᐤ *Daniels* ᐁ ᐋᐸᒋᐦᑖᒋᐠ᙮ ᐁᐊᐧᑯ ᐊᓇ ᑳ ᑮ ᐯ ᓈᑎᑎᓭᐦᐅᐟ ᐊᓇ ᓅᓯᓯᒼ ᐊᓇ [ᐊᑳᐋᐧᐨ ᐯᐦᑖᑲᐧᐣ], ... *Round dance* ᐁ ᑮ ᐯ ᓂᑐᒥᒋᐠ, ᐁᑯᑌ ᓂᑮ ᐃᑐᐦᑖᐣ᙮ ᐆᑕ ᒦᓇ *round dance* ᐊᓂᒪ ᑳ ᓂᑐᒥᑲᐃᐧᔮᐣ, ᐁᑯᑕ ᒦᓇ ᓂᑮ ᐃᑐᐦᑖᐣ, *Hobbema* ᐁᐊᐧᑯ, *you know*᙮ [JO: *mhm.*] ᓂᑮ ᓂᑕᐃᐧᑲᓇᐋᐧᐸᐦᑳᐣ *round dance*᙮

ᑲᔮᐣ ᒫᓇ ᓂᑮ ᓃᒥᐦᐃᑐᐟ, ᒨᐩ ᒫᑲ ᐁᑿ, *you know*, ᒨᐩ ~ ᓂᐦᒋᑿᓇ ᐆᐦᐃ, ᒨᐩ, ᒨᐩ ᒥᔮᐧᓯᓇᐧ, *you know*᙮ ᑲᔮᐣ ᒫᓇ ᓂᑮ ᒥᓈᐧᔮᐟ᙮ ᐁᐩ, ᑫᑕᐦᑕᐍ ᐆᑕ ᐁ ᓃᒥᐦᐃᑐᕽ ᓃᐦᒑᔨᕽ, ᑫᑕᐦᑕᐍ ᑳ ᑌᐺᑎᑲᐏᔮᐟ *number seven* ᐊᓂᒪ ᐁ ᑮ ᐊᔮᔮᐟ ᐊᔭ, ᐊᓂᒪ, ᐊᑭᐦᑖᓱᐏᓇ ᒫᓇ ᐊᓂᐦᐃ, *you know*᙮ ᐁᓴ ᐆᒪ ᐁ ᐅᑕᐦᐅᐍᔮᐟ, ᓂᑮ ᑎᐸᐦᐊᒫᑲᐏᐠ᙮ [ᐹᐦᐱᐤ] ᓇᒨᐩ ᓂᑭᐢᑫᔨᐦᑌᐣ ᐁ ᐅᑕᐦᐅᐍᔮᐟ᙮ ᐁ ᐲᒋᒌᕽ ᒫᓇ ᐊᓂᒪ ᑳ ᓃᒥᐦᐃᑐᕽ [JO: ᐆᐦ, ᐋᐦᐊ᙮], *yeah*, ᐁᑿ ᐊᓂᒪ ᓂᑮ ᐅᑕᐦᐅᐚᐟ, *number seven*᙮ ᐚᐦ, ᒨᐩ ᓂᑭᐢᑫᔨᐦᑌᐣ ᐁ ᐅᑕᐦᐅᐍᔮᐟ᙮ [ᐹᐦᐱᓈᓂᐘᐤ]

[ᓇᑭᐱᒋᑳᑌᐤ]

3
ᒉᐦᑲᑕᐦᐃᑫᐃᐧᐣ

ᐊᔨ ᐆᒪ, ᒥᐢᑕᐦᐃ ᐊᔨ ᓂᒥᔦᐧᔨᐦᑌᐣ *Bingo* ᐁ ᒣᑕᐁᐧᔮᐣ, ᒣᑐᓂ ᐅᑎ᙮ ᓇᒨᔭ ᓂᒥᓂᐦᑳᐧᐣ, ᓇᒨᔭ ᒦᓇ ᓂᐲᐦᑖᐧᐣ ᒫᑲ ᓂᒥᔦᐧᔨᐦᑌᐣ ᐁ ᒣᑕᐁᐧᔮᐣ᙮ ᐁᑯᑌ ᒫᓇ ᓂᓲᓂᔮᒥᐢ ᐊᐢᐱᐣ! [ᐹᐦᐱᓈᓂᐊᐧᐣ] [ᐁᑯᓯ] ᐁ ᐃᑕᒪᐦᒋᐦᐅᔮᐣ, « ᐋᐦ, ᑭᔮᒼ, ᐊᓯᓰᐁᐧᑭᐣ ᐊᓇ, ᓇᒨᔭ ᐊᓇ ᐊᔨᓯᔨᓂᐤ᙮ » ᐯ ᓅᑯᓯᐤ, ᒫᑲ ᐊᔭ ᐊᐊᐧ, ᓲᓂᔮᐤ ᐯ ᐊᔮᐤ; ᐊᔨᓯᔨᓂᐤ ᐱᑯ ᑳ ᐊᐧᓂᐦᐋᐧᔭᕽ ᐊᐢᐱᐣ ᐁᐊᐧᑯ, ᒫᑲ ᐃᐧᔭ ᓲᓂᔮᐤ ᑕᐦᑐ ᑮᓯᑳᐤ ᐯ ᐊᔮᐤ, *it's a paper*᙮ ᐁᑯᓯ ᒫᓇ ᐁ ᐃᑌᔨᐦᑕᒫᐣ᙮ ᐊᔨᓯᔨᓂᐤ ᑳ ᐊᐧᓂᐦᐃᐦᐟ ᐊᐢᐱᐣ ᐁᐊᐧᑯ, ᒨᐩ ᐄᐧᐦᑳ-ᑭᐋᐧᐸᒫᓇᐤ ᒫᑲ ᐃᐧᔭ ᓲᓂᔮᐤ ᐁ ᐊᔮᐋᐧᔭᕽ ᐁ ᐁᐧᐱᓈᔭᕽ, ᑳᐃᐧ ᐊᓇ ᑭᐋᐧᐸᒫᓇᐤ ᓲᓂᔮᐤ᙮ ᐁᑯᓯ ᒫᓇ ᐁ ᐃᑌᔨᐦᑕᒫᐣ᙮ ᐁᐩ, ᓂᒥᔦᐧᔨᐦᑌᐣ ᐁ ᒣᑕᐁᐧᔮᐣ, ᒣᑐᓂ ᐅᑎ᙮

Regina ᓂᑮ ᐊᔮᐣ *nineteen - 1966* ᑳ ᑮ ᐅᐦᒋ ᓯᐯᐧᐦᑌᔮᕽ ᐆᑕ ᓂᑭᓭᔨᓃᒼ ᐁ ᑮ ᐅᑕᐦᐅᐁᐧᐟ, *ah, ah, twelfth of, ah, twelfth of July, 1966,* ᐁ ᑮ ᐅᑕᐦᐅᐁᐧᐟ *big money, a thousand dollars* ᐁᑯᐢᐲᕽ ᑲᔮᐢ ᒥᐢᑕᐦᐃ ᓲᓂᔮᐤ᙮ ᑳ ᑮᐢᑭᓇᒫᐦᐟ ᐅᑕᑐᐢᑫ ~ ᐊᔨ, ᓂᑮᐢᑭᓇᒫᑲᐃᐧᓈᐣ *welfare* ᐁ ᓂᐢᑎᔮᕽ ᓂᑕᐋᐧᓯᒥᓴᐠ᙮ ᓂᑭᓭᔨᓃᒼ ᐱᑯ ᑕ ᐊᑐᐢᑫᐟ ᐁᑲᐧ ᓂᑖᓂᐢ

ᑮ ᐊᑐᐢᑫᐤ *at the hospital, nurs*ᐊ ᐁ ᐄᐧᒋᐦᐋᐟ ᒨᔭ ᐃᐧᔭ ᐅᐦᒋ ᐊᔨ, ᒨᔭ ᐃᐧᔭ ᐅᐦᒋ *nurs*ᐃᐃᐧᐤ ᒫᑲ *help, you know,* ᑮ ᐊᔭᑐᐢᑫᐤ᙮ *In a suite, 11 block Albert Street* ᓂᑮ ᐊᔮᓈᐣ, ᑮ ᐊᔮᐤ ᓂᑖᓂᐢ᙮

ᓂᑭᓭᔨᓃᐨ ᐊᐊᐧ ᐅᒥᓯ ᐃᑌᐧᐤ, « ᑭᑐᐢ ᑭᑖᓂᐢ, » ᐃᑌᐧᐤ, « ᑲ ᓂᑕᐃᐧ ᐄᐧᒑᔮᒫᓇᐤ, » ᐃᑌᐧᐤ᙮ « ᑭᑲ ᐸᒥᐦᒋᑳᐣ ᐁᑯᑕ, ᑲ ᑮᓯᑌᐳᐣ, ᑲ ᐯᐦᑲᐢᒋᑳᐣ, ᐃᐧᔭ ᑕ ᓂᑕᐃᐧ ᐊᑐᐢᑫᐤ᙮ »

ᑖᐯᐧ᙮ ᓂᑌᐹᐧᑖᐤ ᐊᐊᐧ ᓂᑖᓂᐢ᙮ ᐊᔨ ᓂᑎᑖᐤ, « *Barbara,* » ᓂᑎᑖᐤ, « ᓂᐄᐧ ᓂᑕᐃᐧ ᐊᔮᓈᐣ ᐁᑯᑌ ᓂᑮᐢᑭᓇᒫᑲᐃᐧᓈᐣ *welfare* ᐁ ᐃᓯ ᓂᐢᑎᔮᕽ᙮ » « ᐋᐦᐊᐩ, » ᐃᑌᐧᐤ, « ᐯ ᐊᔮᐠ᙮ »

Way up ᓄᑌ ~, *suite* ᓄᑌ *way upstairs*᙮ ᐁᑯᑌ ᑖᐯᐧ ᓂᑎᐢᐱᒋᓈᐣ᙮ *1966* ᐁ ᐃᐢᐱᒋᔮᕽ ᐆᑌᓈᕽ᙮ ᓂᑭᓭᔨᓃᐨ ᐁᑲᐧ ᓂᑯᓯᐢ ᐊᑐᐢᑫᐊᐧᐠ *chickens* ᐁ ᑕᓯᐦᑲᐋᐧᒋᐠ, *[Broad] Street* ᐆᒪ᙮ ᐁᑯᑕ ᑮ ᐅᐦᒋ ᓰᓂᔮᐦᑫᐤ᙮ *1967* ᓂᓂᑐᓄᐣ ᐁᑲᐧ ᐋᐧᐢᑳᐦᐃᑲᐣ, ᓂᒥᐢᑫᐣ; ᓂᒥᐢᑫᐣ ᐋᐧᐢᑳᐦᐃᑲᐣ *10 block McTavish* ᐁᑯᑕ; ᐁᑯᑕ ᐁᑲᐧ ᓂᑎᐢᐱᒋᓈᐣ᙮

ᐦᐋᐤ, ᐁᑯᑕ ᐁᑲᐧ, *a nun* ᐁᑲᐧ ᐊᓂᑕ ᐊᓂᒪ ᐊᔭ *Elphinstone* ᐁᑯᑕ ᐊᐊᐧ *Sister* ᓂᓇᑲᔮᐢᑲᐋᐧᐤ᙮ ᓂᓂᑕᐃᐧ ᑲᑫᐧᒋᒫᐤ ᒪᐦᑎ ᑕ ᑮ ᐄᐧᒋᐦᐃᐟ *a little bit work,* ᑌᐱᔮᕽ ᐸᐦᑫᐧᓯᑲᐣ ᑕ ᐄᐧᒋᐦᐃᐟ, ᐊᐁᐧᑳ ᐱᒥᐩ᙮ « ᐁᐦᐊ, » ᐃᑌᐧᐤ, « *We'll look after you.* ᐁᐦᐊ᙮ » ᐁᑯᓯ ᑖᐯᐧ, ᓂᓂᑕᐃᐧ ᐊᑐᐢᑳᐣ ᐁᑲᐧ ᓃᐢᑕ᙮ ᑖᐯᐧ ᒫᓇ ᐸᐦᑫᐧᓯᑲᓇ ᓂᒥᔨᐠ, *pastry* ᓂᒥᔨᐠ, ᐱᒥᐩ ᓂᒥᔨᐠ ᑕᒦᒋᓱᔮᕽ᙮ ᐋᐦ, ᓂᒦᒋᓱᓈᐣ᙮

ᓂᓂᑐᓄᐣ ᐁᑲᐧ ᐊᑐᐢᑫᐃᐧᐣ; ᑳ ᒥᐢᑲᒫᐣ *eighteen - eighteen - 1821 Scarth Street* ᐁᑯᑕ ᓂᒥᐢᑫᐣ᙮ ᑮ ᐸᓈᑎᓯᐊᐧᐠ *Violet, Dorothy,* ᐁᑲᐧ ᓂᔭ, ᓂᑮ ᓂᐢᑎᓈᐣ᙮ *Second floor* ᐁ ᐊᐢᑖᔮᕽ *shop* ᐁ ᑲᐢᑭᑳᐧᓲᔮᕽ᙮ ᐁ ᐯ ᐊᑖᐁᐧᒋᐠ ᒫᓇ ᒨᓂᔮᐊᐧᐠ᙮ ᑖᐯᐧ ᑫᑕᐦᑕᐁᐧ ᑳ ᓂᑐᒥᑯᔮᐦᑯᐠ ᒨᓂᔮᓴᐠ *Co-op company downstairs*᙮ *Meeting* ᐁᑲᐧ ᐁ ᐄᐧ ᐅᑎᓇᐦᑭᐠ ᐆᒪ *little shop* ᐁ ᐅᔫᐦᑖᔮᕽ᙮ « ᐊᐦᐋᐨ, » ᐃᑌᐧᐊᐧᐠ ᐆᑭ *Violet Fourhorns*

ᑮ ᐃᑖᐤ ᐁᑲᐧ *Dorothy Francis* ᐁᑲᐧ ᓂᔭ, ᓂᒪᓯᓇᐦᐃᑳᓈᐣ ᐁᑲᐧ᙮ *Co-op* ᐅᑎᓇᐟ ᐆᒪ *our shop* ᓂᑕᐃᐧ ᐊᐢᑖᐤ ᐋᐧᐢᑳᐦᐃᑲᓂᕽ ᐁᑳᐧᓂ ᑲᐦᑭᔭᐤ ᑮᑲᐧᐩ ᐁᑲᐧ *machine* ᐁᑯᑕ ᐁᑲᐧ ᐁ ᐊᑐᐢᑫᔮᕽ ᐁᑯᑕ ᐊᓂᒪ *five dollars and thirty-five cents an hour* ᓂᑲᐢᑭᐦᒋᑳᓈᐣ, ᐅᑭᒫᐤ ᐁᑲᐧ ᐁᑯᑕ᙮ ᑮ ᐸᓈᑎᓯᐤ ᒦᓇ ᓂᑑᑭᒫᒥᓈᐣ᙮

ᐁᑯᓯ ᐁᑲᐧ, ᐊᐧᐦᐋᐧ, ᓂᒫᒋ ᓲᓂᔮᐦᑳᓈᐣ᙮ ᓲᓂᔮᐊᐧᓯᓇᐦᐃᑲᓇ *every two weeks*᙮ ᐋᐧᐦᔭᐤ, ᐋᐧᐦᔭᐤ ᓂᑮ ᐊᔮᐣ ᓂᑮ ᐋᐦᑐᑳᐣ ᐊᔨᐢ *17 block Connaught Street, way out, four miles* ᐁ ᐅᐦᑖᐴᔪᔮᐣ, *by bus* ᒫᓇ ᐊᐊᐧ᙮ ᓂᑖᓂᐢ ᐃᐧᔭ ᐊᐊᐧ ᐊᑐᐢᑫᐤ ᐊᔨᐢ, ᐋᐦᑯᓰᐃᐧᑲᒥᑯᕽ ᐃᐧᔭ᙮ ᑫᔮᐱᐨ ᐊᑐᐢᑫᐤ᙮

ᐊᐧᐦᐋᐧ ᐦᐊᐩ, ᑫᑕᐦᑕᐁᐧ ᑳ ᒥᐢᑲᒫᐣ ᐆᒪ *Bingo* ᒥᑐᓂ ᐁ ᐊᑎ ᒥᔦᐧᔨᐦᑕᒫᐣ, ᐊᐧᐦᐋᐧ ᐦᐊᐩ! ᐊᐧᐦᐋᐧ ᓂᑖᐦᐃᑐᐦᑖᐣ᙮ ᓂᑭᓴᔨᓃᐟ ᒦᓇ ᐊᐊᐧ᙮ ᐋᐦ, ᓂᒥᔦᐧᔨᐦᑌᓈᐣ *Bingo*, ᐊᐧᐦᐋᐧ ᐦᐊᐩ᙮

ᐁᑯᓯ ᐁᑲᐧ, ᐊᐧᐦᐋᐧ, ᓂᑖᐦ ᐅᒋᐱᑎᑯᐣ ᒫᓇ ᐆᐦᐃ ᓂᐢᑳᑕ ᐃᔨᑯᕽ ᐁᑎᑫᐧ ᐆᒪ ᐁ ᐊᐱᔮᐣ *in a machine* ᐁ ᑲᐢᑭᑳᐧᓯᔮᐣ᙮ ᓂᐯᑕᒫᐠ ᐊᔨ, ᐆᒪᔨᑯᕽ ᐁᑎᑫᐧ ᐁ ᐃᐢᐱᐦᒑᐠ ᐊᔨ, *a bottle, tube*᙮ « ᐁᐊᐧᑯ ᑕ ᐋᐸᒋᐦᑖᔭᐣ ᐆᒪ, » ᐃᑌᐧᐤ, « *cramp* ~, ᐆᑭ *your cords* ᐆᑭ ᑳ ᐄᐧᓴᑫᔨᒪᒋᐠ, » ᓂᑎᐠ᙮ « ᐁᐦᐊ᙮ » ᐄᐦ, ᓂᑕᐢᑖᐣ ᒫᓇ ᐆᐦᐃ *my markers in a washroom*᙮ *My washroom kind of cold*᙮ ᐆᑌ, ᓂᑕᐢᑖᐣ ᑲᐦᑭᔭᐤ ᑮᑲᐧᐩ᙮ ᐊᐧᐦᐋᐧ! *Any time* ᐁᑲᐧ *my bus eight o'clock* ᑕ ᐯ ᑕᑯᐸᔨᐠ *any time; I have my lunch in a ~, on a table*᙮ ᐋ, ᐋᐦᐊ ᑫᑕᐦᑕᐁᐧ ~ ᐅᐦᒋᑕᐤ ᑕ ᓯᐯᐧᐦᑌᔮᐣ᙮ ᒥᐢᐳᓯᐣ; ᐅᐦᒋᑕᐤ ᒫᑲ *my bus half a block* ᐆᑕ, *street* ᐆᑕ ᐁ ᐱᒪᒧᐠ, ᐁᑯᑕ ᑳ ᐊᔮᔭᐣ᙮

ᐋ, ᐊᐧᐦᐋᐧ, ᓂᑐᒋᐱᑎᑯᐣ ᑖᐋᐧᔨᕽ ᓂᐯᐃᐧᓂᓈᐣ ᐊᐢᑌᐤ ᓂᓃᐦᑕᑯᓰᐣ ᐆᑌ᙮ *Half asleep* ᐆᒪ, ᐊᐧᐦᐋᐧ, ᓂᑐᒋᐱᑎᑯᐣ᙮ ᐊᐧᐦᐋᐧ, ᓂᑕᓯᑲᐣ ᐆᑭ ᐋᓴᐩ ᓂᑭᑲᓯᑳᓈᐣ ᒫᑲ ᐊᐧᐦᐋᐧ ᐁᑲᐧ, *half asleep* ᐆᒪ ᓂᑐᑎᓀᐣ ᐊᔨᐢ *I think* [ᒨᐩ ᐯᐦᑕᐚᐤ ᐊᔨᐢᐠ ᐁ ᒪᑌᐧ ᐹᐦᐱˣ] ᓂᓯᓱᐯᐦᐃᑲᐣ ..., ᑳ ᐋᐢᑌᐸᔨᔮᐣ᙮ [ᐹᐦᐱᓈᓂᐘᐣ]

ᐁᑯᓯ ᓂᑖᐱᓰᐦᑲᐧᓯᐣ᙮ ᓂᑕᐱᐣ᙮ ᐋ, ᐘᐦᐚ ᓂᑌᔨᐦᑌᐣ ᓂᑕᑭ ᐅᑎ *my old man* ᑳᐦ ᐊᑖᐍᐢᑕᒪᐏᐟ ᒪᐢᑭᐦᑭᐩ ᒣᑐᓂ ᓂᒥᔦᐢᑳᑯᐣ᙮ [ᐹᐦᐱᓈᓂᐘᐣ] *Half asleep* ᐆᒪ *you know*; ᒣᑐᓂ ᐁᑲᐧ ᓂᑕᑎ ᐋᐱᓰᐦᑲᐧᓯᐣ᙮ ᐋ, ᐊᐑᓇ ᐆᒪ *green marker*! ᓂᐢᑳᑕ ᐆᐦᐃ! [ᒥᓯ ᐹᐦᐱᓈᓂᐘᐣ]

ᐘᐦᐚ ᐦᐊᐩ! ᑲ ᐑᐦᑕᒪᐘᐠ ᓂᑭᓭᔨᓃᐟ᙮ ᓂᑮ ᑯᐢᑖᐤ ᓂᑭᓭᔨᓃᐟ᙮ ᓈᐯᐘᐠ ᑳ ᐋᔮᐦᒋᐠ [*sic; cf.* ᑳ ᐋᔮᐏᐦᒋᐠ] ᑯᐢᑖᐘᐠ ᐁ ᐊᐤ~᙮ [ᐹᐦᐱᓈᓂᐘᐣ] ᓂᑭᓭᔨᓃᐟ ᓂᑮ ᑯᐢᑖᐤ᙮ ᓂᑑᐢᑭᓈᐤ, « *Old man,* » ᓂᑎᑖᐤ, « ᒫᒋᑰᒋ ᑎᔂᑖᓯᔮᐣ᙮ » ᓂᑎᐢᑯᓈᐤ ᐊᐘ ᓂᑕᓯᑲᐣ, ᐘᐦᐚ, ᓂᐢᑳᑕ ᐆᐦᐃ᙮ *Greeeen* ᒣᑐᓂ ᐁ ᐃᓯᓈᑲᐧᐦᑭ᙮

« ᐊᐦᐊᐦᐋᐋ, ᐁᑯᓯ ᐃᓯ ᓯᐍᐦᑌ, ᓂᔮ! » [ᐹᐦᐱᓈᓂᐘᐣ]

ᒨᔭ ᐊᐦᔮ ᓂᑭᑎᒫᑭᓈᐠ᙮ [ᐹᐦᐱᓈᓂᐘᐣ]

4
ᑳ ᐋᑕᔫᐦᑫᕽ

ᑲᔮᐢ, ᓂᑮ ᐯᐦᑕᐚᐘᐠ ᒫᓇ ᑫᐦᑌ ᐊᔭᐠ ᐁᑯᑐᐘ ᐆᒪ, ᑳ ᐯ ᑲᑵᒋᒥᐟ ᓅᓯᓯᐨ, ᐋᑕᔫᐦᑫᐏᐣ᙮ ᓂᑮ ᓂᑐᐦᑌᓈᐣ ᑲᔮᐢ, ᐁ ᓴᑲᐦᐱᑕᐢᑎᒷᒋᐠ ᑫᐦᑌ ᐊᔭᐠ ᐘᔭᐑᑎᒥᕽ ᐁ ᐊᓴᒫᒋᐠ ᐅᑌᒥᐚᐘ ᐁ ᐊᑿᓇᐦᐋᒋᐠ, ᐁᑿ, ᐊᐑᓇ ᐊᓇ ᑳ ᐲᐦᑐᑳᐦᐟ, ᐁᐘᑯ ᐊᓇ ᑮᓯᑌᐳᐤ᙮

ᐁᑿ ᐁ ᑮᓯ ᒦᒋᓱᕽ, « ᐦᐋᐨ, ᑭᓭᔨᓂᐤ, ᐯ ᐋᑕᔫᐦᑫ ᐆᑕ, » ᑮ ᐃᑗᐘᐠ ᒫᓇ ᑫᐦᑌ ᐊᔭᐠ᙮ ᑿᔭᐢᐠ ᐊᓂᒪ ᐁ ᐃᑑᑕᒣᐠ ᐋᑕᔫᐦᑫᐏᐣ ᑳ ᓂᑑᐢᑲᒣᐠ᙮ ᑮ ᐃᑣᓂᐤ ᑲᔮᐢ, ᑮ ᐃᑣᓂᐤ ᒫᓇ ᑫᐦᑌ ᐊᔭᐠ ᑲᔮᐢ, ᐋᑕᔫᐦᑫᐏᐣ, ᐊᐏᔭᐠ ᓈᓂᑕᐤ ᐁ ᐃᓯ ᐊᔮᐟ, ᐁ ᓂᑐᐦᑕᕽ, ᑖᐱᐢᑰ-, ᑖᐱᐢᑰ- ~ ᐊᐘ ᑳ ᐋᑕᔫᐦᑫᐟ ᑖᐱᐢᑰ- ᐁ ᓂᑐᑕᒫᑫᐢᑕᒪᐚᐟ ᒥᔽᔮᐏᐣ, ᒥᔪᒪᐦᒋᐦᐅᐏᐣ, ᑖᐱᐢᑰ- ᐁ ᐊᔭᒥᐦᑖᑯᓯᐟ, ᑖᐱᐢᑰᐟ ᐁ ᑭᑐᑖᐟ ᑖᐱᐢᑰ- ᒪᓂᑐᐘ ᐁᐘᑯ ᐋᑕᔫᐦᑫᐏᐣ ᑲᔮᐢ᙮ ᐁᑯᓯ ᑮ ᐃᐢᐸᔨᐤ᙮ ᐁ ᑮ ᐯᐦᑕᒫᐣ ᐊᓂᒪ᙮

ᓇᒨᔭ, ᓇᒨᔭ ᓂᔭ, ᒨᐩ ᓂᔭ ᐁᑿᔮᐠ ᐁ ᐑᐦᑕᒫᑕᑯᐠ᙮ ᐁ ᑮ ᐯᐦᑕᒫᐣ ᑖᓂᓯ ᐁ ᐃᑖᑕᔫᐦᑫᒋᐠ ᑫᐦᑌ ᐊᔭᐠ᙮ ᓂᑮ ᐊᐱᐣ ᒫᓇ ᐊᐍᑳ ᒌ ᐁ ᐏᔪᑎᐦᑕᐱᓯᓂᔮᐣ ᐁ ᓂᑐᐦᑕᐘᑭᐠ ᑫᐦᑌ ᐊᔭᐠ ᑳ ᑮ ᐏᔫᐦᑯᒥᔮᐣ

ᐁᑲᐧ ᑳ ᑮ ᐏᔦᒧᓰᒥᔮᐣ᙮ ᓂᒧᓰᑦ ᐁ ᐻᒋᐢ ᑮ ᐃᑖᐤ᙮ ᐁᑲᐧ ᓅᐦᑯᑦ ᐊᔭ, ᓂᑮ ᐃᓯᔭᐦᑳᑖᓈᐣ *Isabelle Eashappie*, ‘ᓭᐯᐣ’ ᒫᓇ ᓂᑮ ᐃᑖᓈᐣ ᓅᐦᑯᑦ ᐅᒫᒥᐦᑴᐤ, ᐅᒫᒥᐦᑴᐤ ᑮ ᐏᔦᐦᑯᒥᔮᐣ, ᓅᐦᑖᐏᐩ ᐅᑳᐐᓭ, ᐅᑳᐏᔭ ᒦᓇ, ᐅᒫᒥᐦᑴᐘᐠ᙮ ᑮ~ ᐊᔭ ᐊᓇ, ᑮ ᐻᓰᒧᐤ ᓅᐦᑯᑦ ᐁᑲᐧ ᓂᓯᑯᐢ ᐯᔭᐠ ᐅᑖᓂᓭ ᐁᑯᑕ ᒫᓇ ᐁ ᐱᒥᓯᓂᔮᕽ, ᐁ ᓂᑐᐦᑕᒫᕽ ᑭᓭᔭᓂᐤ ᐁ ᐋᒋᒧᐟ᙮ « ᐊᐦᐋᑦ, » ᐁᐘᑯ ᐆᒪ ᑲ~, ᑭᓭᔭᓂᐤ, « ᑳ ᐐ ᐋᑕᔦᐦᑫᔮᐣ, » ᑮ ᐃᑘᐤ ᒫᓇ ᐊᐘ ᑭᓭᔭᓂᐤ᙮ ᐁᑯᓯ ᐁᑲᐧ ᐁ ᓂᑐᐦᑖᐦᐟ ᑳᐦ ᑮᓯ ᐃᑖᐢᑯᓂᑫᑗᐏ ᑖᐱᐢᑰᐨ ᐆᒪ ᑳ ᐃᑑᑕᒣᐠ ᐆᑕ, ᐁᑯᓯ ᑮ ᐃᑑᑕᒷᐠ᙮ ᐅᐢᐻᑲᓇ ᑮ ᐋᐸᒋᐦᐁᐘᐠ, ᒫᑲ ᑭᓇᐌᐦᑖᐐᓈᓇᐤ ᑭᔮᓇᐤ ᐋᐱᐦᑕᐤ ᓇᐘᒋᑯ ᑭᒨᓂᔮᐏᑑᑌᓈᓇᐤ ᒨᔭ ᒫᑲ ᓈᓂᑕᐤ, ᐯᔭᑲᐧᐣ᙮ ᐯᔭᑲᐧᐣ, ᐯᔭᑯ ᐅᐢᐻᑲᐣ᙮

ᐦᐋᐤ, ᐊᓄᐦᐨ ᑳ ᐐ ᐱᒥ ᐋᒋᒧᐢᑖᑕᑯᐠ᙮

ᑮ ᒪᒫᐦᑖᐏᓯᐤ ᐁᓭ ᑭᒧᓰᒥᓇᐤ ᐐᓭᐦᑫᒑᕽ ᑮ ᐃᑖᐤ᙮ ᑮ ᒪᒫᐦᑖᐏᓯᐤ ᐁᓭ, ᑲᐦᑭᔮᐤ ᑮᑲᐧᐩ ᑮ ᐅᔦᐦᑖᐤ᙮ « ᐦᐋᑦ, ᐁᑯᑐᐘ, ᐁᑯᓯ ᑲ ᐃᑖᐸᒋᐦᑖᐣ ᐆᒪ᙮ » ᐊᐦᐴ ᒪᐢᑭᐦᑭᔭ, ᑮ ᐐᐦᑕᒫᑫᐤ᙮ « ᐅᒉᐱᕽ, ᐁᑯᓯ ᑳ ᑮ ᐃᑖᐸᒋᐦᑖᔦᐠ, » ᑮ ᐃᑘᐤ ᐁᓭ ᐐᓭᐦᑫᒑᕽ᙮ « ᐁᐘᑯ, ᒥᓯ ᑳᑭᑫ ᐁ ᐅᐦᐱᑭᐦᑭ, ᑭᔮᑦ ᑰᓇ ᑳ ᐊᔮᐟ ᐊᐦᒋ ᐱᑯ ᐁ ᐯ ᐅᐦᐱᑭᐦᑭ ᐆᑌ᙮ ᒪᐢᑭᐦᑭᔭ ᑳ ᐊᑎ ᑮᓯᐸᑳᐠ ᐋᓭᐩ, ᑭᐚᐸᐦᑌᓈᓇᐤ ᐋᓭᐩ ᑫᔮᐱᐨ ᐊᓂᐦᐃ ᒣᑻᐨ ᐆᒪ ᐁ ᐯ ᓭᑭᑭᐦᑭ ᐊᓂᐦᐃ, ᓇᒨᐩ ᐁ ᓂᐴᒪᑲᐦᑭ ᐆᑌ᙮ ᐃᐢᑯ ᑕ ᐊᐢᑮᐏᐠ᙮ » ᐁᑯᓯ ᒫᓇ ᐁᓭ ᑮ ᐃᑘᐤ ᐐᓭᐦᑫᒑᕽ᙮

• • • •

ᐯᔭᑻᐤ ᐁᓭ ᐐᓭᐦᑫᒑᕽ ᐁ ᐸ ᐱᒧᐦᑌᐟ, ᐁ ᐱᒧᐦᑌᐟ ᐐᓭᐦᑫᒑᕽ᙮ ᐘᐦᐚ ᐦᐊᐩ, ᒥᑐᓂ ᐁᓭ ᐅᐦᑯᒪ ᐊᑳᐚᑕᒪᐍᐤ ᐁ ᓈᐦ ᓇᐘᒦᔭᐟ ᐆᒪ ᐊᔭ, ᑳᐦᑫᐘᐠ᙮ ᐘᐦᐚ, ᓅᐦᑌ ᒦᒋᐤ ᐁᓭ, ᒨᐩ ᒫᑲ ᑮ~, ᒥᓯ ᒥᐢᑎᔭᓂᐤ ᐊᔭᐢᐠ ᒥᓯ ᑭᓭᔭᓂᐤ ᐊᐘ ᐐᓭᐦᑫᒑᕽ᙮ ᒨᔭ ᐐ ᐊᓭᒥᐠ ᐅᐦᑯᒪ᙮ ᐘᐦᐚ, ᒥᑐᓂ ᓅᐦᑌᐦᑲᑌᐤ᙮ ᐋᐦ, ᐁᑯᓯ ᓇᑲᑌᐤ ᐆᐦᐃ ᐅᐦᑯᒪ᙮ ᐋᐤ, ᐸᐹᒧᐦᑌᐤ᙮ ᑮ ᐱᒧᐦᑌᐢᑭᐤ ᐊᔭᐢ ᐊᐘ ᐐᓭᐦᑫᒑᕽ᙮ ᐘᐦᐚ, ᒥᑐᓂ ᓅᐦᑌᐦᑲᑌᐤ᙮ ᐘᐦᐚ! ᐅᑭᓂᔭ ᐁᓭ ᑳ ᐚᐸᒫᐟ, ᒥᑐᓂ ᐁ ᒫᐦ ᒥᐦᑯᓯᔭᐟ, ᐁᑯᓂ ᐁᓭ

ᐁᑲᐧ ~, ᓅᐦᑌᐦᑲᑌᐤ᙮ ᐁᑯᓂ ᐁᓴ ᐁᑲᐧ ᐅᑭᓂᔭ ᐆᐦᐃ ᒣᑐᓂ ᒥᓯ ᒧᐁᐧᐤ᙮ ᒥᑐᓂ ᐅᑎ᙮

« ᐊᐦᐋᒼ, ᓂᓰᒥᑎᐠ, ᒥᑐᓂ ᓂᑮᐢᐳᐣ ᐁᑲᐧ᙮ ᑖᓂᓯ ᐆᒪ ᐁ ᐃᓯᔨᐦᑳᓱᔦᐠ? »

« ᐋᐦ, ᐅᑭᓂᔭᐠ᙮ »

« ᐋᐦᐊ, ᐁᑯ ᒌ ᐱᑯ? ᐅᐦᒋᑕᐤ ᑳ ᐊᔨᓯᔨᓃᐃᐧᕽ ᓈᐦ ᓃᓱᐃᐧᐦᑳᓱᓈᓂᐃᐧᐤ, ᓇᒨᔭ ᓇᔦᐢᑕᐤ ᐅᑭᓂᔭᐠ, ᓂᓰᒥᑎᐠ, ᑕ ᑮ ᐃᓯᔨᐦᑳᑎᓱᔦᐠ᙮ »

ᐯᔭᐠ ~, ᐊᐧᐋᐧᓀᔨᐦᑕᒪᐧᐠ ᐁᓴ ᐆᑭ ᐆᑭ ᐅᑭᓂᔭᐠ ᑖᓂᓯ ᑕ ᐃᓯᔨᐦᑳᑎᓱᒋᐠ᙮ ᐅᒥᓯ ᐁᓴ ᐯᔭᐠ ᐊᐊᐧ ᑳ ᐃᑌᐧᐟ ᒥᓯ ᐅᑭᓂᐩ ᐊᐊᐧ, « ᐋᐦ, ᓂᐢᑌᓴ, ᐅᑫᔭᑭᒋᐢᑫᔫᓴᐠ ᓂᑎᑲᐃᐧᓈᐣ᙮ » [ᐹᐦᐱᓈᓂᐊᐧᐣ]

« ᐋᐧᐋᐧᐦᐋᐋ, ᐊᐧᐦᐋᐧ, ᑖᐯᐧ ᑭᒫᔨᐦᑳᓱᓈᐋᐧᐤ! »

« ᐋ, ᐊᓂᒪ ᑳ ᒥᓯ ᒧᐃᐧᔮᕽ, ᑳ ᒥᓯ ᒦᒋᓱᔭᐣ, ᐊᑎ ᐊᐧᔭᐄᐧᔭᓂ ᐆᒪ ᑭᑲ ᒫᔨ ᐃᑑᑖᑯᐣ ᐊᓂᒪ ᐆᑌ [ᐁ ᐃᓯᓂᐢᑫᐟ]᙮ ᒣᑐᓂ ᑭᑲ ᒥᓯ ᑫᔭᑭᓯᐣ᙮ »

« ᐋᐦ, ᓂᑕᑭᓴ ᐁᑎᑫᐧ ᐆᑭ ᐅᑫᔭᑭᒋᐢᑫᐦᐃᐁᐧᔫᓴᐠ᙮ » ᓯᐯᐧᐦᑌᐤ, ᐱᒧᐦᑌᐤ᙮

ᐊᐧᐦᐋᐧ! ᓅᒪᑫᓰᐢ ᐁᓴ ᐁ ᐊᑎ ᐊᔮᐟ᙮ ᐊᐧᐦᐋᐧ, ᑳ ᑳᐦ ᑫᔭᑭᓯᐟ ᐆᑌ [ᐹᐦᐱᓈᓂᐊᐧᐣ], ᐱᔨᐢᐠ ᐁᓴ ᐋᑯᐱᑕᒼ ᐆᒪ ᐆᑌ ᐆᒪ ᐃᑌ ᐊᓂᒪ ᑳ ᐊᐧᔭᐄᐧᐟ᙮ [ᐹᐦᐱᓈᓂᐊᐧᐣ] ᐱᒧᐦᑌᐤ᙮

ᐊᐧᐦᐋᐧ! « ᐊᐧᐦᐋᐧ, ᓅᐦᑯᒼ ᐆᑕ ᑳ ᐱᒥ ᐊᔦᑎᐢᑭᐟ, ᐁᐊᐧᑯ ᑳ ᑮ ᐊᑳᐋᐧᑕᒪᐊᐧᐠ ᑳᐦᑫᐊᐧᐠ᙮ » ᐊᑎ ᒫᑖᐦᐁᐤ ᐆᐦᐃ ~ ᐃᐧᔭ ᐆᒪ ᑳ ᒫᑖᐦᐃᓱᐟ᙮ [ᐹᐦᐱᓯᓈᓂᐊᐧᐣ] ᑳ ᐹᐢᑌᔨᐠ ᐁᓴ ᑳᐦᑫᐊᐧᑯᐢ᙮ ᐸᑯᓀᔮᔨᐤ ᐆᑕ᙮ ᐊᑎ ᐅᑎᓇᒼ᙮ « ᐁᐦᐋᐦᐊ, ᓅᐦᑯᒼ ᐁᓴ ᑳᐦ ᐊᑎ ᐸᑎᓇᕽ ᐅᑳᐦᑫᐊᐧᑯᒥᐢ, ᐁᐊᐧᑯ ᑳ ᑮ ᐊᑳᐋᐧᑕᒪᐊᐧᐠ᙮ » ᐊᑎ ᐅᑎᓇᒼ ᐁᓴ ᐊᐊᐧ

ᐑᓴᐦᑫᒑᕽ ᐁᑿ ᐁ ᐊᑎ ᒦᒋᐟ ᐁᑿ ᐆᒪ᙮ ᐘᐦᐚ, ᒣᑐᓂ, ᒣᑐᓂ ᐊᑎ ᑮᐢᐳᐤ᙮

ᑫᑕᐦᑕᐍ ᐁᓴ ᐱᔦᓰᓴ, « ᐑᓴᐦᑫᒑᕽ ᐅᒥᑭᐩ ᒦᐄᐄᒋᐤ! » [ᐹᐦᐱᓈᓂᐘᐣ] ᑳ ᐃᑘᔨᐟ ᐁᓴ᙮ « ᐑᓴᐦᑫᒑᕽ ᐅᒥᑭᐩ ᒦᐄᐄᒋᐤ! »

« ᐚ, ᓂᓰᒥᑎᐠ, ᑖᓂᑕ ᐃᑕ ᐑᓴᐦᑫᒑᕽ ᐅᒥᑭᐩ ᑫ ᒦᒋᐟ? ᓅᐦᑯᐨ ᐆᒪ ᐅᑳᐦᑫᐘᑯᒥᐢ ᑳ ᒦᒋᔮᐣ᙮ »

ᐚ, ᐋᐦᒋ ᐱᑯ ᓈᐦ ᓂᑲᒧᐘᐠ ᐆᑭ ᐱᔦᓰᓴᐠ ᑳ ᐊᑎ ᓂᓯᑕᐏᓇᕽ ᐁᓴ ᐆᒪ ᐆᑌ ᐃᑌ ᑰᐦ ᐘᔭᐑᕽ ᐁ ᐚᑎᐘᐣ~ ᐊᔨ, ᓇᐘᒋᑯ ᐁ ᐅᓵᐚᐠ ᐆᒪ ᐁᐘᑯ ᐊᓂᒪ ᑳ ᐊᑎ ᐸᐦᑭᐦᑎᑖᐟ ᐁᓴ ᐆᒪ ᐆᐦᐃ ᐅᑭᓂᔭ ᐅᓵᐨ ᐁ ᑮ ᑭᔭᑭᓯᐟ᙮ [ᐹᐦᐱᓈᓂᐘᐣ]

« ᐘᐦᐚ! ᐁ ᑖᐻᒋᐠ ᐁᓴ ᐆᑭ ᓂᓰᒪᐠ᙮ ᐁᒋᑲ ᐆᒪ ᑖᐻ ᓂᒥᑭᐩ ᑳ ᒦᒋᔮᐣ᙮ » [ᒥᓯ ᐹᐦᐱᓈᓂᐘᐣ; ᐑᐢᑕ ᐹᐦᐱᐤ]

ᐁᑯᓯ! ᐦᐋ, ᐦᐋᐨ! ᐁᑯᓯ ᒫᓇ ᑮ ᐊᐩ ᐃᓯ ᐋᑕᔫᐦᑳᓂᐏᐤ, ᐁᐘᑯ ᐯᔭᐠ᙮ ᑖᓂᒪᔨᑯᕽ ᑕ ᐲᑭᐢᑵᔮᐣ? [ᐹᐦᐱᓈᓂᐘᐣ]

[ᑮᐦᑤᐨ ᐊᐘ ᐹᐦᐱᐤ]

« ᐑᓴᐦᑫᒑᕽ ᐅᒥᑭᐩ ᒦᐄᐄᒋᐤ! »

5
ᓀᐦᐃᔭᐤ ᐃᓰᐦᒋᑫᐃᐧᓇ

[1. ᑳᑮᓯᒧᐃᐧᐣ]

ᐋᐦᐋᐤ, ᐊᓄᐦᐨ ᑳ ᑮᓯᑳᐠ, ᓅᓯᓯᒼ ᐆᑕ ᐁ ᐯ ᐊᐢᐯᔨᒧᑐᑕᐃᐧᐟ, ᓃᐢᑕ ᐁ ᑭᑕᒫᑫᔨᒪᐠ ᐁ ᐄᐧ ᑲᑫᐧ ᐄᐧᒎᐦᑲᒪᐊᐧᐠ ᑮᑲᐧᐩ᙮ ᐊᐊᐧ ᐯᔭᐠ ᐅᐢᐹᐧᑲᐣ ᑳ ᑕᐦᑯᓇᐠ, ᐁᐊᐧᑯ ᐊᓇ ᐁ ᐄᐧ ᑭᑐᑕᐠ ᑰᐦᑖᐄᐧᓇᐤ ᑭᓭᒪᓂᑐᐤ ᐊᓄᐦᐨ ᑳ ᑮᓯᑳᐠ᙮ ᐁᑯᓯ ᒫᓇ ᑮ ᐃᑑᑕᒪᐊᐧᐠ ᑫᐦᑌ ᐊᔭᐠ ᑳ ᑮᐢᑭᓴᒫᐦᒋᐠ ᑮ ᐹᐦ ᐲᑭᐢᑳᐧᑌᐊᐧᐠ ᐆᐦᐃ ᒋᐢᑌᒫᐊᐧ᙮ ᐁᑯᓯ ᐁ ᐄᐧ ᐱᒥ ᑑᑕᒫᐣ ᐊᔨᐢᐠ ᑲᔮᐢ ᓅᐦᒌᐣ, ᑲᔮᐢ ᓅᐦ ᐯ ᐯᐦᑌᐣ ᑮᑲᐧᐩ, ᑖᓂᓯ ᐁ ᑮ ᐯ ᐃᑑᑕᐦᑭᐠ ᑫᐦᑌ ᐊᔭᐠ, ᐁᐊᐧᑯᓂᐠ ᐁ ᑮ ᐯ ᑭᐢᑭᓄᐦᐊᒪᐃᐧᒋᐠ ᐁ ᑮ ᐯ ᑲᑫᐧ ᑭᐢᑫᔨᐦᑕᒫᐣ ᑮᑲᐧᐩ᙮

ᐦᐋᐤ, ᓅᐦᑖᐄᐧᓈᐣ ᐊᓄᐦᐨ ᑳ ᑮᓯᑳᐠ, ᐊᐊᐧ ᐯᔭᐠ ᐅᐢᐹᐧᑲᐣ ᐁ ᐱᒥ ᑕᐦᑯᓇᐠ ᓅᓯᓯᒼ ᑮᑲᐧᐩ ᐁ ᐄᐧ ᐱᒥ ᐄᐧᐦᑕᒪᐊᐧᐠ; ᓇᒨᔭ ᑮᑲᐧᐩ ᐁ ᐄᐧ ᐱᒥ ᑭᔮᐢᑭᔮᐣ᙮ ᒪᓂᑐᐤ ᓂᓂᑐᑖᐠ ᐁ ᐱᒥ ᑕᐦᑯᓇᐠ ᐊᐊᐧ ᐯᔭᐠ ᐅᐢᐹᐧᑲᐣ, ᐁᑯᑌ ᑲ ᐱᒥ ᐋᐧᐦ ᐄᐧᒋᐦᐃᑯᔮᕽ ᑮᑲᐧᐩ, ᑮᑲᐧᐩ ᐁ ᐱᒥ ᒪᒫᔩᔮᐣ, ᑕ ᐱᒥ ᒥᔭᐧᐢᑖᐤ ᓅᐦᑖᐄᐧᓈᐣ ᑭᓭᒪᓂᑐᐤ ᐁᑳᔭ ᑮᑲᐧᐩ ᑕᒫᔨ ᐃᑑᑕᐊᐧᐠ ᓅᓯᓯᒼ ᐊᓄᐦᐨ ᑳ ᑮᓯᑳᐠ᙮ ᐁᑯᓯ ᐁ ᐱᒥ ᐃᓯ ᐊᐢᐯᔨᒧᑐᑕᐃᐧᐟ ᑳ ᐱᒥ ᑕᐦᑯᓇᐠ ᐊᐊᐧ

ᒋᐢᑌᒫᐤ᙮ ᐊᐩ ᐦᐊᐩ, ᐁ ᐱᒥ ᐃᑘᔮᐣ ᐊᓅᐦᐨ ᐁ ᐐ ᐱᒥ ᐹᐦ ᐲᑭᐢᑵᔮᐣ ᑮᒁᐩ ᑳ ᐱᒥ ᑲᑵᒋᒥᐟ᙮

[2. ᓂᐹᑵᓯᒧᐎᐣ]

ᑲᔮᐢ ᑮ ᓂᐹᑵᓯᒧᓈᓂᐎᐤ, ᑮ ᑭᐦᒉᔨᐦᑖᑿᐣ ᓂᐹᑵᓯᒧᐎᐣ᙮ ᐁᐗᑯ ᒥᓯ ᒦᑭᐚᐦᑊ ᑳ ᑮ ᐃᓯᔨᐦᑳᑌᐠ, ᑭᐦᒋ ᒦᑭᐚᐦᑊ, ᐁᑯᑕ ᑳ ᓂᐹᑵᓯᒧᕽ᙮ ᐁᑯᓯ ᐁ ᐊᑎ ᐴᔪᒋᐠ, ᐁᑯᓯ ᐁᑿ ᑮ ᒪᑐᑎᓵᓂᐦᑫᐗᐠ, ᓀᒥᑕᓇᐤ ᒥᐢᑎᑿ ᑮ ᐋᐸᒋᐦᐁᐗᐠ ᒪᑐᑎᓵᐣ ᐁ ᐅᔩᐦᑖᒋᐠ᙮ ᐁ ᑳᔩᐦᑲᓴᐦᑭᐠ ᐊᓂᐦᐃ ᐸᑭᐗᔮᓇ ᐊᔨᐢᐠ ᐆᒪ ᒨᔭ ᑲᓈᑎᓯᓈᓂᐎᐤ ᑳ ᐃᐢᑵᐎᕽ; ᒨᐩ ᓈᓂᑕᐤ ᑮ ᑑᒋᑳᑌᐤ ᐁᐗᑯ ᑕᒫᒥᔮᐧᑳᒋᒧᕽ, ᑕᒫᒥᔮᐧᑳᒋᒥᐦᐟ ᐊᐎᔭᐠ, ᐁᑳ ᑲ ᑮ ᑳᔩᐦᑲᓯᑳᑌᐗ᙮ ᑮ ᐋᐸᑕᓇᐧ ᒧᐢᑐᓱ ᐐᐦᑲᐢᑿ ᐁ ᐯᐦᑭᐦᑲᓴᒥᕽ ᐆᐦᐃ, ᐁᑯᓂ ᐆᐦᐃ ᐍᐱᓈᓱᓇ ᑳ ᐃᓯᔨᐦᑳᑌᑭ᙮ ᐁᐗᑯ ᐊᓂᒪ ᐁ ᐯ ᑭᐢᑫᔨᐦᑕᒫᐣ ᑲᔮᐢ; ᑲᔮᐢ ᐃᔩᐦᒋᑫᐎᐣ᙮ ᐁ ᑮ ᓃᓯᑭ ᐁᐗᑯᓂ ᒪᐎᒧᐢᒋᑫᐎᓇ ᑳ ᓂᐹᑵᓯᒧᕽ ᐁᑿ ᒦᓇ ᑳ ᒪᑐᑎᓯᕽ ᐁᑯᓂ ᐁ ᑮ ᑭᐢᑫᔨᐦᑕᒫᐣ᙮ ᐁᑯᑕ ᑮ ᐅᐦᒋ ᐱᒫᑎᓯᐗᐠ ᐊᔨᓯᔨᓂᐗᐠ, ᒪᑐᑎᓵᓂᕽ ᐁ ᐲᐦᑐᑿᐦᐃᐦᐟ ᐊᐎᔭᐠ ᐁᑳ ᑳ ᒥᔮᐧᔮᐟ, ᑮ ᒥᔪ ᑑᑖᐠ ᐁᓴ ᐊᓂᒪ ᒪᑐᑎᓵᐣ, ᐁᑯᓯ ᒫᓇ ᑮ ᐃᑣᓂᐤ, ᐁᐗᑯ ᐁ ᑮ ᐯ ᐯᐦᑕᒫᐣ᙮ ᐁᐗᑯ ᓅᓯᓯᒼ ᐁ ᐯ ᑲᑵᒋᒥᐟ᙮

ᐯᔭᒁᐤ ᐯᔭᐠ ᐊᐢᑭᐩ ᐊᔨᐢᐠ ᒋᒪᒋᑳᑌᐤ, ᑮ ᒋᒪᑖᐗᐠ ᒫᓇ ᑲᔮᐢ ᑭᓭᔨᓂᐗᐠ ᐁᐗᑯ ᐆᒪ ᒪᑐᑎᓵᐣ ᑳ ᐃᑕᒥᕽ ~ ᐊᐩ! ᐆᒪ ᓂᐹᑵᓯᒧᐎᐣ, ᓂᐗᓂᑐᓈᒧᐣ᙮ ᒪᑐᑎᓵᐣ ᐎᔭ ᐹᑐᐢ ᑳ ᐴᔪᐦᑭ ᐁᑯᑕ ᑳ ᑳᔩᐦᑲᓯᑳᑌᑭ ᐆᐦᐃ ᐍᐱᓈᓱᓇ᙮ ᐁᑯᓯ ᑫᐦᑌ ᐊᔭᐠ ᓀᐓ ᑎᐱᐢᑳᐤ ᑮ ᑲᓇᐍᔨᐦᑕᒷᐠ ᐁᑯᓯ ᐁ ᓂᑕᐎ ᐸᑭᑎᓇᐦᑭᐠ, ᐁ ᓂᑕᐎ ᐊᑯᑖᒋᐠ᙮ ᐁᑯᓯ ᑳᐦ ᐱᒥ ᐃᓯ ᐃᑑᑕᐦᑭᐠ ᑲᔮᐢ ᑫᐦᑌ ᐊᔭᐠ, ᐁᐗᑯ ᐆᒪ ᐁ ᐱᒥ ᐐᐦᑕᒪᐗᐠ ᓅᓯᓯᒼ, ᑲᔮᐢ ᐃᔩᐦᒋᑫᐎᐣ ᐁᐗᑯ ᐁ ᑮ ᐯ ᑭᐢᑫᔨᐦᑕᒫᐣ᙮

ᐁ ᑮ ᐯ ᐃᑖᒧᕽ ᐊᓂᒪ, ᐁ ᑮ ᐯ ᐃᑖᒧᕽ ᐊᓇ ᒥᐢᑎᐠ ᑖᐚᔨᕽ ᑳ ᒋᒪᓲᐟ᙮ 'ᑭᒧᓲᒥᓇᐤ' ᑮ ᐃᓯᔨᐦᑳᓱᐤ ᐁᐗᑯ ᐊᓇ ᑳ ᓂᐹᑵᓯᒧᕽ ᐊᓇ ᒥᐢᑎᐠ᙮ ᐁ ᑮ ᒥᔪᐧᔨᐦᑕᐦᑭᐠ ᑖᐱᐢᑰᐨ ~ ᐁᑯᑕ ᐅᐦᒋ ᐊᔨᓯᔨᓂᐤ

ᐁ ᑮ ᐅᐦᒋ ᐱᒫᑎᓯᐟ ᓈᓂᑕᐤ ᑳ ᐃᓯ ᐊᔮᐟ᙮ ᐁ ᑮ ᑲᑳᐧᑕᑭᐦᑖᐟ ᐊᔨᓯᔨᓂᐤ ᐁᑯᑕ ᑮ ᐅᐦᒋ ᐱᒫᑎᓯᐤ, ᐁᐊᐧᑯ ᐁ ᑮ ᓇᓈᐢᑯᒧᒋᐠ ᑫᐦᑌ ᐊᔮᐠ᙮

ᐁᐊᐧᑯ ᐅᐦᒋ ᓂᐹᑫᐧᓯᒧᐃᐧᐣ ᑳ ᐆᐦ ᐃᓯᔨᐦᑳᑌᐠ; ᓀᐅᐧ ᑎᐱᐢᑳᐤ ᐊᓇ ᑰᐦ ᐃᓰᐦᒋᑫᐟ ᓇᒨᔭ ᐅᐦᒋ ᒥᓂᐦᑫᐧᐤ ᓂᐱᐩ, ᓇᒨᔭ ᐅᐦᒋ ᒦᒋᓱᐤ ᓀᐅᐧ ᑎᐱᐢᑳᐤ᙮ ᑮ ᐋᐦ ᐃᔨᓂᑐ ᐃᓰᐦᐅᐤ ᒦᓇ ᒪᐢᑭᓯᓇ, ᐆᐦᐃ ᐃᔨᓂᑕᐧᐢᑭᓯᓇ ᑮ ᑭᑭᐢᑲᒼ ᐁᑲᐧ ᒦᓇ ᑮ ᐊᑲᐧᓇᐦᐅᐤ ᐆᑌ ᐁ ᑕᐦᑯᐱᑕᕽ ᐁ ᐸᑲᐧᐦᑌᐦᐅᐟ ᐊᑯᐦᐠ᙮ ᐁᐊᐧᑯ, ᐁᐊᐧᑯ ᑳ ᐃᓰᐦᒋᑫᐟ ᓃᓱ ᑮ ᑕᐦᑯᓀᐤ ᐁᐧᐁᐧᐢᑌᐦᐊᒫᓇ᙮ ᐁᑲᐧ ᐁᐊᐧᑯ ᐁ ᐃᓰᐦᒋᑫᐟ ᐁᑲᐧ ᐆᑕ ᒦᓇ ᑮ ᐃᑕᐦᐱᓱᐤ ᐸᑭᐊᐧᔮᐣ ᐅᐢᑎᑳᐧᓂᕽ, ᐁ ᓰᑐᐢᑎᑳᐧᓀᐦᐱᓱᐟ ᐁᐊᐧᑯ ᐊᓇ ᑳ ᐃᓰᐦᒋᑫᐟ᙮ ᓇᒨᔭ ᑯᓂᑕ ᐅᐦᒋ ᐃᓯ ᐸᐹᒧᐦᑌᐤ ᐊᔨᐢ ᐆᒪ ᑳ~, ᒨᔭ ᒥᔮᐧᓯᐣ ᐊᐧᔭᐄᐧᑎᒥᕽ ᐊᐊᐧ ~; ᐅᐢᑭᓃᑭᐢᑫᐧᐊᐧᐠ ᐆᑭ, ᐁ ᑮ ᑯᐢᑕᒥᕽ ᑕ ᐱᐢᑎᐢᑲᕽ ᑮᑲᐧᐩ ᐊᐊᐧ ᑳ ᐱᒧᐦᑌᐟ ᐊᐊᐧ ᑳ ᐃᓰᐦᒋᑫᐟ᙮ ᐁ ᑮ ᑯᐢᑕᒥᕽ ᐁᐊᐧᑯ ᑲᔮᐢ᙮

ᐊᓄᐦᐨ ᐁᑲᐧ! ᓇᒨᔭ ᐋᑕᐃᐧᔭ, ᓇᒨᔭ ᐋᑕᐃᐧᔭ ᐊᐃᐧᔭᐠ ᐁ ᐋᓀᐧᔨᒥᐦᐟ ᒫᑲ ᑕ ᑮ ᒪᓈᒋᐦᑖᕽ ᐯᔭᑲᐧᐣ ᐁᑯᓯ ᑕ ᑮ ᑲᑫᐧ ᐃᓯ ᑑᑕᒥᕽ᙮ ᐁᑯᓯ ᐁ ᑮ ᐯ ᐃᓯ ᑭᐢᑫᔨᐦᑕᒫᐣ ᑲᔮᐢ, ᐁ ᑮ ᐯ ᐋᐧᐸᐦᑕᒫᐣ ᒦᓇ ᐁᑲᐧ ᒦᓇ ᐁ ᑮ ᐯ ᐯᐦᑕᐊᐧᑭᐠ ᑫᐦᑌ ᐊᔮᐠ ᐁᐊᐧᑯ ᐆᒪ ᑳ ᐸ ᐲᑭᐢᑳᐧᑕᒫᐣ ᐊᓄᐦᐨ᙮ ᓇᒨᔭ ᐁ ᑭᔮᐢᑭᔮᐣ, ᑭᓭᒪᓂᑐᐤ ᓂᓂᑐᐦᑖᐠ ᐁ ᐱᒥ ᐄᐧᐦᑕᒪᐊᐧᐠ ᐊᐊᐧ ᓅᓯᓯᒼ, ᐁ ᐯ ᑲᑫᐧᒋᒥᐟ, ᐁ ᐯ ᐅᑎᓇᕽ ᓂᐲᑭᐢᑫᐧᐃᐧᐣ᙮

ᒫᑲ ᑐᓂ ᓂᑕᑲᐦᑫᔨᐦᑌᐣ ᐁ ᑫᐦᑌ ᐊᔨᐃᐧᔮᐣ, ᐊᔦᓈᓀᒥᑕᓇᐤ ᐊᔨᐋᐧᐠ ᓂᔮᓇᐣ ᐁ ᐃᑕᐦᑐᐱᐳᓀᐧᔮᐣ, ᑫᔮᐱᐨ ᓅᓯᓯᒪᐠ ᐁ ᐄᐧᒉᐊᐧᑭᐠ, ᑫᔮᐱᐨ ᐁ ᐄᐧᑕᐱᒪᑭᐠ, ᑫᔮᐱᐨ ᐁ ᑲᑫᐧᒋᒥᒋᐠ ᑮᑲᐧᐩ, ᑫᔮᐱᐨ ᑮᑲᐧᐩ ᐁ ᐱᒥ ᑭᐢᑫᔨᐦᑕᒫᐣ᙮ ᓇᒨᔭ ᐁ ᐃᑌᐧᔮᐣ ᐁ ᐃᔨᓃᓯᔮᐣ ᒫᑲ ᓀᒪ ᓈᐊᐧᐩ ᐁ ᑮ ᐯ ᐯᐦᑕᒫᐣ ᑮᑲᐧᐩ ᐁᐊᐧᑯ ᑫᔮᐱᐨ ᐁ ᐱᒥ ᑲᓇᐁᐧᔨᐦᑕᒫᐣ᙮

ᓇᒨᐩ ᓅᐦ ᐯ ᑭᐢᑭᓄᐦᐊᒫᑯᓯᐣ, ᓇᒨᔭ ᓂᔭ ᐁ ᐅᐦᒋ ᐃᑑᑕᒫᐣ᙮ ᓂᑳᐃᐧᐩ, ᐁᑳ ᑮ ᐋᐧᐱᐟ ᓂᑯᑖᐧᓯᐠ ᐁ ᐃᑕᐦᑐᐱᐳᓀᐧᔮᐣ, ᐊᔦᓈᓀᐤ ᐁ ᐃᑕᐦᑐᐱᐳᓀᐧᔮᐣ ᑕ ᑮ ᐲᐦᑐᑫᐧᔮᐣ ᒧᓂᔮᓈᕽ ᒨᐩ ᓅᐦ ᑲᐢᑭᐦᑖᐣ᙮ ᓂᑳᐃᐧᐩ ᐁ ᑮ ᐸᒥᐦᐊᐠ ᓃᐢᑕ ᐊᔨᐢᐠ ᓂᑳᐃᐧᐩ ᓂᑮ ᓵᐁᐧᔨᒫᐤ᙮ ᐁ ᑮ ᐯᔭᑰᓴᓂᐃᐧᔮᐣ, ᓂᒥᓴᐠ ᓂᐢᑐ

ᐁ ᑮ ᐊᐧᓂᐦᐊᑭᐠ᙮ ᓂᑳᐃᐧᐩ ᐁ ᑮ ᐸᒥᐦᐊᐠ, ᓅᐦᑖᐃᐧᐩ ᒦᓇ ᐁ ᑮ ᐸᒥᐦᐊᐠ᙮ ᐁ ᐸᒥᐦᐋᔮᕽ ᓂᑳᐃᐧᐩ ᐁᑳ ᐋᐧᐱᐟ; ᐁ ᑮ ᒥᓯ ᓵᑭᐦᐊᐠ ᓂᒫᒫ, ᓂᑳᐃᐧᐩ ᐁ ᑮ ᒥᓯ ᓵᑭᐦᐊᐠ᙮

ᐊᓅᐦᐨ ᐁᑲᐧ ᑳ ᐯᔭᑯᔮᐣ, ᓃᐢᑕᓇᐤ ᑕᐦᑖᐤ ᐊᐢᑭᐩ ᓂᑭᓭᔨᓃᒼ ᐊᐢᐱᐣ ᐁ ᑮ ᐊᐧᓂᐦᐊᐠ᙮ ᑮ ᑭᐦᑫᔨᐦᑕᒼ ᒪᐃᐧᒧᐢᒋᑫᐃᐧᐣ, ᑮ ᓃᑳᓃᐢᑕᒼ ᒪᐃᐧᒧᐢᒋᑫᐃᐧᐣ ᐁᐊᐧᑯ, ᐁᐊᐧᑯ *John Rockthunder* ᑳ ᑮ ᐃᓯᔨᐦᑳᓱᐟ᙮ ᐁᑯᓯ ᐁᑲᐧ ᓂᔭ ᐆᒪ ᑳ ᐃᓯᔨᐦᑳᓱᔮᐣ *Mary Louise Rockthunder, Mrs. Rockthunder* ᐊᐊᐧ ᑳ ᐹᐦ ᐲᑭᐢᑫᐧᐟ, ᑰᐦᑯᒥᐋᐧᐤ ᐁ ᐊᑎ ᑭᐢ~, ᐁ ᐊᑎ ᓅᑐᑫᐃᐧᐟ, ᒫᑲ ᑫᔮᐱᐨ ᓂᓅᐦᑌ ᐄᐧᒋᐦᐋᐊᐧᐠ ᓅᓯᓯᒪᐠ ᑮᑲᐧᐩ ᑫᑫᐧᒋᒥᑖᐧᐃᐧ ᓂᑲᑫᐧ ᐄᐧᐦᑕᒫᐋᐧᐊᐧᐠ ᑮᑲᐧᐩ ᐁ ᒥᔮᐧᓯᐠ᙮

ᑖᓂᓯ ᓂᔭ ᐁ ᐃᑌᐧᔮᐣ? « ᑳᐃᐧᔭ! », « ᑳᔭ ᐁᑯᓯ ᑑᑕ! », « ᓇᒨᔭ ᒥᔮᐧᓯᐣ ᐁᑯᓯ᙮ » ᐁᑯᓯ ᐁ ᐱᒥ ᐃᑕᑭᐠ ᓅᓯᓯᒪᐠ ᑳ ᐱᒥ ᑮᑲᐧᐩ ᐄᐧᐦᑕᒪᐊᐧᑭᐠ᙮ ᐁ ᐱᒥ ᑯᐢᑕᒫᐣ ᑮᑲᐧᐩ ᐊᔨᐢᐠ ᓂᑮ ᐯ ᑭᐢᑫᔨᐦᑌᐣ ᐁᐊᐧᑯ, ᓈᐊᐧᐩ ᐁᑯᓯ ᐁ ᑮ ᐯ ᐃᑎᑲᐃᐧᔮᕽ, « ᐁᑳᐩ ᐁᑯᓯ ᐃᑑᑕ! », « ᑭᐦᑫᔨᒼ ᑫᐦᑌ ᐊᔭ! », « ᓴᐁᐧᔨᒼ ᑫᐦᑌ ᐊᔭ! » ᓂᑮ ᐃᑎᑲᐃᐧᓈᐣ᙮ ᐁᐊᐧᑯ ᓅᓯᓯᒼ ᐊᐊᐧ ᐁ ᐸᑭᑎᓇᒪᐊᐧᐠ ᑲ ᐄᐧᐦᑕᒫᑯᔦᐠ ᐁᐊᐧᑯ ᐆᒪ ᐁ ᒥᔮᐧᓯᐠ ᐲᑭᐢᑫᐧᐃᐧᐣ, « ᐁᑳᐩ ᐁᑯᓯ ᐃᑑᑕ! » ᐁᑯᓯ ᑮ ᐃᑖᐧᓂᐤ ᑲᔮᐢ᙮

ᐁᐊᐧᑯᔨᑯᕽ ᐁᐊᐧᑯ ᐱᑕᒫ ᓂᐄᐧ ᑮᐢᑭᓈᐣ ᓂᐲᑭᐢᑫᐧᐃᐧᐣ ᐊᓅᐦᐨ ᑳ ᑮᐢᑭᑳᐠ᙮

[3. ᐊᐃᐧᔭᐠ ᑳ ᓇᐦᐃᓂᐦᐟ]

ᐦᐋᐤ, ᑯᑕᐠ ᐁᑲᐧ᙮ ᓅᓯᓯᒼ ᐊᐊᐧ ᑳ ᑲᑫᐧᒋᒥᐟ᙮

ᑲᔮᐢ, ᑲᔮᐢ ᑳ ᐸᓈᑎᓯᒋᐠ ᐊᔨᓯᔨᓂᐊᐧᐠ, ᑮ ᐅᔩᐦᒋᑳᑌᐤ ᒪᐢᑭᒧᒋᐢ, ᐁ ᐊᓴᒧᐱᑕᕽ, ᐁ ᐊᓴᒧᐱᑌᐠ᙮ ᐁᑯᑕ ᐄᐧᔮᑲᓂᐢ ᑮ ᐊᐢᒋᑳᑌᐤ ᐁᑲᐧ ᒦᓇ ᓇᐸᑭᔮᑲᓂᐢ ᐁᑲᐧ ᒦᓇ ᒨᐦᑯᒫᓂᐢ, ᐁᑲᐧ ᒦᓇ ᐸᐦᑫᐧᓯᑲᐣ ᐁᑲᐧ ᒦᓇ ᑮᑲᐧᐩ ᐃᐧᔮᐢ ᐊᔨᐢ᙮ ᐁᑯᑕ ᑮ ᐲᐦᑕᓯᐊᐧᑖᐊᐧᐠ ᓅᑐᑫᐧᐊᐧᐠ ᐁ ᐊᓴᒧᐱᑕᐦᑭᐠ,

ᐆᑌ ᐃᑌᐦᑫ ᑭᐦᒋᓂᐢᑮᕽ ᐁ ᐊᐢᑖᒋᐠ ᐁ ᓃᒫᐦᐋᒋᐠ ᐆᐦᐃ ᑳ ᓇᑲᑎᑯᒋᐠ ᐅᑕᐋᐧᓯᒥᓯᐋᐧᐊᐧ, ᐆᐦ, ᐁᑳ ᒌ ᐅᑭᓭᔨᓃᒥᐋᐧᐊᐧ ᐁ ᓃᒫᐦᐋᒋᐠ᙮ ᐁᑯᓯ ᒦᓇ ᑲᔮᐢ ᓂᑮ ᐃᓯ ᐋᐧᐸᐦᑌᐣ ᒦᓇ ᐁᐊᐧᑯ᙮ ᐁᐊᐧᑯ ᒦᓇ ᐊᐊᐧ ᓅᓯᓯᒼ ᑳ ᑲᑫᐧᒋᒥᐟ, ᐁᐊᐧᑯ ᒦᓇ ᐆᑕ, ᐁᐊᐧᑯ ᒦᓇ ᑳ ᐆᐦ ᑕᓯᐦᑕᒫᐣ᙮

ᐁ ᑮ ᐯ ᐋᐧᐸᐦᑕᒫᐣ ᐊᓂᐦᐃ᙮ ᐁ ᑮ ᐯ ᐋᐧᐸᐦᑕᒫᐣ, ᓂᑮ ᓂᑕᐤ ᑯᐢᑯᐋᐧᑕᐱᐣ ᓅᐦᑯᒼ ᐃᐧᔩᒣᐊᐧᑭ, ᐁ ᐃᐢᑫᐧᐃᐧᐨ ᑮ ᐃᑖᐤ ᓅᐦᑯᒼ, *Mrs. Little Sioux* ᑮ ᐃᑖᐤ᙮ ᐅᒫᒥᐦᑫᐧᐤ, ᐁ ᐋᑲᔮᓰᒧᕽ *Isabelle Eashappie* ᑮ ᐃᓯᔨᐦᑳᓱᐤ ᓅᐦᑯᒼ, ᑮ ᐹᐧᓰᒧᐤ᙮ ᑮ ᐹᐧᓰᒧᐊᐧᐠ ᓅᐦᑯᒪᐠ ᓃᓱ, ᓅᐦᑖᐃᐧᐩ ᐅᑳᐃᐧᔭ ᐁᑲᐧ ᐅᑳᐄᐧᓴ; ᑮ ᐹᐧᓰᒧᐊᐧᐠ ᓅᐦᑯᒪᐠ ᒫᑲ ᑮ ᓀᐦᐃᔭᐁᐧᐊᐧᐠ᙮

ᐄ, ᐁᑳᐧᓂ ᓂᓯᑯᐢ, ᐁ ᑮ ᐯᔭᑰᓴᓂᐃᐧᐟ ᓂᓯᑯᐢ ᐁᐊᐧᑯᓂ ᐆᐦᐃ ᐅᑖᓂᐢ~; ᐆᐦᐃ ᐅᑳᐃᐧᔭ ᐆᐦᐃ *Isabelle Eashappie* ᐊᐊᐧ ᓂᓯᑯᐢ᙮ ᐁᑲᐧ ᒫᓇ ᐁ ᑮ ᐊᐱᔮᕽ, ᐁ ᓂᑐᐦᑕᒫᕽ, ᐁ ᓂᑐᐦᑕᐋᐧᔮᐦᑯᐠ ᑖᓂᓯ ᐃᑌᐧᑖᐧᐃᐧ᙮ ᐁᐊᐧᑯ ᐊᓂᒪ ᑳ ᑲᑫᐧᒋᒥᐟ ᐊᐊᐧ ᓅᓯᓯᒼ ᐁᑯᓯ ᐁ ᑮ ᐃᐢᐸᔨᐠ; ᐁ ᑮ ᓃᒫᐦᐃᐦᐟ ᐊᐃᐧᔭᐠ ᑳ ᑭᑎᒫᑲᐢᑲᓯᐁᐧᐟ, ᑲᔮᐢ ᐁᐊᐧᑯ ᐃᓰᐦᒋᑫᐃᐧᐣ, ᓀᐦᐃᔭᐤ ᐃᓰᐦᒋᑫᐃᐧᐣ᙮

ᐁᑲᐧ ᒦᓇ ᐄᐧᐦᑲᐢᑲᐧ ᐁᑯᑕ ᒦᓇ ᑮ ᐊᐢᒋᑳᑌᐊᐧ᙮ ᐁ ᐊᐢᑕᒫᐦᐟ ᐊᐊᐧ ᐁᑳ ᑳ ᐱᒫᑎᓯᐟ ᐁ ᑕᐦᑯᓇᒨᐦᐃᐦᐟ᙮ ᐁ ᑮ ᑲ ᑭᑎᒫᑲᔨᐦᑎᕽ ᑲᔮᐢ, ᒥᑐᓂ ᐁ ᑮ ᑭᑎᒫᑲᔨᐦᑎᕽ ᐁ ᑮ ᓀᐦᐃᔭᐄᐧᐦᑖᐧᕽ ᑲᔮᐢ᙮ ᐊᓅᐦᐨ ᐁᑲᐧ ᐸᐦᑳᐣ ᑕ ᐊᑎ ᒪ ᒨᓂᔮᐄᐧᐦᑖᐧᕽ, ᒫᑲ, ᒫᑲ ᑐᓂ ᒨᐩ, ᓇᒨᔭ ᓂᑕᑎ ᐊᐢᐯᔨᐦᑌᐣ ᓂᔭ ᑕ ᑲᑫᐧ ᐁᐧᐱᓇᒥᕽ ᑭᓀᐦᐃᔭᐄᐧᐦᑖᐧᐃᐧᓂᓇᐤ᙮

ᓇᐊᐧᐟ ᑕᓵᑭᐦᑖᕽ ᐁᐊᐧᑯ, ᓇᒨᔭ ᐄᐧᐦᑳᐨ ᒥᓴᐋᐧᐨ ᑭᑲ ᒨᓂᔮᐃᐧᓈᓇᐤ᙮ ᒥᓴᑳᒣ ᐃᐢᑯ ᑕ ᐱᒫᑎᓯᔭᕽ ᑲ ᓀᐦᐃᔮᐃᐧᓈᓇᐤ; ᐁᑯᓯ ᒫᓇ ᑮ ᐃᑖᐧᓂᐤ᙮

ᓂᓵᑭᐦᑖᐣ ᓀᐦᐃᔮᐃᐧᐃᐧᐣ, ᓂᓵᑭᐦᑖᐣ, ᓂᓵᑭᐦᑖᐣ ᐄᐧᐦᑲᐢᑲᐧ, ᒧᐢᑐᓱ ᐄᐧᐦᑲᐢᑲᐧ ᓂᓵᑭᐦᑖᐣ᙮ ᐁᑯᑐᐊᐧ, ᐁᑯᑐᐊᐧ ᐁ ᑮ ᐯ ᐅᐦᒋ ᐅᐦᐱᑮᔭᕽ, ᐁ ᑮ ᐯ ᐅᐦᒋ ᐅᐦᐱᑮᔭᕽ ᑲᔮᐢ, ᐁᑲᐧ ~, ᑳ ᒦᔮᐦᑲᓯᑫᕽ ᐁᑲᐧ ᑳ ᒪᐃᐧᒧᐢᒋᑫᕽ, ᑮ ᒪᐃᐧᒧᐢᒋᑫᐊᐧᐠ ᑲᔮᐢ ᑫᐦᑌ ᐊᔭᐠ᙮

ᐊᐦᐴ ᒦᑭᐋᐧᐦᐸ, ᑮ ᒪᓯᓇᐦᐃᑳᑌᐊᐧ, ᐁᑯᑕ ~, ᑳ ᑖᐦ ᑕᐦᑐ ᐊᔭᒥᐦᐁ ᑮᓯᑳᐤ ᐁ ᑮ ᒪᐃᐧᒧᐢᒋᑫᕽ, ᐁ ᓂᑐᑕᒫᑫᐢᑕᒫᐦᒋᐠ ᐊᐋᐧᓯᓴᐠ ᐱᒫᑎᓯᐃᐧᐣ, ᒥᔮᐧᔮᐃᐧᐣ᙮ ᑖᐯᐧ ᑮ ᐊᑎᒪᒥᔮᐧᔭᐊᐧᐠ, ᓇᒨᐩ ᐄᐧᐦᑳᐨ ᐆᒪ ᑳ ᐃᓯ ᐊᔮᕽ ᐊᓄᐦᐨ ᑳ ᐃᑌᐧᕽ 'ᑭᑑᒪᓂᒎᓯᒥᐣ' ᑳ ᐃᑌᐧᕽ, *cancer* ᑳ ᐃᑕᐦᑭᐠ, ᓇᒨᐩ ᐄᐧᐦᑳᐨ ᑮ ᐅᐦᒋ ᐯ ᐊᔮᓂᐃᐧᐤ᙮

ᒪᑖᐧᐣ ᒌ ᓀᐦᐃᔭᐄᐧᐦᑖᐧᐃᐧᐣ ᐁ ᑮ ᐱᒥᑎᓴᐦᐊᒥᕽ ᑰᐦ ᑮ~ ᐁᑳ ᐁᑯᑐᐃᐧ ᑰᐦ ᑮ ᑲᐦᒋᑎᓇᒥᕽ᙮ ᓂᑮ ᒥᓂᐦᑳᐧᓈᐣ ᓂᐱᐩ, ᑭᒥᐊᐧᓈᐳᐩ ᓂᑮ ᒥᓂᐦᑳᐧᓈᐣ, ᐊᔭ ᐊᐊᐧ ᑳ ᐃᑎᐦᐟ ᐊᐊᐧ ᐊᔭ, ᐊᔭ ᑰᓇ ᓂᑮ ᒥᓂᐦᑳᐧᑖᓈᐣ ᐁᑲᐧ ᒦᓇ ᒥᐢᑲᐧᒥᐩ ᒦᓇ ᓂᑮ ᒥᓂᐦᑳᐧᑖᓈᐣ᙮ ᑭᒥᐊᐧᓈᐳᐩ ᐋᐧᐢᑳᐦᐃᑲᓂᕽ ᐁᑯᑕ ᓂᑮ ᐅᐦᒋ ᒥᓂᐦᑳᐧᓈᐣ᙮

ᐊᐩ, ᐁᑲᒫ ᐲᐦᒑᔨᕽ ᑳᐦ ᐊᐧᔭᐄᐧᕽ, ᐊᓄᐦᐨ ᐁᑲᐧ ᐲᐦᒑᔨᕽ ᐊᐧᔭᐄᐧᓈᓂᐃᐧᐤ᙮ ᑭᑯᐢᑌᓈᓇᐤ ᐁᑲᐧ ᐊᓂᒪ ᓂᐱᐩ ᑕᒥᓂᐦᑫᐧᔭᕽ᙮ ᐁᑲᐧ ᒦᓇ ᐊᐊᐧ ᑰᓇ, ᓇᒨᐩ ᑭᑖᐸᒋᐦᐋᐧᓇᐤ᙮ ᒨᓂᔮᐤ ᑲᐦᑭᔭᐤ ᑮᑳᐧᐩ ᐁ ᐊᐢᑖᐟ ᒪᐢᑭᐦᑭᐩ, ᐁ ᐱᒫᐸᐦᑌᐠ ᑳ ᑎᐱᐢᑳᐠ, ᓇᒨᔭ ᒥᔪᓯᐤ ᐊᓇ ᑰᓇ ᑭᑕᒥᓂᐦᑳᐧᑎᐦᐟ ᑭᑲ ᐋᐦᑯᓰᐢᑳᑯᐣ ~ ᓂᑯᐢᑖᐤ ᐊᓇ ᓃᐢᑕ ᑰᓇ; ᐁ ᑮ ᒥᓂᐦᑫᐧᔮᐣ ᒫᓇ ᑲᔮᐢ᙮ ᐊᐦᐴ ᐊᓄᐦᐨ ᐋᐧᐳᓴᐧᐠ ᓂᑯᐢᑖᐊᐧᐠ; ᐁᑯᓂᐠ ᒦᓇ, « ᑳᔭ ᒧᐃᐧᐦᑯᐠ; ᐊᐩ ᐊᐢᑖᐊᐧᐠ ᑮᑳᐧᐩ ᒨᓂᔮᐊᐧᐠ᙮ ᒨᔭ ᐁ ᒥᔪᓯᐟ ᐊᓇ ᐋᐧᐳᐢ ᑕ ᒧᐃᐧᐦᐟ᙮ » ᓂᓴᑭᒥᑲᐧᐠ, ᓇᒨᐩ ᓂᑲᐢᑭᐦᑖᐣ ᐋᐧᐳᐢ ᑎᑕ ᒧᐊᐧᐠ ~ ᐋᐧ, ᐁ ᑖᐯᐧᒋᐠ ᒫᑲ᙮ ᐊᐢᑖᐊᐧᐠ ᐊᔨᐢ ᐆᒪ ᒨᓂᔮᐊᐧᐠ *spray*᙮

ᐊᓄᐦᐨ ᑳ ᑮᓯᑳᐠ ᐁᐊᐧᑯ ᐊᓂᒪ ᐁ ᐋᐧᒋᒧᐢᑕᐊᐧᐠ ᓅᓯᓯᒼ ᐊᐊᐧ ᐁ ᐯ ᑲᑫᐧᒋᒥᐟ ᑮᑳᐧᐩ ᓀᐦᐃᔭᐄᐧᐦᑖᐧᐃᐧᐣ ᑲᔮᐢ᙮ ᑮ ᐯ ᒥᔮᐧᓯᐣ, ᑮ ᐯ ᒥᔪ ᐄᐧᒉᐦᑐᐊᐧᐠ ᐊᔨᓯᔨᓂᐊᐧᐠ, ᓇᒨᐩ ᐄᐧᐦᑳᐨ ᐅᐦᒋ ᐯ ᓂᓯᐊᐧᓈᒋᐦᐃᑐᐊᐧᐠ, ᑮ ᐯ ᒥᔪ ᐄᐧᒉᐦᑐᐊᐧᐠ, ᑮ ᓂᐦᑏᐦᑳᑎᑐᐊᐧᐠ ᐱᔩᐦᑐᑫᐧᐦᑭ, ᐁ ᐊᓴᐦᑐᕽ᙮ ᐊᓄᐦᐨ ᐁᑲᐧ ᑭᑯᐢᑌᓈᓇᐤ ᐁᑯᓯ ᑕ ᐃᑑᑕᒪᕽ, ᑭᑯᐢᑌᓈᓇᐤ ᐊᐃᐧᔭᐠ, « ᐄ, ᑮᑳᐧᐩ ᐊᐊᐧ ᓂᑲ ᐱᐢᒋ ᐊᓴᒥᐠ, » ᐁᑯᓯ ᐊᓄᐦᐨ ᑭᑎᑌᔨᐦᑌᓈᓇᐤ᙮ ᑲᔮᐢ ᓇᒪ ᑮᑳᐧᐩ ᐁᐊᐧᑯ᙮ ᑮᓂᐦᑏᐦᑳᓂᐃᐧᐤ ᐊᐦᐴ ᑳᐦᑫᐊᐧᐠ ᐁᑯᑕ ᐁ ᑮᓯᓴᒥᕽ, ᐁ ᒦᒋᕽ, ᐃᔨᓂᑐ ᐸᐦᑫᐧᓯᑲᐣ, ᐱᒥᐩ

ᐁ ᐊᐢᐸᐦᒋᑫᕽ, ᑲᔮᐢ ᐁᐘᑯ᙮ ᑭᔪᑳᑐᐏᐣ ᐁᐘᑯ, ᐁ ᑮ ᐃᓯ ᓇᓈᐢ~, ᐁ ᓴᑲᐦᐱᑕᐢᑎᒣᐧᕽ, ᐁ ᒧᐢᒋ ᐆᑖᐹᓯᕽ᙮ ᐊᓄᐦᐨ ᐁᑲᐧ ᑮᑲᐧᐩ ᐁᑎᑫᐧ ᑳ ᐚᐸᒋᐦᑖᔮᕽ, ᒥᐢᒋᑯᐘᒋᐢ ᑭᐸᐹᒧᐦᑕᐦᐃᑯᓈᓇᐤ ᐚᐦ ᐚᐦᔮᐤ ᐁ ᐃᑐᐦᑕᐦᐃᑯᔮᕽ᙮ ᐁᐘᑯᓂ ᐆᐦᐃ ᑳ ᐃᑕᒫᐣ, ᓴᐦᑫᐢ ᐊᐘ ᑳ ᐃᑕᐠ, ᐚᐦ ᐚᐦᔮᐤ ᐁ ᐃᑐᐦᑕᐦᐃᑯᔮᕽ᙮ ᐊᓄᐦᐨ ᐁᑲᐧ ᒦᓇ ᐁᐘᑯᓂᐠ ᒥᓴᑎᒪᐧᐠ ᒨᐩ ᐚᐸᑎᓯᐘᐠ᙮ ᐁᐘᑯ ᒦᓇ ᐁ ᑭᐢᑫᔨᐦᑕᒫᐣ᙮ ᐸᐦᑳᐣ, ᐊᓄᐦᐨ ᐆᒪ ᑖᓂᑕᐦᑖᐧᐤ ᐊᐢᑭᐩ ᐊᐢᐱᐣ᙮

[ᐊᒋᔭᐤ ᑳ ᓇᑭᐱᑕᒥᕽ]

ᐁᑲᐧ ᒦᓇ ᐯᔭᑲᐧᔭᐠ ᒦᓇ, ᐯᔭᑲᐧᔭᐠ ᒦᓇ ᒨᔭ ᓂᑖᒋᒧᐣ ᒫᑲ ᓂᐑ ᐑᐦᑌᐣ; ᐁᐘᑯ ᐆᒪ ᐊᔨᓯᔨᓂᐤ ᑲᔮᐢ, ᑲᔮᐢ ᑳ ᐸᓈᑎᓯᐟ ᐊᔨᓯᔨᓂᐤ ᓀᐓ ᑮᓯᑳᐤ ᑮ ᑭᔪᑲᐚᐤ ᐁ ᓂᑕᐤ ᐊᐢᑕᒫᐦᐟ ᒋᐢᑌᒫᓴ, ᐁ ᓂᑕᐤ ᐑᒋ ᐲᐦᑖᐧᒥᐦᐟ, ᐁᑯᑌ ᐁ ᓂᑕᐏ ᒪᐑᐦᑳᑎᐦᐟ᙮ ᐁᑯᓯ ᒦᓇ ᑮ ᐃᑑᒋᑳᑌᐤ᙮ ᓇᒨᔭ, ᓇᒨᔭ ᑲᒫᐟ ᒦᓇ ᒣᐢᑲᓈᕽ ᐅᐦᒋ ᐱᒥᑖᐹᓯᐘᐠ ᐊᔨᐢ ᒥᓴᑎᒪᐧᐠ ᑮ ᐚᐸᑎᓯᐘᐠ ᐁᑯᑕ, ᐁ ᑕᐢᑲᒥᑖᐹᓯᕽ ᐁ ᓂᑕᐤ ᓇᐦᐊᐢᑖᕽ ᐆᒪ ᒥᔭᐤ᙮ ᓀᐓ ᑎᐱᐢᑳᐤ ᑮ ᑭᔪᑲᐚᐤ ᐱᑯ ᐊᓇ ᐊᐏᔭᐠ ᐅᐚᐦᑯᒫᑲᓇ ᐁ ᓂᑕᐏ ᐊᐦᐃᒥᐦᐟ ᒋᐢᑌᒫᓴ, ᐁ ᓂᑕᐤ ᐲᐦᑖᐧᐦᐃᐦᐟ, ᐁ ᑳᑮᓯᒧᑐᑖᐦᐟ ᑫᐧᔭᐢᐠ ᑕ ᐃᓯ ᓯᐯᐧᐦᑌᐟ᙮

ᐁᑲᐧ « ᐁᑳᐩ ᒥᑐᓂ ᒥᐢᑕᐦᐃ ᒫᑐᐠ ᑳ ᓇᑲᑎᑯᔦᐠ ᐊᐏᔭᐠ, » ᑮ ᐃᑖᐧᓂᐤ ᒦᓇ ᒫᓇ᙮ ᓀᐓ ᑎᐱᐢᑳᐤ, ᐁᐘᑯ ~ ᐁᑯᑕ ᐁ ᒪᐑᐦᑳᑎᐦᐟ ᐊᔨᓯᔨᓂᐤ, ᐅᓵᒼ ᒥᐢᑕᐦᐃ ᑳ ᒪᐑᐦᑳᑕᐟ ᓇᑭᐢᑳᐠ ᐁᓴ ᐊᓂᐦᐃ᙮ ᐊᐑᓂᐘ ᑳ ᐑ ᑲᓇᐌᔨᒥᑯᐟ, « ᐊᐦᐋᐤ, ᓅᐦᑕᒋᐌ, ᑮᐌ, ᑫᔮᐱ- ᑭᒪᑌᐧ ᒪᐑᐦᑳᑎᑲᐏᐣ᙮ » « ᑲᑳᐧᑕᑭᐦᐚᐘᐠ, » ᐃᑖᐧᓂᐤ ᒫᓇ ᑭᓀᐧᐢ ᒥᐢᑕᐦᐃ ᑳ ᒫᑐᐟ ᐊᔨᓯᔨᓂᐤ᙮ ᒫᑲ ᐊᔨᐢ ᐋᔨᒪᐣ, ᐋᔨᒪᐣ ᐊᔨᓯᔨᓂᐤ ᑳ ᐘᓂᐦᐃᐦᐟ, ᐅᐦᒋᑕᐤ ᐱᑯ ᑎᑕᒫᑐᕽ᙮ ᐅᐦᒋᑕᐤ ᐋᔨᒪᐣ ᒫᑲ ᐁᐘᑯ ᐊᓂᒪ ᑲᔮᐢ ᐲᑭᐢᑫᐧᐏᐣ᙮ « ᓀᐓ ᑎᐱᐢᑳᐤ ᐱᑯ ᑭᑕ ᒪᐑᐦᑳᑎᐦᐟ ᐊᔨᓯᔨᓂᐤ᙮ » ᐁᑯᓯ ᒦᓇ ᒫᓇ ᑮ ᐃᑌᐧᐘᐠ ᐊᔨᓯᔨᓂᐘᐠ ᑲᔮᐢ᙮ ᐁᐘᑯ ᒦᓇ ᒫᓇ ᐁ ᑮ ᐯᐦᑕᒫᐣ᙮

ᐁᑯᓂ ᐆᐦᐃ ᑳ ᐯᐦᑕᒫᐣ ᓇᒨᔭ ᐁ ᑭᔮᐢᑭᔮᐣ, ᐁ ᑮ ᐯᐦᑕᐊᐧᑭᐠ ᑫᐦᑌ ᐊᔭᐠ ᒥᑐᓂ ᓂᑮ ᓂᑐᐦᑕᐋᐧᐊᐧᐠ᙮ ᐁᐊᐧᑯ ᐊᓂᒪ ᑳ ᐃᑕᒫᐣ, ᓂᓀᐦᐃᔭᐋᐧᑎᓯᐣ, ᓂᓀᐦᐃᔭᐋᐧᑎᓯᐣ ᒥᑐᓂ, ᒥᑐᓂ ᓂᒥᒋᒥᓀᐣ ᓀᐦᐃᔭᐋᐧᑎᓯᐃᐧᐣ ᐊᔨᐢ ᐁᑯᓯ ᓂᑮ ᐯ ᐃᓯ ᐅᐦᐱᑭᐣ, ᓂᑫᐦᑌ ᐊᔨᒪᐠ ᐁᑯᓯ ᓂᑮ ᐯ~᙮

ᑳ ᑮ ᐃᐧᔫᐦᑖᐃᐧᔮᐣ ᑮ ᓂᐹᑫᐧᓯᒧᐃᐧᓂᐦᑫᐤ, ᐁᑲᐧ ᑳ ᑮ ᐃᐧᔫᐦᑯᒥᔮᐣ ᐁᑯᓂᐠ ᑮ ᒪᐃᐧᒧᐢᒋᑫᐊᐧᐠ ᐆᑌ ᐅᐦᒋ *Moose Mountain* ᑭᓭᔨᓂᐤ ᑮ ᐊᔮᐤ᙮ ᐁᑯᑌ, ᐁᑯᑌ ᓅᐦᑯᒼ ᐄᐧᐢᑕᐋᐧᐤ ᒦᑭᐋᐧᐦᐸ ᑮ ᐅᐦᑎᓇᒪᐧᐠ ᐁᑯᑕ ᐁ ᒪᐃᐧᒧᐢᒋᑫᒋᐠ᙮ ᐊᐦᐴ ᓃᐢᑕ ᓰᓰᑲᐧᐣ ᑳᐦ ᐊᔮᐊᐧᐠ; ᒪᐢᑭᒧᒋᐢ ᓂᑮ ᐊᔮᐣ, ᓂᓯᑯᐢ ᒦᓇ ᑮ ᐊᐩ~, ᐁ ᐲᐦᑐᑫᔮᕽ᙮ ᓇᑲᒧᓇ ᐊᓂᐦᐃ, ᐊᐦᐴ ᑫᔮᐱᐨ ᑫᐢᑫᔨᐦᑕᒫᐣ, ᒪᐃᐧᒧᐢᒋᑫᐊᐧᑖᒧᓇ ᐃᓯᔨᐦᑳᑌᐊᐧ᙮ ᐁᑯᑌ ᐁ ᑮ ᐊᔮᐟ ᑭᓭᔨᓂᐤ ᐆᑌ *Moose Mountain* ᐊᓇ ᑭᓭᔨᓂᐤ ᐁ ᑮ ᑭᐢᑭᓇᐧᐦᐊᒪᑫᐟ᙮ ᒪᒑᐯᐢ ᑮ ᐃᓯᔨᐦᑳᓱᐤ ᓂᒧᓲᒥᓈᐣ, ᐁᐊᐧᑯ ᐊᓇ ᑫᔮᐱᐨ, ᑫᔮᐱᐨ ᒫᓇ ᓂᑭᐢᑭᓯᐣ ᐊᓇ ᓂᒧᓲᒼ ᒪᒑᐯᐢ ᑳ ᑮ ᐃᑎᐦᐟ, ᒦᑭᐋᐧᐦᐸ ᐁ ᑮ ᐅᓰᐦᑖᐟ, ᐁ ᑮ ᒪᓯᓇᐦᐊᒨᐦᑫᐟ᙮ ᐁᑯᑐᐊᐧ ᓂᑮ ᐋᐦ ᐊᔮᓈᐣ ᐆᑕ᙮

ᐁᐊᐧᑯ ᐴᓂᐸᔨᐤ, ᐁᐊᐧᑯ ᐊᓂᒪ ᐃᓯ ᒪᐃᐧᒧᐢᒋᑫᐃᐧᐣ, ᒫᑲ ᐃᐧᔭ ᑫᔮᐱᐨ ᑳ ᓂᐹᑫᐧᓯᒧᕽ ᑫᔮᐱᐨ ᐃᐧᔭ ᐁᐊᐧᑯ, ᑫᔮᐱᐨ ᐋᐸᒋᐦᑖᓂᐃᐧᐤ ᐃᐧᔭ ᐁᐊᐧᑯ᙮ ᒫᑲ ᑲᔮᐢ ᒪᒑᐯᐢ ᐁᐊᐧᑯ, ᐁᐊᐧᑯ ᑳᑭᑫ ᑳ ᑮ~, ᑕᐦᑖᐧᐤ ᐊᔭᒥᐦᐁᐤ ᑮᓯᑳᐤ ᑳ ᑮ ᐊᐢᑖᒋᐠ ᑫᐦᑌ ᐊᔭᐠ ᐄᐧᐦᑯᐦᑫᐃᐧᐣ, ᓇᑲᒧᐃᐧᐣ, ᒪᐃᐧᒧᐢᒋᑫᐃᐧᐣ ᑮ ᐃᓯᔨᐦᑳᑌᐤ ᐁ ᓇᑲᒧᕽ᙮ ᐊᐦᐴ ᓂᔭᓈᐣ ᐊᐋᐧᓯᓴᐠ ᐆᑭ ᓂᑮ ᑭᐢᑫᔨᐦᑌᓈᐣ ᐊᓂᐦᐃ ᓇᑲᒧᓇ, ᒫᒑᐯᐢ ᐅᓇᑲᒧᓇ ᐆᑌ ᐅᐦᒋ ᐊᔨ ᐁᐊᐧᑯ ᐊᐊᐧ *Moose Mountain* ᐊᓇ ᑭᓭᔨᓂᐤ᙮ ᑲᐦᑭᔭᐤ ᐃᐧᔭ ᑭᐢᑫᔨᒣᐤ ᐊᓂᐦᐃ ᑳ ᑮ ᐃᓯᔨᐦᑳᓱᐟ ᓂᒧᓲᒥᓈᐣ ᒫᒑᐯᐢ᙮ ᐁᐊᐧᑯ ᐊᓂᒪ ᓅᓯᓯᒼ ᐊᐊᐧ ᐁ ᐄᐧᐦᑕᒪᐊᐧᐠ, ᐁ ᑲᑫᐧᒋᒥᐟ ᑰᐦ ᐄᐧᐦᑕᒪᐊᐧᐠ ᐊᔨᐢᐠ ᓂᑮ ᐯ ᑭᐢᑫᔨᐦᑌᐣ ᐁᐊᐧᑯ ᒦᓇ ᐊᓂᒪ᙮ ᐊᓂᒪ ᒪᐃᐧᒧᐢᒋᑫᐃᐧᐣ ᑳ ᐃᑕᒥᕽ᙮

[ᐊᒋᔭᐤ ᑳ ᓇᑭᐱᑕᒥᕽ]

[4. ᓀᐦᐃᔭᐚᑎᓯᐏᐣ]

ᐦᐋᐤ, ᐯᔭᐠ ᑮᑿᐩ ᒦᓇ, ᐯᔭᐠ ᑮᑿᐩ ᒦᓇ ᓅᓯᓯᒼ ᐆᑌ ᐁ ᓅᐦᑌ ᐐᐦᑕᒪᐘᐠ, ᐁ ᓅᐦᑌ ᑭᐢᑫᔨᐦᑕᕽ᙮ ᐋᑕᐏᔭ ᐅᐦᒋᑕᐤ ᐋᒋᒧᐏᐣ, ᐅᐦᒋᑕᐤ ᐲᑭᐢᑵᐏᐣ, ᐅᐦᒋᑕᐤ ᑕ ᐲᑭᐢᒁᑕᒫᐣ ᐊᔨᐢᐠ ᓂᑲᑵᒋᒥᐠ᙮ ᑖᐱᐢᑰᐨ ~, ᓂᔭ ᓂᑲ ᐋᒋᒥᓲᐣ, ᓂᔭ ᓂᑲ ᐋᒋᒥᓲᐣ᙮

ᑖᐱᐢᑰᐨ ᐊᐘ ᓂᑳᐏᐩ *Catholic* ᐁ ᑮ ᐐᒉᐚᐟ ᐁᑿ ᒦᓇ ᐃᔨᓂᑐ ᐊᔨᓯᔨᓃᐏᐏᐣ ᑳ ᐊᔭ~, ᐊᔨ ᐆᒪ ᑖᐱᐢᑰᐨ ᑳ ᓂᐹᑵᓯᒧᕽ ᑮ ᑭᐦᒋ ᐃᑌᔨᐦᑕᒼ ᒫᑲ ᑮ ᐊᔭᒥᐦᐋᐤ ᓂᑳᐏᐩ᙮ ᐁᑯᓯ ᐁᑿ ᐊᐘ ᐊᔭᒥᐦᐁᐏᔨᓂᐤ ᑳ ᐅᐢᑯᑖᑳᐟ, ᐁᐘᑯ ᐆᒪ ᓂᑮ ᐐᐦᑕᒫᑯᓈᐣ᙮ ᑫᑕᐦᑕᐍ, ᓇᒨᔭ ᒪᓈᐦᑐᐘᐠ ᐊᔨᐢ ᒨᓂᔮᐘᐠ ᑳ ᐃᑎᐦᒋᐠ, ᑫᑕᐦᑕᐍ ᓈᓂᑕᐤ ᐃᓯ ᒪᒫᔨᓂᐠ~, ᓈᓂᑕᐤ ᐃᓯ ᐊᐏᔭᐠ ᓇᑲᑎᐢᑭ ᐊᐦᐴ ᑭᑭᓴᔨᓃᒼ ᐊᐍᑳ ᐸᐦᑳᐣ ᐊᐏᔭᐠ ᑭᐚᐦᑰᒫᑲᐣ, « ᐁᑳᐩ ᐋᐸᒋᐦᑖ ᐁ ᑮᐦᑳᓈᑿᕽ ᐊᔨᐏᐣ ᑕ ᑭᑭᐢᑲᒪᐣ, ᐁ ᑲᐢᑭᑌᐚᐠ, » ᓂᑮ ᐃᑎᑯᓈᐣ᙮ ᐦᐋᒼ, ᐁᐘᑯ ᐁᑯᑕ ᐁ ᑮ ᑭᐢᑭᓄᐦᐊᒫᑯᔮᕽ ᐊᐘ *Catholic* ᐊᐘ, *priest* ᑳ ᐃᑎᐦᐟ ᐊᔭᒥᐦᐁᐏᔨᓂᐤ ᑳ ᐃᑎᐦᐟ᙮ ᓂᑳᐏᐩ ᑮ ᓵᑭᐦᑖᐤ ᓴᐢᑲᒧᐏᐣ᙮ ᐁᑯᓯ ᑫᔮᐱᐨ ᐁᐘᑯ ᓃᐢᑕ ᓂᐐᒉᐦᑌᐣ, ᑫᔮᐱᐟ ᓂᓴᐢᑲᒧᐣ᙮ ᐯᔭᐠ ᐊᐢᑭᐩ ᐆᒪ ᓂᐸᑕᐦᐁᐣ ᒨᐩ ᓂᑎᑐᐦᑖᐣ ᐁᑯᑐᐘ᙮

ᐁᑯᓯ ᐁᑿ ᓅᐦᑖᐏᐩ ᑳ ᐘᓂᐦᐋᔮᕽ *nineteen -, 1932, seventh of January* ᓅᐦᑖᐏᐩ ᑳ ᐸᓈᑎᓯᐟ᙮ ᐦᐋ, ᑲᐦᑭᔭᐤ ᓂᑮ ᑲᐢᑭᑌᐏᔩᐦᐅᓈᐣ, ᓅᓯᓯᒪᐠ ᑲᐦᑭᔭᐤ, ᑲᐦᑭᔭᐤ ᐁ ᐃᐦᑕᓯᔮᕽ ᓂᑮ ᑲᐢᑭᑌᐏᔩᐦᐅᓈᐣ ᐁᑿ ᓀᐓ ᑎᐱᐢᑳᐤ ᓂᑳᐏᐩ ᓇᒨᔭ ᐅᐦᒋ ᔩᑲᐦᐅᐤ, ᓇᒨᐩ ᐅᐦᒋ ᒥᑯᐢᑳᒋᐦᑖᐤ ᐍᐢᑕᑲᔭ ᓀᐓ ᑎᐱᐢᑳᐤ, ᐁᐘᑯ ᓀᐦᐃᔭᐤ ᐃᔩᐦᒋᑫᐏᐣ᙮ ᐁ ᑮ ᐅᑎᓇᕽ ᐁᐘᑯ ᓀᐦᐃᔭᐤ ᐃᔩᐦᒋᑫᐏᐣ᙮ ᐹᑐᐢ ᐁ ᓀᐓ ᑎᐱᐢᑳᐠ ᑮ ᐯ ᔩᑲᐦᐅᐠ ᑫᐦᒋᐚᐠ ᐅᒫᐦᑯᓴ ᑮ ᐯ ᔩᑲᐦᐅᐠ᙮ ᑮ ᐯ ᒉᐢᑯᒦᐦᐃᐠ ᒦᓇ, ᐁ ᑮᐦᑳᓈᑿᓂᔨᐠ ᐸᑭᐘᔮᐣ ᑮ ᑲᐢᑭᒁᑕᒫᐠ, ᐁᑯᓯ, ᐁᑯᓯ ᓃᐢᑕ ᒦᓇ ᓂᑮ ᐊᑎ ᒥᔨᑲᐏᐣ ᑕ ᑭᑭᐢᑲᒫᐣ ᑮ ᒉᐢᑯᑕᔨᐏᓂᓴᐦᐃᐠ~, ᓃᐢᑕ ᒦᓇ ᓂᑮ ᒉᐢᑯᑕᔨᐏᓂᓵᐣ, ᐁ ᑮᐦᑳᓈᑿᐦᑭ ᓂᑮ ᑭᑭᐢᑫᐣ ᓅᐦᑖᐏᐩ ᑳ ᐘᓂᐦᐋᔮᕽ᙮

ᐦᐋᐤ, ᐊᓄᐦᐨ ᐁᑲᐧ, ᓂᑭᓭᔨᓃᒼ ᑳ ᐊᐧᓂᐦᐊᐠ, — ᑳ ᐊᐧᓂᐦᐊᐠ ᐁᑲᐧ ᑳ ᑮ ᐅᑭᓭᔨᓃᒥᔮᐣ ᐊᐊᐧ ᐊᓄᐦᐨ *John* ᐊᐊᐧ ᑳ ᐃᑕᐠ ᑳ ᑮ ᐸᓈᑎᓯᐟ *John Rockthunder* — ᑳ ᐊᐧᓂᐦᐋᐧᔮᕽ ᑲᐦᑭᔭᐤ ᓅᓯᓯᒪᐠ, ᑲᐦᑭᔭᐤ ᓂᑕᐋᐧᓯᒥᓴᐠ ᑲᐦᑭᔭᐤ ᑮ ᑲᐢᑭᑌᐃᐧᔫᐦᐅᐊᐧᐠ. ᑮ ᑲᐢᑭᑌᐃᐧᔫᐦᐅᐊᐧᐠ ᓀᐅᐧ ᑎᐸᐢᑳᐤ. ᐁᐊᐧᑯ ᐁᑎᑫᐧ ᐁ ᑮ ᐱᒥᑎᓴᐦᐅᒋᐠ ᐆᒪ ᑳ ᐃᓯ ᐊᔭᒥᐦᐋᐧᔮᐣ *Catholic* ᐊᔨᐢ ᐁᑯᑐᐊᐧᕽ ᓂᐄᐧᒉᐦᑌᐣ ᑫᔮᐱᐨ. ᓀᐦᐃᔮᐃᐧᐃᐧᐣ ᒦᓇ ᓂᐄᐧᒉᐦᑌᐣ ᓇᒨᔭ ᓂᐸᑭᑎᓀᐣ ᒦᓇ ᑳ ᒪᐃᐧᒧᐢᒋᑫᕽ ᐁ ᐃᑐᐦᑌᔮᐣ, ᓂᐄᐧᒉᐦᑌᐣ ᐁᑯᑐᐊᐧ. ᒫᑲ ᓂᑳᐃᐧᐩ, ᓂᑳᐃᐧᐩ ᐁᐊᐧᑯ ᑯᐦᒋ ᒥᒋᒥᓇᒫᐣ, ᓂᑳᐃᐧᐩ ᐁᑯᓯ ᐁ ᑮ ᐃᓯ ᐊᔭᒥᐦᐋᐟ. ᐁ ᑮ ᓵᑭᐦᑖᐟ ᓃᓯ ᓀᐦᐃᔮᐃᐧᐃᐧᐣ ᐁᑲᐧ ᐆᒪ ᒦᓇ, ᐆᒪ ᒦᓇ ᑳ ᐅᐢᑯᑖᑲᐟ ᑳ ᐃᓯ ᐊᔭᒥᐦᐋᕽ *Catholic* ᑳ ᐃᑌᐧᕽ, *Catholic priest* ᐁᑯᓂ ᑮ ᐄᐧᒉᐁᐧᐤ. ᐁᐊᐧᑯ ᐊᓂᒪ ᐁᑯᓯ ᒦᓇ ᐁ ᑮ ᐃᐢᐸᔨᐠ.

ᐁ ᑮ ᓀᐅᐧ ᑎᐸᐢᑳᐠ ᓅᐦᑖᐃᐧᐩ ᐁ ᑮ ᐊᐧᓂᐦᐋᐧᔮᕽ ᐁᐊᐧᑯ ᑳ ᐃᑕᒫᐣ, ᑮ ᐯ ᔫᑲᐦᐋᐧᐤ ᓂᑳᐃᐧᐩ, ᑮ ᐯ ᒣᐢᑯᑕᔨᐃᐧᓂᓴᐦᐋᐤ. ᓂᔭ ᒦᓇ ᓂᑮ ᐯ ᒣᐢᑯᑕᔨᐃᐧᓂᓴᐦᐃᑲᐃᐧᐣ ᑳ ᑮ ᐊᐧᓂᐦᐋᐧᔮᕽ ᓅᐦᑖᐃᐧᐩ. ᐁᑯᓯ ᓂᑮ ᓇᓈᐢᑯᒧᓈᐣ ᐁ ᐃᑑᑖᑲᐃᐧᔮᕽ. ᐁᑯᓯ ᐁᑲᐧ ᐁ ᔫᑲᐦᐅᐦᐟ ᓂᑳᐃᐧᐩ ᑲᐧᔭᐢᐠ ᐁᐧᐢᑕᑲᔭ, ᑮ ᐄᐧᑎᓯᐤ ᓂᑳᐃᐧᐩ. ᐁᑯᓯ ᓇᒨᔭ ᐄᐧ ᐅᐦᒋ ᑮᐢᑭᓴᒼ ᐁᐧᐢᑕᑲᔭ.

ᑲᔮᐢ ᑮ ᑮᐢᑭᓴᒪᐧᐠ; ᓀᐅᐧ, ᓀᐅᐧ ᒥᒋᐦᒌᐢ ᑮ ᑮᐢᑭᓴᒪᐧᐠ ᐆᑌ ᐁ ᒫᔨᐸᔨᐟ ᐊᔨᓯᔨᓂᐤ. ᐁᐊᐧᑯ ᒦᓇ ᐁ ᑭᐢᑫᔨᐦᑕᒫᐣ ᒫᓇ ᑲᔮᐢ. ᑲᔮᐢ ᐃᔫᐦᒋᑫᐃᐧᐣ ᐁᐊᐧᑯ, ᐁᑯᓯ ᐁ ᑮ ᑑᑕᐦᑭᐠ. ᒨᔭ ᒦᓇ ᑮ ᐁᐧᐱᓂᑳᑌᐊᐧ ᑯᓂᑕ, ᑯᓂᑕ ᐆᒪᑐᐊᐧ ᐊᔭ, ᐊᐢᑮᕽ ᐊᓂᐦᐃ ᒣᐢᑕᑲᔭ. ᑮ ᓴᐢᑲᐦᐃᑳᑌᐊᐧ, ᑮ ᑯᐢᒋᑳᑌᐊᐧ ᑭᓀᐱᐠ ᑲ ᑳᐦᒋᑎᓇᕽ ᑕ ᐊᐧᒋᐢᑕᐧᓂᐦᑫᐟ. « ᑳ ᐊᐧᒋᐢᑕᐧᓂᐦᑳᑫᐟ ᐁᓴ ᑭᓀᐱᐠ ᒣᐢᑕᑲᔭ ᑭᑌᐃᐧᐢᑎᑳᐧᓀᐢᑭᐣ, » ᑮ ᐃᑌᐧᐊᐧᐠ ᒫᓇ ᑲᔮᐢ. ᑲᔮᐢ ᑮᑲᐧᐩ ᓂᑮ ᑖᐯᐧᐦᑌᓈᐣ ᓀᐦᐃᔭᐤ ᐲᑭᐢᑫᐧᐃᐧᐣ.

ᐊᓄᐦᐨ ᐁᑲᐧ ᑭᑲ ᐴᓂᐸᔨᐤ ᐁᐊᐧᑯ, ᒫᑲ ᐅᐦᒋᑕᐤ ᓅᓯᓯᒼ ᐁ ᑲᑫᐧᒋᒥᐟ ᐅᐦᒋᑕᐤ ᑯᐦ ᐄᐧᐦᑕᒫᐣ ᐁ ᑭᐢᑫᔨᐦᑕᒫᐣ ᐁᐊᐧᑯ ᒦᓇ ᐊᓂᒪ ᑲᔮᐢ, ᐁᑯᓯ ~, ᑲᔮᐢ ᐆᐦᐃ ᐲᑭᐢᑫᐧᐃᐧᓇ ᐁ ᐯ ᑲᑫᐧᒋᒥᐟ ᐁᐊᐧᑯ ᐅᐦᒋ ᑯᐦ ᐄᐧᐦᑕᒪᐊᐧᐠ.

ᐁ ᑮ ᐯ ᐚᐸᐦᑕᒫᐣ ᐊᓂᐦᐃ, ᐁ ᑮ ᐯ ᓂᑐᐦᑕᒫᐣ ᒦᓇ ᐁᐘᑯ ᐅᐦᒋ ᑰᐦ ᐊᐩ ᐋᒋᒨᔮᐣ: ᑫ ᓃᑳᓂᐏᐠ ᓀᒪ ᑕ ᐊᑎ ᑲ ᑭᐢᑫᔨᐦᑕᐦᑭᐠ ᐆᑭ ᐊᐚᓯᓴᐠ᙮

ᐁᑿ ᒦᓇ ᑳ ᑮᓯᐢᑵᐏᐟ ᐃᐢᑵᓯᐢ ᑮ ᐯᔭᑯᑲᐦᐚᐤ᙮ ᓂᑮ ᐯᔭᑯᑳᐣ ᒥᑖᑕᐦᐟ ᑎᐱᐢᑳᐤ ᐁ ᑮᓯ ᐅᐦᐱᑮᔮᐣ᙮ ᐅᐦᐱᒣ ᓂᑮ ᐑᑭᐣ᙮ ᐋᑕᐏᔭ ᓅᒋᑵᓯᐤ ᐁᑯᑕ ᓂᑮ ᐑᑭᒫᐤ᙮ ᐁᑿ ᒫᑲ ᑮᑭᓴᐹ ᐑᐸᐨ ᐁ ᐘᔭᐑᔮᐣ ᓇᒨᔭ ᐁ ᓅᐦᑌ ᑲᓇᐚᐸᒪᐠ ᐊᔨᓯᔨᓂᐤ, ᐁᑯᓯ ᐁ ᑮ ᐃᑎᑲᐏᔮᐣ᙮ ᐁ ᐯᔭᑯᑫᔮᕽ ᐚᐢᑳᐦᐃᑲᓂᐢ ᓅᐦᑖᐏᐩ ᐁ ᑮ ᐅᓰᐦᑖᐟ ᐚᐢᑳᐦᐃᑲᓂᐢ᙮ ᓂᑮ ᐯᔭᑯᑳᐣ ᒥᑖᑕᐦᐟ ᑎᐱᐢᑳᐤ ᐁ ᑮᓯ ᐅᐦᐱᑮᔮᐣ᙮ ᐁᑯᓯ ᒦᓇ ᐁᐘᑯ ᐁ ᑮ ᐃᓰᐦᒋᑫᕽ᙮

ᐊᓅᐦᐨ ᐁᑿ ᐁᐘᑯ ᓂᔭᓈᐣ ᐆᑕ ᐆᒪ ᑳ ᐊᔮᔮᕽ ᐸᔨᐻᐟ's, ᐴᓂᐸᔨᐤ᙮ ᒫᑲ ᑯᑕᑭᕽ ᐊᐢᑮᐦᑲᓂᕽ ᐆᑌ ᒫᓇ ᓂᑭᔦᑳᐣ ᐆᑌ ᐆᒪ *Hobbema* [ᒪᐢᑿᒌᓯᕽ] ᑫᔮᐱᐨ ᐁᑯᓯ ᐃᓰᐦᒋᑫᐘᐠ᙮ ᒥᑖᑕᐦᐟ ᑎᐱᐢᑳᐤ ᑲᓇᐍᔨᒣᐘᐠ ᐅᐢᑭᓃᑭᐢᑵᐘ ᑳ ᑮᓯᐢᑵᐏᔨᐟ᙮ ᒥᑖᑕᐦᐟ ᑎᐱᐢᑳᐤ ᐁ ᐃᐢᐸᔨᐠ ᓰᑲᐦᐍᐘᐠ ᐁᑯᑕ ᐁᑿᔮᐨ ᐁ ᐯᐦᑭᐦᐋᒋᐠ, ᐁ ᐯᐦᑲᔨᐏᓂᓴᐦᐋᒋᐠ᙮ ᐁᐘᑯ ᒦᓇ ᐁ ᒥᔦᑑᑕᐦᑭᐠ, ᐁᑿ ᐁ ᒥᓯ ᐍᐱᓈᓱᒋᐠ, ᒥᐢᑕᐦᐃ ᑮᑿᐩ ᐁ ᒣᑭᒋᐠ, ᐁ ᓂᑐᒫᒋᐠ ᐊᔨᓯᔨᓂᐘ; ᐁ ᒦᒋᓱᕽ ᐃᐢᑵᓯᐢ ᑳᐦ ᑮᓯ ᐅᐦᐱᑭᒋ, ᐁ ᑮᓯᐢᑵᐏᐟ᙮ « ᐁ ᑮᓯ ᐅᐦᐱᑭᐟ » ᑮ ᐃᑙᓂᐤ ᒫᓇ ᑲᔮᐢ᙮ ᐁᐘᑯᓂ ~, ᑫᔮᐱᐨ ᐁᑯᓯ ᑑᑕᒷᐠ ᐁᑯᑌ, ᒥᑐᓂ ᒫᓇ ᓂᒌᐦᑫᔨᐦᑌᐣ, ᒥᑐᓂ ᒫᓇ ᓂᒥᔽᔨᐦᑌᐣ ᐁᑯᑌ ᑳ ᐃᑐᐦᑌᔮᐣ᙮

ᑳ ᐯᔭᑯᑫᐟ ᐃᐢᑵᓯᐢ, ᐁ ᓇᓈᑕᐏᐦᐅᕽ; ᑭᓂᑕᐤ ᓇᓈᑕᐏᐦᐅᐣ ᓈᓂᑕᐤ ᑳ ᐃᑕᒪᐦᒋᐦᐅᔭᐣ ᑭᓯᓂᑯᓂᐠ, ᑮ ᓯᐦᑴᑕᒼ ᐊᓂᒪ ᐅ~, ᓯᐦᑯᐏᐣ ᐅᐦᒋ ᐁ ᓇᓈᑕᐏᐦᐃᐢᐠ ᑳ ᑮᓯᐢᑵᐏᐟ ᐊᓇ ᐅᐢᑭᓃᑭᐢᑵᐤ᙮ ᓂᒥᔨᑲᐏᐣ ᓰᑲᐦᐅᐣ, ᑫᔮᐱᐨ ᓂᑲᓇᐍᔨᐦᑌᐣ ᐊᓂᒪ ᓰᑲᐦᐅᐣ ᐁ ᑮ ᑮᓯ ᐅᐦᐱᑭᐟ ᐊᓇ ᓅᓯᓯᒼ, ᐁ ᒥᔨᑲᐏᔮᐣ ᐁᐘᑯ ᑕ ᑲᓇᐍᔨᐦᑕᒫᐣ᙮ ᑫᑕᐦᑕᐍ ᒫᓇ ᓂᓰᑲᐦᐚᑳᐣ ᐊᓂᒪ ᓰᑲᐦᐅᐣ᙮ ᐁ ᑮ ᑮᓯ ᐅᐦᐱᑭᐟ ᐊᓇ ᓅᓯᓯᒥᓈᐣ᙮

ᐁᑯᓯ ᑫᔮᐱᐨ ᐃᓰᐦᒋᑫᐘᐠ ᐆᑌ ᐅᐲᒪ [ᒪᐢᑿᒌᓯᕽ] ᑳ ᐃᑐᐦᑌᔮᐣ ᒫᓇ᙮ ᐁᑯᑌ ᐊᔨᐢ ᒫᓇ ᓂᑎᓯ ᐊᐩ ᑭᔦᑲᐚᐘᐠ ᓂᐚᐦᑰᒫᑲᓇᐠ ᐁᑯᑌ ᐁ ᒥᐦᒉᑎᒋᐠ᙮ *Rocky Mountain House* ᒦᓇ ᐁᑯᑌ ᒦᓇ ᒫᓇ ᓂᑎᑐᐦᑖᐣ,

ᐁᑯᑌ ᒦᓇ ᓂᐚᐦᑰᒫᑲᓇᐠ ᐁ ᐋᔮᒋᐠ᙮ ᐁ ᑮ ᐅᒥᓯᔮᐣ ᐁᑯᑌ ᐁ ᑮ ᐋᔮᐟ ᐁ ᐐᒋ~, ᐯᔭᑲᐧᐣ ᐁ ᐃᓯᔨᐦᑳᓱᔮᕽ ᐊᓇ ᓂᒥᐢ, ᐐᐢᑕ *Mary Louise* ᐁᑲᐧ ᓃᐢᑕ ᐁᑯᓯ ᐁ ᐃᓯᔨᐦᑳᓱᔮᐣ᙮ ᓂᑮ ᐘᓂᐦᐚᓈᐣ ᓃᓵᐧᐢᑭᐩ ᐊᐢᐱᐣ ᐊᓇ ᓂᒥᐢ᙮ ᐁᑯᑌ ᒦᓇ ᓂᑮ ᐃᑐᐦᑖᐣ᙮ ᐯᔭᑲᐧᐣ ᐁ ᓀᐦᐃ~, ᓀᐦᐃᔭᐤ ᑖᐱᐢᑰ-ᐃᓲᐦᒋᑫᐘᐠ, ᓀᐦᐃᔭᐤ ᐃᓲᐦᒋᑫᐘᐠ ᐊᓂᒪ ᑳ ᐚᑐᑕᒫᐣ ᐊᓅᐦ-, ᐅᔮᑲᓂᐢ ᐁ ᑮ ᓃᒫᐦᐚᒋᐠ ᓂᒥᓴ, ᐁ ᓃᒫᐟ ᓂᒥᐢ᙮ ᓂᑮ ᓂᑕᐏ ᐊᑕᒥᐢᑲᐚᐤ ᓂᒥᐢ ᐊᓇ᙮ ᓇᒨᔭ ᒦᓇ ᑌᐦᑕᐢᒋᑳᑌᔨᐤ ᐏᔭᐤ, ᒧᐢᒌᔨᕽ ᐆᑕ ᐁ ᐱᒥᓯᒥᐦᐟ᙮ ᓀᐦᐃᔭᐤ ᐃᓲᐦᒋᑫᐏᐣ ᐁᐘᑯ᙮ ᐁᑲᐧ ᐊᓅᐦ- ᑮᔭᓇᐤ ᑕᐦᑯᐦ- ᐱᒥᓯᐣ ᐊᐏᔭᐠ ᑳ ᐸᓈᑎᓯᐟ, ᒫᑲ ᐊᔨᐣ ᒨᓂᔮᐘᐠ ᐅᑎᓲᐦᒋᑫᐏᓂᐚᐤ ᐏᔭ ᐁᐘᑯ ᐁᑐᑵ ᑰᐦ ᐃᓲᐦᒋᑫᕽ᙮ ᐁᑯᓯ ᒦᓇ, ᐁᐘᑯ ᒦᓇ ᐊᓂᒪ ᑲᔮᐢ ᒦᓇ ᐁᐘᑯ ᐁᑯᓯ ᐁ ᑮ ᐯ ᐃᓯ ᑭᐢᑫᔨᐦᑕᒫᐣ᙮

ᐊᐏᔭᐠ ᑳ ᐸᓈᑎᓯᐟ ᓇᒨᔭ ᒥᑐᓂ ᒣᐢᑲᓈᕽ ᐅᐦᒋ ᐱᒧᐦᑎᒋᑳᑌᐤ ᒥᔭᐤ᙮ ᓇᒨᐩ ᐐᐦᑳ- ᓅᐦ ᐃᑖᐱᓈᐣ ᐊᐚᓯᓴᐠ, « ᐁᑳᐏᔭ ᐃᑖᐱᐠ, » ᐁ ᑮ ᐃᑎᑲᐏᔮᕽ ᒫᓇ, ᓇᒨᔭ ᓅᐦ ᐃᑖᐱᓈᐣ ᒫᑲ ᒫᓇ ᓂᑮ ᐯᐦᑌᐣ ᐁᑯᑐᐏ ᐁ ᐱᒥᑖᐸᐚᓯᒋᐠ ᒨᐩ ᑲᒑᐟ ᒣᐢᑲᓈᕽ, ᐯᔮᐦᑕᐠ ᐁ ᐱᒧᐦᑕᑖᒋᐠ ᐊᓂᒪ ᒥᔭᐤ, ᒫᑲ ᐁᑲᐧ ᐊᓅᐦ- ᐊᔨᐣ ᓴᐦᑫᓯᕽ ᐴᓯᐦᑖᐘᐠ᙮ ᒨᓂᔮᐘᐠ ᐁᑲᐧ ᐊᓅᐦ- ᐸᒥᓇᒪᐧᐠ ᐊᐏᔭᐠ ᐁᑳ ᑳ ᐱᒫᑎᓯᐟ᙮

ᐁᐘᑯ ᒦᓇ ᐊᓂᒪ ᐁ ᐋᒋᒧᐢᑕᐘᐠ ᐊᐘ ᓅᓯᓯᑦ ᐊᔨᐣ ᓂᑲᑵᒋᒥᐠ ᑕ ᐋᒋᒧᐢᑕᐘᐠ, ᐱᑯ ᑎᑕ ᐋᒋᒧᐢᑕᐘᐠ, ᓅᐦᑌ ᑭᐢᑫᔨᐦᑕᑦ ᐁᐘᑯ ᐆᒪ ᐋᒋᒧᐏᓇ ᐆᐦᐃ ᑲᔮᐢ, ᑲᔮᐢ ᐋᒋᒧᐏᓇ ᑰᐦ ᐊᐩ ᐋᒋᒧᐢᑕᐘᐠ ᐁᑯᓯ ᑳ ᑮ ᐃᓯ ᑭᐢᑫᔨᐦᑕᒫᐣ᙮ « ᑲᑵ ᒥᔪ ᐚᐦᑰᐦᑐᐠ, ᑲᑵ ᒥᔪ ᐐᒉᐦᑐᐠ, » ᐁ ᑮ ᐃᑎᑲᐏᔮᕽ ᒦᓇ ᒫᓇ᙮ « ᐁᑳᐏᔭ ᒫᔨ ᐐᒉᐦᑐᐠ, ᒥᔼᓯᐣ ᑕ ᒥᔪ ᐐᒉᐦᑐᔦᐠ᙮ » ᓂᑮ ᐯ ᒥᔪ ᐐᒉᐦᑐᓈᐣ᙮ ᒨᐩ ᐐᐦᑳ- ᓅᐦ ᐯ ᒫᔨ ᐐᒉᐦᑐᓈᐣ ᑲᔮᐢ ᓂᑮ ᓴᐍᔨᐦᑐᓈᐣ, ᑳᓂᑲᓈ ᑫᔮᐱ-ᐁᑯᓯ ᐃᐢᐸᔨᐠ, ᑳᓂᑲᓈ ᓴᐍᔨᐦᑐᕽ, ᐁᑲᐧᔨᑯᕽ ᐁ ᑲᑳᐧᑕᑭᐦᑖᔭᕽ ᐱᑯ ᑮᑲᐧᐩ ᐊᑎ ᐊᐩ ᐃᓯ ᐋᐦᑯᓯᐏᐣ ~, ᐁ ᐊᑎ ᐅᑎᐦᑕᒪᕽ ᒫᑲ ᐊᔨᐣ ᑭᑎᓯᒦᒋᓯᐏᓂᓇᐤ ᐁᐘᑯ ᑳ ᐃᑑᑖᑯᔭᕽ᙮ ᑲᔮᐢ ᐃᐢᑯᑌᐤ ᑭᑮ ᐊᓴᒥᑯᓇᐤ

ᐁᑲᐧ ᒦᓇ ᑭᑮ ᓂᐯᐦᐃᑯᓇᐤ ᐃᐢᑯᑌᐤ, ᒥᐦᑕ ᑭᑮ ᐴᓀᓈᓇᐤ ᐁ ᓂᐹᔭᕽ
ᑭᑮ ᐅᐦᑕᑖᐦᑌᓈᓇᐤ ᒥᐢᑎᑲᐧ ᐁ ᓂᐹᔭᕽ, ᑭᑮ ᒥᔪ ᑑᑖᑯᓈᓇᐤ᙮

ᐁᑲᐧ ᐊᓅᐦᐨ ᐆᒪ ᑳ ᐊᐢᑮᐃᐧᐠ, ᐊᓅᐦᐨ ᐆᒪ ᑳ ᐃᓯ ᑭᐢᑫᔨᐦᑕᒫᐣ
ᓇᓴᐢᑕᐤ ᐚᓯᑲᐣ ᐁ ᒥᔮᐦᑕᒪᕽ ᑳ ᑎᐱᐢᑳᐠ᙮ ᑮᑳᐧᐩ ᑫ ᒥᔪ ᑑᑖᑯᔭᕽ?
ᓇᓴᐢᑕᐤ ᐚᓯᑲᐣ ᓇᒪ ᑮᑲᐧᐩ ᐃᐢᑯᑌᐤ ᐁ ᒥᔮᐦᑕᒪᕽ, ᓇᒪ ᑮᑲᐧᐩ ᐃᐢᑯᑌᐤ
ᐁ ᐊᓴᒥᑯᔭᕽ᙮ ᐁᐊᐧᑯ ᐁ ᐊᓴᒥᑯᔭᕽ ᐚᓯᑲᐣ᙮ ᑳ ᐄᐧ ᑮᓯᑌᐳᔭᕽ
ᐋᓴᐩ ᐁ ᐲᒥᓇᒪᕽ ᐁᑯᑌ ᐁ ᐅᐦᒋ ᒦᒋᓱᔭᕽ ᐊᓅᐦᐨ ᐁᑲᐧ ᐁᑯᓯ ~, ᐁᑯᓯ
ᐁ ᐃᓯ ᒦᒋᓱᔭᕽ ᐊᓅᐦᐨ᙮ ᒫᑲ ᑳᔭᐢ ᐊᐧᔭᐄᐧᑎᒥᕽ ᐊᐦᐴ ᐁ ᑮ ᓇ ᓂᐦᑏᐦᑫᕽ,
ᐁ ᑮ ᐸᑳᐦᑖᑯᑫᕽ ᑲᔮᐢ ᐊᐧᔭᐄᐧᑎᒥᕽ ᐃᐢᑯᑌᐤ ᐁ ᐋᐸᒋᐦᑖᕽ, ᐁᑯᓯ
ᐁ ᐃᓯ ᒦᒋᓱᕽ᙮ ᐊᐧᔭᐄᐧᑎᒥᕽ ᒦᓇ ᐸᐦᑫᐧᓯᑲᐣ ᐁ ᑮᓯᓱᐦᐟ ᐁ ᒧᐋᐧᔭᕽ᙮
ᐁᑲᐧ ᐊᓅᐦᐨ ᐱᓯᓯᐠ ᑕ ᐊᑖᐁᐧᔭᕽ ᐸᐦᑫᐧᓯᑲᐣ᙮ ᐯᔭᐠ ᑮᓯᑳᐤ ᐊᐃᐧᔭᐠ
ᓂᔮᑖᒋ ᐸᐦᑫᐧᓯᑲᓇ ~, ᐋᑎᐦᐟ ᓂᐢᑐᒥᑕᓇᐤ ᐁ ᐅᑎᓈᒋᐠ ᐸᐦᑫᐧᓯᑲᓇ᙮
ᓇᒨᔭ ᐁ ᓇᐋᐧᒦᒋᐠ ᐃᐢᑫᐧᐊᐧᐠ ᐃᔮᔭᐤ ᐆᐦᐃ ᐊᑖᐁᐧᐃᐧᓇ᙮ ᑲᐦᑭᔭᐤ
ᑮᑲᐧᐩ ᑭᒫᔨ ᑑᑖᑯᓈᓇᐤ᙮ ᓇᒨᔭ ᑮᑲᐧᐩ ᐁ ᐊᑖᒧᑕᒫᐣ᙮ ᒫᑲ ᐁᑯᓯ ᐁᑲᐧ
ᐁ ᐊᑎ ᐃᓯ ᐊᔮᔭᕽ, ᐁ ᐊᑎ ᑭᑎᒫᑭᓯᔭᕽ, ᐁ ᐊᑎ ᒫᔨ ᑑᑖᑯᔭᕽ ᐁᐊᐧᑯ ᐆᒪ
ᐚᓯᑲᐣ ᑳ ᐃᑌᐧᕽ᙮ ᐁ ᑮ ᒥᔪᐢᑳᑯᔭᕽ ᐃᐢᑯᑌᐤ, ᐁᑲᐧ ᒦᓇ ᓂᐱᐩ, ᒥᐢᑲᐧᒥᐩ
ᐁ ᑮ ᒥᓂᐦᑳᐧᑖᔭᕽ, ᑰᓇ ᐁ ᑮ ᒥᓂᐦᑳᐧᑖᔭᕽ ᑭᑮ ᒥᔪ ᑑᑖᑯᓈᓇᐤ᙮

ᓂᐦᑎᐩ ᐁ ᑮ ᒥᓂᐦᑫᐧᒋᐠ ᑫᐦᑌᐊᔭᐠ, ᐊᐋᐧᓯᓴᐠ ᓂᐱᐩ; ᓇᒨᐩ ᐄᐧᐦᑳᐨ, ᓇᒨᐩ
ᐄᐧᐦᑳᐨ ᓂᐦᑎᐩ ᐅᐦᒋ ᒥᓂᐦᑫᐧᐊᐧᐠ ᐊᐋᐧᓯᓴᐠ ᐃᔮᔭᐤ ᓂᐱᐩ ᐁ ᑮ ᒥᓇᐦᐃᐦᒋᐠ᙮
ᐁᐊᐧᑯ ᒦᓇ ᐊᓂᒪ ᐊᓅᐦᐨ ᐁᑲᐧ, ᐊᓅᐦᐨ ᐁᑲᐧ ᐃᔮᔭᐤ ᓂᐦᑎᐩ, ᑳᐢᐱᓯᑲᐣ
ᑳ ᐋᐧᐸᒋᐦᑖᒋᐠ, ᑲᐦᑭᔭᐤ ᑮᑲᐧᐩ ᑭᑕᑎᒫᔨ ᑑᑖᑯᓈᓇᐤ᙮ ᓇᒪ ᑮᑲᐧᐩ
ᐁ ᐊᑖᒧᑕᒫᐣ ᒫᑲ ᐊᓅᐦᐨ ᐁᑲᐧ ᐁ ᐊᑎ ᐃᓯ ᑭᐢᑫᔨᐦᑕᒫᐣ ᐁᐊᐧᑯ ᐆᒪ
ᑰᐦ ᐊᐧ ᐄᐧᐦᑕᒪᐊᐧᐠ ᐊᐊᐧ ᓅᓯᓯᑦ ᐊᓅᐦᐨ ᑳ ᑮᓯᑳᐠ ᐁ ᐄᐧ ᐋᐧᑕ ᑲ ᑲᑫᐧ ᐄᐧᒋᐦᐊᐧᐠ
ᐆᒪ ᐅᓀᐦᐃᔭᐃᐧ ᐲᑭᐢᑫᐧᐃᐧᓇ᙮

ᐁᑲᐧ ᒦᓇ ᐁᑯᓯ ᐆᒪ ᐊᓅᐦᐨ ᑳ ᐋᑐᑕᒫᐣ, ᐊᐃᐧᔭᐠ ᑳ ᐸᓈᑎᓯᐟ,
ᐅᐋᐧᐦᑰᒫᑲᓇ ᑳ ᐊᐧᓂᐦᐋᐧᐟ, ᓀᐅᐧ ᑎᐱᐢᑳᐤ ᓇᒨᐩ ᐅᐦᒋ ᓰᑲᐦᐅᓈᓂᐃᐧᐤ᙮
ᑮ ᓂᑕᐤ~, ᑮ ᐅᑎᓇᑦ ᐊᐊᐧ ᐃᐢᑫᐧᐤ ᐊᔨ ᐆᒪ ᓰᑲᐦᐅᐣ ᐁᑲᐧ ᒦᓇ ᐸᑭᐊᐧᔮᐣ

ᒥᐢᑯᑖᑲᐩ, ᒪᐢᑭᓯᓇ, ᐊᓯᑲᓇᐠ, ᐲᐦᑕᐊᐧᔨᐃᐧᓂᓴ, ᐁ ᖨᐃᐧ ᑎᐱᐢᑳᐠ ᑮ ᓂᑕᐃᐧᔩᑲᐦᐁᐧᐤ ᐅᒑᐦᑯᓴ ᐁ ᑮ ᒫᔨᐸᔨᔨᐟ ᐁ ᒣᐢᑯᑕᔨᐃᐧᓂᓴᐦᐋᐧᐟ ᖨᐅᐧ ᑎᐱᐢᑳᐤ ᑳᐦ ᐃᐢᐸᔨᔨᐠ᙮ « ᓂᑕᐃᐧ ᐁᐧᐱᓇᒧᐦᑲᐣ ᐆᐦᐃ ᐊᐦᔩ ᒌ ᑭᑳᐦ ᓴᐢᑲᐦᐁᐧᐣ, » ᑮ ᐃᑌᐤ᙮ ᐁᑯᓯ ᖨᐅᐧ ᑎᐱᐢᑳᐤ ᐁ ᑮ ᑭᑎᒫᑭᓰᐦᐅᐧᐟ ᐊᓇ ᐃᐢᑫᐧᐤ ᐅᓈᐯᒪ ᐁ ᑮ ᐊᐧᓂᐦᐋᐧᐟ ᐊᐁᐧᑳ ᒌ ᐅᑕᐋᐧᓯᒥᓴ᙮

ᐁᐊᐧᑯ ᒦᓇ ᐊᐊᐧ ᓅᓯᓯᐨ ᐁ ᑲᑫᐧᒋᒥᐟ ᐁᐊᐧᑯ ᒦᓇ ᑯᐦ ᐄᐧᐦᑕᒫᐣ ᐆᑕ, ᑰᐦ ᒫᒥᐢᑰᑕᒫᐣ᙮

ᐊᐦᐋᐧᐨ, ᐁᐊᐧᑯᔨᑯᕽ ᐁᐊᐧᑯ᙮

6
ᐅᒉᐱᐦᑿ, ᒪᐢᑭᐦᑭᔭ ᐁᑿ ᒦᓂᓴ

JO: ᓃᐱᓯᔭ, ᓃᐱᓯᔭ, ᑖᓂᓯ ᐁᐘᑯᓂ ᐁ ᑮ ᐊᔨ ᐃᓯ ᐋᐸᒋᐦᑖᕽ?

MLR: ᓃᐱᓯᔭ, ᓃᐱᓯᔭ ᐁ ᑮ ᐃᑖᐸᒋᐦᑖᕽ ᑲᔮᐢ ᐁ ᑮ ᑭᐢᑫᔨᐦᑕᒫᐣ, ᓂᐱᓯᔭ ᐁ ᑮ ᑲᐘᐦᐊᐦᑭᐠ ᐊᔨᓯᔨᓂᐘᐠ ᐁ ᑮ ᐊᑖᐚᑫᒋᐠ; ᒋᒪᒉᓴ ᐁ ᑮ ᐅᓰᐦᒑᒋᐠ, ᓃᐱᓯᔭ᙮ ᐁ ᑮ ᐅᐦᒋ ᒦᒋᓰᐧᑕᐦᑭᐠ᙮ ᑲᔮᐢ ᐁᐘᑯ ᐱᒫᒋᐦᐅᐎᐣ᙮

••••

JO: ᐁᑿ ᒦᓇ ᒥᐦᑯᐯᒥᓇ? ᒥᐦᑯᐯᒪᐠ᙮

MLR: ᒥᐦᒁᐯᒥᓇ᙮

JO: ᐋᐦᐊ, ᒥᐦᒁᐯᒥᓇ᙮

MLR: ᒥᐦᒁᐯᒥᓇ, ᒥᐦᒁᐯᒥᓈᐦᑎᑿ᙮

ᑲᔮᐢ ᐊᔨᓯᔨᓂᐘᐠ ᒥᐦᒁᐯᒪᒁᐦᑎᑿ ᑮ ᐃᓯᔨᐦᒁᑕᒪᐧᐠ, ᐁ ᑮ ᐅᑎᓇᐦᑭᐠ ᐊᓂᒪ ᑳ ᒥᐦᒁᐠ ᐁ ᑮ ᑳᐢᑲᐦᐊᐦᑭᐠ ᐁᑿ ᐊᔨ ᐊᓂᒪ ᑳ ᐊᐢᑭᐦᑕᒁᐠ ᐊᓂᒪ ᐁᑿ ᐁ ᑮ ᑳᐢᑲᐦᐊᐦᑭᐠ᙮ ᐁᑿ

ᑳᐦ ᑳᐢᑲᐦᐊᐦᑳᐧᐃᐧ ᐁ ᑮ ᐊᔨ~ ᐊᔮᒋᐠ ᑖᐱᐢᑰᐨ ᓴᑯᓇᐦᑭᐠ ᐁ ᐹᓴᐦᑭᐠ᙮ ᐁᑯᓯ ᐁᑲᐧ ᑳᐦ ᐹᓴᐦᑳᐧᐃᐧ ᐁᑯᓯ ᐁᑲᐧ ᐁ ᓯᑯᓇᐦᑭᐠ ᒋᐢᑌᒫᐤ ᐁᑲᐧ ᓇᐸᑭᐸᐠ ᓂᑮ ᐃᓯᔨᐦᑳᑖᓈᐣ ᒋᐢᑌᒫᐤ ᐁ ᑮ ᐲᑭᓂᓵᐧᒋᐠ ᑫᐦᑌ ᐊᔭᐠ᙮ ᐁᑯᑕ ᐁᑲᐧ ᐁ ᑕᑯᓈᒋᐠ ᐊᐢᐹᐢᑯᓯᑲᐣ ᑮ ᐃᓯᔨᐦᑳᑌᐊᐧᐠ᙮ ᐁᐊᐧᑯ ᐊᐊᐧ ᓇᐸᐠ~, ᐁᐊᐧᑯ ᐊᓇ ᑳ ᑲᑫᐧᒋᒥᔮᐣ ᐊᓇ ᒥᐦᑳᐧᐯᒪᑳᐧᐦᑎᑲᐧ᙮ ᐁᑯᓯ ᐁ ᑮ~, ᐁᑯᓯ ᐊᓂᒪ ᐁ ᑮ ᐃᑖᐸᒋᐦᐋᒋᐠ ᑲᔮᐢ ᑭᓭᔨᓂᐊᐧᐠ, ᑫᐦᑌ ᐊᔭᐠ᙮

• • • •

JO: ᐋ, ᐊᐊᐧ ᓲᑳᐋᐧᐦᑎᐠ ᑳ ᐃᓯᔨᐦᑲᑕᒋᐠ ᐆᑭ ᐊᔨ, *the TH dialect Cree;* ᓰᓯᐹᐢᑳᐧᐦᑎᐠ *[sic]*᙮

MLR: ᓰᓯᐹᐢᑲᐧᑖᐧᐦᑎᐠ ᓂᑮ ᑭᐢᑫᔨᐦᑌᐣ ᒫᓇ ᑲᔮᐢ᙮ ᐁ ᑮ ᓂᑕᐃᐧ ᐋᐧᑭᒋᐠ ᑫᐦᑌ ᐊᔭᐠ ᐊᔨ ᐆᒪ ᐁ ᓂᑕᐃᐧ ᐅᓰᐦᑖᒋᐠ ᓰᐃᐧᓂᑲᐣ; ᓰᐃᐧᓂᑲᐣ ᐊᔨ ᓰᓯᐹᐢᑲᐧᑖᐧᐦᑎᐠ ᐁ ᐅᐦᒋᑲᐃᐧᐯᐦᐃᑫᒋᐠ ᐁᑲᐧ ᐁ ᒫᐊᐧᒋᐦᑖᒋᐠ ᑮᑭᓭᐹ ᐆᒪ ᓂᐱᐩ, ᓰᓯᐹᐢᑲᐧᑖᐧᐳᐩ ᑮ ᐃᓯᔨᐦᑲᑕᒪᐧᐠ ᒫᓇ, ᐁ ᑮ ᐅᓰᐦᑖᒋᐠ ᓰᐃᐧᓂᑲᐣ᙮ ᑲᔮᐢ ᓰᐃᐧᓂᑲᐣ ᐁ ᑮ~ .... ᐊᐧᐢᑲᐧᐩ, ᐊᐧᐢᑲᐧᐩ ᒫᓇ ᑮ ᐅᓰᐦᑖᐊᐧᐠ, ᐁᑯᑕ ᐁ ᐲᐦᒋ ᓰᑭᓇᐦᑭᐠ ᐁᐊᐧᑯ ᐆᒪ, ᓂᐱᐩ ᑳᐦ ᑮᓯ ᑮᓯᓴᐦᑳᐧᐃᐧ᙮ ᑖᐱᐢᑰᐨ, ᑖᐱᐢᑰᐨ ᓇᒥᓈᐢ ᐁ ᐅᓰᐦᑖᒋᐠ, ᐁᑯᓯ ᐁᑲᐧ ᐁ ᐊᑎ ᐊᐢᑖᒋᐠ, ᐁ ᐋᐦᑲᐧᑎᐦᑖᒋᐠ, ᐁ ᒫᐊᐧᒋᐦᑖᒋᐠ, ᐱᐳᐦᑭ ᐁᐊᐧᑯ ᐁ ᐄᐧ ᒦᒋᒋᐠ, ᐁ ᐄᐧ ᓰᐃᐧᐹᐧᑕᐦᑭᐠ᙮ ᐊᐁᐧᑳ ᒦᓇ ᓈᓂᑕᐤ ᑳ ᐃᑕᐦᑲᒥᑲᕽ ᑖᐱᐢᑰᐨ ᑳ ᒪᐃᐧᒧᐢᒋᑫᕽ, ᐁᑯᑕ ᐁ ᐃᑐᐦᑕᑖᒋᐠ, ᐁ ᐋᐧᐢᑳ ᐃᑎᓯᓇᒥᕽ ᐁᐊᐧᑯ ᐆᒪ ᐹᐦ ᐯᔮᐠ ᐁ ᐅᑎᓇᒥᕽ ᐁ ᒦᒋᕽ ᐁᐊᐧᑯ ᐆᒪ ᐁ ᑮ ᐅᓰᐦᑖᒋᐠ ᐊᓂᒪ ᑫᐦᑌ ᐊᔭᐠ ᐁᑲᐧ ᐊᓂᒪ ᑰᐦ ᐃᓯᔨᐦᑳᓱᒋᐠ ᐊᓂᑭ ᓰᓯᐹᐢᑲᐧᑖᐧᐦᑎᑲᐧᐠ᙮

• • • •

JO: ᐋ, ᑕᑲᐧᐦᐃᒥᓈᓈᐦᑎᑲᐧᐠ ᒫᑲ?

MLR: ᑕᑲᐧᐦᐃᒥᓈᓈᐦᑎᑲᐧᐠ; ᑕᑲᐧᐦᐃᒥᓈᓈᐦᑎᐠ ᑳ ᐃᑎᐦᐟ, ᑕᑲᐧᐦᐃᒥᓈᓇ ᐁᑯᑕ ᐁ ᑮ ᐅᐦᑎᓇᒥᕽ ᐁ ᒪᐃᐧᓱᕽ ᐁ ᑕᑲᐧᐦᐊᐦᑭᐠ ᓈᑐᑫᐊᐧᐠ

ᐊᓯᓃᕽ, ᑮ ᑲᐢᑭᑌᓯᐊᐧᐠ ᒫᓇ ᐊᓯᓂᔭᐠ ᐁᑯᑕ ᐁ ᑕᑲᐧᐦᐊᐦᑭᐠ [MLR ᐸᓯᒋᐦᒉᐦᐊᒫᐤ ᑖᐱᐢᑰᐨ ᐁ ᑕᑲᐧᐦᐃᒥᓄᐟ]᙮ ᐁᐊᐧᑯ ᐁᑲᐧ ᐁ ᒦᒋᒥᐦᑫᒋᐠ ᐱᐳᐦᑭ ᐁᑲᐧ ᐁ ᐄᐧᒦᒋᒋᐠ ᐊᓂᐦᐃ ᑕᑲᐧᐦᐃᒥᓈᓇ ᐁ ᑕᑯᓇᐦᑭᐠ, ᐁ ᐱᐦᑳᒋᐊᐧᓴᐦᑭᐠ ᓂᐱᐩ ᐁᑯᑕ ᐁ ᐊᐢᑖᒋᐠ, ᐁ ᐱᐦᑳᒋᐊᐧᐦᑌᑭ ᐆᐦᐃ ᑕᑲᐧᐦᐃᒥᓈᓇ᙮ ᓰᐃᐧᓂᑲᐣ, ᓰᐃᐧᓂᑲᐣ ᐁᑯᑕ ᑕᑯᓇᒪᐧᐠ ᓰᓯᐹᐢᑲᐧᐟ ᐊᓂᒪ ᑳ ᑮ ᐅᓰᐦᑖᒋᐠ, ᓯᑲᐧᑕᐦᐊᒪᐧᐠ ᐁᑯᑕ ᐁ ᑕᑯᓇᐦᑭᐠ᙮ ᐁᑯᓯ ᐁᑲᐧ ᐱᒥᐩ ᐁᑲᐧ ᐁᑯᑕ ᐁ ᑕᑯᓇᐦᑭᐠ ᐁᑲᐧ ᐁᑲᐧ ᐁ ᒦᒋᒋᐠ ᐁ ᑮ ᒥᔮᐧᓯᑭ ᐊᓂᐦᐃ ᑕᑲᐧᐦᐃᒥᓈᓇ᙮ ᐁᑯᓯ ᐁ ᑮ ᐃᑖᐸᒋᐦᐋᒋᐠ, ᐁ ᑮ ᐃᑖᐸᒋᐦᑖᒋᐠ ᑕᑲᐧᐦᐃᒥᓈᓇ᙮

JO: *Ah, were there any other ways they used that tree?*

MLR: ᑕᑲᐧᐦᐃᒥᓈᓈᐦᑎᐠ, ᑕᑲᐧᐦᐃᒥᓈᓈᐦᑎᐠ ᐁᑯᑕ ᒦᓇ ᐁ~, ᒪᐢᑭᐦᑭᐩ ᐊᓇ, ᒪᐢᑭᐦᑭᐩ ᐊᓇ ᑕᑲᐧᐦᐃᒥᓈᓈᐦᑎᐠ ᒫᑲ ᓄᒪ ᐅᒉᐱᕽ ᓄᒪ᙮ ᐅᒉᐱᕽ ᑫᐦᑌ ᐊᔭᐠ ᑲᔮᐢ ᑮ ᒪᒥᔭᐚᐧᑳᒌᐊᐧᐠ ᐁ ᐅᑎᓇᐦᑭᐠ ᒪᐢᑭᐦᑭᐩ ᒨᓇᐦᐃᑳᐦᑎᑲᐧ ᑮ ᐋᐸᒋᐦᑖᐊᐧᐠ ᐁ ᐅᑎᓇᐦᑭᐠ᙮ ᐃᑖᒥᕽ, ᐃᑖᒥᕽ ᐊᓇ ᐅᒉᐱᕽ, ᐊᓇ ᑕᑲᐧᐦᐃᒥᓈᓈᐦᑎᐠ, ᑭᐦᒋ ᒪᐢᑭᐦᑭᐩ ᐊᓂᒪ᙮ ᐊᐃᐧᔭᐠ ᐁ ᒥᓂᐦᑫᐧᐟ, ᒥᔦᐢᑳᑯᐤ ᐊᓂᒪ, ᒫᑲ ᓇᒨᔭ ᐁ ᐯᔭᑯ ᑕᑯᓇᒥᕽ ᑮᑲᐧᐩ ᐁ ᑕᑯᓇᒥᕽ ᒪᐢᑭᐦᑭᐩ, ᒨᔭ ᒫᑲ ᑫ ᐄᐧᐦᑕᒫᐣ ᑮᑳᐧᐩ᙮ ᐁᑯᓯ ᐁ ᑮ~᙮

• • • •

JO: ᐊᐧᐢᑲᐧᔮᐦᑎᑲᐧ ᒫᑲ?

MLR: ᐊᐧᐢᑲᐧᔮᐦᑎᑲᐧᐠ, ᑲᔮᐢ, ᐁᐊᐧᑯᓂ ~ ᐁᑯᓂ ᑮ ᐋᐸᒋᐦᑖᐊᐧᐠ ᑫᐦᑌ ᐊᔭᐠ᙮ ᒌᑲᐦᐃᑳᐦᑎᑲᐧ ᐁ ᐅᓰᐦᑖᒋᐠ, ᐁ ᒪᓈᒋᐠ, ᐁ ᐋᐦ ᐅᑎᓇᐦᑭᐠ ᐁᑯᑕ ᐁ ᐲᐦᑐᐦᑯᑕᐦᑭᐠ ᐁᑲᐧ ᐁ ᐹᓴᐦᑭᐠ᙮ ᒌᑲᐦᐃᑳᐦᑎᐠ ᐁ ᒪᐢᑲᐃᐧᓯᐟ ᐊᓇ ᐊᐧᐢᑲᐧᔮᐦᑎᐠ᙮ ᐊᐧᐢᑲᐧᔮᐦᑎᐠ ᐁᑯᑕ, ᐁᑯᓂ ᒌᑲᐦᐃᑳᐦᑎᑲᐧ ᐁ ᑮ ᐅᓰᐦᑖᒋᐠ, ᐊᐁᐧᑳ ᒦᓇ ᒌᐢᑕᐦᐃᑲᐣ, ᒌᐢᑕᐦᐃᑲᐣ ᐆᒪ ᑳ~, ᐁᐊᐧᑯ ᒦᓇ ᐊᓂᒪ ᐁ ᑮ~, ᐋ,

ᐁᑯᑕ ᐁ ᑮ ᑖᐱᐦᑎᑖᒋᐠ ᐊᓇ ᐊᐧᐢᑲᐧᔮᐦᑎᐠ ᐅᐦᒋ᙮ ᑮ ᑭᐦᒋ ᐋᐧᐸᑕᓇᐧ ᐊᓂᐦᐃ ᐄᐧᐢᑕᐋᐧᐤ ᑲᔮᐢ ᐁᐊᐧᑯ᙮

JO: ᐋᐦᐊ, ᑫᐧᔭᐢᐠ᙮

• • • •

JO: ᐋ, ᑳᑭᑫᐸᑲᐧ ᒫᑲ?

MLR: ᑳᑭᑫᐸᑲᐧ, ᑲᔮᐢ ᓂᑮ ᐯᐦᑌᐣ, ᓇᒨᔭ ᒉᑐᓂ ᐁᐊᐧᑯ ᓂᑭᐢᑫᔨᐦᑌᐣ᙮ ᑳᑭᑫᐸᑲᐧ ᑮ ᐃᑌᐧᐊᐧᐠ ᒉᑐᓂ ᒦᓇ, ᓈᓂᑕᐤ ᒦᓇ ᐁᐊᐧᑯ ᐁ ᑕᑯᓇᐦᑭᐠ᙮ ᐊᐃᐧᔭᐠ ~ ᓂᑮ ᐃᑖᐧᓈᐣ ᒫᓇ, ᐊᓅᐦᐨ ᐁᑲᐧ ᐊᔨ ᑳ ᐃᓯᔨᐦᑳᑕᒉᐠ, *cancer* ᑳ ᐃᑕᒥᕽ, ᑳ ᐋᐧᐸᐦᑕᒉᐠ *cancer* ᐆᒪ, ᐁᒋᑳᓂ ᐊᓂᒪ ᐁᑯᑐᐊᐧᕽ᙮ « ᐁ ᐅᒦᓂᒥᐟ » ᑮ ᐃᑖᐧᓂᐤ ᒫᓇ, « ᐁ ᐅᒦᓂᒥᐟ. » ᑖᐱᐢᑰᐨ, ᑖᐱᐢᑰᐨ ᐁᑳ ᑮ ᑮᐦᑫᐟ ᐊᔨᐢ, ᑭᑭᐢᑫᔨᐦᑌᐣ « ᐆᒪ ᐃᑕ ᑳ ᐲᑯᐸᔨᐟ, ᐁᑯᑕ ᐁ ᐊᑯᐱᓯᐟ, » ᑮ ᐃᑖᐧᓂᐤ ᒫᓇ, ᒫᑲ ᐁ ᑕᑯᓇᒥᕽ ᑮᑲᐧᐩ, « ᐁ ᒥᐍᐢᑳᑯᐟ, » ᑮ ᐃᑖᐧᓂᐤ ᒫᓇ᙮ ᑖᐱᐢᑰᐨ ᐁ ᓂᐸᐦᐃᐦᐟ ᐊᓇ ᐊᔭ ᒪᓂᒎᐢ ᐊᓇ, *cancer* ᑳ ᐃᑕᒉᐠ, ‘ᐆᒪ ᒪᓂᒎᓴ ᑳ ᒧᐃᐧᑯᐟ ᐊᐃᐧᔭᐠ᙮’ ᐁᑯᑕ ᐊᓇ ᑳᑭᑫᐸᐠ ᐁ ᑮ ᑕᑯᓂᑳᓯᐟ᙮

• • • •

JO: ᑳ ᒥᐦᒉᑖᐧᓂᐢᑫᐧᔮᐠ ᒫᑲ?

MLR: ᑳ ᒥᐦᒉᑖᐧᓂᐢᑫᐧᔮᐠ, ᐁᐦ, ᐱᑯ ᐃᓯ ᒦᓇ ᐁᐊᐧᑯ ᐊᓂᒪ ᐁ ᐃᑖᐸᑕᕽ ᑮ ᐃᑌᐧᐊᐧᐠ ᒫᓇ ᑫᐦᑌ ᐊᔭᐠ, ᐱᑯ ᐃᑕ ᒦᓇ ᐁᑲᐧ ᐊᓂᒪ ᒪᐢᑭᐦᑭᐩ ᐁ ᑕᑯᓂᑳᑌᐠ, ᓈᓂᑕᐤ ᐆᒪ ᑫ~, ᑖᐱᐢᑰᐨ ᑮᑲᐧᐩ ᒪᐢᑭᐦᑭᐩ ᑳ ᐅᓲᐦᑖᔭᐣ ᐁᑯᑕ ᑕᑯᓂᑳᑌᐤ, ᒨᐩ ᒫᑲ ᓈᓂᑕᐤ ᑕ ᑮ ᐃᑌᐧᔮᐣ, *you know*᙮ ᒥᑐᓂ ~, ᑌᐱᔮᕽ ᐁ ᑭᐢᑫᔨᐦᑕᒫᐣ ᐁ ᒥᐍᓯᐟ ᒦᓇ ᐁᐊᐧᑯ ᐊᓇ, ᐁᐊᐧᑯ ᐊᓇ ᑳ ᒥᐦᒉᑖᐧᓂᐢᑫᐧᔮᐠ᙮ ᓇᒨᐩ ᐄᐧᐦᑳᐨ-ᑳᐦ ᑮᓯ ᐊᑭᐦᑌᐣ ᐊᓂᐦᐃ ᑕ ᒨᓇᐦᐊᒪᐣ, ᑕ ᒨᓇᐦᐊᒪᐣ ᒥᑐᓂ ᐃᑖᒥᕽ ᑕ ᐃᓯ ᒨᓇᐦᐊᒪᐣ ᑕ ᐊᐧᔭᐄᐧᐦᑕᑖᔭᐣ ᐆᒪ ᑳ ᒥᐦᒉᑖᐧᓂᐢᑫᐧᔮᐠ

ᑕ ᐹᐦ ᐸᐃᐧᐦᑎᑖᔭᐣ, ᑕ ᐯᐦᑭᐦᑖᔭᐣ᙮ ᓇᒎᐩ ᐄᐧᐦᑳᐨ ᑳᐦ ᑮᓯ ᐊᑭᐦᑌᐣ ᐃᔨᑯᕽ *roots*, ᐃᔨᑯᕽ ᐁ ᓴᑳᐦᑲᐧᓃᐃᐧᑭ, ᒎᐩ ᑳᐦ ᑮᓯ ᐊᑭᐦᑌᐣ, ᐁᐊᐧᑯ ᐅᐦᒋ ᑰᐦ ᐃᓯᔨᐦᑳᑌᐠ ᑳ ᒥᐦᑫᑖᐧᓂᐢᑫᐧᔮᐠ᙮ ᒎᐩ ᑳᐦ ᑮᓯ ᐊᑭᐦᑌᐣ, ᒣᑐᓂ ᐱᑯ, ᑖᐱᐢᑰᐨ ᐆᐦᐃ ᑫᐢᑕᑲᔭ, ᑭᑭᐢᑫᔨᐦᑌᐣ? [JO: ᐋᐦᐊ᙮] ᐃᔨᑯᕽ *roots*᙮ ᐃᔨᑯᕽ, ᒎᐩ ᑳᐦ ᑮᓯ ᐊᑭᐦᑌᐣ ᐄᐧ ᑲᑫᐧ ᐊᑭᐦᑕᒪᐣ ᑳᐦ ᐹᐧᑕᐄᐧᐦᑖᐣ᙮ ᑮᐢᐱᐣ ᑲᑕᐊᐧ ᑕ ᒎᓇᐦᐊᒪᐣ, *you know*, ᐁᑳᐩ ᑕ ᐲᑯᐁᐧᐸᐦᐊᒪᐣ ᓰᐢᑳᐧᐟ ᑕ ᒎᓇᐦᐊᒪᐣ ᑕ ᐹᐦ ᐸᐃᐧᐦᑎᑖᔭᐣ ᑕ ᑲᑫᐧ ᐊᑭᐦᑕᒪᐣ ᑖᒪᔨᑯᕽ ᐊᓂᐦᐃ ~, ᑖᒥ~ ᒣᐢᑕᑲᔭ ᐊᓂᐦᐃ, ᐋᔨᒪᐣ᙮

• • • •

JO: ᐁᑲᐧ ᒦᓇ ᐆᒪ ᐯᔭᐠ ᑳ ᐃᑌᐧᔮᐣ ᐋᓂᐢᑯᐊᐧᐢᑯᓴ?

MLR: ᐋᓂᐢᑯᐊᐧᐢᑯᓴ, ᐁᑯᓂ ᒦᓇ, ᐁᑯᓂ ᒦᓇ ᐁ ᑭᐦᒋ ᐋᐸᑕᐦᑭ, ᒣᑐᓂ ᐅᑎ ᐁ ᑭᐦᒋ ᐋᐸᑕᐦᑭ ᐱᑯ ᐃᑌ ᐁ ᐋᐸᒋᐦᑖᔭᐣ᙮ ᒫᑲ ᒣᑐᓂ [ᒎᐩ ᑲᐧᔭᐢᐠ ᐯᐦᑖᑲᐧᐣ] ᐸᐦᑳᐣ ᐁ ᑕᑯᓂᑳᑌᐠ ᒪᐢᑭᐦᑭᐩ, ᐋᓂᐢᑯᐊᐧᐢᑯᐢ ᐁᑯᑕ ᐄᐧᒋᐦᐃᐁᐧᐤ᙮

• • • •

JO: ᐋ, ᐁᑲᐧ ᒦᓇ *tiger lily, or* ᐅᑭᓂᐩ ᐋᐧᐱᑲᐧᓂᐩ ᒪᐢᑭᐦᑭᔭ?

MLR: ᐅᑭᓂᐩ ᐋᐧᐱᑲᐧᓂᐩ ᒪᐢᑭᐦᑭᔭ, ᐅᑭᓂᐩ ᐋᐧᐱᑲᐧᓂᐩ ᒪᐢᑭᐦᑭᔭ᙮ ᐁᐊᐧᑯ ᐊᓂᒪ ᐅᑭᓂᐩ ᐋᐧᐱᑲᐧᓂᐩ ᒪᐢᑭᐦᑭᔭ, ᐸᑲᐦᑲᑦ ᐁᐊᐧᑯ ᑳ ᐄᐧᐦᑕᒫᑖᐣ ~

JO: ᐋᐦᐊ, *tiger lily*᙮

MLR: ᐁᐦᐊ, ᐁᐊᐧᑯ ᑳ ᐄᐧᐦᑕᒫᑖᐣ ᑳ ᒦᒋᕽ᙮ ᐊᐃᐧᔭᐠ ᐁ ᓅᐦᑌ ᒦᒋᐟ, ᓂᑕᐃᐧ ᒎᓇᐦᐃᑳᑌᐤ ᐁ ᒪ ᒦᒋᔭᐣ ᒫᑲ ᐃᑖᐧᓂᐤ ᒫᓇ ᐁ ᓇᓈᑕᐃᐧᐢᑳᑯᔭᐣ ᑲᔮᐢ ᐃᐧᔭ, *you know*᙮ ᑖᐱᐢᑰᐨ ᐁ ᓇᓈᑕᐃᐧᐦᑖᔭᐣ *your system, like, you know*᙮

••••

JO: ᐋ, ᐋᒧᐤ ᐊᔭ ᒫᑲ?

MLR: ᐊᓂᐦᐃ ᒌ ᐋᒧᐃᐧ ᒪᐢᑭᐦᑭᔭ ᑳ ᐃᑎᑖᐣ?

JO: ᐋᐦᐊ᙮

MLR: ᐁ ᐃᑐᐦᑌᔮᐣ ᐁ ᓃᐱᕽ ᐁ ᐸᐸᒎᐦᑌᔮᐣ ᓵᑳᕽ, ᑫᑕᐦᑕᐁᐧ ᑭᒌᓯᐠ ᐋᒧᐤ᙮ ᐁ ᐋᐧᐸᐦᑕᒪᐣ ᐊᓂᒪ ᒪᐢᑭᐦᑭᐩ ᐊᓂᒪ, ᐊᓂᒪ ᑳ~ ᐋᐧᐱᑲᐧᓃᐢ, ᑭᑑᑎᐦᑎᓀᐣ ᐁᐊᐧᑯ ᑭᓯᑯᐱᑌᐣ ᐊᐦᐴ *your spit* ᑫᐦᒋᐋᐧᐠ, ᐁᑯᑕ ᐁ ᐊᑯᓇᒪᐣ ᐃᑌ ᑳ ᒌᓯᐢᐠ ᐋᒧᐤ, ᒨᐩ ᓈᓂᑕᐤ ᑭᑎᓯ ᐊᔭ~, ᑭᑎᓯ ᐹᑭᐸᔨᐣ ᐁᑲᐧ, ᐁᑯᓯ ᒦᓇ ᐁᐊᐧᑯ ᐁ ᐃᑖᐸᐸᑕᕽ᙮ ᓂᑮ ᑭᐢᑫᔨᐦᑌᐣ ᒫᓇ, ᑲᔮᐢ ᓅᐦᒌᐣ᙮ ᐁᑯᓯ ᐁᑲᐧ ᐆᒪ *eighty-three* ᐁ ᐃᑕᐦᑐᐱᐳᓀᔮᐣ, ᑲᔮᐢ ᓂᑮ ᐯ ᐯᐦᑕᐋᐧᐊᐧᐠ ᑫᐦᑌ ᐊᔭᐠ᙮ ᓃᐢᑕ ᒫᓇ ᓂᑮ ᐋᐸᒋᐦᑖᐣ ᑳ ᒌᓯᐟ ᐋᒧᐤ; ᑫᑕᐦᑕᐁᐧ ᑭᐢᑳᑎᕽ ᑭᒌᓯᑲᐧᐠ, "ᐁ", ᑭᒥᐢᑫᐣ ᐁᐊᐧᑯ, ᑭᓯᑯᐱᑌᐣ ᐁᑲᐧ ᑭᒦᑦ~, ᐁ ᐅᑭᒦᑦ~, ᐅᑭᐣ~ ᐊᔨ *you spit* ᐊᓂᒪ ᐁ ᐅᐦᒋ ᒥᔪᒪ~, ᐁ ᓵᐳᐸᒋᑳᑫᔭᐣ, ᑭᑕᑯᓀᐣ, ᑭᑖᐢᑌᐸᔨᐣ᙮ ᒨᐩ ᑭᒉᐢᑎᓯᑯᐣ ᐊᔨᐋᐧᐠ᙮

••••

JO: ᐋ, ᐸᓴᑯᒉᐱᐊᐧ? [*sic*] ᐸᓴᑯᒉᐱᐦᑲᐧ? ᐸᓴᑯᒉᐱᐦᑲᐧ᙮

MLR: ᐁᑯᓂ ᐃᐧᔭ ᐊᐃᐧᔭᐠ « ᐁᑳ ᑳ ᒥᔮᐧᐢᐱᓀᐟ » ᐃᑖᐧᓂᐤ ᒫᓇ, ᑖᐱᐢᑰᐨ ᐆᒪ ᐊᔨ, ᑭᑲ ᐃᑌᐧᔭᕽ ᑲ ᒪᒐᐦᐱᓀᐟ ᐊᐃᐧᔭᐠ ᐁᑯᑕ ᐁ ᑕᑯᓂᑳᑌᐠ ᑯᑕᑲ ᒫᑲ ᒪᐢᑭᐦᑭᔭ᙮

JO: ᐋᐦᐊ, ᑫᐧᔭᐢᐠ᙮

MLR: ᐋᐦᐊ, ᐁ ᒥᓂᐦᑫᐧᕽ ᐁ~, ᓯᓯᓀ ᓵᐠ~, ᓯᓯᓀ ᒉᐢᑲᓈᕽ ᒫᓇ ᐅᐦᐱᑭᓇᐧ ᐊᓂᐦᐃ᙮

••••

JO: ᑭᓭᐱᑰᒥᓇ ᒫᑲ?

MLR: ᐋᐋ, ᑭᓭᐱᑰᒥᓇ, ᐁᐊᐧᑯᓂ ᐃᐧᔭ, ᐋᐦ, ᒨᔭ ᐃᐧᔭ ᐁᑯᓂ ᐊᐃᐧᔭᐠ ᐄᐧᐦᑳᐟ ᑕᐅᑎᓇᕽ᙮ ᑖᐱᐢᑰᐨ ~

JO: ᒫᔨᐢᑳᑯᐤ᙮

MLR: ᐁ ᑮ~ ᒫᔨᐢᑳᑯᐣ, ᑖᐱᐢᑰᐨ ᐊᔨ, *you know*, ᒨᐩ ~, ᓂᑮ ᐅᐦᒋᒥᑲᐃᐧᓈᐣ ᐊᐦᐴ ᑕ ᑕᐦᑭᓇᒫᕽ, *you know*᙮ ᓇᓈᑐᕽ ᓂᑮ ᐃᑎᑲᐃᐧᓈᐣ, ᑲ ᐅᒥᑭᒋᐦᒑᐣ ᐊᐦᐴ, *you know*᙮ [JO: ᐆᐦ᙮] *Yeah*, ᑲᔮᐢ ᑫᐦᑌ ᐊᔭᐠ ᐁᑯᓯ ᓂᑮ ᐃᑎᑯᓈᓇᐠ, « ᑳᐃᐧᔭ ᑕᐦᑭᓇ, ᐁ ᒫᔮᑕᐦᑭ ᐊᓂᐦᐃ᙮ » ᐊᐦᐴ ᑲ ᐅᒥᑭᐨ~, *you know*, ᑲ ᒥᔨᑯᐣ *rash*᙮ *You know*᙮

••••

JO: ᐋ, ᑳᓴᑫ~, ᑳᓴᑫᐊᐧᐢᐠ?

MLR: ᑳᓴᑫᐊᐧᐢᐠ, ᐊᐃᐧᔭᐠ ᐁᑳ ᑳ ᓂᐦᑖ ᒦᒋᓱᐟ, ᐁᑯᑐᐊᐧ ᐁ ᐊᓴᒥᐦᐟ, ᐁ ᑕᑯᓂᑳᑌᐠ ᒪᐢᑭᐦᑭᐩ ᑯᑕᐠ, *you know*᙮ ᐁᑯᓯ ᒦᒋᓱᐤ᙮ ᒦᓅᐢᑰᐦᑖᐧᐤ, ᒪᐢᑭᐦᑭᐩ ᐊᔨᐢᐠ᙮

••••

JO: ᐋ, *and* ᐱᐦᐁ~, ᐱᐦᐁ~, ᐱᐦᐁᑯ~

MLR: ᐱᐦᐁᑯᒉᐱᕽ᙮

JO: ᐋᐦᐊ, ᐱᐦᐁᑯᒉᐱᕽ᙮

MLR: ᐱᐦᐁᑯᒉᐱᕽ, ᐋ, ᐁᐊᐧᑯ ᒦᓇ ᐁ ᒥᔮᐧᓯᐠ, ᐁᐊᐧᑯ ᒦᓇ ᐊᓂᒪ ᐁ ᒥᔮᐧᓯᐠ, ᐊᐃᐧᔭᐠ ᑖᐱᐢᑰᐨ ᑳ ᓵᐳᐢᑳᐃᐧᓯᐟ, *you know*, ᑖᐱᐢᑰᐨ ᑳ ᐋᐧᐦ ᐊᐧᔭᐄᐧᐟ, ᒫᑲ ᐁ ᑕᑯᓂᑳᑌᐠ ᒪᐢᑭᐦᑭᐩ ᑭᑭ ᑯᑕᐠ᙮

••••

JO: ᐄᐧᐦᑲᐢᑲᐧ?

MLR: ᐄᐧᐦᑲᐢᑲᐧ, ᐃᐧᔭ ᐁ ᒥᔭᐦᑲᓯᑳᑫᔭᐣ᙮ ᑳ ᒥᔮᐦᑲᓯᑫᕽ, ᑖᐱᐢᑰᐨ ᐆᒪ ᓂᔭ ᑮᑭᓭᐹ, ᑮᑭᓭᐹ ᓂᓭᐢᑲᐦᐁᐣ, ᓂᒥᔮᐦᑲᓱᓱᐣ, ᓀᐋᐧᐤ ᐅᒥᓯ ᐃᓯ ᓂᒥᔮᐦᑲᓱᓱᐣ᙮ ᐁᑲᐧ ᐁ ᐊᐧᓂᐦᑫᔮᐣ ᑮᑭᓭᐹ, ᐁ ᐅᑖᑯᓯᐠ ᓂᓭᐢᑲᐦᐁᐣ᙮ ᑲᓇᑫ ᐯᔭᑳᐧᐤ ᐯᔭᐠ ᑮᓯᑳᐤ ᑭᑮ ᐃᑎᑲᐃᐧᓈᓇᐤ ᑕ ᐋᐸᒋᐦᑖᔭᕽ ᐊᓂᐦᐃ, ᐄᐧᐦᑲᐢᑲᐧ᙮ ᐁᑳ ᑳ ᓂᐦᑖ~, ᐁᑳ ᐃᐧᔭ ᑳ ᓂᐦᑖ ᐊᔨ~; ᑖᐱᐢᑰᐨ ᐆᒪ ᐁᑳ ᑳ ᓂᐦᑖ ᑲᑮᓯᒧᐟ ᐊᐃᐧᔭᐠ, ᑭᐄᐧᒋᐦᐃᑯᐣ ᐁᓴ ᐊᓂᐦᐃ ᑭᑎᑌᐧᐢᑕᒫᑯᐣ ᐆᑌ, « ᑮᑳᐧᐩ ᐊᓂᒪ ᐁ ᓂᑕᐁᐧᔨᐦᑕᒪᐣ ᑭᑎᑌᐧᐢᑕᒫᑯᐣ, » ᑮ ᐃᑌᐧᐊᐧᐠ ᒫᓇ ᑫᐦᑌ ᐊᔭᐠ ᐊᓂᑭ᙮ ᑖᐯᐧ ᐊᓂᒪ, ᐋᑎᐦᐟ ᓇᒨᐩ ᓂᐦᑖ ᐊᔭᒥᐦᑖᑯᓯᐊᐧᐠ; ᓇᒨᔭ ᑭᓂᐦᑖ ᐊᔭᒥᐦᑖᑯᓯᐣ᙮ ᑳ ᐊᔭᒥᐦᑖᑯᓯᕽ ᐊᓂᒪ, *you pray, you* can *pray*᙮ ᑭᔭ ᒫᑲ ᑭᐄᐧᒋᐦᐃᑯᐣ᙮ ᑭᐄᐧᒋᐦᐃᐠ ᐁᓴ ᐊᓇ ᐄᐧᐦᑲᐢᐠ, ᐁᑯᓯ ᒫᓇ ᐃᑖᐧᓂᐤ᙮

• • • •

JO: ᐄᐧᐦᑫᐢ ᒫᑲ?

MLR: ᐄᐧᐦᑫᐢ, ᐁᐊᐧᑯ ᒦᓇ ᐁ ᒥᔪ ᐋᐸᑎᓯᐟ ᐱᑯ ᐃᑕ, ᐱᑯ ᐃᓯ ᐃᓯ, ᐱᑯ ᐃᑕ ᑭᑖᐸᒋᐦᐋᐤ ᐄᐧᐦᑫᐢ᙮ ᐊᐦᐴ, ᐊᐦᐴ ᐊᔨ, ᐃᑖᐧᓂᐤ ᒫᓇ ᐊᐃᐧᔭᐠ ᐊᔨ, ᐊᔭ ᑳ ᐋᔮᐟ, ᐁᑳ ᑳ ᑮ ᒥᔪ ᔦᐦᐁᐟ ᑖᓂᓯ ᑳ ᐃᓯᔨᐦᑳᑕᒣᐠ ᐊᓂᒪ? *Asthma* ᐊᐃᐧᔭᐠ ᑳ ᐋᔮᐟ, ᐄᐧᒋᐦᐃᐠ ᐁᓴ ᐊᓂᒪ, ᑳᓰᐦᑲᐦᑌᐤ ᐆᑌ ᐊᓂᒪ ᑮᑲᐧᐩ ᑳ ᑭᐱᐢᑳᑯᔭᐣ ᐸᓴᑯ ᐊᔨ ᐊᔨᐢ ᐊᓂᒪ ᐆᑌ ᐁ ᓇᑭᐸᔨᐠ *in your throat*, ᑭᑯᐦᑖᑲᓂᕽ ᐆᑌ᙮ ᑭᐄᐧᒋᐦᐃᐠ ᐁᓴ ᐊᓇ ᐄᐧᐦᑫᐢ, ᐯᐦᑭᐦᑲᓴᒼ ᐊᓂᒪ ᐊᔨ, ᐃᑖᐧᓂᐤ ᒫᓇ᙮

• • • •

JO: ᐋ, ᒥᑌᐦᐃᒥᓇ, ᐊᐦᐴ ᒌ ᐅᑌᐦᐃᒥᓇ?

MLR: ᐅᑌ~, ᐅᑌᐦᐃᒥᓇ?

JO: ᐋᐦᐊ, ᑖᓂᓯ ᐃᐧᔭ ᐁᑯᓂ ~ ?

MLR: ᐅᑌᐦᐃᒥᓇ, ᐅᑌᐦᐃᒥᓇ ᐆᐦᐃ ᑳ ᐃᑕᒉᕽ ᐏᔭ ᐁᑯᓂ ~᙮

JO: *Strawberries.*

MLR: *Strawberries* ᐏᔭ ᐁᑯᓂ ᐁ ᒦᒋᕽ; ᐁ ᒦᒋᕽ, ᐁ ᐸᑳᐦᑖᔭᐣ, ᐏᔭ ᐁᑯᓂ᙮

JO: ᒨᐩ ᒌ ᐏᔭ ᐊᓂᐦᐃ, ᐋ, *roots*, ᑭᑖᐸᒋᐦᑖᐣ ᐏᔭ ᐁᑯᓂ?

MLR: ᐅᑌᐦᐃᒥᓇ, ᐁᐘᑯ ᒦᓇ ᐊᐏᔭᐠ ᐅᑌᐦᐋᐢᐱᓀᐟ, ᐃᑛᓂᐤ ᒫᓇ᙮ ᐁᐘᑯᓂ ᐊᓂᐦᐃ ᐅᑌ~, ᐊᐦ, ᐏᔭ ᐆᒪ ᐊᓂᒪ ᐅᒉᐱᕽ, ᐅᑌᐦᐃᒥᓂᒉᐱᕽ᙮ ᐊᐏᔭᐠ ᐅᑌᐦ ᑳ ᐑᐢ~, ᑳ ᒫᐦ ᒨᓯᐦᐅᐟ ᐁ ᓵᓵᑿᐦᑕᕽ ᐃᑛᓂᐤ ᒫᓇ ᐁᐘᑯ᙮ ᐁᐘᑯ ᐏᔭ ᒫᓇ ᓂᐯᐦᑌᐣ ᐁ ᐯᔭᑰᓂᑳᑌᐠ, *you know*, ᒨᐩ ᓈᓂᑕᐤ ᐏᔭ ᐁᐘᑯ ᐁ ᐑᐦᑕᒫᑖᐣ, *you know*᙮

••••

JO: ᒦᓂᓯᐦᑫᐢ᙮

MLR: ᒦᓂᓯᐦᑫᐢ, ᑲᔮᐢ ᓂᑮ ᐃᑖᐸᒋᐦᑖᓈᐣ, ᓂᑮ ᑖᐦ ᑌᐏᐦᑕᐘᑫᐸᔨᓈᐣ ᒫᓇ ᐁ ᐸᑳᐦᑖᕽ ᐊᓂᒪ ᒥᓂᓯᐦᑫᐢ ᐁᑿ ᐁ ᓰᐢᑰᐹᑎᓇᒪᐣ ᐁ ᐯᐦᑭᐦᑖᔭᐣ [ᒨᐩ ᑿᔭᐢᐠ ᐯᐦᑖᑿᐣ] ᐁᑯᑕ ᐁᑿ ᐁ ᐲᐦᒋ ᓰᑭᓇᒪᐘᐟ ᐊᐚᓯᐢ ᑳ ᐑᓴᑫᔨᐦᑕᕽ ᐅᐦᑕᐘᑲᐩ; ᒥᔪᐢᑳᑯᐤ᙮ ᑖᓂᑕᐦᑛᐤ ᓂᑮ ᐋᐸᒋᐦᑖᐣ ᓃᐢᑕ᙮ ᑳ ᐹᐦ ᐸᑳᓯᒧᕽ ᒫᓇ ᐆᒪ ᑳ ᓃᐱᕽ ᐲᐦᒋᐦᑕᐘᑫᔮᐹᐚᐣ, ᐁᑯᑕ ᒫᓇ ᐑᓴᑫᔨᐦᒋᑳ~, ᐑᓴᑫᔨᐦᑕᒷᐠ ᐊᐚᓯᓴᐠ᙮ ᑭᒥᔪᐢᑳᑯᐣ ᐊᓂᒪ ᐊᔨ, ᐁᐘᑯ ᐊᓂᒪ, ᐊᓂᒪ ᐊᔨ, ᒦᓂᓯᐦᑫᐢ ᓂᑎᓯᔨᐦᑳᑌᓈᐣ ᐁ ᓀᐦᐃᔭᐍᕽ᙮

••••

JO: ᐋ, ᓃᐱᒥᓈᓇ᙮

MLR: ᓃᐱᒥᓈᓇ᙮ ᓃᐱᒥᓈᓇ, ᓃᐱᒥᓈᓇ ᑳ ᐃᑘᕽ ᐁᑯᓂ ᒦᓇ ᒫᓇ ᑳ ᐃᑘᒋᐠ ᐅᒉᐱᐦᑿ ᑮᑿᐩ ᒪᐢᑭᐦᑭᐩ ᒦᓇ ᐁᑯᑌ ᐁ ᐋᐸᑕᕽ,

ᒥᓂᐦᑫᐧᐃᐧᐣ ᑮᑲᐧᐩ ᒦᓇ, ᓈᓂᑕᐤ ᑳ ᐃᑖᐢᑊ~, *you know*, ᐁᑳ ᑳ ᒥᔪᒪᐦᒋᐦᐅᔭᐣ, ᓃᐱᒥᓈᓇ, ᐅᒉᐱᕽ ᒫᑲ, *you know*᙮

• • • •

JO: ᐋ, ᐅᑭᓃᐋᐧᐦᑎᑲᐧ; ᐅᑭᓃᐋᐧᐦᑎᑲᐧ?

MLR: ᐅᑭᓃᐋᐧᐦᑎᑲᐧᐠ᙮ ᐅᑭᓃᐋᐧᐦᑎᑲᐧᐠ, ᐁᑯᓂᐠ ᐊᓂᑭ ᒦᓇ ᐸᑲᐦᑲᐟ ᒦᓇ ᓈᓂᑕᐤ ᒦᓇ ᐁᑯᓂᐠ ᐃᑖᐸᑎᓯᐊᐧᐠ᙮ ᒫᓇ ᓂᑮ ᐯᐦᑌᐣ ᐅᑭᓃᐋᐧᐦᑎᑲᐧᐠ ᐁ ᐋᐸᑎᓯᒋᐠ᙮ ᑖᓂᓯ ᑲᓂ ᐆᒪ ᑳ ᑮ~? ᐅᑭᓃᐋᐧᐦᑎᑲᐧᐠ, ᐆᐦ, ᐋᐧᐦᐊᐩ! ᓂᑮ ᐯᐦᑌᐣ ᐊᓂᑭ ᒫᓇ ᓈᓂᑕᐤ ᐁ ᐃᑖᐸᑎᓯᒋᐠ᙮ ᐅᑭᓃᐋᐧᐦᑎᑲᐧᐠ ᐊᓂᑭ, ᒫᑲ ᐅᒉᐱᕽ ᓄᒪ; ᑭᑭᐢᑫᔭᐦᑌᐣ ᓈᓂᑕᐤ ᐁ ᐃᑖᐸᑕᕽ᙮

• • • •

JO: ᐊᔭ ᒫᑲ, ᐋ, ᐊᔫᐢᑲᐣ~, ᐊᔫᐢᑲᓇᐋᐧᐦᑎᑲᐧ [*sic*]?

MLR: ᐊᔫᐢᑲᓈᐦᑎᑲᐧᐠ [JO: ᐋᐦᐊ᙮], ᐁᑯᓂᐠ ᒦᓇ ᐊᓂᑭ ᐅᒉᐱᕽ ᒦᓇ ᐁᐊᐧᑯ ᐊᓂᒪ ᒪᐢᑭᐦᑭᐩ ᒦᓇ ᐁᐊᐧᑯ ᐁ ᑕᑯᓇᒥᕽ᙮ ᑮᑲᐧᐩ ᒪᐢᑭᐦᑭᐩ ᑮ ᑕᑯᓇᒪᐧᐠ, ᒨᐩ ᒫᑲ ᓂᑭᐢᑫᔭᐦᑌᐣ ᑖᓂᓯ ᐁ ᐃᓯᔭᐦᑳᑕᒥᕽ᙮

JO: ᐊᔫᐢᑲᓈᐦᑎᑲᐧ [*sic;* ᐊᔫᐢᑲᓇᐠ] ᒫᑲ?

MLR: ᐊᔫᐢᑲᓈᐦᑎᑲᐧᐠ [*sic;* ᐊᔫᐢᑲᓇᐠ], ᐁᑯᓂᐠ ~ ᐁᑯᓂᐠ ᒦᓇ, ᐁ~ ᐊᔭ, ᐁ ᑮᓯᓱᐦᒋᐠ ᐊᓂᑭ ᐊᔫᐢᑲᓈᐦᑎᑲᐧᐠ [*sic;* ᐊᔫᐢᑲᓇᐠ], ᒦᒋᒫᐳᕽ ᐁ ᑕᑯᓂᐦᒋᐠ ᑮ ᐃᑌᐧᐊᐧᐠ ᒫᓇ ᑲᔮᐢ᙮ ᐊᔫᐢᑲᓇᐠ, *wild ones* ᐆᑭ ᒌ, *wild ones*, ᐊᔫᐢᑲᓈᐦᑎᑲᐧᐠ᙮ ᐄ, ᐁᑯᑐᐊᐧ ... ᑮ ᑕᑯᓄᐊᐧᐠ ᒫᓇ ᑫᐦᑌᐊᔭᐠ᙮ ᐁ ᓯᑯᓵᐧᒋᐠ, *you know*, ᐁ ᐸᑳᓯᒫᒋᐠ, ᒦᒋᒫᐳᕽ ᐁ ᑕᑯᓈᒋᐠ ᑮ ᐃᑌᐧᐊᐧᐠ ᒫᓇ᙮

• • • •

JO: ᐋ᙮ ᐸᓴ~ *bulrushes? Bulrushes,* ᐸᓯᒎᐤ? ᐸᓯᒎᓇᐠ? [*sic;* ᐸᓯᐦᑳᓇᐠ] *You know* ᐊᓂᐦᐃ, ᐋ, *bulrushes?*

MLR: ᐆᐦ, ᐁᐊᐧᑯ ᐊᓂᒪ, ᒪ ᒌ ᑳ~ [ᒨᐩ ᑲᐧᔮᐢᐠ ᐯᐦᒑᑲᐧᐤ]᙮ [JO: ᐋᐦᐊ᙮] ᐦᐊᐩ, ᑲᔮᐣ ᐊᓂᐦᐃ ᐁ ᑮ ᐋᐸᒋᐦᐋᒋᐠ ᐆᑭ ᐯᐲᓴᐠ, ᐊᐋᐧᓯᓴᐠ ᑳ ᓂᐦᒑᐃᐧᑭᒋᐠ, ᐁ ᐱᓯᓈᒋᐠ ᐆᑭ ᐃᐢᑫᐧᐊᐧᐠ ᐁᑲᐧ ᐊᐊᐧ ᒥᐢᑎᐠ *a rotten one* ᐁᑲᐧ ᐖᐢᑭᐦᑕᑭᓯᐤ ᐊᔦᐢᐠ ᒦᓇ, ᐁᑯᑕ ᐁ ᑕᑯᓈᒋᐠ᙮ ᐆᑕ ᐁ ᑮᓯᐦᐱᑖᒋᐠ ᐊᐋᐧᓯᓴ ᐆᑕ ᐅᑖᓯᔻᓂᔦˣ, ᑲᔮᐣ ᐁᐊᐧᑯ; ᐁᑲᐧ ᐊᓂᐦᐃ ᑳ ᓵᐳᐯᔦᐟ ᐊᓂᐦᐃ ᑮ ᐁᐧᐱᓀᐊᐧᐠ ᒫᓇ᙮ ᑲᔮᐣ ᐁᐊᐧᑯ ᐊᓂᑭ ᐁᑯᓯ ᐁ ᑮ ᐃᑖᐸᑎᓯᒋᐠ᙮ ᒫᑲ ᐊᔦ, ᓇᒨᔮ ᐃᐧᔭ ᐁᑯᓯ ᑕ ᐊᑎ ᐃᓯ ᐋᐸᒋᐦᐋᒋᐠ, ᐁ ᑮ ᓴᑯᓈᒋᐠ *in the oven;* ᐁ ᒣᐢᑎᓵᐧᒋᐠ ᑖᐱᐢᑯᐨ ᑮᑲᐧᐩ ᒪᓂᒎᐣ ᐁᑯᑕ ᑕ ᑮ ᐃᐦᑕᑯᐟ, *you know*᙮ ᐁᑯᓯ ᒨᐩ ᑮᑲᐧᐩ ᑮ ᐅᐦᒋ ᐃᐦᑕᑯᐤ ᒪᓂᒎᐣ *you know, to* ~, ᑕ ᓴᓴᐢᑫᔦᐦᑖᑯᓯᐟ ᑕ ᑖᐦᑲᐧᒥᑯᐟ ᐊᐋᐧᓯᐣ, ᒨᐩ᙮ ᑮ ᒥᔦ ᐸᒥᓀᐊᐧᐠ ᐊᓂᐦᐃ ᒫᓇ ᐊᔦᐢᐠ ᐊᐋᐧᓯᓴᐠ ᐁ ᑭᑲᐦᐱᑎᐦᒋᐠ, ᐁ ᑮᓯᐦᐱᑎᐦᒋᐠ, *you know*᙮

••••

JO: ᐋ, ᑕᑲᐧᐦᐃᒥᓈᐦᑎᑲᐧ; ᐋᓴᐩ ᒌ?

MLR: ᐋᓴᐩ ᐃᐧᔭ ᐁᑯᓂ᙮

JO: ᐆ᙮

MLR: ᐋᓴᐩ ᑭᑮ ᐄᐧᐦᐟ~, ᑭᑮ ᑲᑫᐧᒋᒥᐤ ᑕᑲᐧᐦᐃᒥᓈᐦᑎᑲᐧ, *ya*᙮

••••

JO: ᐋ, ᓵᐳᒥᓈᐦᑎᑲᐧ ~

MLR: ᓵᐳᒥᓈᐦᑎᑲᐧ, ᒨᐩ ᓈᓂᑕᐤ ~

JO: ~ ᐊᐦᐴ ᒌ ᓵᐳᒥᓇᐠ?

MLR: ᒨᐩ ᓈᓂᑕᐤ ᐃᑖᐸᑕᓈᐧ᙮ ᐸᑲᐦᑲᐣ᙮

JO: ᐋ, ᓵᐴᒥᓇᐠ ᒫᑲ?

MLR: *Ya*, ᓵᐴᒥᓇᐠ? ᑭᒧᐢᒋ ᒧᐋᐧᐊᐧᐠ, ᒫᑲ ᑭᑲᑳᐧᐦᔭᑭᐦᐃᑲᐧᐠ [ᐹᐦᐱᐤ]
ᒣᑐᓂ ᑭ~, ᒣᑐᓂ ᐊᔨ ᑭᐢᑮᓯᑲᐧ ᒫᔨ ᐃᑑᑕᒪᐧᐠ᙮

• • • •

JO: ᐄᐧᐦᑳᐨ ᒌ ᐊᔨ, ᐋ, *mushrooms* ... ᑮ ᒧᐋᐧᐊᐧᐠ?

MLR: ᐁᐦᐊ᙮

JO: *Wild mushrooms*?

MLR: ᐁᐦᐊ, ᐁᐦᐊ᙮ ᒧᐋᐧᐊᐧᐠ ᒦᓇ ᐁᑯᓂᐠ, ᐁᐦᐊ᙮

JO: ᑖᓂᓯ ᑭᔨ ᐁ ᐃᓯᔨᐦᑳᑕᒋᐠ?

MLR: *Mushrooms*? ᐁᐩ ᐦᐁᐩ, ᑖᓂᓯ ᐁᑎᑫᐧ ᓂᑲ ᐃᓯᔨᐦᑳᑖᐊᐧᐠ
ᐁ ᓀᐦᐃᔭᐁᐧᕽ᙮

JO: ᐋᑎᐦᐟ ᐆᑭ ᐊᔨ, ᐊᔩᐠ~, ᐊᔩᑭ ᓅᓈᒥᑲᓂᓴᐠ᙮

MLR: ᐊᔩᐠ~, ᐊᔩᐠ~, ᐊᔩᑭᑖᓴᐠ ᐋᑎᐦᐟ ᒌ? [ᐹᐦᐱᐊᐧᐠ]

JO: ᐊᔩᑭ ᓅᓈᒥᑲᓂᓴᐠ᙮

MLR: ᐊᔩᑭ ᓅᓈᒥᑲᓂᓴᐠ, *yeah*, ᐁᑯᓯ ᒫᓇ ᓂᑮ ᐯᐦᑌᐣ ᐁ ᐃᓯᔨᐦᑳᓱᒋᐠ
ᑖᓂᓯ ᐁᑎᑫᐧ ᒫᑲ ᐁ ᐃᑖᐸᑎᓯᒋᐠ᙮ [ᐹᐦᐱᐊᐧᐠ]

JO: ᐊᔨᐢᐠ ᐋᑎᐦᐟ ᐊᓂᑭ ᐊᔨ *they're poisonous, huh*?

MLR: ᐋᐦᐊ, ᐋᑎᐦᐟ ᐊᓂᑭ ᐱᐢᒋᐳᐃᐧᐊᐧᐠ᙮ « ᑳᔭ ᒥᑯᐢᑳᒋᐦᐃᐠ, »
ᑮ ᐃᑖᐧᓂᐤ ᒫᓇ᙮ [ᐹᐦᐱᐊᐧᐠ]

• • • •

JO: ᐋ, ᒉᐢᑿ᙮ [ᐁ ᑲ ᑭᑐᐍᐘᑭᐸᔨᐠ] ᐁᑯᓯ ᐊᓂᒪ ᐁᑎᑵ᙮ ᐁᑯᓯ᙮ ᐦᐋᐤ᙮ ᑭᓇᓈᐢᑯᒥᑎᐣ᙮

MLR: ᐋᐦᐊ, ᐋ᙮

ᐁᐦᐊ, ᐁᑿ ᓂᔭ ᐆᒪ ᑳ ᐯ ᐑᒋᐦᐊᐠ ᐊᐘ ᓅᓯᓯᐨ ᐁ ᓴᐍᔨᒪᐠ, ᑳᓂᑲᓈ ᑵᔮᐢᐠ ᐱᒧᐦᑌᐟ, ᐱᒧᐦᑖᑕᕽ ᐅᑕᑐᐢᑫᐏᐣ, ᐁᑯᓯ ᐁ ᐃᓯ ᐸᑯᓭᔨᒪᐠ᙮ ᓇᒨᔭ ᓃᐢᑕ ᑮᑿᐩ ᒥᑐᓂ ᒥᐢᑕᐦᐃ ᓂᑭᐢᑫᔨᐦᑌᐣ ᒫᑲ ᑳᔮᐢ ᐁ ᐯ ᐅᐦᒌᔮᐣ ᑮᑿᐩ ᐁ ᐯ ᐯᐦᑕᒫᐣ ᑳ ᑲᑵ ᐯ ᐑᒋᐦᐊᐠ ᓅᓯᓯᐨ ᐆᑕ᙮ ᐱᑕᓀ ᒫᑲ ᒥᓴ~, ᒥᔮᐧᓯᓂᔨᐠ ᐅᑕᑐᐢᑫᐏᓂᐚᐤ ᐏᔭ ᐁᑿ ᐅᐑᒉᐚᑲᓇ, ᐁᑯᓯ ᐁ ᐯ ᐃᓯ ᐚᐦ ᐑᒋᐦᐊᐠ ᓅᓯᓯᐨ ᐊᓄᐦ- ᑳ ᑮᓯᑳᐠ᙮ ᓂᓇᓈᐢᑯᒧᐣ ᐆᑕ ᐁ ᐯ ᐚᐸᐦᑕᒫᐣ ᐃᑕ ᐁ ᐊᔮᐟ, ᐁ ᒥᔭᐧᐱᐟ, ᑳᓂᑲᓈ ᒥᓴᑳᒉ ᐁᑯᓯ ᐊᑎ ᐃᓯ ᑲᓇᐍᔨᐦᑕᕽ ᐆᒪ ᐅᑎᐢᑯᑌᐨ, ᐁᑯᓯ ᐁ ᐃᓯ ᓂᑐᑕᒫᑫᐢᑕᒪᐚᐠ ᓅᓯᓯᐨ, ᐁ ᓴᐍᔨᒪᐠ, ᐁ ᓵᑭᐦᐊᑭᐠ, ᓂᔭ *Mary Louise Rockthunder from Piapot's*᙮

kayās nōhcīn

I Come from a Long Time Back

1
kayās ēkwa anohc
LONG AGO AND TODAY

The following was recorded on May 10, 1995, at the home of Mary Louise Rockthunder on Piapot First Nation, Saskatchewan, in the presence of Jean Okimāsis [JO] *and Doreen Oakes* [DO].

In this first part of that day's recording Mary Louise compares a more traditional way of life on the Reserve with living in town and life today. In particular, she tells about her family background, her parents, her own family, and traditional values of miyo-wīcēhtowin / *good relations.*

hāw, anohc kā-kīsikāk, nōsisimak ōta ē-pē-kakwēcimicik, niya, *Mary Louise Rockthunder*. anohc kā-kīsikāk māka, ē-miywēyihtamāhk ē-wāpahtamāhk ē-miywāsik ē-wī-askihtakwaskamikāk, ē-wī-nīpinisiyāhk kānikanā nōsisiminānak, nitawāsisiminānak kwēyask k-ōhpikicik, ēkāy kīkway ta-māyātahk ōtē kē-nīkānīyik. ēkosi ē-pim-īsi-nitotamān anohc. nitawāsimisak ōt ē-kakwēcimicik ōta nēhiyawipwātināhk ayisk ōma ē-ohcīyān ōta kā-pāh-pīkiskwēyān kā-wī-ācimostawakik ōki.

[1. niwāhkōmākanak]

kayās, nōhtāwiy ..., kīskacawēhamās kī-isiyihkāsow ēkwa nīsta *Mary Louise Bangs* nikī-isiyihkāson. ēkosi nikī-nis--, nikī-nēwinān nimisak, nisto nikī-wanihāwak, niya piko ē-pimātisiyān. nikī-nistinān nōhtāwiy ēkwa niya ēkwa nikāwiy, namōya ohci-wāpiw nikāwiy, nikī-pamēyimāw nikāwiy, nikī-pamihāw. namōya nōh-itohtān kiskinwahamātowikamikohk; nikī-itohtān ayēnānēw ē-itahtopiponēyān, māka nōhtāwiy, mōy ohci-nitawēyihtam ta-kiskinwahamākosiyān nikāwiy nāway ta-nakatak, kī-pakwātam nōhtāwiy. ēkosi nikī-pē-kīwān.

hām, anohc ēkwa, nimihtātēn, iyikohk mōniyāw-iyiniw ēkwa anohc, kā-wīcihikoyāhk, nama kīkway niya mistahi kiskēyihtāsowin nitayān, apisīs piko, ēta-- ētataw! māka ēyiwēhk niwīcihison, niwī-kakwē-wīcihison kīkway. ēkosi, ōta ē-kī-tasi-nihtāwikiyān. ēkosi mīna nicawāsimisak kahkiyaw ōt ē-tasi-nihtāwikicik, mētoni ninanāskomāw kōhtāwīnaw anohc — kisē-manitow — kā-kīsikāk. kēkāc kahkiyaw nitawāsimisak ē-ohtinikēyān, nīso nikī-wanihāwak māka; nīso iskwēsisak nikī-wanihāwak. ayēnānēw-- kēkā-mitātaht ta-kī-ayāwakik awāsisak, nīso niwanihāwak, tēpakohp pimātisiwak, niyānan iskwēwak, nīso nāpēwak. kēkāc mētoni nimiy-ōhpikihāwak nitawāsimisak, namōya ē-mamihcimoyān, māk ētokē ē-pē-nitohtawicik tānisi ē-pē-itwēyān, niya nitawāsimisak wiya ēwakonik; namōya ē-nitaw-- namōy nōsisimak ōk ōtē — nōsisimak nisawēyimāwak, mīna kahkiyaw niwāhkōmākanak nisawēyimāwak.

All right, today my grandchildren have come here with enquiries for me, Mary Louise Rockthunder. But today we are happy, we see it is good that the earth is turning green, that we'll be passing through the summer. It is my hope that our grandchildren and our children grow up properly and for there to be nothing bad in their future. This is what I ask for today. My children are here asking me, here at Piapot First Nation where I am from; it's here that I will be speaking and telling these ones my stories.

[1. My Relatives]

Long ago, my father – his name was *kīskacawēhamās* [Hair Cut Short/Bangs] and I too was named Mary Louise Bangs. Well, there were thr-- there were four of us with my older sisters, I lost the three of them and I am the only one living. There were three of us, my father and me and my mother. My mother was blind. I cared for my mother, I tended to her. I hadn't gone to school; I went when I was eight years old but my father didn't want me to go to school and to leave my mother behind. My father hated that. So I came home.

Well, today I feel sorry at how much the Whiteman helps us nowadays. I have nothing of that higher learning, just a little bit, barely at all! But I help myself as well as I can, and I'm going to try to help myself in some way. That's the way I grew up here. And that's the way all of my children are also growing up, I am really grateful to Our Father today – the Creator. Nearly all of my children have come from that, but I lost two of them; I lost two little girls. I should have eigh-- nine children, I lost two of them, seven are living, five woman and two men. I raised nearly all my children well, I'm not bragging, but I guess they listened all along to what I had to say, I mean my own children, not those - not my grandchildren over here – I love my grandchildren, and I love all of my relatives.

ōma k-ēspīhtisīyān, namōy wīhkāc awiyak ē-pē-māy-ītak aspin nipē-ohpikin, namōy wīhkāc nipē-na-nōtinikān -, ē-pē-awāsisīwiyān mīna namōy wīhkāc nōh-pē-nōtinikān. wāwīs ēkwa ōma ē-kēhtē-ayiwiyān nōhtāwiy ē-kakēskimit, "ēkāy awiyak māyi-wīcēw. pikw īta kika-pīhtokwān ēkā awiyak māyi-wīcēwaci. kakwē-miyo-pimātisi," nikī-itik māna nōhtāwiy. ēwako nisakinēn anohc. namōy wīhkāt nimā--, awiyak nānitaw k-ētwēt namōy ninōhtē-na-nitohtēn, nikanawēyihtamāson. mōya wīhkāc kīkway nikakwē-māy-ōhpinēn ē-wī-kakwē-miyo-pimātisiyān. kīkwāy k-ōh-tōtamān? nitawāsimisak, nōsisimak, niwāhkōmākanak ta-kakwē-- wīstawāw --miyotēhēcik anohc kā-kīsikāk ōma k-ēsinākwahk kitaskīnaw, ē-wī-askihtakwaskamikāk. hāw, anohc niwī-pim-ācimon.

kayās ōta ē-ohcīyān, kayās. ē-kī-nihtāwikiyān, nika-wīhtēn māka nika-ākayāsīmon, *nineteen thirteen* ē-kī-nihtāwikiyān, īh, tānimayikohk ōma mēkwāc ētokē? mētoni nitōskinīkiskwēwin anohc. mētoni ē-oskinīkiskwēwiyān anohc ōma kā-kīsikāk. kēyāpic māka, kēyāpic nipapāmohtān, isko pwātawihtāyāni ta-pimohtēyān ētokē nika-apin; nika-apin ētokē nipēwinihk. mōya ēkotowihk ē-nitotamākēyān māk--, namōya ēkotowihk ē-nitawēyihtamān ēkosi ita pēyakwanohk t-āpiyān ahpō ētokē nika-papāmitācimon tānisi - . [*pāhpināniwan*] ēkosi.

ēkwa ōta, ōta ē-kī-tasi-nihtāwikiyān, nīhcāyihk ōm ōta *down the valley* ē-kī-tasi-nihtāwikiyān. ēkospīhk kayās *nineteen thirteen, sixteenth of Feb--* āh, āh, āh, *October* kā-kī-nihtāwikiyān, *nineteen thirteen.* iyikohk ōma anohc k-ēspīhtisīyān. ēkwa tānisi ē-kī-pē-isi-wāpahtamān anoht nōsisimak niwī-ācimostawāwak.

namōya -, namōya niya ākwāskam ōta ta-kī-- ta-kī-itwēyān ōta nōhtāwiy namōya ākwāskam ōta ē-kī-ohcīt, ē-kī-mosci-pīhtokwahiht ētokē nōhtāwiy *Bangs*; ōtē ē-ohcīt *Turtle Mountain, Monta-- oh, States* ēkotē ē-ohcīt nōhtāwiy. ēkotē ētokē anima askiy ē-tipēyihtamān nīsta. nikī-ohtisinān *nineteen - nineteen thirty-six* nikī-māc-ōhtisinān anima askiy, nikī-nistinān niya ēkwa

As old as I am I have never said anything bad to anyone, since I grew up I have never fought, as a child I never fought anyone. Especially now as I am old, my father counselled me, "Don't be on bad terms with anyone. You will be able to enter anywhere if you are not on bad terms with anyone. Try to live a good life," my father used to tell me. I cling to that today. Never ..., if anyone says anything bad, I don't want to listen, I keep it to myself. I never try to bring up anything bad, as I am trying to live a good life. What would I do that for? [I want] my children, my grandchildren, and all my relatives as well, to try to be good-hearted. Today, the way our land will look, the earth is going to be green. All right, today now I am going to be telling a story.

I am from here for a long time back, long ago. I was born ... I will tell it but I will say it in English, I was born in nineteen thirteen, oh, how much is that I wonder? I am a very young woman today. But still, I still walk about, until I am unable to walk, then I guess I will just sit. Maybe I will sit on the bed. I am not asking for that kind of thing, I don't want that kind of thing, to be sitting thus in one place; or perhaps I will crawl around, how.... [*laughter*] That's it.

And here, here where I was born and raised; it was down here in the valley that I was born and raised. At that time long ago, nineteen thirteen, it was on the sixteenth of Feb--, uhh, October that I was born in nineteen thirteen. That's how far I have reached in age today. And today I am going to tell my grandchildren about what I have seen.

Not ... I shouldn't really be saying here, my father was not really from here, he was accepted as a member here, my father Bangs. He was from Turtle Mountain, Monta-- [North Dakota], oh, my father was from over there in the States. I guess I, too, own some land there. We received payment, in nineteen -, in nineteen thirty-six we started getting paid from that land. The three of us, me and nikā--, nikāwiy ēkwa nitānis ēkwa niya nikī-nistinān ē-ohtisiyāhk anima askiy. ēkotē nistam okimāhkān, nimosōm, *Albert Firstchief* kī-isiyihkāsow, ēwako ana otaskiy. nōhtāwiy ēw-- ēkoni nōhtāwiy ohtāwiya *Rainsky* kī-itāw ēsa nimosōm; *Rainsky* ohtāwiya ōhi *Fra-- Albert Firstchief* ēwakw āna nimosōm nitāniskōhpicikan ēwako. ēkotē askiy ētokē apisīs nikanawāpamikon māka niwī-kakwēcihkēmon ōtē, *States* anima ē-wī-kakwēcihkēmoyān kīkwāy anima iyinito-sōniyāw kā-kī-otihtikoyāhk. askiy wiya nitipēyihtēn ēkotē mōy wīhka-- mōy māka mētoni nikiskēyihtēn.

ēkosi, ēkosi ōta nikī-- nikī-tasi-nihtāwikin nōhtāwiy ōta kī-pīhtokwahāw ayisk payipwāt's ōta. ōtē nīhcāyihk nitisiyihkātēnān, ēkotē ē-kī-tasi-nihtāwikiyān. ēkwa nimosōm ē-pwācis kī-itāw, *Little Sioux* kī-itāw nimosōm. ēkwa nōhkom, nōhkom *Isabelle* kī-itāw nōhkom, sapēn nikī-itānān māna nōhkom ē-nēhiyawihkāsot; wiya ēwako omāmihkwēw kī-nihtā-- *ahsinipwān* [*Assiniboine*] kī-isi-pīkiskwēw. kī-pwāsīmow nōhkom, ēkosi māna nikī-kiskinwahamākonān niya ēkwa nisikos, ē-kī-pwāsīmoyāhk ē-kī-itēyihtamāhk ē-kī-isi-nisitohtawāyāhk nōhkom, māka kayās kā-nakasit nōhkom, *a hundred and four* kī-itahtopiponwēw nōhkom ē-kī-panātisit, kēyāpic kī-kakāyiwātisiw nōhkom. kānikanā k-ōtihtamān, kānikanā nōhkom naspitawak kāyakwāki-- mōy, mōy māka mētoni ta-naspitawak mōy ayisk ohci-wāpiw, māka wiya niya niwāpin ayisk. māka ayisk mōniyāw k-ōh-wāpiyān ē-kī-pāh-pīhtonahk niskīsikwa ōhi, ē-kī-wīcōhkamawit.

ēkwa mīna, ōma nīsta ōma ōta kā-- kā-ayāyān ōta nīsta mīna mōniyāw ē-itāmoyān ē-nānapācihit. nīsta namōya kwēyask miywāsin, mōy nitēh ōma pīwāpisk nīsta ayisk, *a pacer* ē-ayāyān nitēhihk. māka niwīcihikon, ninanāskomāw mōniyāw-iyiniw ē-kī-wīcōhkamawit, *a pacer* ē-ayāyān. *Two years* ēkwa ēkosi ē-ayāyān nīsw-āskiy ēkwa ōma, ē-kik-- ē-kikiskamān ōma. *My will* nikī-osīhtān ōta āhkosīwikamikohk, *my will* nikī-nitaw-ōsīhtān. panātisiyāni ē-nitawēyihtamān ta-kēcikonahkik ēkosi masinahikātēw *my will* anima ēwako ē-kī-osīhtāyān. kīspin ayisk takohtēyāni ōtē tānitē kā-tēpwāsit manitow takohtahici ēkotē, my - ... my mother and my daughter and me, the three of us received benefits from that land. There, the first chief, my grandfather, he was named Albert Firstchief, that was his land. My father ... well, my father's father, I understand he was called Rainsky. And Rainsky's father, that was Albert Firstchief and he was my great-grandfather. There is a little bit of land that looks after me monetarily, but I was going to ask, over here in the States I was going to ask about that payment which reached us. For I do own land over there, I've never ... I don't really know about it.

So, so I was born and raised here, my father was taken here as a member of Piapot [Reserve]. Over here, we just call it *nīhcāyihk* [down the hill], that's where I was born and raised. And my grandfather was called ē-*pwācis*, my grandfather was called Little Sioux, and my grandmother, my grandmother was called Isabelle, we used to call my grandmother *sapēn* naming her in the Cree way. She was an Assiniboine woman, she could ... she spoke Assiniboine. My grandmother spoke Assiniboine, so she used to teach us, me and my auntie. In our minds we spoke Assiniboine as we understood my grandmother. But it was a long time since my grandmother left me, she was a hundred and four years old when she passed away. She was still very hard-working. If only I would reach that, if only I could resemble my grandmother's industri-- No, but not to really resemble her because she was blind. Because I at least have my sight. But then it is because of a white man that I can see, as he peeled these eyes of mine [i.e., he removed cataracts from my eyes], helping me.

And also, I too am here, I'm also here having run to a white man to patch me up. For me too, it wasn't proper, not my heart, because it is metal, I have a pacer [i.e., pacemaker] in my heart, but it helps me. I thank the Whiteman for helping me with this, as I have a pacer. Two years now that I've had it, it's two years now ... that I've been wearing it. I made my will here at the hospital. I went and made my will. When I die, I want them to take it off, so it is written in my will, the one that I made. Because if I arrive over here where the Creator calls me, if he takes me over there, takohtēyāni mōy ka-cīhkēyihtam ōma pīwāpisk ōta nāskikanihk kā-kikamok, nika-pē-nīhtaciwētisahok, nika-kwātakihtān ōta, ēwak ōhci k-ōh-kī-- osi-ī-- --wiyascikēyān.

[**2. kayās pimācihowin**]

hām ēkwa, kayās ayisiyiniwak tānisi ē-kī-isi-pimācihocik, mētoni kī-miyw-āyāniwiw kayās. kahkiyaw kīkway ē-kī-mīcihk, ayi ōma *wild meat* k-ētamihk tāpiskōc mōsowiyās kī-mīcināniwiw ēkwa mīna apisimōsis kī-mowāw; kāhkēwakwa nikī-osīhtānān. namōy ānim ōt-- namōy ānim ē-ohci-osi-- ēkota ōcēwak ē-ohc-āyācik ē-kī-kaskāpasahkik nōtokwēwak, kī-yīkatēyāpasowak. ēwako ētikwē anima *spray* wīstawāw ē-kī-itōtahkik nōtokwēwak kayās. kī-osīhtāwak kāhkēwakwa ēkwa mīna yīwahikana mīna kī-osīhēwak kēhtē-ayak, ē-osīhtācik pimīhkān k-ētamihk. wīhkway, nōhkom māna wīhkway kī-kaskikwātam ēkota ē-asiwahāt ōhi - ōma pimīhkān ōma ē-kaskipitahk.

ēkwa nimosōm awa tānisi kāh-isīhcikātamokwē māna apoya kī-tahkonēw; kī-sipwēhtēw māna ē-sipwēhtatācik ōma kīkwāy ētok ōma pimīhkān ōma, ēkotē ē-nitaw-astācik. matwān cī māna ē-kī-ayahahkik mōy nikāh-kiskēyihtēn, māka nikī-kiskēyihtēn māna pīwāpisk, pīwāpisk anima mistikowas ēkota māna ē-kī-astācik anima ayi pimīhkān. ēkwa kā-at-ākwā-pipohk nānitaw ētokē, nānitaw ētokē k-āpihtā-pipohk, niyanān āpihtā-piponi-pīsim nititwānān, *January* ēwako; ēkota māna ē-kī-nātahkik anima nōhkom ēkwa ē-mīciyāhk tāpiskōc mētoni anohc ē-kī-kīsihtāhk. tāpiskōc, tāpiskōc ōma anohc *canning* kā-tōtamahk ēkosi ē-kī-tōtahkik māka *Indian way* wīstawāw. namōy nōh-āhkosīskākonān anima, namōy wīhkāt nōh-ayānān *cancer* wāsakāmē ōma ati-- ēwako nēma, nāway nēma *nineteen - nineteen twenty* awasitē. namōya wīhkāc kīkway *cancer* awiyak t-āyāt. namōy wīhkāc awiyak ta-miyiwit, nama kīkway. ma kīkway awiyak *whooping cough* kā-itwēhk, ma kīkway. mistahi sōskwāc ē-kī-ohpikiyāhk, sōskwāc ē-kī-ma-miyw-āyāhk.

k-āti-tipiskāk, k-āti-tipiskāk tāpiskōc awa kimosōminaw kā-kīs-āwasēwēt, ēwako ētokw ānima k-ētamahk anohc *six o'clock* when I arrive He won't like this metal attached here on my chest. He will send me back down and I will have a very difficult time here, that is why I made these arrangements.

[**2. Life Long Ago**]

So now, the people of long ago and the way they lived, everyone was very healthy long ago. Everything was eaten, ah, this "wild meat" as they call it, like moose meat was eaten and deer was also eaten; we made dried meat. There wasn't ... There were no flies there as the old ladies smudged and they were turned away by the smoke. That must have been their "spray," the old women were doing that too, long ago. They made dried meat and also the old people made pounded dried meat, for making what is called *pimīhkān* [pemmican]. A bladder, my grandmother used to sew a bladder and put these inside - she tied up that pemmican.

And my grandfather, whatever activity he was engaged in, he used to carry a shovel; he used to leave, they'd be taking along this, what, this pemmican, I guess, which they were going to cache. I wondered if perhaps they went and buried it, I wouldn't know. But I do know that it was metal, it was a metal box where they would put that, ah, pemmican. Then when it was getting on in winter, I guess, perhaps when it was around midwinter – we used to call it the Mid-Winter Moon, that was January – they used to go get it from there and then my grandmother [and us], we'd eat it, and it was just like it had been made that day. Like, it's like when we do the canning today, that's the way they too did it, but the Indian way. That never made us sick, we never had that cancer, that which is [now] all around, that one, not back then, in nineteen - nineteen twenty and earlier. There was never any kind of cancer for anyone to have. No-one ever had tuberculosis, there was none of that. No-one got that "whooping cough" as it is called, there was none of that. We simply grew up, and we just had good health.

When night approached, when it was getting dark, like when our Grandfather had disappeared [i.e., when the Sun set], that must ēwako k-ētamahk kiyānaw, kī-tipahākēwak pīsimwa kēhtē-ayak. ē-at-āwasēwēt "pīhtokēk, pēyahtak-- pēyakwanohk ayāk wāskāhikanihk!" tāpiskōc nikī-- namōy nōh-itēyihtēn tāpwē ōki nikakwātakihikwak nikēhtē-ayimak, namōy nōh-itēyihtēn. "nipāk, kē-wāpahk kīkisēpā wīpac ka-waniskāyēk. ka-papāmi-mētawānāwāw kē-wāpahk," nikī-itikawinān māna. tāpwē ē-at-ōtākosiki nikī-kawisimonān ē-nipāyāhk, ē-na-nipāyāhk. wiyāpahki, "ahā, mīcisotān." nimīc--, nikī--, namōya kīkway wiya *porridge* ma kīkway, ē-iyinito-mīcisoyāhk mīcimāpoy ē-kist-- ē-mīciyāhk kīkway ōhi otisīhkāna. ahpō kāh-mīciyāhk ayi *wild turnips, on a hill* māna ihtakonwa. mistaskosīmina māna nikī-isiyihkātēnān ēkwa ē-mōnahahkik ōki kēhtē-ayak ē-sikwatahahkik, ē-pāsahkik, mīcimāpōhk ē-pakā--. wahwā, wīhkasin mīcimāpoy *wild turnip* ēwako k-ētamihk kiyānaw anoht *turnips* k-ētamahk.

ēkwa ōma kā-pāh-pīkiskwātitakok anohc, namōya kīkway, ma kīkway ē-māyātahk, ē-miywāsik ē-pē-nitōskamēk ēwako k-ōh-wīhtamātakok, nōsisim awa kiya mīna nōsisim kōhkomiwāw kā-pē-ācim--, namōya wiya ē-kiyāskiyān ē-tāpwēyān ōma k-ētwēyān. mōy nikāh-kī-kiyāskin ōma k-ētācimostātakok, ēkosi ē-kī-pē-isi-ohpikiyāhk nāway nēma.

[**3. anohc māyinikēwin**]

anohc ēkwa, niwāpahtēn tānisi anohc ē-ispayik, nitawāsimisak, nōsisimak, nitāniskōhpicikanak, tānisi anohc ē-isi-ohpikicik, kā-tipiskāk okīsikāmiwak anohc awāsisak, ēwak ōhci k-ōh-māh-māyinikēcik kitawāsimisinawak kōsisiminawak. wiyāpahki kā-pēhtamahk ē-kī-nipahiht kōsisiminaw, kitawāsimisinaw kī-tahkamāw, miyātoyahk ēkota. āta anima ē-ohcimāwasoyahk, mōy māka nisitohtamwak anoht, anohc tānisi k-ēs-ōhpikicik anohc. kisāstaw, kisāstaw anohc ōma nawacikw āpisīs ē-māy-ōhpikihk, namōy tāpiskōt nēma kayās, mistahi kayās kī-miywāsin. namōy wīhkāc māmihk ayisiyiniw ohci-kīskwēpēw.

kīkwāy k-ētwēhk ē-kīskwēpēhk, ē-ka-kīskwēt awiyak. "ahām," kī-itwēwak māna kēhtē-ayak, "anaha [*sic:* ana nāha] kā-wāpamat be what we refer to today as six o'clock, that's what we mean now; but the elders used the sun to measure time. As the Sun was setting, "Go inside, be care-- stay in one place, in the house!" Like I ... I hadn't thought, "my elders are being mean to me," I never thought that. "Sleep! When it is daylight you will arise early in the morning. You will go about and play when it is daylight," we used to be told. Sure enough, as it was evening, we went to bed and we'd be sleeping. When morning came, "Okay, let's all eat." We ea--, we ... there was no porridge, nothing like that. We just ate soup, ... ah, we ate things like these turnips. We even ate wild turnips that used to grow on the hill. We used to call them *mistaskosīmina* ["big-grass-berries"] and these elders would dig them, crush them by pounding, dry them; put them ... in soup. Oh my, that soup was delicious, that which was called "wild turnip," that which we call "turnips" nowadays.

And this which I am speaking to you about today, there was nothing, there was nothing bad at all, you came to ask about the good and that is what I am telling you. This is my grandchild, and you also are my grandchild, your grandmother has come to tell ... I am not telling lies, I am telling the truth in what I say. I couldn't lie about what I will tell you about, that is how we grew up, ah, back then.

[**3. Today's Problems**]

Now today, I see what is happening; my children, my grandchildren, my great-grandchildren, how they grow up today. When the dark night is the daytime of the children of today. That's why they get into trouble, our children and our grandchildren. In the mornings we hear that our grandchild has been killed, our child was stabbed and we are crying at that. Although we warn our children, they don't understand today, it's how they grow up today. It's as if today they're growing up somewhat poorly, it wasn't like that long ago.
It was really good long ago. The Downstream People had never gotten drunk.

What does that say, *ē-kīskwēpēhk* [being drunk]? That someone is crazed. "Okay," the elders used to say, "that one you see who is kā-minihkwēt, matwān cī kitāh-miywēyihtam ana ōmatowahk ta-pakamahoht ostikwānihk, kapē-kīsik isko ē-āwasēwēt ta-papā-ka-kīskwēt, nama kīkway ta-kiskēyihtam, namōya tāh-miyo-- tāh-miyonākwan ēwako," kī-itwēwak māna kayās, wiyāpamātwāwi awiya nawaciko ēkosi kā-wī-is--. kayās ētokē kī-oy-osīhtāwak māna kīmōc kīkway, namōy nikāh-kī-mamihcihtēn ēwakw ānima. kīkway ētokē māna kī-minahisowak ōki. ēkosi anima māna kāh-itwēcik, "namōy tāh-cīhkēyihtam ta-pa-pakamahoht ostikwānihk ayi ta-papā-ka-kīskwēt," ēkotowa ayisk anima kā-kīskwēpēhk, k-ētwēhk. ayi kiyitihp anima namōya ē-miywāsik, namōya ē-miywāpāwatāyan ēwakw ānima okīskwēyāpamohk kā-minihkwēhk. nikiskēyi-- nikī-pa-pē-minihkwān nīsta kayās, mōy māka mistahi, nikī-pa-pōyonān. nikī-pē-minihkwānān apisīs, mōya mistahi kāh-ka-kīsi-- ēkosi nikī-pakitinēn. kayās kā-pōni-minihkwēyān, nikisēyinīm mīna kayās. kayās mīna kā-pōni-pīhtwāyān.

pīhtwāwin ōma, ēwako mīna kā-nipahikohk pīhtwāwin, ayisiyiniw mistahi k-ōtinahk. ōtē ōma, kihpanak [*sic*: kōhpanak] ōki, kitimahāwak, kikitimahtān kiyēhēwin. īh, tānima-- tānitowahk ē-āpacihtamōhikawiyahk anohc *spray* anohc mōniyāwak ka-miyo-yēhēyahk. ēkotowahk nitāpacihtān, *spray* nitōnihk nitāpacihtān, māka ōma niya *my heart* k-ōh-miyikawiyān, ta-kakwē-miyokotēk ōma *my cord* ōtē. nitāpacihtān anima nīswāw, nīswānis-- ayi, ayi, nitispitamāson *air, you know,* ēwakw ānima nimiyo-tōtākon, māka wiya niya anima ayi ōma ētokē nitēh ohci.

ēwako anima anohc ē-pim-ācimostātakok, kayās mistahi kī-miywāsin, mēton ōti kayās. anohc ēkwa awāsisak, ma kīkway kinitohtākonawak, ayis pahkān isikiwak, pahkān kitisi-ohpikihānawak, namōy tāpiskōc kayās. namōya ē-mamihcimoyān ōma ē-pē-kiskēyihtamān anima k-ōh-ācimostātakok, *you know*, tānisi ē-pē-ispayik anohc ēkwa kā-takohtēyahk anohc ēkwa niwāpahtēn nīsta. tahto-kīsikāw kēkāt nimōskotēhān nōsisimak ohci, nitawāsimisak. pēyak nīsta nitawāsimis, mōy tāpwē kīkway ē-tāpwēhtahk, ē-isi-- ē-ihtasiyāhk drinking, I wonder if that one would like it if he were to be hit on the head, to go around crazed all day until sunset. He would know nothing, that would not look good," they used to say long ago, whenever they saw someone who was more or less going to be that way .... I guess they used to make something secretly long ago, I wouldn't brag about that. I wonder what these ones used to give themselves to drink. That is what they would say: "He would not enjoy being repeatedly hit on the head and wandering about crazed." Because that's what being drunk was like, it was said. Ah, that's your brain, it's not right, you didn't properly hydrate it, that is that dizziness when drunk. I know ... I too came to drink long ago, but not a lot, and we quit. We drank a bit, not a lot would we ..., so we left it. I stopped drinking long ago, and my old man also a long time ago. And a long time ago I also quit smoking.

Smoking, that too, one can be killed by smoking, if a person takes too much of it. Over here, these lungs of yours, they are mistreated, you are damaging your breathing. Look, which ... what kind of spray are we made to use today by the white people in order to breathe well. I use that kind [i.e., an inhaler], I use that spray in my mouth, but for me I was given it for my heart, to try and make my cord over here work right. I use that twice, two time--, ah, ah, I open my air passages, you know, that benefits me. But for me I guess that is mainly for my heart.

That is what I am telling you today. Long ago, it was really good, really wonderful long ago. Now today, the children, they don't listen to us at all, because they develop differently, we raise them differently, not like in the old days. It's not that I am bragging, but I have come to know about what I am telling you, you know, how things have come to be today and how we have arrived here today and what I, too, see. Every day, I almost cry in my heart for my grandchildren, my children. One of my own children, she doesn't really believe in anything, although, in our family, we all love her, āta ana ē-sawēyimāyāhk ē-sākihāyāhk ana āta. ēkā sawēyimāyāhk namōy nikāh-kitotānān, kiyām nikāh-itēyihtēnān, māka ē-sawēyimāyāhk pēyak nīsta nitawāsimis; niya, niya, niya, nitohpikihcikan, ēwakw ānima. namōya mētoni ātawiya mitoni mistahi tita-- tita-mōhcowit māka nawaciko sasīpihtam. kīkway māka anima kā-wīhtamāht wāpahtam: " 'kāwiya', kīkwāy anima, 'kāwiya'?". wāpamēw awīniwa anihi nawaciko ayiwāk ēsa ē-tipēyimikot, simākanis ayis anohc kitipēyimikonaw ēkwa anohc kā-kīsikāk. nānitaw k-ēsi-ma-māyinikēhk āsay ēkota simākanis. "miy-ōkimāw" kititēyihtēnānaw, namōya. nānitaw ē-ay-itinikēhk, āsay ōta, pē-ayāw, ēkwa kinitotamākonaw awīna kā-ma-māyinikēt ta-wīcōhkamawāyahk sōniyānāhk [*sic;* okimānāhk] ohci.

tānitē kē-ohtinak sōniyāw? namōy nitatoskān, nikēhtē-ayiwin. kīkway piko ē-pēhtāyān nimasinahikan ta-otihtikoyān, ēwako piko niya. kayās ēyiwēhk nikī-sōniyāhkēsin. anoht niwī-kakwē-sōniyāhkān, ētataw māka nikaskihtān ē-sōniyāhkēyān. nisōniyāhkēsin mōy - mōy māka ēwakoyikohk, nikaskihtān māka apisīs ē-wāpamak ana mōniyās kā-takahkēyimācik itowa sōniyāwa. ēwakoni ayis wiyawāw tēkahkēyimācik, mōniyāwak ōki.

[*aciyaw ē-nakipitamihk*]

[**4. payipwātināhk**]

nika-māci-- nika-māc-ācimon kīkway ē-pē-isi-ka-kiskēyihtamān. kayās, kayās niyanān ēkosi ē-kī-pē-itācihoyāhk ōk āwāsisak kā-pē-wīhtamawakik. ēyiwēhk nikī-pē-mī-- kī-pē-miyokiwak awāsisak, ta-kī-itwēyān, ē-kī-pē-miyokicik. namōya wīhkāc awiyak nōh-pēhtēnān: "ēwakw āna misiwanāci-- misiwanācihiwēw, nipahtākēw." mōy wīhkāc nōh-- nōh-- nōhci-pēhtēnān, mēton āyis kī-kostēwak mōniyāw-iyiniwa ōki niyanān iyikohk kā-pē-ispīhtisīyān. ahpō māna kā-pētisāpamakik niya ē-iskwēsisiwiyān kāh-tapasīyān, nikī-sēkwāmon nānitaw atāmihk ēkāy ta-wāpamit mōniyās. ē-kī-isi-kostāyāhkok mōniyāwak, maskimota ē-kī-kostamāhk. kī-tahkonamwak ayis māna maskimota ōhi. kēyāpic anima nikanawēyihtēn anima itowahk kā-kī-kostamān ē-iskwēsisiwiyān anim āyi, anima, tāpiskōc we cherish her. If we didn't love her, we wouldn't talk to her, but we do love that one, and me too, that child of mine, me, my own, one that I raised, that's the situation. She doesn't really get crazy but she is somewhat stubborn. She sees what is being told to her: "'*kāwiya*' [Don't], what is that '*kāwiya*'?" She sees the one who has control of her, because the police do have control of us today. If there is any wrongdoing, already the police are there. "Good officer," we think of this, but no. If anything is going on, already he comes here and asks us who is the evildoer and for us to help him out on behalf of the bank [*sic;* government].

Where would I get money? I don't work, I am old. The only thing is that I wait for my [pension] cheque to reach me. That's all I have. Long ago I made a bit of money. Today I try to make money but I am barely able to earn money. I make a little bit but not hardly enough; I am able to a little but I go and see that white man, the kind that really like money [i.e., pawn shop], because that's what they really like, these white people.

[*pause in recording*]

[**4. At Piapot Reserve**]

I will start ... I will start ... I will start telling about things that I have come to know – from long ago, how we made a living a long time ago – which I have come to tell these children about. Anyway, we ... the children grew well, I should say, they developed well. We never heard tell of anyone: "that one is destructive, a murderer." We had never ever heard that, because they were very afraid of white people, those who were the same age as I am. Whenever as a child I noticed them approaching I would run away to hide under something so the white man wouldn't see me. We were so afraid of the white man, we were afraid of [medical] bags, because they used to carry these bags. I still keep that kind [of bag] that I used to be afraid of as a little girl, that, ah, just like a big purse, it is a big, black *big purse*, misāw, *black one*. kēyāpic nikanawēyihtēn *for souvenir* ē-itwātamān. ē-kī-nipahi-kostamān anima māna, maskihkīwiyiniw māna ē-kī-kostak, nikī-sēkwāmon mān āyi atāmihk ōmatowahk nipēwinihk. ēkwa anohc awāsisak mōniyāw-iyiniw kā-pē-takohtēt mōniyās, kā-wīhkwēkāpawicik awāsisak ē-kitotācik mōniyāsa. mōy anima kīkway niyanān kayās, nikī-kostānānak mōniyāsak.

anohc ēkwa namōy kīkway ta-kostahkik awāsisak. ākayāsīmowak ayisk, nisitohtamwak ayis, māka niyanān mōy nōh-āh-ākayāsīmonān, iyikohk awāsisak kā-kī-pē-ay-- mōy māh-mihcēt ē-ohc-āyāwācik awāsisa, *parents*, mōy wiya māh-mihcēt, ātiht nēwo, nisto piko ātiht. īh, tāpiskōc ōma niya nikī-nēwin piko, *four, four - three sisters, but* kī-panātisiwak nītisānak, ēkwa ātiht kī-nīsōsēwak nayēstaw. ēkwa ētokē ana kayās nikī-pa-pēhtēn kim-- nimosōm-- nimosōminān, okimāhkān ōta, ēwako ana kā-kī-mihcētoskwēwēt, mitātaht wīwa, ē-kī-mitātahtoskwēwēt ana *Chief* payipwāt kī-itāw, ē-kī-okimāhkāniwit, mitātaht iskwēwa ē-kī-wīkimāt. ēkosi, ēkosi kī-itwēw māna kā-kī-oyōhtāwīyān. namōya ē-kī-mihcētōsēt ana ayi, okimāhkān ana. ayēnānēw piko otawāsimisa ē-kī-ihtasiyit iyikohk mihcēt ē-kī-ayāwāt ...

> — matwān cī ana kisēyiniw ē-kī-ohtamin--, ē-kī-ayi-- ēy, māskōc ana kisēyiniw ē-kī-tiyawīt, *you know*, tita-papā-wīcēwāt ōho otiskwēma; ēkwa ahpō ētokē mīna ēkot--, ahpō cī kī-kāh-kāhkwēyihtowak anik īskwēwak. [*pāhpināniwan*] namōya anima ta-pāhpihk, ka-pāhpihtānāwāw. —

ēkosi anima māna kāh-itwēhk, ayēnānēw piko ē-kī-ihtasicik awāsisak ēkwa *ten wifes* ē-kī-ayāwāt. ēkwa ana *the old -* māmawaci-wīwimāw ana, ēwako kākikē kā-papā-wīcihiwēt, nānitaw kā-isitāpāsowiht, kā-nikohtēwiht, ēkosi ēsa kāh-pōsit ēwako. ēwako ēsa kī-papā-wīcihiwēw, kihci-wīwimāw ana. ēkwa ōk ōtē kēkā-mitātaht ēwakonik ē-kīsitēpocik, ē-paminawasocik kahkiyaw kīkway kāhkēwak ē-osīhtācik, mihta ē-āwat-- ē-āwacitāpēcik, ē-nikohtēcik. omiht-- mihtikowāhpa kayās one. I still keep it for a souvenir, as I call it. I used to be deadly afraid of that, I used to fear the doctor. I used to flee underneath this kind of bed. And now today, the children, when a white person arrives, the children stand around the white man talking to him. There was nothing like that for us long ago. We were afraid of white men.

Today now there is nothing for children to be afraid of. Because they speak English, because they understand it, but us, we didn't ever speak English, as many children as they ... they didn't have many children, parents, not very many [per family]; some four, some only three. See, just like me, we were only four, four, four ... three sisters ... but my siblings passed away, and instead some had two children. And I guess there was that one long ago, I heard ... my grandfather, our grandfather, the chief here, that one who had many wives, ten wives, he had ten wives, that Chief *payipwāt* [Piapot] as he was called, he had been the chief and he married ten women. So that's what my late father used to say. He didn't have many children, that one, ah, that chief. There were only eight children though he had so many ...

> — I wonder if perhaps that old man was kept bus--, see, that old man was probably very busy, you know, to go about accompanying these women of his. And perhaps there would also be ... or else they would get jealous of each other, those women. [*laughter*] There should not be laughter, but you will laugh at that. —

That was what used to be said, there were only eight children and he had ten wives! And that one, the old ... the primary wife, the one who always went along, when going somewhere in the wagon, when going to chop firewood, I understand that that one would be on board. That one apparently went along, that foremost wife. And these ones over here, the nine of them, those ones were cooking, preparing the meals, everything, making dried meat; haul-- hauling firewood, chopping firewood. They would make wooden tipi structures long ago, kī-osīhtāwak māna kī-itwēw nohtā-- kā-kī-wiyōhtāwīyān. ē-cimatācik ayi, mihta, kayās ēwako ēkā t-āyahākoniyiki. ēkwa mīna ēkotē kīkway astāsowikamikohkēcik ē-ā-- omisi ē-itahpitahkik ayi mistikwa [*ē-isiniskēt*]. ēkotē ē-tēhtastācik ayi, omīciwiniwāwa tāpiskōc ōma mōsowiyās, *deer meat*, ēkot ē-astācik, kī-itwēwak māna ē-kī-tāpiti-pēhtawakik māna. ēwakw ānima wīstawāw otastāsowikamikowāw anima *same time* ē-kī-osīhtācik mihta anihi ohci. iskwēwak māk ēs ōki ē-kī-osīhtācik ēwakonik ōk ōki *ten - nine wives* ōk ōtē kā-nakatihcik *behind* ayisk pēyak awa wīcihiwēw kīkwāy papā-nātamowākwē. matwān cī ēwakw āna nawac ētokē ahpō wiya ēwako ē-kī-sākihiht nistam wīwimāw ahpō mīna ēkosi, ēkosi ē-kī-ispayik.

ēkosi māna nikī-itihtēn ayisk māna nikī-ayi---na-nitohtawāwak nimosōm ēkwa mīna nōhkom, awa *Little Sioux* ē-pīhtokwāht ōki kēhtē-ayak ōta niyanān kayās. ēkosi māna nikī-pa-pēhtawāwak ē-tāc-- ē-itācimocik ē-pam-- ē-na-nitohtamān ēkwa ē-pāhpicik māna. kētahtawē māna ē-kī-wawiyasācimot aw āyi, awa nimosōm awa, *Little Sioux* kī-itāw, ē-pwācis kī-itēwak.

ēkwa - tipiyawē wiya awa nōhkom awa ē-kī-- nōh-- nōhtāwiy ayi, tipiyawē okāwīsa, kā-kī-wiyokāwīt nōhtāwiy ē-kī-omisit ōhi. ōk āyi, nōhkom ēwakw āwa; nōhkom ēsa simāk kī-itāw kayās ēwako owīhowin nōhkom nōhtāwiy awa okāwiya, simāk kī-itāw ēsa nōhkom, ēwako tipiyawē nōhkom. ēkwa awa nōhkom, *her sis--* ōhi wīcisāna ōhi *Mrs. Little Sioux* ēwako, māka ēwakw āna kī-itāw nōhkom ē-iskwēwic kī-itāw. kā-iskwē--, ē-- ē-is-- ē-iskwēwit tāpiskōc, ēkosi kī-isiyihkāsow. ēkosi anima ē-kī-- kā-ispayik.

[5. **mīciwin**]

kayās ēwako ōma kā-wīhtamātakok, māka ētikwē nama kīkway nikiyāskin, ē-tāpwēyān ōma k-ētācimoyān ē-kī-pē-nēhiyawi-pimātisihk; ahpō mīna -.

my father said... my late father. They would stand the, ah, firewood up long ago so they would not be covered by snow. And also over there they would build something as a storage structure, tying the poles like this. [*MLR gestures.*] They placed their food on top of that, like moose meat, deer meat, they put it there. They used to say that, I always used to hear them. That was their storage place, while at the same time they were making firewood from those. But it was these women doing this, th-- those ten ... nine wives who were left behind over here, because that one would accompany him about with whatever they were going for. I wonder if that one was perhaps more ... or she was the first wife to be loved, or something like that, and that's how it happened.

That's what I used to hear, because I used to, ah, listen to my grandfather and also my grandmother; Little Sioux had these Elders entering our place long ago. So I used to hear them, ah, as they were telling stories ... I was listening and they were usually laughing. Eventually he would usually start telling funny stories, this one, ah, my grandfather who was called Little Sioux, they called him ē-*pwācis*.

And my actual, ah, this grandmother of mine, ah, my father's actual auntie, she was the older sister of my father's mother. These, well, that was my grandmother; my [own] grandmother was apparently called *simāk* long ago, that was my grandmother's name, my father's mother. My grandmother was apparently called *simāk*, that was my actual grandmother. And this grandmother of mine, her sis-- her sibling, that was Mrs. Little Sioux, but that grandmother of mine was called ē-*iskwēwic*. She was ... ah, ah, like "she who is a little girl," that was her name. That's how it was.

[**5. Food**]

This was long ago which I am telling you about, but I don't think I have told a lie about anything, I am being truthful when I tell about how Cree life was; and also ...

mihta ē-kī-ohtācihohk ēkota ē-kī-ohci-mīcisohk ēkwa mīna ē-kī-kawahikēcik nāpēwak. mētoni kī-misi-sakāw ōm ōta payipwāt's. ēwakw ānima ētokē ē-kī-kitācik ē-- ōh-- mihta ōhi nama kīkway ēkwa kā-ayāki. ē-kī-āh-ispāskwēyāk ēsa ōta māka cimacēsa ōhi ē-kī-osīhtācik ēkoni ē-atāwākēcik. kahkiyaw kīkway ē-atāwēcik: kistikāna, wiyās, ēkwa ōh ōta, kahkiyaw kīkway ōh ōh-- ohpikihcikana ōhi, wāwa mīna ēkota, pimiy — sīkosākana, mōniyāwak ōki k-ōsīhācik — ēkoni ē-oht-atāwēcik. nikī-ma-miywahcikānān māna. ēkwa mīna ē-kī-miyikawiyāhk māna kayās ayi-- kī-itwāniw māna "asahtowin", kiyānaw *rations* kī-itwāniw. ayi māna ē-kī-miyikawiyāhk ayi, aya awa, *bacon* awa. sōskwāc māna pēyak kitapahikan [*sic*: kitipahikan] ē-wēwēkinikātēk ē-miyikawiyāhk. wiyās, sīwinikan, ēkwa ka-- ah, *prunes* ōki, *prunes* ē-kī-asamikawiyāhk. sīwinikan, nihtiy, ēkwa cistēmāw, ē-- t-ēs-āpacihtāhk! wahwā, tāpiskōc ē-kī-nitaw-mis-ātāwēhk māna. ēkoni anihi ē-asamikawiyāhk, ēwakoni anihi ē-mīciyāhk. ēkwa -

āstamita ēkwa, kīkwāy ē-kī-wīcihikawiyāhk, kīkwāy ētikwē pahkwēsikanak māna nikī-wīcihikawinān. *Nineteen twenty-two* ēwako, nikī-wīcihikawinān kāspi-pahkwēsikanak, mētoni ē-kī-maskawisicik. mētoni māka kī-wīhkicisiwak māna, ē-kī-sikwāciwaswakik māna niya ēkwa sōminisak ē-takonakik. nitawāsimisak ōki ē-- ē-- tohtōsāpoy ē-takonahkik. kī-miyo-mīcisowak māna ōki awāsisak. ēwakw ānima ē-sīwipohāwasoyān, ē-mīcisocik ēkota.

ēkwa nikī-miyikawinān mīna sāh-sōskwāt pēyak mistikowas ōma ayi, *canned meat*, kā-pōskwahamahk māna, āskaw nīso mistik-- ē-ihtasiyāhk iyikohk ē-isi-miyikawiyāhk. wahwā, ēkwa māna ē-sāsāpiskisamāhk ēwako. nikī-ati-sikatēyihtēnān anima, *canned meat* anima, kikiskēyihtēn, nikī-misi-miyikawinān anima āskaw *eight boxes* ōhi. matwān cī anihi *twelve* māna ē-kī-asiwatēki, kēhcinā, *twelve*, ēy, 'toni kī--. wahwā, nikī-ma-miyopam-- nikī-miyo-pamihisonān, nikī-miyo--.

anohc ōm ēkwa, sōniyāw piko, sōniyāw pikw ānohc, sōniyāw ē-ayāwat kā-mīcisoyan. ēkwa, ēkwa ēwako ōma

People made a living from firewood, and were able to eat therefrom, and also from the men chopping down trees. There was really a lot of bush here on Piapot's Reserve. I guess that was all consumed, ah, the firewood, there is none of that left now. I understand that there used to be wooded areas on the hills here, but they made pickets and sold those. They bought everything: seeds, meat, and these here, every one of these homegrown items [e.g., vegetables], and eggs as well, lard, – cracklings, those that the white people made – those they bought from them. We used to eat well. And we used to be given, long ago, ah, it was referred to as "rations," we called it rations. Ah, we used to be given, ah, this, it was bacon. There used to be just one portion wrapped up and given to us. Meat, sugar, and ah, there were prunes, prunes were fed to us. Sugar, tea, and tobacco for use. Oh my, it was always like going shopping for a whole lot. Those are what we were fed, those are what we ate. And ...

Later on now, what was it that we were helped with, I don't know what these little biscuits were that we received as help. That was nineteen twenty-two, we received crunchy biscuits that were really hard. But they were always very tasty, I used to boil them into pieces and add raisins. My children, they ... they'd add milk. The children always used to eat well, and I'd be sweetening them up with dessert, and they'd eat from that.

And we were also merely given one box of ah, canned meat that we used to pierce open. Sometimes two box... how much was given depended on the number in a family. Oh my, we used to fry that. We started getting tired of that canned meat, you know as we'd be given a great deal, sometimes there'd be eight boxes. There were perhaps twelve [cans] in each box, I think twelve, eh, very ... We were very, we took good care of ourselves, we were well ...

Today now, it's only money, it's just money today, you have to have money to eat. And now this food, a little, it affects us a bit mīciwin apisīs, apisīs nānitaw kitōtākonānaw, māk āyisk ohtitaw ta-mīciyahk. ēkwa mīna, sīsīpak mīna kayās nikī-mowānānak, ēkwa mīna wēskacānisipak nikī-mowānānak. wāwa nikī-mīcinān, ēwakoyikohk ōma kē-ihkihk ōma *this month* awa, nikī-mīcinān wāwa. ēkwa anohc k-ōhcimikawiyāhk ēkwa, t-ōhcimi-- nōhcimikawinān ēkwa sīsīp ta-mowāyāhk. tānēhk ōhci k-ōhcimikawiyāhk? kīkwāy anima ē-miyosit awa sīsīp, tānēhki ētikwē? kīkwāy māk[a] k-ōhcimikoyāhkok mōniyāwak? *Spray* anima ōta k-āstācik *in a field*, kā-kistikēcik *spray*. ēkota ōhci sīsīpak ē-mīcisocik, mōya miyopayiw ōtē wiyawiwāhk t-āti-mowāyahkok sīsīpak. anohc ēkwa mōy nikaskihtānān, ēkwa ē-wīhkicisicik aniki sīsīpak. mētoni! mīcimāpoy, pahkwēsikan kā-takonat, pahkwēsikan, mitoni awāsisak māna ē-kīspocik. anohc ēkwa namōy kīkway nipakitinamākawinān kā-ayisiyinīwiyāhk ta-mowāyāhk pisiskīs, ahpō *deer* mīna ahpō ētokē nōhcimikawinān ēkwa ta-mowāyāhk, mēkwāc ōma; ayisk mīcisow, papā-mīciw ōma *spray* wīsta pistahtam. ēkota ētokē ahpō āhkosiwin nikāh-kī-ohci-kāhcitinēnān. īh, anohc ōma wāposwak māna ē-kī-miywēyimakik, nawaciko ēkwa nikostāwak, anima ē-āh-itwēhk, *you know*, nānitaw isi tāpwē, *you know*, ōma *spray* wīstawāw piko kīkway mīciwak, *grass* ayisk ōki wāposwak. nikostāwak mīna ēwakonik nīsta, namōya, namōya āta ē-kihc-ītēyimoyān, *but* nayēstaw ēwako ohci. kīspin ēkā ēkosi kī-ispayik, kēyāpic ōma wāposwak - nikī-nihtā-tāpakwān māna kayās māka ēkwa mōy nikāh-kaskihtān ta-tāpakwēyān. pahkisiniyān nānitaw ēkota nikāh-pa-pimisinin, namōya ayisk miywāsinwa nihcikwana, ōma *arthritis* ē-ayāyān, ēkwa ē-saskahohtēyān.

[**6. mīnisa, pahkwēsikan ēkwa nihtiy**]

wahwā, nīpinohk ōma, mīnisa ōta mētoni ē-kakwāyakēyatiki, mētoni ē-nōhtē-mīciyān mīnisa, mētoni omisi ē-itāskiskotēki. *Walker* nitayān, aya ē-kī-miyit anima, *Jean* aya, ākacac [*Akachuk*], ayi, ē-kī-wīcihit. ēwakw ēkwa mahti, ōta ēkwa *my apron* nikāh-kipwahpitēn, nitāyītahpitēn. ninātawāpin mahti t-ētakotēk, sēhkēs ta-pē-itakocihk, mōy awiyak. nisipwēhtān ēkwa ōta ōma sakāhk kisiwāk, ēwako ōma *walker*. wahwā, mīnisa omisi somehow but we have to eat it. And also, we also ate ducks long ago and we'd eat mud hens. We ate eggs, those were readily available during this month [May], so we ate eggs. Now today, we are forbidden, ah, we are prevented now from eating duck. Why are we warned against this? What is that, the duck is fine. But why do the white people warn us against them? It is the spray that they put in a field, spray where they are planting. The ducks eat from there. It's not doing good in their bodies and for us then to be eating the ducks. Today we are not able to, but those ducks are quite delicious. Very much so! In soup, where you add flour, and bannock, the children are always full. Today now we First Nations people aren't allowed to eat small animals, or deer even, I guess we are prevented from eating it, presently. Because it eats, it goes about eating and it, too, accidentally eats the spray. I guess we could even catch some illness from there. Well, today, these rabbits that I used to like, now I'm rather afraid of them, that is what's said now, you know, what if it is true, you know, this spray, they too eat everything, grass, these rabbits. I too am afraid of these ones. No, although I am not thinking highly of myself, but it's just from that. If that wasn't happening, the rabbits would still ... I used to be good at setting snares long ago, but now I wouldn't be able to set snares. If I fell somewhere, I would just lie there, because my knees are not good, I have arthritis and I walk with a cane.

[6. Berries, Bannock and Tea]

Oh my! In the summer there are a tremendous number of berries here, I really want to eat berries, they are just hanging thick and heavy like this. I have a walker, ah, she gave it to me, Jean, ah, Akachuk, she helped me. So now, let's see, I would tie my apron closed here, I tie it on both sides. I look around to see if anything is speeding along, if a car was approaching, there's no-one. I start off to this bush nearby; with this walker. Wow! The berries are ē-itāskiskotēki. mētoni ēkwa ē-mawisoyān ēkwa, wahwā, miscahīs, wahwā! nipē-pīhtokwān ēkwa oyākan nipiy nisīkinēn, ē-māyātahki waskicipayinwa, ēwakoni ēkwa niwēpinēn ēkwa, niwēpinēn ōma nipiy. wahwā, nisāsāpiskisēn ēkwa mīnisa, iyinito-pahkwēsikan mīn āwa mētoni miyohkasow ayisk ēyiwēhk ninihtā-nawacīn kēyāpic. ēwak ōma *muscles* k-ōh-ayāwakik iyikohk ē-māh-- ē-māh-mākonak *bannock*. [*pāhpināniwan*]

ēkosi ēkwa *bannock*, ēkwa awa iyinito-pahkwēsikan nikāh-kīskiswāw. ēy! ē-ma-mowak ēkwa mīnisa ōhi, *you know*. mōy āwiyak, nikēcikonēn ōhi nīpitihkāna ē-kostamān t-ātisamān, *you know*, mōy āwiyak. mētoni nikīspon mīnisa ē-mīciyān. ēkwa wiyāsis ōma ē-takwahtamān wiyās, *you know*.

nihtiy: kīkway ayis ōma mīna ē-pakwātamān niya. nikī-āpacihtān māna nihtiy anihi kā-asiwatēki maskimocisihk mistahi nikī-nayēhtāwispitēn māna, tāpiskōc māna pakiwayānis ē-- ē-kiki-minihkwēyān ē-kī-ispitamān ōma nihtiy. wā, nikwēskīn nitawāc. *Loose tea* ēkwa nima-minihkwān kayās ohci. ma kīkway ēwako - ma kīkway - ma kīkway ta-- tit-ēspitaman pakiwayānis ēkota, namōya ayisk - *loose tea* anima nitatāwān. *Blue Ribbon* mān ānima ēwakw ānima nitatāwān, nima-minihkwān ēwako. māka mīskot niwīnihikon anihi aya *leaves, you know,* māka māna kwēyask ē-wēpinamān anita māna ayi, anima ayi ita kā-kisīpēkiyākanēyān, ēkota ispayinwa. niwēpinēn māka māna, *you know. Loose tea* ōma ē-ma-minihkwēyān.

[**7. mawimoscikēwina**]

ēkosi anima k-āy-itācimostātakok kayās kī-miywāsin. ēkwa mīna nikāwiy, nikāwiy kī-- kiyē-- mōy ohci-wāpiw. mētoni kī-miywēyihtam, kī-sākihtāw ōma pāhkw-āyamihāwin, *Catholic* ōma k-ētwēyahk, ēkwa mīna ōma nēhiyawi-ayamihāwin kī-sākihtāw. omisi māna nikī-itik, "nitānis, ē-nīsiki ōhi piko kimawimoscikēwininawa," kī-itwēw māna. "ōma ayi, pāhkw-āyisak ōki — pāhkw-āyisak k-ētihcik *Catholic* aniki — ēkwa ōma kā-- ōma kā-nipākwēsimohk ēkwa mīna kā-matotisihk, nīso anihi ēwakoni kiyānaw," ē-kī-itwēt māna. ēwako ohci hanging thick and heavy like this. So now I am picking berries, oh my, quite a lot, really! I come inside and pour water in a bowl, the bad berries float to the top. I throw those ones out, and I throw out the water. Oh my! Then I fry the berries, and the bannock also bakes nicely because I can still bake well. This is the reason I have muscles, from kneading the bannock so much. [*laughter*] That's good.

So now the bannock, I would bake real bannock. Hey, I was eating that and these berries, you know. There was no-one around, I took out my dentures as I was afraid to stain them, you know, there was no-one around. I get really full eating berries. And a little bit of meat, eating meat with it, you know.

Tea! For that's another thing that I don't like. I used to use the tea that was in little bags but I really didn't like the flavour of it, it seemed like I was drinking through cloth, or that's what the tea tasted like. Oh my, I changed instead. I have been drinking loose tea for a long time. There is none ... nothing ... there is none of that cloth taste there, because there's no ... I buy that loose tea. Blue Ribbon is the one that I usually buy, I drink that. But on the other hand, it is untidy for me, those, ah, those leaves, you know. But I usually throw those in there, ah, where I am washing dishes, that's where they go. I generally throw them away, you know. It's loose tea that I drink.

[**7. Ways of Worship**]

So it is that what I am telling you about, it was nice long ago. And also my mother, my mother was, she was blind. She really liked and embraced Catholicism, we say "Catholic," and she also loved the Cree way of praying. This is what she used to tell me: "My daughter, there are only two ways that we pray," she used to say. "The one ... these are Catholics – the Catholics are called *'pahkw-āyisak'* – and the Thirst Dance and sweatlodge way, these are the two that are ours," she always used to say. For this reason k-ōh-sākihtāyān, kākikē nikī-itohtahāw nikāwiy *communion* k-ētohtēt nikī-wīcēwāw *communion* ē-otinahk. kēkāt tahtwāw ayamihēwi-kīsikāw ē-kī-pīhtokwēyāhk *church* ōta. kī-miywēyihtam nikāwiy ēkotowi ē-isi-ayamihāt kī-sākihtāw ēkwa mīna ōma nēhiyāwiwin mīna kī-sākihtāw, nīso.

ēkwa k-ētikot ēkwa ayamihēwiyiniw iskwēyāc kā-pē-pīhtokākoyāhk, wīhtamāk, "nawac, nawac *once a year* piko kī-otinaman ōma ayi, ta-nitawi-saskamoyan," kī-itik. "tānita ta-otinaman, *Easter time*. ēkota t-ōtinaman, pēyakwāw kanakē. ēkwayikohk kikitimākisin ēkā ē-wāpiyan," kī-itik nikāwiy. "kiwāpamik ētokē manitow ēkā ē-wāpiyan, pēyakwāw piko pēyakwāw otina, ta-saskamoyan." ēkosi nikī-itōtēnān nikāwiy. pēyakwāw, pēyak - pēyak pīsim pēyakwāw ē-ayamihāyāhk nikī-nitawi-saskamonān nikāwiy.

hām, kēyāpic, kēyāpic aspin nikāwiy ē-kīs-- ē-kī-isi-kiskinwahamawit kēyāpic nikanawēyihtēn anima, kēyāpit nisaskamon. ispī mēyopayiki *communion* nititohtān, *confession* ōma, kikiskēyihtēn, nititohtān pēyakwāw. mēyopayiki ita nititohtān, pēyakwāw. ēkwa ōma mīna kā-- kā-mawimoscikēhk pikw īspī wiya - pikw īspīhk wiya ēwako nititohtān. [*mōy kwayask pēhtākwan*] ōma kiyānaw kā-ay--. tāp-- tāpiskōc kā-nipākwēsimohk ēkwa mīna ēkosi ōma kā-ayi--, kā-mawimoscikēhk wiya ēwako nititohtān, mōya katāc pēyakwāw pēyak-askiy. māka wiya ana nikāwiy ē-kī-pimitisahwak anima pēyak-askiy piko - pēyak ask--, kētahtawē nikī-itohtānān *not every Sunday* māka māna *every Sunday* nikī-itohtahāw ē-sakāpēkinak ē-itohtēyāhk nitawi-saskamot, ta-nitaw-saskamoyāhk. ēkosi ē-kī-isi-ayamihāt nikāwiy.

hām, ēkwa ōki nicawāsimisak, ēkosi ē-isi-wīhtamawakik, ēwako sakinamwak. sākihtāwak ōki *Catholic* nicawāsimisak miywēyihtamwak. ēkwa mīna ōma kā-nipākwēsimohk, kā-nēhiyawi-mawimoscikēhk mīna sākihtāwak, wīcēhtamwak mīna ēwako, ē-nīsiki piko.

I hold to these, I always took my mother, when she'd go to communion, I would accompany her as she took communion. Almost every time it was Sunday, we'd enter the church here. My mother liked that way of prayer, she loved that, and she also loved the Cree culture, both of them.

And then the priest said to her, when he finally came to our house, he told her, "It would be better, better if you'd only take it once a year, ah, to go for communion," he said to her. "When should you take it? Easter time. Take it then, at least once. You are poor enough being blind," he said to my mother. "The Creator must see that you are blind; just once, take communion just once." So, we did that, my mother and me. Once, once each month we'd go to church and we took communion, my mother and me.

Well, still, still the way my mother taught me, I still keep that, I still take communion. When things go well, I go to communion, and confession, you know, I go once. If things go well, I go once. And also whenever there is a gathering to ask for blessing, whenever that is, I go. This is our [*inaudible*], like when there is a Thirst Dance, and also when, ah, when there are ceremonial prayers, I go for that, and not necessarily just once each year. But I followed my mother with that once a year, one year ... Eventually we went not absolutely every Sunday, but usually I took her every Sunday, leading her along so she'd go for communion, for us to go for communion. That's the way my mother prayed.

Well, and these children of mine, that's what I tell them, they hold onto this. My children hold onto being Catholic, they like it. And also the Thirst Dance, when there are Cree ceremonies as well, they hold to that, they follow that as well, the two ways only.

kētahtawē pē-nakīwak ōta, kīkwāyak ētokē, *preachers* ōta. namōya nikaskihtān ēkotē t-ē-- t-ēsi-wīcēwakik, ātawiya wīstawāw ēsa ē-miyo-nitotahkik kīkway, *you know*, māka wīstawāw pahkān, wīstawāw - *but* wīstawāw pahkān. ēkosi māna ē-itēyihtamān, mōy ē-pakwātakik, *you know, but* ma kīkway niya ēkota wīstawāw ayisk pahkān. nīsta ōki nitawāsimisak ē-isi-wīhtamawakik, itōtamwak ēwako. ēwako ōma kētahtawē saskamowak ōki ēkwa mīna ōma kā-ayi-- tāpiskōc *Christmas, midnight mass* itohtēwak ōki nikotwāw. āskaw niwīsāmikwak nititohtahikwak *midnight* ōma ē-itohtēyāhk, ē-mawimoscikēhk ayisk anima mīna ēwako, *you know*, kayās. kayās ēwakoni anihi nīso, nīso ayamihāwina ē-kī-ayāyāhk.

[**8. pimātisiwin wayawītimihk ēkwa askīhkānihk**]

ēkosi anima mētoni ē-takahkēyihtamān ōma ē-pē-isi-kakwēcimiyēk, āta mistah āyi, kwayask ē-kakwē-wīcihitakok. kayās, tānisi ē-kī-pē-pa-pamihohk, ahpō māna wayawītimihk mīna ē-kī-wa-wīkihk mīkiwāhpihk. anohc ēkwa sēsēskēyihtākwan awiyak ta-piscipayihtāt kīki, mitoni ta-nipahiskōhisk ēkota, anohc ēkwa ēwako. ēkosi ē-ispayik, ēha. wayawītimihk ē-kī-na-nipāhk, kā-nipāyan piyēsīsak ē-pēhtawacik kā-ati-wāpahk. ēkwa ē-kotawēyan pīhcāyihk, kocawānāpiskos ē-wī-pas--, ōma ē-nitohtamahk *fire*. āh, kī-miywāsin kayās, anohc ēkwa namōya. wahwā, mitoni. ēkwa mīna kayās mīna māna ē-kī-nawacīyāhk kāhkēwak ōma ayi, *dry meat*, ē-nawacīyāhk, *we roast it*, wahwā, ēkwa pimiy ēkota, iyinito-pimiy. wahwā, ēkwa *bannock* mētoni māna ē-kī-wīhkasik tāpiskōc ōma *dry meat*, kā-pāsamihk ōma kāhkēwak. mētoni māna nikī-takahkēyihtēnān.

anohc ēkwa pahkān. kīkwāy ocakisīsa ēkwa anih āyi kā-kīsisahkik? otākosīhk ēkosi nikī-nitawi-itōtēnān. ēkwa mīna kīkwāy ētokē wāwāpiskāsinwa ēkoni mīna ē-nawacīyāhk anihi. wahwā, wīhkasinwa wiya ātawiya. [JO: *"Marshmallows?"*] ēkotowa, awāsisak, kiyām mētoni ē-pihkahtēki kī-sāh-sōpahtamwak, nīsta mīna ēkosi ē-isi-mīciyān ayisk wīhkasinwa. [*pāhpināniwan*] wahwā! wawiyatēyihtākwan ōma anohc kā--

At one time, they came stopping here, whatever they were, some preachers here. I was not able to go with them, although they too appeared to petition well for things, you know, but they were different again, they as well ... but they, too, were different. That's what I think, it's not that I hate them, you know, but there's nothing there for me because they are different again. I, too, tell my children this, they do it. There are times they take communion, these ones, and also they ... like at Christmas, they go to midnight mass, any special time. Sometimes they invite me, they take me and we go to midnight [mass], because those were also the prayers, you know, long ago. Those were the two long ago, we had these two ways of worship.

[**8. Life Outdoors and on the Reserve**]

I am very pleased that you have come to ask me – although I am trying my best to help you – how long ago one took care to make a living, even living outdoors in a tipi. Nowadays there is a fear that someone might accidentally drive into your lodge and crush you to death there, that's how it is today. That's how it happens, yes. Sleeping outside, when you are sleeping you hear the birds as dawn approaches. And you make a fire inside, a little stove is going to ... you listen to the fire. Oh, it was nice long ago, and now today, not. Oh my, it really was. And also long ago we would roast ***kāhkēwak***, ah, dry meat, we roasted it, we roast it, oh my, and the grease there, rendered fat grease. Wow, and bannock, it would really taste good just like this, the dry meat, the ***kāhkēwak*** when it was dried. We really used to like that.

Today it is different. What are those little sausages [i.e., wieners] that they cook now? Yesterday we went and did that. And also whatever those little white things are, we roasted those too. Oh my, they did taste good though. [JO: *"Marshmallows?"*] That kind; the children, never mind that they are burnt, they slurp them up. I too ate them like that because they are delicious. [*laughter*] Oh my! It's funny today ...

āhh, ēkwa mīna awāsisak anohc. wahwā! mōya kīkway kayās ēwako. ōhi cēhcapācikanisa, āāh, ē-ati-pimakocihkik. wahwā, tānispīhk ētokē piko ta-āpocikwānīcik, ta-nipahisihkik. ma kīkway kayās. kīkwāy māna niyanān ē-kī-āpacihtāyāhk? mistik ē-kīskatahamāhk, miscikos, takwahiminānāhcikos, ēwako ē-papā-tēhtapiyāhk tāpiskōc tāpwē. kayās ēwakw ānima, ēkwa anohc ka-- oskātisiwāwa konita k-ētakotē-- [*pāhpināniwan*]. ēwakw ān-- kayās nimētawēwininān niyanān miscikosa ē-kī-tēhtapātamāhk āhk ītāp tāpiskōc misatim ana ē-papāmipahtāyāhk. [*pāhpināniwan*] wahwā, ēwako wawiyatēyihtākwan.

mētoni ēkos ānima, anohc ēkwa mīna wiya āta wiya ēkwa pahkān mīna ōma anohc nitat-ītēyihtēn ōma ōta k-āyāyāhk payipwāt*'s*. mitoni kāmwātan ōta. nama kīkway ē-- mōy ākwāskam awiyak. niya wiya ē-isi-kiskēyihtamān, *you know*, ti-- ta-misi-sās-- awiyak ta-sasīhtēyihtamān ōma *next door*, mōya. mētoni sōskwāc *at night*, ma kīkway *no noise*, kwayask nina-nipānān. mōy kīkway ēkwa mīna - sōskwāc ayi *nice and quiet* kā-itwēhk, sōskwāc mitoni miywāsin askīhkānihk awiyak t-āyāt. ēkota ayisk ōma ē-ohtaskānēsiyahk askīhkānihk. māka ayisk kīkwāy k-ētwēyān, sōniyāw ēkwa anohc, ēwako ōma k-ōh-ayāyēk ōtēnāhk, kitatoskānāwāw ayis, sōniyāw ē-kaskihāyēk. anohc ēkwa sōniyāw kā-pīkiskwēt, kiyawāw ōma anohc k-ōhpikiyēk. ēkwa māka niyanān ōma kā-kēhtē-ayiwiyāhk, ma kīkway ēwako, *you know*, namōy-- ēwak ōhci ētokē ōta 'toni k-ōh-takahkēyihtamān niya, *you know*, kinwēsīs ōma kā-kī-sipwēhtēyāhk ōta ohci *nineteen sixty-six* kā-kī-ohci-piciyāhk.

[**9. sōniyāhkēwin**]

kīkwāy anima kā-kī-ohci-piciyāhk? kī-mētawāniwiw māna wayawītimihk *cars* ē-nitawi-mētawēyāhk *bingo* ē-nitaw-mētawēhk. kayās ēwakw ānima wayawītimihk ē-tasi-mētawēhk. *Edenwold* ōta, ēkotē nititohtānān nikisēyinīm niwīcēwāw, nipōsihikawinān, ē-mohci-pō-- ē-mosci-mostohtēyāhk māka nipōsihikawinān. ēkwa ayi piko ē-osōniyāmiyāhk, *fourteen dollars* piko ē-ayāwāyāhk kā-nitaw-mētawēyāhk *Edenwold. Nineteen - nineteen sixty-six, twelfth of May - July, July*, namōya wiya *May. July* ē-mētawēhk *Edenwold*

Oh, and also the children today! Oh my! There was none of that long ago. These bicycles, ah, they go by so fast. Wow! One wonders when they will tumble head first, and fall to their death. There was none of that long ago. What did we used to use? We cut down a branch, a little stick, a chokecherry branch, we would ride around on that like it was real. That was long ago, and today their little legs are just going.... [*laughter*] That ... our play long ago for us was riding on little sticks pretending like it was a horse as we were running about. [*laughter*] Oh my, that is so funny.

That was the way that it was, and today now it's alright that it is different, I start to think here where we are at Piapot Reserve. It's really calm here. There is nothing ... No-one is over-anxious. As for me, that's how I know it, you know, for someone to be ... for me to be stressed about next door, no. At night there is absolutely no noise, we sleep properly. And there is nothing ... ah, it's just nice and quiet, as they say, it's just really nice for someone to be on the reserve. Because that's where we come from, the reserve. But what else can I say? Money is the thing, that is why you are in town, because you work, earning money. Nowadays money talks, for you who are growing up today. But now for us who are elderly, there is none of that, you know, not ... Perhaps that is why I am really happy, you know, it's been a little while since we left from here, it was nineteen sixty-six that we moved from here.

[**9. Making Money**]

For what reason did we move? There used to be games outside, we'd go in cars to play, people would go play bingo. That was long ago, when people played outside. Here in Edenwold, we went there, I accompanied my old man, we were given a ride, we just ... we were on foot walking but we got a ride. And, ah, we had only a bit of money, we only had fourteen dollars when we went to play in Edenwold. It was nineteen - nineteen sixty-six, the twelfth of May ... July, it was July, not May. There was a sports day here in ōta. ēkotē ē-mētawēhk, nikisēyinīm k-ōtahowēt *thousand dollars*. wahwah! nipē-kīwānān. nipē-kīwānān *a thousand* ē-ayāwāyāhk, nīhcāyihk ēkotē ē-ayāyāhk. nō-- nikisēyinīm kī-atoskēw kiskinwahamātowikamikohk ē-wēpahikēt, ē-atoskēt anita ē-pēhkihcikēt. nīst-- nīstanaw tahtwāpisk ē-miyiht, ē-tipahamāht *every two weeks* ēwako, *twenty dollars* ē-miyiht. kī-wēhtakihcikāniwiw ayisk kayās.

īh, ē-- ē-kiskēyihtahkik ōki *welfare*, niyanān *welfare*, niya ēkwa *Johnny* ēkwa *Marie* ē-nistiyāhk. kā-kīskisokawiyāhk *our welfare*, namōy nōh-miyikawinān. ēkosi k-ētwēt *old man*, "nitakisa awa *thousand dollars*," itwēw. "kiyām, picitān," itwēw. "ka-nitawi-wīc-āyāmānaw *Barbara*." kī-atoskēw anita *eleven block Albert Street* awa *Barbara*, kī-atoskēw ayihk āhkosīwikamikohk. *Nurse* ōma ē-itatoskēt. namōya wiya ē-*nursi*wit, *you know*, māka ē-wīcihāt *nursa*. ēkosi nititāw awa *Barbara*, "ka-pē-wīc-āyāmitinān, misawāc kitatoskān, nika-pēhkascikān niya ēkwa mīna nika-kīsitēpon ēkwa mīna ka-astamātinān ta-mīciyahk, ta-mīciyahk, ta-mīciyan," nititāw. "ēha," itwēw. "ēkosi ispī miskamāni wāskāhikan, ēkospī nika-sipwēpicinān," nititāw. "ōta nikakwē-ayānān ōtēnāhk," nititāw. "ēha," itwēw. tāpwē nitawi-atoskēw.

ēkwa mīna awa kisēyiniw miskam *chickens* ē-atoskātācik wiya ēkwa nikosis, *Johnny* awa, awa *Johnny Rockthunder, my son* awa, *you know*. ēkota kī-atoskēwak *chickens* ē-- ē-- --pimi-atoskātācik, *you know*, kā-pimakocihkik *chickens* ēkotowa, kī-sōniyāhkēwak. ēkosi ēkwa ē-pōyot, ē-pōyot ēkwa awa nikisēyinīm nikosis mīna. wahwā, niyaskotam ēkwa. pitamā nitēpwātēn ayi wāskāhikan mahti ta-miskamān. nimiskēn pēyak, ēkota *hundred and ten* nitikawin ta-tipahamān. ēkotē nitispicinān.

ēkotē ēkwa ē-ispiciyāhk, wahwā, nama kīkway ēkwa sōniyāw kā-pīkiskwātak pēyak, āh, *Sister* ē-kiskēyimak, *at Sacred Heart. I phone her* ēwako. ēwako tāpwē nipē-- nipē-āsitēmik. "ahām," itwēw. "pē-atoskē ōta," itwēw. "namōya māka wiya *by the hour*," itwēw. "ka-mosci-tipahamātin sōniyāw ēkwa mīna

Edenwold in July. Playing there, my old man won a thousand dollars. Wow! We came home. We came home and had a thousand dollars, we were down there in the valley. My ... my old man worked in the school, sweeping up, he worked there cleaning. Twe-- He was given twenty dollars, he was paid every two weeks, receiving twenty dollars. Because things were cheap long ago.

Well, the welfare people knew, our welfare, me and Johnny and Marie, the three of us, our welfare was cut off, we didn't receive it. So the old man said, "So much for this thousand dollars," he said. "Never mind, let's move," he said. "We will go and stay with Barbara." She worked [*sic;* lived] there at eleven block Albert Street, did Barbara, she worked there at the, ah, hospital. She worked as a nurse. She wasn't a nurse, you know, but she helped the nurses. So I said to Barbara, "We will come to stay with you, you work at any rate. I will clean up and I will also cook and we will set aside something for all of us to eat, for us to eat, for you to eat," I told her. "Yes," she said. "So when I find a house, we'll move out at that time," I said to her. "We are trying to stay here in town," I told her. "Yes," she said. Then she went to work.

And the old man found something, they were working with chickens, he and my son, Johnny, this Johnny, ah, Johnny Rockthunder, this son of mine, you know. They worked there, working along on the chickens, you know, when the chickens moved by on that kind [conveyor belt], they made money from that. But then he quit, my old man quit then and my son too. Oh my, it was my turn now. First of all, I called hoping to find a house. I found one, there I was told to pay a hundred and ten [dollars]. We moved over there.

Then moving over there, oh my, there was really no money and I spoke to one, ah, Sister that I knew at Sacred Heart. I phoned that one. Sure enough she called me back. "Okay," she said. "Come work here," she said. "But it won't be by the hour," she said. "I will give you some money, and kika-mosci-miyitin kīkway ta-mīciyan tāpiskōc kīkway ōma pimiy ēkwa sāsikanak ōki ēkwa mīna pahkwēsikan ēkwa mīna awa aya, ōhi sīwihkasōsak. ēwakonik kikāh-kīwēhtahāwak ēkwa *a little bit money*," itwēw. tāpwē, k-ētohtēyān. tāpwē ē-otākosik kā-pē-kīwēhtahicik misi-pōsihcikēwak nāway. pimiy ē-misi-miyicik, *Sisters* ōki, *you know*. tānitē wētinamowākwē, matwān cī aniki kā-kiskinohamāhcik nēk āyamihēwihkānak ēkotē ohci. nimisi-pē-- nipē-- nimisi-pē-kīwētonawān kīkway ta-misi-mīciyāhk, pahkwēsikan, *pastry, cakes* ōki nanātohk. nihtiy mīna nimiyik, kāspisikan mīna pēyak nimiy--. wahwā, mētoni ēkwa mīna awa sōniyās awa ōta, mētoni nimiywācihonān. ēkwa ōmayikohk ēkwa wiyāpahki māna ē-itohtēyān ē-mostohtēyān *Sacred Heart*, ēkwa āh, *ten block McTavish* ē-ayāyān ēkotē ohci ē-mostohtēyān. *St. Mary's* anima, āh, ēkotē ē-itohtēyān *every morning*.

piyisk nitati-mihcētinān iskwēwak ē-atoskēyāhk. mihcēt ēkota nōh-kiskēyimāwak ōki *young people* ōki, oski-iskwēsisak ōki; ē-atoskēyāhk, ē-wiyēsamāhk ōhi maskisina. ēkwa mīna *jack-shirts* ōhi ē-wiyēsamāhk, ēkwa mīna *mukluks* ē-wiyēsa--, ē-ati-kaskikwātāyāhkok. piyisk mētoni mistahi kīkway sōniyāhkēw aw āya *Sister*. ati-sōniyāhkēw, nitipahamākonān mōy wiya *by the hour* sōniyāsa omis īsi. kahkiyaw kīkway ahpō piko mīna manisikanisa mīna misi-nātitisaham mitoni ē-miywāsiki. ēkoni mīna pāh-pēyak ē-miyikoyāhk, ēkoni anihi *seven dollars* ē-tipahamāhk anihi manisikanisa pahkēkin ohci. tipiyawē ōhi kēyāpic anima misi-manisikanis ōta nitāpacihtān kā-kaskikwāsoyān. mitoni nimiyo-sōniyāhkānān.

ēkosi ēkwa, ēkosi ēkwa, ispimihk ēkwa kā-āhtokēyāhk ēkwa *eighteen twenty-one Scarth Street. Scarth Street,* ēkota ēkwa mīna kā-atoskēyāhk. mitoni ēkwa, niya *ēkwa Mrs. Fourhorns, Violet* itāw. ēkwa mīna kī-panātisiw pēyak aya *Dorothy Francis*, ahpw ētokē *you know her*, *that's the one*, ēkwa niya, ninistinān. nikaskikwāsonān ispimihk — [*ē-īkatē-itwēt*, MLR: *"coffee wī-minihkwēyēko..."*] — nikaskikwāsonān. wahwā, mitoni piko! nimāh-miyikawinān ōhi kīkway ōhi itāp-- itāpacihcikana ahpō piko *aprons* ōhi ta-kikiskamāhk kā-kaskikwāsoyāhk, ... kā-kaskikwāsoyāhk. wahwā, mitoni nitakahkācihonān.

I will give you something to eat, things like lard and cracklings, and also bannock and also this, ah, these baked sweets. You can take those home and a little bit of money," she said. "Certainly," and I went. Sure enough that evening when they brought me home, they put lots of stuff in the back. They gave me a lot of lard, these Sisters, you know. Wherever she got it from, I wonder if it was from those ministers over there. I greatly ... I came, I came home with a great deal for us to eat, bannock, pastry, cakes of all kinds. She also gave me tea and one [tin] of coffee ... Oh my, and there was this money here, we were really living well with this amount. And every morning I would go walking, just on foot, to Sacred Heart, and ah, I was at ten block McTavish and I walked from there. It was St. Mary's, ah, that I went to every morning.

Eventually there started to be a lot of us women working. I knew many of these young people from there, these young girls; we were working, cutting out patterns for moccasins. And also we cut out patterns for these "jack-shirts," and also mukluks, we cut ..., and we began sewing them. Finally, she made a great deal of money, did this, ah, Sister. She started making money, and she paid us but not by the hour, small change like this. Just everything, and she also sent for scissors which were very nice. She gave those to each of us, we paid seven dollars for those leather scissors. I still use my own big scissors here when I am sewing. We really made good money.

So then, so then, we moved up to eighteen twenty-one Scarth Street. And there at Scarth Street we were also working. Really then, me and Mrs. Fourhorns, she was called Violet. And also the late Dorothy Francis, perhaps you know her, that's the one, and me, the three of us. We sewed upstairs – [*aside*, MLR: "If you want to drink coffee..."] – we sewed. Oh my, just really! We would be given these items, these tools or even these aprons for us to wear when we were sewing ... when we sewed. Wow, we made a great living.

kētahtawē k-ō-wiyasiwēhk. "wī-oyasiwāniwiw," itwāniw. wī-oyasiwēw *Co-op Company* itwēwak ōki *Violet* wiyawāw, *Violet*. kiskēyihtam awa wiya nistim awa ōta *Violet*, aya awa *Fourhorns*. kiskēyihtam anima kahkiyaw, namōya ōma ē-kiyāskīwācimoyān, kwēyask ē-ācimoyān. tāpwē, *Co-op* anima k-ōtinahk ōma *shop* ōma k-āyāyāhk. *Co-op* kī-otinam, *by the hour* ēkwa ē-wī-miyikawiyāhk. "ēha," nititwānān. ahām ēkwa nētē k-ēspiciyāhk ēkwa āh, āh, *Victoria Avenue, way up east*, ēkwa nētē ē-ayāyān nēma ayi *Connaught Street, seventeen block, west side* ē-ayāyāhk, wāhyaw. *Four miles* ē-itohtēyān māna. mōy wiya ē-pimohtēyān, *bus* ē-pōsiyān. k-ōtinahk ēkwa *company* aw ānima, *by the hour* ēkwa *five dollars* nitikawinān ē-wī-tipahamākawiyāhk. tāpwē.

mitoni misi-- misi-*machines* pē-pāh-pīhtokwatāniwiw kaskikwāsonākana, nikāh-kocīhikawinān, nikāh-kaskihtānān. mētoni ēkwa iskwēwak misahkamik ēkota ē-otinihcik ēkwa ayis ēkwa *by the hour* ēkwa ē-isi-miyikawiyāhk, *company* awa ē-miyikoyāhk, āh, *Co-op*. āāh, nitatoskānān, *eight o'clock* nimātatoskānān, *four o'clock* nipōyonān. *Bus* māna nitōtināw nīsta, *four miles* ē-itohtēyān *every morning. Every morning* anima ēkota ē-ohtohtēyān ayi ē-kakwē-sōniyāhkēyān. piyis ēkwa, āh, *five dollars and thirty cents* kā-miyikawiyāhk. piyisk ēkwa *thirty-five cents* niyahki-miyikawinān, *five thirty-five* niyahki-miyikawinān. āh, nisōniyāhkānān 'toni, *every two weeks* nimiyikawinān *money*.

ēkota ēkwa iyikohk ē-sīsko-- kahkiyaw kīkway ē-osīhtāyāhk, *mukluks*, pakwahtēhona, *beadwork*, kahkiyaw kīkway ē-wiyēsamāhk *jack-shirts*, āhh! wahwā, misi-mistikowata māna awa ē-kī-- ēwako awa nitōkimāminān *Roger* kī-itāw, *Roger, Howard; Roger* māka kī-itāw. ēwako māna ē-kipahahk ōhi mistikowata, nitatoskēwininān ōma ē-sipwētisahahk. kahkiyaw kīkway yiyīkastisak mīna, ēkwa mīna kā-māsihkēcik anihi ē-pē-atoskēmocik ayi, *jackets* anihi, *fringes* ōki. ēwakonik aniki mīna ē-kī-misi-osīhtamawāyāhkok anihi *jackets*, kīh-kāh-kikiskamwak māna ... pahkēkinwē-*jackets*, niyanān anihi ē-kī-osīhtāyāhk. ē-kī-atoskēmocik māka wiya ē-ohtisit awa nitōkimāminān, *you know*, māka mētoni mistahi nikī-sōniyāhkēstamawānān. *Company* ēwako wīsta ayisk ē-otōkimāmit anihi, *you know*, ēkwa nīstanān awa nitōkimāminān.

Eventually there was to be a decision. "There is going to be a decision," it was said. The Co-op Company will make a decision, Violet and them were saying, Violet. She knows, this niece of mine here, Violet, ah this one, Fourhorns, she knows all that. I am not telling a fabricated story, I am telling it properly. Sure it was true, the Co-op took over the shop we were at. The Co-op took it over and now we were going to be paid by the hour. "Yes," we said. So now we were to move over there, ah, ah, to Victoria Avenue, way up east, and I was over there, ah, at Connaught Street, seventeen block, we were on the west side, far away. I used to go four miles. I wasn't walking, I took the bus. When the [Co-op] company took over, we were told we were going to be paid by the hour, five dollars. Sure enough.

Really big, big machines were brought in, sewing machines, we were tested on them and we were able to do it. So now there were a whole lot of women hired, since now we were being paid by the hour, this company was giving us that, the Co-op. Oh, we worked, we started at 8 o'clock, we quit at four o'clock. I also used to take the bus, going four miles every morning. Every morning I would go from there, trying to make money. Finally then, ah, we were given five dollars and thirty cents. Then finally we were given a raise to thirty-five. We got a raise to five thirty-five. Oh, we really made money, we received money every two weeks.

Then there was so much ... We made everything, mukluks, belts, beadwork, we cut patterns for everything, jack-shirts, oh! Oh my, usually these large boxes, ... that boss of ours, he was called Roger, Roger, Howard; but he was called Roger. That's the one who would always close the boxes and send our work away. Everything, gloves as well, and also those wrestlers would come to place orders for ah, jackets, with these fringes. Those ones as well, we made a lot of those jackets, they would always wear those ... leather jackets, we made those. They ordered those, but that boss of ours made a lot from there, you know, we made a great deal of money for him. But he, too, had the company as his boss, you know, and he was our boss.

wahwā, mitoni piko nikī-- nikī-miyopayinān anima iyikohk isko nīsta *sixty-five year old* kā-kī-pōyoyān. *My last, my last day* nikī-nitaw-ātoskān *sixty-five.* kā-pē-miyit nitōkimām ayi asiwacikan asisīwēkin ēkota pē-astāw, "*For your birthday,*" nitik. kīkwāy ētokē, *I thought* niya *a card* ē-miyit, *you know*, nitohtamahkamikisin ōtē; *las-- my last day* ōma ē-nitaw-atoskēyān. ēkwa ōma niyōhtēnēn ōma *my -* kīkwāy kā-pē-miy-- awīn āwa mitātahtomitanaw tahtwāpisk, *a hundred* ēs ōma *for my birthday*. wahwā, nitatamihik ēkot ēkwa ohci ē-wāh-wāstinamawak, "*Thank you,*" ēkotē ohci ē-itak, *you know*, ē-nanāskomak ē-tipahamawit, ē-miyit ōma *for my birthday* awa nitōkimāminān. ēkosi iskwēyāc ēkwa nikī-itik, "namōya ē-pakitinitān," nitik, "kīspin nānitaw ōta ispayiki kinakacihtān kīkway, kika-tēpwātikawin, kika-pē-ayi--, kika-pē-otinēn *a little bit work* kika-tipahamākawin," ē-tāpwēt māka.

ēkwa, ēkosi ēkwa nētē nititohtān ēkwa nēm āyi, *Grey Nuns* nēma nikī-isiyihkātēnān, *Grey Nuns* mān ēwako ōma, *Pasqua* ēkwa. ēkotē nitapin *x-ray* ē-nitawi-otinamān, āsay ē-kī-kīsatoskēyān, ōma ayiw anita *shop* anima āsay ē-kī-pōyo--. ēkota awa *x-ray man* awa, mitoni nitakahkēyimik, *you know*, mitoni nipāh-pīkiskwātik, nikakwēcimik tānisi, niwāh-wīhtamāk tānisi ōki ayisiyiniwak, nikāh-kiskēyimimāwa, *you know*.

ēkwa ōma itwēw, "kēyāpic cī ōma *shop* ē-pimipayihtāt?" itwēw. ēkoni ōhi wīhēw ōho ōta nistima ōhi *Violet* awa. "namōya ēkwa niya," nititāw. "nikī-pōyon," nititāw, "*but* nitōtinēn māka kēyāpic *a little bit work* ēkotē ohci," nititāw. "*Mr. Rogers* ana nitōkimām." "ēwako ana ē-kī-kitotak," itwēw. "ēkwa ōma ē-kī-wīhtamawit ēkwa ōma ē-isiyihkāsoyan *Mary Louise Rockthunder*, kiya ēcik ōma," nitik. "ēha," nititāw. "kiya cī k-ōtinaman ayi," itwēw, "ayi apisīs atoskēwin wayawītimihk?" nitik. "ēha," nititāw, "niya." "ayi," itwēw, "ē-nōhtē-atotitān," itwēw. "mētoni misahkamik ōta kīkway nitayānān," itwēw, "*nurses* ēkwa mīna *doctors* ōki, ē-pāh-pīkopayiniyiki ayi," itwēw, "ēkotowahk ōhi," itwēw, "ōh ōkikiskikaniwāwa tāpiskōc ōma ayi *jacket* ōma, *ripping*,

Oh my, we were just really ... we did so well until I, too, was sixty-five when I quit. My last, I went and worked my last day at sixty-five. My boss came and gave me a packet; an envelope, he placed there. "For your birthday," he told me. I wonder what it is? I thought he was giving me a card, you know, I was busy over here; las... it was my last day working. Then I opened this ... my ... what did he come to give .... but here was a hundred dollars, a hundred apparently just for my birthday. Oh my, he made me happy and from there I was waving at him, "Thank you," I told him because of that, you know, I was grateful to him for paying me, for giving me this for my birthday, this boss of ours. So then at last he said to me, "I am not letting you go," he said to me. "If anything happens here that you can handle, you'll get a call, you'll come and ... you'll come take a little bit of work and you'll be paid," he said and he meant it.

And so now I went over there and that, ah, we called that the Grey Nuns [Hospital], that used to be Grey Nuns, now it's Pasqua. I sat over there going to take an x-ray – I had already retired, this ah, I had already quit there from that shop – there was this x-ray man there, he really liked me, you know, he would talk with me a lot, he asked me how things were, he would tell me how these people ..., I knew them, you know.

And he said this: "Does she still run the shop?" he said. It was that one he named here, that niece of mine, Violet. "I don't anymore," I told him. "I quit," I told him, "but I still take a little bit of work from there," I told him. "My boss is Mr. Rogers." "That is the one I spoke to," he said, "and he told me this, that your name is Mary Louise Rockthunder, so I guess that's you," he said to me. "Yes," I said to him. "Are you the one that takes, ah," he said, "ah, a little work on the side?" "Yes," I said to him, "That's me." "Ah," he said. "I want to ask you to do something," he said. "We have a whole lot here," he said, "the nurses and the doctors as well, their things get torn now and again," he said. "Those kinds of things," he said, "those uniforms of theirs, like, ah, jackets, this, ripping, and ēkwa mīna otāsiwāwa, *patching*, ēkwa mīna omaskisiniwāwa, *patching*," itwēw. "ēkotowahk ē-nōhtē-atotitāhk," itwēw. "mōy cī, namōy cī nānitaw otinaman?" itwēw. "tāpwē," nititāw. "ēkosi anima ē-itatoskēyān," nititāw. "nikāh-kī-otinēn," nititāw. "māka kika-itōtēn," nititāw, "kīspin, kīspin awiyak ē-wī-atosit kahkiyaw masinahikana otayiwiniwāwa awīn āna omaskisina, ēkota kik-ākostahēn," nititāw. "*You paste it* ēkota, kahkiyaw. ēkosi ati-kīsihtāyāni kahkiyaw ōhi ēkota nika-ati-kikamohtān, *which ones* anihi." "ēkosi nika-itōtēn," itwēw. "kik-ētohtatamātin, *you wait for me about, oh, about* nīso-kīsikāw ōta ohci," itwēw. "*You wait -*." nikakwēcimik, "tānitē oht-- ē-ayāyān?" — nētē nikī-ayān *2nd Avenue*, nētē nēma ayi *street* anima. — "ēkotē nitayān," nititāw ēkwa mīna *my phone number* nitōtinēn, nimiyāw, ēwako mīna otinam. "*I phone you*," itwēw, "mayaw wī-sipwēhtēyāni." "*Okay*."

tāpwē, kētahtawē kā-pē-sēwēpicikēt *next day*: "kē-wāpahk, kē-wāpahk *you wait for me*," itwēw, "*about four o'clock*," itwēw. "nika-kīsatoskān ōta," itwēw, "*half past four. You wait for me*." "ēha, ēha," nititāw, "ka-pēhitin." ayisk nika-miywēyihten *bingo, any time* ta-sōniyāhkēyān *for my bingo, you know*. tāpwē! kā-takopayik ōta *nice* ayi, ayi, ayi ōma *van* mitoni wahwā, pē-- pē-ma-matwēhikēw ēwako awa, ēwako awa *x-ray man* awa, ninisitawēyimāw. "nipētān ōta anihi," itwēw, "kā-wī-atotikawiyan," itwēw. "nika-nātēn," itwēw. "mōya cī nān-- ...?" "pē-pīhtokwatā!" nititāw. wahwā, misi-mistikowas mētoni anima ē-misāk kā-pē-pīhtokwēta-- pē-- pē-astamawit. wahwā, tān ōt āni a-mīsahikēyān! ahpō mitāsak māka ōki aya *buckskin pantses* ōki, kikiskēyihtēn, *hide* ōma, *you know*. ēkwa mīna ōhi *jackets* ē-āh-*rip*iwiki. "ēwakoni ōhi," itwēw. "kahkiyaw masinahikana kikamowa owīhowiniwāwa," itwēw. "ē-at-īsi-kīsihtāyan, ēkos īsi ati--" "ēh, kiwīhtamātin ē-wī-at-ākwahamān," nititāw. tāpwē. ēkwa miyācikwāsoyān ēkwa, nikīsihtān pēyak nitati-akostahēn anihi, ohpimē nitat-āsiwatān kahkiyaw ōhi. "ēkwa mayaw kīsihtāyani," itwēw, "*you phone me*," itwēw. "kahkiyaw nika-māwasakwasinahēn tānisi ē-itakihcikēyan," itwēw. niwīhtamawāw tānisi ē-itakihcikēyān. kīkway ōma, apisīs kīkway ē-pīkopayik ... [*matwē-sēwēpicipayin*] also their pants, patching, and also their moccasins, patching," he said. "We'll hire you to do that kind of thing," he said. "Isn't it, would it be fine for you to take it on?" he said. "Sure," I told him. "That's the kind of work I do," I told him. "I could take it," I told him. "But you will do this," I told him, "if, if someone wants to hire me, records will be kept for all their clothing, whose shoes, etc., you'll fasten that there," I told him. "You paste it there, for all of them. So as I finish all of those things, I will attach it there, which ones are which." "I will do that," he said. "I will bring it to you, you wait for me for about, oh, about two days from now," he said. "You wait ...." He asked me, "where fro..., are you [living]?" – I was over there on 2nd Avenue, that was over there at, ah, that street. – "That is where I am," I told him and I also took my phone number and I gave it to him, and he took that as well. "I'll phone you," he said, "as soon as I'm going to leave." "Okay."

Sure enough, all of a sudden he called next day. "Tomorrow, you wait for me tomorrow," he said, "about four o'clock," he said. I will finish work here," he said, "at about half past four. You wait for me," he said. "Yes, yes," I told him, "I'll wait for you." Because I will enjoy bingo, and any time I can make money for my bingo, you know. For sure! When it arrived here, a nice ah, ah, ah, van, really, oh my. He comes ... that one was knocking, it was that x-ray man, I recognized him. "I brought these here," he said, "which you are being hired to do," he said. "I will pick them up," he said, "if that's all righ...?" "Bring them inside," I told him. Oh my, what a big box, it was really big which he brought in and set there for me. Oh my, how I was going to be patching! Even pants, but these, ah, there were these buckskin pants, you know, it was hide, you know. And also these jackets that had been ripped. "Those are the ones," he said. "All the labels are attached with their names," he said. "As you're getting finished ... that's the way to ...." "Ah, I did tell you that I'll be attaching them," I told him. Right. And now I started sewing, I finish one and fasten one of those on, and I continue putting all of those in the bag off to the side. "And as soon as you're finished," he said, "you phone me," he said. "I will tally everything up for how much you will be charging," he said. I told him how much I was charging. If it's something, something with a little apisīs ē-pīkopayik kīkway ēyiwēhk apisīs tāpiskōc *seven dollars*, ēkwa mistahi kīkway ē-pīkopayik miscahīs. nitati-masinahēn ēkota nitati-masinahēn, nitati-masin-- nimasinahikān ayis wiya, *you know*. "ēkosi mayaw kīsihtāyani," itwēw, "*you phone me*," itwēw. ninakatamāk ayis *phone number*.

mayaw ē-kīsihtāyān ka-ta-- āsay kā-pē-takopayit. wahwā *two hundred and fifty* nikī-sōniyāhkān, *two hundred and fifty* nayēstaw *repairing work* ē-itōtamān. *You know*, ē-mīsahikēyān ōma. ēkosi māka anima *two fifty*, *lots* ē-kī-osīhak, *you know*, nīkihk ē-ma-- namōya awiyak tipahikēsimoyān ēkosi, tēpiyāhk nimīsahikēwin, *you know*, ātiht apisīs, *you know*, *seven dollars* ēwakoni maskisina mīna apisīs ātiht māka māh-mistahi, *you know, ripping* mistahi ēwako anima. māka kahkiyaw kīkway ayis nitayān, *you know*, anima tāpiskōc ayi sāponikan ēkwa mīna *threa--*, an āyi, *string* mīn ānima, *you know*. kahkiyaw kīkway, *pliers*, manisikanisa, mētoni sōskwāc nitapin *one room* anima ē-ayāyān ēkwa mīna anima akoskiwahikan ēwako nitati-āpacihtān ēkwa ē-kaskikwāsoyān, *no time* nikīsihtān. *Two fifty* kā-pē-miyit kahkiyaw ōma ē-māwasakopēhahk tānimēyikohk ē-- ē-kī-- wīstawāw --tipahikēhihcik aniki *people*, awīn āna kā-atosit, *you know*. ēkwa kā-pē-sēwēpayik *phone* ē-atamihā-- ē-atami-- ē-ataminācik aniki kā-wīn-- ōko kā-wīcihakik, *you know*. mētoni ēyiwēhk nikī-sōniyāhkān ēkospīhk, māka *bingo* ayisk mistahi ē-miywēyihtamān. [*pāhpiw*] namōya nipīhtwān, namōya mīna niminihkwān, *you know*. [*pāhpiw*]

[*aciyaw ē-nakipitamihk*]

[**10. ninīkihikwak**]

nikī-pē-pēyako-pimātisin, nimisak ayisk nisto kā-ācimostātakok kī-panātisicik. nikī-pēyakon ēkwa māna nōhtāwiy awa ē-kī-isit, "kīkway tōta ōta, kaskikwāso, kakwē-osīhtā t-ākwanahoyan. kaskikwāso, nitānis, ēkwa mīna kīkway ōta tōtamaw kikāwiy ē-wī-nakatamān. mihta nitastān ōta, kipētamātināwāw ta-pōnamēk. kikāwiy nākatohkē, kāya, ēkāya nāh-nakacipah. ēkwa mīna namōya miywāsin ta-papā-kāh-kiyokēyan. pētisāpamā-- pē-itis--." konita māna ē-kī-sēkimit nōhtāwiy, "pētisāpamikawiyani damage [*a telephone rings*], something with a little damage, it's like seven dollars, and anything damaged worse, a bit more. I started writing it there, I started writing it, I started writ... because I can write, you know. "As soon as you're finished," he said, "you phone me," he said. For he left me his phone number.

As soon as I finished for him to ... he arrived soon after. Oh my, I made two hundred and fifty dollars, two hundred and fifty for just doing the repair work. You know, I was patching. So that was two-fifty, I made lots, you know, at my home ...
I didn't have anyone else to rely on in that way, it was merely my mending, you know, some needed only a little, you know, seven dollars for those ones, shoes also, a little bit, but some needed more, you know, ripping, that was more. But I had everything, you know, things like needles, and threa... and, ah, string as well, you know. Everything, pliers, small scissors, really I just sat in one room that I had, and also that patching glue, I started using that and I was sewing. I was finished in no time. He came to give me the two-fifty, as he figured out how much those people ... they too ... were charged, those who asked me for it, you know. Then the phone would be ringing as they were hap..., hap... and they were pleased, those ... the ones that I had helped, you know. I really made a fair amount of money at that time. But it was because I really liked bingo. [MLR *laughs*.] I didn't smoke, and I also didn't drink, you know. [MLR *laughs*.]

[*pause in recording*]

[10. My Parents]

I grew up as the sole one living, because my three older sisters, who I told you about, had died. I was alone, and my father used to say to me, "Do something here, sew, try to make a blanket for yourself. Sew, my daughter, and also do something here for your mother, as I will be leaving. I have put firewood here, I brought it for you to burn. Take care of your mother, don't, don't take off on her.
And it is also not good for you to go around visiting. Come to see ..., come thus ...." My father used to say things to frighten me

nētē iskwāhtēmihk, 'kīkwāy piyē-nātahk awa?' kik-ētikwak. namōy ka-pēhtawāw awiyak," t-ēsit, "iskwāhtēmihk kika-nīpawin kiya, kika-na-nīpawin. ēkāy ēkosi tōta! pēyakwanohk kakwē-ayā, kikāwiy kanawēyim." nikī-sēkimik māna ē-kī-isi-kiskinwahamawit nōhtāwiy, *you know*, konita māka ētokē māna ē-kī-isi-sa-sēkimit anima, *you know*.

ēkosi māna mōy--, ēkosi, ēkosi nikī-wī-kakwē-itōtēn, kispēw *eight year old* ē-ayāyān. *Nine year old* ēkwa, ē-kī-tēhcikāpawiyān māna miscikowacis *bannock* māna ē-nawacīyān, iyinito-*bannock* awa nikāwiy ē-osīhtamawak. nikī-nihtā-nawacīn pahkwēsikan, ē-- ayēnānēw ē--, kēkā-mitātaht ē-itahtopiponēyān, *bannock* nikī-osīhāw iyinito-pahkwēsikan ē-nawacīyān kā--. mihta ayis mīna ē-pōnamāhk. mihta ē-- ē-mana--, mōy ē-nōhtē-mēstisosoyān, *you know*, nitaspinikān kīkway. kīkwāy ētokē nōhtāwiy kāh-astamawit ātawiya ēkota, kīkwāy ētokē kāh-astāt? matwān cī ana ēkwa astisihkān kā-ayāwāyahk, matwān cī ēkotowahk ana, mōy nikiskēyihtēn.

ēkwa awa nimāmā māna ē-wayawīhtahak, *washroom* ayisk wayawītimihk ōmatowahk ē-kī-osīhtāhk. ē-sakāpēkinak nikāwiy ē-wayawīhtahak. kā-tipiskāk mīna kā-wī-nīpā-wayawīt, piko ta-waniskāyān ē-tēpwāsit, piko ta-postayawinisēyān ē-sakāpēkinak ē-wayawīt. ēwako nikāwiy ē-kī-isi-pē-paminak. anohc kā-kīsikāk namōy nimihtātēn nikāwiy ē-kī-pamihak. namōya wīhkāt nōh-kisī-kitotāw nikāwiy. namōy wīhkāt nōh-kisiwāhik nikāwiy. ēy, manitow ninitohtāk, ēkosi ē-kī-isi-pamihak nikāwiy. mōy wīhkāt nōh--, mōy wīhkāt na-- ta-kakw-- ta-kakwē-kisīmit nikāwiy, namōya. ē-kī-kitimākinawak ēkā ē-wāpit nikāwiy. nikī-- anohc ēkwa nimiywēyihtēn ē-kī-isi-pamihak nikāwiy, ēkā wīhkāc ē-kī-pē-kisī-kitotak ē-kī-pē-isi-nakasit.

nōhtāwiy, wīpac nikī-nakatikonān. nōhtāwiy, kayās kā-panātisit ēwako *nineteen thirty-two, seventh of January* nōhtāwiy kā-wanihāyāhk, ēkwa nimāmā kēhcinā *after about - about five years,* niyānan askiy kēhcinā nikāwiy ēkā cī, *or* ēkā cī nikotwāsik askiy nikāwiy kā-kī-- āhh --kī-askowāt nōh-- okisēyinīma, nikāwiy awa, *you know*. ēkosi.

needlessly. "When you are seen over there at the door, 'What is this one coming for?' they will say about you. You won't hear anyone," he'd say to me, "you'll stand there by the door, you'll be left standing there. Don't do that! Try to stay in one place, take care of your mother." My father used to frighten me while teaching me like that, you know, but I guess he was just scaring me for nothing, you know.

So usually not ..., so, so I was going to try to do that, despite the fact that I was only eight years old. Then at nine years old I would stand on a box to bake bannock, I was making plain bannock for my mother, I was good at baking bannock, at eight, nine years of age, I made bannock, baking ordinary bannock, because we'd also burn the firewood. The firewood, with care, ... I didn't want to burn myself, you know, I used potholders. I wonder what my father left there for me to use, I wonder what he put there? I wonder if it was the oven mitt that we have now, perhaps it was that kind, I don't know.

And I would take my mother outside, because the washroom was the kind that was built outside. I would lead my mother when taking her out to the toilet. At night she would need to go out in the dark, I'd have to get up when she called me, I'd have to get dressed to lead her out to the toilet. That's how I looked after my mother. To this day I do not regret that I took care of my mother. I never spoke to my mother in anger. My mother never made me angry. Hey, the Creator listens to me, that's how I looked after my mother. I never ..., my mother ... never tried ... tried to speak to me so as to make me angry, no. I looked on my mother with compassion as she was blind. I was ... now today I am very happy that I took care of my mother like that, and I had never spoke to her in anger, that is the way she left me.

My father, he left us early. My father, he died long ago in nineteen thirty-two. The seventh of January is when we lost my father, and my mom I believe after about ..., about five years, five years I believe it was for my mom, or else, or else it was six years when my mother followed my fa... her old man, that was my mother, you know. That's it.

ēkospī ē-kī-ohci-pēyakoyān, *nineteen thirty-eight* ē-kī-ohci-pēyakoyān, ē-kī-ohci-pēyako-pimācihoyān ōmatowihk wāskāhikan ē-kī-ayāyān. ēkosi ēkota ohci nikī-pa-pēyakwācihon. piyisk awa kā-kī-ma-miskawak nikisēyinīm, ēkota ē-kī-ohci-wa-wīcēwak *nineteen thirties, my old man* awa. ēkospīhk ē-ohci-pēyakwācihoyāhk.

ēkospīhk ē-kī-- ē-kī-isit ōma, ēkāy ta-kakwē-wēpinamān niwāskāhikan ē-wī-nakasit. kēyāpic nikanawēyihtēn niwāskāhikan ē-kī-isi-kiskinwahamawit kēyāpic nitōtēn. "namōya ākwāsk--," nōhtāwiy ē-kī-isi-kiskinwahamawit, "namōya ākwāskam papā-ka-kiyok--." kētahtawē nikiyokān, kikiskēyiht--, kētahtawē, kētahtawē, māka kwayask ē-kiyokēyān. namōya kīkway ē-nitaw-māyātahk ē-pēhtamān mīna namōya kīkway ē-nōhtē-ma-māy-ācimoyān, ē-nōhtē-nitohtamān kīkway ta-pāhpihk tēpiyāhk, *you know*.

[**11. miyo-wīcēhtowin**]

ēwako ohci kahkiyaw ayisiyiniw k-ōhci-miyo-wīcēwak. namōya awiyak nimāyi-wīcēwāw. namōya nānitaw ninēpēwisin t-ētohtēyān. namōy wīhkāc awiyak nipē-kīhkāmik, namōy wīhkāc awiyak nikīhkāmāw. namōy wīhkāc nima-māy-ācimon, namōya ē-mamihcimisoyān, *you know*, *but* ēkosi ē-kī-pē-itācihoyān ē-ācimostātakok, ēkosi ta-kakwē-itōtamēk kīstawāw. pikw āwiyak wiyāpamāyēko ta-kakwē-wāhkōmāyēk āta ēkā ē-nisitawēyimāyēk awiyak. nawac ēwako ka-miyohtahikonāwāw, ēkosi māna nikī-pē-itikawin ēkwa *same time* mīna ē-kakēskimitakok, *you know*. pikw āwiyak, ēkāwiy āwiyak nēpēwisīstāhk! namōya miywāsin ta-nēpēwisihk ayis namōya kikiskēyimānaw awīn āna ē-wāpamāyahk, ta-kakwē-kitotāyahk nawac ēkosi ta-isi-miywēyihtam: "'ēwako kā-kī-kitosit ēkotē kā-kī-wāpamak,' kētahtawē kik-ētik," nikī-itikawin māna nīsta. tāpwē anima ēkosi ē-ispayik. ēkosi nitōtēn anohc.

pikw āwiyak, nōsisimak kā-wāpamicik kā-pē-sakikwēnicik ē-pē-ocēmicik. mētoni anima ē-miywēyihtamān ē-sawēyimicik nōsisimak. niya mīna ē-sawēyimakik. namōya awiyak

Since then I have been alone, nineteen thirty-eight, I have been by myself, I have lived by myself in a house like this one. So from then on I was by myself. Finally, I found my old man, I had been with him from the nineteen thirties, this old man of mine. We had been on our own since then.

At that time, he [my father] ... he told me, try not to throw away my house when he was going to leave me [i.e., pass on]. I still keep my house just as he had taught me, and I still do it. "Not very mu...," my father taught me, "You shouldn't go around visiting very much. Eventually I visited, you know..., eventually, at one time, but I went visiting politely. I didn't hear anything bad, and I didn't want to talk about anything bad either. I wanted to listen to something just for the laughter, you know.

[11. Good Relations]

That's why I get along with all people. There is no-one that I get along poorly with. I am not ashamed to go anywhere. No-one has ever scolded me, I never scold anyone. I don't ever tell bad things, I don't brag about myself, you know, but that's how I have lived, that I am telling you about, so that you, too, can try to do the same. Whenever you see anyone, you should try to relate to them even though it is someone that you don't recognize. That will guide you well, that is what I used to be told, and at the same time that is how I am counselling you, you know, for everyone. Don't be bashful with anyone! It is not good to be bashful because we don't know who that is who we see, we should try to speak to them, they will like that better: "'That one spoke to me when I saw her over there,' he'll eventually say about you," I, too, used to be told. That's how it really happened. So I do that today.

Everyone, when my grandchildren see me, they come give me a hug and kiss me. I am very happy that my grandchildren love me. I love them too. I don't hesitate to tell anything to anyone, that nimanā-wīhtamawāw kīkway, ē-miywāsiniyik oti kīkway kikiskēyihtēn namōya wiya ē-māyātahk kīkway. mihcētiwak nōsisimak. āta mīna ēkā ē-nisitawēyimakik nōsisimak aniki, ahpō mōniyāwak nōsisimak. "āh, *Kohkom, Grandma*!" pikw īta nitikwak ē-nisitawēyimicik mōniyāsak ayisk mihcēt ninakayāskawāwak. mihcēt nikitotāwak mōniyāsak. ēkotowahk mīna ōma ē-papā-wītapihkēmoyān, awāsis kā-kakēskimiht, kikiskēyihtēn, kā-wīhkwēpihk anima ēkot ānima mīna ē-papā-pīhtokwēyān, ē-papā-wīcōhkamawakik ōki nōsisimak. niya ayisk ēkwa piko nikēhtē-ayiwin. namōya ēkosi ē-isi-nitotamawakik t-ēsi-s-- t-ēsi-wī-- t-ēsi-sīhkimicik māka nīsta ē-kakwē-wīcōhkamawakik, ēsitwāwi ta-wīcōhkamawakik niwīcōhkamawāwak nōsi--, ēkota ōma kā-wīhkwēpihk anima ōki nōs--.

ēkwa mētoni nimiywēyihtēn kā-kitotak, kā-kitot-- ninēhiyawān māna, piko t-ētwēstamawiyēk nititāwak māna awiyak ē-nihtā-- ē-nihtā-nēhiyawēt nik-ētwēstamāk. pēyak māna ōta *Mr. Lavallee* ana, *Alphonse*, ēwako māna nititwēstamāk ana nitihkwatim, ōma ē-kwēskastāt, *you know, how*, ē-ākayāsīmot. niwīhtamawāwak tānisi ē-itēyihtamān, ati-wīhtam. ēkwa nititāwak namōya ēwako iyikohk ē-- ōki mōniyāwak, niwītapimānānak *lawyers* ōki, ēkwa mīna ōki *welfare people*, nanātohk isi. niwīhtamawāwak ēkota, nititāwak, namōya ōma ē-nihtā-ākayāsīmoyān. nitākayāsīmototawāwak, "namōya ē-nihtā-ākayāsīmoyān. mētoni ē-papakā-ākayāsīmoyān. ēwakoyikohk ē-kī-itohtēyān kiskinwahamātowikamikohk, ma kīkway nikiskēyihtēn. konita nitāh-ākayāsīmon, māka nikostēn māna ta-wanitonāmoyān," nititāwak. "*A little bit* ōma tāpiskōc kā-- kā-misi-- kā-misi-pīkiskwēhk ōma *high words* ēkota ninakāsinin." nititāwak. "māka niwī-nēhiyawān, māka nāha nika-itwēstamāk." "ēha," nitikwak, "ta-kī-pīkiskwēyan ōma t-ākayāsīmoyan," nitik māna *lawyer* ōta, "kinihtāwān." "mōya," nititāw. "mōya kiwīhtamātināwāw nānitaw isi, nānitaw isi wanitonāmoyāni nika-māyi-itōtēn." "*Okay, okay, okay, Grandma, okay*."

is if it is good, you know, not anything bad. My grandchildren are numerous. Although there are those who I don't recognize, even white grandchildren. "Oh, Kohkom, Grandma!" these white folks say to me everywhere, recognizing me, for I am comfortable with them. I speak with many white people. That kind of thing, as I go about sitting with people, when children are counselled, you know, and when sitting in a [talking] circle, there, too, I go in to help out these grandchildren of mine. Because I am now just an elderly person. I am not asking them for that, to... to thus ..., to urge me in that way, but I, too, try to help them, to do what they say to me, to help them out, I help out my grand... there in the talking circle, those grand[children of mine].

Now, I really like it when I speak to them, when I speak ... I usually speak Cree. "You will have to interpret for me," I tell them, and usually someone who speaks Cree really well will interpret for me. There is one here, a Mr. Lavallee, Alphonse, that one usually interprets for me, that nephew of mine, he translates it properly, you know, how, as he speaks English. I tell them what I think, and he tells it accordingly. And I tell them, "It's not so much ...," – these white people, we sit with these lawyers, and also these welfare people, all sorts of people. I tell them there, I say to them, "I don't speak English well." I tell them in English, "I'm not a good English speaker. I really only have a thin amount of English. As I only went to school for a short time, I know nothing. I could speak English, but I am afraid to misspeak," I say to them. "A little bit, but like when there is high speech, high words, there I am stumped," I say to them. "But I am going to speak Cree, and that one there will interpret for me." "Yes," they tell me. "You should speak, you should speak English," the lawyer here always tells me, "you speak well." "No," I tell him. "No, I tell you all something, if I misspeak about that, I will do ill." "Okay, okay, okay, Grandma, okay."

ēkwa māna ēkwa awa *Alphonse* māna nititwēstamāk, ē-kwēskastāt kwēyask ē-wīhtamawak awa nōsisiminān kā-pē-itohtahiht. "īīh," nititāw māna, māka ēkwa ē-ākayāsīmoyān māna ē-ākayāsīmototawak ēwakw āwa. "nitohtawik," nititāwak māna. "apisīs niwī-pīkiskwān, namōya mistahi ē-wī-kitotak awa nōsisim." nitākayāsīmototawāw, "tānisi ē-isi-cīhkēyihtaman, ta-cīhkēyihtaman," ē-itak māna. "wāpahta iyikohk, tānimēyikohk ōta ē-apiyāhk. *You know why we come here, we want to help you*, ta-nitohtawiyāhk, ta-kakwē-sawēyimiyāhk, ē-sawēyimitāhk. kīspin ēkā ē-sawēyimitāhk namōya ōta nikāh-ayānān. tānisi ōma kā-itōtaman? pakitina ēwako! nawat ta-miyohtahikoyan ta-kiskinwahamākosiyan. namōya ta-miywāsin kīko-- kiya *Dojack* anima t-ētohtēyan, namōya ēwako ta-miywāsik kiya ohci, nawat ta-nitohtawiyāhk, nawat ta-kakwē-kwēskinaman kimāmitonēyihcikan. manitow kika-wīcihik ēkosi isi kika-miyokin ahpō cī kika-miyo-sōniyāhkān ahpō cī kika-- kika-āpaciho-- kā-āpacihtāyan wayawītimihk *car* ahpō cī kika-kaskihtamāson. ēkāy kit-ōtinaman anima ē-māyātahk, ēkāy kīkway ta-cīstahisoyan. nawac omisi isi ta-kitimākihtawiyāhk ē-sākihitāhk ōma, *we love you, that's why we here*," nititāwak māna aniki awāsisak. yāh-nāmiskwēwiwak, āskaw pē-ispayihowak ē-mātocik, kikiskēyihten, ē-ocēmicik. nīsta māna nimāton ayisk nimōskomikwak, tāpiskōc ē-mōskomoyān ē-miywēyihtamān tāpiskōc ē-wī-tāpwēhtahkik. tānitahto ēkosi nititōtaw-- niwīcihiwān.

nānitaw kā-wāpamakik aniki awāsisak kā-pēcāstamohtēcik. kiyām *a lot of people* ōtē pēcāstamohtēcik ē-pē-sakikwēnicik, "*Grandma, you here*." ē-pē-ocēmicik. īīh, tānisi māna ē-itēyihtamān, *my heart*, mistahi māna nimiyotēhān, wāwīs ētokē manitow. wāwīs ētokē manitow sawēyimēw anihi ē-itōtamiyit, ahpō ētokē mitonēyihtam, "hām, nōsisim nika-kwēskināw, pahkān t-ētēyihtam." wiy-- ahpō ē-- ahpō ētokē ēkosi itēyihtam manitow, ahpō niya ēkosi ē-itēyihtamān nimōsihtān anima māna, *I feel it*, kā-pē-sakikwēnicik. kānikanā ēkos īsi miyokicik k-ētāyāhkok, tāpwēhtahkik, ēkosi māna ē-itēyihtamān.

So whenever now this Alphonse interprets for me, he converts it properly as I tell our grandchild who has been brought. "Well!" I usually say, but then I'm usually speaking English, I speak English to that one. "Listen to me, all of you," I say to them. "I am going to speak a little bit, I'm not going to say a lot to this grandchild of mine." I speak English to him or her, "However you are happy, you should be happy," I usually tell her. "Look at this number, how many of us are sitting here. You know why we come here, we want to help you, to listen to you, for you to love us, as we love you. If we didn't love you, we would not be here. Whatever you did. Leave that! School will take you to a better way of life. It won't be good for you to go to the [Paul] Dojack [Centre], that won't be good for you, better for you to listen to us, better to try and change your way of thinking. The Creator will help you and thus you will grow well, or you will earn a salary, or you will ... you will use ... when you use a car outdoors, you will manage on your own. You shouldn't take anything bad [i.e., drugs], you shouldn't inject yourself with anything. Better to listen with pity to us as we love you, we love you, that's why we are here," I usually say to those children. They nod their heads, "ya", and sometimes they come to me, crying, you know, and kiss me. I, too, usually cry, because they make me cry, it's like I make myself cry in happiness, as it seems they are going to believe. How often have I done... have I helped others in that way.

Whenever I see those children come walking towards me, regardless whether there are a lot of people, they come walking over here to come and hug me, "Grandma, you're here." They come and kiss me. Oh my! How can I express my thoughts, my heart, I get a warm feeling in my heart, the Creator must feel even moreso. God must love those even more for doing that, perhaps he thinks about it, "Okay, I will turn my grandchild, she will think differently." He... or..., maybe the Creator thinks that. Even I am thinking that way when I feel that way, I feel it, when they come to give me a hug. I wish that they grow as well as we have told them, and that they believe, that's what I usually think.

īh, anohc ōma mīna nikī-itohtān ōta *last week* ōta ōtēnāhk. ēkosi ōma ē-itapiyāhk ē-wāsakāpiyāhk. nikī-pīkiskwān mīna, mōy āwiyak - mōy awiyak kitā-- mōya awiyak - mōy awiyak ta-nēpēwisīstawak, namōya. namōya, namōya ninēpēwisin ayisk ē-miywāsik anima, *you know*. kīkwāy ta-nēpēwihikoyān ta-māy-ītak ayisiyiniw. hām, ta-māy-ītak ayisiyiniw kit-ētohteyān nētē, namōy nikāh-kaskihtān t-ētohtēyān niya ayisk nikāh-nēpēwihison ēwakw ānima kā-itwēhk. "ēkāy awiyak kakwē-māyī-- māyiwī-- --māyi-isi. ēkā kīkway ē-māyātaniyik kīc-āyisiyiniw tit-ētat. namōya miywāsin. nawac ē-miywāsik t-ētat, nama kīkway ka-nēpēwihikon pikw īta ka-pīhtokwān." ēkosi nikī-itikawinān māna kā-kakēskwēcik ōki kēhtē-ayak, ē-tāpwēcik. kīspin ayisiyiniw ēkā kwayask ē-isitēhēt, ēkā kwayask ē-isi-pamināt owīcēwākana, nēpēwihow ana. mōy kaskihtāw t-ētohtēt mihcētinānihk, mōy kaskihtāw ta-kitotāt ayisiyiniwa, kositonāhkēmow, kosit-- kostēw, "kī-pēhtam ētokē awa ē-kī-itak," ēkosi itēyihtam, ēkā kwayask kā-pimātisit ayisiyiniw.

namōya ē-mamihcimoyān ōma k-ētwēyān kwayask ē-wīhtam-- ē-wīhtamān tānisi ē-ispayik kā-nēhiyāwiyahk. pikw īta ē-itohtēhk, nawac, nawac, nawac kitōtōtēmin ayisiyiniw, nawac kiwāhkōmik ayisiyiniw. ēwakw ānima kā-itwēhk "ē-otōtēmihk", ē-wāhkōmisk kwayask kā-nēhiyāwihk. māka mētoni kwayask ē-pīkiskwēyan, tāpiskōc ōma kā-ākayāsīmoyēk *high words*. "ē-otōtēmihk," namōy kinisitohtēnāwāw māka ē-wāhkōmisk ēwakw ānima kā-itwēhk. ēkota mān ānima k-ētamān kā-nēhiyawēhk, apisīs mīna ē-āh-ispi-pīkiskwēhk, ātiht namōy nisitohtamwak, pēyakwan ōma kā-ākayāsīmoyēk ē-ispi-pīkiskwēt awiyak. ēkota māna nīsta nitā-- nitā-- nitācisinin, *you know*, ēkwa. [*pāhpināniwan*]

[*ēkosi pitamā*]

Oh, and now I went here last week into town. This is how we sat, we sat in a circle. I spoke too, nobody ...nobody to .... I'm not shy with anyone, no. No, I'm not shy, because that's not good, you know. What would embarrass me would be to say something bad about a person. Okay, to say something bad about a person and to go over there, I personally would not be able to because I would shame myself, that is what is said, "Try not to ... poorly ... to speak ill to anyone. Nothing bad should be said to your fellow human being. It's not good. It's better for you to say something nice to someone, nothing will shame you and everywhere is open to you." That is what we used to be told when the Elders were counselling, and they were right. If a person doesn't have a good heart, and doesn't treat his or her partner properly, they shame themselves. He is not able to go to gatherings, she is unable to speak with people, their words come back to haunt them, it comes back ... he is afraid of them, "She may have heard what I said about her," that's what he thinks, the person who is not living right.

I am not bragging in what I am saying, I am telling it correctly, how it is for us being Cree. Everywhere one goes, the more, more, the more people will relate to you, the more people will treat you as a relative, that's what it means, making relationships and treating you as kin, when properly being Cree. But I am speaking correctly, like when you use high words in English, "Making relations." You don't understand that, but "as she takes you as kin," that's what that means. That's what I mean when speaking Cree, and someone is speaking a bit of the elevated language, some don't understand it the same as when English is spoken and someone speaks elevated language, that is where I, too, am usually st-- st-- stumped, you know, now. [*laughter*]

[*That's it for now.*]

2
nēhiyawiskwēw opimohtēhowin
A CREE WOMAN'S LIFE

This is the second part of the narration recorded on May 10, 1995, at the home of Mary Louise Rockthunder on Piapot First Nation, in the presence of Jean Okimāsis [*JO*] *and Doreen Oakes* [*DO*].

After a break following the recording of one side of a cassette tape, Mary Louise continued to tell of humorous events in her own life and to impart her knowledge of Cree culture and language.

[1. ē-wawiyatācimohk]

... ēkwa mān ōki, mayaw kīkway kā-kakwēcimicik, ēkosi ē-mātācimostawakik, ēkosi māna ē-wī-nipahāhpicik, ē-tāh-tēpwēyāhpicik māna. [*pāhpināniwan*] "mahti pē-kiyokēhkan nētē nōhkom kika-pē-nātitinān ici, pē-mīcisohkan." "ēha," nititāw ana nōs-~, ōtē ē-kiyokēyāhk ōta ayāw ana nōsisim, aya, 'māya' isiyihkāsow, *Lorraine Bear* isiyihkāsow nōsisim ana, ēkotē ē-kī-kiyokēyān ēkwa okāwiya kī-panātisiyiwa, *Mrs. ~ Blanche* ana, *you know, she passed away* kayāsēs, māka *Lorraine* awa pimātisiw, ēkota anima ē-kiyokēyān.

"nikāwīs," itwēw aw āya, *Blanche*, maht ācimo anima," itwēw, " kā-kī-wāh-wawiyēsiyinīhkēyan," — 'toni ayisk nēhiyawēwak, — "kā-kī-wāh-wawiyas-~ , kā-kī-wāh-wawiyas-itōtaman, mahti ēwako ācimo." "ēha" nititāwak, "kahkiyaw ōma kiyawāw misawāt nōsisimak, nāha piko nitihkwatim, namōya māka nānitaw pēhtawici tēpiyāhk kita-pāhpit ōma kā-wī-ācimoyān." ēkw ēkwa ōma ē-ācimoyān ēkwa, wāāhway, ēkwa iyikohk kā-wī-nipahāhpihicik mētoni ē-māh-mōskwāhpicik ē-wawiyas-~, ē-wawiyasihtawicik tānisi ōma ē-ay-itinikēyān.

> — tāpwē ayis ōma, ōma k-ēspīhtisīyān kā-ācimostātakok, ma kīkway, ma kīkway ē-ayamihcikēyān. nitayamihcikān, namōya mīna ~ nitayamihcikān, ninisitawinēn ātiht mōy māka kacāt [*sic*; *cf.* katāc] ninōhtē-ayamihcikān. konita kīkway nitat-īsi-na-nawatinēn, kikiskēyihtēn, anima ayis kacāt ayamihcikēyān, āh, kiyām ēkosi. —

īh, niwāh-wan-ōtinēn kīkway ēkoni ōhi wawēsīhowin-āyisa ēwako anima kā-pāh-pisci-astāyān; mihcēt kīkway ōma ē-pisci-tōtamān ēwako māka kā-ācimostātakok kā-sisopēkahoyān anima ayi, *marker* ani, *bingo marker* ēwako ē-pisci-tōtamān ēkwa mīna anima kā-sisopēkahoyān ōta nistikwānihk ayi anima *toothpaste*, ēkwa mīna mōya ē-ayamihtāyān. ēkwa mīna awa nitānis awa *Barbara* ēwako kā-ācimoyān ē-ayi-~ ē-ka-kanawēyihtamāhk ōma *suite*, niwāpamāw māna awa nitānis kā-wī-sipwēhtēt

[1. Telling Funny Stories]

... and generally as soon as these ones ask me something I just begin telling them stories. So then they'll really have a good laugh, they usually laugh out loud. [*laughter*] "Please come visit me over there later, Grandma, we'll come get you then, come eat then." "Yes," I tell this grand--, we're visiting over here, my grandchild is here, ah, she is called *māya*, Lorraine Bear is her name, that one is my grandchild, I visited over there and her mother had passed away, that was Mrs. - Blanche, you know, she passed away a while ago, but that one, Lorraine is alive, that's where I was visiting.

"Auntie," said this one, ah, Blanche, "tell a story about that," she said, "the time when you made funny mistakes," – because they really can speak Cree – "when you did some funny things, how about telling about that." "Okay," I told them. "After all, you are all my grandchildren. Just that one is my nephew, never mind if he hears me, he can just laugh at what I am going tell." So then I am telling stories and, ohhh my, they are killing themselves laughing at me, they were laughing so much they were crying, they found it fun-- they thought the way I was telling the story of my activities was funny.

> — Because this is true, at my age, that which I tell you about, I don't, I don't read at all; I went to school, but I don't read, I recognize some, but it's not necessary for me to read. I catch some and I begin to recognize, you know, that which I have to read, but never mind. —

Ooh, I am taking the wrong things, those cosmetic items that I was mistakenly using. There are many things that I do wrong, such as that time I was telling you about when I painted myself with that marker, that bingo marker that I mistakenly applied and also when I plastered my head with that toothpaste and I wasn't reading. And this daughter of mine, Barbara, that one I told you about when we were keeping this suite, I would watch this daughter of mine, when she was preparing to leave, and she'd be ē-*spray*iwit ōma ostikwān ayis, ayis aya ta-titipawēhikēt tāpiskōc; niwāpamāw māna ē-*spray*iwit ōma, ōma ost--.

> — ēkw ōma ēwakonik pēyakwan ōki *Joe Carrier* nitihkwatim awa ēkwa mīna nistim awa *Alice Carrier* kā-kī-itiht owīkimākana ōhi, *couple* ōki. ēwakonik ōki ē-pē-nātikoyāhkok. ēkwa *Barbara* wīsta wī-wīcihiwēw, kayās māna ōh āyaha *purses* ōta kikī-tāpiskēnāwāw ē-miywāsiki, tāpiskōc *saddle* ōta ēkotowa, ēkotowa, atoskēw ayis māka wīsta ēkwa ē-wī-nitawi-mētawēt. —

īh, niwāpamāw māna awa nitānis ē-sisopātahk ōma ostikwān, ē-*spray*iwit ōma, ē-sisopātahk. mētoni māna wīhkimākostikwānēw; ēkospī nīsta nēscakāsa nawaciko nikī-wī-kakwē-mōniyāskwēwēwahikēsin, ē-kīskahamāyān, anohc ēkwa namōya, nipakwātēn ēkosi t-ēsīhoyān ayis nitati-kēhtē-ayiwin, mōy ēkosi, nawat ē-apihkēyān nimiywēyihtēn. niwāpamāw māna ōma ē-*spray*iwit ***her hair*** ōta, "mahti nika-kimotamawāw," ***in the bedroom*** nētē tatahkamikisiw. [*matwē-sēwēpicikāniwan.* MLR: "otina."] tatahkamikisiw ēkota [MLR: *"I have no time* wiya niya," *sēwēpicikan anima kā-itahk*], tatahkamikisiw, niwāpamāw māna ē-*spray*iwit ōm ōstikwān; īh, "nika-kimotamawāw." ninitawi-pīhtokwān *washroom*. īh, kakwāyakakotēwa ōhi ōtē *containers* ōhi nanātohk ē-isinākwahki, ātiht ē-kaskitēwāki. īh, tān ēwako ētikwē kē-otinamān? pēyak [*pāhpināniwan*] pēyak nitōtinēn, ē-misāk. wahwā, nipasakwāpin, niwāpamāw māna ē-itōtahk. misiwē, 'toni misiwē, tāpwē mēton āyi, sīhtawāwa nēstakaya. "kiyipa, ***mom***," itwēw, "āsay ōma ***outside*** kipēhikawin," itwēw, "āyimāc ē-wī-pōsihikawiyahk." "ahām." pē-wayawīw. "***Mmm mmm," she told me, "you put too much.***" īih, ē-kiskēyihtahk ē-kimotamawak [*pāhpināniwan*], ē-kiskēyihtahk ē-kimotiyān. "ahām, ēkosi sēmāk." "wahwā ***mom, you put too much.***" "kīkwāy ***too much*** māka ē-astāyān?" "***You put too much house spray,***" k-ēsit. ***House spray*** ēsa ōma kā-sisop-- [*pāhpināniwan*] kā-sisopātamān nistikwān, namōy nikiskē-- "tānita, tān ēwako wētinaman, tān ēwako?" "āstam, mācikōtitāk." ***Washroom, a black tube*** anima, ***house spray*** ēsa ōma kā-sisopātamān nistikwān. wahwā! [*pāhpināniwan*] spraying this on her head because, because she would curl her hair, like. I used to see her spraying it on her head.

> —And it was the same for those ones, Joe Carrier, this nephew of mine, and also his wife, my niece, the late Alice Carrier, this couple. Those ones were coming for us. And Barbara was also going to help others. Long ago the style of those, ah, purses that you wore around the neck, they were nice, like a saddle here, that kind, that kind. Because she is working but she too was going to go play [bingo].—

Oh, I would see my daughter spraying her head, she'd be spraying, she was spraying it. Her head would smell so nice. At that time, I too was sort of trying to have my hair like the white women, having a haircut; nowadays, no, I don't like dressing like that because I am getting old. Not like that, I prefer braiding my hair. I would see her spraying her hair here, "Let's see, I'll steal it from her," in the bedroom over there, she will be busy. [*A telephone rings.* MLR: "Take it."] She will be busy there [MLR: "I have no time, me," *speaking of the phone*], she will be busy. I used to see her spraying her hair. Well! "I will steal it from her." I go into the washroom. Oh, there were a whole lot of those containers on the shelf, all kinds of containers, some black ones. Oh my! I wonder which one I should take? One [*laughter*], I took one, a large one. My goodness, I close my eyes, I would see her doing that. All over, really all over, and my hair was really very stiff. "Hurry up, mom," she said. "They are already waiting for you outside," she said. "We'll barely make our ride." "Okay." She comes out. "Oh no," she tells me, "you put too much." Geez, she knows I stole from her [*laughter*], she knows I am a thief. "Okay, let's go." "Oh my, mom, you put too much." "What did I put too much of?" "You put too much house spray,'" she said to me. I guess it was house spray that I used [*laughter*] to spray my head, I didn't kno-- "Where, which one did you take, which one?" "Come on, let me show you." In the washroom, it was that black tube, it appears that it was house spray that I sprayed on my head. My goodness! [*laughter*] mētoni ē-wī-nipahāhpit. konita mīna ēkwa anima ē-kimotiyān. [*pāhpināniwan*] ēkāy anima ē-ayamihcikēyān, *you know*. wahwā, nīsta mīna ēkota nikī-pāhpin, ē-kimotiyān anima; mōy nitayamihcikān, konita nitis-ōtinēn *spray* anima, *house spray* ēsa anima kā-sisopātamān, tāpwē māka sītaw. [*pāhpināniwan*] wahwā, mitoni nima-māyinikēskin, mitoni ē-isi-tōtamān.

ēwako mīna anima nikisēyinīm ana, ēwako mīna ē-kī-takahkāpamak māna ē-wīhkimākostikwānēt, ēwakw ānim āy-- anima; tānisi ētikwē māna ē-kī-isiyihkātēk ē-kaskitēwāk *tube* mān ānima ostikwāniwāhk nāpēwak ē-āpacihtācik. ēwakw ānima ē-kimotiyān ē-itakihcikēyān kā-wan-ōtinamān anima ayi *toothpaste* ēsa ōma kā-mis-āstāyān k-ācimostātakok. āhh, mētoni kā-misi-kakwāyakihoyān ōma *bingo* ē-wī-tēpwēhk, pitamā mīna ē-nitawi-kisīpēkistikwānēyān. wahwā! *Foam, no towel*, ma kīkway aniki *paper towels, nothing*. āhh, *my shirt* ēkwa k-āpacihtāyān ēkwa.

> — nikostāw ayisk nikisēyinīm ta-kisī-kitosit, nikī-kostāw ana. ayisk - ayisk kā-wīkimat nāpēw kikostāw, *you know*, ayisk kikihci-wīkimāw, *you know*, kikī-asotēn tānisi ē-wī-tōtaman ē-kakwēcimisk, ē-kakwēcimisk kā-wīkihtahisk ana, "kiwī-tōtēn cī tānisi -," ē-itisk ana. "ēha, nika-tōtēn. *I will, I will*," kititwān ē-asotamawat awa mīna manitow. āh, tāpwē. kikostāw ana nāpēw; niya nikī-kostāw, kīkway nānitaw t-ēsi-kisiwāhak, *you know*, tāpitaw ētikwē ē-nitawēyihtamān ayi kita-miywātisit, kikiskēyihtēn, ē-kakwē-tēpiyawēhak omis īsi, ēkwa kā-wī-kisī-kitosit tāpiskōc māna ē-kī-ca-cihcipipayiyān, *you know*, ē-kī-isi-kostak. nikī-kostāw, ē-tāpwēyān nikī-kostāw. —

īh, anima, anima *bingo* anima ē-tōtākoyān kā-tōskinak, "kiyāmapi." ha, tānisi māk-- īh, anima, ē-kisīpēkistikwānēyān nikimotiwin ēkā ē-ayamihcikēyān. [*pāhpināniwan*]

She was really going to laugh herself to death. I didn't really have to steal that. [*laughter*] It was that I didn't read, you know. Oh my, I too laughed that I was stealing that and I could not read. I just took that spray, and it was house spray which I sprayed, but it was really stiff. [*laughter*] Oh my, I really make mistakes whenever I do something.

Then there was that old man of mine, too, and I admired him, his hair always smelled nice, it was that, I don't know what it is called, it's a black tube that men would use on their heads. That's what I stole, thinking that what I mistakenly took was ah, here it was toothpaste which I put on in great amounts on, as I was telling you about. Ohh, I was really being rushed for they were going to start calling bingo, but in the meantime I had to go and wash my hair. Oh my! There was foam, and no towel, none of those paper towels, nothing. Ohh, so now I used my shirt.

> – because I was afraid of him, afraid for my old man to scold me, I was scared of him. Because, because when you are married to a man, you fear him, you know, because you married him in the church, you know, you promised how you are going to act, when he asks, when that one who performs the marriage questions you, "Are you going to do what [he tells you]?" he says to you. "Yes, I will do it. I will, I will," you say, and you are promising him and God as well. Ah, it's true. You are afraid of that man, I was afraid of him, to do something to make him angry, you know? I guess I was always wanting him to, ah, to be kind, you know, I was trying to soothe his temper in this way, and when he was going to speak angrily to me, it was like I was quivering, you know, I feared him that way. I was afraid of him, I truly feared him. –

Ah, that, that's bingo that does that to me, when I nudged him, "Be quiet." Hah, but that's how my theft led to my washing my hair, as I can't read. [*laughter*] wahwā, anima mīna kā-sisopēkahoyān k-ācimostātakok, [w]ahwā, ēkw ānima mīna wawiyēs anima mīn ēwako. īh, anima ē-wī-a---nitaw-ātoskēyān nitōcipitikon ēkosi ēkwa piko maskihkiy nikī-atāwēstamāk anima *green medicine*. ā, mitoni ēkwa *half asleep* k-ōtinamān, ē-misi-ocipitikoyān mētoni ēkwa niskāta ōhi, ēkwa ē-ati-āpisihkwasiyān awīna ōma nikī-tahkonēn *bingo marker*, mētoni kā-māh-misi-askihtakokātēyān. [*pāhpināniwan*] wahwā! nikakwāyakihison; māka nitāstē-ayān, ē-miywāsik ētikw ānima nitāstēskākon, tahkikamāpoy ayisk, tahkikamiw [JO: "āha."], nipōn-ocipitikon. ēkosi ēkwa ta-nitaw-atoskēyān, *my bus any time coming* māka *snowing* pēskis, kimiwa--, ma-mispon. āhh, wahwā, ta-nitaw-koskonak nikisēyinīm, nikiskēyihtēn ta-kisī-kitosit, wahwā hay, "āh!" tāpwē nikisī-kitotik. pikw ēkosi k-ēsi-pōsiyān ē-askihtakokātēyān anima; nētē k-ētohtēyān nitōkimām kēkāc kā-nipahi-pāhpit, nitōkimāskwēm mīn āwa. wāhwā, kēkāc nikī-nipahāwak *bingo marker* ē-nanātawihwākēyān māk āyisk nikī-miyoskākon, ē-miywāsik anima. [*misi-pāhpināniwan*] wāhay!

namōya ōma ē-kiyāskīw-ācimoyān, ē-tāpwēyān, misiwē misawāc nipēhtākawin. ahpō ōk ōtē ōtēnaw-iyiniwak, ōko kihc-ōkimāwak, kahkiyaw anima kiskēyihtamwak, nipēhtākwak. ōki mīna nitawāsimisak, ē-wawiyatēyihtahkik nayēstaw ē-pāhpihikawiyān, mitoni nitakahkēyihtēn, ayisk māka nikī-ma-māyinikēskin ēkā ē-nihtā-ayamihcikēyān.

[**2. kiskinwahamātowin**]

ēwako k-ētamān ē-āyimahk ēkā kā-ayamihcikēt ayisiyiniw, ēwak ōhci k-ōh-itakik, "itohtēk kiskinwahamātowikamikohk, kīkway ta-kiskēyihtamēk," nititāwak awāsisak ē-tāpwēyān. ēkotowahk ayisk ēkwa pisisik mōniyāwak ēkwa kiyawāw ēwakw ānima mōniyāsak ē-kis--, ta-kis--, ē-kiskinwahamākoyēkok kīkway. niyanān kayās nama kīkway, kī-wēhcasin itēyihtākwan māk ēcikāna ē-kī-kitimahisoyāhk, *you know*, anohc ēkwa, kitimākan. niya ohci, nikiskēyihtēn niya, ētataw kā-ākayāsīmoyān, nikaskihtān ē-pīkiskwēyān mōy māka *high words* ōhi, nipwātawihon ēkota. *But* ēkwa mīna apisīs nikiskēyihtēn t-ēs-āyamihcikēyān,

Oh my, and also that time I painted myself, which I told you about, oh my, and that too was another funny episode. See, that was when I was going to go to work and I got cramps so then he bought medicine for me, that green medicine. Ah, I applied it when I was half asleep, I was having really terrible cramps on my legs, and then as I was emerging from sleep, what is this!? I was carrying a bingo marker, and had very, very green legs. [*laughter*] Oh my! I really mistreated myself, but I recovered, that must have been good for it relieved me, because it was cold liquid, the cold water [JO: "Yes."] stopped my cramps. So then I had to go to work, my bus was coming at any time, but at the same time it was snowing, rainin--, snowing. Ohh, my goodness, I went to wake up my old man, I knew he would speak angrily to me. Oh my goodness gracious, "Ahh!" for sure he spoke angrily to me and I just had to get on the bus with my green legs. I went over there, my boss nearly died laughing, my boss-lady too. Oh my, I nearly killed them using a bingo marker to doctor myself, but because it cured me, that's all right. [*laughter*] Oh goodness!

I am not telling false stories, I am telling the truth; I am heard everywhere. Even these ones over here, the town-folk, these ones in high positions, all of them know it, they hear me. And these children of mine, they think it is funny that I am just laughed at. I really like that, but I did things wrong all the time because I didn't read well.

[**2. Education**]

I will say that, it is difficult when a person can't read, that's why I tell them, "Go to school, to learn something," I say to my children and I'm telling the truth. Because that kind of thing is for the Whiteman and for you, that's what the white people ... they are teaching you something. For us, there was none of that, it is thought that it was easy, but here it was that we were making it hard on ourselves, you know, and today it is pitiful. For myself, I know it, I barely speak English, I am able to speak but not the high words, that stumps me. But still, I do know how to read a little, apisīs mōya mistahi. kīkwāy ohci kōh-kiskēyihtamān ka-wīhtamātināwāw, kīkwāy kōh-ākayāsīmoyān nika-wīhtēn mīna ēwako, kika-wīhtamātināwāw mīna ēwako.

nitawāsimisak ē-kiskinwahamawihcik. nitawāsimisak, niyānan iskwēwak nitayāwāwak, ēkwa kahkiyaw ē-ākayāsīmocik ēkwa ātiht ē-nēhiyawēcik. kīkway ē-mamāyīyān pīkiskwēwinihk nikwēskiwēpinikwak, nikwēskastamākwak. "ēkosi anima t-ētwēyan, māmā, kiwanitonāmon." hāw, ēkota nikiskēyihtēn kīkwāy, tānisi kita-kī-itwēyān, nitati-kiskēyihtēn ēkota, ēkonik ōki ē-kiskinwahamawicik ēkwa mīna nīciskwēsisak kayās nistam ēwako, ēwako ōma *a,b,c,d* ēkwa mīna *1,2,3* nikī-kiskinwahamākwak ē-pē-kīwēcik *from Lebret,* nīciskwēsisak. ēkota nikī-ohci-kiskēyihtēn ēwako. ēkwa ōma ē-at-īsi-kēhtē-ayiwiyān nitawāsimisak ēkwa nikwēskinikwak, ēkonik niwīhtamākwak kīkway kā-wī-mamāyīyān. nikaskihtān ē-ākayāsīmoyān, nikaskihtān ē-pīkiskwēstamāsoyān, ahpō okimānāhk nikaskihtān ē-itohtēyān ē-nitaw-pīkiskwēstamāsoyān ē-ākayāsīmoyān. māka niwīhtamawāwak ita ēkā ka-nisitohtawakik *high words* ōhi, māka kwēskastāwak ēkotowa, ēkosi ē-ititān, ēkota nōh-ayi-kiskēyihtēn. ēkosi, ēkosi ē-isi-nayēhtāwīyān. ēkwa mīna nikāh-kiskinohamākān ōma ninihtā-nēhiyaw-ayamihcikān, ninihtā-nēhiyaw-- ... [MLR: "Margaret! ..... oh."] āh, nihtā--, nihtā-ayamihc--, [ni]nihtā-ayamihcikān ōma ē-nēhiyawēhk, anihi ayi anihi, *half, half-diamond* anima [JO: "ōh, *Syllabics.*"], ēwakw ānima. [JO: "āha."] ninihtā-ayamihcikān [JO: "ōōh!"], ninihtā-ayamihcikān, ninihtāwasinahikān ninihtā-ayamihcikān ē-nēhiyawēhk. nikāh-kiskinohamākān ōma, nikāh-sōniyāhkān, māka ēwako piko ōma ē-itwēyān, *you know.*

tāpiskōc ōma: ‘ahām, kē-wāpahk ēkotē pē-itohtēhkan, ēwako wīkiwāhk,’ tit-ētastāyān. ‘ ᐊᐦᐋᑦ, ᐆᑌ ᐯ ᐃᑐᐦᑌᐠ ᐚᑭᐚᕽ. ’ "hām, ōta tāh-masinaham awiyak ta-mōniyāwipēhahk. ēkosi ōma ē-itwēt awa." [*e.g.*, ᐊ = a] [JO: "mhm."] kinisitohtēn k-ētamān? [JO: "āha."] "ēkota ka-ohci-kiskēyihtēn ta-mē-- ta-- t-āyamihtāyan ōma. māka ēkosi ē-ititān, ‘ahām, ēkotē pē-itohtēhkan ēwako wīkiwāhk.’ " [JO: "mhm."] māk āyisk nikāh-- nihtāwasinahikēyān nikāh-masinahēn ēkosi ōma ē-itwēyān, māka ēwako nisākohikon.

a bit, not much. How I came to know it, I will tell you, why I can speak English, I will tell that as well, I will tell you all that as well.

My children taught me. My children, I have five girls and all of them speak English and some speak Cree. When I make mistakes in my speech, they correct me, they set me right. "That's how you say it, Mom, you said it wrong." Okay, now I know what, how I should say it, I start to learn from that, and those are the ones teaching me, and also my fellow girls first long ago, with that a, b, c, d, and also 1, 2, 3, that they taught me when they came back from Lebret, my fellow girls. That is where I learned it from. And now that I am getting older, my children correct me now, those ones tell me when I'm making a poor job of it. I am able to speak English, I am able to speak for myself, even at band council I am able to go there and speak for myself in English. But I tell them where I don't understand them and these high words but they restate those ones. So that's why I told you I don't know it. That's, that's how I have a hard time. On the other hand, I could teach and I can read Cree [syllabics] well, I am able to in Cree ... [MLR: "Margaret! ..... oh."] ... ah, able to -, able to read -, I read well in Cree, those, ah, those half, half-diamond [JO: "Oh, syllabics."], that's it. [JO: "Yes."] I read well [JO: "Ohh."], I read well, I write well, I am able to read in Cree. I could teach this, I could make money but I am just saying that, you know.

Like this: I would write down, 'Okay, in the morning come over there, to that one's home.' '*ahām, ōtē pē-itohtēk wīkiwāhk.*' "Okay, someone could write it using the English symbols. That is what this one means." [e.g., ᐊ = a] [JO: "Mhm."] You understand what I mean? [JO: "Yes."] From there you will learn how - to read this. But it is as I said to you, 'Okay, come over there to that one's house.' [JO: "Mhm."] But because I could - I am able to write, I could write it just as I say it, but that [English writing] defeats me.

JO: āha. nihtā-- nihtāwasinahikēw wīst āwa.

masinahikēw?

JO: āha.

ēkotowa cī kā-kiskēyihtaman?

DO: āha.

ēkotowa anihi mētoni ē-nakacihtāyān, mētoni 'toni ē-nihtā-- ē-nihtā-masinahikēyān, ēkwa ē-nihtā-- ē-nihtāwipēhikēyān [JO: "āha."], kahkiyaw ē-kiskēyihtamān, kahkiyaw ōki mīn ōki, ōki mīn ōk āyakak, ōk ā--, ōk āyi, ōki cahkipēhikanisak [JO: "āha."], kahkiyaw ayisk ōta ta-wīcihiwēcik kahkiyaw. īh, tāpiskōc awa: ᐚ, ᐱ, ᑎ, ᑭ, ᒋ, ᒥ, ᓂ, ᓯ, ᔨ; ᔨ awa. [JO: "āha."] ēkosi anima ē-is-āyi-- kikiskēyihtēn? [DO: "Ya."] ē-is-āyamihcikēhk, ēha. nikāh-kiskinwahamākān ōma, nikāh-kiskinwahamākān, *but* ēwako ninayēhtāwīn t-āt-ītastāyān anima tahta-- t-āta-- tānisi anima ē-itwēyān. [JO: "mhm, mhm, *yeah*, kwayask."]

JO: ē-kī--, awīna ē-kī-kiskinwahamāsk?

kā-kī-wiyohtāwiyān, kā-kī-wiyohtāwiyān, āh — āsay cī pimakotēw? — kā-kī-wiyohtāwiyan ē-kī-kiskinwahamawit kī-nihtāwipēhikēw, ē-nēhiyawipēhikēt, ē-nēnihāw-- ē-nēhiyaw-ayamihcikēt, ēkwa nikī-apinān ē-tipiskāk, *two nights* nikī-apinān. pēyak, pēyak nīciskwēsis wīsta ēkota, kī-panātisiw māka, ē-kiskinwahamākoyāhk nōhtāwiy. nikī-kiskēyihtēn, *two nights* āsay nikī-nihtāwasinahikān. [JO: "ōōh."] wēhcasin anima, cī? wēhcasin, wēhcasin.

[3. wāhkōhtowin]

JO: ēkwa *Turtle Mountain* kōhtāwiy ē-kī-ohcīt?

ēkotē ē-kī--, ēwako kā-ācimostātān, kā-wiyohtāwiyān awa ē-kī-omosōmit *Albert Firstchief* kī-isiyihkāsow nimosōm ēkotē, omosōma awa -, mācikōcicān, niya ōma ēkwa awa nōhtāwiy ēkwa nōhtāwiy ohtāwiya ēkwa awa nimosōm ohtāwiya ōhi *Albert Firstchief* ēwako. *Albert Firstchief* okosisa ōhi *Rainsky*, ēkota ohci

JO: Yes. This one also writes well.

She writes?

JO: Yes.

You know about this kind?

DO: Yes.

These are the kind that I am skilled at, really, I can really - I can write well, and I can - I am good at drawing them [JO: "Yes."], I know all of these, all of these ones too, these ones and also ... these things, ah, these syllabics [JO: "Yes."], because all of them have to help out here, all of them. Hey, it's like this: *'wā, pi, ti, pi, ci, ni, mi, si, yi;* this is *yi.'* [JO: "Yes."] It's like that, as it, ah, you know? [DO: "Ya."] as it is read, yes. I could teach this, I could teach it, but it would be awkward for me to start setting down that - to set it -, how I am saying it. [JO: "Mhm, mhm, yeah, right."]

JO: Who taught you?

My late father, my late father, ah – is it already running? – my late father taught me, he wrote well, he was a good writer, he read Cree and we sat at night, two nights we sat. One, one of my sisters was there too. She has died, but my father taught us. I learned it, after two nights I could already write well. [JO: "Ohh."] It's easy, isn't it? It's easy, it's easy.

[3. Kinship]

JO: And your father was from Turtle Mountain?

It was over there, that's what I had told you, my late father had a grandfather who was named Albert Firstchief, my grandfather over there, it was his grandfather, let me show you. This is me and this is my father and my father's father and this is my grandfather's father, that's Albert Firstchief. Albert Firstchief's son was Rainsky nōhtāwiy *Bangs* kī-isiyihkāsow, ēkot ōhc ōma niya *Mary Louise.* īh, ēkwa awa nōhtāwiy awa *Fred, Fred Rainsky* ta-kī-isiyihkāsot *but* kī-mōhcowiwak kayās nēhiyawak, mōy ohci-nakat-- mōy ohci-nākatohkēwak *last names*, mōy ohc-- mōy ohc-ōtinamwak ēkotowa, owīhowiniwāw kī-āpacihtāwak. īh, ēwakw āwa nōhtāwiy awa *Bangs* ē-isiyihkāsot, ē-ati-kē--, ē-ati-- ayi ōma, ē-ati-masinahikāsoyān okimāwiwin, nīsta ēkwa *Bangs* nitāpacihtān. nikī-āpacihtān *his name* anima, *his nickname* anima kā-āpacihtāyān, kīskacawēhamās, ēwako anima kā-āpacihtāyān, *Bangs, Mary Louise Bangs*, niya ēwako. īh, *Rainsky* ana ta-kī-itiht nōhtāwiy, ta-kī-āpacihtāt ōhi ohtāwiya owīhowiniyiw, awēkā cī awa, *Albert* awa, *Firstchief* ta-kī-āpacihtāt awa *Rainsky, Firstchief* ohcitaw ta-kī-āpacihtāyāhk, kikiskēyihtēn? [JO: "āha."]

ēkotē ōma ōtē askiy ē-tipēyihtamān; ē-itēyihtamān tānēhki ohci k-ōh-kī-ohtisiyāhk, ē-nistiyāhk, niya ēkwa nikāwiy ēkwa nitānis, ē-nistiyāhk. ēkotē ē-kī-ohtitisahamākawiyāhk sōniyāw. ē-kī-awihiwēt ēsa nimosōm ayi [*oscoscocasiw*, MLR: *"Excuse me."*], ē-kī-awihiwēt ēsa ayi, ayi, *to rent* ayi, tāpiskōc misatimwak ita kā-asiwasocik, ēkwa mīna ita kā-mētawēcik kā-kwāskwēnitowēcik, *golf ground*, ē-kī-awihiwēt ēsa nimosōm. ēkwa mīna ita kā-nōcikinosēwēcik sākahikan, ē-kī-awihiwēt ēsa okimāhkān ēwako; ē-nōcikinosē-- *renting, rent*. ēkwa wāskāhikanisa mīn ōhi kā-sisonēstēki sonēsa-- sisonēkamīhk, *you know*, sisonē sākahikanihk. ēkosi ēsa ē-kī-is-āwihiwēt nimosōminān. ēwakw āwa sōniyāw awa ē-kī-māwasakōt *Washington* ōtē ayi, nētē okimānāhk ēwakw āwa kā-kī-miyikawiyāhk anima askiy. ēkw āwa kā-kī-omosōmiyān, *Albert Firstchief*, ē-kī-masinahamōhiht ēsa, kayās. kayās ēwako *law*, pīwāpisk ē-napakāk, ē-sōhkahk pīwāpisk, ēkota ē-masinahamoht iyikohk *sections* ē-ayāt awa nimosōm *Albert Firstchief*. *Fifty-five, two fives* ēsa ē-kī-masinahamoht; matwān cī anima *fifty-five sections* ē-kī-ayāt nimosōm, askiy. ēwakw āwa *Albert Firstchief*, iyikohk, iyikohk ta-kī-tipēyihtahk awa *Albert Firstchief, fifty-five section*[*s*] ē-kī-sakahamoht askiy. itāmihk ēsa anima, kēyāpic ētikwē kikamon anima ēkotē anima askīhk.

and from there my father was named Bangs, and from there it's me, Mary Louise. See now this father of mine he should have been called Fred, Fred Rainsky but they were silly long ago, the Cree, they didn't leav-- they didn't pay attention to last names, they didn't - they didn't take that kind, they used their own names. See that was my father's name, Bangs, I started -, I sta--, ah, I was listed in the records and I too use Bangs, I used his name, that was his nickname that I used, ***kīskacawēhamās***, that is what I used, Bangs, Mary Louise Bangs, that's me. See, my father he should have been called Rainsky, he should have used his father's name, this one, or else because of Albert, Rainsky should have used Firstchief, we should have used Firstchief, you know? [JO: "Yes."]

It is a fact that I own land over here; I think about why we had received payment, the three of us, me and my mother and my daughter, the three of us. We had received money in the mail from over there. It appears that my grandfather had leased, ah [*coughing a bit,* MLR: "Excuse me."], I guess he loaned, ah, rented, ah, like a place where the horses are enclosed [pasture], and also where they play golf, a golf ground, my grandfather had leased it out. And also a lake where fish were caught [fishing resort?], it appears the chief had leased that, a fishin-- ... renting, rent. And there were also these cabins set along - along the shoreline, you know, along the lake. So it appears that's how our grandfather had leased it out. It was that money that was collected over in Washington, ah, over there where they govern, it was that land that was given to us and my [great-]grandfather Albert Firstchief, I guess he had been made to consign it long ago. That was the law back then, a flat iron, a strong iron was inscribed there, the number of sections that my late [great-]grandfather Albert Firstchief had. Fifty-five, I understand that two fives had been written; I wonder if that was fifty-five sections of land that my [great-]grandfather had. It was this Albert Firstchief, so much, Albert Firstchief must have owned that much, fifty-five sections of land were signposted. I understand it would be underground, I guess it is still attached there on that land.

kayās nōhcīn

JO: wīhkāc cī ēkotē -?

namōya wīhkāc ōma nititohtān, mōy kī-- mōy āwiyak nikiskēyihtēn ta-wīcōhkamawit.

[*aciyaw ē-nakipitamihk*]

niya wiya anima ēkotē nōhtāwiy anima ēkotē ē-kī-ohcīt, niwāhkōmākaninānik ōki. ēkwa, ōma mēkwāc ē-kiskēyimakik aniki kahkiyaw ē-isiyihkāsocik nimosōm ēkwa nōhkominān.

[*aciyaw ē-nakipitamihk*]

ōtē anima astēw nīst āyi, ah, *States* anihi nimasinahikana, ēkotē anima astēwa. *Nineteen, nineteen forty-five* ēkospīhk kā-misi-nōtinitohk, kā-nōtinikēcik mōniyāsak, ēkospīhk nikī-pē-itisahamākawin ayi masinahikan, *letter* nikī-pē-itisahamākawin.

> —*Jean*, namōy ta-tāpwēhtaman mētoni ē-kī-sāpwāstēk *like this, like this* [*ē-kitowēyēkihcikēt*], mētoni ē-kī-sāpwāstēk. [JO: *"Oh, yeah, I remember those."*] ē-kī--, ē-kī-āyimahk *paper* ispīhk kā-nōtinitohk. tēpiyāhk anihi *letters* anihi ē-ayamihtāhk, tānisi ētikwē kāh-itastēk. —

kahkiyaw anihi ē-kī-wanihtāyān. kahkiyaw nimasinahikana ē-kī-wanihtāyān, kahkiyaw ē-kī-kanawēyihtamān ēkwa ōma nika-miyw-āpacihtān. ēkwa ōma pēyakwāw ē-nitōskamān ēkotē isi, namōy ōhci-kiskēyihtamwak osām namōya mistahi kīkway ayi, kiskēyihtāsowin nōh-astānān anima, kikiskēyihtēn? [JO: "āha."] tēpiyāhk, tēpiyāhk ē-kī-isi-nātitisahwak ana sōniyāw, ē-kī-isi-- ē-kī-isi-kiskinwahamākēyān, kī-nātitisahwāw. ē-nātitisahoht, ē-pē-itisahoht sōniyāw *Agency at the Fort* [*Qu'Appelle, SK*].

namōya niya nōh-wīcēkawin. nayēstaw nimosōm ē-kī-pistiskawak, kā-kī-wiyohtāwiyān ēsa ē-kī-okosisihkāht ōhi ē-kī-- ōhi nōhtāwiya. ōmatowi ēsa ē-kī-astācik *in a paper* ōma

JO: Have you ever gone there -?

I have never gone, it didn-- I don't know anyone who would help me with it.

[*break in recording*]

For me, that's the place, that's where my father came from, these relatives of ours and I currently know how all of those ones are named, my grandfather, and our grandmother.

[*break in recording*]

It is over here, mine too, ah, in the States, those papers of mine are over there. In nineteen, nineteen-forty-five at the time of the great war, when white people were fighting, that was the time I was sent ah, a letter, a letter was sent to me.

> —Jean, you wouldn't believe it was really transparent, like this, like this [*the sound of rustling paper*], it was really transparent. [JO: "Oh, yeah, I remember those."] The paper was difficult [to use] during the war. You could just barely read the letters, I wonder how it could be written. —

I lost all of those. I lost all of my letters, I kept all of them and I would put them to good use now. One time I inquired about them over there, they didn't know anything about them because we hadn't set down enough information, you know? [JO: "Yes."] I just, I had just sent for that money, as I had, it was sent as I had instructed. It was sent, the money came to the Agency at the Fort [Qu'Appelle, SK].

I was unaccompanied. I just happened to bump into that grandfather of mine, the one that had taken my late father as a son, ... my father. That was apparently set in a paper that showed that ē-tāpāhkōmāt ōhi, ōh āyi nōhtāwiya. nikī-pistiskawāw ana nimosōm wīsta kī-tipahamawāw. nōhtāwiya nayēstaw ē-kī-tāpāhkōmāt, ēkwa nikāwiy, nimosōm ēkwa nikāwiy, wiyawāw piko kī-itohtēwak *Agency* [*Fort Qu'Appelle, SK*] ē-nātācik anihi sōniyāwa. māka nikī-tipahamākawin nīsta, nitānis ēkwa niya; nikī-nistinān ana sōniyāw ē-miyikawiyāhk ēkotē ana ē-ohcīt, nikāwiy, ēkwa nimosōm wīsta, *Little Sioux,* namōy āna tipiyaw ē-wāhkōmak *Little Sioux*, mōy tāpwē. tēpiyāhk nōhkom ē-kī-wīkimāt; kinisitohtēn cī? [JO: "āha, āha."] namōya wiya, nōhkom awa, awa aya, aya, ē-iskwēwic kā-kī-itiht tipiyawē nōhkom, nōhtāwiy anihi *his aunt,* okāwīsa tipiyawē, nōhtāwiy ē-kī-oyokāwīt *her sister* anihi nimā--, *you know*, kikiskēyihtēn? [JO: "*Yeah*, āha."] nōhtāwiy okāwiya *her sister* ōhi, *Mrs. Little Sioux*. ēkoni awa ē-kī-wīkimāt awa nōhkom awa, ōh āya *Little Sioux*, mōy tāpwē nimosōm ana, *you know.* [JO: "āha."] awa piko tipiyawē nōhkom awa, *the old lady* awa, aya, kā-kī-wiyōhtāwiyān okāwīsa, ēkosi anima ē-kī-ispayik.

nikī-pistiskawāwak aniki, kī-tipahamawāwak; kī-tipahamawāw ana nimosōm. māka ēkwa ana nimosōm, mōya awiya ēkwa owāhkōmākana, namōya awiya pimātisiyiwa. pēyak ē-kī-ohpikihācik, ēwako piko, mōy māka ēkota wiya kī-ohtisiw. mōy ēkosi ispayiw.

niya pikw ānima, niya piko ēkw ēkwa ē-pimātisiyān. ēkwa ē-manā-tōtamān, *you know*, ayis ōm īyikohk nitihtasin, tāpiskōc tēpakohp ōm ēkwa nitihtasin. kahkiyaw nitawāsimisak, nīso - pēyak nikosis *Charlie* itāw, ēkwa pēyak *Johnny* itāw. ēkwa pēyak aya, aya itāw *Irene,* ēkwa awa pēyak āh, awa, aya awa, āh *Pearl*, aya awa *Pearly*, ēkwa - *No, Alice, Alice* awa nitānis. tāpiskōc ōmisi nikē-itwān, aya awa, *Charlie* awa, ēkwa *Alice,* ēkwa ēkwa aya, awa *Margaret,* ēkwa aya, *no, Irene, Margaret, Barbara,* ēkwa aya, aya *Marie, no, Johnny* ēkwa *Marie*; ēkosi ē-ihtasicik; awa ōta nikosis awa *Johnny*, ōhi ē-osīmit ōhi *Marie*wa. nitānis ēkwa awa nipēpīsim nīsta *thirty-nine* itahtopiponēw, *Marie* ēwako. ēkwa awa, awa, awa nistamōsān *sixty-one* itahtopiponēw, *sixty-one Alice*, ēwako *my first one*, ēwako nistamōsān.

[*aciyaw ē-nakipitamihk*]

he had adopted that, ah, my father. I bumped into that grandfather and he too was being paid. The one who had adopted my father, and my mother, my grandfather and my mother, only those ones went to the Agency [Fort Qu'Appelle, SK] to get that money. But I was paid as well, my daughter and me. The three of us were given that money, that is where my mother is from, and my grandfather too, Little Sioux, he's not my blood relation, Little Sioux, not really. He just married my grandmother; do you understand? [JO: "Yes, yes."] Not my own grandmother, this, ah, ah, my own grandmother had been called *ēiskwēwic* — that was my father's aunt, my father's actual aunt. That was my father's mother's sister, my mo..., you know, you know? [JO: "Yeah, yes."] My father's mother's sister was that Mrs. Little Sioux. That's the one that this grandmother of mine was married to, ah, Little Sioux, that one is not really my grandfather, you know. [JO: "Yes."] Just this one, my own grandmother, this old lady, ah, this was my late father's aunt, that's what happened.

I bumped into those ones, they were being paid, that grandfather of mine was being paid. But now my grandfather does not have any relatives, none are living. The one that they had raised, just that one, but he did not get anything. It doesn't work that way.

It's just me, I am the only one living now. And I act with care, you know, because I have descendants, like the seven in my family. All of my children, two ... one son of mine is called Charlie and one is called Johnny. And one, ah, ah, she is called Irene, and this one, ahh, this one, ah, this one, oh, Pearl, ah, this is Pearly, then ... no Alice, this daughter of mine Alice. I will say it like this: ah, there is Charlie, and Alice, and then, ah, it is Margaret, and ah, no Irene, Margaret, Barbara, and ah, ah Marie, no, Johnny and Marie. That's my family here. This son of mine here is Johnny, and Marie, his younger sibling, my daughter is now, my baby, she is thirty-nine years old, that's Marie now. And this one, the, my firstborn, is sixty-one years old, Alice is sixty-one, that's my first one, that's my firstborn.

[*pause in recording*]

[**4. nanātohk kā-ohpikihki**]

JO: *Cactuses* anihi, atimosi--, atimosita.

ayi ēsa anihi kā-kāsāki isiyihkātēwa. [JO: "kā-kāsāki, ōh."] kā-kāsāki, *yeah* [JO: "ōh, āhā."], kā-kāsāki. ēkoni anihi kā-askihtakwāki, kā-kāsāki isiyihkātēwa ēs ānihi. [JO: "ōh."] kā-askihtakwāki anihi kā-kāsāki, ēkoni. ēkwa mīna pēyakwan ēkota mīna -, ēkota mīna pēyakwan a--, ēkota mīna pēyakwan wēhpikihki anih āyi, ayi anihi, ēkoni mīna kā-nōhtē-wīhtamātān anihi, mīna ēkoni ahpw ētikwē awiyak tāh-nōhtē-kiskēyihtam, ayi - aay, tānisi ē-isiyihkāsot, ēy, hēy! niwanihkān anima, niwanihkān nānitaw nistikwānihk -

JO: acimomēyisimina?

acimomēyisimina! [*pāhpināniwan*] kikiskēyihtēn mīna ēkoni, cī?

JO: otākosīhk kikī-wīhtamawin.

āh, acimomēyisimina, kāsāwa māna pē-sākikinwa anihi, wīhkasinwa māna acimomēyisimina, māk āyi - ispatināhk ohpikinwa.

JO: āha. ēkoni anihi, āha.

acimomēyisa wīhkasinwa kā-takwākik māna, kikiskēyihtēn? ē-papā-otinamihk, kāsāwa patihtakonāyēk, kikiskēyihtēn, *stem* ē-ohc-ōcipitaman, kā-kī-- wīhkasinwa. namōya māka nānitaw kī-isi-kīsisikātēwa, wīninākwanwa ta-kīsisamihk, *you know*. pasakwāwa mīna. [*pāhpināniwan*]

JO: ana ē-kakwēcimit, "*There's a willow,*" itwēw [MLR: "ēha."], nawaciko wāpiskāwa [MLR: "ēha."] ēkwa mīna anihi nīpiya mīna wāpiskāwa, ēkwa mīn ānihi, *ah*, "*white berries*," itwēw. [MLR: "ēha."] tānisi kani -

[4. Various Plants]

JO: Those are cactuses, cac-... cacti.

Ah, yes, those ones are called *kā-kāsāki*. [JO: "Sharp ones, oh."] Sharp ones, yeah [JO: "Oh, yes."], sharp ones. Those are the green ones that are called *kā-kāsāki*, I understand. [JO: "Oh."] Those are ones that are green, those *kā-kāsāki*. And it's the same there as well, it's also the same, it's the same there when they grow those, ah, those ones, those are the ones I want to tell you about, and maybe someone wants to know, ah, well, oh, what are they called, oh shoot! I forget that, it's gone clear out of my head.

JO: Cactus berries [*literally*, "little dog turd berries"].

Cactus berries! [*laughter*] You also know about those ones, do you?

JO: You told me yesterday.

Ah, cactus berries, they are generally sharp when they begin to poke out, they are always tasty those little cactus berries, but ah -, they grow in the hills.

JO: Yes. Those are the ones, yes.

"Little dog turds" are tasty in the fall, you know? One goes around picking them up, they are sharp if you mishandle them by the stem, you know, when you're pulling the stem, they - they taste good. But there is no way to cook them, they look dirty when they are cooked, you know. They are sticky as well. [*laughter*]

JO: She was asking you, "There's a willow," she said [MLR: "Yes."], which is sort of white [MLR: "Yes."] and the leaves are also white, and there are those "white berries," she said. [MLR: "Yes."] How were -

ēkoni anihi mīna, ēkoni anihi mīna wīhcikātēwa ē-isiyihkātēki; wāpiskāwa ēkwa ē-pōskwahtaman *green* isinākwanwa. [JO: "*āhā.*"] ēkwa ōma ē-wīhtamawit *Alice* -, — mācikōc ōma ayamihtā, ēwakw āni ē-masinahamawak tānisi kāh-kī-itwān, ē-itak.

JO: okama-- okām--

okāminakasīwāhtikwak [JO: "okam--"], okāminakasīwāhtikwak. kikiskēyimāwak aniki kīkwāyak okāminakasīwāhtikwak? [JO: "mōya."] okāminakasiyak? ayi māna, sakāhk māna mitoni ohpikiwak okāminakasiyak, mān-- kāh-kinwāwa māna ē-kāsāki, ēkot-- ēkotowa mistik ana. [JO: "*Oh, thorns.*"] ēha, ēkotowa. [JO: "*Thorn trees.*"] ēkotowa, māh-misāwa mān āyi. [JO: "āha. *Red berries.*"] ēkotowa mihkwāwa, ēkoni anihi, okāminakasīwāhtikwak ēwakonik, okāminakasīwāhtikwak.

JO: maht ēsa, *do you have a* -

cēskwa, ōta nitayān ... [*matwē-tahcipicikēw*] ....

okāminakasīwāhtikwak: pēyak ēkota manisi-- [*mōy kwayask pēhtākwan*] cēskwa. cēskwa, cēskwa, cēskwa. okāminakasīwāhtikwak, okāminakasīwāhtikwak, misikitiwak māna, mitoni kāh-kinwāwa mān āyi, tāpiskōc ayi, sāponikana, ēkota, ēkota sākamowak māna ē-mihkosicik *berries* tāpiskōc, māka pihēkosiwak ayi kā-mowacik tāpiskōc ē-pihēkwāk. ēkonik aniki okāminak-- okāminak--, tānisi? [JO: "okāminasīwāhtik--"] okāminak--, ay say! [JO: "okāminasīwāhtikwak" (*sic*)] ā, okāmin--, ēy, ēkosi anima.

DO: ēkwa niyanān kēhtinā okiniyak isiyihkāsowak.

Yeah, ēwakonik kiya aniki pahkān, okiniyak kā-itacik ...

DO: pahkān cī?

... cimisisiwak māna.

Those ones too, those too are told about, they have a name; they are white and when you bite them open they look green. [JO: "Yes."] This is what Alice told me – Could you read this? I am writing this for her how you would say it, I told her that.

JO: *okama-- okām--*

okāminakasīwāhtikwak [JO: "*okam--*"], thornberry bushes. You know what those thornberry bushes are? [JO: "No."] Thorns? Ah, usually, they generally grow in the bush, the thorns, they are usually long and sharp on that kind of tree. [JO: "Oh, thorns."] Yes, that kind. [JO: "Thorn trees."] That kind, they are generally quite big, ah. [JO: "Yes. Red berries."] That kind, those ones are red, those thornberry bushes, thornberry bushes.

JO: Let's see, do you have a -

Wait, I have it here ... [*the sound of unzipping*] ....

Thornberry bushes: pull one off there [*inaudible*], wait. Wait, wait, wait. Thornberry bushes, thornberry bushes are usually large and they are generally really long, ah, like ah, needles. There, it is there that the red berries stick to, like, but they are rough and scaly when you eat them, they seem scaly. Those ones are thorn--, how [JO: "Thornberr--"] thorn- ... oh heck! [JO: "Thorberries" (*sic*)] Ah, thorn-- hey, those ones.

DO: And for us I believe they are called rosehips.

Yeah, yours are different than those, the ones you call rosehips ...

DO: They are different?

... are generally short.

JO: *Those are small ones.* [DO: "ōh."] [MLR: "ēwakonik."] *There's other thorn berries* mīna.

kotak mīna, cimisisiwak wiya aniki okiniyak k-ētacik. [JO: "*mhm.*"] [DO: "*mm.*"] ayi ay-isiyihkāsowak māna okēyakiciskēhiwēsīsak [*tēpwēyāhpināniwan*], kā-misi-mowacik kikēyakiciskān. tāpwē kā-wa-- kā-w-- ē-misi-mowacik ē-wayawīyan, nānākēs kimōsihtān ē-wī-kēyakiciskēyan, *you know*. [*pāhpināniwan*] ēkonik aniki okēyakiciskēhiwēsīsak itāwak. [*tēpwēyāhpināniwan*] ēkosi isiyihkāsowak, tāpwē!

JO: maht ēsa nika-masinahēn, tānisi kanihk, o--?

okēyakiciskēhiwēsīsak [*pāhpināniwan*], okēyakiciskēhiwēsīsak itāwak aniki, okāminakasiyak ēwakonik. [DO: "*oh?*"] namōya, mōya, mōya, mōya [DO: "okiniyak."], okiniyak ēwakonik, okinīwāhtikwak wiya isiyihkāsowak aniki, miscikosak aniki, okinīwāhtikwak ēwakonik; okinīwāhtikwak, ēkota kikamowak aniki okēyakiciskēhiwēsīsak. [*pāhpināniwan*]

JO: okēyakicis-- kē [hi] wē [MLR: "sīsak"] sī [MLR: "sak"] sak. [MLR: "ēha."] [*misi-pāhpināniwan*]

māka ayis kinōhtē-- [*aciyaw ē-nakipitamihk ēkosi mōya masinahikātēw*] ... ē-isiyihkātēk kīkway. [JO: "*Ya.*"] 'toni ē-wawiyatēyihtākwahk aniki okiniyak, okinīwāhtikwak itāwak aniki; okiniyak aniki kā-sākikicik mitoni kā--, māka apisāsinwa ayi, *pins, you know*, apisāsinwa māka mētoni kāsāwa, *you know.* māka namōya ta-misi-mowacik aniki ayis okiniyak kikēyakiciskēskākwak, masāniwiwak aniki, *you know*, masāniwiwak. māka mistahi ē-takonaman pimiy, namōy ēkosi kititiskākwak. *You put* -

JO: tānisi māka ē-isi-ayi--,

ē-isi-kīsiswacik? [JO: "āha."]

JO: Those are small ones. [DO: "Oh."] [MLR: "Those ones."] There's also other thorn berries.

Another one also, for those you call rosehip [bushes] are short. [JO: "mhm."] [DO: "hm. "] Ah, they are usually called *okēyakiciskēhiwēsīsak* ["little butt-itch makers"] [*burst of laughter*], when you eat a lot of them you get an itchy anus. Really, when you eat a lot of them and you go to the bathroom, later on you will feel it and you're going to have an itchy anus, you know. [*laughter*] Those are the ones referred to as *okēyakiciskēhiwēsīsak*. [*burst of laughter*] That's their name, really!

JO: I will have to write that down, how is that again?

okēyakiciskēhiwēsīsak [*laughter*], they are referred to as "little butt-itch makers," those are those thornberries. [DO: "Oh?"] No. No, no, no [DO: "Rosehips."], those are rosehips, for they are called wild rose bushes, those bushes, those are those wild rose bushes; they are attached there on those wild rose bushes, "the little butt-itch makers." [*laughter*]

JO: *okēyakicis-- kē* [*hi*] *wē* [MLR: "*sīsak*"] *sī* [MLR: "*sak*"] *sak*. [MLR: "Yes."] [*much laughter*]

But it's because you want - [*short break in recording and so unwritten*] ... what something is called. [JO: "Ya."] It sounds really funny, how those rosehips, those wild rose bushes are called. Those are rosehips which grow forth, really, but they are small, ah, the pins, you know, they are small but they are very sharp, you know. But you shouldn't eat lots of those because rosehips will make your anus itchy, those are [like] nettles, you know, they are nettles. But if you add a lot of grease to them, it won't affect you like that. You put -

JO: But how do you -?

Cook them? [JO: "Yes."]

ay, kisikwahwāwak, kisikwahwāwak ēkwa kikēcikopitēn *stems* anihi ayisk *leaves* omisi itamonwa, ēkoni kahkiyaw, tāpiskōc *apples*. kahkiyaw kimanipitēn anihi, mētoni kipēhkihāwak kikisīpēkināwak kwēyask, kisākamitēwāpōhk, ahpw ētikwē *worms* ēkota kikamowak wayawīyāpāwēwak ēwakonik, kinwēsīs ē-akwamo-- ē-asiwahacik nipīhk ē-kisitēk. ēkosi ēkwa kipās-- kipāhkwahwāwak, ēkosi ēkwa kitisi-pakāsimāwak pimīhk, kisikwahwāwak ayisk, kisikwahwāwak aniki pimiy māka kitakonēn ēkwa sīwinikan, mistahi wīhkitisiwak. wīhkitisiwak aniki, nēhiyawi-*fruit* anima, *you know*. [DO: "mhm."]

JO: *But how do you take out those seeds?*

ēkos īsi kikīsisēn, ēkos īsi. [JO: "ōh."] ēwako k-ōh-tōminaman ēwako k-ōh--, kīspin anima pīhcāyihk aniki nayēstaw ē-āpacihacik, ēkā ē-tōminaman anima, ēkota kā-kēyakiciskēskāskik. mētoni kikāh-pāh-pīkopitēn kicisk kiya. [*kinwēs misi-pāhpināniwan*] māka wiya misi-tōminacik, namōya kitāhkohikwak, *you know*, ayis tōmisiwak.

JO: āha, nōhkom ana ē-kī-ācimot mān āyi, āh, ohkoma ētikwē māna ē-kī-ayi-- ē-kī-papā-mōminēcik ēkwa māka ohkomiwāwa - [MLR: "ēha."] māka mōy - mōy kī-wīhtam tānisi ē--

ē-itihkwaswācik.

JO: *Yeah* [MLR: "ēkos ānima -."], tāpiskōc ē-kī-- mōya, mōya kī-kīsiswēw.

namōya, kīsiswāwak aniki, ē-sikwahwacik.

JO: ēkwa ē-kī-sēkonahkik *in a bag*.

ēha; wiyawāw ētikwē pahkān, niyanān māna wiya kā-is-āsamikawiyāhk kā-kī-wiyohkomiyān, kī-nitaw-mawisow anihi mān--, mōy wiya cīpokiniyak aniki. cīpokiniyak ātiht [JO: "āha."], cīpokiniyak cīposiwak, māka aniki kā-wāwiyēsicik ēkotowa.

Well, you crush them, you crush them and you pull those stems off because the leaves run like this, all of those, just like apples. You pull all of them off, you really clean them, you wash them properly in hot water. Maybe there will be worms clinging on and those will float out when you immers-- have put them in hot water for a little while. So then you dr-- you dry them, so then you boil them in grease. Because you crush them, you crush them but you add grease and sugar, they are really delicious. They are tasty, that's Cree fruit, you know. [DO: "Mhm."]

> JO: But how do you take out those seeds?

You cook them like that, just like that. [JO: "Oh."] That's why you grease them, that's why - if that's inside there and you just use them without greasing it, that's where they will give you an itchy anus. You would really scratch your anus raw. [*long period of laughter*] But if you grease them well, they won't aggravate you, you know, because they are greasy.

> JO: Yes, my grandmother used to tell about, ah, oh, her grandmother who I guess, ah, they used to go about eating berries off the bush, but their grandmother [MLR: "Yes."], but she didn't - she didn't tell how -

the way that they cooked them?

> JO: Yeah [MLR: "Just like that -."], like -, no, they were not cooked.

No, they were cooked when they were crushed.

> JO: And they stuffed them in a bag.

Yes. I guess they did it differently. As for us, when we were being fed by my late grandmother, she went berry-picking for those, not those pointy rosehips. Some of them are pointed rosehips [JO: "Yes."], the *cīpokiniyak* are pointed, but it was the kind that are round.

kī-misi-mawisow māna nōhkom; ēkwa anihi kahkiyaw anihi *stems* anihi kahkiyaw ē-kī-wēpināt ēkwa kisākamitēwāpōhk ē-akohcimāt. "tānēhki k-ōh-akohcimacik ōki," ē-itāyāhk māna nōhkom. "ayi aniki ta-wayawīyāpāwēcik ātiht mohcēsak pīhcāyihk kikamowak, ē-wayawīyāpāwēcik, waskicikipayiw ēkonik kiwēpināwa-- kiwēpināwak, wēpināwak. ēkwa, ēkwa, ēkwa ē-ati-kīsiswacik ēkwa, pimiy ēkota kitakonēn, pimīhk ēkwa ē-kīsiswacik ē-nipahihkasaman anima ayi, anima t-ōh-kēyakiciskēyan ē-nipahihkasaman," anima i-- kī-itwēw māna. ēkwa ēkosi sīwinikan ē-takonaman, kitaspahcikān wīhkicisiwak mētoni wīhkicisiwak. ēkwa mōy, mōy kikēyakiciskēskākwak pimiy ē-misi-takonaman, *you know*. māka wiya ēkā ē-takonaman pimiy, kikēyakiciskān kipāh-pakopitēn kicisk. ēkwa kitāpacihtān *after, vaseline, you know,* ē-tōmiciskēyan. [*pāhpināniwan*] wahwā!

DO: wīsahkēcāhk.

awas, ēkāy! [*pāhpiw*] ēkāya tasim wīsahkēcāhk, ka-pē-nānitaw-itōtākonaw ōta ta-pē-pīhtokēw aya, aya, osikiyāwīs. [*pāhpināniwan*]

[**5. tānisi k-ōh-isiyihkāsocik pisiskiwak**]

osikiyāwīsak! wah, osikiyāwīsak ayis ōki nihtā-nōtiskwēwēwak. wayawītimihk k-āyāhk ēsa iyāyaw ē-kakwē-kīminikēcik ayis, *you know*. ēkwa ēsa māna ēkosi ōm [*ē-isiniskēt*] ē-tōtahkik osikiyāwīsak, tāpiskōc ē-ākawāsonamācik ē-kakwē-wāpamiskik tān--, ēkw ēsa māna omisi [*ē-isiniskēt*] ē-tōtahkik. tāpiskōc ē-tahkiniskik, [ki]kiskē--, ē-miyāhtahkik ocihcīsiwāw itwāniw māna, ē-kīminikēskicik ayis aniki osikiyāwīsak. ēkosi it-- itaci awiyak 'osikiyāwīs!', ē-kīminikēskit ana. [*pāhpināniwan*]

ēkwa mīna, ēkwa mīna, ēkwa mīna kā-kīhkāwitohk, kētahtawē awiyak kikīhkāmik, kina-nitohtawāw awiyak ē-kīhkāmisk kicawās--, kiwīkimākan awēkā cī mīna kotak awiyak, *you know,* kiyām ta-nitohtawat nānitaw ē-itisk awiyak. nānitaw omis ītiski, 'atim' itiski, ēkāy ka-kisīmik, ēkāy- ēkāy ka-kisiwāsiyan,

My grandmother used to pick lots of berries; and all of those stems, she'd throw all of those out and then she soaked them in hot water. "Why do you soak these ones?" we used to say to my grandmother. "Well, in order to separate out some little worms that might be clinging inside, they will float out, and come to the surface, those you throw - you throw them out, they are thrown out. And then, then you started to cook them, and you add the grease in there, and when they are cooked in the grease you kill that, ah, that which would give you an itchy anus is cooked to death by that," she used to say. Then finally you add in sugar, you eat it as a condiment, it is delicious, really delicious. Then they don't, they do not give you an itchy anus if you add in a lot of grease, you know. But if you don't add in the grease, you get an itchy anus and you scratch your bum raw. And afterwards you have to use vaseline, you know, to grease your bum. [*laughter*] Oh my!

DO: *wīsahkēcāhk.*

Go on, don't! [*MLR laughs.*] Don't invoke *wīsahkēcāhk*, he might come and do something to us, he will come in here ah, ah, as a lizard. [*laughter*]

[5. Why Animals Have Such Names]

Lizards! Oh, because these lizards are known for coming after women. Because it appears they prefer to try to molest, you know, when people are outdoors. And it appears that lizards do this [*MLR gestures*], like they are shading their eyes in trying to see you whe--, and they do like this. [*MLR gestures.*] It's like they are poking you, you kn-- it is said that they smell their little hands because they are always attempting molestation, those lizards. So if you name someone 'lizard!', that one is a pervert. [*laughter*]

And also, and also, and also when quarrelling and someone suddenly scolds you, you are just listening to someone scold you, your chil-- your spouse or someone else, you know, you just listen to whatever that one says to you. Maybe if she says something like this to you, if he calls you "dog," don't let him anger you, don't, don't ē-mamihcimisk anima. tāpiskōc miton āyi ē-mīhkawikīyan, *you know*, tāpiskōc awiyak ē-- ē-ati-sipwēpahtāt, tāpiskōt ta-- āh - tak--, t-ātimat, tāpiskōc *you* - t-ātimat ē-itikawiyan, tāpiskōc ē-mīhkawikīyan ē-itisk anima awiyak. 'atim' itiski, mōy ta-- mōy ta-kisiwāsiyan, tāpiskōt niya kititēyihtēn, "acimosis ē-asp-- ē-aspi-kīhkāmit," ē-itēyihtaman, namōya. tāpiskōc anima ē-mamihcimisk, *you know*, itēyihtam wiya awa ayisiyiniw ē-mis-ītahk anima "ē-kīhkāmak 'atim' k-ētak." mōya! ē-mamihcimisk anima, ē-itisk anima ē-mīhkawikīyan, *you know?* [JO: "*Ooooh.*"] kinisitohtēnāwāw cī 'ē-atimat awiyak'? [DO: "*Mhm.*"]

ēkwa mīna ana 'minōs' kā-itiht; minōs kititānaw pōsīs; minōs kititānaw. ē-tāpwēmāyahk ana minōs k-ētāyahk wīhowin ayis anima minōs. ōta ē-itinat oskātisihk, ē-pakiciwēpinat, mīnōw ana, kikiskēyihtēn? mīnokocin [JO: "*Ooooh.*"], nīpawakocin, mīna ēwakw ānima, ēha, ēkos ānima mīn ē-itwēhk. ēkwa mīna sīsīp ē-wāpamat, "īīh, nāha sīsīp!" ē-itwēyan kwēyask anima ē-wīhat ana sīsīp. kikiskēyihtēn tānisi ana ē-isiyihkāsot 'sīsīp' k-ētiht, sīsīpak ōki. kikiskēyihtēn tānēhk ōh-isiyihkāsot, sīsīp? [JO: "namōya."] kā-wī-ohpahot, pisisik ē-sīpīt [*ē-isiniskēt*], *see!* [JO: "ōh."] kinisitohtēn? [JO & DO: "āha."]

ēkwa mīna, tānis āna mīna, tānis āna mīna k-ōh-isiyihkāsot an āya, 'sihkos' k-ētāyahk, sihkos, *a weasel,* tānis ānima? sihkos ana tānisi ana ē-wī-isiyihkātat? 'sihkos' k-ētat? mōy kinisitohtēn? [DO: "mōya."] ka-wīhtamātin kīkwāy anima. sihkos awa *weasel* kinosiw, namōya ana ē-owiyawit nayēstaw mētoni ē-sīkosit ana, *you know*. ē-sīkosit ana sihkos, nama kīkway ōtē ayi, namōy mistahi kīkway ōtē ē-ayāt. [DO: "*Oh, yeah.*"] ē-sīkosit 'sihkos' k-ētāyahk. ōki *weasels* ōki kāh-kinosiwak, namōya aniki tāpwē kīkway ōtē ē-ayācik. ē-sīkosit, kinisitohtēn? [JO: "āha." DO: "*Yeah.*"] īh, ēwako mīna anima takahk-ācimowin, *you know.* 'sihkos' k-ētāyahk anima ēkwa, ē-sīkosit anima ē-itwēyahk, kwēyask anima ē-wīhāyahk, *you know.* tāpwē aniki kāh-kinosiwak, ma kīkway ōtē ē-asiwatēyik, ētataw, ētataw apisīs piko; 'sīkōs' ē-itāyahk, ē-sīkosit [*pāhpināniwan*] [JO: "*Geez*, tāpw ēsa."]

let yourself be angry as she is praising you. It's like you're a really fast runner, you know, like someone who can take off at a run, like ah, for you to catch up to her, like what is being said of you is that you are overtaking him, it's like someone is telling you that you are a really fast runner. When he says "dog" to you, not, you shouldn't be angered, it seems to me, you think: "She is scolding me badly like a puppy," that's what you think, but no. It's like he is praising you, you know, this person thinks that he is making a statement, "I am scolding him by calling him 'dog.'" No! He's praising you by calling you that, as it means you are a fast runner, you know? [JO: "Ooooh."] Do you understand '*ē-atimat awiyak*' [that you are overtaking someone]? [DO: "Mhm."]

And also the one that is called "cat": we call the cat *minōs*, we call it *minōs*. It's right that we call it *minōs* because that's its name, *minōs*. You hold it here [upside down] by its legs and let it go, it rights itself, you know? It lands properly [JO: "Ooooh."], it recovers its natural standing position, and that's it, yes, that's what is said. And also you see a duck, you say, "Hey, that duck over there!", you are correct to name it *sīsīp*. You know how that one is called, when it is called *sīsīp*, those ducks. You know why it is called *sīsīp*? [JO: "No."] When it is going to fly up, it always stretches [MLR *gestures*], see! [JO: "Oh."] You understand? [JO & DO: "Yes."]

And also how that one, why is that other one called, ah, when we say *sihkos*, sihkos, a weasel, how is that? For that weasel, what are you calling it that for, when you say *sihkos*? You don't understand it? [DO: "No."] I'll tell you what it is. The weasel, *sihkos* is long, it doesn't have a body, it is just really empty, that one, you know. That weasel is empty, there is nothing over here, ah, it doesn't have much of anything over here. [DO: "Oh, yeah."] The one we call *sihkos* is empty. These weasels are just length, they really don't have anything over here. It's empty, you understand? [JO: "Yes." DO: "Yeah."] See, that is also a great story, you know. When we call it *sihkos*, that's what it is, we mean that it is empty, and we are right to name it that, you know. They are really long and there's nothing inside here, or instead, rather just a little, we call it "the empty one," as it is empty. [*laughter*] [JO: "Geez, is that right!"]

ēkos ānima mīna, ēwakw ānima mīna, ēkw ānima mīna ācimowin anima, ēkos ānima mīna. īh, ana minōs ana, ē-tāpwēmiht ana. oskātihk kocihāhkan, oskātihk ka-napwē--, omisi kik-ētināw, ka-pakiciwēpināw, ta-kwēskīw, 'mīnōs', ē-mīnōt! kinisitohtēn cī? [DO: "āha." JO: "āha".] ēkos ānima, ēkos ānima mīn ē-itwēhk anima. ēwakw ānima mīna, ēwakw ānima mīna ācimowin ē-wawiyatēyihtākwahk, *you know.*

sīsīp mīn āna, 'sīsīp' k-ētāyahk, ē-sīpīskit ana [*ē-isiniskēt*], kiwāpamāw pisisik ē-sīpīt [DO: "āha."] 'sīsīp' kititānaw. ēwakw ānima mīna, ēwākw ānima mīna takahk-ācimowin [JO: "*mhmmm.*"] [*pāhpināniwan*] okēyakicis-- kēyakiciskēsīsak, okēyakiciskēhiwēsīsak .... [*pāhpināniwan*] [*ostostotam.*] wawiyatēyihtākwan!

[**6. akohpa ēkwa pwēkiciminak**]

ēkwa mīna ōma kā-miyit ōma kā-atamihit ana k-ētitān. "kitatamihin" k-ētak ōma, t-ākwanahoyān ayis ōma ē-nitawēyimit ta-kīsōhkwāmiyān. mōy kacāc nika-mwēstācīhkawāwak pwēkiciminak ta-mowakik. [*tēpwēyāhpināniwan*] nika-kīsōhkwāmin kwayask.

JO: mācikōtitān, *is it* - tānisi ōma kā-isiyihkātēk?

DO: *Foot warmer.*

JO: *Oh. Foot warmer* isiyihkātēw ōma [MLR: "āha, āha."], *it will warm your feet.* [MLR: "ēha, ēha."] [*pāhpināniwan*]

ēkosi isiyihkātēw; māka ēkwa mīna ōta ta-kīsōskākoyān ōta, ēkwa kīspin mitoni ē-nōhtē-kīsōhkwāmiyān, *beans* nika-misi-kīsiswāwak. mōy konita nika-akwanahon, *you know*. māka wiya ōma, mōy kacāc *beans* [*pāhpiw*], mōy kacāc pwēkiciminak ta-mowakik. [*pāhpināniwan*] kitatamihin.

wahwā hay!

JO: kēhcināc awa ē-pāhpihit.

So then as well, there's also that, there's also another story, there's another one. See, there's that *minōs* which is spoken of properly. Test it out on its legs, you bend it at the legs - you hold it like this and you let it go, it will turn that *minōs*, as it's agile! Do you understand? [DO: "Yes." JO: "Yes."] That's, That is also what is said. That too, that is also a funny sounding story, you know.

And that duck which we call *sīsīp*, that one is always stretching [*MLR gestures*], you see it stretching all of the time. [DO: "Yes."] We call it "the stretcher." That one as well, that one is also a great story [JO: "mhMMM"]. [*laughter*] Little itch-- little butt-itchers, little butt-itch makers .... [*laughter*] [*MLR coughs.*] That is amusing!

[**6. Blankets and Beans**]

And there is this which she gave me, so that I am grateful to her, I was telling you. "Thank you," I told her, so I can cover myself, because she wanted me to sleep warmly. It's not necessary for me to bother with eating beans. [*loud laughter*] I will have a proper warm sleep.

JO: Let me show you, is it - what is it that it is called?

DO: Foot warmer.

JO: Oh, this is called a foot warmer [MLR: "Yes, yes."], it will warm your feet. [MLR: "Yes, yes."] [*laughter*]

That is what it is called, but now it will also warm me here, and if I really wanted to sleep warm, I will cook a lot of beans. I won't cover up for nothing, you know, but now beans are not necessary [*MLR laughs*], it won't be necessary for me to eat beans ["fart-berries"]. [*laughter*] I thank you.

Oh my goodness gracious!

JO: This one certainly makes me laugh.

ēha, ēkosi. [*pāhpiw*]

wawiyatēyihtākwan anima ācimowin, mētoni misahkamik kīkway ōma kikāh-ācimostātināwāw, mētoni kapē-kīsik nikāh-pāh-pīkiskwān kīkway ta-wīhtamātakok, ē-miywāsik oti, mōy wiya ē-māyātahk, ē-wawiyatēyihtākwahk mīna ēkwa ē-pāhpihk. ē-wawiya-- ē-wawiyatēyi--, ē-wawiyas-ācimohk takahkēyihtākwan, kipāhpin ayis.

[7. ē-pāh-pakamahikēt]

īh, ōki nōsisimak ōki, mōniyāwak ōki, wahwā, mistahi mīna nikī-pāhpin ōma. pikw īta māna ōm āyis ē-pōsiyān, ōma -, ōm āy--, pikw īta ē-pōsiyān ayis nimiywēyihtēn *bingo*. kīspin k-ōsōniyāmisiyān, ahwā, āsa[y] k-āt-ōtākosik, ōma māna mēkwāc mōya nikī-miyo-pimohtān, ētataw nipa-pimohtān. māka kē-- mitoni k-- nikotwāsik - nikotwāsik tipahikan, nikotwāsik k-āt-īspayik mētoni niyahkīn ōtē ē-papāmohtēyān, *bingo* ayis ōma t-ētohtēyān; mētoni niyahkikocinin namōya awiyak ēkwa niwīcōhkamāk. ēkwa, ēkwa, ēkwa ta-kakwē-*hitchhike*iwiyān ēkwa, tāpwē! nikaskihon ōtēnāhk ta-itohtēyān, māka ē-cipahikēsiyān kwēyask, *you know*, ē-kakwē-miyak kīkway, *gas money* awa, iyikohk wēsōniyāmisiyān āskaw *twenty, ten dollars*, *five dollars*, iyikohk - iyikohk ē-tēpēyimoyān iyikohk ē-[o]sōniyāmiyān.

ēkwa, nikosis awa māka naniwē-- ninanōyacimik nawaciko māna ē-isit nikosis awa *Johnny* awa, "māmā!" "kīkwāy? kīkwāy?" nititāw. "wahwā, *you hitch-- you hitchhike* māna pisisik," itwēw, "*bingo all the time* pikw ītē ē-pōsiyan. pikw īta kāh-kī-nipān ātawiy," ītwēw, "nikiskēyihtēn wiya pikw īta ta-nipāyan," itwēw, "namōy nānitaw," itwēw, "ayis *you hitch-- you hitchhiking all the time*," nitik ē-ākayāsīmot. "ēha."

> — ē-pimipayiyāhk ōma sēhkēsihk. cimatēwa ōta *number six* ayi nīso inito-macēkinohkāna, kiwāpahtēnāwāw? [DO & JO: "āha."] —

Yes, that's the way. [*MLR laughs.*]

That is a very funny story, there are really a lot of things that I could tell you about, I could really keep speaking all day telling you things, and good things, not bad stuff, funny sounding things and there'd be laughter. Funny - humour-- telling funny stories is wonderful, because you laugh.

[7. Dabbing]

See, these grandchildren of mine, these white people, oh my, I really laughed a lot. Because I always get rides everywhere and, ah, I get rides all over, because I like bingo. If I have a little bit of money, oh my, right away come evening time, although I was not able to walk well at the time, I could barely walk. But, really, at six - at six o'clock, as it approaches six I really pushed myself to get walking because I have to go to bingo. I really forged ahead, with no-one helping me then. And then, and then I was trying to hitchhike and sure enough! I managed to go to town, but I chipped in a bit as appropriate, you know, trying to give some gas money, as much of the little money I have, sometimes twenty, or ten dollars, five dollars, as much as I can afford of the money I have.

And this son of mine would tease - he would tease me. This son of mine always kind of says to me, this one, Johnny, "Mom!" "What? What?" I say to him. "Oh my goodness, you hitch-- you hitchhike all the time," he says, "bingo all the time, getting rides all around. You could sleep anywhere," he said, "although I know you could sleep anywhere," he said, "that's all right," he said, "because you're hitchhiking all the time," he told me in English. "Yes."

> — We're driving along in the car. There are set up here on number six [highway], ah, two imitation tipis, you've seen them? [DO & JO: "Yes."] —

"māmā," itwēw, "kētahtawē pimi-nīpā-- pimi-nīpāhtēyani," itwēw, "kakwē-pīhtokēyāhtawīhkan ōma mēnikan," itwēw, "ēkota ka-nitawi-nipān," itwēw, "namōy āwiyak nānitaw k-ētik." [*pāhpināniwan*] ēkwa - ēkwa mīna ē-ati-pāhpihit ēwako, tāpiskōt tāpwē ta-pīhtokēyān ōma misi--, nika-sākikātēsinin, nikinosin ayisk. [*pāhpināniwan*] wāhay, nawaciko mān ē-isit, ē-pāhpihit māk ānima, *you know*.

āh, ēkosi māna - ēy, *bingo* ē-miywēyihtamān, *you know*. ē-- tēpiyāhk ē--, āskaw - āskaw ayi, nikī-miyopayin ōma namōy kayās. *Fifth of March* kā-miyo--, kā-takahkipayiyān, ātawiya ninōtikēwin, *you know*, māka kēyāpic nitakahkipayin, ēēh! [*pāhpināniwan*] mōya, kwēyask ōma ē-is-- ē-itinikēyān, *you know*.

ayi, nistim awa pēyak ōta, "*Auntie*," itwēw, "pēyak cī akohp kitatāmitin?" itwēw. ēkotowa ōma, *you know*. "āha," nititāw, "*forty* ayis ōhi." "pēyak nik-ōtinēn." wahwā, *I phone her now, I phone*, "nistim," nititāw, "akohpa ōta astēwa, pē-nawasawāpamow *which one you like*, ka-pē-otinēn," "ēha," itwēw, "*you wait for me,*" ē-nōhtē-itohtēyān *bingo*. "tāpwē," itwēw. āsay ōta *car*, hā, hā namōy.., āsay mēkwāc ayi *my - springtime, you know*. ēkos ōma ē-isi-pēhkastēk nīkis. namōya wī-pē-pīhtikwēw, nētē nīpawiw anima ayi, *carpet* anima ē-aspikā--, namōy ē-nōhtē-kētaskisinēt; "wahwā, nisikosē, tān ēwako?" anit ōhi astēwa. "āh, piko pikw ānima," nititāw, "otinamani, anima ka-miyokwātēw." *Half* ōhi māna ō--, ōmatowa, kikiskēyihtēn? [JO: "āha."] omis īsi, mitoni nimi-- nimiyo--, nimiyokwātēn. "ēwak ōm," ītwēw. nawaciko, nawaciko *green* isinākwan. "ēwako." *Forty dollars* nipē-miyik.

ahh, ēkw ē-nitaw-sipwēhtēyān, wahwā, k-āti-sipwēhtēt mayaw sēmāk *phone* -

> — ayis nitayān *phone; I have to have a phone here* ōm ōhci, *you know*, kā-is-āyān [otēh ē-itahk, *pacemaker*] —

"Mom," he said, "if you're walking along in the dark sometime," he said, "try to climb in through the fence and you can go sleep there," he said. "Nobody will say anything to you." [*laughter*] And he started laughing at me. It was as though I could just go inside - I'd be lying down with my legs sticking out, because I'm tall. [*laughter*] Oh my, he always kind of talks to me like that, laughing at me, you know.

Ah, so that's the way it - hey, I just really like bingo, you know. At any rate, ah, sometimes, sometimes ah, I had some luck not long ago. Fifth of March, I was ... I had things go very well although I am an elderly woman, you know, but I still get lucky, ennh! [*laughter*] No, I act properly, you know.

Ah, this one niece of mine here, ah, "Auntie," she said, "Can I buy one blanket from you?" she said. This kind here, you know. "Yes," I told her, "these are forty." "I will take one of them." Oh wow, I phone her now, I phone, "My niece," I said to her, "the blankets are here, come and have a look and choose which one you like, you'll come and take it." "Yes," she said. "You wait for me," as I was wanting to go to bingo. "For sure," she said. And already there's a car here, ha, well, not ... already then, ah, my ..., it's springtime, you know. So that's why my little home was clean. She wouldn't come in, she was standing over there, ah, on the carpet as it - she didn't want to take her shoes off. "Oh my, Auntie, which one of those?" They were sitting there. "Ah, whichever one you take," I told her, "it will be sewn really well." Half of these were of this kind, you know? [JO: "Yes."] In this way, I - I sew - I sew them really well. "That's that one," she said. It was sort of, it looked sort of green. "That one." She came to give me forty dollars.

Ah, and I went to leave, oh my, as soon as she started to leave, right away the phone -

> — because I have a phone. I have to have a phone here because of my condition, you know [referring to her heart and pacemaker] —

sēmāk nitēpwātāw awa nikosis. "*Johnny*," nititāw, "*you pick me up*," nititāw, "*I have a little bit money here.*" "*Okay,*" itwēw, "*You wait for me, about half an hour's time.*" "*Okay.*" āsay ōta nikosis *half an hour outside*; āsay wiya nikīsi-pēhkihon, nipēhkihon māna, *you know*, mōniyānāhk ayis. ahh, [ni]nitaw-pōsin, nitati-wīcēwāwak; nēma ēkwa ayi *Queen City* ēkwa ē-itohtēyāhk *bingo*.

ēkā kā-pīhtwāhk nitati-nahapin, *first table* anima māna kā-ati-pīhtikwēhk, wiyawāw wāhyaw nētē; mōy āwiyak ayis -, namōy āwiyak nimiciminik, nikaskihon ē-ati-pīhtikwēyān, nitaw-āpin ēkota. īh, *forty dollars* awa nitayāwāw, *ten* nimiyāw, *thirty* ēkwa piko nitayāwāw, *cards* ē-tipahamān *thirty*, nitaw-nahapin. āh, ōtē *behind* āpihtawikosisānis ninisitawēyimāw, *behind* apiw. ēkwa ōma ē-wī-māci-mētawēhk ōma *Queen* anihi māna *yellow ones* anihi, ē-wī-māci-mētawēhk aspin nīso ē-kī-atāwēyān *two dollars* ohci, *three dollars* ohci 52 *Bonanzas* ē--, āh, ēkwa nika-māci-pakamahikān ēkwa wī-māci-mēta--, ahh, ninitonēn *my paper*, namwāc kīkway! ēēy!! ēsa kāh-mōsāhkinahkik ōki owēpahikēwak aniki māna *paper* k-ōtinahkik; ahh, nama kīkway *my paper*, kahkiyaw ēsa masaskonamwak!

wahwā! ōtē awa āpihtawikosisān nōsisim awa, "nōhkom," nitik māna. "*Kohkom, what you doing now?*" itwēw. "*You know what,*" nititāw, "*I lost all my paper here*," nititāw. tāpwē, nama kīkway astēw, *you know*, ahpō, *you know just my purse* ōta ēkwa *my kerchief* ōta, nama kīkway, moscāyihk mīna nama kīkway, namōya ninihtā-ka-kayēyisin, *you know*, ma kīkway. ma kīkway, kahkiyaw ēsa kāh-mōsāhkinahkik. "*Here's this girl, call her,*" nitik, "ahpō ētikwē kī-otinam." *I call this girl now, I call her, "Come here!"* wahwā! āsay ōta, "tānisi, *Grandma*?" itwēw. "*You know what,*" nititāw, "*I lost all my paper* ōta," nititāw. "tānimayikohk kāh-ohc-ōtinaman ayi *Bonanzas*," nitik "namōya mistahi," nititāw, "*just five dollars' worth, two dollars' worth of yellow ones, Queen* anihi," nititāw, "ēkwa wiya *three dollars' worth of 52.*" "hay," itwēw, "*I'll help you, fif-- ah, three dollars' worth* ayi," itwēw, "ōh āyi 52." *So* ōta pē-astāw *six, six* ayis. "ēkwa anihi

I immediately call my son. "Johnny," I say to him, "you pick me up," I tell him, "I have a little bit of money here." "Okay," he says. "You wait for me, about half an hour's time." "Okay." And already after a half an hour here's my son outside, I had already finished cleaning myself up, I usually clean up, you know, to be among the white people. Ah, I go to get into the car, I head out with them, that now, ah, now we're going to the Queen City for bingo.

I usually sit at the first table where there is no smoking, at the entrance, and they are far away over there; so there is no-one, ... no-one is holding me back, I am able to enter and I go and sit there. See, I have forty dollars, I gave him ten, now I only have thirty, I pay thirty for cards and I go and sit down. Ah, behind me over here I recognize a little Métis man, he is sitting behind. And then the game is going to begin, that was "Queen," those are usually the yellow ones, the game is going to start and I had purchased two, for two dollars, and for three dollars, 52 Bonanzas - Ah, then I will start dabbing and the game begin-- Oh, I look for my paper, there's nothing at all! Hey! Apparently they had gathered it up, those sweepers who usually take the papers. Ah, none of my papers were there, they had apparently gathered them all up.

Oh my! Over here is this Métis, my grandchild. "Grandmother," he says to me. "Grandma, what are you doing now?" he says. "You know what," I say to him, "I lost all my papers here," I tell him. There was really nothing there, you know, or, you know, just my purse is here and my kerchief is here, but nothing else. On the floor too, nothing. I am not a deceitful person, you know, there was nothing. There was nothing, they had apparently gathered all of it up. "Here's this girl, call her," he tells me. "Maybe she took them." I call this girl now, I call her. "Come here!" Oh my! And here she is, "What is it, Grandma?" "You know what," I tell her, "I lost all my paper here," I tell her. "How much did you spend on, ah, Bonanzas," she says to me. "Not much," I tell her, "just five dollars' worth, two dollars' worth of yellow ones, that's 'Queen,'" I tell her, "and three dollars' worth of fifty-two." "Aw," she says, "I'll help you, fif-- ah, three dollars' worth, ah," she said, "of these 52s." So here she *yellow ones* kinitawē--" āsay māka wī-māci-mētawēwak ēkwa, nī-- otatamihit [*sic*: otamihit] nīso, *you know, two dollars* ohci ayi, *ya,* nīso pakahkam.

āsay ēkota kā-pē-takohtēt pēyak iskwēs aspin ē-nācipahtwāt *yellow ones* ē-wī-miyit. kā-pē-wīcēwāt aw ō-- ēwakw āw ōkimāw ana kā-okimāhkān-- anita, āh, *manager* ētikwē ōta nīpawiw ēkwa nikakwēcimik, *"Grandma, what's wrong with you?"* nitik, *"You lost something?" "Yeah," I told him, "I lost all of my paper,"* nititāw, "kahkiyaw otinamwak aniki iskwēsisak, *I don't know which one*," nititāw. pēyak nipē-wāpahtahik *but "my marker red* niya," nititāw, "*all blue* anihi," nititāw. *"Well,"* itwēw, *"what do you -, if you want,"* itwēw, *"I replace it for you,"* itwēw, *"that money, how much you -* kā-ōt-- kā-isi-mēstinikēyan," nitik. *"Just five dollars."* namōy āyiwāk ninōhtē-itāw. "*Five dollars." "Okay,"* itwēw. *This girl, "Help her,"* itwēw; "*I need ayi,"* nititāw, "*two dollars* kēyāpic ohci," nititāw. tāpwē āsay. ēkosi ēkwa *five dollars* ohc ānihi. miywēyihtam awa ōta āpihtawikosisān. "wahwā!" itwēw, itēw ōhi okimāwa. "ēwako anima kā-pakwātamān," itwēw, itwēw awa āpihtawikosisān, "ta-kī--, ōki otatoskēwak kā-wī-pēhkihcikēcik, ta-kī-- ta-kī-kakwēcimācik anihi, *which ones* anihi ēkā ē-nitawēyihtamiyit." āhci piko awa kisēyiniw otōskinī--, nāpēw aw ītwēw, āsay māka niwīcihikwak. *"Well, that's okay,"* itwēw awa aya *manager* awa. "*You*, ēkosi cī?" niya "ēkosi," nititāw.

ēkwa ē-pē-pakamahikēyān ēkwa ēwak ōm āyi ōhi *52s* ēkwa. nēma nikanawāpahtēn nētē. wahwā, *sixty-seven* ōta, namōya tēpwācikātēw. *sixty-eight* mīna. nīso nimanēsin. "īhī," nitēyihtēn. *I know this girl,* pēyak awa *Linda* isiyihkāsow. *I call her, "Come here,"* nititāw, *"come and help Kohkom here."* "kīkwāy?" nitik "mahti ōhi *check it* ōhi," nititāw. "*My pa-- my 52* ōmatowi, tāpiskōc *I need just two*," nititāw. nīso ayisk ē-patahamān. ēkwa, wiyāpahtahk ēkwa ēkw āwa, *you know*, niwīcōhkamāk ōhi. pēyak ēkota pē-nīpawiw, "wāh! kī-tēpwācikātēw anima *sixty-eight,"* itēw ōhi iskwēsisa. "ahh, tāpwē," itwēw, "*Grandma, you need just one."* [*ostostotam*] *"You need just one, sixty-- sixty-seven* piko." pēyak ninitawēyihtēn.

comes and puts down six, because six -, "And those yellow ones you want -." But they were already going to start playing, and she's pre-occupying me with the two, you know, for the two dollars, ah, ya, I guess it was two.

Now this one young lady has already arrived there having run off to get the yellow ones to give to me. She came with that bo--, that manager, that one in charg-- there, ah, I guess it was that manager standing here and he asks me, "Grandma, what's wrong with you?" he said to me, "You lost something?" "Yeah," I told him. "I lost all of my paper," I told him. "Those girls took all of it, I don't know which one," I told him. He came and showed me one, but "My own marker is red," I told him, "and those are all blue," I told him. "Well," he said, "What do you - if you want," he said, "I will replace it for you," he said, "that money, how much did - did you spend," he said to me. "Just five dollars." I didn't want to tell him more, "Five dollars." "Okay," he says. This girl, "Help her," he says. "I need, ah," I said to him, "two more dollars," I told him. Sure enough already. So that's the five dollars worth. The Métis man was happy. "Oh wow!" he said, he said to the manager, "That's what I hate," he says, this Métis says, "they sh... these workers, when they are going to clean up they should ask people which ones they don't want." Continuing on, this old man's young m-- the man was saying, but they already helped me. "Well, that's okay," he said, ah, the manager. "Are you all right?" "It's all right," I told him.

And I come now to dab at those, ah, 52s. I look at that one over there. Oh my, sixty-seven isn't called. Nor is sixty-eight. I am short of two. "Whoa," I think. I know this one girl, called Linda. I call her, "Come here," I say to her, "come and help Kohkom here." "What?" she says to me. "Can you please check these," I say to her. "My pa--, my 52 card, it seems I need just two," I tell her. I had missed two. And then she spots them then, you know, she helps me with those. The one who came to stand there. "Whoa! They called that sixy-eight," he tells that girl. "Oh, it's true," she says, "Grandma, you need just one." [*MLR coughs.*] "You need just one, only sixty-- sixty-seven." I need one.

[*mōy kwayask pēhtākwan*] *next table* apiwak. nitakwanahēn ēkwa ōma ēkwa *my purse on top*; mēton ēkwa nikanawēyihtēn. wahwā, *N-34* pē-wayawīw, *N-45*; mōy kīkway '*O*'. kētahtawē kā-pē-kwēskipayihot "*Grandma, Mrs. Rockthunder, you need, you need, that's your number!*" nitik, ē-wāpahtahk [*ostostotam*] *sixty-seven.* "āsay pēyak *one winner,*" itwēw awa. "kēyāpic pēyak," kā-misi-tēpwēyān. *A thousand dollars* [JO: "*Oooo.*"] [*mōy kwayask pēhtākwan*]... --oyāni *forty dollars* ōmatowa nimisi-wīcihikon, *thirty* ē-kī-osōniyāhkēsiyān. *Forty*, māka ē-kī-wīcihtāsoyān *ten dollars.*

ēkosi nipē--, nīso nipē-tipahamākwak ōta, *five hundred a piece* tahkonēwak, *you know*, nipa-pēyakwapin ayisk. [JO: "mhm."] ōta nipē-tipahamāk awa. ēkwa awa kā-kī-wīcihit awa nōsisim, "*Come here,*" nititāw, "*I'm going to help you, a little money for you, twenty dollars,*" "*No, Grandma,*" itwēw, "*keep it, keep it,*" nitik. "namōya," nititāw, "*for your smokes,*" nititāw, "*You help me lots.*" "*Okay, Okay.*" pē-otinēw *twenty dollars.* mōniyās awa: "*Grandma, me too, I smoke*," ē-nanōyacimit mōniyās awa [*pāhpināniwan*], ē-māh-mēkiwak ōma sōniyāwa. [*pāhpināniwan*]

ēkosi ē-kīsi-tipahamawit, ē-tipahamawit mēkwāc ēkwa, awīn āwa āsay ōta nikosis *Johnny* kī-nīpawiw, ē-pē-nāsit ēkwa ayisk niwīcēwāwak, ē-kī-nakasicik ōma wāhyaw. [*pāhpināniwan*] ē-wawiyatēyimak, niwayawīnān. [*pāhpināniwan*] mētoni ēkwa nikihc-ītēyimikwak ōma ē-misi-otahowēyān. [*pāhpināniwan*]

[**8. ē-pimohtēhot**]

īh, *fifth of - fifth of March* anima kā-kī-otahowēyān, *fifth of March* kā-kī-otahowēyān, kahkiyaw masinahikātēw nētē. tāpiskōc mīn ānita anihi kahkiyaw kīkway nimasinahēn māna, *you know*, ōma tānisi ē-ay-itahkamikisiyāhk. ōtē nikī-itohtahikawin mīn ōpīma ēkwa mīna iyikohk ē-mēstinikēyān, kahkiyaw masinahikātēw. ēkotē ayisk māna ē-itohtēyān, *Hobbema.* kayās māna nikī-otināw *plane*, mōya māk ēkwa, *you know,* āhkwakisow ēkwa ayisk. kayās wiya *a hundred and seventy* māna *one way*, *plane* awa, *you know?*

[*Inaudible*] they are sitting at the next table. I cover it then with my purse on top of it; I'm really looking after it now. Oh my, N-34 comes out, N-45; nothing "O." All of sudden, she quickly turns back around. "Grandma, Mrs. Rockthunder, you need, you need, that's your number!" She tells me seeing [*MLR coughs*] sixty-seven. "There's already one winner," this one tells me. "Still one more," I yelled out loudly. A thousand dollars [JO: "Oooo."] [*inaudible*] - that forty dollars really helped me, thirty, as I had made a little money. Forty, but I helped out with ten dollars.

So I came, two came here to pay me, they carried five hundred apiece, you know. As it was, I was sitting by myself. [JO: "Mhm."] This one came here to pay me. And then this grandchild of mine who had helped me, "Come here," I say to her, "I'm going to help you, a little money for you, twenty dollars." "No, Grandma," she says, "keep it, keep it," she tells me. "No," I tell her, "for your smokes," I tell her, "You help me lots." "Okay, Okay." She comes and takes twenty dollars. And this young white person, "Grandma, me too, I smoke," this young white person is teasing me [*laughter*], as I was giving away money. [*laughter*]

So he finished paying me, and then while they are paying me, who else but my son Johnny should already be standing here, coming to get me because I was accompanying them, and they had left me far behind. [*laughter*] I found him funny, and we went outside. [*laughter*] They were really thinking highly of me now t hat I had won big. [*laughter*]

[**8. Travels**]

See, it was the fifth of - the fifth of March when I had won, it was the fifth of March when I won, everything is written down over there. It's like that there too, I usually write all of those things down, you know, what I am doing. I am taken over to Hobbema [now Maskwacis, Alberta] and the amount that I spend is all written down. Because I usually go over there to Hobbema. Long ago I used to take a plane, but not now, you know, because it is expensive now. In the past it used to be a hundred and seventy for a one-way trip, by plane, you know?

[JO: "āha."] nistwāw ēkotowa nipōsin ōt ōhci, *an hour and ten minutes* āsay nētē ayi, *Edmonton* takwakotēw. aciyaw piko ē-apiyān, *you know*, namōya kinwēs. māka ēkwa māna namōya, *bus* nitōtināw āskaw, āskaw *car* awiyak nipōsihik, *you know.*

JO: āskaw mān ānima *seat sale* ayāwak. [MLR: "ēha."] wēhtakihtēw.

ēkos ānima āskaw. ayi anima, ispīhk kā-pē-kīwēyān, mwēhc ānima *New Year's Day, on the first,* kā-- kā-- *next day* tāpiskōc kā-wī-pē-kīwēyān, *New Year's Day* kā-pē-kīwēyān, mētoni ē-āhkwakihtēki ēkwa ēkota anima ayi, anih āya *fare money* ana, *you know*. nakacā, misahkamik ē-mēstinahkik anihi kā-- kā-wēhtakihtēyiki, ēkwa ohcitaw t-ōtinamān anima kā--, *first class* ayi, anim āyi masinahikan nikī-otinēn ē-pē-kīwēyāpōyoyān, *plane* ē-pē-kīwēyān. nānahi-kēswān mīna ēkota ē-otahowēyān *that night, fifty-two hundred* ē-ispayit aya *Bonanzas*, māka nikī-nistinān, ta-kī-nēwiyāhk māk āwa pēyak ma kīkway *forty-six* ē-ayāt. nisto piko niyanān kwēyask, ēkos āna *fifty-two, fifty-two hundred* ana sōniyāw; *seventeen hundred and thirty-three dollars and thirty-three cents a piece* nikī-miyikawinān [JO: "*Ooooh.*"], ē-nistiyāhk. hā, akihcikēyan ēwakoyikohk [JO & DO: "*Mhm.*"], ēwakoyikohk nisto. *Fifty-two hundred,* ēwakw ānima ē-kī-misi-otahowēyān ēkotē mīna, *you know.* kīh-pēyakoyān mistahi nika-kī-otahowān. *Lions* aniki ē-osīhtācik anima *bingo* ēkospīhk, ēkwa awa nītim ē-nitawi-nātāt anihi sōniyāwa, *Lloyd Buffalo* itāw. "niya nika-nātāw, nītim," itwēw. "pē-askowin," nitik. *Lions* ōki mitoni māna *yellow* k-ēsīhocik [JO: "āha."], tipahamawit, ē-miyit anihi sōniyāwa. "ē-otahowēt aw," ītwēw, "*from Regina,*" itwēw. "*Well,*" itwēw, "*first class* kik-ōtinēn *plane here.*" "ēkotowa māka ana ē-kī-pē-pōsit," itēw awa nītim. "ēkotowa ana ē-kī-otināt, ēkwa mīna ēkotowa t-āti-kīwēt ōma ē-wī-otināt ēkotowa ocawāsimisa ē-wī-kakwē-otihtāt *New Year, New Year's Day,*" itēw. īh, tāpwē anima nikī-otināw ana [*ostostotam*] *a hundred - okay,* kēkāt *two hundred* pakahkam kā-kī-tipahikēyān anima āyi, kikiskēyihtēn, ē-āhkwakihtēk ē-mēstinamihk anihi ayi masinahikana, opōsiwak ōki ē-mēstinahkik.

[JO: "Yes."] I boarded that three times from here, an hour and ten minutes and already over there, ah, it arrives in Edmonton. I'm sitting for only a short time, you know, not long. But not usually nowadays, I take the bus sometimes, sometimes someone drives me, you know.

JO: Sometimes they have a seat sale. [MLR: "Yes."] It's cheap.

It is like that sometimes. Ah, when I was coming home, right on New Year's Day, on the first, the next day, like when I am going to come home, when I'm coming home on New Year's Day, then that's really expensive there, ah, that, ah, it's that fare money, you know. Holy, they had run out of those cheap ones and I had to take that - I took a first class, ah, ticket when I was coming back home, coming home on the plane. And coincidentally I also won there that night, fifty-two hundred as it happened, ah, Bonanzas, but there were three of us, there would have been four of us but one didn't have forty-six. Only three of us got that fifty-two properly, so that fifty-two hundred dollars; we were given seventeen hundred and thirty-three dollars and thirty-three cents apiece [JO: "Oooooh."], the three of us. Ha, you count that much [JO & DO: "Mhm."], that amount, three [ways]. Fifty-two hundred, that was my big victory over there, too, you know. Were I to have been alone, I could have won a great deal. That was the Lions that made that bingo then and my cousin went to get the money, his name is Lloyd Buffalo. "I will get it, cousin," he said. "Follow me," he told me. The Lions usually dress in yellow [JO: "Yes."], he paid me, he gave me that money. "This one is a winner," he said, "from Regina," he said. "Well," he said, "You will take a first class plane here." "That's what she took to get here," my cousin told him. "That's what she took and that's what she will be going home in, she'll be taking that kind as she tries to reach her children for the New Year, on New Year's Day," he told him. See, for sure, I took that [*MLR coughs*] a hundred - okay, I guess it was almost two hundred that I paid, you know, it's expensive paying for those tickets, passengers are going broke.

[*aciyaw ē-nakipitamihk*]

nītim an ēwakw āna, ē-kī-oyociwāmit awa kā-kī-wīcēwak. ēkwa aniki ēkotē wāhkō--, ē-kī-wāhkōmāt awa kā-kī-oyokisēyinīmiyān, *Rabbits* aniki. *Rabbits* itāwak ē-kī-wāhkōmāt kā-kī-wīcēwak awa *John*, kisēyiniwa anihi *Joe Rabbit* kī-itāw, kī-panātisiw māka, *you know.* ēkwa ēkoni ēwako māna ōma kōh-itohtēyān ēkotē, nitihkwatimak aniki ēkwa mīna nistimak, māka nikisēyinīm ana ē-kī-wāhkōmāt, *you know*. māka mētoni ninakayāskawāwak, *you know*, ēkwa mīna mētoni nisawēyimikwak. wiyawāw ōki nitawāsimisak ē-wāhkōmācik, *you know*. [JO: "*Mhm.*"]

kākikē ēkotē nititohtān, ēkotē ōma ē-kī-itohtēyān ōma, ōtē *north*. ēkwa mīn ōm ōtē aya, aya ana, ēkonik aniki tānis ē-isiyihkāsot ana kā-- kā-aya--, ana kā--, anohc kā-wīhat ana, āh, wahwā hay, niwanihkān. *Carrieres* aniki kā-wāhkōmācik anihi ētikwē - [JO: "*Daniels.*"] *Daniels!* [JO: "āha."] *Henry* itāw ana, *Henry Daniels* itāw ana kā-kī-pē-nātitisahot. ōtē ana okimāhkān ayi - [JO: "kotakak aniki kēscināc."] kot--, pahkān, pahkān. [JO: "āha, pahkān."] wīstawāw *Daniels* ē-āpacihtācik. ēwakw āna kā-kī-pē-nātitisahot ana nōsisim ana [*mōy kwayask pēhtākwan*] .... *Round dance* ē-kī-pē-nitomicik, ēkotē nikī-itohtān. ōta mīna *round dance* anima kā-nitomikawiyān, ēkota mīna nikī-itohtān, *Hobbema* ēwako, *you know*. [JO: "*Mhm.*"] nikī-nitawi-kanawāpahkān *round dance.*

kayās māna nikī-nīmihiton, mōy māk ēkwa, *you know*, mōy - nihcikwana ōhi, mōy, mōy miywāsinwa, *you know*. kayās māna nikī-minw-āyān [*sic; cf.* nimiyw-āyān]. ēy, kētahtawē ōta ē-nīmihitohk nīhcāyihk, kētahtawē kā-tēpwātikawiyān *number seven* anima ē-kī-ayāyān aya, anima, akihtāsowina mān ānihi, *you know.* ēsa ōma ē-otahowēyān, nikī-tipahamākawin. [*pāhpiw*] namōy nikiskēyihtēn ē-otahowēyān. ē-pīcicīhk mān ānima kā-nīmihitohk [JO: "ōh, āha."], *yeah*, ēkw ānima nikī-otahowān, *number seven*. wāh, mōy nikiskēyihtēn ē-otahowēyān. [*pāhpināniwan*]

[*nakipicikātēw*]

[*pause in recording*]

That one is my brother-in-law. My late partner had him as a brother [parallel cousin], and they were relate-- my late old man was related to them, those Rabbits. They are called Rabbits, who he was related to, my late partner, John; that old man was called Joe Rabbit, but he passed away, you know. And they're the reason that I go over there, my nephews and also my nieces, but it was my old man who was related to them, you know. I was really comfortable with them, you know, and those ones really love me. These children of mine are related to them, you know. [JO: "Mhm."]

I always go there, that's where I went, over here to the north. And also over here, ah, ah, that, those ones, what is that one's name, that - the one who - the one that, the one you named today, oh, for goodness sakes, I forget. The Carrieres are related to them, I guess. [JO: "Daniels."] Daniels! [JO: "Yes."] That one's name is Henry, he is called Henry Daniels, the one who sent for me. That one is the chief over here, ah [JO: "Those are other ones, I think."] Oth-- different, different. [JO: "Yes, different."]
They too use the name Daniels, and that one who sent for me is my grandchild [*inaudible*].... They had come to invite me to a round dance, and I went over there. I was invited to a round dance here as well and I went there, that's Hobbema, you know. [JO: "Mhm."] I went to watch the round dance.

I used to dance long ago, but not now, you know, no - these knees of mine, no, they are not good, you know. Long ago, I used to be healthy. Hey! There once was a dance here down in the valley, all of a sudden I was called, "number seven" was the number I usually had, you know. And it appears that I won, I was paid. [*MLR laughs.*] I didn't know I won. That dance was the ***pīcicīwin*** [JO: "Oh, yes."], yeah, and I won that, number seven. Whoa! I didn't know I won. [*laughter*]

[*recording stopped*]

3
cahkatahikēwin
BINGO

Told on March 23, 2001, at the Cree Language Retention Committee's Language Teachers' Workshop in Saskatoon, Saskatchewan.

This text adds to Mary Louise's tales of work and bingo from the preceding texts.

ayi ōma, mistah āyi nimiywēyihtēn *Bingo* ē-mētawēyān, mēton ōti. namōya niminihkwān, namōya mīna nipīhtwān māka nimiywēyihtēn ē-mētawēyān. ēkotē māna nisōniyāmis aspin! [*pāhpināniwan*] [ēkosi] ē-itamahcihoyān, "āh, kiyām, asisīwēkin ana, namōya ana ayisiyiniw." pē-nōkosiw, māka -, m--, aya awa, sōniyāw pē-ayāw; ayisiyiniw piko kā-wanihāyahk aspin ēwako, māka wiya sōniyāw tahto-kīsikāw pē-ayāw, *it's a paper*. ēkosi māna ē-itēyihtamān. ayisiyiniw kā-wanihiht aspin ēwako, mōy wīhkāc kiwāpamānaw māka wiya sōniyāw ē-ayāwāyahk ē-wēpināyahk, kāwi ana kiwāpamānaw sōniyāw. ēkosi māna ē-itēyihtamān. ēy, nimiywēyihtēn ē-mētawēyān, mēton ōti.

Regina nikī-ayān *nineteen - 1966* kā-kī-ohci-sipwēhtēyāhk ōta nikisēyinīm ē-kī-otahowēt, *ah, ah, twelfth of ah, twelfth of July, 1966,* ē-kī-otahowēt *big money, a thousand dollars* ēkospīhk kayās mistahi sōniyāw. kā-kīskinamāht otatosk--, otatoskē-- ayi, nikīskinamākawinān *welfare* ē-nistiyāhk nitawāsimisak. nikisēyinīm piko ta-atoskēt ēkwa nitānis kī-atoskēw *at the hospital, nurs*a ē-wīcihāt mōya wiya ohci ayi, mōya wiya ohci *nurs*iwiw māka *help, you know*, kī-ay-atoskēw. *In a suite, 11 block Albert Street* nikī-ayānān, kī-ayāw nitānis.

My, my -, nikisēyinīm awa omisi itwēw, "kitos kitānis," itwēw, "ka-nitawi-wīc-āyāmānaw," itwēw. "kika-pamihcikān ēkota, ka-kīsitēpon, ka-pēhkascikān, wiya ta-nitaw-ātoskēw."

tāpwē. nitēpwātāw awa nitānis. ayi nititāw, "*Barbara*," nititāw, "niwī-nitaw-āyānān ēkotē nikīskinamākawinān *welfare* ē-isi-nistiyāhk." "āhay," itwēw, "pē-ayāk."

Way up nētē -, *suite* nētē *way upstairs*. ēkotē tāpwē nitispicinān. *1966* ē-ispiciyāhk ōtēnāhk. nikisēyinīm ēkwa nikosis atoskēwak *chickens* ē-tasīhkawācik, [*Broad*] *Street* ōma. ēkota kī-ohci-sōniyāhkēw. *1967* ninitonēn ēkwa wāskāhikan, nimiskēn; nimiskēn wāskāhikan *10 block McTavish* ēkota; ēkota ēkwa nitispicinān.

Ah, I really like playing bingo, a whole lot! I don't drink, and I also don't smoke, but I like to play. There goes my money again! [*laughter*] That's how I feel, "Oh, never mind, it's only paper, it's not a person." ... but it appears ... ah, the money comes; when we lose a human being, that one is gone, but as for money it comes every day, it's a paper. That's what I usually think. When a person is lost, they are gone and we will never see them again, but when we have money and throw it away, we will see that money come back again. That's what I always think. Hey, I like to play, a whole lot.

I was in Regina, it was nineteen ... 1966 when we left from here, my old man had won on the twelfth of ah, the twelfth of July, 1966. He won big money, a thousand dollars was big money at that time long ago. When his work was cut off, his work, ah, we were cut off welfare, the three of us with our children. My old man had to work and my daughter worked at the hospital helping the nurses. She was not, ah, she was not a nurse but she helped, you know, she was working. We lived in a suite, 11 block Albert Street, at my daughter's place.

My, my ... this old man of mine said this: "Speak to your daughter," he said. "We will go and stay with her," he said. "You will manage things there, you will cook, you will clean, and she will go to work."

For sure, I called my daughter, ah, I told her, "Barbara," I said to her, "we are going to come stay there, our welfare is cut off, the three of us." "Yes," she said, "come stay."

The suite over there, it was way upstairs there and for sure we moved there. We moved into town in 1966. My old man and my son worked, working on chickens. It was on [Broad] Street. He made his money there. Then in 1967 I looked for a house and I found it; I found a house there on 10 block McTavish. So then we moved there.

hāw, ēkota ēkwa, *a nun* ēkwa anita anima āya *Elphinstone* ēkota awa *Sister* ninakayāskawāw. ninitawi-kakwēcimāw mahti ta-kī--, ta-kī-wīcihit *a little bit work*, tēpiyāhk pahkwēsikan ta-wīcihit, awēkā pimiy. "ēha." itwēw, "*We'll look after you*. ēha'." ēkosi tāpwē, ninitaw-ātoskān ēkwa nīsta. tāpwē māna pahkwēsikana nimiyik, *pastry* nimiyik, pimiy nimiyik ta-mīcisoyāhk. āh, nimīcisonān.

ninitonēn ēkwa atoskēwin; kā-miskamān *eighteen - eighteen - 1821 Scarth Street* ēkota nimiskēn. kī-panātisiwak *Violet, Dorothy*, ēkwa niya, nikī-nistinān. *Second - second floor* ē-astāyāhk *shop* ē-kaskikwāsoyāhk. ē-pē-atāwēcik māna mōniyāwak. tāpwē kētahtawē kā-nitomikoyāhkok mōniyāsak *Co-op company downstairs*. *Meeting* ēkwa ē-wī-otinahkik ōma *little shop* ē-osīhtāyāhk. "ahām," itwēwak ōki *Violet Fourhorns* kī-itāw ēkwa *Dorothy Francis* ēkwa niya, nimasinahikānān ēkwa. *Co-op* otinam ōma *our shop* nitaw-āstāw wāskāhikanihk ēkw āni kahkiyaw kīkway ēkwa *machine* ēkota ēkwa ē-atoskēyāhk ēkota anima *five dollars and thirty-five cents an hour* nask-- nikaskihcikānān, okimāw ēkwa ēkota. kī-panātisiw mīna nitōkimāminān.

ēkosi ēkwa, wahwā, nimāci-sōniyāhkānān. sōniyāwasinahikana *every two weeks*. wāhyaw, wāhyaw nikī-ayān nikī-āhtokān ayis *17 block Connaught Street, way out, four miles* ē-ohtāpōyoyān, *by bus* māna awa. nitānis wiya awa atoskēw ayis, āhkosīwikamikohk wiya. kēyāpic atoskēw.

wahwā hay, kētahtawē kā-miskamān ōma *Bingo* mitoni ē-ati-miywēyihtamān, wahwā hay! wahwā nitāh-itohtān. nikisēyinīm mīna awa. āh, nimiywēyihtēnān *Bingo*, wahwā hay.

ēkosi ēkwa, wahwā, nitāh-ocipitikon māna ōhi niskāta iyikohk ētikwē ōma ē-apiyān *in a machine* ē-kaskikwāsoyān. nipētamāk ayi, ōmayikohk ētikwē ē-ispīhcāk ayi, *a bottle*, *tube*. "ēwako ta-āpacihtāyan ōma." itwēw, "*cramp--*, ōki *your cords* ōki kā-wīsakēyimacik." nitik. "ēha." īh, nitastān māna ōhi *my markers in a washroom. My washroom kind of cold*. ōtē, nitastān kahkiyaw

Well, and there, then there was a nun there at, ah, Elphinstone, I was familiar with this Sister there. I went and asked her if she could help me with a little bit of work, just to help me with flour, or lard. "Yes," she said, "we'll look after you, yes." So for sure, I too went and worked, and truly she used to give me flour, and she'd give me pastry, and she'd give me lard for us to eat. Well, we ate.

And I looked for work. I found it at eighteen ... eighteen ... 1821 Scarth Street, I found it there. They have passed on, Violet and Dorothy, and with me, there were three of us. We had a shop on the second floor, sewing. White people used to come and shop. For sure eventually we were invited by the white folks from Co-op company downstairs. Then there was a meeting as they were going to take that little shop that we made. "Okay," said these ones, Violet Fourhorns was her name, and Dorothy Francis and me, we signed then. Co-op took this shop of ours and went and put it in a house, and everything was machines there and we worked there and earned $5.35 an hour, and a boss was there. That boss of ours also passed away.

So then, oh my, we started making money, [receiving] cheques every two weeks. Far away, I was far away, because I moved house to 17 block Connaught Street, way out, I used to travel four miles by the bus. As for my daughter, she worked, she was at the hospital. She still works.

Oh my goodness, eventually I discovered bingo and really started liking it, oh my goodness! Oh my, I would go. My old man as well. Hey, we liked bingo, oh my goodness.

So then, oh my, I would usually get cramps in my legs, I guess from sitting so much at a machine sewing. He brought me, ah, I guess it was a bottle or tube this size. "This is for you to use," he said, "for your cords [i.e., tendons] that you find painful," he said to me. "Yes." See, I used to put these markers of mine in the washroom. My washroom was kind of cold. I put everything over kīkway. wahwā! *Any time* ēkwa *my bus eight o'clock* ta-pē-takopayik *any time; I have my lunch in a, on a table*. ā, āhā kētahtawē - ohcitaw ta-sipwēhtēyan. misposin; ohcitaw māka *my bus half a block* ōta, *street* ōta ē-pimamok, ēkota kā-ayāyān.

ā, wahwā, nitocipitikon tāwāyihk [ni]nipēwininān astēw ninīhtakosīn ōtē. *Half asleep* ōma, wahwā, nitocipitikon. wahwā, nitasikan[ak] ōki āsay nikikasikanān māka wahwā ēkwa, *half asleep* ōma nitotinēn ayis *I think* [*mōy pēhtawāw ayisk ē-matwē-pāhpihk*] nisisopēhikan ..., kā-āstēpayiyān. [*pāhpināniwan*]

ēkosi nitāpisihkwasin. nitapin. ā, wahwā nitēyihtēn nitak ōti *my old man* kāh-atāwēstamawit maskihkiy mētoni nimiyoskākon. [*pāhpināniwan*] *Half asleep* ōma *you know*; mētoni ēkwa nitat-āpisihkwasin. ā, awīn ōma *green marker*! niskāta ōhi! [*misi-pāhpināniwan*]

wahwā hay! ka-wīhtamawak nikisēyinīm. nikī-kostāw nikisēyinīm. — nāpēwak kā-ayāhcik [*sic*; cf. kā-ayāwihcik] kostāwak ē-aw-- [*pāhpināniwan*] — nikisēyinīm nikī-kostāw. nitōskināw, nitōskin--, "*Old man*," nititāw, "mācikōci tiyōtāsoyān." nitiskonāw awa nitasikan, wahwā, niskāta ōhi. *Greeeen* mētoni ē-isinākwahki.

"ahahāā, ēkos īsi sipwēhtē, niyā!" [*pāhpināniwan*]

mōy āhpō nikitimākināk. [*pāhpināniwan*]

here. Oh my! Any time now, my bus would be arriving at eight o'clock, any time; I have my lunch in a ... on the table. Ah, yes, all of a sudden, I had to leave. It is snowing a bit, but of course my bus was half a block from where the street was running here, that's where I was.

Oh, oh my, I get a cramp in the middle of our bed, and I climb down on this side. I was half asleep, oh my, I get a cramp. Oh goodness, these stockings of mine, I already had my stockings on, but oh my now, I was half asleep, I take what I think is [*inaudible due to laughter*], my salve .... Then I was relieved. [*laughter*]

So then I'm fully awake. I sit up. Oh, oh my, I thought it was a good thing that my old man had bought the medicine for me, it really did me good. [*laughter*] I was half asleep, you know, but now I'm waking up. Oh, what is this, green marker! These legs of mine. [*much laughter*]

Oh my goodness, I had to tell my old man. I was afraid of my old man. – When one has a man, they are feared - [*laughter*] – I was afraid of my old man. I wake him up, my ... "Old man," I said to him, "look at what I've done to myself." I pulled up my stocking, oh my, these legs of mine. They looked really greeeeen.

"Ahaha, leave like that, go on!" [*laughter*]

He didn't even feel sorry for me. [*laughter*]

4
kā-ātayōhkēhk
TELLING A SACRED STORY

This was told and recorded on March 23, 2001, at the CLRC Language Teachers' Workshop in Saskatoon, Saskatchewan, to which Mary Louise was driven by Jean and Arok.

The latter section, the ātayōhkēwin *itself, is the story that Mary Louise refers to above in text 2, section 4, in her discussion of* okiniyak. *This portion of the current text was originally published as* "wīsahkēcāhk omikiy mīciw / Wīsahkēcāhk Eats His Scab" *in* wawiyatācimowinisa / Funny Little Stories, *edited by Arok Wolvengrey, Regina: University of Regina Press, 2007.*

kayās, nikī-pēhtawāwak māna kēhtē-ayak ēkotowa ōma, kā-pē-kakwēcimit nōsisim, ātayōhkēwin. nikī-nitohtēnān kayās, ē-sakahpitastimwēcik kēhtē-ayak wayawītimihk ē-asamācik otēmiwāwa ē-akwanahācik, ēkwa ha-- awīn āna kā-pīhtokāht, ēwakw āna kīsitēpow.

ēkwa - ēkwa ē-kīsi-mīcisohk, "hām, kisēyiniw, pē-ātayōhkē ōta," kī-itwēwak māna kēhtē-ayak. kwayask anima ē-itōtamēk ātayōhkēwin kā-n-- kā-nitōskamēk. kī-itwāniw kayās, kī-itwāniw māna kēhtē-ayak kayās, ātayōhkēwin, awiyak nānitaw ē-is-āyāt, ē-nitohtahk, tāpiskōc, tāpiskōc ē-- tāpiskōc ē-- awa kā-ātayōhkēt tāpiskōc ē-nitotamākēstamawāt miywāyāwin, miyomahcihowin, tāpiskōc ē-ayamihtākosit, tāpiskōt ē-kitotāt tāpiskōc manitowa ēwako ātayōhkēwin kayās. ēkosi kī-ispayiw. ē-kī-pēhtamān anima.

namōya, namōya niya, mōy niya ēkwayāk ē-wīhtamātakok. ē-kī-pēhtamān tānisi ē-itātayōhkēcik kēhtē-ayak. nikī-apin māna awēkā cī ē-wiyotihtapisiniyān ē-nitohtawakik kēhtē-ayak kā-kī-wiyōhkomiyān ēkwa kā-kī-wiyomosōmiyān. nimosōm ē-pwācis kī-itāw. ēkwa nōhkom ayi, nikī-isiyihkātānān *Isabelle Easbappie*, sapēn māna nikī-itānān nōhkom omāmihkwēw, omāmihkwēw kī-wiyōhkomiyān, nōhtāwiy okāwīsa, okāwiya mīna, omāmihkwēwak. kī-- ayi ana, kī-pwāsīmow nōhkom ēkwa nisikos pēyak otānisa ēkota māna ē-pimisiniyāhk, ē-nitohtamāhk kisēyiniw ēhā-- ē-ācimot. "ahām," ēwak ōma ka--, kisēyiniw, "kā-wī-ācimostā-- kā-wī-- kā-wī-ātayōhkēyān," kī-itwēw māna awa kisēyiniw. ēkosi ēkwa ē-nitohtāht kāh-kīsi-itāskonikētwāwi tāpiskōc ōma kā-itōtamēk ōta, ēkosi kī-itōtamwak. ospwākana kī-āpacihēwak, māka kinayēhtāwīnānaw kiyānaw āpihtaw nawaciko kimōniyāwi-tōtēnānaw mōya māka nānitaw, pēyakwan. pēyakwan, pēyak-ōspwākan.

hāw, anohc kā-wī-pimi-ācimostātakok.

Long ago, I would hear the elders tell the kind of thing that my grandchild is asking about, the sacred story. We listened long ago, while the elders tied their horses outside and fed them and covered them, and, ah, whoever's home was entered, that one cooked.

Then ... then when the meal had been eaten, "Okay, old man, come and tell a sacred story here," the elders would say. You were doing the right thing asking for a sacred story. It was said long ago, the elders would say in the old days of a sacred story, when someone was in a poor condition, and was listening to a sacred story, it was like ... just like ... it was like the one telling the sacred story was asking, on behalf of the ill person, for good health, feeling healthy, it was like he was praying, like he was talking to the Creator with that sacred story, long ago. That was what happened. I heard that.

No, not me, it is not me only now telling this to you. I heard how the elders told sacred stories. I would sit or else I would lie on my belly listening to the elders, my late grandmother and my late grandfather. My grandfather was called ē-*pwācis* (Little Sioux). And my grandmother, ah, we called her Isabelle Eashappie, *sapēn* we used to call my grandmother, an Assiniboine. My grandmother was an Assiniboine woman, my father's aunt was Assiniboine, his mother too, they were Assiniboine women. They, ah, that grandmother of mine, she spoke Assiniboine, and one of my aunt's daughters, we used to lie there listening to the old man, as he was telling a story. "Okay," said this one old man, "I am going to tell, ... it's ... it's a sacred story I am going to tell," is what this old man used to say. So then he was listened to when they had finished smoking the sacred pipe, just like what you do here, they did that. They used a pipe, but we have a difficult time, we are more or less halfway doing things the Whiteman way, but that's okay, it's the same. It's the same, a single pipe.

Okay, today I am going to tell you all a story.

kī-mamāhtāwisiw ēsa kimosōminaw, wīsahkēcāhk kī-itāw. kī-mamāhtāwisiw ēsa, kahkiyaw kīkway kī-osīhtāw. "hām, ēkotowa, ēkosi k-ētāpacihtān ōma." ahpō maskihkiya, kī--, kī--, kī-wīhtamākēw. "ocēpihk, ēkosi kā-kī-itāpacihtāyēk," kī-itwēw ēsa wīsahkēcāhk. "ēwako, misi-kākikē ē-ohpikihki, kiyām kā-- kōna k-āyāt āhci piko ē-pē-ohpikihki ōtē. maskihkiya k-āti-kīsipakāk āsay, kiwāpahtēnānaw āsay kēyāpic anihi mēkwāc ōma ē-pē-sākikihki anihi, namōy ē-nipōmakahki ōtē. isko ta-askīwik," ēkosi māna ēsa kī-itwēw wīsahkēcāhk.

• • • •

pēyakwāw ēsa wīsahkēcāhk ē-pa-pimohtēt, ē-pimohtēt wīsahkēcāhk. wahwā hay, miton ēsa ohkoma akāwātamawēw ē-nāh-nawacīyit ōma ayi, kāhkēwak. wahwā, nōhtē-mīciw ēsa, mōy māka kī--, misi-mistiyiniw ayisk misi-kisēyiniw awa wīsahkēcāhk. mōya wī-asamik ohkoma. wahwā, mitoni nōhtēhkatēw. āh, ēkosi nakatēw ōhi ohkoma. āw, papāmohtēw. kī-pimohtēskiw ayis awa wīsahkēcāhk. wahwā, mitoni nōhtēhkatēw. wahwā! okiniya ēsa kā-wāpamāt, mitoni ē-māh-mihkosiyit, ēkoni ēsa ēkwa -, nōhtēhkatēw. ēkoni ēs ēkwa okiniya ōhi mētoni misi-mowēw. miton ōti.

"ahām, nisīmitik, mitoni nikīspon ēkwa. tānis ōma ē-isiyihkāsoyēk?"

"āāh, okiniyak."

"āha', ēko cī piko? ohcitaw kā--, kā-ayisiyinīwihk nāh-nīsowihkāsonāniwiw, namōya nayēstaw okiniyak, nisīmitik, ta-kī-isiyihkā--, ta-kī-isiyihkātisoyēk."

pēyak -, wawānēyihtamwak ēs ōk ōki okiniyak tānisi t-ēsiyihkātisocik. omisi ēsa pēyak awa k-ētwēt mis-ōkiniy awa, "āāh, nistēsē, okēyakiciskēsīsak nitikawinān." [*pāhpināniwan*]

He was spiritually gifted, was this grandfather of ours, and he was called Wīsahkēcāhk. He was gifted, and he made everything. "Okay, that kind, that's the way you use this." Even medicines, he - he - he told about them. "The root, that's the way you use it," Wīsahkēcāhk would apparently say. "That one, those are growing eternally; regardless if there is snow there, it's still growing over here. When plants start to lose their leaves, we will still see these growing forth, they never die. Up to a year." That is what Wīsahkēcāhk used to say.

• • • •

Once upon a time Wīsahkēcāhk was walking along, he was walking Wīsahkēcāhk was. Oh my goodness, it seems he was really craving that which his grandmother would roast, umm, ***kāhkēwak*** [dried meat]. Oh my, he wanted to eat it, but she didn't .... Because he was a very big man, this old man Wīsahkēcāhk, his grandmother wasn't going to feed him. Gee whiz, he was really hungry. Well, so he left his grandmother. So then he wandered about. But that's Wīsahkēcāhk for you, he's always walking. My goodness, but he was very hungry. Well! Then he spotted some rosehips, and they were really red, so those were the ones now, for he was hungry. So then he really gobbled up great quantities of those rosehips. A great many.

"All right, my little brothers, now I'm really full. What are you called?"

"Oh, rosehips."

"Yes, but only that? It's compulsory that, among people, there be two names, so my little brothers, you should not call yourselves by the name 'rosehips' alone."

One -, these here rosehips were at a loss for what other name they had. Then this one large rosehip spoke up saying: "Oh, elder brother, we are called Little Butt Itchers." [*laughter*] "wāāhāā, wahwā, tāpwē kimāyiyihkāsonāwāw!"

"āā, anima - anima kā-misi-mowiyāhk, kā-misi-mīcisoyan, ati-wayawīyani ōma kika-māy-ītōtākon anima ōtē [*ē-isiniskēt*]. mētoni kika-misi-kēyakisin."

"āāh, nitakisa ētikw ōki okēyakiciskēhiwēsīsak." sipwēhtēw, pimohtēw.

wahwā! nōmak-- nōmakēsīs ēsa ē-at-āyāt. wahwā, kā-kā--, kā-kāh-kēyakisit ōtē [*pāhpināniwan*], piyisk ēsa pīkopitam ōm ōtē ōm ītē anima kā-wayawīt. [*pāhpināniwan*] pimohtēw.

wahwā! "wahwā, nōhkom ōta kā-pim-āyētiskit, ēwako kā-kī-akāwātamawak kāhkēwak." ati-mātāhēw ōhi - wiy ōma kā-mātāhisot. [*pāhpisināniwan*] kā-pāstēyik ēsa kāhkēwakos. pakonēyāyiw ōta. at-ōtinam. "ēhāha, nōhkom ēsa kāh-ati-patinahk okāhkēwakomis, ēwako kā-kī-akāwātamawak, at-ōtinam ēsa awa wīsahkēcāhk ēkwa ē-ati-mīcit ēkw ōma. wahwā, mētoni, mētoni ati-- ati-kīspow.

kētahtawē ēsa piyēsīsa, "wīsahkēcāhk omikiy mīīīciw!" [*pāhpināniwan*] kā-itwēyit ēsa. "wīsahkēcāhk omikiy mīīīciw!"

"wā, nisīmitik, tānita ita wīsahkēcāhk o-- omikiy kē-mīcit. nōhkom ōma okāhkēwakomis kā-mīciyān."

wā, āhci piko nāh-nikamowak ōki piyēsīsak kā-ati-nisitawinahk ēsa ōm ōtē itē kōh-wayawīhk ē-- ē-wātiwan-- ē-wā--wā-- ayi, nawaciko ē-osāwāk ōma ēwakw ānima kā-ati-pahkihtitāt ēsa ōma ōh ōkiniya osām ē-kī-kiyakisit. [*pāhpināniwan*]

"wahwā! ē-tāpwēcik ēsa ōki nisīmak. ēcik ōma tāpwē nimikiy kā-mīciyān." [*misi-pāhpināniwan; wīsta pāhpiw*]

"Oho, my goodness, you have a truly hideous name!"

"Ah, since you ate so many of us, since you ate such a great amount, when nature calls it's going to have quite a bad effect on you over here. [*MLR gestures.*] You will really get very itchy."

"Aah, there's nothing to these Little Butt Itchers." He merely left and walked on.

My goodness! I guess he had been on his way for a while. Oh my, by then he kept itching over here [*laughter*], and eventually he tore [a scab] loose over here from where he voids. [*laughter*] And on he walked.

Well! "Goodness, my grandmother was leaving tracks along here, the one who's dried meat I wanted." He started tracking her, but it was himself that he was tracking. [*MLR chuckles.*] Here [he found] a small piece of dry ***kāhkēwak***. It had a hole here in the middle of it. He picked it up. "Oh yes, my grandmother must have dropped a piece of her dried meat, the stuff I had wanted." Wīsahkēcāhk took it and started eating it right then. Oh my, really, he started getting very full.

All of a sudden, some birds were singing, "Wīsahkēcāhk eeeats his own scab!" [*laughter*] "Wīsahkēcāhk eeeats his own scab!"

"Whoa, my little brothers, from where might the scab come that Wīsahkēcāhk would eat? It's my grandmother's dried meat that I'm eating."

Well, nevertheless these birds kept singing and he started to recognize this from over here where one voids, the hole ... ah, that which he had let drop was somewhat orange and it was due to the rosehips that he was itchy. [*laughter*]

"Oh no! These younger brothers of mine are telling the truth. It appears that I was really eating my own scab." [*great laughter*] [*MLR laughs as well.*]

kayās nōhcīn

ēkosi! hā, hām! ēkosi māna kī-ay-is-ātayōhkāniwiw, ēwako pēyak. tānimayikohk ta-pīkiskwēyān? [*pāhpināniwan*]

[*kīhtwām awa pāhpiw*]

"wīsahkēcāhk omikiy mīīīciw!"

That's it. All right. That's how this sacred story is always told, this is one of them. How long should I speak? [*laughter*]

[MLR *laughs again*]

"Wīsahkēcāhk eeeats his own scab!"

5
nēhiyaw-isīhcikēwina
CREE CUSTOMS

This four-part text was recorded on February 22, 2002, at the home of Mary Louise Rockthunder at Piapot First Nation.

One of the important teachings that Mary Louise had to share, which was barely touched on in her other recordings, was her knowledge of traditional Cree customs and sayings. Thus, we are particularly grateful that Mary Louise made this final recording for Jean.

[**1. kākīsimowin**]

ahāw, anohc kā-kīsikāk, nōsisim ōta ē-pē-aspēyimototawit, nīsta ē-kitamākēyimak ē-wī-kakwē-wīcōhkamawak kīkway. awa pēyak ospwākan kā-tahkonak, ēwakw āna ē-wī-kitotak kōhtāwīnaw kisē-manitow anohc kā-kīsikāk. ēkosi māna kī-itōtamwak kēhtē-ayak kā-kīskisamāhcik kī-pāh-pīkiskwātēwak ōhi cistēmāwa. ēkosi ē-wī-pimi-tōtamān ayisk kayās nōhcīn, kayās nōh-pē-pēhtēn kīkway, tānisi ē-kī-pē-itōtahkik kēhtē-ayak, ēwakonik ē-kī-pē-kiskinohamawicik ē-kī-pē-kakwē-kiskēyihtamān kīkway.

hāw, nōhtāwīnān anohc kā-kīsikāk, awa pēyak ospwākan ē-pimi-tahkonak nōsisim kīkway ē-wī-pimi-wīhtamawak; namōya kīkway ē-wī-pimi-kiyāskiyān. manitow ninitotāk ē-pimi-tahkonak awa pēyak ospwākan, ēkotē ka-pimi-wāh-wīcihikoyāhk kīkway, kīkway ē-pimi-mamāy--, ē-pimi-mamāyīyān, ta-pima-mi--, ta-pimi-miywastāw nōhtāwīnān kisē-manitow ēkāya kīkway ta-māyi-itōtawak nōsisim anohc kā-kīsikāk. ēkosi ē-pimi-isi-aspēyimototawit kā-pimi-tahkonak awa cistēmāw. ay hay, ē-pim-ītwēyān anohc ē-wī-pimi-pāh-pīkiskwēyān kīkwāy kā-pimi-kakwēcimit.

[**2. nipākwēsimowin**]

kayās kī-nipākwēsimonāniwiw, kī-kihcēyihtākwan nipākwēsimowin. ēwako misi-mīkiwāhp kā-kī-isiyihkātēk, kihci-mīkiwāhp, ēkota kā-nipākwēsimohk. ēkosi ē-ati-pōyocik, ēkosi ēkwa kī-matotisānihkēwak, nēmitanaw mistikwa kī-āpacihēwak matotisān ē-osīhtācik. ē-kāsīhkasahkik anihi pakiwayāna ayisk ōma mōya kanātisināniwiw k-ēskwēwihk; mōy nānitaw kī-tōcikātēw ēwako ta-māmiywākācimohk, ta-māmiywākācimiht awiyak, ēkā ka-kī-kāsīhkasikātēwa. kī-āpatanwa mostoso-wīhkaskwa ē-pēhkihkasamihk ōhi, ēkoni ōhi wēpināsona k-ēsiyihkātēki. ēwakw ānima ē-pē-kiskēyihtamān kayās; kayās isīhcikēwin. ē-kī-nīsiki ēwakoni mawimoscikēwina kā-nipākwēsimohk ēkwa mīna kā-matotisihk ēkoni ē-kī-kiskēyihtamān. ēkota kī-ohci-pimātisiwak ayisiyiniwak,

[**1. A Prayer**]

Yes, today my grandchild is here placing her trust in me and, as I also have compassion for her, I am going to try to help her with something. While I am holding this one pipe I am going to speak to Our Father, the Creator on this day. That is what the elders did when they were presented with tobacco; they spoke with this tobacco. This is what I am going to do as I am from a long time back, I have heard things from long ago, how the old people did things, these are the ones who taught me and I have tried to learn something of that.

Yes, Our Father, today I hold this one pipe as I am going to tell my grandchild some things. I am not going to tell lies, the Creator is listening to me as I carry this one pipe so that he will help us with something. If I mis--, if I make mistakes in anything I do, Our Father, the Creator will make it right, so that I will not harm my grandchild today. So she is relying on me as I hold this tobacco. I am expressing my gratitude today as I am going to be speaking about what she is asking me.

[**2. Thirst Dance**]

Long ago the Thirst Dances were held; the Thirst Dance was highly respected. That was called the big-lodge, the great-lodge, the Thirst Dance was held in there. As they finished, then they built a sweatlodge; they used forty trees building the sweatlodge. They were purifying those cloths because there may be some impurity due to the presence of women. Nothing was done to cause offense, for anyone to be offended, lest [the cloths] become impure. Buffalo sage was used for cleansing these, these which are called *wēpināsona* [ceremonial cloths]. That is what I have come to know from long ago; the customs of the past. There were two of those ceremonies, the Thirst Dance and the sweatlodge, those are the ones that I know. The people were given life through that;

matotisānihk ē-pīhtokwahiht awiyak ēkā kā-miyw-āyāt, kī--, kī-miyo-tōtāk ēsa anima matotisān, ēkosi māna kī-itwāniw, ēwako ē-kī-pē-pēhtamān. ēwako nōsisim ē-pē-kakwēcimit.

pēyakwāw pēyak-askiy ayisk cimacikātēw, kī-cimatāwak māna kayās kisēyiniwak ēwako ōma matotisān k-ētamihk - ay! ōma nipākwēsimowin, niwanitonāmon. matotisān wiya pātos kā-pōyohki ēkota kā-kāsīhkasikātēki ōhi wēpināsona. ēkosi kēhtē-ayak nēwo tipiskāw kī-kanawēyihtamwak ēkosi ē-nitawi-pakitinahkik, ē-nitawi-akotācik. ēkosi kāh-pimi-īs--, kāh-pim-īsi-itōtahkik kayās kēhtē-ayak, ēwako ōma ē-pimi-wīhtamawak nōsisim, kayās isīhcikēwin ēwako ē-kī-pē-kiskēyihtamān.

ē-kī-pē-itāmohk anima, ē-kī-pē-itāmohk ana mistik tāwāyihk kā-cimasot. kimosōminaw kī-isiyihkāsow ēwakw āna kā-nipākwēsimohk ana mistik. ē-kī-miywēyihtahkik, tāpiskōc ē-kī--, ēkota ohci ayisiyiniw ē-kī-ohci-pimātisit nānitaw k-ēs-āyāt. ē-kī-kakwātakihtāt ayisiyiniw ēkota kī-ohci-pimātisiw, ēwako ē-kī-nanāskomocik kēhtē-ayak.

ēwak ōhci nipākwēsimowin k-ōh-isiyihkātēk: nēwo tipiskāw ana k-ēsīhcikēt namōya ohci-minihkwēw nipiy, namōya ohci-mīcisow nēwo tipiskāw. kī-āh-iyinito-isīhow mīna maskisina ma-- ōhi iyinitwaskisina kī-kikiskam ēkwa mīna kī-akwanahow ōtē ē-tahkopitahk ē-pakwahtēhot akohp. ēwako, ēwako k-ēsīhcikēt nīso kī-tahkonēw ē-- wēwēstēhamāna. ēkwa ēwako ē-isīhcikēt ēkwa ōta mīna kī-itahpisow pakiwayān ostikwānihk, ē-sītostikwānēhpisot ēwakw āna k-ēsīhcikēt. namōya konita ohc-īsi-papāmohtēw ayis ōma kā--, mōya miywāsin wayawītimihk awa -; oskinīkiskwēwak ōki, ē-kī-kostamihk ta-pistiskahk kīkway awa kā-pimohtēt awa k-ēsīhcikēt. ē-kī-kostamihk ēwako kayās.

anohc ēkwa! namōya ātawiya, namōya ātawiya awiyak ē-ānwēyimiht māka ta-kī-manācihtāhk pēyakwan ēkosi a person with ill health was taken into the sweatlodge. I understand that sweatlodge helped him, that was what was said, I heard that. That is the information my grandchild has come to ask me.

It was erected only once a year, the old men of long ago used to build this which is referred to as a sweatlodge – Oh! I said the wrong thing – this Thirst Dance lodge. The sweatlodge was used after the Thirst Dance was finished, to cleanse the ceremonial cloths. Then the elders kept them for four nights and then from there they went to release them, going to hang them up. That is what the elders used to do long ago. This is what I am telling my grandchild, the customs from the past as I came to know them.

People fled to find refuge, they came to find refuge in that pole which was erected in the center. That pole at the Thirst Dance lodge was referred to as "Our Grandfather." They were happy -, it was as if -, if a person had an illness of some kind they would be healed, an afflicted person would be restored to health through that, and the elders were grateful for that.

This is the reason why this is called the Thirst Dance: the person who was performing this rite did not drink water for four days, he did not eat for four nights. He dressed traditionally and for shoes he wore moccasins and he covered himself here by tying a blanket around his waist like a belt. That one who was performing this rite held two [wings as] fans, and the ceremonialist also tied a cloth here around his head, the one performing this rite would be supporting his own head. He did not go walking about just anywhere because, ah -, it was not good outside for this one -; in the presence of these young women, it was feared that this one who is performing the rite would accidentally step on something [which would taint his ability] while walking. That was feared long ago.

Nowadays! Although there is not, it's not as though anybody is being rejected, but it [ritual] must be respected and it should be ta-kī-kakwē-isi-tōtamihk. ēkosi ē-kī-pē-isi-kiskēyihtamān kayās, ē-kī-pē-wāpahtamān mīna ēkwa mīna ē-kī-pē-pēhtawakik kēhtē-ayak ēwak ōma kā-pa-pīkiskwātamān anohc. namōya ē-kiyāskiyān, kisē-manitow ninitohtāk ē-pim--, ē-pimi-wīhtamawak awa nōsisim, ē-pē-kakwēcimit, ē-pē-otinahk nipīkiskwēwin.

māka 'toni nitakahkēyihtēn ē-kēhtē-ayiwiyān, ayēnānēmitanaw ayiwāk niyānan ē-itahtopiponwēyān, kēyāpic nōsisimak ē-wīcēwakik, kēyāpic ē-wītapimakik, kēyāpic ē-kakwēcimicik kīkway, kēyāpic kīkway ē-pimi-kiskēyihtamān. namōya ē-itwēyān ē-iyinīsiyān māka nēma nāway ē-kī-pē-pēhtamān kīkway ēwako kēyāpic ē-pimi-kanawēyihtamān.

namōy nōh-pē-kiskinohamākosin, namōya niya ē-ohci-itōtamān. nikāwiy, ēkā kī-wāpit nikotwāsik ē-itahtopiponwēyān, ayēnānēw ē-itahtopiponwēyān ta-kī-pīhtokwēyān mōniyānāhk mōy nōh-kaskihtān. nikāwiy ē-kī-pamihak nīsta ayisk nikāwiy nikī-sawēyimāw. ē-kī-pēyakōsāniwiyān nimisak nisto ē-kī-wanihakik. nikāwiy ē-kī-pamihak, nōhtāwiy mīna ē-kī-pamihak. ē-pamihāyāhk nikāwiy ēkā wāpit; ē-kī-misi-sākihak nimāmā, nikāwiy ē-kī-misi-sākihak.

anohc ēkwa kā-pēyakoyān, nīstanaw tahtwāw askiy nikisēyinīm aspin ē-kī-wanihak. kī-kihcēyihtam mawimoscikēwin, kī-nīkānīstam mawimoscikēwin ēwako, ēwako *John Rockthunder* kā-kī-isiyihkāsot. ēkosi ēkwa niya ōma k-ēsiyihkāsoyān *Mary Louise Rockthunder*, *Mrs. Rockthunder* awa kā-pāh-pīkiskwēt, kōhkomiwāw ē-ati-kis--, ē-ati-nōtokēwit, māka kēyāpic ninōhtē-wīcihāwak nōsisimak kīkway kēkwēcimitwāwi nikakwē-wīhtamawāwak kīkway ē-miywāsik.

tānisi niya ē-itwēyān? "kāwiya!", "kāya ēkosi tōta!", "namōya miywāsin ēkosi." ēkosi ē-pim-ītakik nōsisimak kā-pimi-kīkway-wīhtamawakik. ē-pimi-kostamān kīkway ayisk nikī-pē-kiskēyihtēn ēwako, nāway ēkosi ē-kī-pē-itikawiyāhk, "ēkāy ēkosi itōta!", "kihcēyim kēhtē-aya!", "sawēyim kēhtē-aya!" nikī-itikawinān. ēwako nōsisim awa ē-pakitinamawak done that same way. That is how I knew it to be long ago, and I saw it and I also heard the elders speak about what I am talking about today. I am not telling lies, the Creator is listening to me as I -, as I am telling this grandchild of mine what she came to ask me; as she has come to record my speech.

But I am really very happy, now that I am elderly at eighty-five years old, that I am still with my grandchildren, I still sit with them, they still ask me things, and that I still have some knowledge. I am not saying I am intelligent but I still keep that which I heard in the past.

I have never been to school; it was not my doing that when I was six years old my mother was blind, I should have gone into the white world when I was eight years old but I couldn't. I looked after my mother as I, too, loved my mother. I was an only child as I lost my three older sisters. I looked after my mother, I looked after my father as well. We tended to my mother who was blind. I loved my mom a lot, I really loved my mother.

Today I am by myself; I lost my old man twenty or so years ago. He thought highly of traditional prayer. He was a leader of prayer, that one, that one who was named John Rockthunder. So then I am called Mary Louise Rockthunder; Mrs. Rockthunder is the one who is speaking, your grandmother is - she is becoming an old lady, but I still want to help my grandchildren whenever they ask me something, I try to tell them something good.

What do I say? "Don't!" "Don't do that!" "That is not the right way." That is what I say to my grandchildren when I tell them something. I am afraid of things because I know from experience, since that is what we used to be told in the past, "Don't do that!" "Respect elders!" "Cherish elders!" we were told. I give permission ka-wīhtamākoyēk ēwako ōma ē-miywāsik pīkiskwēwin, “ēkāy ēkosi itōta!” ēkosi kī-itwāniw kayās.

ēwakoyikohk ēwako pitamā niwī-kīskinēn nipīkiskwēwin anohc kā-kīskikāk.

[**3. awiyak kā-nahiniht**]

hāw, kotak ēkwa. nōsisim awa kā-kakwēcimit.

kayās, kayās kā-panātisicik ayisiyiniwak, kī-osīhcikātēw maskimocis, ē-asamopitahk, ē-asamopitēk. ēkota wiyākanis kī-ascikātēw ēkwa mīna napakiyākanis ēkwa mīna mōhkomānis, ēkwa mīna pahkwēsikan ēkwa mīna kīkway wiyās ayis. ēkota kī-pīhtasiwatāwak nōtik--, nōtokwēwak ē-asamopitahkik, ōtē itēhkē kihciniskīhk ē-astācik ē-nīmāhācik ōhi kā-nakatikocik otawāsimisiwāwa, ōh, ēkā cī okisēyinīmāwa ē-nīmāhācik. ēkosi mīna kayās nikī-isi-wāpahtēn mīna ēwako. ēwako mīna awa nōsisim kā-kakwēcimit, ēwako mīna ōta -, ēwako mīna k-ōh-tasihtamān.

ē-kī-pē-wāpahtamān anihi. ē-kī-pē-wāpahtamān, nikī-nitaw-koskowātapin nōhkom wiyīcēwaki, ē-iskwēwic kī-itāw nōhkom, *Mrs. Little Sioux* kī-itāw. omāmihkwēw, ē-ākayāsīmohk *Isabelle Easbappie* kī-isiyihkāsow nōhkom, kī-pwāsīmow. kīpwāsīmowak nōhkomak nīso, nikāwiy -, nōhtāwiy okāwiya ēkwa okāwīsa; kī-pwāsīmowak nōhkomak māka kī-nēhiyawēwak.

ī, ēkw āni nisikos, ē-kī-pēyakōsāniwit nisikos, ēwakoni ōhi otānis--; ōhi okāwiya ōhi *Isabelle Easbappie* awa nisikos. ēkwa māna ē-kī-apiyāhk, ē-nitohtamāhk, ē-nitohtawāyāhkok tānisi itwētwāwi. ēwakw ānima kā-kakwēcimit awa nōsisim ēkosi ē-kī-ispayik; ē-kī-nīmāhiht awiyak kā-kitimākaskasiwēt, kayās ēwako isīhcikēwin, nēhiyaw-isīhcikēwin.

ēkwa mīna wīhkaskwa, ēkota mīna kī-ascikātēwa. ē-astamāht awa ēkā kā-pimātisit ē-tahkonamōhiht. ē-kī-ka-kitimāk-āyihtihk to this one, my grandchild, to tell you that this is good to say, "Don't do that!" That is what was said long ago.

That is all for now, I will conclude my speech for today.

[3. When Someone Is Buried]

Okay, now for another one. My grandchild has come to ask me.

Long ago, long ago when people died, a little bag was made, it was tied into a bundle by gathering the material and tying it, it was gathered and tied. A little cup was put in there along with a little plate and also a little knife and bannock and meat of any sort which was available. The old women placed them there in a bag and tied it up, and placed it on this side, the right-hand side giving this one, their child or their old man who had died, a lunch to take along. That is also what I saw long ago. That is what my grandchild here has asked me, that is why I am talking about it.

I saw these things. I saw them happening, I would go and sit quietly when I went with my grandmother, ē-*iskwēwic* as she was called, my grandmother who was called Mrs. Little Sioux. My grandmother was a Nakoda woman and her English name was Isabelle Eashappie, she spoke Nakoda [Assiniboine]. Two of my grandmothers spoke Nakoda, my mother -, my father's mother and his aunt; my grandmothers spoke Nakoda but they also spoke Cree.

You see, this aunt [second cousin] of mine, my aunt was an only child, and this one daugh--, this one's mother was *Isabelle Eashappie*, that aunt of mine. We would sit listening, listening to what they were saying. That is what this grandchild of mine came to ask me, that is what happened; food was given to the poor departed one to take along as a lunch. That was the old custom, a Cree custom.

And also sweetgrass, that was also put there; it was placed there for this deceased one to take along. Long ago people were very kayās, mitoni ē-kī-kitimāk-āyihtihk ē-kī-nēhiyawīhtwāhk kayās. anohc ēkwa, pahkān ta-ati-ma-mōniyāwīhtwāhk. māka, māka 'toni mōy, namōya nitati-aspēyihtēn niya ta-kakwē-wēpinamihk kinēhiyawīhtwāwininaw.

nawat ta-sākihtāhk ēwako, namōya wīhkāc misawāc kika-mōniyāwinānaw. misakāmē isko ta-pimātisiyahk ka-nēhiyāwinānaw; ēkosi māna kī-itwāniw.

nisākihtān nēhiyāwiwin, nisākihtān, nisākihtān wīhkaskwa, mostoso-wīhkaskwa nisākihtān. ēkotowa, ēkotowa ē-kī-pē-ohc-ōhpikiyāhk, ē-kī-pē-ohc-ōhpikiyāhk kayās, ēkwa -, kā-miyāhkasikēhk ēkwa kā-mawimoscikēhk, kī-mawimoscikēwak kayās kēhtē-ayak.

ahpō mīkiwāhpa, kī-masinahikātēwa, ēkota ē-tas--, kā-tāh-tahtw-āyamihē-kīsikāw ē-kī-mawimoscikēhk, ē-nitotamākēstamāhcik awāsisak pimātisiwin, miywāyāwin. tāpwē kī--, kī-ati-ma-miyw-āyāwak, namōy wīhkāc ōma kā-is-āyāhk anohc kā-itwēhk 'kitōmanicōsimin' k-ētwēhk, *cancer* k-ētahkik. namōy wīhkāc k-ōhci-pē-ayāniwiw.

matwān cī nēhiyawīhtwāwin ē-kī-pimitisahamihk k-ōh-kī--, k-ōh-kī-- ēkā ēkotowi k-ōh-kī-kahcitinamihk. nikī-minihkwānān nipiy, kimiwanāpoy nikī-minihkwānān, aya awa kā-itiht awa aya, aya kōna nikī-minihkwātānān ēkwa mīna miskwamiy mīna nikī-minihkwātānān. kimiwanāpoy wāskāhikanihk ēkota nikī-ohci-minihkwānān.

ay, ēkamā pīhcāyihk kāh-wayawīhk, anohc ēkwa pīhcāyihk wayawīnāniwiw. nikōst--, kikostēnānaw ēkwa anima nipiy ta-minihkwēyahk. ēkwa mīna awa kōna, namōy kitāpacihānaw. mōniyāw kahkiyaw kīkway ē-astāt maskihkiy, ē-pimāpahtēk kā-tipiskāk; namōya miyosiw ana kōna kita-minihkwātiht kika-āhkosīskākon. nikostāw ana nīsta kōna; ē-kī-minihkwēyān māna kayās. ahpō anohc wāposwak nikostāwak; ēkonik mīna, "kāya mowihkok; ay-astāwak kīkway mōniyāwak.

compassionate, there was a great deal of compassion in Cree culture long ago. Nowadays it is different, we are beginning to be like the Whiteman. But, but it is -, not really, I don't -, I, myself, am beginning not to trust the attempt to throw away our Cree ways.

It would be better to cherish that; we will never be of the white society anyway. We will always, for the whole of our lives, be Cree. That is what was said.

I cherish being Cree, I love it, I cherish the sweetgrass, and I love the buffalo sage. That kind, that is the kind of thing we grew up with, we grew up with that long ago and - the smudging and prayer ceremony; the elders prayed long ago.

Also the tipis were painted with designs there that - every Sunday, there were prayer ceremonies, asking for life for the children, for good health. They surely were healthy and there was never this condition that we have today, when they say "*kitōmanicōsimin*" ["you have bugs"], that which they name "cancer." That was never the case.

I wonder whether following the Cree culture would - would - if it prevented one from contracting that kind of disease. We drank water, we drank rainwater, ah, that which is called, ah, snow, we got drinking water from that and also from ice. We drank rainwater draining of off the house.

It was not acceptable for one to go to the toilet indoors, today one does go to the toilet indoors. I am afraid--, we are afraid to drink the water now. And we also don't use the snow now. The Whiteman applies all kinds of chemicals, carried along in the smoky air at night; that snow is not good for drinking, it will make you ill -, I, too, am afraid of snow; I used to drink it long ago. Even now I am afraid [to eat] of rabbits. "Don't eat those. White people are adding something.

mōya ē-miyosit ana wāpos ta-mowiht." nisēkimikwak, namōy nikaskihtān wāpos tita-mowak - ā, ē-tāpwēcik māka. astāwak ayis ōma mōniyāwak *spray*.

anohc kā-kīsikāk ēwakw ānima ē-ācimostawak nōsisim awa ē-pē--, ē-pē-kakwēcimit kīkwāy nēhiyawīhtwāwin kayās. kī-pē-miywāsin, kī-pē-miyo-wīcēhtowak ayisiyiniwak, namōy wīhkāc ohci-pē-nisiwanācihitowak, kī-pē-miyo-wīcēhtowak, kī-nihtīhkātitowak piyīhtokwēhki, ē-asahtohk. anohc ēkwa kikostēnānaw ēkosi ta-itōtamahk, kikostēnānaw awiyak, "ī, nika--, kīkway awa nika-pisc-āsamik," ēkosi anohc kititēyihtēnānaw. kayās nama kīkway ēwako. kīnihtīhkāniwiw ahpō kāhkēwak ēkota ē-kīsisamihk, ē-mīcihk, iyinito-pahkwēsikan, pimiy ē-aspahcikēhk, kayās ēwako. kiyokātowin ēwako, ē-kī-isi-nanās--, ē-sakahpitastimwēhk, ē-mosci-ōtāpāsohk. anohc ēkwa kīkwāy ētikwē k-āpacihtāyahk, miscikowacis kipapāmohtahikonānaw wāh-wāhyaw ē-itohtahikoyahk. ēwakoni ōhi kā-itamān, sēhkēs awa kā-itak, wāh-wāhyaw ē-itohtahikoyahk. anohc ēkwa mīna ēwakonik misatimwak mōy āpatisiwak. ēwako mīna ē-kiskēyihtamān. pahkān, anohc ōma tānitahtwāw askiy aspin.

[*aciyaw ē-nakipitamihk*]

ēkwa mīna pēyakwayak mīna, pēyakwayak mīna mōya nitācimon māka niwī-wīhtēn; ēwak ōma ayisiyiniw kāyās, kayās kā-panātisit ayisiyiniw nēwo kīsikāw kī-kiyokawāw ē-nitaw-astamāht cistēmāsa, ē-nitaw-wīci-pīhtwāmiht, ēkotē ē-nitawi-mawīhkātiht. ēkosi mīna kī-itōcikātēw. namōya, namōya kacāt mīna mēskanāhk ohci-pimitāpāsowak ayis misatimwak kī-āpatisiwak ēkota ē-- ē-taskamitāpāsohk ē-nitaw-nahastāhk ōma miyaw. nēwo tipiskāw kī-kiyokawāw pikw ān āwiyak owāhkōmākana ē-nitaw-āhimiht cistēmāsa, ē-nitaw-pīhtwāhiht, ē-kākīsimototāht kwēyask t-ēsi-sipwēhtēt.

ēkwa "ēkāy mitoni mistahi mātok kā-nakatikoyēk awiyak," kī-itwāniw mīna māna. nēwo tipiskāw, ēwako - ēkota

That rabbit is not good for eating." They frightened me, and I am unable to eat rabbit, oh, but they are telling the truth. Because the Whiteman applies spray.

Today I am telling this to my grandchild here who has come to ask me about Cree ways of long ago. It was nice, people got along well, they never destroyed one another, they got along well, they made tea for each other as soon as one came in the door, they fed each other. Nowadays, we are afraid to do that. We are afraid somebody [will say], "Oh, I will -, this one might accidentally feed me something--". That is what we think now. There was nothing like that long ago. Tea was made, even dried meat would be cooked and eaten, bannock, using lard as a spread, that was the way it was long ago. That was visiting one another, thus were -, they would harness their horses, they would go in a wagon. Nowadays I don't know what we use, a little box takes us around, taking us to far-off places. These are the ones I am talking about, I mean the car which takes us long distances. And today those horses are not used. That is also what I know, it has been different now for I don't know how many years.

[*pause in recording*]

And there is one more thing, there is one thing I did not talk about but I will tell about it; it was about people long ago. Long ago when a person passed away that deceased person was visited for four days in a row, to go to put down some tobacco for them, to have a smoke with them, and to mourn them with tears. That is what was also done. They purposefully did not use the road, for horses were used and they would drive cross-country to go and bury this body. For four nights anyone could visit anybody's relative's grave to go and place tobacco for them, to give them a smoke, and to pray for them to have a good journey.

And "Don't cry too much when somebody dies," used to be said as well. That was for four nights that one wept for a person there;

ē-mawīhkātiht ayisiyiniw, osām mistahi kā-mawīhkātat nakiskāk ēsa anihi. awīniwa kā-wī-kanawēyimikot, “ahāw, nīhtaciwē, kīwē, kēyāpic kimatwē-mawīhkātikawin.” “kakwātakihāwak,” itwāniw māna kinwēs mistahi kā-mātot ayisiyiniw. māka ayis āyiman, āyiman ayisiyiniw kā-wanihiht, ohcitaw piko tita-mātohk. ohcitaw āyiman māka ēwakw ānima kayās pīkiskwēwin. “nēwo tipiskāw piko kita-mawīhkātiht ayisiyiniw.” ēkosi mīna māna kī-itwēwak ayisiyiniwak kayās. ēwako mīna māna ē-kī-pēhtamān.

ēkoni ōhi kā-pēhtamān namōya ē-kiyāskiyān, ē-kī-pēhtawakik kēhtē-ayak mitoni nikī-nitohtawāwak. ēwakw ānima kā-itamān, ninēhiyawātisin, ninēhiyawātisin mitoni, mitoni nimiciminēn nēhiyawātisiwin ayis ēkosi nikī-pē-is-ōhpikin, nikēhtē-ayimak ēkosi nikī-pē--.

kā-kī-wiyōhtāwīyān kī-nipākwēsimowinihkēw, ēkwa kā-kī-wiyōhkomiyān ēkonik kī-mawimoscikēwak ōtē ohci *Moose Mountain* kisēyiniw kī-ayāw. ēkotē, ēkotē nōhkom wīstawāw mīkiwāhpa kī-ohtinamwak ēkota ē-mawimoscikēcik. ahpō nīsta sīsīkwan kāh-ayāwak; maskimocis nikī-ayān, nisikos mīna kī-ay--, ē-pīhtokēyāhk. nakamona anihi, ahpō kēyāpic kēskēyihtamān, mawimoscikēwatāmona isiyihkātēwa. ēkotē ē-kī-ayāt kisēyiniw ōtē *Moose Mountain* ana kisēyiniw ē-kī-kiskinwahamakēt. macāpēs kī-isiyihkāsow nimosōminān, ēwakw āna kēyāpic, kēyāpic māna nikiskisin ana nimosōm macāpēs kā-kī-itiht, mīkiwāhpa ē-kī--, ē-kī-osīhtāt, ē-kī-masinahamōhkēt. ēkotowa nikī-āh-ayānān ōta.

ēwako pōnipayiw, ēwakw ānima isi-mawimoscikēwin, māka wiya kēyāpic kā-nipākwēsimohk kēyāpic wiy ēwako, kēyāpic āpacihtāniwiw wiya ēwako. māka kayās macāpēs ēwako, ēwako kākikē kā-kī--, tahtwāw ayamihēw-kīsikāw kā-kī--, kā-kī-astā--, kā-kī-astācik kēhtē-ayak wīhkohkēwin, nakamowin, mawimoscikēwin kī-isiyihkātēw ē-nakamohk. ahpō niyanān awāsisak ōki nikī-kiskēyihtēnān anihi nakamona, macāpēs onakamona ōtē ohci ayi ēwakw āwa *Moose Mountain* ana kisēyiniw. kahkiyaw wiya kiskēyimēw anihi kā-kī-isiyihkāsot nimosōminān macāpēs. ēwakw ānima nōsisim awa ē-wīhtamawak, ē-kakwēcimit if you weep too much then that will stop the deceased person['s journey]. Whoever it is who is going to keep them [will say], "Okay, go back down, go home. They are still weeping for you." "They suffer," is what is said of the fact that people cry too much. But then it is difficult, it is hard to lose someone; it is natural to cry. Of course it is difficult but that was the old saying. "One is to weep for the departed for only four nights." That is also what people said long ago.

That is what I used to hear. These are the things that I heard, I am not telling lies, I heard the elders and I really listened to them. That is what I mean, I live a Cree life, I really live as a Cree, I really hold onto the Cree culture because that is the way I grew up, that is the way my elders -

My late father held the Thirst Dance, and also my late grandmother would carry on the prayer ceremony with this old man from Moose Mountain [White Bear]. Over there, my grandmother, they too got tipis from over there, praying there. Even I would have a rattle; I had a little bag, my paternal aunt also - we used to go in. Those songs, I still know them, they are called *mawimoscikēwatāmona* [prayer songs]. There was an old man over [t]here in Moose Mountain and he was teaching. That grandfather of ours was named *macāpēs* [Badfellow]. Even now I still remember that my late grandfather *macāpēs* made tipis, he would paint them for people. That was the kind we had here.

That [practice] has stopped, that way of praying, but the Thirst Dance is still held, it still is, the Thirst Dance is still used. But long ago that was *macāpēs*, he's the one who always - every Sunday the--, they would - the elders would put on a feast, with song, it was called a prayer ceremony with singing. Even us children knew those songs, *macāpēs*' songs, this old man from over here in Moose Mountain. That grandfather of ours *macāpēs* knew all of them. That is what I am telling my grandchild, as she has asked me, that is why I am telling her because I have k-ōh-wīhtamawak ayisk nikī-pē-kiskēyihtēn ēwako mīn ānima. anima mawimoscikēwin k-ētamihk.

[*aciyaw ē-nakipitamihk*]

[**4. nēhiyawātisiwin**]

hāw, pēyak kīkway mīna, pēyak kīkway mīna nōsisim ōtē ē-nōhtē-wīhtamawak, ē-nōhtē-kiskēyihtahk. ātawiya ohcitaw ācimowin, ohcitaw pīkiskwēwin, ohcitaw ta-pīkiskwātamān ayisk nikakwēcimik. tāpiskōc -, niya nik-ācimison, niya nik-ācimison.

tāpiskōc awa nikāwiy *Catholic* ē-kī-wīcēwāt ēkwa mīna iyinito-ayisiyinīwiwin kā-aya--, ayi ōma tāpiskōc kā-nipākwēsimohk kī-kihc-ītēyihtam māka kī-ayamihāw nikāwiy. ēkosi ēkwa awa ayamihēwiyiniw k-ōskotākāt, ēwak ōma nikī-wīhtamākonān. kētahtawē, namōya manāhtowak ayis mōniyāwak kā-itihcik, kētahtawē nānitaw isi mamāyinik--, nānitaw isi awiyak nakatiski ahpō kikisēyinīm, awēkā pahkān awiyak kiwāhkōmākan, "ēkāy āpacihtā ē-kīhkānākwahk ayiwin ta-kikiskaman, ē-kaskitēwāk." nikī-itikonān. hām, ēwako ēkota ē-kī-kiskinohamākoyāhk awa *Catholic* awa, *priest* kā-itiht ayamihēwiyiniw kā-itiht. nikāwiy kī-sāki--, kī-sākihtāw saskamowin. ēkosi kēyāpic ēwako nīsta niwīcēhtēn, kēyāpit nisaskamon. pēyak-askiy ōma nipatahēn mōy nititohtān ēkotowa.

ēkosi ēkwa nōhtāwiy kā-wanihāyāhk *nineteen--, 1932, seventh of January* nōhtāwiy kā-panātisit. hā, kahkiyaw [ni]kī-kaskitēwisīhonān, nōsisimak kahkiyaw, kahkiyaw ē-ihtasiyāhk nikī-kaskitēwisīhonān ēkwa nēwo tipiskāw nikāwiy namōya ohci-sīkahow, namōy ohci-mikoskācihtāw wēstakaya nēwo tipiskāw, ēwako nēhiyaw-isīhcikēwin. ē-kī-otinahk ēwako nēhiyaw-isīhcikēwin. pātos ē-nēwo-tipiskāk kī-pē-sīkahok kēhciwāk ocāhkosa kī-pē-sīkahok. kī-pē-mēskocīhik mīna, ē-kīhkānākwaniyik pakiwayān kī-kaskikwātamāk, ēkosi, ēkosi nīsta mīna nikī-ati-miyikawin ta-kikiskamān kī-mēskotayiwinisēhik--, nīsta mīna nikī-mēskotayiwinisān, ē--, ē-kīhkānākwahki nikī-kikiskēn nōhtāwiy kā-wanihāyāhk.

knowledge of that also. That traditional prayer ritual as it was called.

[*pause in recording*]

[**4. Cree Life**]

All right, one more thing, one more thing I want to tell my grandchild over here, as she wants to know. It has to be told anyway, it has to be put in words, it is necessary for me to talk about this because she has asked me. It is like ..., I will tell about myself, I will tell about myself.

For instance, my mother followed the Catholic [way] and also what the First Nations - ah ..., like the Thirst Dance, she really thought highly of that but my mother also prayed [as a Christian]. So then this "robe-wearing" priest told us this. At some point, because they are not respectfully careful with one another, those who are called *mōniyāwak* [white people], eventually something goes wro--, when someone leaves you [in death], even your husband or the -, or even another relative, "You shouldn't wear any bright-coloured clothing, just black," he said to us. Okay, that is what this Catholic priest taught us, the one called a priest, the one called *ayamihēwiyiniw*. My mother love--, she held to Holy communion. So I continue with that too, I still take communion. I missed one year, I did not attend that.

So now when we lost my father; it was nineteen--, 1932, seventh of January that my father passed away. Ah, we all wore black, all of my grandchildren, all of our family were dressed in black and for four nights my mother did not comb her hair, she did not bother with her hair for four nights, as is the Cree custom. She followed that Cree custom. Afterwards, as soon as four nights had passed, her sister-in-law came to comb her hair. She also had her change into clothes that she had sewn for her from bright-coloured material. So, that is what I, too, was given to wear, she had me change my clothe-, I, too, changed my clothes, I wore bright clothing at the time we lost my father.

hāw, anohc ēkwa, nikisēyinīm kā-wanihak, — kā-w--, nikis--, kā-wanihak ēkwa kā-kī-okisēyinīmiyān awa anohc *John* awa kā-itak kā-kī-panātisit *John Rockthunder* — kā-wanihāyāhk kahkiyaw nōsisimak, kahkiyaw nitawāsimisak kahkiyaw kī-kaskitēwisīhowak. kī-kaskitēwisīhowak nēwo-tipiskāw. ēwako ētikwē ē-kī-pimitisahocik ōma k-ēsi-ayamihāyān *Catholic* ayis ēkotowahk niwīcēhtēn kēyāpic. nēhiyāwiwin mīna niwīcēhtēn namōya nipakitinēn mīna kā-mawimoscikēhk ē-itohtēyān, niwīcēhtēn ēkotowa. māka nikāwiy, nikāwiy ēwako k-ōhci-miciminamān, nikāwiy ēkosi ē-kī-isi-ayamihāt. ē-kī-sākihtāt nīso nēhiyāwiwin ēkwa ōma mīna, ōma mīna k-ōskotākāt kā-isi-ayamihāhk *Catholic* kā-itwēhk, *Catholic priest* ēkoni kī-wīcēwēw. ēwakw ānima ēkosi mīna ē-kī-ispayik.

ē-kī-nēwo-tipiskāk nōhtāwiy ē-kī-wanihāyāhk ēwako k-ētamān, kī-pē-sīkahwāw nikāwiy, kī-pē-mēskotayiwinisahāw. niya mīna nikī-pē-mēskotayiwinisahikawin kā-kī-wanihāyāhk nōhtāwiy. ēkosi nikī-nanāskomonān ē-itōtākawiyāhk. ēkosi ēkwa ē-sīkahoht nikāwiy kwayask wēstakaya, kī-wītisiw nikāwiy. ēkosi namōya wī-ohci-kīskisam wēstakaya.

kayās kī-kīskisamwak; nēwo, nēwo micihcīs kī-kīskisamwak ōtē ē-māyipayit ayisiyiniw. ēwako mīna ē-kiskēyihtamān māna kayās. kayās isīhcikēwin ēwako, ēkosi ē-kī-tōtahkik. mōya mīna kī-wēpinikātēwa konita, konita ōmatowa aya, askīhk anihi mēstakaya. kī-saskahikātēwa, kī-koscikātēwa kinēpik ka-kāhcitinahk ta-wacistwan--, ta-wacistwanihkēt. "kā-wacistwanihkākēt ēsa kinēpik mēstakaya kitēwistikwānēskin," kī-itwēwak māna kayās. kayās kīkway nikī-tāpwēhtēnān nēhiyaw-pīkiskwēwin.

anohc ēkwa kika-pōnipayiw ēwako, māka ohcitaw nōsisim ē-kakwēcimit ohcitaw k-ōh-wīhtamān ē-kiskēyihtamān ēwako mīna anima kayās, ēkosi --, kayās ōhi pīkiskwēwina ē-pē-kakwēcimit ēwak ōhci k-ōh-wīhtamawak. ē-kī-pē-wāpahtamān anihi, ē-kī-pē-nitohtamān mīna ēwak ōhci k-ōh-ay-ācimoyān: kē-nīkāniwik nēma t-āti-ka-kiskēyihtahkik ōki awāsisak.

Now, more recently when I lost my husband, – when, when I lost my late old man, this one that I call John, when John Rockthunder had passed away – when we lost him, all my grandchildren and all my children, they all wore black. They wore black clothing for four nights. Perhaps it was that they were following me in the way I pray as a Catholic because that I still follow that way. I also follow the Cree way, I didn't let go of it, I attend the prayer ceremonies when they are held, I follow those things. But my mother, it was for my mother that I held on to it as that was how she prayed. She loved the two, the Cree way and also this one, the "robe-wearer" way of prayer, that which is called Catholic, the Catholic priest, she followed those. That is the way it happened as well.

When it was four nights since my father passed on, I mentioned that someone came to comb my mother's hair, and had my mother change her clothes. I, too, was made to change my clothes when we lost my father. So we were thankful that they did that for us. So then my mother's hair was combed; she surely had thick hair so they did not cut her hair.

Long ago they cut it. When a person suffered misfortune they would cut off four, a measurement of four fingers width. That is also something I know from long ago. That was the custom they did long ago. Also they did not throw that hair just anywhere, anywhere on the ground. They were set afire; they were afraid that a snake would get ahold of it to make a nest. "When a snake makes a nest with your hair you are prone to have headaches," they used to say long ago. We believed in the old Cree sayings.

And now that will stop but that is what my grandchild is asking me and I have to tell about it as I know that was how it was long ago, so ..., she came to ask about these Cree sayings that is why I am telling her about them. I saw them and I listened to them and that is also why I am telling about them: in the future the children will get to know about them.

ēkwa mīna kā-kīsiskwēwit iskwēsis kī-pēyakokahāw. nikī-pēyakokē--, nikī-pēyakokān mitātaht tipiskāw ē-kīs-ōhpikiyān. ohpimē nikī-wīkin. ātawiya nōcikwēsiw ēkota nikī-wīkimāw. ēkwa māka kīkisēpā wīpac ē-wayawīyān namōya ē-nōhtē-kanawāpamak ayisiyiniw, ēkosi ē-kī-itikawiyān. ē-pēyakokēyāhk wāskāhikanis nōhtāwiy ē-kī-osīhtāt wāskāhikanis. nikī-pēyakokān mitātaht tipiskāw ē-kīs-ōhpikiyān. ēkosi mīna ēwako ē-kī-isīhcikēhk.

anohc ēkwa ēwako niyanān ōta ōma kā-ayāyāhk payipwāt's, pōnipayiw. māka kotakihk askīhkānihk ōtē māna nikiyokān ōtē ōma *Hobbema* kēyāpic ēkosi isīhcikēwak. mitātaht tipiskāw kanawēyimēwak oskinīkiskwēwa kā-kīsiskwēwiyit. mitātaht tipiskāw ē-ispayik sīkahwēwak ēkota ēkwayāc ē-pēhkihācik, ē-pēhkayiwinisahācik. ēwako mīna ē-miyo-tōtahkik, ēkwa ē-misi-wēpināsocik, mistahi kīkway ē-mēkicik, ē-nitomācik ayisiyiniwa; ē-mīcisohk iskwēsis kā--, kāh-kīs-ōhpikici, ē-kīsiskwēwit. "ē-kīs-ōhpikit" kī-itwāniw māna kayās. ēwakoni -, kēyāpic ēkosi tōtamwak ēkotē, mitoni māna nicīhkēyihtēn, mitoni māna nimiywēyihtēn ēkotē k-ētohtēyān.

kā-pēyakokēt iskwēsis, ē-nanātawihohk; kinitaw-nanātawihon nānitaw kā-itamahcihoyan kisinikonik, kī-sihkwātam anima o--, sihkowin ohci ē-nanātawihisk kā-kīsiskwēwit ana oskinīkiskwēw. nimiyikawin sīkahon, kēyāpic nikanawēyihtēn anima sīkahon ē-kī-kīs-ōhpikit ana nōsisim, ē-miyikawiyān ēwako ta-kanawēyihtamān. kētahtawē māna nisīkahwākān anima sīkahon. ē-kī-kīs-ōhpikit ana nōsisiminān.

ēkosi kēyāpic isīhcikēwak ōtē ōpīma k-ētohtēyān māna. ēkotē ayis māna nitis-ay-kiyokawāwak niwāhkōmākanak ēkotē ē-mihcēticik. *Rocky Mountain H--, Rocky Mountain House* mīna ēkotē mīna māna nititohtān, ēkotē mīna niwāhkōmākanak ē-ayācik. ē-kī-omisiyān ēkotē ē-kī-ayāt ē-wīci--, pēyakwan ē-isiyihkāsoyāhk ana nimis, wīsta *Mary Louise* ēkwa nīsta ēkosi ē-isiyihkāsoyān.

And also when a girl became a woman she was made to live by herself. I lived alon--, I lived in isolation for ten nights when I reached adulthood. I lived away [from everyone]. Although at least I stayed with an elderly woman there. But then in the morning I went out [to go to the bathroom] early because I didn't want to look at people. That is what I was told. We lived by ourselves in a little cabin; my father had built a small cabin. I lived by myself for ten nights when I reached adulthood. That is how another custom was performed.

Today now, for us who live here in Piapot, that has stopped. But at another reserve where I usually go to visit over here in Hobbema [now Maskwacis, Alberta] they still perform this custom. They keep a young girl for ten nights when she reaches womanhood. When ten nights have gone by they comb her hair, and only then do they cleanse her and give her a change of clean clothing. That is a good thing they do also, and they make cloth offerings, they give away lots of gifts to people they invite; they have a meal when a girl is finished growing, when she reaches womanhood. "She is an adult," they used to say long ago. Those are -, they still do that over there and I like that very much, I really enjoy going over there.

When a young girl lives by herself, there is a healing power; you go and get healed, wherever you are not feeling well she rubs you, she spits on that -, she heals you with saliva, that young lady who is reaching womanhood. I was given a comb when my grandchild reached adulthood, and I still keep that. That was given to me to keep. I sometimes used that comb to comb my hair. She became a woman that grandchild of ours.

They still do that over here in Hobbema [now Maskwacis, Alberta], where I go. I usually go over there to visit my relatives who are great in number over there. Rocky Mountain -, I also go to Rocky Mountain House, usually. My relatives are over there too. I had an older sister over there that -, that older sister and I have the same name, she, too, is Mary Louise and I also have the same name.

nikī-wanihānān nīsw-āskiy aspin ana nimis. ēkotē mīna nikī-itohtān. pēyakwan ē-nēhi--, nēhiyaw tāpiskōc isīhcikēwak, nēhiyaw-isīhcikēwak anima kā-ātotamān anohc, oyākanis ē-kī-nīmāhācik nimisa, ē-nīmāt nimis. nikī-nitawi-atamiskawāw nimis ana. namōya mīna tēhtascikātēyiw wiyaw, moscāyihk ōta ē-pimisimiht. nēhiyaw-isīhcikēwin ēwako. ēkwa anohc kiyānaw tahkohc pimisin awiyak kā-panātisit, māk āyis mōniyāwak otisīhcikēwiniwāw wiya ēwako ētokwē k-ōh-isīhcikēhk. ēkosi mīna, ēwako mīna anima kayās mīna ēwako ēkosi ē-kī-pē-isi-kiskēyihtamān.

awiyak kā-panātisit namōya mitoni mēskanāhk ohci-pimi--, ohci-pimohticikātēw miyaw. namōy wīhkāc nōh-itāpinān awāsisak, "ēkāwiya itāpik," ē-kī-itikawiyāhk māna, namōya nōh-itāpinān māka māna nikī-pēhtēn ēkotowi ē-pimitāpāsocik mōy kacāt mēskanāhk, pēyāhtak ē-pimohtatācik anima miyaw, māka ēkwa anohc ayis sēhkēsihk pōsihtāwak. mōniyawak ēkwa anohc paminamwak awiyak ēkā kā-pimātisit.

ēwako mīna anima ē-ācimostawak awa nōsisim ayis nikakwēcimik ta-ācimostawak, piko tit-ācimostawak, nōhtē-kiskēyihtam ēwako ōma ācimowina ōhi kayās, kayās ācimowina k-ōh-ay-ācimostawak ēkosi kā-kī-isi-kiskēyihtamān. "kakwē-miyo-wāhkōhtok, kakwē-miyo-wīcēhtok," ē-kī-itikawiyāhk mīna māna. "ēkāwiya māyi-wīcēhtok, miywāsin ta-miyo-wīcēhtoyēk." ē-kī-pē-miyo-wīcēhtonān [*sic, cf.* nikī-...nān]. mōy wīhkāc nōh-pē-māyi-wīcēhtonān kayās nikī-sawēyihtonān, kānikanā kēyāpic ēkosi ispayik, kānikanā sawēyihtohk, ēkwayikohk ē-kakwātakihtāyahk piko kīkway ati-ay-isi-āhkosiwin ē-ati--, ē-at-ōtihtamahk māka ayis kitisi-mīcisowininaw ēwako kā-itōtākoyahk. kayās iskotēw kikī-asam--, kikī-asamikonaw ēkwa mīna kikī-nipēhikonaw iskotēw, mihta kikī-pōnēnānaw ē-nipāyahk kikī-ohtatāhtēnānaw mistikwa ē-nipāyahk, kikī-miyo-tōtākonānaw.

We lost my older sister two years ago now. I went over there too. They perform similar Cree customs, like the Cree custom that I spoke about today where a dish of food was prepared for the deceased to take along, my older sister took food along. I went to bid farewell to that older sister of mine. Her body was not placed up on anything, they lay her on the floor. That is a Cree custom. And now for us the deceased is placed on top of something, but then perhaps that is the Whiteman's custom that is followed. That too, that is also something that I know from long ago.

When someone passed away the roads were not followed while transporting the body. We children never looked; "Don't look," we were always told; we didn't look but I heard that sound from the wagon but purposefully not on the road. They carefully transported that body; but now today, they put it in a car. The white people take care of the funeral when someone passes on today.

That is also what I am telling this grandchild of mine because she asked me to tell her, so I have to tell her these stories about long ago that she wants to know about, these stories I am telling her of the things that I know from the past. "Try to have good relations, try to get along with one another," is what we were always told. "Don't have poor relations with each other, it's good for you to get along well." We got along with each other. We never had disagreements long ago, we cherished one another, and it would be good if it were still like that, it would be good if there were mutual compassion, we are suffering enough as it is what with all these different diseases that we are coming in contact with but it is our diet that is doing this to us. Long ago the fire fed you - it fed us and it also put us to sleep, we burned wood as we slept, we breathed in that wood while we slept and it did us good.

ēkwa anohc ōma kā-askīwik, anohc ōma k-ēsi-kiskēyihtamān nayēstaw wāsikan ē-miyāhtamahk kā-tipiskāk. kīkwāy kē-miyo-tōtākoyahk? nayēstaw wāsikan nama kīkway iskotēw ē-miyāhtamahk, nama kīkway iskotēw ē-asamikoyahk. ēwako ē-asamikoyahk wāsikan. kā-wī-kīsitēpoyahk āsay ē-pīminamahk ēkotē ē-ohci-mīcisoyahk anohc ēkwa ēkosi ē--, ēkosi ē--, ēkosi ē-isi-mīcisoyahk anohc. māka kāyas wayawītimihk ahpō ē-kī-na-nihtīhkēhk, ē-kī-pakāhtākokēhk kayās wayawītimihk iskotēw ē-āpacihtāhk, ēkosi ē-isi-mīcisohk. wayawītimihk mīna pahkwēsikan ē-kīsisoht ē-mowāyahk. ēkwa anohc pisisik ta-atāwēyahk pahkwēsikan. pēyak kīsikāw awiyak niyātāci pahkwēsikana -, ātiht nistomitanaw ē-otinācik pahkwēsikana. namōya ē-nawacīcik iskwēwak iyāyaw ōhi atāwēwina. kahkiyaw kīkway kimāyi-tōtākonānaw. namōya kīkway ē-atāmotamān. māka ēkosi ēkwa ē-ati-is-āyāyahk, ē-ati-kitimākisiyahk, ē-ati-māyi-tōtākoyahk ēwako ōma wāsikan kā-itwēhk. ē-kī-miyoskākoyahk iskotēw, ēkwa mīna nipiy, miskwamiy ē-kī-minihkwātāyahk, kōna ē-kī-minihkwātāyahk kikī-miyo-tōtākonānaw.

nihtiy ē-kī-minihkwēcik kēhtē-ayak, awāsisak nipiy; namōy wīhkāc, namōy wīhkāc nihtiy ohci-minihkwēwak awāsisak iyāyaw nipiy ē-kī-minahihcik. ēwako mīna anima anohc ēkwa, anohc ēkwa iyāyaw nihtiy, kāspisikan kā-āpacihtācik kahkiyaw kīkway kitati-māyi-tōtākonānaw. nama kīkway ē-atāmotamān māka anohc ēkwa ē-ati-isi-kiskēyihtamān ēwako ōma k-ōh-wa-wīhtamawakawa nōsisim anohc kā-kīsikāk ē-wī-āta-ka-kakwē-wīcihak ōma onēhiyawi-pīkiskwēwina.

ēkwa mīna ēkosi ōma anohc kā-ātotamān, awiyak - awiyak kā-panātisit, owāhkōmākana kā-wanihāt, nēwo tipiskāw namōy ohci-sīkahonāniwiw. kī-nitaw--, kī-otinam aw īskwēw ayi ōma sīkahon ēkwa mīna pakiwayān miskotākay, maskisina, asikanak, pīhtawayiwinisa, ē-nēwi-tipiskāk kī-nitawi-sīkahwēw ocāhkosa ē-kī-māyipayiyit ē-mēskotayiwinisahāt nēwo tipiskāw kāh-ispayiyik. “nitawi-wēpinamohkan ōhi ahpō cī

And now, this year, what I know of it today, it is only electric heat that we smell at night. In what way will it do us any good? Smelling electricity exclusively, we smell nothing of the fire, there is no fire to feed us. It is that electricity feeding us. Whenever we are going to cook we turn it on; we eat from there nowadays and, and so -, that -, that is the way we eat today. But long ago, even tea was prepared outdoors, in the past water was boiled outdoors using fire, that's the way meals were eaten. We cooked bannock and ate it outdoors too. And today we're always having to buy bread. One day whenever a person goes for bread ... some buy thirty loaves. Women don't bake instead there are these bought ones. Everything is doing us ill. I am not putting blame on anything but that is how we are now, we are becoming poor, this thing that is called electricity is harming us. Fire did us good, and water, melted ice gave us water to drink, snow gave us water to drink; it did us good.

The elders drank tea, the children water; the children never, never drank tea. They were given water to drink instead, and that's something about nowadays. Now today, instead of tea they use coffee; everything is harming us. I am not putting blame, but now, I am getting to know the ways of today and this is why I am telling this grandchild of mine today as I am trying to help her with her Cree sayings.

And again I am speaking this way about someone, when someone passes on, when one loses a relative, the hair was not combed for four nights. She went and -, the woman took, ah, this comb, and a cotton dress, moccasins, stockings, underclothes, when four nights had passed she went to comb the hair of that sister-in-law or cousin who had suffered a loss; she had her change her clothes after four nights had passed. "Go and throw kikāh-saskahēn," kī-itēw. ēkosi nēwo tipiskāw ē-kī-kitimākisīhot ana iskwēw onāpēma ē-kī-wanihāt awēkā cī otawāsimisa.

ēwako mīna awa nōsisim ē-kakwēcimit ēwako mīna k-ōh-wīhtam--, k-ōh-wīhtamān ōta, k-ōh-māmiskōtamān.

ahām, ēwakoyikohk ēwako.

them away or you can burn them," she told her. So for four nights after she lost her husband or a child that woman dressed poorly.

This is what this grandchild of mine asked me and that is why I have told..., that's why I have told this here, why I have discussed it.

All right. That's enough for this topic.

6
ocēpihkwak, maskihkiya ēkwa mīnisa
ROOTS, HERBS AND BERRIES

Recorded at the home of Jean Okimāsis,
Regina, SK,
and thus introduced:

"Today is November 23rd, 1997, and I'm here with Mary Louise Rockthunder, who is going to tell me something about roots and herbs and the uses of the different parts of plants; either for medicines or just for eating. hāw. ... maht ēsa. ..."

JO: nīpisiya, nīpisiya, tānisi ēwakoni ē-kī-ā--, ē-kī-ayi---isi-āpacihtāhk?

MLR: nīpisiya, nīpisiya ē-kī-itāpacihtāhk kayās ē-kī-kiskēyihtamān, nīpisiya ē-kī-kawahahkik ayisiyiniwak ē-kī-atāwākēcik; cimacēsa ē-kī-osīhtācik, nīpisiya. ē-kī-ohci-mīciswātahkik. kayās ēwako pimācihowin.

• • • •

JO: ēkwa mīna mihkopēmina? mihkopēmak.

MLR: mihkwāpēmina.

JO: āha, mihkwāpēmina.

MLR: mihkwāpēmina, mihkwāpēmināhtikwa.

kayās ayisiyiniwak mihkwāpēmakwāhtikwa kī-isiyihkātamwak, ē-kī-otinahkik anima kā-mihkwāk ē-kī-kāskahahkik ēkwa ayi anima kā-askihtakwāk anima ēkwa ē-kī-kāskahahkik. ēkwa kāh-kāskahahkwāwi ē-kī--ayi---ayācik tāpiskōc sēkonahkik ē-- ē-pāsahkik. ēkosi ēkwa kāh-pāsahkwāwi ēkosi ēkwa ē-sikonahkik cistēmāw ēkwa napakipak nikī-isiyihkātānān cistēmāw ē-kī-pīkiniswācik kēhtē-ayak. ēkota ēkwa ē-takonācik aspāskosikan kī-isiyihkātēwak. ēwakw āwa napak--, ēwakw āna kā-kakwēcimiyan ana mihkwāpēmakwāhtikwa. ēkos ē-kī--, ēkos ānima ē-kī-itāpacihācik kayās kisēyiniwak, kēhtē-ayak.

• • • •

JO: ā, awa sōkāwāhtik kā-isiyihkātacik ōki ayi, *ah, the TH dialect Cree*; sīsipā--, sīsipāskwāhtik [*sic*].

MLR: sīsipāskwatwāhtik nikī-kiskēyihtēn māna kayās. ē-kī-nitawi-wīkicik kēhtē-ayak ayi ōma ē-nitawi-osīhtācik

JO: Willows. Willows, how were those ones - how were they used?

MLR: Willows, the way willows were used long ago, I know, the people cut them down and sold them; they made pickets of the willows. They fed themselves from those. That was a way of life long ago.

• • • •

JO: And also red willows? Red willow?

MLR: Red willows.

JO: Yes, red willows.

MLR: Red willows, red willow bushes.

Long ago the people called them *mihkwāpēmakwāhtikwa*, they took that red part and scraped it off and then the green part also they scraped off. Then, when they had finished scraping them, they -, ah, had, like putting it in the oven and drying it. So then when they had dried it, they then crushed it up by hand for tobacco and we called it *napakipak* [flat-leaf], that tobacco that the elders cut into bits. From there they added *aspāskosikan* [tobacco-mixture], as they called it. That was that flat -, that's what you were asking about, those red willow branches. That's how - that's how they used it long ago, the old men, the elders.

• • • •

JO: This "sugar tree" as these TH dialect Cree called it; maple, sugar maple tree -.

MLR: The sugar maple tree, I used to know about it long ago. The elders went to camp, ah, they went to make sugar; sugar, sīwinikan; sīwinikan ayi sīsipāskwatwāhtik ē-ohcikawipēhikēcik ēkwa ē-māwacihtācik kīkisēpā ōma nipiy, sīsipāskwatw--, sīsipāskwatwāpoy kī-isiyihkātamwak māna, ē-kī-osīhtācik sīwinikan. kayās sīwinikan ē-kī-- .... waskway, waskway māna kī-osīhtāwak, ēkota ē-pīhci-sīkinahkik ēwak ōma, nipiy kāh-kīsi-kīsisahkwāwi. tāpiskōc, tāpiskōc naminās ē-osīhtācik, ēkosi ēkwa ē-at-āstācik, ē-āhkwatihtācik, ē-māwacihtācik, pipohki ēwako ē-wī-mīcicik, ē-wī--, ē-wī-sīwipwātahkik. awēkā mīna nānitaw k-ētahkamikahk tāpiskōc kā-mawimoscikēhk, ēkota ē-itohtatācik, ē-wāskā-itisinamihk ēwako ōma pāh-pēyak ē-otinamihk ē-mīcihk ēwak ōma ē-kī-osīhtācik anima kēhtē-ayak, ēkw ānima k-ō-isiyihkāsocik aniki sīsipāskwatwāhtikwak.

• • • •

JO: ā, takwahiminānāhtikwak māka?

MLR: takwahiminānāhtikwak; takwahiminānāhtik k-ētiht, takwahimināna ēkota ē-kī-ohtinamihk ē-mawisohk ē-takwahahkik nōtokēwak asinīhk, kī-kaskitēsiwak māna asiniyak ēkota ē-takwahahkik. [*pasicihcēhamāw tāpiskōc ē-takwahiminēt*] ēwak-- ēwakw ēkwa ē-mīcimihkēcik, pipohki ēkwa ē-wī-mīcicik anihi takwahimināna, ē-takonahkik ē-pihkāciwasahkik nipiy ēkota ē-astācik, ē-pihkis--, ē-pihkāciwahtēki ōhi takwahimināna. sīwinikan, sīwinikan ēkota takonamwak sīsipāskwat anima kā-kī-osīhtācik, sikwatahamwak ēkota ē-takonahkik. ēkosi ēkwa pimiy ēkwa ēkota ē-takonahkik ēkw ēkwa ē-mīcicik ē-kī-- ē-kī-miywāsiki anihi takwahimināna. ēkosi ē-kī-itāpacihācik, ē-kī-itāpacihtācik takwahimināna.

JO: *Ah, were there any other ways they used that tree?*

MLR: takwahiminānāhtik, takwahiminānāhtik ēkota mīna ē--, maskihkiy ana, maskihkiy ana takwahiminānāhtik ah, they drained the sap of the sugar maple tree and in the morning they gathered this liquid, maple sugar, they used to call it maple sugar syrup, they would make sugar; long ago sugar was ...; birch, they used to make birch [containers] and they'd pour this water in there when they were finished cooking it. Like, it was like they were making molasses and then they'd begin putting it away, freezing it and storing it, as they were going to eat it in the winter, going to - they are going to eat something sweetened. Or else when something was going to happen like a ceremony, they would take it there, and it would be passed around, this would be taken by each one to eat a bit. It was this which the elders had made, that is what they are called, those sugar maple trees.

• • • •

JO: And how about chokecherry trees?

MLR: Chokecherry trees; the one called *takwahiminānāhtik*, chokecherries were obtained there, the old women picked and crushed them on a stone, the stones were black, there where they crushed them. [*MLR claps her hands like crushing berries*] Tha-- then with that they would make a meal, in the winter and when they were going eat those chokecherries in winter, they'd added them, putting them in the water there to boil apart, boiling - those chokecherries would boil apart. Sugar, they added sugar there, that's the maple sugar which they made, they crushed it and added it in there. So then grease was added in there and then they ate it, those chokecherries were good. That is how they used them, how they used the chokecherries.

JO: Ah, were there any other ways they used that tree?

MLR: The chokecherry tree, the chokecherry tree there also ... that was medicine, the chokecherry tree was medicine, but māka nēm ōcēpihk nēma. ocēpihk kēhtē-ayak kayās kī-ma-miyawākācīwak ē-otinahkik maskihkiy mōnahikanāhtikwa kī-āpacihtāwak ē-otinahkik. itāmihk, itāmihk ana ocēpihk, ana takwahiminānāhtik, kihci-maskihkiy anima. awiyak ē-minihkwēt, miyoskākow anima, māka namōya ē-pēyako-takonamihk kīkway ē-takonamihk maskihkiy, mōya māka kē-wīhtamān kīkwāy. ēkosi ē-kī--.

• • • •

JO: waskwayāhtikwa māka?

MLR: waskwayāhtikwak, kayās, ēwakoni - ēkoni kī-āpacihtāwak kēhtē-ayak. cīkahikanāhtikwa ē-osīhtācik, ē-manīcik, ē-āh-otinahkik ēkota ē-pīhtohkotahkik ēkwa ē-pāsahkik. cīkahikanāhtik ē-maskawisit ana waskwayāhtik; waskwayāhtik ēkota, ēkoni cīkahikanāhtikwa ē-kī-osīhtācik, awēkā mīna cīstahikan, cīstahikan ōma kā--, ēwako mīna anima ē-kī--, ā, ēkota ē-kī-tāpihtitācik ana waskwayāhtik ohci; kī-kihc-āpatanwa anihi wīstawāw kayās ēwako.

JO: mhm, kwēyask.

• • • •

JO: ā, kākikēpakwa māka?

MLR: kākikēpakwa, kayās nikī-pēhtēn, namōya mētoni ēwako nikiskēyihtēn. kākikēpakwa kī-itwēwak, mētoni mīna - nānitaw mīna ēwako ē-takonahkik. awiyak - nikī-itwānān māna, anohc ēkwa ayi k-ēsiyihkātamēk, *cancer* k-ētamihk, kā-wāpahtamēk *cancer* ōma, ēcikāni anima ēkotowahk. "ē-omīńimit," kī-itwāniw māna, "ē-omīńimit." tāpiskōc, tāpiskōc ēkā kī-kīhkēt ayis, kikiskēyihtēn, "ōm īta kā-pīkopayit, ēkota ē-akopisot," kī-itwāniw māna, māka it was that root there. The root, the elders long ago took particular care in taking that medicine using digging sticks to take them. Underground, that was the root underground, that chokecherry tree is an important medicine. Someone drinking it is cured, but it is not the sole ingredient, something is added to the medicine, but I'm not going to tell what. That's how it -

• • • •

JO: And birch trees?

MLR: Birch trees, long ago, those ones, the elders used those. They made axe handles by harvesting them, they would take them and peel them there with a knife and then dry them. The birch tree is strong for an axe-handle; that's the birch tree, they made those axe-handles, or else the hay-fork also, it was a hay-fork that, ah, it was also that, ah, they fit handles from that birchwood; those ones too were very useful long ago.

JO: Mhm, right.

• • • •

JO: Ah, how about *kākikēpakwa*?

MLR: I heard of *kākikēpakwa* long ago, I don't really know that one. They said *kākikēpakwa,* really also, they added that to other herbs as well. Someone - we used to say and what you nowadays, ah, name "cancer," as it is called, and when you saw this cancer, evidently it was that kind [which was used]. "She has internal sores," it used to be said, "she has internal sores." It's like, because it seemed like she couldn't heal. You know, "it is here where the skin is broken, she is bandaged there," ē-takonamihk kīkway, "ē-miyoskākot," kī-itwāniw māna. tāpiskōc ē-nipahiht an āya manicōs ana, *cancer* k-ētamihk, ōma manicōsa kā-mowikot awiyak. ēkota ana kākikēpak ē-kī-takonikāsot.

• • • •

JO: kā-mihcētwāniskwēyāk māka?

MLR: kā-mihcētwāniskwēyāk, ēh, pikw īsi mīna ēwakw ānima ē-itāpatahk kī-itwēwak māna kēhtē-ayak, pikw īta mīna ēkw ānima maskihkiy ē-takonikātēk, nānitaw ōma kē--, tāpiskōc kīkway maskihkiy k-ōsīhtāyan ēkota takonikātēw, mōy māka nānitaw ta-kī-itwēyān, you know. mitoni -, tēpiyāhk ē-kiskēyihtamān ē-miyosit mīna ēwakw āna, ēwakw āna kā--, kā-mihcētwāniskwēyāk. namōy wīhkāc kāh-kīs-akihtēn anihi ta-mōnahaman, ta-kī--, ta-mōnahaman mitoni itāmihk t-ēsi-mōnahaman ta-wayawīhtatāyan ōma kā-mihcētwāniskwēyāk ta-pāh-pawihtitāyan, ta-pēhkihtāyan. namōy wīhkāc kāh-kīs-akihtēn iyikohk roots, iyikohk ē-sakāhkwanīwiki, mōy kāh-kīs-akihtēn, ēwak ōhci k-ō-isiyihkātēk kā-mihcētwāniskwēyāk. mōy kāh-kīs-akihtēn, mētoni piko, tāpiskōc ōhi kēstakaya, kikiskēyihtēn? [JO: "āha."] iyikohk *roots*. iyikohk, mōy kāh-kīs-akihtēn wī-kakwē-akihtaman kāh-pwātawihtān. kīspin katawa ta-mōnahaman, *you know,* ēkāy tap-- ēkāy ta-pīkowēpahaman sōskwāt ta-mōnahaman ta-pāh-pawihtitāyan ta-kakwē-akihtaman tāmayikohk anihi -, tāmi-- anihi mēstakaya anihi; āyiman.

• • • •

JO: ēkwa mīna ōma pēyak kā-itwēyan āniskowaskosa?

MLR: āniskowaskosa, ēkoni mīna, ēkoni mīna ē-kihc-āpatahki, mēton ōti ē-kihc-āpatahki pikw ītē ē-āpacihtāyan. māka it used to be said, but something would be added, "she is healed by that," they used to say. It seemed that, ah, bug was killed, the one that is called cancer, or "when someone is eaten by this bug." That's the medicine where that *kākikēpak* was added.

• • • •

JO: And how about *kā-mihcētwāniskwēyāk*?

MLR: *kā-mihcētwāniskwēyāk* is one that has all kinds of uses, the elders used to say, that's one medicine that is added in everywhere, somewhere where - for instance any remedy you make it is in there but I should not say anything, you know. Really -, it is enough that I know that that one is also a good one, that one which, which has many hair-like strands as roots. You will never be able to finish counting those for you to dig, you'd - you would have to dig really deep to be able to dig them out those *kā-mihcētwāniskwēyāk* and to shake it out, to clean off the dirt. You will never be able to finish counting them, there are so many roots, so many that are tangled, you will never finish counting them, that's why it is called "*kā-mihcētwāniskwēyāk*." You can never finish counting them, it really just seems like your hair, you know? [JO: "Yes."] So many roots. You cannot finish counting so many, if you were going to try count them you would not be able to. If you were to dig them properly, you know, so that you don't break them off, you just have to dig them up to shake them out in order to try to count how many of those, how many - as with hair; it is difficult.

• • • •

JO: And then also this one that you mentioned, *āniskowaskosa*?

MLR: Horsetails, those also, those ones are also very useful, they are really so useful and it was used everywhere. But really mētoni [*mōy kwayask pēhtākwan*] pahkān ē-takonikātēk maskihkiy, āniskowaskos ēkota wīcihiwēw.

• • • •

JO: ā, ēkwa mīna *tiger lily*, *or* okiniy wāpikwaniy maskihkiya?

MLR: okiniy wāpikwaniy maskihkiya, okiniy wāpikwaniy maskihkiya. ēwakw ānima okiniy wāpikwaniy maskihkiya, pakahkam ēwako kā-wīhtamātān - ...

JO: āha, *tiger lily*.

MLR: ēha, ēwako kā-wīhtamātān kā-mīcihk. awiyak ē-nōhtē-mīcit, nitawi-mōnahikātēw ē-ma-mīciyan māka itwāniw māna ē-nanātawiskākoyan kayās wiya, *you know*. tāpiskōc ē-nanātawihtāyan *your system, like, you know*.

• • • •

JO: ā, āmow aya māka?

MLR: anihi cī āmowi-maskihkiya k-ētitān?

JO: āha.

MLR: ē-itohtēyan ē-nīpihk ē-papāmohtēyan sakāhk, kētahtawē kicīsok āmow. ē-wāpahtaman anima maskihkiy anima, anima kā-- wāpikwanīs, kitōtihtinēn ēwako kisikopitēn ahpō *your spit* kēhciwāk, ēkota ē-akonaman itē kā-cīsosk āmow, mōy nānitaw kitis-āya--, kitisi-pākipayin ēkwa, ēkosi mīna ēwako ē-itāpatahk. nikī-kiskēyihtēn māna, kayās nōhcīn. ēkosi ēkwa ōma *eighty-three* ē-itahtopiponēyān, kayās nikī-pē-pēhtawāwak kēhtē-ayak. nīsta māna nikī-āpacihtān kā-cīsot āmow; kētahtawē kiskātihk kicīsokwak, hēh, kimi-- kim-- kimiskēn ēwako, kisikopitēn ēkwa kimīm--, ē-okimīm--, okin-- ayi *you spit* anima being added to [*inaudible*] different medicines, *āniskowaskos* helps out in that way.

• • • •

JO: Ah, and then the tiger lily, or rose-flower medicines?

MLR: Rose-flower medicines, rose-flower medicines. That's the rose-flower medicines that I told you about - ...

JO: Yes, tiger lily.

MLR: Yes, that's the one I told you was eaten. Anyone who wants to eat it, it can be dug up and you eat it but it is said that it will do you good, that was long ago though, you know. It is like you are healing your system, like, you know.

• • • •

JO: Ah, what about the bee?

MLR: Is it the bee-medicines that I told you of?

JO: Yes.

MLR: As you are going in summer wandering about in the bush, suddenly a bee stings you. You'll see that medicine, that one that - a little flower, you take that and you crush it or even just your spit, holding it on there where the bee stung you, you won't have any - then you won't swell, that's how that one is used. I had that knowledge, I come from a long time back. So now I am eighty-three years old, I had heard the elders long ago. I, too, used to use that when a bee stung; suddenly they sting you on your leg, hey, you find that one, you crush it up and you, on the sore -, ah, your spit is good ē-ohci-miyoma--, ē-sāpopacikākēyan, kitakonēn, kitāstēpayin. mōy kimēstisokon ayiwāk.

• • • •

JO: ā, pasakocēpiwa [*sic*]? pasakocēpihkwa? pasakocēpihkwa.

MLR: ēkoni wiy āwiyak ēkā kā-miywāspinēt itwāniw māna, tāpiskōc ōma ayi, kik-ētwēyahk ka-macahpinēt awiyak ēkota ē-takonikātēk kotaka māka maskihkiya.

JO: mhm, kwēyask.

MLR: āha, ē-minihkwēhk ē--. sisonē sāk--, sisonē mēskanāhk māna ohpikinwa anihi.

• • • •

JO: kinēpikōmina māka?

MLR: āā, kinēpikōmina, ēwakoni wiya, āh, mōya wiya ēkoni awiyak wīhkāt t-ōtinahk. tāpiskōc -

JO: māyiskākow.

MLR: - ē-kī-- māyiskākow, tāpiskōc ayi, *you know*, mōy -, nikī-ohcimikawinān ahpō ta-tahkinamāhk, *you know*. nanātohk nikī-itikawinān, k-ōmikicihcān ahpō, *you know*. [JO: "ōōh."] *Yeah*, kayās kēhtē-ayak ēkosi nikī-itikonānak, "kāwiya tahkina, ē-māyātahki anihi." ahpō k-ōmikic--, *you know*, ka-miyikon *rash*. *You know*.

• • • •

JO: āā, kāsakē--, kāsakēwask?

for - you moisten it with that and put it on, and you get relief. It doesn't burn you anymore.

• • • •

JO: Ah, *pasakocēpiwa* [*sic*]? *pasakocēpihkwa*? *pasakocēpihkwa*.

MLR: That is for someone who was a "not good" illness, as it is said, like this, ah, we would say when someone has a venereal disease, that is added there with other herbs.

JO: Mhm, right.

MLR: Yes, one drinks it. Along the lak-- those ones generally grow along the road.

• • • •

JO: And how about *kinēpikōmina*?

MLR: Ahh, as for those *kinēpikōmina* ["snakeberries"], oh, no-one should ever take those. Like -

JO: It is bad for them.

MLR: - they -, it will harm them, like, ah, *you know*, no - we were forbidden even to touch them, you know. We were told all sorts of things, you would get scabby hands even, you know. [JO: "Ohh."] Yeah, long ago the elders said that to us, "Don't touch them as those ones are bad." You will even have scab--, you know, it will give you a rash. You know.

• • • •

JO: Ah, *kāsakē--*, *kāsakēwask*?

MLR: kāsakēwask, awiyak ēkā kā-nihtā-mīcisot, ēkotowa ē--, ē--, ē-asamiht a-- ē-takonikātēk maskihkiy kotak, *you know.* ēkosi mīcisow. mīnoskōhtwāw, maskihkiy ayisk.

• • • •

JO: ā, *and* pihē--, pihē--, pihēko--

MLR: pihēkocēpihk.

JO: āha, pihēkocēpihk.

MLR: pihēkocēpihk, ā, ēwako mīna ē-miywāsik, ēwako mīn ānima ē-miywāsik, awiyak tāpiskōc kā-sāposkāwisit, *you know*, tāpiskōc kā-wāh-wayawīt, māka ē-takonikātēk maskihkiy kiki kotak.

• • • •

JO: wīhkaskwa.

MLR: wīhkaskwa, wiya ē-miyāhkasikākēyan. kā-miyāhkasikēhk, tāpiskōc ōma niya kīkisēpā, kīkisēpā nisaskahēn, nimiyāhkasoson, nēwāw omis īsi nimiyāhkasoson. ēkwa ē-wanihkēyān kīkisēpā, ē-otākosik nisaskahēn.

kanakē pēyakwāw pēyak kīsikāw [ki]kī-itikawinānaw ta-āpacihtāyahk anihi, wīhkaskwa. ēkā kā-nihtā--, ēkā wiya kā-nihtā-ayi--; tāpiskōc ōma ēkā kā-nihtā-kākīsimot awiyak, kiwīcihikon ēs ānihi kititwēstamākon ōtē, "kīkwāy anima ē-nitawēyihtaman kititwēstamākon," kī-itwēwak māna kēhtē-ayak aniki. tāpwē anima, ātiht namōy nihtā-ayamihtākosiwak; namōya kinihtā-ayamihtākosin. kā-ayamihtākosihk anima, *you pray, you can pray*. kiwīc--, kiya māka kiwīcihikon. kiwīcihik ēsa ana wīhkask, ēkosi māna itwāniw.

MLR: Licorice, for someone who has no appetite, that kind -, they are fed that, added to other medicine, you know. So they eat. They are restored [i.e., to a healthy appetite], because it is medicine.

• • • •

JO: Ah, and *pihē--, pihē--, pihēko--*

MLR: *pihēkocēpihk.*

JO: Yes, *pihēkocēpihk.*

MLR: *pihēkocēpihk,* ah, that one is also good, that's also good, when someone has diarrhea, you know, like when someone keeps going out to the toilet, but the medicine is taken along with another herb.

• • • •

JO: Sweetgrass?

MLR: Sweetgrass, that is for smudging. When you smudge, like I do in the morning, I light it in the morning, I smudge myself, four times like this I smudge myself and if I forget in the morning, I light it in the evening.

At least once each day we are told to use that, sweetgrass. If one does not - if someone is not able -, ah, like when someone is not able to pray, it evidently helps you and that speaks on your behalf over here, "whatever it is that you want, it speaks on your behalf," they used to say, those elders. It's true, some are not practiced at prayer; you are not able to be heard in prayer. That's when you will be heard in prayer, you pray, you **can** pray. You are help-- but it helps you. That sweetgrass helps you, that's what is said.

• • • •

JO: wīhkēs māka?

MLR: wīhkēs, ēwako mīna ē-miyw-āpatisit pikw īta, pikw īs īsi, pikw īta kitāpacihāw wīhkēs. ahpō, ahpō ayi, itwāniw māna awiyak ayi, aya kā-ayāt, ēkā kā-kī-miyo-yēhēt tānisi kā-isiyihkātamēk anima? *Asthma* awiyak kā-ayāt, wīcihik ēsa anima, kās-- kāsīhkahtēw ōtē anima kīkway kā-kipiskākoyan pasakw-āyi ayis anima ōtē ē-nakipayik *in your throat,* kikohtākanihk ōtē. kiwīcihik ēsa ana wīhkēs, pēhkihkasam anima ayi, itwāniw māna.

• • • •

JO: ā, mitēhimina, ahpō cī otēhimina?

MLR: otē--, otēhimina?

JO: mhm, tānisi wiya ēkoni - ?

MLR: otēhimina, otēhimina ōhi k-ētamihk wiya ēkoni -.

JO: *Strawberries.*

MLR: *Strawberries* wiya ēkoni ē-mīcihk; ē-mīcihk, ē-pakāhtāyan, wiya ēkoni.

JO: mōy cī wiy ānihi o-- ā, *roots* kē-- kitāpacihtān wiya ēkoni?

MLR: otēhimina, ēwako mīna awiyak otēhāspinēt, itwāniw māna. ēwakoni anihi otē--, ah, wiy ōm ānim ōcēpihk, otēhimin--, otēhiminicēpihk, awiyak otēh kā-wīs--, kā-māh-mōsihot ē-sāsākwahtahk itwāniw māna ēwako. ēwako wiya māna nipēhtēn ē-pēyakōnikātēk, *you know*, mōy nānitaw wiya ēwako ē-wīhtamātān, *you know*.

• • • •

JO: And what about *wīhkēs* [ratroot]?

MLR: That ratroot is also very useful everywhere, in every way, you can use ratroot just anywhere. Or, even ah, it is generally said that when someone, ah, has that when they can't breathe well, what do you call that? When someone has *asthma*, that apparently helps them, it clears it out that stuff over here which blocks you up, that sticky stuff, because it gets lodged over here in your throat, over here in your throat. That ratroot apparently helps you, that burns it clean, ah, it was always said.

• • • •

JO: And *mitēhimina* or else *otēhimina* [strawberries]?

MLR: *otē--, otēhimina*?

JO: Mhm, how about those - ?

MLR: *otēhimina*, these which you call *otēhimina*, well as for these -

JO: Strawberries.

MLR: As for strawberries, those are eaten, they are eaten, you just boil those ones.

JO: Aren't those, ah, do you use those roots, though?

MLR: Strawberries, that too if someone has a heart ailment, it is said. Those straw-- ah, as for that root, strawberry-- strawberry root, anyone having pain in their heart -, the one feeling that, they chew it into small pieces, it was said about that one. For that one, I would hear that it is used on its own, but I won't say anything more about it, you know.

• • • •

JO: mīnisihkēs.

MLR: mīnisihkēs, kayās nikī-itāpacihtānān, kah--
nikī-tāh-tēwihtawakēpayinān māna ē-pakāhtāhk anima mīnisihkēs ēkwa ē-sīskōpātinaman ē-pēhkihtāyan [*mōy kwayask pēhtākwan*] ēkota ēkwa ē-pīhci-sīkinamawat awāsis kā-wīsakēyihtahk ohtawakay; miyoskākow. tānitahtwāw nikī-āpacihtān nīsta. kā-pāh-pakāsimohk mān ōma kā-nīpihk pīhcihtawakēyāpāwān, ēkota māna wīsakēyihcikā--, wīsakēyihtamwak awāsisak. kimiyoskākon anim āyi, ēwakw ānima, anima ayi, mīnisihkēs nitisiyihkātēnān ē-nēhiyawēhk.

• • • •

JO: ā, nīpimināna.

MLR: nīpimināna. nīpimināna, nīpimināna k-ētwēhk ēkoni mīna māna k-ētwēcik ocēpihkwa kīkway maskihkiy mīna ēkotē ē-āpatahk, minihkwēwin kīkway mīna, nānitaw k-ētāsp--, *you know* kā--, ēkā kā-miyomahcihoyan; nīpimināna, ocēpihk māka, *you know*.

• • • •

JO: ā, okinīwāhtikwa; okinīwāhtikwa?

MLR: okinīwāhtikwak. okinīwāhtikwak, ēkonik aniki mīna pakahkam mīna nān--, nānitaw mīna ēkonik itāpatisiwak. māna nikī-pēhtēn okinīwāhtikwak ē-- ē-āpatisicik. tānisi kani ōma kā-kī--? okinīwāhtikwak, ōh, wāhay! nikī-pēhtēn aniki māna nānitaw ē-itāpatisicik. okinīwāhtikwak aniki, māka ocēpihk nēma; kikiskēyihtēn nānitaw ē-itāpatahk.

• • • •

• • • •

JO: *mīnisihkēs* [Seneca root]?

MLR: Seneca root, we used it long ago, we would suddenly get earaches, and that seneca root would be boiled and you strained it to clean it [*inaudible*] and then you would pour it in [the ear] for a child who had pain in their ear; it made them feel good. How many times did I, too, use that! When people were swimming a lot in summer and water gets in the ear, and there's usually pain felt -, children feel pain. That makes you feel better, ah, that's the one, that, ah, we call it *mīnisihkēs* in Cree.

• • • •

JO: Ah, *nīpiminâna* [highbush cranberries]?

MLR: Cranberries. Cranberries, those that were called '*nīpiminâna*', they also used to say the roots were something that was used as a medicinal drink, as something to relieve - you know, when you're not feeling well; cranberries, the roots though, you know.

• • • •

JO: Ah, *okinīwâhtikwa* [*sic*]; wild rose bushes?

MLR: Wild rose bushes. Those wild rose bushes are perhaps in some -, those are also useful somehow. I used to hear that wild rose bushes are useful. I forget how they were -? Wild rose bushes, well, for goodness sake! I used to hear that those were useful in some way. Those wild rose bushes, but that root; you know, it is useful in some way.

• • • •

JO: ayi māka, ā, ayōskan--, ayōskanawāhtikwa [*sic*]?

MLR: ayōskanāhtikwak [JO: "āha."], ēkonik mīn āniki ocēpihk mīna ēwako anima maskihkiy mīna ēwako ē-takonamihk. kīkway maskihkiy kī-takonamwak, mōy māka nikiskēyihtēn tānisi ē-isiyihkātamihk.

JO: ayōskanāhtikwa [*sic*; ayōskanak] māka?

MLR: ayōskanāhtikwak [*sic*; ayōskanak], ēkonik - ēkonik mīna, ē--, ē-- ayi, ē-kīsisohcik aniki ayōskanāhtikwak [*sic*; ayōskanak], mīcimāpōhk ē-takonihcik kī-itwēwak māna kayās. ayōskanak, *wild ones* ōki cī, *wild ones,* ayōskanāhtikwak. ēy, ēkotowa ē-takon-- kī-takonēwak māna kēhtē-ayak. ē-sikop--, ē-sikoswācik, *you know*, ē-pakāsimācik, mīcimāpōhk ē-takonācik, kī-itwēwak māna.

• • • •

JO: ā. pasa-- *bulrushes? Bulrushes*, pasicān? pasicānak? [*sic*; cf. pasihkānak] *You know* anihi, ā, *bulrushes*?

MLR: ōh, ēwakw ānima, ma cī kā-- [*mōy kwayask pēhtākwan*]? [JO: "āha."] hay, kayās anihi ē-kī-āpacihācik ōki pēpīsak, awāsisak kā-nihtāwikicik, ē-pīsinācik ōki iskwēwak ēkwa awa mistik *a rotten one* ēkwa yōskihtakisiw ayisk mīna, ēkot ē-takonācik. ōta ē-kīsōhpitācik awāsisa ōta otāsiyāniyihk, kayās ēwako; ēkwa anihi kā-sāpopēyit anihi kī-wēpinēwak māna. kayās ēwako aniki ēkosi ē-kī-itāpatisicik. māk āyi, namōya wiya ēkosi ta-ati-isi-āpacihācik, ē-kī-sēkonācik *in the oven*; ē-mēstiswācik tāpiskōc kīkway manicōs ēkota ta-kī-ihtakot, *you know*. ēkosi mōy kīkway kī-ohci-ihtakow manicōs, *you know, to* -, ta-sēsēskēyihtākosit ta-tahkwamikot awāsis, mōy. kī-miyo-paminēwak anihi māna ayisk awāsisak ē-- ē-kikahpitihcik, ē-kīsōhpitihcik, *you know*.

JO: How about, ah, raspberri--, *ayōskanāhtikwa*[*k*] [raspberry bushes]?

MLR: Raspberry bushes [JO: "Yes."], with those ones as well it's the root that is medicinal and it is added in as an ingredient. They added it into some medicine, but I don't know what it was called.

JO: Raspberry bushes [*sic*; raspberries]?

MLR: Raspberry bushes [*sic*; raspberries], those too, ah, they were cooked too, those raspberry bushes [*sic*; raspberries] and added into a soup, they used to say long ago. Raspberries, the wild ones? The wild raspberry bushes. Well, they added - they old people used to add that kind in. They tear-- they cut them into bits, you know, and boil them, and add them into soup, they used to say.

• • • •

JO: Ah, bull-- bulrushes? Bulrushes, *pasicān*? *pasicānak*? [*sic*; cf. *pasihkānak*]. You know those, ah, bulrushes?

MLR: Oh, that one, is it the one that [*inaudible*]? [JO: "Yes."] Well, long ago the babies used those, when children were born, the women would break those into small pieces and this tree, a rotten one, because it was soft wood, they added that in there. Here they would wrap the children warmly in their diapers, that was long ago; and when they were wet they used to throw those away. Those were used in that way long ago. But, ah, they didn't just start using them in that way, they placed them in the oven; burning them up, like if there was some kind of bug that was there, you know. Thus there would be no bug to - you know, to be frightening or for the child to be bitten, no! They always handled those well because children would be bundled up with that, and wrapped up warmly, you know.

• • • •

JO: ā, takwahiminâhtikwa; āsay cī?

MLR: āsay wiy ēkoni.

JO: ō.

MLR: āsay kikī-wīht--, kikī-kakwēcimin takwahiminâhtikwa, *ya*.

• • • •

JO: ā, sāpōminâhtikwa -

MLR: sāpōminâhtikwa, mōy nānitaw -,

JO: - ahpō cī sāpō-- sāpōminak?

MLR: mōy nānitaw itāpatanwa. pakahkam.

JO: ā, sā-- sāpōminak māka?

MLR: *Ya*, sāpōminak? kimosci-mowāwak, māka kikwah-- kikakwāhyakihikwak [*pāhpiw*] mētoni ki--, ki--, mēton āyi kiskīsikwa māyi-itōtamwak.

• • • •

JO: wīhkāc cī ayi, ā, *mushrooms* ... kī-mowāwak?

MLR: ēha.

JO: *Wild mushrooms*?

MLR: ēha, ēha. mowāwak mīna ēkonik, ēha.

JO: tānisi kiya ē-isiyihkātacik?

• • • •

JO: Chokecherry bushes; Did we already -?

MLR: We did those ones already.

JO: Oh.

MLR: I already told--, you asked me about chokecherry bushes, ya.

• • • •

JO: Ah, *sāpōmināhtikwa* [gooseberry bushes] -

MLR: Gooseberry bushes, there is nothing -

JO: - or rather gooseber-- *sāpōminak* [gooseberries]?

MLR: They are not useful. I guess.

JO: How about gooseberries?

MLR: Ya, gooseberries? You just ate them raw, but they will give you a bad time [*MLR laughs*] when, really you - you - ah, they are really bad for your eyes. [i.e., they make you wince].

• • • •

JO: Were they ever, ah, oh, mushrooms, were they eaten?

MLR: Yes.

JO: Wild mushrooms?

MLR: Yes, yes. Those ones were also eaten, yes.

JO: What do you call them?

MLR: *Mushrooms?* ēy hēy, tānisi ētikwē nika-isiyihkātāwak ē-nēhiyawēhk.

JO: ātiht ōki ayi, ayīk--, ayīki-nōnācikanisak.

MLR: ayīk--, ayīk--, ayīkitāsak ātiht cī? [*pāhpiwak*]

JO: ayīki-nōnācikanisak.

MLR: ayīki-nōnācikanisak, *yeah*, ēkosi māna nikī-pēhtēn ē-isiyihkāsocik tānisi ētikwē māka ē-itāpatisicik. [*pāhpiwak*]

JO: ayisk ātiht aniki ayi *they're poisonous, huh?*

MLR: āha, ātiht aniki piscipowiwak "kāy--, kāya mikoskācihik," kī-itwāniw māna. [*pāhpiwak*]

• • • •

JO: ā, cēskwa. [*ē-ka-kitowēyēkipayik*] ēkos ānim ētikwē. ēkosi! hāw. kinanāskomitin.

MLR: āha, ā.

ēha, ēkwa niy ōma kā-pē-wīcihak awa nōsisim ē-sawēyimak, kānikanā kwēyask pimohtēt, pimohtātahk otatoskēwin, ēkosi ē-isi-pakosēyimak. namōya nīsta kīkway mitoni mistahi nikiskēyihtēn māka kayās ē-pē-ohcīyān kīkway ē-pē-pēhtamān kā-kakwē-pē-wīcihak nōsisim ōta. pitanē māka miyo--, miywāsiniyik otatoskēwiniwāw wiya ēkwa owīcēwākana, ēkosi ē-pē-isi-wāh-wīcihak nōsisim anohc kā-kīsikāk. ninanāskomon ōta ē-pē-wāpahtamān ita ē-ayāt, ē-miywapit, kānikanā misakāmē ēkosi ati-isi- --, isi--, isi-kanawēyihtahk ōma otiskotēm ēkosi ē-isi-nitotamākēstamawak nōsisim, ē-sawēyimak, ē-sākihakik, niya *Mary Louise Rockthunder from Piapot's.*

MLR: Mushrooms? Oh, hey, I wonder what I would call them in Cree.

JO: Some of these, ah, frog--, *ayīki-nōnācikanisak* ["frog soothers"]?

MLR: Frog-- frog--, are some called *ayīkitāsak* ["frog-pants"; i.e., pitcher plants]? [*laughter*]

JO: *ayīki-nōnācikānisak*.

MLR: *ayīki-nōnācikanisak*, yeah, I used to hear them called that, but I wonder how they were used. [*laughter*]

JO: Because some of those are, ah, they're poisonous, eh?

MLR: Yes, some of those are poisonous, "Don't, don't mess with them," that is what was said. [*laughter*]

• • • •

JO: Ah, hold on. [*the sound of rustling papers*] I guess that's it. That's it! Okay. I am grateful to you.

MLR: Yes, ah.

And I came to help this grandchild of mine who I love, may she walk a good path, carrying her work well, that is what I wish for her. I don't really know very much but I come from long ago and I would hear things along the way with which I am trying to help my grandchild here, may it be good, may their work go well, her and her partner. In this way I've come to help my grandchild today. I am grateful I have come here to see where she lives, that she lives well, may it always be that she look after her home fire, that's what I ask on behalf of this grandchild of mine who I cherish, I love them. I am Mary Louise Rockthunder from Piapot's.

Cree-English Glossary

Stem-Class Codes

INM Indeclinable Nominal – a non-nominal (usually verbal) structure used to form names in place of a noun

IPC Indeclinable Particle – a free particle

IPH Indeclinable Particle Phrase – two or more particles combined into a Phrase

IPJ Indeclinable Interjection – a particle used as a holophrastic utterance (i.e., an exclamation unto itself) outside of clausal syntax

IPN Indeclinable Prenoun – a particle which must be attached to a Noun

IPV Indeclinable Preverb – a particle which must be attached to a Verb

NA Animate Noun – a noun classed as animate within the Cree system of grammatical Gender
- **NA_1** – class 1 is the basic or regular paradigm
- **NA_2** – class 2 end in Vowel-Glide sequences
- **NA_3** – class 3 end in Consonant-/w/ sequences
- **NA_4** – class 4 consist of single-syllable stems, some of which also end in Consonant-/w/ sequences (i.e., NA_{4w})

NDA Dependent Animate Noun – an inalienable animate noun which must take person-marking prefixes (e.g., kinship terms, body parts, etc.). Note: NDAs can occur in all of the subtypes of NA stems (see above)

NDI Dependent Inanimate Noun – an inalienable inanimate noun which must take person-marking prefixes (e.g., body parts and some special items). Note: NDIs can occur in all of the subtypes of NI stems (see below)

NI Inanimate Noun – a noun classed as inanimate within the Cree system of grammatical Gender
- **NI$_1$** – class 1 is the basic or regular paradigm
- **NI$_2$** – class 2 end in Vowel-Glide sequences
- **NI$_3$** – class 3 end in Consonant-/w/ sequences
- **NI$_4$** – class 4 consist of single-syllable stems, some of which also end in Consonant-/w/ sequences (i.e., NI$_{4w}$)
- **NI$_5$** – class 5 end in /t/ (alternating with /s/) stems (a very small, irregular class)

PR Pronoun – a grammatical particle used as a shortcut to refer to a larger noun or noun phrase
- **PrA** Animate Pronoun – a pronoun used to refer to an animate referent
- **PrI** Inanimate Pronoun – a pronoun used to refer to an inanimate referent

VAI Animate Intransitive Verb (classes 1, 2 and 3) – intransitive verbs with an animate actor/subject
- **VAI$_1$** – class 1 is the basic or regular paradigm
- **VAI$_2$** – class 2 are n-final stems
- **VAI$_3$** – class 3 are intransitive verbs that inflect like VTI$_1$

VII Inanimate Intransitive Verb (classes 1 and 2) – intransitive verbs with no animate actor/subject
- **VII$_1$** – class 1 are impersonal verbs (i.e., no plurals)
- **VII$_2$** – class 2 are all others (both Vowel-final and n-final stems)

VTA Transitive Animate Verb (classes 1, 2, 3, and 4) – transitive verbs with an animate actor/subject and an inanimate goal/object
- **VTA$_1$** – class 1 is the basic or regular paradigm
- **VTA$_2$** – class 2 end in Vowel-Glide sequences
- **VTA$_3$** – class 3 end in Consonant-/w/ sequences
- **VTA$_4$** – class 4 end in /t/ (alternating with /s/) stems

VTI Transitive Inanimate Verb (classes 1, 2, and 3)
- **VTI$_1$** – class 1 is the basic or regular paradigm
- **VTI$_2$** – class 2 end in /ā/ and inflect like VAI$_1$
- **VTI$_3$** – class 3 end in /i/ and inflect like VAI$_1$

For further information on these parts of speech, notes on the format of the glossary, and Cree grammar in general, please see the Introduction to this volume, and/or consult language teaching materials such as:

Okimāsis, Jean. 2021. *nēhiyawēwin: paskwāwi-pīkiskwēwin / Cree: Language of the Plains*. Regina: University of Regina Press. (Also available as open online resources at: https://www.uregina.ca/oer-publishing/titles/cree.html).

Ratt, Solomon. 2016. *māci-nēhiyawēwin / Beginning Cree*. Regina: University of Regina Press.

Wolvengrey, Arok. 2001. *nēhiyawēwin: itwēwina / Cree: Words*. Regina: University of Regina Press.

or consult the online Plains Cree Grammar pages, maintained by Arok Wolvengrey, available at: http://plainscree.atlas-ling.ca/grammar/.

Another useful online tool that can be consulted for more information on individual words and their grammatical forms is the *itwēwina* dictionary at: https://itwewina.altlab.app/.

-awāsimis- NDA$_1$ child; fetus [cf. **awāsis-**; 1sPoss singular: *nicawāsimis* or *nitawāsimis* "my child"]

-āskikan- NDI$_1$ chest, breastbone; bosom

-cāhkos- NDA$_1$ female cross-cousin; sister-in-law, brother's wife [used by a female speaker only]

-cakisīs- NDI$_1$ small intestine; sausage

-cihcīs- NDI$_1$ finger; little hand

-cisk- NDI$_1$ anus; rear end

-ēscakās- NDI$_1$ hair, short hair; lock of my hair [generally plural]

-ēstakay- NDI$_2$ hair, head of hair [generally plural]

-hcikwan- NDI$_1$ knee

-hpan- NDA$_1$ lung [also: **-ohpan-**]

-htawakay- NDI$_2$ ear

-(t)iskwēm- NDA$_1$ wife, woman, (female) lover [cf. **iskwēw-**; 1sPoss singular *nitiskwēm* "my wife"]

-iyaw- NDI$_1$ body; corpse [singular: *miyaw* "corpse, dead body"; 3sPoss: *wiyaw* "his/her body"]

-iyitihp- NDI$_1$ brain [singular: *miyitihp*]

-īci-ayisiyiniw- NDA$_2$ fellow human, fellow person

-īcisān- NDA$_1$ sibling

-īciskwēsis- NDA$_1$ sister, fellow little girl [cf. **iskwēsis-**]

-īk- NDI$_4$ home, dwelling, house

-īkis- NDI$_1$ small home; cabin

-īpitihkān- NDI$_1$ false tooth, denture, [plural:] dentures

-ītimw- NDA$_3$ cross-cousin of the opposite gender; [male speaker:] daughter of father's sister or daughter of mother's brother; sister-in-law (i.e., wife of male sibling or parallel cousin); [female speaker:] son of father's sister or son of mother's brother; brother-in-law (i.e., husband of female sibling or parallel cousin)

-ītisān- NDA$_1$ sibling; brother or sister

-īw- NDA$_4$ wife [3sPoss, obviative: *wīwa* "his wife"]

-kāwiy- NDA$_2$ mother

-kāwīs- NDA$_1$ parallel aunt; mother's sister, father's brother's wife; stepmother; godmother; "my dear mother"

-kēhtē-ayim- NDA$_1$ elder; parent, grandparent

-kisēyinīm- NDA$_1$ old man, husband

-kohtākan- NDI$_1$ throat; gullet, esophagus

-kosis- NDA$_1$ son; parallel nephew (i.e., son of sibling of same gender); [male speaker:] brother's son; [female speaker:] sister's son

-māmā- NDA mom, mother

-mis- NDA$_1$ older sister; older female parallel cousin (i.e., daughter of mother's sister or daughter of father's brother)

-mosōm- NDA$_1$ grandfather, grandpa, grand uncle;

[reference extended to all related males of grandfather's generation:] respected male elder

-nāpēm- NDA$_1$ husband, (male) lover [cf. **nāpēw-**]

-nīkihikw- NDA$_3$ parent; blood relative

-ohkom- NDA$_1$ grandmother; [reference extended to all related females of grandmother's generation:] respected female elder [e.g., 1sPoss singular: *nōhkom*]

-ohtāwiy- NDA$_2$ father; [Christian:] Heavenly Father [e.g., 1sPoss singular: *nōhtāwiy*]

-(t)ōkimām- NDA$_1$ chief, leader, boss; superior; king [cf. **okimāw-**; 1sPoss singular: *nitōkimām*]

-(t)ōkimāskwēm- NDA$_1$ leader, boss, boss-lady; boss's wife; chieftess; superior; queen [cf. **okimāskwēw-**; 1sPoss singular: *nitōkimāskwēm*]

-ōsisim- NDA$_1$ grandchild; [reference extended to any young person when used by an elder] [e.g., 1sPoss singular: *nōsisim*]

-pēpīsim- NDA$_1$ baby [cf. **pēpīsis-**]

-sikos- NDA$_1$ aunt, cross-aunt; father's sister, paternal aunt; mother's brother's wife; mother-in-law

-sīm- NDA$_1$ younger sibling (brother or sister), younger parallel cousin

-skāhtikw- NDI$_3$ forehead

-skāt- NDI$_1$ leg

-skātis- NDI$_1$ small leg

-skīsikw- NDI$_3$ eye

-skotākay- NDI$_2$ coat, jacket; dress; skirt

-sōniyāmis- NDA$_1$ bit of money, poor wages [cf. **sōniyās-**]

-stikwān- NDI$_1$ head; mind; head of hair

-stim- NDA$_1$ niece, cross-niece (i.e., daughter of sibling of opposite gender); daughter-in-law; [male speaker:] sister's daughter; [female speaker:] brother's daughter

-tānis- NDA$_1$ daughter; parallel niece (i.e., daughter of sibling of same gender); [male speaker:] brother's daughter; [female speaker:] sister's daughter

-tāniskōhpicikan- NDA$_1$ ancestor, descendant; great-grandparent, great-grandchild

-tās- NDA$_1$ pair of pants, trousers; leggings

-tāsiyān- NDA$_1$ diaper; [historically:] loincloth, breechclout

-tēh- NDI$_1$ heart; [figuratively:] heart, soul

-tēm- NDA$_1$ dog; horse

-tihkwatim- NDA$_1$ nephew, cross-nephew (i.e., son of sibling of opposite gender); [male speaker:] sister's son; [female speaker:] brother's son; son-in-law

-tōn- NDI$_1$ mouth

-wāhkōmākan- NDA$_1$ relative

-wīcēwākan- NDA1 spouse; companion, partner, buddy, friend
-wīkimākan- NDA1 spouse, wife, husband; housemate

a

acimomēyis- NI1 cactus berry, red berry from a cactus [literally: "little dog-feces"]
acimosis- NA1 pup, puppy; small dog
aciyaw IPC for a short while, a short time, a little while
ah IPJ ho! [discourse particle signifying surprise; formed by sharp intake of breath]
ah- VTA5 put s.o. (s.w.), place s.o.; set s.o. down
ahahāā IPJ oh for goodness sakes
ahā IPJ ya; okay; agreed [cf. **ahām, ahāw, āw**]
ahām IPJ okay then; okay already, hurry up [cf. **ahā, ahāw, āw**]
ahāw IPJ okay; ready, let's go; now indeed [cf. **ahā, ahām, āw**]
ahpō IPC even, possibly; or, or else
ahpō cī IPH or else, or is it?
ahpō ētikwē IPH maybe, perhaps [cf. **ahpō ētokē**]
ahpō ētokē IPH maybe, perhaps [cf. **ahpō ētikwē**]
ahwā IPJ oh my! wow! good gracious; really; [emphatic:] so [cf. **wahwah, wahwā**]
akāwātamaw- VTA2 desire (it/him) from s.o., desire (it/him) for s.o., covet (it/him) from s.o.; envy s.o. over (it/him), begrudge (it/him) to s.o.
akihcikē- VAI1 count, count things
akiht- VTI1 count s.t.; add up s.t.
akihtāsowin- NI1 counting, the act of counting; phone number
akohcim- VTA1 put s.o. into water (e.g., a baby), soak s.o. in water, immerse s.o. in water
akohp- NI1 blanket
akon- VTI1 hold s.t. in place, stick s.t. on (it)
akopiso- VAI1 have a compress tied on oneself, have a poultice on; put on medicine, tie on a bandage
akoskiwasikan- NI1 sealing wax; object used to apply glue, paste, wax
akostah- VTI1 sew s.t. on (as trimming)
akotā- VTI2 hang s.t. up; hang up one's own snare, set one's own snare
akwah- VTI1 paste s.t. on (the wall)
akwanah- VTI1 cover s.t. up
akwanah- VTA1 cover s.o. up
akwanaho- VAI1 wrap oneself in a blanket, cover oneself up, be covered; use (it) as a cover
ana PrA that, that one
anaha PrA that yonder, that one yonder [also: **nāha**]
ani IPC indeed, surely; then
anihi PrA that, that one; those, those ones
anihi PrI those, those ones
aniki PrA those, those ones
anima PrI that, that one

anima **IPC** it is that; the fact that
anita **IPC** there, at that place
anohc **IPC** now, today [cf. **anoht**]
anohc kā-kīsikāk **IPH** today
anoht **IPC** now, today [cf. **anohc**]
api- **VAI**$_1$ sit, sit down, be present; be available; be there, be situated; be at home, stay at home
apihkē- **VAI**$_1$ braid, braid hair; weave, make a net; knit, do knitting
apisāsin- **VII**$_2$ be small
apisimōsos- **NA**$_1$ deer, red deer; mule deer
apisīs **IPC** a little, a little bit
apoy- **NA**$_2$ paddle; shovel, spade
asahto- **VAI**$_1$ feed one another
asahtowin- **NI**$_1$ rations; feeding one another
asam- **VTA**$_1$ feed s.o., feed (it) to s.o., give s.o. food, serve s.o. food; hand out rations to s.o.
asamopit- **VTI**$_1$ close s.t. (e.g., pouch) with a gathering string
ascikātē- **VII**$_2$ be placed
asikan- **NA**$_1$ sock, stocking
asiniy- **NA**$_2$ rock, stone
asisīwēkinw- **NA**$_3$ paper
asiwacikan- **NI**$_1$ pouch, pocket; purse, suitcase; storage container, receptacle, bin; can, jar, vessel
asiwah- **VTA**$_1$ put s.o. inside (a bag or box), enclose s.o.
asiwaso- **VAI**$_1$ be inside, be closed in, be enclosed, be contained within; live inside, dwell inside; be locked up, be imprisoned
asiwatā- **VTI**$_2$ put s.t. inside (a bag or box), enclose s.t.
asiwatē- **VII**$_2$ be inside, be closed in, be contained, be enclosed; be placed inside
askihtakokātē- **VAI**$_1$ have green legs
askihtakwaskamikā- **VII**$_1$ the earth is green, be green earth, be the earth in spring
askihtakwā- **VII**$_2$ be green; be blue, be blue-green
askiy- **NI**$_2$ land; region, area; earth, world; settlement, colony, country; Métis colony; [plural:] fields under cultivation, pieces of farmland, the lands
askīhk **IPC** on the land; in the earth, on the earth; reserve
askīhkān- **NI**$_1$ reserve; band
askīwi- **VII**$_1$ be one year, be summer; be land, be earth
askow- **VTA**$_2$ follow s.o., follow behind s.o.
asot- **VTI**$_1$ promise s.t.
asotamaw- **VTA**$_2$ promise (it/him) to s.o.
aspahcikē- **VAI**$_1$ eat a relish with one's food
aspāskosikan- **NA**$_1$ leaves or bark mixed with tobacco
aspēyiht- **VTI**$_1$ rely on s.t.
aspēyimototaw- **VTA**$_2$ rely on s.o.
aspi- **IPV** badly
aspi-kīhkām- **VTA**$_1$ scold s.o. badly
aspin **IPC** away, off, from a distance, in departing, ago; since then, the last I knew; back then, so long

ago; gone for good, gone for the present; since; just; presumably, evidently

aspinikē- **VAI$_1$** hold things with a pot holder; use a pot holder

astamaw- **VTA$_2$** put (it/him) on s.o.; apply (it/him) to s.o.; place (it/him) for s.o., bet with s.o.

astā- **VTI$_2$** put s.t. there, place s.t. there

astāsowikamikohkē- **VAI$_1$** build a storage building; make a cache

astāsowikamikw- **NI$_3$** storage building; cache

astē- **VII$_2$** be there, sit there; be placed, be in place; be piled up; be out (e.g., leaf)

astisihkān- **NA$_1$** oven mitt

atamih- **VTA$_1$** make s.o. smile; please s.o., make s.o. glad; make s.o. grateful, make s.o. indebted; treat s.o. well

ataminā- **VAI$_1$** be appreciative, be grateful, be thankful

atamiskaw- **VTA$_2$** greet s.o., send greetings to s.o.; say hello to s.o.; shake hands with s.o.; hug s.o. in greeting, kiss s.o. in greeting; bid s.o. farewell

atām- **VTA$_1$** buy (it/him) from s.o., buy for s.o.

atāmihk **IPC** beneath, under, underneath; inside (e.g., clothing); deep down

atāmot- **VTI$_1$** put blame on s.t.

atāwākē- **VAI$_1$** sell, sell things

atāwē- **VAI$_1$** buy, trade; buy s.t., trade s.t.

atāwēstamaw- **VTA$_2$** buy (it/him) for s.o.

atāwēwin- **NI$_1$** purchase; buying; [plural:] groceries, supplies

ati- **IPV** start to, begin to, beginning; progressively, proceed to, going on, progressing; on the way

atim- **VTA$_1$** catch up to s.o., overtake s.o.

atimosit- **NI$_1$** cactus, prickly-pear cactus [literally: "dog foot"]

atimw- **NA$_3$** dog; horse; beast of burden

atis- **VTI$_1$** tan s.t., dye s.t.

atoskāt- **VTA$_4$** work at or on s.o.

atoskē- **VAI$_1$** work, do work

atoskēmo- **VAI$_1$** employ people (e.g., for magic/medicine); get people to do things, hire people; ask to have s.t. repaired

atoskēwin- **NI$_1$** work, labour, employment, job; contract; industry

atot- **VTA$_4$** make a request of s.o., ask s.o. to do something; engage s.o. for something, employ s.o.; command s.o.

awa **PrA** this, this one

awas **IPJ** go on! go away! away with you! get out of my way!

awasēwē- **VAI$_1$** go behind an obstacle to vision, out of sight, disappear from view; the sun sets

awasitē **IPC** go on; go away; on, to the farther side (in time or space); beyond, farther over there

awāsis- **NA$_1$** child

awāsisīwi- **VAI$_1$** be a child

awēkā **IPC** or else, if you prefer

awēkā cī **IPH** or else

awihiwē- **VAI1** lend (it/him) to people; rent (it/him) out to people
awiya **PrA** someone
awiyak **PrA** someone, somebody
awīna **PrA** who, whose
awīna ōma **IPH** what is this!
awīniwa **PrA** who, whose
ay **IPJ** hey!
ay hay **IPJ** thank you
ay say **IPH** oh geez
ay- **IPV** [grammatical preverb: ongoing, continuing]
ay-astā- **VTI2** keep s.t. in place
ay-itinikē- **VAI1** be doing things thus
aya **IPC** ah, well, hmm
aya- **IPV** ah, well, hmm
ayah- **VTI1** cover s.t. with earth, bury s.t.; hoe s.t., hill s.t.
ayaha **PrI** those, those ones; thingamajigs [hesitatory particle replacing plural inanimate nouns]
ayahākonē- **VII2** be covered in snow, be covered by shovelled snow
ayakak **PrA** those, those ones; thingamajigs [hesitatory particle replacing plural animate nouns]
ayamihā- **VAI1** pray, say prayers; hold a church service, celebrate mass, attend mass, go to church; participate in a religious rite; follow a religion
ayamihāwin- **NI1** prayer, Christian prayer; praying, saying prayers, litany; church service; religious rite, religious observance; religion, religious denomination; the Roman Catholic church, Christian church
ayamihcikē- **VAI1** read, read things; go to school
ayamihēwi-kīsikā- **VII1** be Sunday, be the Sabbath [literally: "prayer-day"]
ayamihēwihkān- **NA1** minister, vicar; monk, brother; seminary student
ayamihēwiyiniw- **NA2** priest, minister, preacher, missionary, member of the clergy; Catholic priest
ayamihtā- **VTI2** read s.t.
ayamihtākosi- **VAI1** be heard in prayer, sound like one is praying
ayā- **VII2** be, be there, exist
ayā- **VAI1** be, be there, be located there; live there, stay there; exist
ayā- **VTI2** have s.t., own s.t.; have s.t. on
ayāw- **VTA1** have s.o., own s.o.; be pregnant with s.o., give birth to s.o.
ayēnānēw **IPC** eight, 8
ayēnānēwimitanaw **IPC** eighty, 80
ayētiski- **VAI1** leave tracks
ayi **NI4** one, thing [generally in compounds]
ayi **IPC** ah, well, hm
ayi- **IPV** ah, well, hm
ayihk **IPC** ah [often a hesitation for a locative form]
ayis **IPC** because, for; so be, cannot be changed

ayisiyiniw- NA2 person, human being; [plural:] people
ayisiyinīwi- VAI1 be a person, be a human being
ayisk IPC because, for
ayiwāk IPC more, more than, greater than, in excess, further; excessively, overly; [in numeral phrases:] plus
ayiw- NI2 one, thingy [hesitation for an inanimate noun]
ayiwin- NI1 article of clothing; [plural:] clothing, apparel
ayīk- NA1 frog, toad
ayīki-nōnācikanis- NI1 mushroom
ayīkitās- NA1 pitcher plant [literally: "frog-pants; frog-leggings"; Lat. *Sarracenia purpurea*]
ayōskan- NA1 raspberry
ayōskanāhtikw- NA3 raspberry bush [Lat. *Rubus* sp.]

ā

ā IPJ well
ā IPJ ah, oh [also: **āh**]
ācimiso- VAI1 tell about oneself, tell a story about oneself, talk about oneself; [figurative:] confess oneself, confess
ācimo- VAI1 tell, tell a story; tell news, give an account, narrate; tell one's own story
ācimostaw- VTA2 tell a story to s.o., tell news to s.o.; tell s.o. about (it/him), give s.o. an account
ācimowin- NI1 story, true story, account, report; news; what is being told
ācisin- VAI2 be blocked
āh IPJ ah, oh, och! well! [also: **ā**]
āh- IPV [grammatical preverb: intermittent, repeatedly; again and again; here and there]
āha IPJ yes; as I told you [cf. **ēha, ēha'**]
āhay IPJ yes; agreed
āhā IPJ yes; agreed [cf. **āha, ēha, ēha'; ahāw, hāw, āw**]
āhā IPJ oho!, holy!
āhci piko IPH still, nevertheless; despite the odds; in spite of; all the more
āhki itāp IPH as if, pretendingly
āhkoh- VTA1 give s.o. a sharp pain, give s.o. a great deal of pain; hurt s.o.
āhkosiwin- NI1 illness, sickness, disease
āhkosīskaw- VTA2 make s.o. sick
āhkosīwikamikw- NI3 hospital
āhkwakihtē- VII2 be expensive, cost dearly; cost more, be worth a top-up amount
āhkwakiso- VAI1 be expensive or costly
āhkwatihtā- VTI2 freeze s.t.; let s.t. freeze
āhtokē- VAI1 move camp, move one's camp elsewhere
ākacac- NA1 Akachuk [personal name]
ākawāsonamā- VAI1 shade one's own eyes
ākayāsīmo- VAI1 speak English
ākayāsīmototaw- VTA2 speak English to s.o.

ākwā- IPV quite a lot; well on its way, in progress of time

ākwāskam IPC really, rather; overanxious; [in negative clauses:] not really, not as much

āmow- NA_2 bee, honeybee; wasp

āmowi-maskihkiy- NI_2 bee medicine, bee-sting medicine

āniskowaskos- NI_1 horsetail; bullrush, reed

ānwēyim- VTA_1 refuse s.o., reject s.o.

āpacih- VTA_1 use s.o., make use of s.o. (e.g., porcupine quills), find s.o. useful; cure s.o.

āpacihtamōh- VTA_1 make s.o. use (it/him), give (it/him) to s.o. to use; use (it/him) for s.o., use (it/him) on s.o.

āpacihtā- VTI_2 use s.t., make use of s.t.

āpatan- VII_2 be used, be useful

āpatisi- VAI_1 be used, be useful; be required

āpihtaw IPC half, ½, in half, halfway

āpihtawikosisān- NA_1 Métis, Métis person

āpihtawikosisānis- NA_1 small Métis person, young Métis person

āpihtā- IPV half

āpihtā-pipon- VII_1 be midwinter

āpihtā-piponi-pīsimw- NA_3 Mid-Winter Moon; January

āpisihkwasi- VAI_1 awaken from sleep, revive from sleep; come fully awake; awaken from a nightmare

āpocikwānī- VAI_1 somersault, do a somersault

āsay IPC already; without delay

āsay cī IPH already? are you ready?

āsitēm- VTA_1 call s.o. back, respond back to s.o.

āskaw IPC once in a while, from time to time, sometimes

āstam IPJ come here!

āstamita IPC later, more recently; on this side, closer; on the hither side (in time or space); this way over

āstē-ayā- VAI_1 recover from illness, be gradually restored, have one's condition improve

āstēpayi- VAI_1 feel better (in health); be healed, recuperate

āstēskaw- VTA_2 make s.o. feel better, improve s.o.'s health; settle s.o.

āta IPC although, even though, in vain; on the other hand

āta wiya IPH though, although; nonetheless, anyway

āta- IPV although, on the other hand; in vain

ātawiya IPC though, although; nonetheless, anyway

ātayōhkē- VAI_1 tell a sacred story or legend

ātayōhkēwin- NI_1 sacred story, legend

ātiht IPC some

āw IPJ ah, oh

āw IPJ all right, okay, fine, let's go

āwacitāpē- VAI_1 pull s.t., drag s.t. home (e.g., wood), haul s.t. dragging

āyiman- **VII2** be difficult
āyimāc **IPC** with difficulty, barely, scarcely
āyītahpit- **VTI1** tie s.t. tightly, fasten s.t. firmly

c

ca- **IPV** [grammatical particle: ongoing, continuing]
cahkipēhikanis- **NA1** syllabic symbol; Cree syllabic final, diacritical mark in the Cree syllabary; [plural:] the Syllabics, the Cree syllabary
cēhcapācikanis- **NI1** bicycle, small bike
cēskwa **IPC** wait, wait a minute; presently, yet; soon; in the future; [in negative constructions:] not yet
cihcipipayi- **VAI1** operate a wheeled vehicle; ride a bicycle
cimacēs- **NI1** fence post, picket
cimacikātē- **VII2** be erected, be set up (e.g., sweatlodge)
cimaso- **VAI1** stand upright (e.g., tree), stand erect
cimatā- **VTI2** place s.t. upright, plant s.t. upright; stand s.t. up, erect s.t.
cimatē- **VII2** stand upright (e.g., tipi), stand erect; be erected
cimisisi- **VAI1** be short of stature; be very short
cipahikēsi- **VAI1** pay a bit, pay a small amount; measure a small amount
ciscēmās- **NA1** tobacco, small amount of tobacco, a small pouch of tobacco
cistēmāw- **NA2** tobacco [also: **kistēmāw-**]
cī **IPC** [question marker: "is it the case that"; enclitic follows questioned element in initial position; sometimes also used as tag question marker]
cīhkēyiht- **VTI1** like s.t., approve of s.t., be happy with s.t.; be eager for s.t., eagerly participate in s.t.; be proud of s.t.
cīkahikanāhtikw- **NI3** axe handle
cīpokiniy- **NA2** pointed rosehip, pointed rose-bush berry
cīposi- **VAI1** be pointed; be a pear (i.e., fruit)
cīstahikan- **NI1** hay fork; spear, lance, harpoon; tent peg; awl; inoculation needle
cīstahiso- **VAI1** give oneself an injection; inject oneself (e.g., drugs)
cīsw- **VTA3** sting s.o. (i.e., a bee), prick s.o.

ē

ē- **IPV** [grammatical preverb: complementizer; defines a changed conjunct clause]
ē-iskwēcic **INM** Girlie; maternal aunt of Mary Louise Rockthunder [personal name]
ē-pwācis **INM** Little Sioux, the grandfather (father's mother's older sister's husband) of Mary Louise Rockthunder [personal name]

ēcika ana IPH what is that!; so that's it
ēcika ani IPH as it turns out, apparently, evidently, indeed; so that's it; so be
ēcika ōma IPH what is this!; and so it appears
ēēh IPJ [expression indicating someone is joking around; produced with considerable nasalization]
ēh IPJ well
ēha IPJ yes [cf. **āha, ēha'**]
ēha' IPJ yes [cf. **āha, ēha**]
ēhāhā IPJ hey; well, look at that [expressive interjection of discovery]
ēkamā IPC there is not, it is not the case
ēkā IPC no; not; don't; not to [negator in certain conjunct clauses]
ēkā awiyak IPH no-one, nobody
ēkā cī IPH or, or maybe
ēkā kīkway IPH nothing, not, not at all, not any
ēkā wiya IPH it is not the case [emphatic negator in conjunct clauses]
ēkā wīhkāc IPH never, not ever
ēkāwiya IPC no; not; don't, don't you dare [negator in conjunct and imperative clauses]
ēkāy IPC not; don't [negator in conjunct and imperative clauses]
ēkāy kīkway IPH nothing, not, not at all, not any
ēkāya IPC not; don't [negator in conjunct and imperative clauses]
ēko cī IPH is that it?; is that the one?
ēkoni PrA this, this is the one; those, those are the ones (previously mentioned)
ēkoni PrI those, those are the ones (previously mentioned)
ēkoni anihi PrI those are the ones (previously mentioned)
ēkoni ōhi PrI those are the ones (previously mentioned)
ēkonik PrA those, those are the ones (previously mentioned)
ēkonik aniki PrA those are the ones (previously mentioned)
ēkosi IPC so, thus, in that way; right, alright; there, that's it, that is all; well; enough; later
ēkosi isi IPH just so, like that; thus, in that way; that is how it is
ēkospī IPC then; at that time; in the past
ēkospīhk IPC then, at that time; since
ēkota IPC there, right there; at that very place
ēkotē IPC over there; a place in that direction
ēkotowa IPC of that kind, like that
ēkotowahk IPC of that kind, like that
ēkotowi IPC in that place, a place like that, in such a place

ēkotowihk IPC in that place, a place like that, in such a place
ēkwa IPC and, also; then; now; let's go
ēkwa ani IPH it was then; well, that's it [concluding statement]
ēkwa mīna IPH and now; also
ēkwayāc IPC only now, for the first time; just then, only then, not until then
ēkwayāk IPC only now, for the first time; just then, only then, not until then
ēkwayikohk IPC that much, to that extent, up to that point; enough; not so, not as [negative comparative]
ēkwāni IPC that's the end, that's all
ēsa IPC I understand; apparently, reportedly, so it appears, evidently; this one; because of something [information received from others; reference to time past]
ētataw IPC barely, scarcely, barely enough; not hardly [commenting on someone's inability to do something due to a hindrance of some kind]
ētikwē IPC apparently, I guess, I suppose, supposedly, presumably; maybe, perhaps; about (doubtful) [dubitative; personal inference]
ētokē IPC I wonder, I don't know [dubitative; personal inference]
ētokwē IPC maybe, I guess, presumably, perhaps; about (doubtful) [dubitative; personal inference]
ēwako PrA this (previously mentioned), that one; the same one
ēwako PrI this (previously mentioned), that one; the same one
ēwako ana PrA that is the one (previously mentioned) [also: *ēwakw āna*]
ēwako ani IPH and so after that [also: *ēwakw āni, ēwakwāni*]
ēwako anima PrI that is the one (previously mentioned) [also: *ēwakw ānima*]
ēwako awa PrA this is the one (previously mentioned) [also: *ēwakw āwa*]
ēwako ohci IPC that's the reason, that's why [also: *ēwak ōhci*]
ēwako ōma PrI this same one (previously mentioned) [also: *ēwak ōma*]
ēwakoni PrA this, this is the one; those, those are the ones (previously mentioned)
ēwakoni PrI those, those are the ones (previously mentioned)
ēwakoni anihi PrI those, those are the ones (previously mentioned) [also: *ēwakon ānihi*]
ēwakonik PrA those, those are the ones (previously mentioned)

ēwakonik aniki PrA those, those are the ones (previously mentioned)
ēwakonik ōki PrA these, these are the ones (previously mentioned)
ēwakoyikohk IPC that much, to that extent; that's enough
ēy IPJ hey! [introductory]; my goodness! [exclamatory]
ēy hēy IPJ oh hey, what is that?
ēyiwēhk IPC anyway, nevertheless; to a fair extent, as well as may be, better than nothing; so-so; despite shortcomings

h

ha IPJ ha, so [interjection; can be used when something happens to someone despite repeated warnings]
hay IPJ whoa, well, oh my [expression of frustration]
hā IPJ oh! hah! there!
hām IPJ now then; all right, okay! [hortatory, indicating readiness or impatience]
hāw IPJ now then; ready, all right, let's go, come on; see here; well [hortatory, indicating readiness or impatience]
hēh IPJ hey [exclamatory, denotes surprise]
hēy IPJ hey [introductory; exclamatory]

i

ici IPC then, later, afterward, subsequently
ihkin- VII2 happen, occur, take place
ihtako- VAI1 exist, be there; be born (e.g., infant)
ihtakon- VII2 exist, be there
ihtasi- VAI1 have a family, be so many in a family; be so many
inito- IPN common, plain, ordinary [cf. **iyinito-**]
isi IPC so, thus, this way; there; to, towards, in the direction of, in such direction
isi- IPV so, this way, thus, such; there, thither, in such direction
isi-ayā- VAI1 be thus, be in such a state, be in such shape; be thus in health, be unwell, be in poor health, be out of sorts
isi-mawimoscikēwin- NI1 such a ceremony
isi-mīcisowin- NI1 diet, eating in such a way
isiki- VAI1 grow so, grow in such a way
isinākwan- VII2 look thus, give such an appearance (e.g., colour, etc.), appear so
isiniskē- VAI1 have one's own arm thither or thus, move one's hand so, make such a gesture with one's hand; make hand signs, use sign language
isitēhē- VAI1 have such a heart, be thus predisposed to compassion
isiyihkāso- VAI1 be named thus, be called so, have such a name

isiyihkāt- **VTI$_1$** call s.t. thus, give s.t. such a name; use such a name for s.t.

isiyihkāt- **VTA$_4$** call s.o. thus, give s.o. such a name; use such a name for s.o.

isiyihkātē- **VII$_2$** be called thus, have such a name

isiyihkātiso- **VAI$_1$** call oneself so, name oneself so

isīhcikāt- **VTI$_1$** do things thus for s.t., proceed thus for s.t.

isīhcikē- **VAI$_1$** do things thus, proceed thus, settle things thus; make things thus, shape things thus; perform a ceremony thus, perform such a ritual; make a feast or banquet; throw a party

isīhcikēwin- **NI$_1$** culture; ritual, such rite; the doing so, what is thus done, such activities; act; feast, banquet; resource

isīho- **VAI$_1$** be thus dressed, be thus equipped; dress oneself so

isko **IPC** so far, to such a point, to such an extent; as far as, up until, until; this far

iskon- **VTA$_1$** pull s.t. up so far, hold s.o. up to such an extent

iskotēw- **NI$_2$** fire, hearth-fire, home-fire; embers

iskwāhtēm- NI$_1$ door

iskwēs- **NA$_1$** teenage girl, little girl

iskwēsis- **NA$_1$** girl, little girl, female infant

iskwēsisiwi- **VAI$_1$** be a little girl

iskwēw- **NA$_2$** woman, female, adult female

iskwēwi- **VAI$_1$** be a woman, be female, reach womanhood, become a woman

iskwēyāc **IPC** last, at last, finally; to the end, to the last, at the end of it all; the last one, the last time; youngest

ispatinaw- **NI$_2$** hill; hilly region

ispayi- **VAI$_1$** be thus affected, have such an experience; be thus afflicted; fare thus; go, go there; ride, drive, travel thus or there; move along

ispayi- **VII$_2$** take place thus, occur thus; go thither or thus, travel there; have passed (e.g., days, years), come by, go by; run thus (in a cycle), be there (in a cycle), come around (in a cycle)

ispayiho- **VAI$_1$** throw oneself thither or thus; move toward there quickly

ispayin- **VII$_2$** be, become; go there; happen thus, occur thus, take place thus; run thus (in a cycle), be there (in a cycle), come around (in a cycle), be that time again; come by, go by, have passed (e.g., days, years)

ispāskwēyā- **VII$_2$** be a high, thick-wooded area

ispi- **IPV** high, elevated, advanced

ispi-pīkiskwē- **VAI$_1$** use high speech, speak using advanced language

ispici- **VAI$_1$** move there, move camp thither, move one's household there

ispimihk IPC up, up above; in the air, on high, high up; upstairs

ispit- VTI1 pull s.t. thither or thus, draw s.t. thither or thus, bring s.t. hither; pull a trailer

ispitamāso- VAI1 pull (it/him) thither or thus for oneself

ispī IPC then, at such a time; when; until

ispīhcā- VII2 extend so far, be of such size (e.g., country), reach so far as land; be so big, large, or long

ispīhk IPC then, at such a time; when; until

ispīhtisī- VAI1 be such in age, be so many years old; extend thus

ita IPC there; where; there where; exactly there

itahkamikan- VII2 be an event, a happening; be done thus; happen thus; go on that way, work thus

itahkamikisi- VAI1 do things thus, behave thus; busy oneself thus, work thus, be thus occupied; go on that way

itahpiso- VAI1 be so tied, be harnessed thus

itahpit- VTI1 tie s.t. so

itahtopiponē- VAI1 be so old, be so many winters old

itahtopiponwē- VAI1 be so old, be so many winters old

itakihcikē- VAI1 value things so; fix a price; count so

itakocin- VAI2 hang thus or there, be suspended thus or there; fly thus or there, travel (by motor)

itakotē- VII2 hang thither or thus, be suspended thither or thus; fly thither or thus

it- VTI1 say thus to or about s.t.; call s.t. thus

it- VTA5 say thus to s.o., say thus about s.o.; call s.o. thus

itamahciho- VAI1 feel thus, be in such health

itamon- VII2 hang thus, be thus attached, be mounted thus; run thus (e.g., road); go in such a direction

itapi- VAI1 sit thus or there, be present thus or there; be thus placed; hold office thus or there

itastā- VTI2 place s.t. thus or there

itastē- VII2 be placed thus or there, be located thus or there; be written thus

itatoskē- VAI1 work thus or there

itāciho- VAI1 travel there or thus; lead one's life thus

itācimo- VAI1 tell thus, narrate thus; tell such a story, tell news thus

itācimostaw- VTA2 tell s.o. thus about (it); narrate thus to s.o., tell s.o. such a story, give s.o. such an account

itāmihk IPC beneath, under, underneath; inside (e.g., clothing); deep down

itāmo- VAI1 flee there or thus, seek such refuge

itāpacih- VTA1 use s.o. thus, make such use of s.o., find s.o. thus useful

itāpacihcikan- NI1 such tool, tool of such purpose

itāpacihtā- VTI2 use s.t. thus, make such use of s.t.

itāpatan- VII2 be thus used, be of such use, be useful

itāpatisi- VAI1 be useful, be used thus, be of such use

itāpi- VAI1 look thus or there; take aim thus or there

itāskiskotē- VII2 hang thick and heavy [sic?]

itāskonikē- VAI1 point the pipe or pipestem; hold a pipe ceremony

itātayōhkē- VAI1 tell a sacred story in such a way

itē IPC there, thereabouts, over there, thither, wherever

itēhkē IPC in that direction

itēyiht- VTI1 think thus of or about s.t., regard s.t. thus

itēyihtākwan- VII2 be thus thought of, be thus considered

itēyimo- VAI1 think thus of oneself; think of (it/him) for oneself, have (it/him) in mind for oneself

itihkasw- VTA3 cook s.o. thus

itiht- VTI1 hear s.t. thus

itin- VTA1 move s.o. thither or thus by hand; hold s.o. thus

itinikē- VAI1 act thus, fare thus, do things thus; experience such things; get into such (e.g., deplorable) things

itis- VTI1 cut s.t. thus

itisahamaw- VTA2 send (it/him) to s.o. thus or there; drive (it/him) thither to s.o.

itisahw- VTA3 send s.o. thus or there; drive s.o. thither

itiskaw- VTA2 have such an effect on s.o., leave s.o. thus affected

itohtah- VTA1 take s.o. thus or there, lead s.o. thither; go there with s.o.

itohtatamaw- VTA2 take (it/him) there to or for s.o.

itohtatā- VTI2 take s.t. there, go there with s.t.

itohtē- VAI1 go, go there or thus

itowa IPC this kind, a certain kind

itowahk IPC this kind, a certain kind

itōcikātē- VII2 be done, be done so; be customary

itōt- VTI1 do s.t. thus, do thus, act thus; make s.t.

itōtaw- VTA2 do thus to s.o., treat s.o. thus

itwāt- VTI1 say s.t. so, say s.t. thus

itwē- VAI1 say so, say thus, call (it) so; have such a meaning

itwēstamaw- VTA2 say so for s.o.; speak for s.o.; interpret for s.o.; translate for s.o.; speak on behalf of s.o. (in making a date or betrothal); relay s.o.'s message, transmit s.o.'s message

iyāyaw IPC instead, by preference; first thing, preferably, rather; eagerly, with full intent

iyikohk IPC so much, to such a degree, to such an extent; until, when time comes; more

iyinito- **IPN** common, plain, ordinary {cf. **inito-**}
iyinito- **IPV** common, plain, ordinary, regular
iyinito-ayisiyinīwiwin- **NI1** Indigeneity, being Indigenous
iyinito-isīho- **VAI1** wear ordinary clothing; wear traditional Indigenous clothing
iyinito-pahkwēsikan- **NA1** bannock
iyinito-pimiy- **NI2** ordinary grease; less easily congealed, found especially in association with muscle tissue, and including bone marrow or "marrow-fat"
iyinito-sōniyāw- **NA2** cash, money
iyinitwaskisin- **NI1** moccasin, traditional Indigenous footwear [also: *iyinito-maskisina*]
iyinīsi- **VAI1** be clever, be smart, be intelligent; be wise

ī

ī **IPJ** lo! look! behold!
īh **IPJ** lo! look! behold!
īhī **IPJ** oh my, geez!; enemy in sight!

k

k-ōh- **IPV** [grammatical preverb; defines a changed conjunct clause; often negative (i.e., "who didn't, which didn't, where not, when not"), or reason (i.e., "why")]
k-ōh-kī- **IPV** [grammatical preverb; defines a changed conjunct clause; negative reason (i.e., "why not")]
k-ōskotākāt **INM** Catholic, a Catholic priest [literally: "one with a robe"; also: *kā-oskotākāt*; cf. **oskotākā-**]
ka- **IPV** [grammatical preverb: future "will, shall"; irrealis; infinitive "to, in order to"; optative "ought, should"]
ka- **IPV** [grammatical preverb: ongoing, continuing]
ka-kī- **IPV** can, be able to; may; should, ought to
kacāc **IPC** insistently, deliberately; be opportune [in negative clauses:] necessarily, just in this way
kacāt **IPC** insistently, deliberately; be opportune [in negative clauses:] necessarily, just in this way
kahkiyaw **IPC** all, every; entire, the full amount
kahkiyaw kīkway **PR** everything, all things
kakāyawātisi- **VAI1** be diligent, be hard-working, be of industrious disposition; be active, be agile, be energetic
kakēskim- **VTA1** lecture s.o., counsel s.o., give s.o. advice; preach to s.o.
kakēskwē- **VAI1** preach
kakwāhyakih- **VTA1** do (s.t.) outrageous to s.o., do a terrible thing to s.o., mistreat s.o. greatly; betray s.o., scheme against s.o.

kakwātakih- **VTA1** distress s.o., torment s.o., torture s.o., make s.o. suffer; mistreat s.o., be abusive to s.o., be mean to s.o.; affect s.o. terribly (e.g., as a disease), ravage s.o. (e.g., as a disease)

kakwātakihtā- **VTI2** suffer, be distressed; suffer because of s.t., have difficulties because of s.t.; experience a crisis (e.g., in the course of an illness)

kakwāyakakotē- **VII2** hang in great numbers

kakwāyakēyatin- **VII2** be in vast numbers

kakwāyakihiso- **VAI1** do (s.t.) outrageous to oneself, do a terrible thing to oneself, mistreat oneself greatly

kakwāyakiho- **VAI1** be in a terrible state, be in a frenzy

kakwē- **IPV** try to, attempt to; circumstances permitting, by divine grace

kakwēcihkēmo- **VAI1** ask, inquire, ask people; ask for s.t., ask questions of people

kakwēcim- **VTA1** ask s.o., ask s.o. a question; make a request of s.o.; ask s.o. about (it/them)

kanakē **IPC** at least; even if only; for a short while

kanawāpahkē- **VAI1** observe, observe people, watch people, watch things

kanawāpaht- **VTI1** look at s.t., observe s.t.; watch s.t., view s.t.

kanawāpam- **VTA1** look at s.o., watch s.o., observe s.o.; look after s.o.

kanawēyiht- **VTI1** keep s.t., preserve s.t., store s.t.; look after s.t., take care of s.t., guard s.o. closely

kanawēyihtamāso- **VAI1** keep (it/him) for oneself; take good care of (it/him) for oneself, look after (it/him) for oneself

kanawēyim- **VTA1** look after s.o., take care of s.o., tend s.o., keep s.o., guard s.o. closely

kanātisi- **VAI1** be clean, be tidy

kani **IPC** oh yes, I just remembered, I had forgotten; of course, come to think, now that I remember

kanihk **IPC** oh yes, I just remembered, I had forgotten; of course, come to think, now that I remember

kapē-kīsik **IPC** all day, all day long, throughout the day

kaskāpas- **VTI1** smoke s.t.; treat s.t. (e.g., hide) with smoke

kaskihcikē- **VAI1** manage things, control things; be able to do things, be competent at things; earn a salary, command an income

kaskih- **VTA1** be able to deal with s.o.; manage s.o., control s.o., convince s.o., make s.o. do something, prevail upon s.o., win s.o. over, succeed in imposing one's will on s.o.;

earn s.o. (i.e., money); be able to seduce s.o.
kaskiho- **VAI1** have the ability to do s.t., be able, be competent; succeed; escape
kaskihtamāso- **VAI1** be able to do for oneself, accomplish (it) for oneself, get (it) for oneself, earn (it) for oneself; deserve what one gets (good or bad); make money for oneself
kaskihtā- **VTI2** manage s.t., control s.t.; be able to do s.t., be competent at s.t.
kaskikwāso- **VAI1** sew, do one's own sewing; sew s.t.; stitch
kaskikwāsonākan- **NI1** sewing machine
kaskikwāt- **VTI1** sew s.t., sew s.t. up
kaskikwātamaw- **VTA2** sew (it/him) for s.o.
kaskikwātē- **VII2** be sewn
kaskipit- **VTI1** tie s.t. shut
kaskitēsi- **VAI1** be black
kaskitēwā- **VII2** be black
kaskitēwisīho- **VAI1** dress in black
katawa **IPC** properly
katāc **IPC** insistently, deliberately; be opportune [in negative clauses:] necessarily, just in this way
kawah- **VTI1** chop s.t. down, fell s.t.
kawahikē- **VAI1** chop down trees
kawisimo- **VAI1** go to bed, lie down; get ready for bed
kayās **IPC** long ago, of old, in earlier days; previously
kayāsēs **IPC** a while ago; quite some time ago, quite long ago, formerly
kayēyisi- **VAI1** cheat, be sly
kā- **IPV** [grammatical preverb; defines a changed conjunct clause; often a relative clause, i.e., "who, which, where, when"]
kā-mihcētwāniskwēyāk **INM** plant unidentified in English [a plant with hair-like roots; literally: "that with many strands, that with much hair"]
kāh- **IPV** would, ought to; could; likely to
kāh- **IPV** [grammatical preverb: intermittent, repeatedly; again and again; here and there; augmentative]
kāhcitin- **VTI1** catch s.t., procure s.t., obtain s.t.; hold s.t., seize s.t.; reach s.t., get s.t. with effort by hand, get s.t. back
kāhkēwakos- **NI1** small piece of dried venison, dried meat
kāhkēwakw- **NI3** dried meat, dried venison; piece of dried meat, sheet of dried meat
kāhkwēyihto- **VAI1** be jealous of one another
kākikē **IPC** forever, at all times, always; for a very long time
kākikēpakw- **NI3** muskeg tea, Labrador tea [literally: "forever-plants"; Lat. *Rhododendron neoglandulosum*; also: *maskēkopakw-*]

kākīsimototaw- VTA2 supplicate s.o., pray to s.o.; chant prayers over s.o., chant prayers for s.o.

kākīsimo- VAI1 pray, plead, chant prayers; supplicate the spirits with humility

kākīsimowin- NI1 prayer, chant; praying, praying in a traditional manner, chanting prayers, supplication of the spirits

kāmwātan- VII2 be quiet, be quiet and peaceful, be serene; be melancholy, be depressing, be sad; be an isolated place

kānikanā IPC may it be that

kāsakēwaskw- NI3 licorice [literally: "greedy-herb; glutton-herb"; Lat. *Glycyrrhiza glabra*]

kāsā- VII2 be sharp

kāsīhkahtē- VII2 burn clear, be cleared by burning

kāsīhkas- VTI1 burn s.t. clear, clear s.t. by burning

kāsīhkasikātē- VII2 be burned clear, be cleared by burning

kāskah- VTI1 scrape s.t., scrape s.t. off

kāspi- IPN crunchy

kāspi-pahkwēsikan- NA1 biscuit

kāspisikan- NI1 coffee

kāwi IPC again; back, in return

kāwiya IPC don't; no; not [used in conjunct and imperative clauses]

kāya IPC no, not; do not, don't [used in conjunct and imperative clauses]

kē- IPV [grammatical preverb; future, conditional: "shall"; defines a changed conjunct clause]

kēcikon- VTI1 take s.t. off (e.g., clothing, glasses)

kēcikopit- VTI1 pull s.t. free, pull s.t. out; take s.t. off by pulling; pull out of s.t.

kēhcinā IPC of course, for sure, for certain; certainly, surely, I assure you; perhaps, maybe

kēhcināc IPC of course, for sure, for certain; certainly, surely, I assure you; perhaps, maybe

kēhciwāk IPC near, nearby; without mediation, by immediate contact

kēhtē-ay- NA4 elder, old one, old person; the old [singular: *kēhtē-aya*]

kēhtē-ayiwi- VAI1 be an elder, be old, be an old person, be in one's old age; get old

kēhtinā IPC of course, for sure, for certain; certainly, surely, I assure you; perhaps, maybe

kēkā-mitātaht IPC nine, 9

kēkāc IPC almost, just about, nearly

kēkāt IPC just about, almost

kēscināc IPC of course, for sure, for certain; certainly, surely, I assure you; perhaps, maybe

kētahtawē IPC at times, sometimes, once in a while; sometime, in the future;

at one time, all at once, suddenly
kētaskisinē- **VAI**$_1$ take off one's own shoes (moccasins, boots, etc.)
kēyakiciskēhiwē- **VAI**$_1$ give people itchy anuses, cause people to have itchy anuses
kēyakiciskēsīs- **NA**$_1$ Little Butt Itcher; legendary second name of rosehips
kēyakiciskēskaw- **VTA**$_2$ give s.o. an itchy bum, make s.o. have an itchy anus
kēyakiciskē- **VAI**$_1$ have an itchy bum, have an itchy anus
kēyakisi- **VAI**$_1$ itch, be itchy
kēyāpic **IPC** still, yet, in continuity, once again, once more, some more, more; furthermore
kēyāpit **IPC** still, more
kihc- **IPV** [see **kihci-**]
kihcēyiht- **VTI**$_1$ respect s.t.; think highly of s.t., hold s.t. in high regard; hold s.t. sacred; be proud of s.t.
kihcēyihtākwan- **VII**$_2$ be respected; be highly thought of; be held sacred; be of the utmost importance; be venerable
kihcēyim- **VTA**$_1$ respect s.o.; think highly of s.o., hold s.o. in high regard, have high esteem for s.o.
kihci- **IPN** great, big
kihci- **IPV** great, big, important; greatly; formally
kihci-āpatan- **VII**$_2$ be very important, be highly useful, be of great use
kihci-itēyiht- **VTI**$_1$ think highly of s.t., have important thoughts
kihci-maskihkiy- **NI**$_2$ important medicine, great medicine
kihci-mīkiwāhp- **NI**$_1$ great lodge, large tipi
kihci-okimāw- **NA**$_2$ king; grand chief; important official; government
kihci-wīkim- **VTA**$_1$ marry s.o. formally, marry s.o. in church
kihci-wīwimāw- **NA**$_2$ favoured wife
kihciniskēhk **IPC** right, the right side; at the right, on the right hand, to the right
kika- **IPV** [grammatical preverb; future; defines a conjunct clause]
kikahpit- **VTI**$_1$ have s.t. tied on, wear s.t. tied on
kikamo- **VII**$_2$ be attached; have a fixed place
kikamo- **VAI**$_1$ cling, stick; be fastened on; have a fixed place (e.g., star)
kikamohtā- **VTI**$_2$ fasten s.t. on, attach s.t.; put s.t. on something
kikamon- **VII**$_2$ be attached, be fastened; be on something
kikasikanē- **VAI**$_1$ wear (one's own) socks, have (one's own) socks on
kiki **IPC** for, with, along with, in addition to
kiki- **IPV** along with
kikisk- **VTI**$_1$ wear s.t.; have s.t. as an intimate possession;

carry s.t. within oneself (e.g., blood)

kikiskikan- **NI**$_1$ article of clothing

kimiwanāpoy- **NI**$_2$ rainwater

kimosōminaw **NDA**$_1$ Our Grandfather, The Sun

kimotamaw- **VTA**$_2$ steal (it/him) from s.o., rob s.o. of (it/him)

kimoti- **VAI**$_1$ steal (it/him); be a thief

kimotiwin- **NI**$_1$ theft, stealing, robbery; thing stolen, swag

kinanāskomitin **IPJ** thank you, I am grateful to you

kinēpikōmin- **NI**$_1$ berry unidentified in English [literally: "snake-berry"]

kinēpikw- **NA**$_3$ snake

kinosi- **VAI**$_1$ be long, be tall

kinwā- **VII**$_2$ be long, be tall

kinwēs **IPC** a long while; for a long time

kinwēsīs **IPC** for a while, for quite a long time

kipah- **VTI**$_1$ close s.t., shut s.t.; obstruct s.t.; close s.t. off, shut s.t. off (e.g., recording device)

kipahikanihk **INM** Fort Qu'Appelle, SK; [literally: "at the enclosure" (i.e., "at the weir; at the fort; at the jail")]

kipiskaw- **VTA**$_2$ block s.o.'s way bodily, stand in s.o.'s way, hinder s.o.

kipwahpit- **VTI**$_1$ tie s.t. shut, tie s.t. closed in (in a sack); pull s.t. closed

kisākamitēwāpoy- **NI**$_2$ hot water

kisāstaw **IPC** sort of, kind of, to appearance, by seeming; roughly like, resembling; it might be, as if, as though

kisē-manitow- **NA**$_2$ the Creator; Great Spirit, God, the compassionate God; [Christian:] Merciful God

kisēyiniw- **NA**$_2$ old man, male elder

kisitē- **VII**$_2$ be hot; be warmed up, be heated up; be a hot compress

kisiwāh- **VTA**$_1$ anger s.o., make s.o. angry

kisiwāk **IPC** near, nearby, close by

kisiwāsi- **VAI**$_1$ be angry, be mad

kisī- **IPV** angrily, in anger

kisī-kitot- **VTA**$_4$ speak to s.o. in anger, speak angrily to s.o.

kisīm- **VTA**$_1$ anger s.o. by speech

kisīpēkin- **VTA**$_1$ wash s.o.; bathe s.o.

kisīpēkistikwānē- **VAI**$_1$ wash one's own head, wash one's own hair

kisīpēkiyākanē- **VAI**$_1$ wash dishes

kiskēyiht- **VTI**$_1$ know s.t., know s.t. of one's own experience; have knowledge; find s.t. out, experience s.t.

kiskēyihtāsowin- **NI**$_1$ information; education, schooling

kiskēyim- **VTA**$_1$ know s.o., know about s.o.

kiskinohamaw- **VTA**$_2$ teach s.o., teach (it) to s.o.

kiskinohamākē- **VAI1** teach, teach things, teach (it) to people

kiskinwahamaw- **VTA2** teach s.o., teach (it) to s.o.

kiskinwahamākē- **VAI1** teach, teach things, teach (it) to people

kiskinwahamākēw- **NA2** teacher

kiskinwahamākosi- **VAI1** learns; be a student, attend school; be taught

kiskinwahamāso- **VAI1** be taught, be in school, attend school, be a student; teach (it to) oneself

kiskinwahamātowikamikw- **NI3** school, schoolhouse

kiskinwahamātowin- **NI1** teaching one another, learning, schooling; education; education system, school board

kiskisi- **VAI1** remember, remember s.t.; recall

kistēmāw- **NA2** tobacco [also: **cistēmāw-**]

kistikān- **NI1** field, arable land; farm; garden; potato; vegetable

kistikē- **VAI1** farm, farm the land; plant things, seed things, do the seeding, do the planting; harvest

kispēw **IPC** even so, even though, despite the fact; nevertheless

kita- **IPV** [grammatical preverb]; future: "will, shall"; infinitive; optative: "ought, should"

kita-kī- **IPV** can, be able to; may; should, ought to

kitatamihin **IPJ** thank you, you make me smile, you please me [cf. **atamih-** VTA1]

kitā- **VTI2** eat all of s.t.; eat s.t. up, devour s.t. completely, eat all of the food; drink all of s.t., finish drinking a bottle of s.t.; drink an entire bottle; consume s.t. entirely

kitimah- **VTA1** be rough on s.o.; treat s.o. badly, treat s.o. cruelly; be mean to s.o., bring misery upon s.o.; ruin s.o., reduce s.o. to ruin, destroy s.o.

kitimahiso- **VAI1** ruin oneself, be mean to oneself, treat oneself badly, treat oneself cruelly; hurt oneself

kitimahtā- **VTI2** be cruel to s.t., be rough on s.t.; treat s.t. badly, treat s.t. cruelly; ruin s.t., reduce s.t. to ruin, destroy s.t.

kitimākan- **VII2** be in a state of destitution, be a poor area; be pitiable, be miserable, be a sorry situation, be an unfortunate situation

kitimākaskasiwē- **VAI1** be the poor departed; depart the world leaving those behind in a pitiful state

kitimākēyim- **VTA1** pity s.o., feel pity for s.o., take pity on s.o., think of s.o. with compassion; feel sorry for s.o.; have sympathy for s.o.; be kind to s.o.; love s.o.; bless s.o.

kitimāki-ayihti- **VAI1** behave pitifully, behave in a pitiful manner

kitimākihtaw- **VTA2** hear s.o. with pity; feel sorry for s.o. upon hearing circumstances; listen to s.o. with pity, listen to s.o. with compassion

kitimākinaw- **VTA2** pity s.o., take pity on s.o., look with pity upon s.o., look with compassion on s.o., feel sorry for s.o.; lovingly tend s.o.; regard s.o. with respect

kitimākisi- **VAI1** be poor; be pitiable, be miserable; be unfortunate, be desolate, be destitute; have an impoverished attitude or lifestyle; have a bad attitude

kitimākisīho- **VAI1** dress pitifully, dress in a pitiful state

kitot- **VTA4** address s.o., talk to s.o., speak to s.o.; lecture s.o.; rebuke s.o., reprimand s.o., bawl s.o. out

kitowēyēkihcikē- **VAI1** make a rustling noise with paper, rustle papers

kitowēyēkipayi- **VII2** rustle noisily (as paper or cloth)

kiya **PrA** you

kiyakisi- **VAI1** itch, be itchy

kiyawāw **PrA** you

kiyām **IPJ** oh well, it's okay, never mind, think nothing of it; so much for this; anyway, rather; let it be, let there be no further delay; please; let's go then; do so; quietly

kiyāmapi- **VAI1** be quiet, keep quiet, sit quietly, sit still

kiyānaw **PrA** we, us, our; you and I, you and we

kiyāskiw **VAI1** lie, tell a lie

kiyāskīwācimo- **VAI1** tell false news, tell an untrue story, tell a tall tale

kiyipa **IPC** quickly; soon; hurry up

kiyokaw- **VTA2** visit s.o.

kiyokāto- **VAI1** visit one another

kiyokātowin- **NI1** visiting one another, exchanging visits

kiyokē- **VAI1** visit, visit people, go visiting, pay a visit

kī- **IPV** [grammatical preverb: in the past; to completion, completely]

kī- **IPV** [grammatical preverb: abilitative, facultative: "can, able to"]

kīh- **IPV** [grammatical preverb: abilitative, facultative: "can, able to"]

kīhkām- **VTA1** scold s.o., revile s.o.; argue with s.o.

kīhkānākwan- **VII2** be clearly visible, look sharp and clear, be seen distinctly; be recognized

kīhkāwito- **VAI1** quarrel with one another, scold one another

kīhkē- **VAI1** have a sore heal up, heal up (i.e., a sore)

kīhtwām **IPC** again, once more; another, the next; next time

kīkisēpā **IPC** in the morning, early in the morning

kīkway **PR** something, thing; [in negative phrases:] anything, any

kīkwāy PrA what
kīkwāy PrI what
kīkwāyak PrA what
kīminikē- VAI₁ touch or feel people sexually, cop a feel
kīminikēski- VAI₁ be a pervert; be always groping, be always molesting
kīmōc IPC secretly, in secret, stealthily, slyly, by stealth; privately, in private
kīsatoskē- VAI₁ retire, finish work
kīsi- IPV finish; completely, to completion; completing, having done
kīsi-ohpiki- VAI₁ be an adult, reach adulthood, be grown up [also: *kīs-ōhpikiw*]
kīsihtā- VTI₂ complete s.t., finish s.t., finish work on s.t.
kīsikā- VII₁ be day, be daylight
kīsipakā- VII₁ the leaves are full-grown, there is full leaf growth
kīsis- VTI₁ cook s.t., bake s.t. to completion, complete s.t. by heat; burn s.t.
kīsisikātē- VII₂ be cooked, be cooked done, be baked
kīsiskwēwi- VAI₁ come to womanhood; have one's first menstruation
kīsisw- VTA₃ cook s.o., cook s.o. (e.g., goose) to completion; bake s.o. (e.g., bread) to completion
kīsitēpo- VAI₁ cook, finish cooking; cook a feast, cook ritual food
kīskacawēhamās- NA₁ Bangs, father of Mary Louise Rockthunder [personal name]
kīskahamā- VAI₁ have a haircut
kīskatah- VTI₁ chop s.t. with an axe, hew s.t. through or off; chop s.t. in two
kīskin- VTA₁ break s.o. off (by hand)
kīskinamaw- VTA₂ break (it/him) off for s.o.
kīskis- VTI₁ cut s.t. through, cut s.t. off
kīskisamaw- VTA₂ cut (it/him) off for s.o.; offer (it/him) (i.e., tobacco) to s.o., cut tobacco as a offering to s.o., present tobacco to s.o.
kīskisw- VTA₃ cut s.o. through or off; play s.o. (i.e., playing card)
kīskwē- VAI₁ be mentally disturbed, be mad, be crazy, be insane, be out of one's mind; be silly
kīskwēpē- VAI₁ be drunk, be crazy from alcohol
kīskwēyāpamo- VAI₁ be dizzy, be disoriented
kīsōhkwāmi- VAI₁ sleep warmly
kīsōhpit- VTA₄ tie s.o. warmly
kīsōskaw- VTA₂ warm s.o., keep s.o. warm with one's body
kīspin IPC if, in case; whether
kīspo- VAI₁ be full, be full of food, have enough to eat, have one's fill
kīstawāw PrA you (pl) too; you (pl) as well; you (pl) by contrast; you yourselves
kīwē- VAI₁ go home, go back, return home

kīwēhtah- **VTA**$_1$ take s.o. home, carry s.o. back home; go home with s.o.

kīwētonawē- **VAI**$_1$ take food home, return home with food

kīwēyāpōyo- **VAI**$_1$ go home (by vehicle; e.g., plane, train), go home by plane, go home by train

kocawānāpiskos- **NA**$_1$ stove, cookstove, camp stove

kocih- **VTA**$_1$ try s.o., test s.o.

kocīh- **VTA**$_1$ make s.o. try

konita **IPC** merely, just for nothing; in vain, vainly, without reason, without purpose, to no purpose; wasted efforts; without further ado; anywhere, at random, in a random place

koscikātē- **VII**$_2$ be feared

kositonāhkēmo- **VAI**$_1$ be afraid to speak to people

koskon- **VTA**$_1$ wake s.o. up, awaken s.o. by hand; startle s.o. by hand

koskowātapi- **VAI**$_1$ sit still, sit quietly

kost- **VTI**$_1$ fear s.t., be afraid of s.t., be scared of s.t.

kost- **VTA**$_4$ fear s.o., be afraid of s.o.

kotak **PrA** other, another

kotak **PrI** other, another

kotaka **PrI** other

kotakak **PrA** other

kotakihk **IPC** in another place, elsewhere

kotawē- **VAI**$_1$ build a fire, make a campfire, make a cooking fire

kōh- **IPV** [grammatical preverb: defines an independent clause; second person, past tense (in negative construction)]

kōhtāwīnaw **NDA**$_2$ Our Father; The Creator; [Christian:] Heavenly Father, Our Father; Our Lord

kōn- **NA**$_4$ snow

kwayask **IPC** right, properly, straight, correct, by rights; honest [cf. **kwēyask**]

kwāskwēnitowē- **VAI**$_1$ play golf; play a ball game (e.g., football, baseball)

kwēskastamaw- **VTA**$_2$ change (it/him) for s.o., alter (it) for s.o., put (it) in another form for s.o.

kwēskastā- **VTI**$_2$ place s.t. turning; change the position of s.t.

kwēskin- **VTI**$_1$ turn s.t. over (the other way)

kwēskin- **VTA**$_1$ turn s.o. over, turn s.o. around to the opposite side; change s.o. around; convert s.o. (e.g., to Christianity)

kwēskipayiho- **VAI**$_1$ turn oneself around, throw oneself around

kwēskiwēpin- **VTA**$_1$ change s.o., turn s.o. around, correct s.o.

kwēskī- **VAI**$_1$ turn, turn about, turn around

kwēyask **IPC** right, properly, straight, correct, by rights; honest [cf. **kwayask**]

m

ma cī IPH is it not the case? was it not? not so?
ma kīkway PR nothing, zero, nil; not, not at all; there is none
ma- IPV [grammatical preverb: ongoing, continuing]
macahpinē- VAI1 have a sexually transmitted disease (STD), have a venereal disease (VD), have a bad disease
macāpēs- NA1 Bad Man, grandfather of Mary Louise Rockthunder [personal name]
macēkinohkān- NI1 imitation tipi
mahti IPJ / IPC well, then, please; come, let's see [hortatory]
mahti ēsa IPH please; let's see
mamāhtāwisi- VAI1 have supernatural power, be gifted spiritually, be spiritually powerful; do magic
mamāyī- VAI1 be poor at something, do something poorly; be inefficient
mamihciht- VTI1 praise s.t.
mamihcim- VTA1 praise s.o., boast about s.o.; adulate s.o.
mamihcimiso- VAI1 brag about oneself, boast about oneself
mamihcimo- VAI1 boast, brag about oneself, be boastful; sing one's own praises
manā- IPV beware of, careful not to, avoid doing; in avoiding, in sparing
manācihtā- VTI2 be careful of s.t., treat s.t. with respect; use s.t. carefully, spare s.t.
manāhto- VAI1 be respectful towards one another, be careful of one another, treat one another with respect
manēsi- VAI1 be in need of something, be in want of something, lack something, run out of something; be poor
manicōs- NA1 insect, crawling insect, bug; little worm
manipit- VTI1 obtain s.t. by pulling; pull s.t. out (e.g., tooth), pull s.t. loose, pull s.t. free, tear s.t. off; pick s.t. (i.e., a plant)
manisikanis- NI1 scissors; small cutting implement
manitow- NA2 spirit, spirit being; God; sacred power, spirit power
manī- VAI1 harvest, pick (plants)
masaskon- VTI1 gather s.t. up wholly
masāniwi- VAI1 be a nettle, be a thistle
masinah- VTI1 write s.t., write s.t. down, record s.t. in writing; sign s.t.; mark s.t. by tool, draw s.t.
masinahamaw- VTA2 write (it) to s.o., write (it) for s.o.; owe (it) to s.o., owe s.o. money, be in debt to s.o.
masinahamōh- VTA1 be indebted to s.o., record a debt to s.o.
masinahamōhkē- VAI1 paint (it; e.g., tipi)) for people

masinahikan- NI$_1$ book; letter, mail; written document, report, paper; magazine; will

masinahikāso- VAI$_1$ be written on; be marked, be pictured on; be drawn, be pictured, be depicted; be recorded historically

masinahikātē- VII$_2$ be written, be written on; have writing, have marks, be marked, be drawn, be pictured, be depicted

masinahikē- VAI$_1$ write, write things, be literate; depict things; take employment; give credit; get credit; owe, go into debt, have debts

maskawisi- VAI$_1$ be firm, be hard; be strong, be powerful

maskihkiy- NI$_2$ medicine; herb, plant; medicinal root; chemicals

maskihkīwiyiniw- NA$_2$ doctor, physician; medicine man, herbalist; shaman

maskimocis- NI$_1$ little bag, small sack; pocket

maskimot- NI$_1$ bag, sack

maskisin- NI$_1$ moccasin; shoe

matotisān- NI$_1$ sweatlodge

matotisānihkē- VAI$_1$ build a sweatlodge, prepare a sweatlodge

matotisi- VAI$_1$ go into a sweatlodge, sweat oneself; hold a sweatlodge, take a steam bath

matwān **IPC** I wonder; can it really be?

matwān cī **IPH** I wonder, I wonder if; I believe; perhaps

matwē- **IPV** audibly, visibly; perceptibly; in full view; in plain sight; noticeably; loudly; heard or seen from a distance

matwē-pāhpi- VAI$_1$ laugh out loud (so as to be heard at a distance)

matwēhikē- VAI$_1$ bang things, hammer things, be heard hammering at a distance

mawimoscikē- VAI$_1$ pray, chant, worship, pray to God, make an entreaty, cry out in prayer, wail

mawimoscikēwatāmon- NI$_1$ prayer song

mawimoscikēwin- NI$_1$ entreaty, worship, praying, prayer to the Great Spirit; religion, form of worship, rite; crying out in prayer, wailing

mawiso- VAI$_1$ pick berries, gather berries; gather food (by hand above ground)

mawīhkāt- VTA$_4$ beg s.o. with tears; cry for s.o., cry out over s.o., mourn for s.o.; be sad to see s.o. go

mayaw **IPC** as soon as; straight, exact, on time

māci- **IPV** begin to, start to; commencement; initially

mācikōc **IPC** look, you will see for yourself that be so; by gosh!

mācikōci **IPC** look, you will see for yourself that be so; by gosh!

mācikōcicān IPC look, let me show you

mācikōtitāk IPC let me show you (pl)

mācikōtitān IPC look, let me show you; you will see; wait and see! lo!

mācikwāso- VAI1 start sewing, begin to sew

māh- IPV [grammatical preverb: intermittent, repeatedly; again and again; here and there]

māh-mihcēt IPC always lots, many again and again; a great many, very numerous

māh-mistahi IPC quite a lot, a great deal

māka IPC but, then; still

mākon- VTA1 press s.o., press hard upon s.o. by hand; press s.o.'s hand; knead s.o. (e.g., bread); push s.o. down

māmawaci-wīwimāw- NA2 first wife, first married among wives, earliest wife

māmihk IPC downriver, downstream; east

māmiskōt- VTI1 talk about s.t., discuss s.t., expound upon s.t., speak of s.t., refer to s.t.

māmitonēyihcikan- NI1 mind; conscience; a thought; troubled mind, worry; [plural:] thoughts

māmiywākācim- VTA1 argue with s.o.; question s.o.; provoke s.o. by speech, offend s.o. by speech

māmiywākācimo- VAI1 question, argue; use provocative language

māna IPC usually, habitually, generally, always; used to

māsihkē- VAI1 wrestle, be a wrestler

māskōc IPC perhaps, maybe, I suppose; probably, it's likely, it's a reasonably likely possibility; undoubtedly

mātatoskē- VAI1 begin to work; begin a new job; enter the workforce

mātācimostaw- VTA2 begin to tell stories to s.o.

mātāhiso- VAI1 come upon one's own track, see one's own footprints; track oneself

māto- VAI1 cry, wail, weep

māwacihtā- VTI2 save s.t., preserve s.t., conserve s.t.; assemble s.t., collect s.t., gather s.t. up

māwasakopēh- VTI1 add s.t. up, record s.t., compile s.t. (as records)

māwasakō- VAI1 collect, gather

māwasakwasinah- VTI1 record s.t., keep records of s.t., compile s.t.

māyātan- VII2 be bad, be evil; be ugly

māyi- IPV bad, evil; badly, evilly, wickedly

māyi-itōt- VTI1 do ill, do a bad thing, do s.t. bad; do ill deeds

māyi-ohpin- VTI1 create s.t. bad; raise s.t. bad (e.g., a topic)

māyi-tōt- VTI1 do a bad thing, impose a curse; do s.t. wrongly; do s.t. evil

māyi-tōtaw- VTA2 do a bad thing to s.o., do evil to s.o., make s.o. sick, put a curse on s.o., do s.o. wrong, harm s.o.; have a bad effect on s.o.

māyi-wīcēhto- VAI1 live in discord with one another

māyi-wīcēw- VTA2 live in discord with s.o.

māyinikē- VAI1 have ill befall him/her, have bad luck, have misfortune; become pregnant out of wedlock; act badly, do harmful things

māyinikēski- VAI1 always act awkwardly, tend to handle things badly, handle things carelessly all the time

māyinikēwin- NI1 wrongdoing, evil deed; bad luck; awkwardness, clumsiness

māyipayi- VAI1 suffer ill, fare ill, fare badly; suffer a death, be bereaved (by the loss of s.o.), have a death in the family

māyiskaw- VTA2 affect s.o. negatively, have an adverse effect on s.o.; make s.o. ill; be not suited to s.o., do not fit in with s.o.

māyiskāko- VTA2 affect s.o. badly, have an adverse effect on s.o.; make s.o. ill, make s.o. react allergically

māyiyihkāso- VAI1 have a bad name, have an ugly name

mēki- VAI1 give, give away; donate; give s.t. away, give (it/him) out as a present; release s.t.; give (s.o.) in marriage

mēkwāc IPC currently, presently, right now; while, during, in the course of, in the meantime, during the time; ago

mēnikan- NI1 fence

mēskanaw- NI2 road, path, trail

mēskocīh- VTA1 change s.o.'s clothes, make s.o. change clothes, attend to s.o.'s dressing (when at the end of a period of mourning)

mēskotayiwinisah- VTA1 change s.o.'s clothes

mēskotayiwinisēh- VTA1 change s.o.'s clothes

mēskotayiwinisē- VAI1 change one's clothes

mēstin- VTI1 use s.t. up, use all of s.t.; spend s.t.

mēstinikē- VAI1 use things up; exhaust things, waste things; spend, spend it all, spend all of one's money on things

mēstisoso- VAI1 burn oneself up, burn oneself badly

mēstisw- VTA3 burn s.o. up

mētawē- VAI1 play; gamble, contest

mētawēwin- NI1 game, contest, sport; dialogue

mētoni IPC very, really, intensively, fully; yes, indeed; truly [cf. **mitoni, 'toni**]

mētoni oti IPH very, really, intensively, fully; yes, indeed; truly

micimin- VTI1 hold s.t. fast, hold on to s.t., hold s.t. in place, grasp s.t.

micimin- VTA1 hold s.o. fast, hold s.o. in place, take hold of s.o., hold on to s.o.
mihcēt IPC many, much; a good number, numerous
mihcēti- VAI1 be numerous, be many, be plentiful
mihcētoskwēwē- VAI1 have many wives
mihcētōsē- VAI1 have many children; have many young ones, have numerous offspring
mihcētwāniskwēyā- VII2 have many hair-like roots
mihkosi- VAI1 be red
mihkwā- VII2 be red
mihkwāpēmakw- NI3 red willow; red osier dogwood
mihkwāpēmakwāhtikw- NA3 red willow tree, red osier dogwood [Lat. *Cornus sericea*]
miht- NI4 piece of wood, piece of firewood
mihtāt- VTI1 regret s.t., be sorry about s.t., grieve over s.t., deplore the loss of s.t.
mihtikowāhp- NI1 wooden lodge
mikiy- NI2 scab [also: **omikiy-**]
mikoskācih- VTA1 bother s.o., annoy s.o., give s.o. trouble; hurt s.o.
mikoskācihtā- VTI2 bother s.t., trifle with s.t., tamper with s.t.
minah- VTA1 give s.o. a drink or broth; give s.o. (it) to drink (e.g., tea, soup, medicine); give s.o. an alcoholic drink, induce s.o. to drink alcohol
minahiso- VAI1 give oneself a drink
minihkwāt- VTA4 drink s.o. (e.g., snow), be provided drink from s.o. (e.g., ice)
minihkwē- VAI1 drink, have a drink, drink s.t.; drink alcohol, abuse alcohol
minihkwēwin- NI1 drink, beverage, alcoholic beverage; drinking, alcohol abuse
minōs- NA1 cat
misahkamik IPC many, a great many; in great number; all
misakāmē IPC entirely, all the way; all the way across the whole area, throughout, in continuity
misatimw- NA3 horse
misawāc IPC anyway, at any rate, in any case; despite, in spite of; whatever might be thought; no doubt be the case
misawāt IPC anyway, at any rate, in any case; despite, in spite of; whatever might be thought; no doubt be the case
misā- VII2 be big, be large
miscahīs IPC a good deal; quite greatly, quite a bit, a fair amount
miscikos- NA1 little tree; sapling
miscikos- NI1 little stick; little pole, rod, rail (e.g., on a drying rack); branch
miscikowacis- NI1 small box
misi- IPV big, greatly; much, a lot; very, extremely, to the extreme

misi- **IPN** big, large, great
misi-kākikē **IPC** forever and ever
misi-mistikowat- **NI**$_5$ large box, trunk
misi-mīkiwāhp- **NI**$_1$ large tipi, large lodge
misi-okiniy- **NA**$_2$ large rosehip
misi-sakā- **VII**$_2$ be a large woodland, be a large grove of trees, be a forest
misikiti- **VAI**$_1$ be big, be large (in height or girth); be a big person
misiwanācihiwē- **VAI**$_1$ destroy (animate) things, damage, spoil things
misiwē **IPC** all over, everywhere, the entire place, on the whole body
misk- **VTI**$_1$ find s.t.
miskaw- **VTA**$_2$ find s.o.
miskwamiy- **NA**$_2$ ice
mispon- **VII**$_1$ snow, be snowing, there is falling snow, there is a snowfall
misposin- **VII**$_1$ snow a little
mistahi **IPC** much, greatly, a great deal, a lot, lots; very, very many; very much so
mistaskosīmin- **NI**$_1$ wild turnip; wild onion
mistikowat- **NI**$_5$ box, trunk
mistikw- **NI**$_3$ stick, log, pole, post, wood, wooden rail; club
mistikw- **NA**$_3$ tree
mistiyiniw- **NA**$_2$ big man, large man; giant
mitātaht **IPC** ten, 10
mitātahtomitanaw tahtwāpisk **IPH** one hundred dollars, $100
mitātahtoskwēwē- **VAI**$_1$ have ten wives
mitēhimin- **NI**$_1$ strawberry, wild strawberry [Lat. *Fragaria glauca*; *Fragaria* sp.]
mitonēyiht- **VTI**$_1$ ponder over s.t.
mitoni **IPC** very, really, intensively, fully, completely, to full degree; quite; much, a lot; well [cf. **mētoni**, **'toni**]
mitoni oti **IPH** very, really, intensively, fully, completely, to full degree
miy- **VTA**$_1$ give (it/him) to s.o.
miyawākācī- **VAI**$_1$ take particular care
miyāhkasikākē- **VAI**$_1$ smudge with something, cense with something, use something as incense; use something as a scented lure (e.g., in trapping)
miyāhkasikē- **VAI**$_1$ smudge with sweetgrass, burn incense, cense things
miyāhkasoso- **VAI**$_1$ smudge oneself with sweetgrass, cense oneself
miyāht- **VTI**$_1$ smell s.t., sniff s.t.
miyiwi- **VAI**$_1$ have an open infection, have discharge, have pus, have an abscess
miyo- **IPN** good; beautiful; valuable
miyo- **IPV** good, well, beautiful; valuable
miyo-ayāwin- **NI**$_1$ good health, prosperity
miyo-āpacihtā- **VTI**$_2$ use s.t. well, make good use of s.t.

miyo-āpatisi- VAI1 have a good use, be properly useful
miyo-okimāw- NA2 good chief, good leader, good officer, good boss
miyo-pimātisi- VAI1 live a good life, be well, keep well, live well, live a proper life, live an exemplary life
miyo-tōt- VTI1 do a good thing, do s.t. good; do kind deeds
miyo-tōtaw- VTA2 do s.o. good, do s.o. a good turn, affect s.o. beneficially, do a charitable deed for s.o.
miyo-wāhkōhto- VAI1 relate to one another well, be good relations to one another
miyo-wīcēhto- VAI1 get along well with one another, get along well together, live in harmony with one another
miyo-wīcēhtowin- NI1 living in harmony together; alliance; co-operative
miyo-wīcēw- VTA2 get along well with s.o.
miyohkaso- VAI1 bake well (e.g., bannock)
miyohtah- VTA1 guide s.o. well
miyoki- VAI1 grow well
miyokotē- VII2 work well, travel well, speed along well [also: *miywakotē-*]
miyokwāt- VTI1 sew s.t. well
miyokwātē- VII2 be well-sewn
miyomahciho- VAI1 feel fine, feel well, feel healthy, be in good health or spirit; feel pleased; fare well
miyomahcihowin- NI1 good health, good feelings
miyonākwan- VII2 be beautiful, look good, have a nice appearance, look prosperous
miyopayi- VII2 go well, go smoothly; work well; work out well; come to pass
miyopayi- VAI1 have good luck; fare well, have things go well, have things go smoothly; work well
miyosi- VAI1 be good, be nice, be pretty, be handsome, be beautiful; be competent
miyoskaw- VTA2 fit s.o. (e.g., clothing) nicely; be well-suited to s.o.
miyoskāko- VTA2 go through s.o.'s body with good affect, do s.o. good (e.g., animate food as actor); fit s.o. well (e.g., pants)
miyotēhē- VAI1 be good-hearted, have a good heart
miyw-āyā- VAI1 be well, be in good health, be in good shape [also: *minw-āyā-*, as in Saulteaux and Swampy Cree]
miywahcikē- VAI1 have good eating, eat well
miywapi- VAI1 sit well; be well-off, be well-situated
miywastā- VTI2 place s.t. well
miywāciho- VAI1 make a good living, live well
miywāpāwatā- VTI2 treat s.t. well with water, nurture s.o. correctly with liquid; wash s.t. well
miywāsin- VII2 be good, be nice, be pretty, be beautiful;

be valuable; [in negative clauses:] be bad, be evil

miywāspinē- **VAI1** have a good disease [typically in negative: "have a not good disease, have a bad disease"]

miywātisi- **VAI1** be good

miywāyāwin- **NI1** good health, prosperity

miywēyiht- **VTI1** be glad, be happy, be pleased; be glad about s.t.; like s.t., think well of s.t., consider s.t. good

miywēyim- **VTA1** like s.o., think well of s.o.; be pleased with s.o., consider s.o. good

mīci- **VTI3** eat s.t.

mīcimāpoy- **NI2** soup, broth

mīcimihkē- **VAI1** make food, prepare food

mīciso- **VAI1** eat, have a meal; feed (e.g., bird); chew one's cud (e.g., ruminant)

mīcisowin- **NI1** meal; eating, eating habits; food, foodstuff, food supply

mīciswāt- **VTI1** eat from s.t., eat off s.t.

mīciwin- **NI1** food, groceries; meal

mīhkawikī- **VAI1** run fast, be a fast runner

mīkiwāhp- **NI1** tipi, lodge

mīna **IPC** and, plus; also, and also, again, furthermore

mīnis- **NI1** berry

mīnisīhkēs- **NA1** Seneca root, Seneca snakeroot, rattlesnake root, mountain flax [Lat. *Polygala senega*]

mīnokocin- **VAI2** speed into the correct position; settle correctly

mīnoskōhtwā- **VAI1** be healed, be restored to health

mīnō- **VAI1** recover, rebound, right oneself

mīsahikē- **VAI1** mend things, patch things, repair things

mīsahikēwin- **NI1** patching, mending, repairing

mīskot **IPC** instead, in return, in exchange; by retaliation

mohcēs- **NA1** small worm; small caterpillar; maggot

moscāyihk **IPC** on the ground; on the floor

mosci- **IPV** just, merely, plainly, simply, directly, singly, without instrumentality, without mediation; without recompense, free; by hand

mostohtē- **VAI1** walk without aid or conveyance; merely walk, travel on foot

mostoso-wīhkaskw- **NI3** sage, prairie sage, buffalo sage [literally: "buffalo-sweetgrass"; Lat. *Artemesia ludoviciana*]

mow- **VTA1** eat s.o. (e.g., bread)

mōhcowi- **VAI1** be mad, be crazy; be stupid, be foolish; be silly, be funny; be promiscuous

mōminē- **VAI1** eat berries from the bush, eat berries as one picks

mōnah- **VTI1** dig s.t., dig for s.t., dig s.t. out; dig roots

mōnahikanāhtikw- **NI3** digging stick, stick for digging roots

mōnahikātē- **VII2** be dug up out of the ground
mōniyānāhk **INM** White society, Canadian society, non-Indigenous society; the White world, the non-Indigenous world
mōniyās- **NA1** a white man; little white man; Canadian; non-Indian, non-First Nations person [plural:] white people; the Whites
mōniyāskwēwēwahikēsi- **VAI1** act a little like a white woman, act a little like a non-Indigenous woman
mōniyāw- **NA2** white man; non-Indian, non-First Nations man; Canadian, Canadian male [plural:] white people; the Whites
mōniyāw-iyiniw- **NA2** Canadian, white person
mōniyāwi-tōt- **VTI1** act as a white man, do things like a white man, act in a White way
mōniyāwipēh- **VTI1** write s.t. in English, write s.t. with the English alphabet, write s.t. with the Roman alphabet
mōniyāwi- **VAI1** be a white man, be White, be a non-Indian; act White
mōniyāwīhtwā- **VAI1** follow Whiteman's way, follow White custom, follow non-Indigenous culture
mōsāhkin- **VTI1** pick s.t., pick s.t. up, gather s.t. up
mōsiho- **VAI1** feel s.t. is coming; have the sensation of feeling; sense that birth is imminent, feel the pangs of childbirth
mōsihtā- **VTI2** feel s.t., sense s.t.; perceive s.t.'s presence, feel s.t. approaching
mōskom- **VTA1** move s.o. to tears by weeping or speaking; make s.o. cry, make s.o. weepy, make s.o. become emotional
mōskotēhē- **VAI1** be very sad; be heartbroken [literally: "have a crying heart"]
mōskwāhpi- **VAI1** laugh so hard one cries; cry from laughing
mōsowiyās- **NI1** moose meat
mōy **IPC** no, not
mōy awiyak **PrA** no-one, nobody
mōy āhpō **IPH** not even
mōy ākwāskam **IPH** not really, not as much
mōy kacāc **IPH** not necessarily
mōy kīkway **PrI** nothing, none
mōy nānitaw **IPH** it's fine, alright; no worries; there is nothing wrong with that
mōy wīhkāc **IPH** never
mōy wīhkāt **IPH** never
mōya **IPC / IPJ** no; not
mōya ahpō **IPH** not even
mōya awiyak **PrA** no-one, nobody
mōya katāc **IPH** not necessarily
mōya wīhkāc **IPH** never
mwēhci **IPC** just; just then, exactly then; just after; just like; exactly
mwēstācīhkaw- **VTA2** bother s.o., annoy s.o., make a nuisance of oneself to s.o., be troublesome for s.o.

n

na- **IPV** [grammatical preverb: ongoing, continuing]

nahapi- **VAI**$_1$ sit down, sit down in one's place, be properly seated

nahastā- **VTI**$_2$ put s.t. away; put s.t. in its place, place s.t. right; store s.t., cache s.t.; bury s.t.

nahin- **VTA**$_1$ bury s.o.; hold a funeral for s.o.; put s.o. in place

nakacā **IPJ** holy cow! oh my goodness! oh my! [expressing surprise and/or disapproval]

nakacihtā- **VTI**$_2$ know well how to do s.t., be familiar with doing s.t., be practised at s.t., be skilled (through experience); be used to s.t.'s ways

nakacipah- **VTA**$_1$ run away from s.o.; leave s.o. alone (behind) by running; outdistance s.o.

nakamo- **VAI**$_1$ sing; sing a ritual song

nakamon- **NI**$_1$ song; ritual song; hymn

nakamowin- **NI**$_1$ song, singing; ritual song

nakat- **VTI**$_1$ leave s.t., abandon s.t., leave s.t. behind; go away from s.t.

nakat- **VTA**$_4$ leave s.o., leave s.o. behind; abandon s.o., leave s.o. alone and helpless; go away from s.o.; leave s.o. behind in death, die leaving s.o. behind

nakayāskaw- **VTA**$_2$ be used to s.o., be familiar with s.o.; be accustomed to s.o., be comfortable with s.o.

nakāsin- **VAI**$_2$ be unable to continue because of blockage; stop, be prevented from proceeding

nakipayi- **VII**$_2$ stop working (automatically), stop suddenly

nakipicikātē- **VII**$_2$ be stopped; be turned off (e.g., machinery, recording device); be pulled to a stop

nakipit- **VTI**$_1$ pull s.t. to a stop; stop the recording

nakiskaw- **VTA**$_2$ meet s.o., encounter s.o.

nakī- **VAI**$_1$ stop, come to a stop; park

nama **IPC** not

nama kīkway **PrI** nothing; not at all; none; there is none

naminās- **NI**$_1$ syrup; molasses

namōy **IPC** not [used in independent clauses]

namōy nānitaw **IPH** fine, I'm fine, all right, okay, nothing wrong; insignificant, of little account; not anything; nowhere

namōy wīhkāc **IPH** never

namōy wīhkāt **IPH** never

namōya **IPC / IPJ** no; not

namōya awiya **PrA** no-one, nobody, not anybody

namōya awiyak **PrA** no-one, nobody, not anybody

namōya ākwāskam **IPC** not really, not as much

namōya kīkway **PrI** nothing, none

namōya nānitaw **IPH** fine, I'm fine, all right, okay, nothing wrong; insignificant, of little account; not anything; nowhere

namōya wīhkāc **IPH** never, not ever

namōya wīhkāt **IPH** never, not ever

namwāc kīkway **PrI** nothing, none; there is absolutely nothing

nanāskom- **VTA$_1$** thank s.o., give thanks to s.o., be grateful to s.o., speak words of thanks to s.o.

nanāskomo- **VAI$_1$** be grateful, be thankful; give thanks, express thanks

nanātawih- **VTA$_1$** treat s.o. (medically), provide healing medicine for s.o.; doctor s.o., heal s.o., cure s.o.

nanātawihiwākē- **VAI$_1$** doctor people with something, use something to doctor people

nanātawiho- **VAI$_1$** treat oneself (medically); doctor oneself, heal oneself; be treated, be doctored, be healed, be cured; take healing medicine

nanātawihtā- **VTI$_2$** treat s.t. (medically), provide healing medicine for s.t.; heal s.t., cure s.t.

nanātawiskaw- **VTA$_2$** have a healing effect on s.o.

nanātawiskāko- **VTA$_2$** have a healing effect on s.o.

nanātohk **IPC** different, variously, all kinds, of various kinds, different items, a variety

nanōyacim- **VTA$_1$** tease s.o. verbally, provoke s.o.; flirt with s.o.

napakā- **VII$_2$** be flat

napakipakw- **NI$_3$** prepared tobacco leaf [literally "flat-leaf"]

napakiyākanis- **NI$_1$** saucer, bread-and-butter plate

naspitaw- **VTA$_2$** resemble s.o., bear a resemblence to s.o., look like s.o.

nawac **IPC** by comparison; better, more; before; instead, rather, somewhat

nawaciko **IPC** sort of, kind of, approximately; more or less; even a little; not fully

nawacī- **VAI$_1$** roast s.t., roast one's food; cook s.t. (i.e., in a wood stove or on a fire)

nawasawāpamo- **VAI$_1$** make one's choice by sight

nawat **IPC** by comparison; better, more; rather

nawatin- **VTI$_1$** grab s.t. in mid-air, seize s.t.; catch s.t. in one's hand

nayēhtāwispit- **VTI$_1$** find s.t. distasteful, dislike the taste of s.t.

nayēhtāwī- **VAI$_1$** be hindered, have a difficult time doing something; be awkward at something

nayēstaw **IPC** only, exclusively; be only that; always; instead of

nācipahtwā- **VTI**$_2$ go for s.t. at a run

nāh- **IPV** [grammatical preverb: intermittent, repeatedly; again and again; here and there]

nāha **PrA** that one yonder, that farther, that one over there

nākatohkē- **VAI**$_1$ take notice, be observant, notice people, pay attention to people; care for people, look after people, attend to people; listen attentively; be courteous, be respectful

nānahi-kēswān **IPC** coincidentally, by chance, at the right moment

nānapācih- **VTA**$_1$ mend s.o., fix s.o. up; doctor s.o., tend to s.o.; tidy s.o. up

nānāhtē- **VII**$_2$ be a mirage, dazzling sunlight

nānākēs **IPC** later, later on

nānitaw **IPC** simply; something; something bad; somewhere, at some undetermined place; anyhow; in some way; [with numbers:] about, approximately, roughly, variously; [in negative clauses:] anything, anything bad

nānitaw isi **IPH** in some way, in any way; in various ways; in a random direction; if by any chance, just in case

nānitaw- **IPV** [in negative clauses:] any

nāpēw- **NA**$_2$ man, male, male adult, male being; husband

nāt- **VTI**$_1$ fetch s.t.; go for s.t., go to get s.t.

nāt- **VTA**$_4$ fetch s.o.; go for s.o., go to get s.o.

nātawāpi- **VAI**$_1$ go to see, take a look around

nātitisah- **VTI**$_1$ send for s.t., order s.t.

nātitisahw- **VTA**$_3$ send for s.o., order s.o. (e.g., chickens) by catalogue; go to fetch s.o. (e.g., horses)

nāway **IPC** in back, behind, at the rear; behind one another; past, in the past

nēhiyaw- **NA**$_2$ Nehiyaw; Cree, Cree man, First Nations person, Indigenous person

nēhiyaw-ayamihcikē- **VAI**$_1$ read Cree, read Cree syllabics; read written Cree

nēhiyaw-isīhcikē- **VAI**$_1$ follow Cree culture, partake of Cree ceremony, follow the Cree way; follow First Nations culture, participate in First Nations ceremony

nēhiyaw-isīhcikēwin- **NI**$_1$ Cree culture, Cree ceremony, the Cree way; First Nations culture, First Nations ceremony

nēhiyawātisi- **VAI**$_1$ have the Cree cultural tradition, live a traditional Cree life

nēhiyawātisiwin- **NI**$_1$ Cree cultural tradition, living a traditional Cree life

nēhiyawē- **VAI**$_1$ speak Cree

nēhiyawi- **IPN** Cree; First Nations, Indigenous, Indian

nēhiyawi- **IPV** Cree, in Cree, in the Cree language; First Nations, Indigenous, Indian

nēhiyawi-ayamihāwin- **NI$_1$** Cree prayer

nēhiyawi-pimātisi- **VAI$_1$** live a Cree life, live as a Cree person

nēhiyawi-pīkiskwēwin- **NI$_1$** Cree speech, the Cree language

nēhiyawihkāso- **VAI$_1$** be called so in Cree, have a Cree name, have an Indigenous name [also: **nēhiyawiyihkāso-**]

nēhiyawipēhikē- **VAI$_1$** write in Cree, write Cree syllabics

nēhiyawipwātināhk **INM** Piapot First Nation, SK; Cree and Dakota reserve; literally: "among the Cree-Dakota"

nēhiyawīhtwā- **VAI$_1$** follow the Cree way, follow Cree culture, follow Cree custom; follow First Nations culture, follow Indigenous culture

nēhiyawīhtwāwin- **NI$_1$** the Cree way, Cree culture, Cree custom; First Nations culture, Indigenous culture

nēhiyāwi- **VAI$_1$** be Cree, be Plains Cree, be a Cree Indian; be an Indigenous person

nēhiyāwiwin- **NI$_1$** being Cree, Cree identity, Creeness; Indigeneity, Indianness

nēki **PrA** those yonder

nēma **PrI** that yonder

nēmitanaw **IPC** forty, 40

nēpēwih- **VTA$_1$** make s.o. ashamed, shame s.o., put s.o. to shame; embarrass s.o.; make s.o. become shy

nēpēwihiso- **VAI$_1$** shame oneself, embarrass oneself

nēpēwiho- **VAI$_1$** be shamed, be embarrassed; be shameful, be embarrassing

nēpēwisi- **VAI$_1$** be bashful, be shy; be ashamed, be shamed, be embarrassed

nēpēwisīstaw- **VTA$_2$** be bashful about s.o.; be shy towards s.o.

nētē **IPC** over there, over yonder, in that direction, thereabouts

nēwāw **IPC** four times; fourth time

nēwi- **VAI$_1$** be four in number

nēwo **IPC** four, 4

nēwo-kīsikā- **VII$_1$** be Thursday; be four days, be the fourth day [literally: "(be) the fourth day"]

nēwo-kīsikāw **IPC** four days, for four days

nēwo-tipiskā- **VII$_1$** be the fourth night, be four nights

nēwo-tipiskāw **IPC** four nights

nihtā- **IPV** able; good at, competent, practised, experienced, doing much of, skillful at, expert at, known as one who does s.t. habitually; well

nihtā-ayamihcikē- **VAI$_1$** be a good reader; read well

nihtā-masinahikē- **VAI$_1$** write well

nihtāwasinahikē- **VAI**$_1$ write well, be an excellent writer
nihtāwē- **VAI**$_1$ be able to talk well; speak well; be an excellent speaker
nihtāwiki- **VAI**$_1$ be born
nihtāwipēhikē- **VAI**$_1$ write well, be highly literate
nihtiy- **NI**$_2$ tea
nihtīhkātito- **VAI**$_1$ make tea for one another
nihtīhkē- **VAI**$_1$ make tea
nikamo- **VAI**$_1$ sing; sing a ritual song
nikohtē- **VAI**$_1$ cut wood, chop wood; get, gather, collect, prepare firewood
nikotwāsik **IPC** six, 6
nikotwāw **IPC** either one, anyone, any, any choice; any time
nipah- **VTA**$_1$ kill s.o.
nipahāhpi- **VAI**$_1$ laugh uproariously, (almost) die laughing
nipahāhpih- **VTA**$_1$ make s.o. laugh uproariously, (almost) kill s.o. with laughter
nipahi- **IPV** really, very, extremely, greatly; deadly, terribly, to the death
nipahihkas- **VTI**$_1$ really cook s.t., thoroughly cook s.t.; bake s.t. to death
nipahisin- **VAI**$_2$ fall to death, be killed by a fall; lie dead; get killed in an accident (e.g., car, airplane, vehicle)
nipahiskōh- **VTA**$_1$ kill s.o. by weight; kill s.o. by overfeeding, overfeed s.o. causing death
nipahtākē- **VAI**$_1$ kill people, murder people
nipākwēsimo- **VAI**$_1$ attend a Sundance, participate in a Sundance, dance the Sundance; attend a Raindance, participate in a Raindance, dance the Raindance; attend a Thirst Dance, participate in a Thirst Dance, dance the Thirst Dance
nipākwēsimowin- **NI**$_1$ Sundance, Raindance; Thirst Dance
nipākwēsimowinihkē- **VAI**$_1$ give a Sundance, hold a Sundance; hold a Raindance; hold a Thirst Dance
nipā- **VAI**$_1$ sleep, be asleep
nipēwin- **NI**$_1$ bed
nipiy- **NI**$_2$ water
nipōmakan- **VII**$_2$ die, be dead
nisikosē! **NDA**$_1$ aunt!, cross-aunt!; father's sister!, mother's brother's wife!; mother-in-law! [vocative]
nisitawēyim- **VTA**$_1$ know s.o., recognize s.o., be acquainted with s.o.
nisitawin- **VTI**$_1$ recognize s.t. by sight
nisitoht- **VTI**$_1$ understand; understand s.t.
nisitohtaw- **VTA**$_2$ understand s.o.
nisiwanācihito- **VAI**$_1$ destroy one another
nistam **IPC** first; at first, before anything else; for the first time, initially, originally

nistam-ayisiyiniw- **NA2** first person, first human being
nistamōsān- **NA1** firstborn, firstborn child
nistēsē! **NDA1** older brother! [vocative]
nisti- **VAI1** be three in number
nisto **IPC** three, 3
nistomitanaw **IPC** thirty, 30
nistwāw **IPC** three times, thrice; third time
nitaki oti **IPH** well, really! it just worked out
nitakisa **IPJ** yeah, right! not by any chance
nitaw- **IPV** go and, go to; engaged in [cf. **nitawi-**, **nitō-**]
nitawāc **IPC** in spite of everything, despite all; in a complete reversal; as the best thing to do; instead
nitawēyiht- **VTI1** want s.t., desire s.t.; need s.t.
nitawēyim- **VTA1** want s.o., desire s.o., desire (it/him) from s.o.
nitawi- **IPV** go and, go to; engaged in [cf. **nitaw-**, **nitō-**]
nitoht- **VTI1** listen to s.t., listen for s.t.; try to hear s.t.
nitohtaw- **VTA2** listen to s.o., listen for s.o.; obey s.o.
nitom- **VTA1** invite s.o., call s.o., beckon s.o.
niton- **VTI1** seek s.t., look for s.t., search for s.t.
nitot- **VTI1** ask for s.t., order s.t. (e.g., in a restaurant)
nitotamaw- **VTA2** ask s.o. for (it/him)
nitotamākēstamaw- **VTA2** make a request for s.o., pray on s.o.'s behalf, ask for (it/him) on s.o.'s behalf
nitotamākē- **VAI1** request things, ask for things, pray for things; demand things
nitō- **IPV** go and, go to; engaged in [cf. **nitaw-**, **nitawi-**]
nitōsk- **VTI1** seek s.t.; make a request for s.t. (e.g., medicine)
niya **PrA** I, me, mine
niya wiya **PrA** for my part, as for me; I myself
niyanān **PrA** we, us, our
niyā **IPJ** go ahead, go on, be off!
niyānan **IPC** five, 5
nīhc-āyihk **IPC** below; down, downward, downstairs, down the hill; in the low place
nīhcāyihk **IPC** below; down, downward, downstairs, down the hill; in the low place
nīhtaciwētisahw- **VTA3** send s.o. downhill
nīhtaciwē- **VAI1** climb down, walk down; go downstairs, descend a hill, stairs, etc.
nīhtakosī- **VAI1** dismount, climb down, get down, get off
nīkānīst- **VTI1** be at the head of s.t., lead s.t.
nīkānī- **VII2** be first, best, favourite; lead, be ahead, be at the head
nīkānīwi- **VII2** be in the future, lie in the future; be ahead, be the future

nīmā- VAI1 pack a lunch, take provisions on the way
nīmāh- VTA1 give s.o. provisions for the journey, make lunch for s.o. to take, make s.o. take a lunch; add (it) to s.o.'s packed provisions
nīmihito- VAI1 dance, join in the dancing; dance a secular dance; [plural:] dance with one another, move about in a dancing motion (e.g., northern lights)
nīpawakocin- VAI1 quickly stand upright; speed into a standing position
nīpawi- VAI1 stand, stand upright, stand erect, stand there, stand fast
nīpā- IPV at night, in the dark
nīpāhtē- VAI1 walk in the dark, come home late at night
nīpiminān- NI1 highbush cranberry [generally plural; Lat. *Viburnum trilobum*]
nīpin- VII1 be summer
nīpinisi- VAI1 camp for the summer, spend the summer
nīpinohk IPC last summer
nīpisiy- NI2 willow, willow bush; willow branch
nīpiy- NI2 leaf; blade of grass; leafy branch; [plural:] leaves; salad
nīsin- VII2 be two in number
nīso IPC two, 2; two together
nīso-askiy IPC two years, for two years [also: *nīsw-āskiy*]
nīso-kīsikāw IPC two days, for two days
nīsowihkāso- VAI1 have two names [also: *nīsoyihkāso-*]
nīsōsē- VAI1 have twins, have two children, have two in a litter
nīsta PrA I, too; I by contrast; I myself
nīsta mīna PrA I, too; I by contrast; I myself
nīstanaw IPC twenty, 20
nīstanān PrA we, too; we by contrast; we ourselves
nīswāw IPC twice, two times; double
nōcikinosēwē- VAI1 fish, go fishing, go for fish; be engaged in fishing
nōcikwēsiw- NA2 old woman, wife
nōh- IPV [grammatical preverb: defines an independent clause; first person, past tense (in negative construction)]
nōhci- IPV [grammatical preverb: first person singular, past tense (in negative construction)]
nōhtē- IPV want to, desire to; lack
nōhtē-mīciso- VAI1 be hungry; want to eat, would like to eat
nōkosi- VAI1 appear, come into view, be visible, become visible, be seen; be born
nōmakēsīs IPC for a little while, after just a little while
nōtikēwi- VAI1 be an old woman [cf. **nōtokēwi-**]
nōtikwēw- NA2 old woman, wife [cf. **nōtokwēw-**]
nōtinikē- VAI1 fight people, put up a fight; take part in war (e.g., World War II)

nōtinito- **VAI1** fight, fight one another
nōtiskwēwē- **VAI1** court a woman
nōtokēwi- **VAI1** be an old woman [cf. **nōtikēwi-**]
nōtokwēw- **NA2** old woman, wife [cf. **nōtikwēw-**]

O

ocēm- **VTA1** kiss s.o.
ocēpihkw- **NI3** root
ocipit- **VTI1** pull s.t., pull s.t. out, pull s.t. off, extract s.t.; move s.t. (e.g., house)
ocipitiko- **VAI1** have a seizure, have fits; have cramps
ohci **IPC** from there, thence, out of; with, by means of; because of, for that reason; for; from then; about
ohci- **IPV** from there, thence; with, by means of; because, for that reason, therefore; [grammatical preverb; past preverb in negative clauses]
ohcikawipēhikē- **VAI1** tap trees, cause the liquid (e.g., sap) to run
ohcimāwaso- **VAI1** scold one's children over something; counsel one's children against improper action
ohcim- **VTA1** scold s.o. over something; stop s.o. from doing something improper
ohcitaw **IPC** on purpose, purposely, deliberately; have to be, be necessary, be requisite; as expected; without fail; by all means; expressly, specifically
ohcī- **VAI1** be from there, come from there; exist thence, therefore
ohpaho- **VAI1** fly up, rise, fly away, fly off, fly from one's perch, lift off by airplane
ohpiki- **VAI1** grow, grow up; be raised
ohpikih- **VTA1** raise s.o., rear s.o., make s.o. grow up
ohpikihcikan- **NI1** plant, grown thing
ohpikin- **VII2** grow, grow up
ohpimē **IPC** off, away, to the side; at another place, elsewhere, somewhere else
ohpin- **VTI1** lift s.t., lift s.t. up, hoist s.t. up, raise s.t.; create s.t.
ohtamahkamikisi- **VAI1** be busy with something, be delayed by something
ohtaskānēsi- **VAI1** come from there, come from that people or nation
ohtatāht- **VTI1** take s.t. into one's own mouth; inhale s.t. (e.g., smoke, incense)
ohtāciho- **VAI1** make one's living from there, that source; travel from there
ohtāpōyo- **VAI1** come from there by vehicle (e.g., train, bus)
ohtin- **VTI1** get s.t. from there, take s.t. from there, obtain s.t. from there, accept s.t. from there
ohtinikē- **VAI1** get things from there, take things from there, obtain things from there

ohtisi- **VAI**$_1$ receive s.t. from there, obtain s.t. (e.g., money) from there, obtain payment from there or thereby; receive benefit from there, profit

ohtitaw **IPC** by nature, of necessity, necessarily, be requisite; for real; expressly, specifically, purposely

ohtitisahamaw- **VTA**$_2$ send (it) to s.o. from there

ohtohtē- **VAI**$_1$ come from there, be coming from there, walk from there; arrive from there

okāminakasiy- **NA**$_2$ thorn-tree, brier; Canada thistle

okāminakasīwāhtikw- **NA**$_3$ thorn-tree

okēyakiciskēhiwēsīs- **NA**$_1$ Little Butt Itcher [legendary second name of rosehips]

okēyakiciskēsīs- **NA**$_1$ Little Butt Itcher [legendary second name of rosehips]

okimāhkān- **NA**$_1$ chief; elected or appointed chief; reserve chief; band council leader; pretend leader

okimāhkāniwi- **VAI**$_1$ be chief, serve as elected chief; be a government-appointed chief

okimānāhk **INM** government, federal or provincial government; Band Council, Band authorities

okimāw- **NA**$_2$ chief, leader, head person, man of high position; king; boss; one's superior; manager

okimāwiwin- **NI**$_1$ chieftaincy; social status; government

okiniy- **NA**$_2$ rosehip, rose-bush berry; thorn berry; tomato

okiniy wāpikwaniy maskihkiy- **NI**$_2$ wild rose flower medicine, medicine made from the flower of the rosehip

okinīwāhtikw- **NA**$_3$ wild rose bush [Lat. *Rosa acicularis*]

okisēyinīmi- **VAI**$_1$ have (s.o. as) a husband, have a living husband, have (s.o. as) one's old man

okīsikāmi- **VAI**$_1$ have a day, be day to one; treat it as if it is daytime

okosisīhkā- **VAI**$_1$ have (s.o. as) a godson, have a male godchild

omanicōsimi- **VAI**$_1$ have cancer [literally: "have little worms"]

omāmihkwēw- **NA**$_2$ Stoney, Assiniboine, Nakoda woman

omikicihcē- **VAI**$_1$ have scabby hands, have sores on one's hands

omikiy- **NI**$_2$ scab, sore; scale; rash; one's scab, one's sore

omisi **IPC** thus, in this way, as follows, like this

omisi isi **IPH** like this, in this way; this is how it is [also: *omis īsi*]

omisi- **VAI**$_1$ have (s.o. as) an older sister

omīńimi- **VAI**$_1$ have internal sores, have open sores, have pus from sores [cf. *miyi* "pus, sore"]

omosōmi- **VAI1** have (s.o. as) a grandfather

opīma **INM** Hobbema, Alberta, former name of Maskwacis, Alberta

opōsiw- **NA2** passenger, traveller

osām **IPC** because, since, for; because of excess

osām **IPC** too much, excessively

osāwā- **VII2** be yellow; be orange; be brown

oscoscocasi- **VAI1** cough a little; cough up a little of something

osikiyāwīs- **NA1** lizard, water dog

osīh- **VTA1** make s.o. (e.g., bread), arrange s.o., prepare s.o. (e.g., porcupine-quill, rattle, etc.)

osīhcikātē- **VII2** be built, be constructed; be made, be prepared

osīhtamaw- **VTA2** make (it/him) for s.o., arrange (it/him) for s.o., prepare (it/him) for s.o.

osīhtā- **VTI2** make s.t., prepare s.t., build s.t.; put s.t. into service, inaugurate s.t.

osīmi- **VAI1** have (s.o. as) a younger sibling

oski-iskwēsis- **NA2** young girl

oskinīkiskwēw- **NA2** young woman (about 14 or 15 years of age); maiden; virgin

oskinīkiskwēwi- **VAI1** be a young woman (about 14 or 15 years of age)

oskotākā- **VAI1** have a coat, dress, robe [e.g., ***k-ōskotākāt***]

osōniyāmi- **VAI1** have money, carry money on oneself

osōniyāmisi- **VAI1** have a little bit of money

ospwākan- **NA1** pipe; ceremonial pipe, sacred pipe

ostostot- **VAI3** cough, have a coughing spell; cough s.t. up, cough s.t. out

otahowē- **VAI1** win, win in gambling

otamih- **VTA1** interrupt s.o., delay s.o., preoccupy s.o.

otatoskēw- **NA2** worker, labourer

otākosin- **VII1** be evening

otākosīhk **IPC** yesterday; the previous evening

otāpāso- **VAI1** ride in a vehicle, drive (a vehicle)

otēhāspinē- **VAI1** have heart disease

otēhimin- **NI1** strawberry, wild strawberry [literally: "heart-berry"; Lat. *Fragaria glauca*; *Fragaria* sp.]

oti **IPC** in fact [emphasises preceding word or phrase]; [cf. **ōti**]

otiht- **VTI1** reach s.t., come to where s.t. is, arrive at s.t., encounter s.t., approach s.t.

otiht- **VTA1** reach s.o., get to s.o.; come upon s.o., approach s.o.

otihtapisin- **VAI2** lie prone, lie face down, lie on one's own stomach face down to the ground; lie on one's own stomach with head propped up on one's own hands [e.g., ***ē-wiyotihtapisiniyān***]

otin- **VTI$_1$** take s.t.; choose s.t., select s.t., pick s.t.; purchase s.t.; steal s.t.; take s.t. over; extract s.t., remove s.t. (e.g., glands in butchering beaver); accept s.t. (e.g., contract); capture s.t., record s.t. on audio-tape

otin- **VTA$_1$** take s.o., take s.o. in (e.g., orphan); choose s.o., select s.o., pick s.o.; purchase s.o.; take s.o. for (it/him), steal s.o.

otisīhkān- **NI$_1$** turnip

otōkimāmi- **VAI$_1$** have (s.o. as) a chief; have (s.o. as) a boss, master

otōtēmi- **VAI$_1$** be friendly; have (s.o. as) a friend or kinsman

owēpahikēw- **NA$_1$** sweeper, janitor

owiyawi- **VAI$_1$** have a body

oy- **IPV** [grammatical preverb: ongoing, continuing]

oyasiwē- **VAI$_1$** make laws; judge

oyākan- **NI$_1$** plate, dish, pan; bowl

oyākanis- **NI$_1$** cup; little plate, small dish

oyociwāmi- **VAI$_1$** have a brother, have a male parallel cousin

oyokāwī- **VAI$_1$** have (her as) a mother [cf. **wiyokāwī-**]

oyokisēyinīmi- **VAI$_1$** have (s.o. as) a husband, have a living husband, have (s.o. as) one's old man

oyomosōmi- **VAI$_1$** have (him as) a grandfather, have a living grandfather

oyōhkomi- **VAI$_1$** have (her as) a grandmother, have a living grandmother [cf. **wiyōhkomi-**]

oyōhtāwī- **VAI$_1$** have (s.o. as) a father [cf. **wiyōhtāwī-**]

Ō

ō **IPJ** oh! [cf. **ōh**]

ō- **IPV** from there, for that reason; with, by means of; [grammatical preverb]

ōcēw- **NA$_2$** fly, housefly; maggot

ōh **IPJ** oh! [cf. **ō**]

ōh- **IPV** [grammatical past preverb in negative clauses: have done]

ōh- **IPV** from there, thence; for that reason; with, by means of; for that reason

ōhi **PrI** these ones

ōhi **PrA** this one, these ones

ōho **PrA** this one, these ones

ōki **PrA** these

ōko **PrA** these

ōma **PrI** this

ōma **IPC** be this; the fact that; then; when; as be, actually [focus marker]

ōma ita **PrI** here it is [also: *ōm īta*]

ōmatowa **IPC** of this kind, like this

ōmatowahk **IPC** of this kind, like this

ōmatowi **IPC** right here, in this place; like this

ōmatowihk **IPC** right here, in this place; like this

ōmayikohk **IPC** this much, to this degree, to this extent, this far

ōta **IPC** here

ōtē **IPC** over here, hither; over there
ōtēnaw- **NI2** camp-circle; town, settlement; city
ōtēnaw-iyiniw- **NI2** person living in a town or city, citizen of a city; [plural:] townsfolk
ōtēnāhk **IPC** in town, in the city
ōti **IPC** that is to say, at any rate [cf. **oti**]

p

pa- **IPV** [grammatical preverb: ongoing, continuing]
pahkān **IPC** different, differently
pahkēkinw- **NI3** hide; tanned hide, dressed hide, finished hide, leather; tent cover
pahkēkinwē- **IPN** leather, tanned hide
pahkihtitā- **VTI2** drop s.t. accidentally, let s.t. fall
pahkisin- **VAI2** fall, fall down; have an airplane accident, crash one's airplane
pahkwēsikan- **NA1** bannock, bread; flour
pakahkam **IPC** I think, I believe; apparently; perhaps, maybe; surely, it's very likely, to judge by appeal
pakamahikē- **VAI1** strike, hit, hammer; box; dab (i.e., at bingo)
pakamahw- **VTA3** hit s.o., pound s.o., strike s.o., beat s.o.
pakamicihcēhamā- **VAI1** clap one's hands
pakāhtākokē- **VAI1** use something to boil water, boil water with something
pakāhtā- **VTI2** boil s.t. in water; immerse s.t. in water
pakāsim- **VTA1** boil s.o. in water; immerse s.o. in water
pakāsimo- **VAI1** bathe, take a bath; swim; be immersed in water
pakiciwēpin- **VTA1** let go of s.o., abandon s.o.
pakitin- **VTI1** let s.t. go; release s.t., set s.t. down by hand; allow s.t., permit s.t.; provide s.t.; leave s.t. behind; put s.t. down on earth, sow s.t., put s.t. in (e.g., seed potatoes)
pakitin- **VTA1** let s.o. go, release s.o.; set s.o. down by hand; let s.o., allow s.o., give permission to s.o., permit (it to) s.o.; set s.o. free; drop s.o. off (e.g., as an airplane); stock a lake with s.o. (e.g., fish)
pakitinamaw- **VTA2** let s.o., allow s.o., allow (it for) s.o.; set (it/him) down for s.o. (by hand), arrange (it) for s.o.; let s.o. have (it/him); sow (it/him) for s.o.; release (it) for s.o.
pakiwayān- **NI1** shirt; blouse
pakiwayānis- **NI1** shirting, cloth; small shirt; small blouse
pakonēyā- **VII2** have a hole in it, have a hole in the middle of it
pakopit- **VTI1** rip s.t. open
pakosēyim- **VTA1** wish s.o. (to get well), wish (it) for s.o.; expect (it) of s.o.
pakwahtēho- **VAI1** have a belt on

pakwahtēhon- **NI1** belt; girdle
pakwāt- **VTI1** hate s.t., dislike s.t., disapprove of s.t.
pakwāt- **VTA4** hate s.o., dislike s.o., disapprove of s.o.
pamēyim- **VTA1** take thought of s.o., care for s.o., watch over s.o.; take charge of s.o.
pamih- **VTA1** take care of s.o., look after s.o., help s.o., give aid to s.o., tend to s.o., serve s.o.; attend s.o. (i.e., in childbirth), serve s.o. as a midwife; guide s.o. (e.g., sleigh); drive s.o. (e.g., horse, car)
pamihcikē- **VAI1** drive, drive one's team; tend things
pamihiso- **VAI1** look after oneself, tend to oneself, wait on oneself, support oneself; attend oneself in childbirth, serve as one's own midwife
pamiho- **VAI1** be well off; be well looked after; look after oneself
pamin- **VTI1** tend to s.t., look after s.t.
pamin- **VTA1** tend to s.o., handle s.o.; foster s.o., support s.o., look after s.o.; guide s.o.; attend s.o. in childbirth, serve as midwife to s.o.
paminawaso- **VAI1** cook, prepare a meal
panātisi- **VAI1** die
papakā- **IPV** thinly, not in depth
papakā-ākayāsīmo- **VAI1** speak only a bit of English, do not speak high English, have a surface knowledge of English, be not fully fluent in English
papā- **IPV** go around, about, all over; here and there
papāmi- **IPV** around, about, all over, here and there, hither and thither
papāmipahtā- **VAI1** run about; run around, be promiscuous
papāmitācimo- **VAI1** crawl around, about
papāmohtah- **VTA1** carry s.o. about, walk s.o. about, take s.o. about, take s.o. here and there
papāmohtē- **VAI1** wander, walk around, walk about, go here and there; run around, be promiscuous
pasako-ay- **NI4** sticky thing
pasakocēpihkw- **NI3** plant unidentified in English [literally "sticky root"]
pasakwāpi- **VAI1** close one's eyes, have one's eyes shut
pasakwā- **VII2** be sticky
patah- **VTI1** miss s.t. (by tool or shot); miss the target, miss the mark
patihtakon- VTA1 mishandle the stem of s.o. (e.g. an animate plant)
patin- **VTI1** drop s.t., miss s.t. by hand
pawihtitā- **VTI2** shake s.t. out, shake the dust off of s.t.
payipwāt- **NA1** Chief Piapot, literally: "Hole-in-the-Sioux"; prominent chief of the *nēhiyawipwātak* or Piapot Band

payipwātināhk **INM** Piapot First Nation, SK [literally: "among Piapot's people"]
pāh- **IPV** [grammatical preverb: intermittent, repeatedly; again and again; here and there]
pāh-pēyak **IPC** each individually, each one; one each; singly, one at a time, one by one
pāhkw-āyamihāwin- **NI**1 Roman Catholic religion; the Roman Catholic church; the Roman Catholic liturgy [also: *pāhko-ayamihāwin*]
pāhkw-āyis- **NA**1 Roman Catholic [also: *pāhko-ayis*]
pāhkwahw- **VTA**3 dry s.o., wipe s.o. dry
pāhpi- **VAI**1 laugh, be laughing, smile
pāhpih- **VTA**1 laugh at s.o., deride s.o.; joke with s.o.; make s.o. laugh
pāhpihtā- **VTI**2 laugh at s.t., deride s.t.
pāhpisi- **VAI**1 smile, laugh a little, giggle, chuckle
pākipayin- **VII**2 swell, be swollen
pās- **VTI**1 dry s.t. (by warmth or heat) (e.g., meat, berries, moss)
pāstē- **VII**2 dry, be dried (in warmth), be dry
pātos **IPC** only later; then, later
pē- **IPV** come and, come to; towards, approaching; hither; thence, from there on down; [towards focus]
pē-ayā- **VAI**1 come to live, come to stay
pē-itohtē- **VAI**1 come walking, come over here
pēcāstamohtē- **VAI**1 come walking hither
pēh- **VTA**1 wait for s.o.
pēhkascikē- **VAI**1 clean up, tidy up
pēhkastē- **VII**2 be cleaned up, be tidied up
pēhkayiwinisah- **VTA**1 clean clothing for s.o., clean s.o.'s clothing
pēhkihcikē- **VAI**1 clean up
pēhkih- **VTA**1 clean s.o., cleanse s.o.
pēhkihkas- **VTI**1 clean s.t. by burning
pēhkiho- **VAI**1 keep oneself clean
pēhkihtā- **VTI**2 clean s.t., cleanse s.t.
pēht- **VTI**1 hear s.t.
pēhtaw- **VTA**2 hear s.o.
pēhtākwan- **VII**2 be audible, be heard; be noisy
pēhtā- **VTI**2 wait for s.t.
pēpīsis- **NA**1 baby
pēskis **IPC** at the same time, simultaneously; also, besides, as well
pētamaw- **VTA**2 bring (it/him) to or for s.o.
pētā- **VTI**2 bring s.t., bring s.t. hither
pētisāpam- **VTA**1 see s.o. coming
pēyak **IPC** one, 1; alone, single, a single one; the only one; a certain one
pēyak-askiy- **IPC** one year; for one year
pēyako- **IPV** alone, only; as one

pēyako-ospwākan- NA$_1$ single pipe, lone pipe [also: *pēyak-ōspwākan*]

pēyakokah- VTA$_1$ isolate s.o., make s.o. dwell alone

pēyakokē- VAI$_1$ dwell alone, live alone, dwell by oneself

pēyakonikātē- VII$_2$ be held apart, be held alone

pēyakosisāniwi- VAI$_1$ be an only son

pēyako- VAI$_1$ be alone; be the only one; be left alone, go alone

pēyakwan IPC same, the same, just the same; similar

pēyakwanohk IPC in one place, in a single place; the same spot, in the same place

pēyakwapi- VAI$_1$ be alone; sit alone, stay alone at home, be alone in the house

pēyakwayak IPC in one place, in a certain place; in the same place; one way, one kind

pēyakwāciho- VAI$_1$ live alone, travel alone

pēyakwāw IPC once, one time, once more; at one time

pēyāhtak IPC / IPJ quietly, gently, softly, slowly, carefully; take it easy

pici- VAI$_1$ move, move camp; move one's belongings and family; travel, go on a trek

pihēkocēpihkw- NI$_3$ plant unidentified in English [literally: "scaly-root"]

pihēkosi- VAI$_1$ be rough, scaly and hard to swallow

pihēkwā- VII$_2$ be rough, scaly and hard to swallow

pihkahtē- VII$_2$ be burnt (as a roast)

pihkāciwahtē- VII$_2$ be boiled to soften, be boiled to reconstitute it

pihkāciwas- VTI$_1$ boil s.t. to soften it, boil s.t. to reconstitute it (e.g., dried chokecherries)

piko IPC only

piko IPC must, have to; for sure, without a doubt

piko ani IPH anyway

piko awiyak PrA everyone, everybody; anyone

piko isi IPH in any manner, no matter how; any way, every way; in any direction

piko isi isi IPH in any manner, no matter how; any way, every way; in any direction

piko ispī IPH any time

piko ispīhk IPH any time

piko ita IPH anywhere, in any place, no matter where; everywhere [also: *pikw īta*]

piko itē IPH anywhere; to any place, no matter whither; all over, everywhere [also: *pikw ītē*]

piko kīkway PrI something or other; anything at all, everything

pimakocin- VAI$_2$ fly past; move along, go by; work, be in working order (e.g., clock, car)

pimakotē- VII$_2$ fly past; run along, operate, work, be in working order, run (e.g., tape recorder)

pimamo- VII$_2$ pass along

pimāciho- **VAI**1 live, make oneself live, make a living (from s.t.), make a life for oneself; travel

pimācihowin- **NI**1 travel, journey; living, way of life, livelihood, earning a living; culture

pimāpahtē- **VII**2 float along as smoke, be smoke blowing a long way

pimātisi- **VAI**1 live, be alive; survive

pimātisiwin- **NI**1 life

pimi- **IPV** along, in linear progression; while moving in linear progression

pimi-ācimo- **VAI**1 tell stories along the way, go along telling stories

pimipayihtā- **VTI**2 run s.t., operate s.t., (e.g., machine, program); keep s.t. up, exercise s.t.; conduct s.t.

pimisim- **VTA**1 lay s.o. down, lay s.o. extended, lay s.o. on the ground or bed, put s.o. to bed

pimisin- **VAI**2 lie, lie down, lie extended; lie confined, lie in childbed

pimitāpāso- **VAI**1 drive about, drive by, drive around, drive along in a vehicle

pimitisah- **VTI**1 follow s.t.; send s.t.; adhere to s.t. (as a religion)

pimitisahw- **VTA**3 follow behind s.o., go behind s.o.; drive s.o. along; send s.o.

pimiy- **NI**2 grease (rendered); lard; shortening; oil; butter; fat; crude petroleum; [plural:] variety of fats, lards, tallow, mazola

pimīhkān- **NI**1 pemmican

pimohtacikātē- **VII**2 be transported, be carried along

pimohtatā- **VTI**2 carry s.t., take s.t. along, travel with s.t., have s.t. along; transport s.t.

pimohtāt- **VTI**1 walk through s.t.; pass through s.t.

pimohtē- **VAI**1 walk, walk along; go along

pimohtēho- **VAI**1 travel; travel through life, live one's life

pimohtēski- **VAI**1 always walk, walk all of the time

pipon- **VII**1 be winter; be one year

piponi-pīsimw- **NA**3 winter month

pisci- **IPV** accidentally, by accident, mistakenly, erroneously, in error

pisci-asam- **VTA**1 feed s.o. (it) by accident

piscipayihtā- **VTI**2 accidentally drive into s.t.

piscipowi- **VII**2 be poisonous

pisisik **IPC** always, all the time, constantly, every time, routinely; mere; nothing else

pisiskiw- **NA**2 animal, beast; wild animal; domestic animal

pisiskīs- **NA**1 small animal

pistaht- **VTI**1 bite s.t. by mistake, accidentally bite s.t.

pistisk- **VTI**1 step on s.t. accidentally, bump or knock into s.t. by mistake

pistiskaw- **VTA2** step on s.o. accidentally, bump or knock into s.o. by mistake, knock s.o. down inadvertently (by foot or body movement)

pitamā **IPC** first, first of all, prior to doing anything else; for a while, for now, just a while; in the meantime

pitanē **IPC** would that, wish that; I wish, I hope

piyē- **IPV** come and, come to; towards, approaching; hither; thence, from there on down; [towards focus]; [changed conjunct form of **pē-**]

piyēsīs- **NA1** bird, small bird

piyis **IPC** eventually, finally, in the end, at last; until

piyisk **IPC** eventually, finally, in the end, at last; until

pīhcāyihk **IPC** inside, indoors

pīhci- **IPV** inside, in, within; in between

pīhcihtawakēyāpāwē- **VAI1** have water poured into one's ear, undergo irrigation of the ear

pīhtasiwatā- **VTI2** put s.t. inside (a bag or box), enclose s.t.

pīhtawayiwinis- **NI1** underclothing, underwear [generally plural]

pīhtikwē- **IPV** indoors; entering [cf. **pīhtokē-**, **pīhtokwē-**]

pīhtohkot- **VTI1** peel s.t. by knife (e.g., tree bark), cut the covering layer off of s.t.

pīhtokaw- **VTA2** enter s.o.'s abode, enter to visit s.o.

pīhtokē- **VAI1** enter, go in [cf. **pīhtikwē-**, **pīhtokwē-**]

pīhtokēyāhtawī- **VAI1** climb inside

pīhtokwah- **VTA1** make s.o. enter, make s.o. go inside, take s.o. inside, enter with s.o., bring s.o. inside; allow s.o. to enter

pīhtokwatā- **VTI2** bring s.t. inside, take s.t. indoors, enter with s.t.

pīhtokwaw- **VTA1** enter s.o.'s home

pīhtokwē- **VAI1** enter, go inside [cf. **pīhtikwē-**, **pīhtokē-**]

pīhton- **VTI1** peel s.t. by hand (e.g., tree bark), take the covering layer off s.t.

pīhtwā- **VAI1** smoke; smoke the pipe, use the pipe; hold a pipe ceremony; be a nicotine addict

pīhtwāh- **VTA1** give s.o. a smoke; give s.o. to smoke; make s.o. smoke

pīhtwāwin- **NI1** smoking; smoking ceremony; cannabis abuse

pīkinisw- **VTA3** cut s.o. into small pieces

pīkiskwāt- **VTI1** speak to s.t., talk to s.t., address s.t.; speak about s.t.; speak about s.t. with concern; speak a prayer over s.t.

pīkiskwāt- **VTA4** speak to s.o., talk to s.o., address s.o.; speak about s.o.

pīkiskwē- **VAI1** speak, talk, use words, make a speech; speak a prayer, pray

pīkiskwēstamāso- VAI$_1$ speak for oneself, do one's own speaking

pīkiskwēwin- NI$_1$ word, expression, phrase; what is being said, speech, talk, conversation; lecture; language; voice; syllable of syllabary

pīkopayi- VAI$_1$ be broken, be torn; break down; be broke, be without monetary funds; go broke, go bankrupt

pīkopayin- VII$_2$ be broken; break down

pīkopit- VTI$_1$ tear s.t., break s.t. (e.g., soil), plough s.t. (e.g., field)

pīkowēpah- VTI$_1$ break s.t. (by prying with a bar)

pīmin- VTI$_1$ twist s.t. by hand, unscrew s.t.; turn s.t. on (e.g., equipment), turn s.t. down (e.g., electric appliance, temperature, etc.)

pīsimw- NA$_3$ sun; moon; month

pīsin- VTA$_1$ break s.o. into little bits by hand

pīwāpiskw- NA$_3$ metal, piece of metal, metal object; steel blade; iron; screen of wire mesh; dollar

postayiwinisē- VAI$_1$ put one's own clothing on, get dressed

pōn- VTI$_1$ build a fire, feed the fire; build a fire with s.t., put (s.t. as) fuel on the fire

pōni- IPV stop, terminate, cease; after

pōnipayi- VII$_2$ stop running, stop operating, stop, cease, cease to exist, come to an end

pōnipayi- VAI$_1$ stop, stop driving

pōsi- VAI$_1$ board, get aboard, embark, be aboard; ride (in a vehicle), ride the train

pōsihcikē- VAI$_1$ load things

pōsih- VTA$_1$ give s.o. a ride; put s.o. on board, make s.o. board (e.g., boat or vehicle), put s.o. on a sleigh, give s.o. a ride on a sleigh

pōsihtā- VTI$_2$ put s.t. on board, load s.t. on

pōsīs- NA$_1$ cat; kitten

pōskwah- VTI$_1$ open s.t. (by making a hole)

pōskwaht- VTI$_1$ bite s.t. open

pōyo- VAI$_1$ stop, cease, quit, give up

pwācis- NA$_1$ little Sioux, little Dakota person, you Dakota person

pwāsīmow- VAI$_1$ speak Assiniboine, Nakoda; speak Dakota, Sioux

pwātawiho- VAI$_1$ fail, be unable; be stumped

pwātawihtā- VTI$_2$ fail of s.t., be thwarted at s.t.; give up trying to fix s.t.

pwēkicimin- NA$_1$ bean [generally plural; literally: "fart-berry"]

S

sa- IPV [grammatical preverb: ongoing, continuing]

sakah- VTI$_1$ nail s.t., nail s.t. on, fasten s.t. on (by tool), attach s.t. by nails

sakahpitastimwē- **VAI1** tie up one's horses, harness one's horses

sakā- **VII2** be bush, there are woods; there is a grove of trees, woodland, forest

sakāhk **IPC** in the woods, in the bush

sakāhkwanīwi- **VII2** have tangled branches

sakāpēkin- **VTA1** lead s.o., hold s.o. (by string or rope in hand)

sakāw- **NI2** bush, woods, grove of trees, woodland, forest

sakikwēn- **VTA1** seize s.o.'s neck (by hand), hold s.o. by the neck, take s.o. by the neck

sakin- **VTI1** hang on to s.t. (by hand)

sasīhtēyiht- **VTI1** worry about s.t., have anxiety over s.t., be uptight about s.t.

sasīpiht- **VTI1** be disobedient, disobey s.t.; be stubborn; fail to listen (to s.t.)

saskah- **VTI1** kindle s.t., ignite s.t, light s.t. (e.g., a lamp); set s.t. on fire

saskahikātē- **VII2** be kindled, be ignited, be set alight, be set on fire

saskahohtē- **VAI1** walk with a cane

saskamo- **VAI1** put (it/him) into one's own mouth; take holy communion; have one's first communion

saskamowin- **NI1** host (e.g., in communion)

sawēyihto- **VAI1** bless one another; love one another

sawēyim- **VTA1** cherish s.o., love s.o., take care of s.o., look out for s.o.; be generous to s.o.; bless s.o.; give s.o. the last sacrament

sāh- **IPV** [grammatical preverb: intermittent, repeatedly, iteratively; again and again; here and there]

sāh-sōskwāt **IPC** just, truly, surely; directly, straight away; simply, without further ado

sākahikan- **NI1** lake

sākamo- **VAI1** stick out

sākih- **VTA1** love s.o., prize s.o., be attached to s.o.

sākihtā- **VTI2** love s.t., prize s.t., be attached to s.t.; be stingy of s.t., be selfish of s.t.

sākikātēsin- **VAI2** lie with one's legs sticking out, lie with legs protruding

sākiki- **VAI1** grow forth, sprout

sākikin- **VII2** grow forth, sprout, emerge from the ground

sākoh- **VTA1** overcome s.o., overpower s.o., overwhelm s.o., defeat s.o.

sāponikan- **NI1** needle

sāpopacikākē- **VAI1** use something to water things; drench things with something

sāpopē- **VAI1** be wet, be drenched, be sodden, be wet throughout; get wet

sāposkāwisi- **VAI1** have diarrhea

sāpōmin- **NA1** gooseberry; currant

sāpōmināhtikw- **NI3** gooseberry bush [Lat. *Ribes hirtellum*]

sāpwāstē- VII2 be transparent
sāsākwaht- VTI1 chew s.t. into small pieces
sāsāpiskis- VTI1 fry s.t.
sāsikan- NA1 rendered fat, incompletely rendered pieces of fat [generally plural]
sēhkēs- NA1 car
sēkim- VTA1 frighten s.o. by speech
sēkon- VTI1 put s.t. under or between; place s.t. beneath the coals; put s.t. into the oven
sēkon- VTA1 put s.o. (e.g., a chicken) into the oven
sēkwāmo- VAI1 flee and hide under something
sēkwamon- VII2 be underneath, run beneath, be attached underneath
sēmāk IPC right now, right away, at once, immediately, instantly
sēsēskēyihtākosi- VAI1 be thought frightening
sēsēskēyihtākwan- VII2 be thought frightening
sēwēpayi- VII2 jingle, rattle; ring (e.g., phone)
sēwēpicikan- NI1 phone, telephone
sēwēpicikē- VAI1 jingle things; ring a bell; make a phone call
sihkos- NA1 weasel; ermine
sihkowin- NI1 spit, spittle, saliva
sihkwāt- VTI1 spit on s.t.
sikatēyiht- VTI1 be bored by s.t.
sikon- VTI1 crush s.t. by hand until small
sikopit- VTI1 tear s.t. to pieces
sikosw- VTA3 cut s.o. up (e.g., tobacco)
sikwahw- VTA3 crush s.o. (by tool) until small; mash s.o. (as food)
sikwatah- VTI1 pound s.t. (by tool with handle) until small, crush s.t. (by pounding)
sikwāciwasw- VTA3 boil s.o. until it falls into small bits, boil s.o. apart, dissolve s.o. in boiling
simākanis- NA1 policeman, officer; [plural:] policemen; soldiers
sinikon- VTA1 rub s.o., stroke s.o.
sipwēhtatā- VTI2 take s.t. away, leave with s.t., depart with s.t.
sipwēhtē- VAI1 leave, go off, depart
sipwēpahtā- VAI1 leave running; run off
sipwēpici- VAI1 move camp away, move away with all one's own goods and family, leave with one's camp, depart with one's camp
sipwētisah- VTI1 send s.t. away, mail s.t. away
sisonē IPC along, alongside, along the edge
sisonēkamīhk IPC along the water; on the waterfront, along the shore
sisonēstē- VII2 be alongside, be situated along (the shore)
sisopāt- VTI1 spray s.t.; lick s.t.; spit s.t. spattering (e.g., in traditional healing, the

practice of chewing herbs which are blown on a patient)

sisopēhikan- NI_1 salve, lotion

sisopēkaho- VAI_1 paint oneself; put salve on oneself, slather it on oneself

sīhkaci- VAI_1 be very thin; be lean

sīhkim- VTA_1 urge s.o., encourage s.o., guide s.o. (by speech); order s.o.

sīhtawā- VII_2 be tight, be stiff

sīhtostikwānēhpiso- VAI_1 bandage one's own head tightly

sīkaho- VAI_1 comb one's own hair

sīkahon- NI_1 comb

sīkahw- VTA_3 comb s.o.'s hair

sīkahwākē- VAI_1 comb one's hair with something, use something to comb one's own hair

sīkin- VTI_1 pour s.t., pour s.t. in; spill s.t.; let it rain (e.g., the Creator)

sīkinamaw- VTA_2 pour (it/him) for s.o. (e.g., tea); pour (it/him) out for s.o.

sīkosākan- NA_1 cracklings; rendered fat; the solids remaining at the end of the process of rendering [generally plural]

sīkosi- VAI_1 be empty

sīpī- VAI_1 stretch

sīpīski- VAI_1 stretch all of the time

sīsipāskwat- NI_1 maple sugar, soft sugar

sīsipāskwatāhtikw- NA_3 sugar maple [Lat. *Acer saccharum*]

sīsipāskwatwāhtikw- NA_3 sugar maple [Lat. *Acer saccharum*]

sīsipāskwatwāpoy- NI_2 sugar maple sap

sīsīkwan- NA_1 rattle

sīsīp- NA_1 duck

sīskōpātin- VTI_1 strain s.t., sift s.t.

sītaw **IPC** stiff

sīwinikan- NA_1 sugar, sweetener

sīwipohāwaso- VAI_1 give one's children something sweet to eat, provide sweets to one's children

sīwipwāt- VTI_1 eat s.t. as a sweet

sōhkan- VII_2 be strongly made, be sturdy, be firm, be solid, be strong; be important; be powerful, have supernatural power

sōkāwāhtikw- NA_3 sugar maple tree

sōminis- NA_1 currant; little grape, raisin

sōniyāhkēsi- VAI_1 make some money, earn a little money, earn some wages

sōniyāhkēstamaw- VTA_2 earn money from s.o., make money for s.o.

sōniyāhkē- VAI_1 earn money, earn wages; make money, create money

sōniyānāhk **INM** at the bank

sōniyās- NA_1 money; change; coin; [singular:] quarter dollar; a quarter, twenty-five cents; a little money, some money

sōniyāw- NA_2 money, wages; gold, silver

sōniyāwasinahikan- NI1 cheque; money order
sōpaht- VTI1 lap s.t. up; lick s.t. off the bone; eat meat off; put s.t. in one's mouth; spit on s.t.
sōskwāc IPC just, regardless, no matter what the consequences; truly, surely; directly, immediately, straight away; simply, without further ado, without delay; [in negative clauses:] at all
sōskwāt IPC just, regardless, no matter what the consequences; truly, surely; directly, immediately, straight away; simply, without further ado, without delay; [in negative clauses:] at all

t

ta- IPV [grammatical preverb: future; irrealis, infinitive]
ta-kī- IPV can, be able to; may; should, ought to
tahcipicikē- VAI1 undo things; unzip
tahkam- VTA1 stab s.o.
tahkikamāpoy- NI2 cold water
tahkikami- VII2 be cold water
tahkin- VTI1 poke s.t. with a finger, elbow, etc.
tahkin- VTA1 poke s.o. with a finger, elbow, etc.
tahkohc IPC top, on top; above
tahkon- VTI1 carry s.t.; grasp s.t., hold s.t.
tahkonamōh- VTA1 make s.o. carry (it/him), make s.o. hold (it/him)
tahkon- VTA1 carry s.o.; grasp s.o., hold s.o.
tahkopit- VTI1 tie s.t. fast, tie s.t. shut, tie s.t. in, tie s.t. up
tahkwam- VTA1 bite s.o.; have s.o. in one's own mouth; hold s.o. fast by mouth
tahto-ayamihēwi-kīsikāw IPC every Sunday
tahto-kīsikāw IPC each day, every day, daily
tahtwāpisk IPC dollar(s); so many dollars
tahtwāw IPC each time, every time; so many times
takahkāciho- VAI1 make a very good living, live very well
takahkāpam- VTA1 really like the look of s.o.; look very favourably on s.o.
takahkēyiht- VTI1 be glad, be pleased; think well of s.t., like s.t., be glad about s.t.
takahkēyihtākwan- VII2 be highly thought of, be thought to be terrific
takahkēyim- VTA1 think well of s.o., like s.o., consider s.o. nice; like s.o.'s ways
takahki-ācimowin- NI1 beautiful story, great story, terrific story
takahkipayi- VAI1 have things go very well, be moving along beautifully
takohtah- VTA1 arrive with s.o.; take s.o. to arrive, bring s.o. to a destination

takohtē- **VAI$_1$** arrive, arrive walking, arrive on foot

takon- **VTI$_1$** add more to s.t., include s.t., add s.t. to something

takon- **VTA$_1$** add on to s.o., add more to s.o., add (it/him) to s.o.; include s.o., enrich (it) with s.o.

takonikāso- **VAI$_1$** be added in (as an ingredient)

takonikātē- **VII$_2$** be added in by hand

takopayi- **VAI$_1$** arrive riding, arrive by horseback, arrive driving, arrive by vehicle

takopayi- **VII$_2$** arrive (e.g., a vehicle)

takwah- **VTI$_1$** crush s.t. (by hand); pound or press s.t. with a heavy weight; crush berries; add s.t. by tool

takwahiminãhtikw- **NA$_3$** chokecherry tree [Lat. *Prunus virginiana*]

takwahiminān- **NI$_1$** chokecherry [generally plural]

takwahiminānāhcikos- **NA$_1$** chokecherry tree branch

takwahiminānāhtikw- **NA$_3$** chokecherry tree

takwahiminē **VAI$_1$** crush berries, crush chokecherries

takwaht- **VTI$_1$** eat s.t. along with something

takwakotē- **VII$_2$** arrive across the sky (e.g., cloud); arrive flying

takwākin- **VII$_1$** be autumn, be fall

tapasī- **VAI$_1$** flee, run away

tasi- **IPV** for such a time, along in time, for the duration; an action at a time; while, at the same time; at that place

tasim- **VTA$_1$** talk about s.o., discuss s.o.; talk at s.o

tasīhkaw- **VTA$_2$** work with s.o., work on s.o., trouble oneself with s.o.; be busy with s.o. (as a doctor with a patient)

tasīht- **VTI$_1$** talk about s.t., discuss s.t.

taskamitāpāso- **VAI$_1$** drive across (e.g., with horse and wagon)

tatahkamikisi- **VAI$_1$** have things to do; be busy there, be busy at s.t.

tāh- **IPV** would, ought to; likely to

tāh- **IPV** [grammatical preverb: intermittent, repeatedly; again and again; here and there]

tān ōt āni **IPH** how much, how great [also: *tāni oti ani*]

tānēhki **IPC** why

tānēhki ētikwē **IPC** I don't know why; I wonder why?

tāni **PrI** which one

tānimayikohk **IPC** how much, to what extent; to such an extent; how far is it

tānisi **IPC** how, in what way

tānispīhk **IPC** when

tānita **IPC** where (in a defined area), where precisely

tānitahto **IPC** how many; so many

tānitahtwāw **IPC** how many times; so many times

tānitē **IPC** where, where over there (in an undefined area), whereabouts, where in general; whither

tānitowahk **IPC** what kind, in what way
tāpakwē- **VAI**$_1$ snare, set snares
tāpāhkōm- **VTA**$_1$ adopt s.o., take s.o. as a relative
tāpihtitā- **VTI**$_2$ fit s.t. in; put a handle on s.t.
tāpisk- **VTI**$_1$ wear s.t. around one's own neck; wear s.t. fitted
tāpiskōc **IPC** like, for instance; just like, as if, in the same way; it seems, seemingly, apparently, similar to; equally
tāpiskōt **IPC** like, for instance; just like, as if, in the same way; it seems, seemingly, apparently, similar to; equally
tāpitaw **IPC** even if; always, all the time
tāpiti- **IPV** always, all the time
tāpwē **IPC** in truth, truly, indeed, really, for sure
tāpwē ēsa **IPH** really?, is that really true?; a little too much
tāpwē- **VAI**$_1$ speak truly, speak the truth, tell the truth
tāpwēht- **VTI**$_1$ believe s.t., agree with s.t.
tāpwēm- **VTA**$_1$ tell the truth about s.o. (generally about personality); convince s.o. to be truthful
tāwāyihk **IPC** in the centre, in the middle; between the places, in the place between
tēhcikāpawi- **VAI**$_1$ stand on something
tēhtapāt- **VTI**$_1$ mount s.t., ride s.t.; sit on top of s.t.
tēhtapi- **VAI**$_1$ mount, be mounted, ride; sit on horseback, be on horseback; sit on top
tēhtascikātē- **VII**$_2$ be placed on top of something
tēhtastā- **VTI**$_2$ place s.t. on top of something
tēpakohp **IPC** seven, 7
tēpēyimo- **VAI**$_1$ agree, agree to do s.t.; be content, be willing
tēpiyawēh- **VTA**$_1$ soothe s.o.'s anger, calm s.o. down from their anger
tēpiyāhk **IPC** the only thing; the most (if any); at least, at any rate, as long as; only if; just, just so, just barely; merely; [in negative phrases:] all but
tēpwācikātē- **VII**$_2$ be called
tēpwāt- **VTI**$_1$ call for s.t.
tēpwāt- **VTA**$_4$ call to s.o., call for s.o., yell at s.o.; publish the marriage banns for s.o.
tēpwē- **VAI**$_1$ call, shout, yell, holler
tēpwēyāhpi- **VAI**$_1$ laugh out loud, guffaw
tēwihtawakēpayi- **VAI**$_1$ get a sudden earache
tēwistikwānēski- **VAI**$_1$ alway have headaches, be plagued by headaches, have migraines
tipah- **VTI**$_1$ pay for s.t., pay s.t.; measure s.t.; make s.t. even by tool
tipahamaw- **VTA**$_2$ pay (it/him) to s.o., pay s.o. for (it/him),

repay a debt to s.o.; pay s.o. a pension

tipahākē- VAI1 measure things with something, measure things against something, use something to measure things, use something as a benchmark; rely on things

tipahikan- NI1 measurement, portion; yardstick; yard; hour

tipahikē- VAI1 pay for things, make a payment; measure

tipahikēh- VTA1 make s.o. pay

tipahikēsimo- VAI1 earn for oneself, make payments on one's own behalf; rely on oneself to earn

tipēyiht- VTI1 own s.t., possess s.t., control s.t., rule s.t.; be master over s.t.; have a voice in the affairs of s.t. (e.g., reserve)

tipēyim- VTA1 own s.o., possess s.o.; control s.o., rule over s.o., govern s.o.; be in charge of s.o., have s.o. in one's clutches; [Christian:] be the Lord over s.o.

tipiskā- VII1 be night, be nighttime; be dark

tipiyaw IPC personally, in person; own; really; in person

tipiyawē IPC one's own, personal; personally, in person; really

tita- IPV [grammatical preverb; irrealis]

titipawēhikē- VAI1 curl hair

tiyawī- VAI1 be busy

tohtōsāpoy- NI2 milk

'toni IPC very, really, intensively, fully, completely, to full degree; quite; much, a lot; well [cf. **mitoni, mētoni**]

tōcikātē- VII2 be done, be done so; be customary

tōmiciskē- VAI1 have salve on one's own anus; have a greasy anus

tōmin- VTI1 grease s.t. up, oil s.t.

tōmisi- VAI1 be greasy, be oily

tōskinē- VTA1 nudge s.o. (with one's own hand or elbow)

tōt- VTI1 do s.t., do s.t. so, act thus

tōtamaw- VTA2 do (it) so for s.o.; do thus to s.o.

tōtaw- VTA2 do (it) so to s.o., do so for s.o.; treat s.o. so

tōtāso- VAI1 do so to oneself

W

wa- IPV [grammatical preverb: ongoing, continuing]

wacistwanihkākē- VAI1 build a nest from something, use something to build a nest

wacistwanihkē- VAI1 build a nest

wah IPJ well; oh!

wahwah IPJ oh my! wow! good gracious; really; [emphatic:] so [cf. **ahwā, wahwā**]

wahwā IPJ oh my! wow! good gracious; really; [emphatic:] so [cf. **ahwā, wahwah**]

wahwā hay IPJ oh my goodness gracious; oh how ridiculous

wani-otin- VTI1 take s.t. by accident, take s.t. as the wrong thing

wanih- **VTA1** lose s.o.; lose s.o. (to death)
wanihkē- **VAI1** forget; forget s.t.
wanihtā- **VTI2** lose s.t.; get relief from s.t.
waniskā- **VAI1** get up, arise from lying, get out of bed; go in, come in
wanitonāmo- **VAI1** say the wrong thing, make an error in speaking, commit a slip of the tongue
waskicipayi- **VAI2** come to the surface
waskicipayin- **VII2** come to the surface
waskway- **NA2** birchbark; birch, birch tree [Lat. *Betula* sp.]
waskwayāhtikw- **NA3** birch tree, birchwood
wawānēyiht- **VTI1** be at a loss (for s.t.), fail to think of s.t.; worry about s.t., be worried; be confused
wawēsīhowini-ayis- **NI1** beauty product
wawiyas-ācimo- **VAI1** tell humorous stories, tell about funny things
wawiyas-itōt- **VTI1** do s.t. humorously, do funny things
wawiyasācimo- **VAI1** tell funny stories
wawiyasiht- **VTI2** hear s.t. as funny, be amused when hearing s.t.
wawiyasihtaw- **VTA2** hear s.o. as funny, be amused when hearing s.o.
wawiyatācimo- **VAI1** tell funny stories
wawiyatēyiht- **VTI1** consider s.t. funny, find s.t. amusing, find s.t. odd, behave oddly
wawiyatēyihtākwan- **VII2** appear funny to all
wawiyatēyim- **VTA1** consider s.o. funny, find s.o. amusing, think s.o. drole, funny; feel joy about s.o.
wawiyēs **IPC** humorous, funny, amusing
wawiyēsiyinīhkē- **VAI1** do humorous things, get oneself into humorous situations
wayawī- **IPV** outside, outdoors; out from inside
wayawī- **VAI1** go out, go outside; go to relieve oneself, go to the toilet
wayawīhtah- **VTA1** take s.o. outside
wayawīhtatā- **VTI2** take s.t. outside, have s.t. go outdoors
wayawītimihk **IPC** outside, outdoors, out of doors
wayawīyāpāwē- **VAI1** float out of the water, be washed out
wā **IPJ** so; well; hey; what?
wāāhāā **IPJ** oh geez, oho!
wāh **IPJ** oh! well!
wāh- **IPV** [grammatical preverb: intermittent, repeatedly; again and again; here and there]
wāh-wāhyaw **IPC** very far; a very long distance; in far places
wāhay **IPJ** oh for goodness sake; wow, oh my! [exclamation of surprise, frustration or disgust]

wāhkōhtowin- NI1 relationship
wāhkōmākan- NA1 relative [cf. **-wāhkōmākan-** NDA1]
wāhkōm- VTA1 be related to s.o., have s.o. as one's relative; use a kin term for s.o.
wāhway IPJ oh my! wow! good gracious; really; [emphatic:] so
wāhwā IPJ oh my! wow! good gracious; really; [emphatic:] so
wāhyaw IPC far, far away
wāpaht- VTI1 see s.t., witness s.t.; have a vision
wāpahtah- VTA1 show (it/him) to s.o.
wāpam- VTA1 see s.o., witness s.o.
wāpan- VII1 be dawn, be first daylight, be early morning; be the next day
wāpikwaniy- NI2 flower; wild rose flower; white flower
wāpikwanīs- NI1 flower
wāpiskā- VII2 be white; be unsmoked (e.g., leather)
wāpiskāsin- VII2 be small and white; be a small white thing
wāpi- VAI1 see, have vision [generally in negative phrases:] be blind
wāposw- NA3 rabbit, hare
wāsakā- IPV around, all around; in a circle around something, in a full circle
wāsakāmē IPC around, in a circuit
wāsakāpi- VAI1 sit in a circle
wāsikan- NI1 electricity, electrical power
wāskā- IPV around, around in a circuit
wāskāhikan- NI1 house [also *wāskahikan-*]
wāskāhikanis- NI1 small house, cabin [also: *wāskahikanis-*]
wāstinamaw- VTA2 wave to s.o., gesture to s.o.
wāwāpiskāsinwa INM marshmallows
wāw- NI4 egg [e.g., singular: *wāwi*]
wāwiyēsi- VAI1 be round, be circular; be full (i.e., moon)
wāwīs IPC especially, particularly; all the more so, better so
wēhcasin- VII2 be easy, be simple; be cheap in price
wēhtakihcikē- VAI1 price things cheaply
wēhtakihtē- VII2 be cheap, be inexpensive
wēpahikē- VAI1 sweep, sweep things, do the sweeping
wēpin- VTI1 throw s.t. away, abandon s.t.
wēpin- VTA1 throw s.o. away, throw s.o. aside; empty s.o. (e.g., pail); leave s.o., abandon s.o., divorce s.o.; throw s.o. down or in (e.g., money in a card game)
wēpināso- VAI1 give cloth offerings (to the spirits)
wēpināson- NA1 ceremonial cloth, cloth offering; draped cloth; flag
wēpinikātē- VII2 be thrown away, be abandoned, be discarded; be lost (e.g., blood)

wēskacānisip- **NA**1 mud hen
wēwēkinikātē- **VII**2 be wrapped
wēwēstēhamān- **NA**1 fan, eagle wing fan, traditional fan
wiya **PrA** he, she, it; him, her, it; his, hers, its
wiya **IPC** for, because
wiya **IPC** this, that; as for, by contrast
wiyasiwē- **VAI**1 make laws; judge; decide
wiyawāw **PrA** they, them, theirs; themselves
wiyākanis- **NI**1 small dish, small bowl, small vessel
wiyās- **NI**1 meat
wiyāsis- **NI**1 bit of meat, piece of meat
wiyēs- **VTI**1 cut s.t. to shape
wiyokāwī- **VAI**1 have (her as) a mother [cf. **oyokāwī-**]
wiyōhkomi- **VAI**1 have (her as) a grandmother, have a living grandmother [cf. **oyōhkomi-**]
wiyōhtāwī- **VAI**1 have (s.o. as) a father [cf. **oyōhtāwī-**]
wī- **IPV** going to; intend to, be about to
wīc-āyām- **VTA**1 live with s.o., be together with s.o., be married to s.o. [also: *wīci-ayām-*]
wīcēht- **VTI**1 go along with s.t.; support s.t., cooperate with s.t.
wīcēhto- **VAI**1 get along with one another; accompany one another; live with one another; join with one another
wīcēw- **VTA**2 get along with s.o.; come along with s.o., accompany s.o., join s.o.; have s.o. along, be with s.o., live with s.o.
wīcēwākan- **NA**1 spouse, wife; friend, companion, buddy, partner [cf. **-wīcēwākan-** **NDA**1]
wīci- **IPV** together with
wīci-atoskēm- **VTA**1 work with s.o.
wīci-pīhtwām- **VTA**1 smoke with s.o., smoke the pipe with s.o.; have s.o. as one's smoking partner
wīcih- **VTA**1 help s.o.
wīcihiso- **VAI**1 help oneself; apply oneself, study for oneself; rely on herself in childbirth
wīcihiwē- **VAI**1 help people, give a helping hand; accompany, go along; be along, be part of a group, join in, take part, participate, be part of something
wīcihtāso- **VAI**1 help out, help with things
wīcōhkamaw- **VTA**2 help s.o., help s.o. by doing (it)
wīh- **VTA**1 name s.o., give a name to s.o.; call s.o. so, mention s.o. by name; rely on s.o., tell (it/him) from s.o.
wīhcikātē- **VII**2 be named, be mentioned; be told
wīhkasin- **VII**2 taste good, be delicious
wīhkaskw- **NI**3 sweetgrass [generally plural; Lat. *Hierochloe odorata*]

wīhkāc **IPC** ever; at times; [in negative clauses:] never
wīhkāt **IPC** ever; at times; [in negative phrases:] never
wīhkēs- **NI1** muskrat root, rat root, sweet flag, water arum, wild ginger [Lat. *Acorus calamus*]
wīhkicisi- **VAI1** taste good, be delicious [cf. **wīhkitisi-**]
wīhkimākostikwānēw **VAI1** have good-smelling hair
wīhkitisi- **VAI1** taste good [cf. **wīhkicisi-**]
wīhkohkēwin- **NI1** banquet
wīhkway- **NI2** bladder; swim bladder (e.g., fish); craw (e.g., bird)
wīhkwēkāpawi- **VAI1** stand all around something
wīhkwēpi- **VAI1** sit all around something
wīhowin- **NI1** name; spirit name
wīht- **VTI1** tell about s.t., report s.t.; decree s.t.; name s.t., mention s.t. by name
wīhtamaw- **VTA2** tell s.o. about (it/him), tell (it/him) to or for s.o.; name (it/him) to s.o.
wīhtamākē- **VAI1** announce; make predications; name (it) to people
wīki- **VAI1** live there, dwell there, have one's own home (there)
wīkihtah- **VTA1** make s.o. marry, arrange for s.o. to be married; unite s.o. in marriage, join s.o. (e.g., a couple) in marriage; take s.o. to be married
wīkim- **VTA1** marry s.o., take s.o. as spouse; be married to s.o.; live with s.o.
wīnih- **VTA1** make s.o. dirty by splashing; dirty s.o. with one's own dirty hands
wīninākwan- **VII2** look dirty
wīpac **IPC** soon, quickly, soon as possible; early
wīsahkēcāhkw- **NA3** Wisahkecahk; Cree culture hero, legendary figure
wīsakēyiht- **VTI1** be hurt by s.t.; be sore, be hurt, feel pain from s.t.
wīsakēyim- **VTA1** be hurt by s.o.; feel pain due to s.o.
wīsām- **VTA1** invite s.o., invite s.o. along, ask s.o. to come along with him/her
wīsta **PrA** he, too; she, too; he, by contrast; she, by contrast; he himself; she herself
wīstawāw **PrA** they, too; they, by contrast; they themselves
wītapihkēmo- **VAI1** sit and speak with people, sit with people to speak with them
wītapim- **VTA1** sit with s.o., sit beside s.o., stay with s.o., be present with s.o.; work together with s.o.; sit by s.o. (in marriage)
wītisi- **VAI1** have long, thick hair
wīwimāw **NA2** wife

y

yahkakocin- **VAI2** increase speed; drive forward, speed forward, make speedy progress

yahki- **IPV** act of pushing forward; increasing, increasingly, adding, more and more

yahki-miy- **VTA**1 give s.o. a raise

yahkī- **VAI**1 push forward, move forward

yēhē- **VAI**1 breathe

yēhēwin- **NI**1 breath; breathing

yiyīkastis- **NA**1 glove

yīkatēyāpaso- **VAI**1 moved aside from the smoke

yīwahikan- **NA**1 pounded dry meat, pounded dry fish; lump of ground dried meat

yōhtēn- **VTI**1 open s.t.; turn s.t. (e.g., television) on

yōskihtakisi- **VAI**1 be a crumbly log, be a rotting tree with soft wood

ABOUT THE SERIES

Our Own Words

University of Regina Press's book series, *Our Own Words*, publishes the personal stories of members from the Indigenous Nations of the Great Plains in their Indigenous language.

The books in the series provide longer, more extensive Indigenous texts for both the intermediate and advanced learners of the Indigenous language, and are presented, where appropriate, in syllabics, standard roman orthography, and English translation.

Series Editor

AROK WOLVENGREY

A linguist noted for his work with Indigenous Languages of the Americas, Arok Wolvengrey is a professor of Algonquian Languages and Linguistics in the Indigenous Languages Program at the First Nations University of Canada in Regina, Saskatchewan, located on Treaty 4 territory.

For more information about publishing in the series, please contact:

Karen May Clark, Senior Acquisitions Editor
University of Regina Press
3737 Wascana Parkway
Regina, Saskatchewan S4S 0A2 Canada
karen.clark@uregina.ca
www.uofrpress.ca

CPSIA information can be obtained
at www.ICGtesting.com
Printed in the USA
LVHW091330020222
710064LV00003B/49

9 780889 778368